Mormonism Under the Microscope

Mormonism Under the Microscope

"Breaking Bad"

Volume 11

by

Joel M. Allred

To the victims of secrets not shared.

To those betrayed by their unexpected exposure to the notorious facts seen to attend the society's difficult past.

To indoctrinated children groomed to become compliant adults.

For those who have risked everything to shout defiance.

Facts are found, not felt.

Knowledge is information bundled in principle.

Truth and freedom are more important than comfort, security, celebrity, acceptance, peace or power.

CONTENTS

Foreword

Foreword

In support of thought:

Thought is subversive . . . revolutionary, destructive and terrible, . . . merciless to privilege, . . . anarchic and lawless, indifferent to authority . . . . Thought looks into the pit of hell and is not afraid . . . . It bears itself proudly . . . as if it were lord of the universe. Thought is great and swift and free, the light of the world, and the chief glory of man.

Bertrand Russell

In support of the private life:

Every spirit builds itself a house; and beyond its house a world; and beyond its world a heaven. ... Adam called his house, heaven and earth. Caesar called his house Rome; you perhaps call yours, a cobbler's trade, or a scholar's garret. Yet line for line and point for point, your dominion is as great as theirs though without fine names. Build, therefore, your own world.

Ralph Waldo Emerson

In support of self-determination:

[L]et the counsel of thine own heart stand:
For there is none more faithful unto thee than it.
For a man's mind is sometime wont to bring him tidings,
More than seven watchmen, that sit above in a high tower.

Ecclesiastes

Introduction

Remembering Joseph

One must seriously consider how a stranger from Ohio could get eleven people in Manchester, New York, then fifty-one other people in Palmyra, New York, to sign group statements harshly critical of Joseph Smith and his family if those statements contained observations known not to be true and were not believed.

Joel M. Allred

For breach of contracts, for the non-payment of debts and borrowed money, and for duplicity with their neighbors, the family was notorious.

Roswell Nichols

With every new success of his son-in-law, Isaac Hales' tongue grew more acid, for he never lost his conviction that the youth was a barefaced impostor.

Fawn McKay Brodie

PITFALLS

Anyone honestly interested in the character of Joseph Smith and his family must soberly assess the affidavits, declarations and statements contained in E.D. Howe's *Mormonism Unvailed* published at Painesville, Ohio, in 1834. No one should disregard scores of contemporaneous assessments offered by men and women of standing in three separate communities in two different states. Dale Morgan described Mormonism's facile dismissal of Howe's influential accounts by taking B.H. Roberts to task. "Even the most responsible of the Mormon historians, B.H. Roberts, simply waved aside the universal testimony of Palmyra concerning their old neighbor – mere idle stories, dark insinuations, anything to discredit the prophet."[1]   Marvin S. Hill, a Mormon scholar, reported that many of the detractors were "'far above the Smiths in social rank and community status' and therefore had little first-hand information about the Smiths and 'probably did not know them well.'"[2] What else could anyone say? Then or now?

More than eighty Manchester, Palmyra (New York) and Harmony (Pennsylvania) residents offered unflattering reminiscences of the Smiths in *Mormonism Unvailed*, a nineteenth-century exposé. Describing the credibility of Howe's witnesses, E.W. Vanderhoof said, "Any old resident of Palmyra or Manchester will recognize among the signatures the names of the best people living at that time in those towns."[3] The 1834 recitals of *respected* citizens who knew Joseph Smith and his family early and in their element may not be simply "waved aside." History supports the proposition that the declarations of the Smith family's on-the-site detractors are far more accurate than the faith-protective recitals of those long after-the-fact never-at-the-scene apologists bound and determined to

---

[1]Brigham H. Roberts, *Comprehensive History of the Church*, 6 vol. (Salt Lake City, 1930), 1:41, quoted in Dale Morgan, *Dale Morgan on Early Mormonism: Correspondence & A New History*, ed. John Phillip Walker, with a Biographical Introduction by John Phillip Walker and a Preface by William Mulder (Salt Lake City: Signature Books, 1986), 239.

[2]Eber D. Howe, "Palmyra Residents Group Statement, 4 December 1833," Eber D. Howe, *Mormonism Unvailed: Or, A Faithful Account of That Singular Imposition and Delusion* (Painesville, OH: E.D. Howe, 1834; reprint, New York: AMS Press Inc., 1977), 261-62, Editorial Note, citing M. Hill (1990), 73-74, quoted in Dan Vogel, ed., *Early Mormon Documents* (Salt Lake City: Signature Books, 1999), 2:48.

[3]Howe, "Palmyra Residents Group Statement, 4 December 1833," *Mormonism Unvailed*, 261-62, Editorial Note, citing Vanderhoof (1907), 136, quoted in Vogel, ed., *Early Mormon Documents*, 2:48.

discredit them.[4] "At no time did he [Joseph Smith] ever squarely meet the question whether he had used his peepstone in the country roundabout Palmyra for treasure seekers of that neighborhood."[5] The Rockwell and Beman families, Luman Walters, Joseph Knight, Josiah Stowell and others were money-diggers with Smith at Palmyra, Manchester, Bainbridge and Colesville, New York. Joseph Smith Sr. accompanied his son to one important adventure in Harmony, Pennsylvania. Martin Harris, like other early disciples, was also "well informed."[6]

For more than a century, *the Church and its scholars denied* the "very prevalent story" that Smith was a money-digging "juggler" practiced to discern things invisible to the natural eye by gazing at a peepstone in a stovepipe hat. Who knew that Joseph Smith was the supernatural leader of superstitious bands of rough, idle, lazy men who dug for buried treasure at night? Smith's critics describe him as having been involved in "the fraudulent, superstitious, and criminal practice of money digging."[7] Today, to those concerned, it is known beyond any reasonable doubt that his activities were dictated by things magic and occult – like digging when the moon was full, or on the eve of the autumnal equinox. Joseph Smith, who practiced his money-digging trade with a forked witch-hazel rod, a

---

[4]The characteristic "Mormon reaction to the Palmyra stories has been the [*ad hominem*] vilification of the affiants, 'a set of blackguards, liars, horse jockeys and drunkards.' See, *e.g.*, Benjamin Winchester, *The Origin of the Spaulding Story*, (Philadelphia, 1840)," quoted in Walker, ed., *Dale Morgan on Early Mormonism*, 371 fn 29. Benjamin Winchester, like various other apologists, didn't know E.D. Howe's testators. Winchester, a convert at the age of fifteen whose exposure to Smith was up close and personal, later changed his mind about Mormonism and did himself denounce the character of Joseph Smith. "What kind of man was Smith? 'I have entertained him for a month at a time, while we lived in Philadelphia, while he was hiding from a mob. There was not a particle of true religion in him.'" (Testimony of Benjamin Winchester, Council Bluffs, Iowa, 27 November 1900 [Spalding Stories Library, Special Collections, accessed 9 September 2013], available from http://www.solomonspalding.com/docs/1900winc. htm; Internet).

[5]Walker, ed., *Dale Morgan on Early Mormonism*, 370-71 fn 26.

[6]Ibid.

[7]James A. Beverley, *Mormon Crisis: Anatomy of a Failing Religion* (Pickering, Ontario, Canada: Castle Quay Books, 2013), 145.

Jupiter talisman, a magic dagger and several different peepstones, believed in treasure-guarding demons.

What the Church for ever so long angrily denied, Martin Harris, a treasured Book of Mormon witness, was quick to admit. "There was a company there in that neighborhood who were digging for money supposed to have been hidden by the ancients. Of this company were old Mr. Stowell – I think his name was Josiah – also old Mr. Beman, also Samuel Lawrence, George Proper, Joseph Smith, Jr., and his father, and his brother Hiram Smith." "They dug for money in Palmyra, Manchester [Bainbridge, Colesville], also in Pennsylvania, and other places. When Joseph found this stone, there was a company digging in Harmony, Pa., and they took Joseph to look in the stone for them."[8] Now the celebrated treasure-seeking seer who also told fortunes with his stone took his act (and his treasure-seeking father) on the road. The Smiths, both father and son, were now involved in interstate commerce. Josiah Stowell made Joseph Smith (and his father) an offer they couldn't refuse.

Philastus Hurlbut

Philastus Hurlbut, who gathered many of the accounts published in *Mormonism Unvailed*, was an excommunicated Mormon. According to one prominent Latter-day Saint historian (Donna Hill), "Hurlbut, who had been excluded by the Methodists for immoralities [the instinctive Mormon approach to critics of any kind[9]], had visited Joseph in his home one day in March 1833, and Joseph had talked to him at length about The Book of Mormon." "He was ordained five days later by Sidney Rigdon . . . ." Hurlbut's membership, though short, was memorable. According to Donna

---

[8]Interview with Martin Harris in *Tiffany's Monthly*, V (July 1859): 164, quoted in Walker, ed., *Dale Morgan on Early Mormonism*, 371-72 fn 35, emphasis added.

[9]"One of the ways we can dismiss certain ideas is to discredit the people who utter them." (Paul James Toscano, *The Sacrament of Doubt* [Salt Lake City: Signature Books, 2007], 22).

Hill, "he was disfellowshipped from the church in June for 'unChristian conduct with women' (afterward more clearly described as using obscene language to a young member) while he was on a church mission in the east."[10] Conversely, Joseph's own language, as remembered by others, "was coarse full of epithets, taunts and braggadocio."[11] And his conduct with young women was not beyond reproach. The recent convert disputed the ruling, argued his appeal and managed to get the finding reversed. "Hurlbut appealed his excommunication on the grounds that he had been absent from the proceedings. Allowed a hearing, he confessed, and was forgiven and restored. Only two days later, however, he was called in again when two brethren accused him of boasting that he had 'deceived Joseph Smith's God.'" That is now described as his mistake. "This was more than the council could tolerate, and Hurlbut, to his great indignation, was cut off from the church."[12]

That is the traditional Mormon account of Hurlbut's disaffection. After his dismissal he was supposed to have become "an enemy of the Mormons,"[13] gathering affidavits and statements antagonistic to Joseph Smith, his mother, father and siblings. Donna Hill reports that Hurlbut "went to Palmyra in the fall of 1833 in search of evidence against Joseph Smith. In two months of diligent work he could not find anything to substantiate the theory that *The Book of Mormon* was written by Solomon Spaulding . . . ."[14] What he managed to find was *about one hundred residents of Palmyra and Manchester who were willing for one reason or another to make*

---

[10]Donna Hill, *Joseph Smith: The First Mormon* (USA: Doubleday & Company, Inc., 1977; reprint, Salt Lake City: Signature Books, 1977, 1982, 1999), 156.

[11]Richard S. Van Wagoner, *Sidney Rigdon: A Portrait of Religious Excess* (Salt Lake City: Signature Books, 1994; paperback 2006), 290.

[12]Hill, *Joseph Smith: The First Mormon*, 156.

[13]Ibid.

[14]There is, notwithstanding Hurlbut's failed efforts to link Solomon Spaulding to the Book of Mormon and Ms. Hill's predictable dismissal, more to the Spaulding theory than meets the Mormon eye. For modern scholarship in support of a linkage, one might look first to the writings of Vernal Holley.

derogatory statements about the Smiths. Hurlbut eagerly collected their signed affidavits."[15]

Ms. Hill (one Joseph's faithful biographers and the sister of yet another Mormon historian, Marvin S. Hill) does not include in her description various Harmony, Pennsylvania, affidavits independently prepared by Emma Smith's family and others (then also published by Howe) because Philastus Hurlbut, who operated principally in Palmyra and Manchester, didn't gather them. While Hurlbut gathered many statements, declarations and affidavits, his compilation did not include the Pennsylvania reports. Emma Smith's family, her father Isaac Hale and others, people acquainted with Joseph Smith in Harmony, authored the Pennsylvania accounts, which also contained "derogatory statements" about Joseph Smith.

Apostle John A. Widtsoe, one of Mormonism's respected scholars, discussed the affidavits collected by Philastus Hurlbut, dismissing the allegations of those who said that Joseph Smith had been a money-digging scryer. "These affidavits were collected by one P. Hurlburt [Hurlbut], of unsavory fame, who had been cast out from the Church for adultery. In revenge he proceeded to write a book against the Mormons, in which these affidavits were included . . . ."[16] (Widtsoe, like others and incorrectly, assumed that Hurlbut gathered the Pennsylvania affidavits). It is the Mormon way to say that an apostate man guilty of adultery can't be trusted to tell the truth and ought not be believed. In that Latter-day Saints conveniently ignore the particularly sordid domestic history of the prophet Joseph Smith (as well as Brigham Young and many others). In the case of Philastus Hurlbut, his work is dismissed

---

[15]Hill, *Joseph Smith: The First Mormon*, 156, emphasis added.

[16]John A. Widtsoe, "What Manner of Boy and Youth Was Joseph Smith?" *Improvement Era*, vol. 49 no. 8 (August 1946), 542. According to Widtsoe (speaking to history in 1946), "The charge that Joseph Smith was a money digger rests first upon the established fact that he once was employed to dig for a 'lost' silver mine. One Josiah Stowell so employed the young man. Joseph Smith has fully acknowledged this employment, which did not last long." (Ibid.).

because it is said that he was morally unclean, angry about the loss of his membership and determined to seek revenge.

Vilification

A recent example of the vilification principle involved Simon Southerton, a former Mormon bishop excommunicated for alleged (and unproven) adultery seven years after he informally left the Church. The alleged offense occurred while the Southertons were separated for about two years, and the excommunication occurred after they had reconciled.[17] Southerton, because he is a molecular biologist, was excommunicated because he wrote a book about DNA in which he denied to Native Americans an Hebraic lineage – a direct attack upon the central principle of the Book of Mormon. Now, because of that particularly fortuitous alleged adultery, it can be said that no one should believe Southerton, an excommunicated adulterer. How much better it is for Mormons to say that the Australian scholar is generally untrustworthy because he is morally infirm than it is to say that he is generally untrustworthy because his scholarship challenged the historicity of the Book of Mormon.

---

[17]Southerton described his "Court of Love" in these terms: "My wife and I left the church 7 years ago in 1998 [but did not request that our names be removed from the records]. We separated in 2003 for a period of almost 2 years. Several months after we separated I met a woman and we were close friends for about a year. She was in the process of leaving the church, lives interstate, and was separated from her husband (now divorced). The relationship ended and about 6 months later my wife and I got back together. We have been together for about nine months [on July 18, 2005] and things are going well." (Simon Southerton, *My Court of Love*, July 18, 2005 [accessed 10 September 2013], available from http://www.mormoncurtain.com/topic_simonsoutherton.html#pub_1293847311;Internet, 1). On August 2, 2005, Southerton reported his excommunication – not for apostasy, he had apostatized – but rather for misconduct (an "alleged 'inappropriate relationship'"). "They did not have," he said, "evidence to support that charge." "I asked if alleged misconduct over 2 years ago between separated adults was more serious than the charge of public apostasy for the last 6 years." He was "assured" that it was. "I was . . . instructed before the meeting that if I attempted to talk about 'DNA' and my apostasy that the council would be immediately shut down and . . . completed in my absence." (Simon Southerton, excommunicated 2 August 2005, Ibid.).

Joseph Smith made many moral mistakes, for one what Emma's cousin Levi Lewis called the attempted seduction of Miss Eliza Winters, Emma's very special friend, in Harmony.[18] For another certain liberties supposed to have been taken with then sixteen-year-old Marinda Nancy Johnson in Hiram, Ohio, an accusation that caused his Ohio neighbors to tar and feather him. A doctor brought to the scene for a surgical solution saved the prophet from permanent disfigurement when he changed his mind and refused to perform a castration. Oliver Cowdery, Joseph's early intimate colleague, later described what he called "a dirty, nasty, filthy affair" involving Joseph Smith and Fanny Alger, a teenage intern in the home he shared with Emma and the children.

Joseph Smith publicly denied that he practiced polygamy until the day he died. But it is now known that he married as many as thirty-four women in twenty-two months,[19] and that he was secretly married to as many as fourteen women who were previously (and simultaneously) legally married to other men.[20] And that he proposed a relationship ("connubial bliss") or plural marriage to other women, some of whom were already married to other prominent Mormon men (priesthood brothers). Four of those women declined a relationship or marriage – Mrs. Orson Pratt, Mrs. Hiram Kimball (whose husband was not a Mormon), Mrs. William Law and Mrs. Robert D. Foster. In addition to those peculiar proposals, Smith informed Miss Nancy Rigdon (Sidney Rigdon's unmarried daughter) that her marriage to him "would not

---

[18]"Levi Lewis [Emma Smith's cousin and a "constable"] states, that he has 'been acquainted with Joseph Smith Jr. and Martin Harris, and that he has heard them both say, adultery was no crime. Harris said he did not blame Smith for his (Smith's) attempt to seduce Eliza Winters &c;' – . . . ." (Levi Lewis Statement, 1834, Vogel, ed., *Early Mormon Documents*, 4:296-97). Martin Harris, an alleged adulterer known to have beaten his wife, had been selected by Smith to be one of the Three Witnesses to the Book of Mormon. Lucy (Mrs. Martin) Harris: "Whether the Mormon religion be true or false, I leave the world to judge, for its effects upon Martin Harris have been to make him more cross, turbulent and abusive to me." (Howe, *Mormonism Unvailed*, 255).

[19]George D. Smith, *Nauvoo Polygamy . . . But We Called It Celestial Marriage* (Salt Lake City: Signature Books, 2008), 621-23.

[20]Ibid.

prevent her from marrying any other person . . . ."[21]   Had those prominent Mormon women accepted proposals of marriage, he would have married eighteen or nineteen women who were or soon would be the wives of other men. Was Joseph Smith not generally untrustworthy? Were his teachings not morally suspect because he was secretly married to more than thirty women – including nine or ten teenagers, two of them fourteen years old, three sets of sisters, then Patty Sessions and her daughter Sylvia – when he repeatedly said that he was not? Calling Simon Southerton tarnished and unworthy of belief in the face of Joseph Smith's tumultuous life is perfectly foolish and desperately partisan.

Joseph Smith hated his enemies and did not hesitate to say so – men like Warren Parrish, Warren Cowdery, Oliver Cowdery, David Whitmer, John Whitmer, Lyman E. Johnson, John Boynton, Martin Harris, Stephen Burnett, Grandison Newell, Philastus Hurlbut, Leonard Rich, Joseph Coe, Symonds Rider, Sylvester Smith, John C. Bennett, George M. Hinkle, Samuel Lucas, Lilburn W. Boggs, William Law, Wilson Law, Charles Foster, Robert D. Foster, Reed Peck, Francis Higbee, John Corrill, and very many others. This list is far from complete. Joseph didn't turn the other cheek, but rather exacted and encouraged revenge. Witness the alleged conspiracy to assassinate Missouri's former Governor, Lilburn W. Boggs (a crime supposed to have been committed by the prophet's bodyguard, the notorious Orrin Porter Rockwell). Witness the alleged threat to put Grandison Newell "out of the way." According to Orson Hyde and Luke Johnson (two of his apostles), Joseph "said destroying Newell would be justifiable in the sight of God, that it was the will of God . . . ."[22] Witness his alleged threat to kill Hiram Kimball for failing to collect a Nauvoo wharfage fee.[23] Should not the same test be applied to the words

---

[21]John C. Bennett, *The History of the Saints: Or, an Expose of Joe Smith and Mormonism* (Boston: Leland & Whiting, 1842; photomechanical reprint of 1842 original, Salt Lake City: Modern Microfilm Company), 242.

[22]D. Michael Quinn, *The Mormon Hierarchy: Origins of Power* (Salt Lake City: Signature Books in association with Smith Research Associates, 1994), 626.

[23]Joseph Smith Jr., *History of The Church of Jesus Christ of Latter-day Saints*, B.H. Roberts, ed., 2d ed., rev., (Salt Lake City: The Deseret Book Company, 1978),

and products of Joseph Smith – who made many moral mistakes, hated his enemies, prevaricated hundreds of times and sought revenge – that Mormons have applied to the words and products of his Painesville, Ohio, detractor Philastus Hurlbut?

Smith's Philastus Hurlbut Prophecy

Joseph Smith predicted the morbid demise of his affidavit attracting tormentor. "[T]he Lord shall destroy him who has lifted his heel against me even that wicked man Docter P. H[u]rlbut he <will> deliver him to the fowls of heaven and his bones shall be cast to the blast of the wind <for> he lifted his <arm> against the Almity therefore [p. 68] the Lord shall destroy him."[24] This prophecy was written in his own hand by a very angry prophet who usually dictated. "Evidently the curse did not immediately overtake Mr. Hurlbut for Ellen Dickinson, who visited him forty-six years later at Gibsonburg, Ohio, found him in tolerable health, even though doddering with age." Hurlbut outlived the prophet who prophesied his morbid demise by more than thirty years. "While it is true his expose sought to undermine the Prophet's character, he was not alone in his accusations. If the affidavits and the eighty or more signatures that he obtained are ignored, the remaining accounts of Joseph's interest in mystic arts still form a formidable challenge to church history."[25]

6:238. "I despise the man who will betray you with a kiss; and I am determined to use up these men, if they will not stop their operations."

[24]Joseph Smith Jr., *The Papers of Joseph Smith: Journal, 1832-1842*, ed. Dean C. Jessee (Salt Lake City: Deseret Book Company, 1989-1992), 1 April 1834, 2:28.

[25]LaMar Petersen, *The Creation of the Book of Mormon: A Historical Inquiry* (Salt Lake City: Freethinker Press, 2000), 53.

WHO WERE JOSEPH'S 1830'S DETRACTORS?

Doctor Philastus Hurlbut[26] had "lived in Kirtland and during the winter and spring had given much in looking up evidence and documents to prove that Mormonism was a delusion."[27] Hurlbut began collecting documents in November and December of 1833.[28] They concerned events and impressions mostly related to the 1820s and early 30s. Joseph and Oliver's *1834-35 History* is thought to have been an attempt at a response to the stinging criticisms leveled at the characters of Joseph Smith, his mother, father and siblings in *Mormonism Unvailed.*

On March, 22, 1831, more than two years before Doctor Philastus Hurlbut gathered his affidavits and statements, and years before they were published in *Mormonism Unvailed*, E.D. Howe's *Painesville Telegraph* received and published a letter challenging the integrity of the Smiths and their followers. The letter dated *12 March 1831* was signed by "ten individuals of the first respectability." These declarants were from Palmyra, New York, and their names were withheld when the letter was published. Dan Vogel thought that Howe's publication of the unsolicited letter in the *Telegraph* may have inspired Hurlbut to undertake to interview "Smith's former neighbors in western New York."[29]

---

[26]Introduction to Philastus Hurlbut Collection, Vogel, ed., *Early Mormon Documents*, 2:13. Hurlbut's first name was "Doctor."

[27]Hurlbut's expeditions to western New York in 1833 and 1834 to interview people familiar with the Smiths were funded by Grandison Newell, Orrin Clapp and Nathan Corning of Mentor, Ohio, and by "many leading citizens of Kirtland and Geauga Co. . . ." Other community leaders who served on a committee which met to examine the evidence Hurlbut had collected included Judge Nehemiah Allen, "who had been an Associate Judge of the county of Cuyahoga, a representative in the Legislature," Dr. George W. Card, a physician, Samuel Wilson, a business man, Jonathan Lapham, an experienced lawyer, and James Briggs, the scribe and a less experienced lawyer. "We met at the house of Mr. W. Corning in Mentor, . . . Doctor P. Hurlbut also met with us." (Vogel, ed., *Early Mormon Documents*, 2:13 [citing James A. Briggs to Arthur B. Deming, 22 March 1866, *Naked Truths About Mormonism* 1 (January 1888):4, Collection, Chicago Historical Society, Chicago, Illinois]).

[28]Vogel, ed., *Early Mormon Documents*, 2:13.

[29]Ibid.

Palmyra/Manchester: Affidavits, Declarations and Statements

Among the *first* of the declarations collected by Hurlbut in Palmyra and Manchester (New York) "was a *group statement* signed by eleven residents of Manchester."[30] These people, unlike the people who wrote to the *Telegraph* in 1831, were published as signators. The statements were probably written by Hurlbut and presented to the signers for ratification. In them are the declarations of some of the about eighty-two witnesses who disparaged the Smiths in editor Howe's critical book. No one should cavalierly dismiss the integrity of eighty witnesses by declaring them bigots, by saying that the man who collected these accounts was an enemy of the Mormon Church, or that the publisher was. The Book of Mormon was presented on the basis of testimony from eleven less respectable witnesses, including people with extraordinary conflicts of interest (Smiths, Cowdery, Whitmers, Hiram Page). All of the Whitmers (including Hiram Page) later left the Church.[31] They voted with their feet. The credentials of the affiants and declarants cited in this section, and of some few others cited in the book, are found at the back of this work at Appendix A.

The eleven residents from tiny rural Manchester reported as follows:

> *We, the undersigned, being personally acquainted with the family of Joseph Smith, sen. with whom the*

---

[30]Manchester Residents' Group Statement, 3 November 1833, Editorial Note, Ibid., 2:18.

[31]Hiram Page was married to Catherine Whitmer. David Whitmer, one of the Three Witnesses to the Book of Mormon, it has long been known, denounced the faith as follows: "If you believe my testimony to the Book of Mormon; if you believe that God spake to us three witnesses by his own voice, then I tell you that in June, 1838, God spake to me again by his own voice from the heavens, and told me 'to separate myself from among the Latter Day Saints, for as they sought to do unto me, so should it be done unto them.' 'In the spring of 1838, the heads of the church and many of the members had gone deep into error and blindness.'" (David Whitmer, *An Address to All Believers in Christ: by A Witness to the Divine Authenticity of The Book of Mormon* [Richmond, MO: n.p., 1887; photographic reprint, Concord, CA: Pacific Publishing Company, 1993], 27).

celebrated Gold Bible, so called, originated, state: that
they were not only a lazy, indolent set of men, but also
intemperate; and their word was not to be depended
upon; and that we are truly glad to dispense with their
society.[32]

Some of E.D. Howe's individual witnesses signed their literate declarations under oath subject to the penalties of perjury in the presence of a justice of the peace or some other officer of the court. Conversely, the statements of the witnesses to the Book of Mormon were not signed or notarized.

Had the Smiths been respected and honorable citizens held in high esteem, how difficult should it have been to find reputable witnesses willing to attach their names in a public way to this damning indictment? To recitals prepared while memories were reasonably vivid and fresh? Here are neighbors in a closely-knit rural community anxious to express low opinions of Joseph Smith and his family. The historic, amended, thoroughly sanitized Smith, rehabilitated in his 1838-39 History, which included the canonized account of the First Vision (the only account known at the time), was a better man than the unamended, less historic, original Smith described in the history Smith and Cowdery jointly prepared in 1834-35. The man described in the *Manuscript History* composed in 1838-39, by himself and others, was supposed to be the most important man on earth.

Recitals

Various respected individuals in the communities where they had lived in squalid poverty knew and remembered the Smiths during their early portentous years. Some of them thought they lacked ambition, weren't religious and seemed slow. The preponderant impression of their New York and Pennsylvania neighbors was that

---

[32]Manchester Residents' Group Statement, November 3, 1833, Vogel, ed., *Early Mormon Documents*, 2:18-21, emphasis added.

they were money-diggers, less than dependable people telling fortunes and seeking elusive treasures for gullible clients with less than sacred "peepstones." E.D. Howe's ten anonymous informants reported in 1831 that the Smiths believed "in witchcraft, ghosts, goblins, &c." Joseph Smith, a combative belligerent man easily provoked, became a "pugnacious prophet." He was involved in altercations before and after the Church was formed, before and after he was married, and as an adult. One of Hurlbut's witnesses described him as "quarrelsome" when "intoxicated"; others just called him "intemperate."

Peter Ingersoll, who met the Smiths in 1822 and lived in their neighborhood until about 1830, became a trusted friend of Joseph Smith. Before Martin Harris provided Joseph with the funds required to travel to Pennsylvania and take up residence with Emma's family, Joseph had drawn close to Peter Ingersoll, "his confident" (confidant) with whom he shared "what daily transpired in the family of Smiths . . . ."[33] After Joseph and Emma moved to Pennsylvania in the fall of 1827, Ingersoll had "not been much in his society." He did however speak to William Smith, Joseph's brother. "While the Smiths were living at Waterloo, William visited my [p. 236] neighborhood, and upon my inquiry how they came on, he replied, 'we do better there than here; we were too well known here to do much.[']"[34] Certain facts "came under my observation,"[35] Ingersoll would later report.

Ingersoll accompanied Joseph and Emma to Pennsylvania in August, 1827 – following their marriage in January 1827 – when the young couple returned to Harmony to move some household furniture belonging to Emma from Harmony to Manchester, things left behind when Emma eloped with Joseph Smith without her father's consent. This was the first time the young couple returned to face the wrath of Emma's offended father. Ingersoll made the

---

[33]Peter Ingersoll Statement, December 2, 1833, Vogel, ed., *Early Mormon Documents*, 2:43.
[34]Ibid., 2:45, emphasis added.
[35]Ibid., 2:40.

trip at Joseph's request ("I was hired by Joseph Smith, Jr.") to help them transport Emma's things.   When Ingersoll returned to Manchester with Joseph and Emma, after Joseph and Emma's fateful first encounter with Emma's father, Isaac Hale, he recounted a small but meaningful detail:

> *On our journey to Pennsylvania, we could not make the exact change at the toll gate near Ithaca. Joseph told the gate tender, that he would "hand" him the toll on his return, as he was coming back in a few days. On our return, Joseph tendered to him 25 cents, the toll being 12½. He did not recognize Smith, so he accordingly gave him back 12½. After we had passed the gate, I asked him if he did not agree to pay double gatage on our return? No, said he, I agreed to "hand" it to him, and I did, but he handed it back again.*[36]

This was a technique Joseph and others in the Mormon leadership perfected over the years. Code words and clever but dishonest distinctions that shaded the truth became early Mormon staples often associated with the secret practice of polygamy.

Joseph, Hyrum, and various other prominent leaders of the early Church ignored many of their creditors and later discharged their substantial debts in bankruptcy proceedings. Joseph Smith Sr. shared a jail cell with Eli Bruce, the former High Sheriff of Canandaigua County and a Mason who had been implicated in the murder of the Masonic martyr, William Morgan. Bruce "was tried and found guilty of conspiracy in Morgan's abduction."[37] Joseph

---

[36]Ibid., 2:43, emphasis retained as underlined and added.

[37]Editorial Note, Eli Bruce Diary, 5 November 1830, reproduced in Vogel, ed., *Early Mormon Documents*, 3:3-4. Bruce Diary, 5 November 1830: "Had a long talk with the father of *the Smith* [Joseph Smith Sr.], who, according to the old man's account, is the particular favorite of Heaven! [p. 266].   To him Heaven has vouchsafed to reveal its mysteries; he is the herald of the latter-day glory. The old man says that he is commissioned by God to baptize and preach the new doctrine. He says that our Bible is much abridged and deficient; that soon the Divine will is

Sr.'s offense? Stiffing his troublesome creditors. Joseph Sr. found himself in debtor's prison for thirty days "because of an unpaid debt of four dollars." *Joseph Capron* became acquainted with Joseph Smith Sr. "in the year of our Lord, 1827." "While they were digging for money," Capron reported, "they were daily harassed by the demands of creditors, which they were never able to pay."[38]

Fifty-one Palmyra residents now signed another statement as follows:

> *We, the undersigned, have been acquainted with the Smith family, for a number of years, while they resided near this place, and we have no hesitation in saying, that we consider them destitute of that moral character, which ought to entitle them to the confidence of any community. They were particularly famous for visionary projects, spent much of their time in digging for money which they pretended was hid in the earth; and to this day, large excavations may be seen in the earth, not far from their residence, where they used to spend their time in digging for hidden treasures. Joseph Smith, Senior, and his son Joseph, were in particular, considered entirely destitute of moral character, and addicted to vicious habits . . . .*
>
> *And in reference to all with whom we were acquainted, that have embraced Mormonism from this neighborhood, we are compeled to say, were very visionary, and most of them destitute of moral character, and without [p. 261] influence in this community; and this may account why they were permitted to go on with their impositions undisturbed. It was not supposed that any of them were possessed*

---

to be made known to all, as written in the *new Bible*, or *Book of Mormon*." (Ibid., emphasis retained).

[38]Joseph Capron Statement, 3 November 1833, Ibid., 2:25.

of sufficient character or influence to make any one
believe their book or their sentiments, and we know of
not a single individual in this vicinity that puts the
least confidence in their pretended revelations.[39]

The Pennsylvania Principals

Isaac Hale, Emma Smith's father and a religious man, signed a
sworn affidavit before a Justice of the Peace in Harmony,
Pennsylvania, on March 20, 1834.[40] "Smith and his father," it said,
"with several other 'money-diggers' boarded at my house while
they were employed in digging for a mine . . . ." "Young Smith gave
the 'money-diggers' great encouragement, at first, but when they
had arrived in digging, to near the place where he had stated an
immense treasure would be found – he said the enchantment was so
powerful that he could not see. They then became discouraged, and
soon after dispersed. This took place about the 17th of November,
1825; . . . ."[41] Smith was nineteen years old at the time. In 1842
Smith said he saw the Father and the Son in 1820. The incident his
father-in-law described occurred in Harmony, Pennsylvania, in
1825, five-and-one-half years after Smith said that he saw the
Father and the Son. After the "money-diggers" scattered, "[Y]oung
Smith made several visits at my house, and at length asked my
consent to his marrying my daughter Emma. This I refused, and
gave him my reasons for so doing; some of which were, that he was

---

[39]Palmyra Residents Group Statement, 4 December 1833, Ibid., 2:48-55,
emphasis added.

[40]Hale's statement was solicited by Philastus Hurlbut, who received it in letter
form as a statement postmarked 22 December 1833. W.R. Hine claimed Hurlbut
wrote to Hale at his suggestion. Martin Harris challenged the statement ("Hale
was old and blind and not capable of writing it"). Hurlbut turned Hale's statement
over to E.D. Howe, who requested Hale draw up "a full narrative of every
transaction" and "attest them before a magistrate." (Editorial Note, Isaac Hale
Statement, 1834, Vogel, ed., *Early Mormon Documents*, 4:282-83). William
Thompson and Davis Dimock, "associate Judges of the Court of Common Pleas" in
"Susquehanna County," attested that Isaac Hale "is a man of excellent moral
character, and of undoubted veracity." (Ibid., 4:288).

[41]Isaac Hale Statement, 1834, Ibid., 4:284.

a stranger, and followed a business that I could not approve; he then left the place." Though that may have seemed to have been the end of that, "Not long after this, he returned, and while I was absent from home, carried off my daughter, into the state of New York, where they were married without my approbation or consent."[42]

Isaac discussed this conduct with Joseph Smith later that same year in the presence of Peter Ingersoll:

> *"You spend your time in digging for money – pretend to see in a stone, and thus try to deceive people." Joseph wept, and acknowledged he could not see in a stone now, nor never could; and that his former pretentions in [p. 234] that respect, were all false. He then promised to give up his old habits of digging for money and looking into stones."*[43]

This was a stunning admission, supremely important even today. The unusual occupation of Smith's precocious youth had been built on smoke and mirrors. At the same time he said that he saw the Father and the Son in 1820 and the Angel Moroni in 1823, he was pretending to tell fortunes and see things invisible to the natural eye by looking at a magic stone. On the occasion of this encounter with Emma's father, Isaac Hale, and in the presence of Peter Ingersoll, Joseph Smith admitted that "he could not see in a stone now, nor never could." Joseph told Peter Ingersoll "that he intended to keep the promise which he had made to his father-in-law: but said he, it will be hard for me, for they will all oppose, as they want me to look in the stone for them to dig money: and in fact it was as he predicted."[44]

Following Joseph's promise "to give up his old habits," and in consequence of a reconciliation of sorts, Joseph and Emma then

---

[42]Ibid., 4:285.
[43]Peter Ingersoll Affidavit, 2 December 1833, Ibid., 2:42-43, emphasis added.
[44]Ibid., 2:43.

later moved from New York to Pennsylvania to live by Isaac Hale, who supported them in various important ways. After a time, after watching Joseph and Martin Harris (who joined Joseph in Pennsylvania) engaged in the translation of the Book of Mormon (Hale was not permitted to see the plates), and after seeing some of the translated words committed to paper by Joseph and his scribe, Isaac Hale was mystified.

> *I enquired whose words they were, and was informed. . . that they were the words of Jesus Christ. I told them then, that I considered the whole of it a delusion, and advised them to abandon it. The manner in which he pretended to read and interpret, was the same as when he looked for the money-diggers, with the stone in his hat, and his hat over his face, while the Book of Plates were at the same time hid in the woods! . . . .*[45]

What he had pretended to do for money he pretended to do for words. What he admitted was false he continued to do. What he "could not see in a stone" while digging for money, he pretended to see in a stone while translating a book.

> *Joseph Smith Jr. resided near to me for some time after this, and I had a good opportunity of becoming acquainted with him, and somewhat acquainted with his associates, and I conscientiously believe from the facts I have detailed, and from many other circumstances, which I do not deem it necessary to relate, that the whole "Book of Mormon" (so called) is a silly fabrication of falsehood and wickedness, got up for speculation, and with a design to dupe the credulous and unwary – and in order that its fabricators might live upon the spoils of those who swallowed the deception.*[46]

---

[45]Isaac Hale Statement, 1834, Ibid., 4:287, emphasis added.
[46]Ibid., 4:287-88, emphasis added.

Isaac Hale was a decent man of common sense. Martin Harris later confirmed the Hales' opposition to Emma's marriage to Joseph. After he gave up the dig in Harmony, Pennsylvania, because "the enchantment was so strong he could not see" in the stone, "He afterwards returned to Pennsylvania again, and married his wife, taking her off to old Mr. Stowels, because her people would not consent to the marriage. She was of age, Joseph was not."[47] Francis M. Gibbons, a secretary to the First Presidency and a biographer to the prophets, would later deny "that Isaac Hale was opposed to Joseph's marriage to his daughter Emma because of his treasure-seeking activities." But Isaac had said, "I refused [Joseph's request to marry Emma], and gave him my reasons for so doing, some of which were, that he was a stranger, and followed a business that I could not approve . . . ." Hale's after-the-fact conclusion was that, "you have stolen my daughter and married her. I had much rather have followed her to her grave." No one ever heard that story in a Mormon Sunday School.

LaMar Petersen described Gibbons' apologetic report. "An assumption has grown within the church that one Philastus Hurlbut was chiefly responsible for the malicious stories directed against the Prophet and that, if his endeavor be exposed as revenge and character assassination, then the matter would be disposed of." "For example," said Petersen, "Francis M. Gibbons, secretary to the First Presidency, in denying that Isaac Hale was opposed to Joseph's marriage to his daughter Emma because of his treasure-seeking activities, stated that Hurlbut wrote Hale's affidavit."[48] In that he was mistaken. While Hurlbut solicited a statement from Isaac Hale, and while E.D. Howe requested that Hale draw up a full narrative of every transaction he had had with his son-in-law and attest to the same before a magistrate, neither Howe nor Hurlbut

---

[47]Martin Harris interview with Joel Tiffany, 1859, Ibid., 2:304. All of this happened *after* Smith had been pronounced *"guilty"* of being a "disorderly person" and an "Impostor" at the Bainbridge trial in March of 1826.

[48]Francis M. Gibbons, *Joseph Smith, Martyr, Prophet of God* (Salt Lake City: Deseret Book Co., 1977), 44, quoted in Petersen, *The Creation of the Book of Mormon*, 52. Philastus Hurlbut did not write the Pennsylvania affidavits reprinted in *Mormonism Unvailed*.

wrote Isaac Hale's statement, nor the statements of any of the other Pennsylvania witnesses.

D. Michael Quinn also discussed the issue raised by Gibbons in Quinn's book *Mormonism and the Magic World View*, concluding as follows: "Hale, in his affidavit, said he refused [to allow Smith to marry Emma] because of the young man's treasure-seeking background."[49] Quinn then proceeded to rebut Gibbons on the Hurlbut thing. "A recent biography of Smith disputes this explanation of Hale's opposition to his marriage proposal because the 'affidavit supposedly executed by Isaac in 1834 . . . was prepared by Philastus Hurlburt' (Gibbons 1977, 44). On the contrary, Isaac Hale published his affidavit in a local (Pennsylvania) newspaper. Hurlbut had nothing to do with it, and E.D. Howe simply reprinted it in *Mormonism Unvailed* . . . ."[50] Joseph Smith – while tapping an inexhaustible resource – explained the antagonism of Emma Hale's family on religious grounds. He was persecuted "mainly because he had asserted that he had seen a vision."[51]

Alva Hale, Emma's brother, said Smith said his gift, "in seeing with a stone and hat, was a gift from God." But on another occasion, Smith told Alva that "this *'peeping' was all* d - - - - d nonsense." Alva Hale said he knew "Joseph Smith Jr. to be an imposter, and a liar, and knows Martin Harris to be a liar likewise."[52] *Nathaniel C. Lewis,* Emma's uncle and a prominent figure in the Harmony Methodist Episcopal Church, was repeatedly told by Smith that he would be permitted to see the golden plates "at the time appointed." "I stated at the time he made the promise, I was fearful 'the enchantment would be so powerful' as to remove the plates, when

---

[49]Isaac Hale Statement, 1834, Vogel, ed., *Early Mormon Documents*, 4:285, cited in D. Michael Quinn, *Early Mormonism and the Magic World View* (Salt Lake City: Signature Books, 1987), 140.

[50]*Susquehanna Register,* 1 May 1834; cited in Quinn, *Early Mormonism and the Magic World View,* 140 fn 12.

[51]Hill, *Joseph Smith: The First Mormon,* 62.

[52]Alva Hale Statement, 1834, Vogel, ed., *Early Mormon Documents*, 4:291-92, emphasis retained.

the time came in which they were to be revealed."[53] When they were not revealed on time as promised, or ever, Lewis concluded that, "These circumstances and many others of a similar tenor, embolden me to say that Joseph Smith Jr. is not a man of truth and veracity; and that his general character in this part of the country, is that of an impostor, hypocrite and liar."[54] Nathaniel C. Lewis further states "he has always resided in the same neighborhood with Isaac Hale, and knows him to be a man of truth, and good judgment."[55]

Levi Lewis, Emma's cousin, says that he also "knows Smith to be a liar; – that he saw him (Smith) intoxicated at three different times while he was composing the Book of Mormon, and also that he has heard Smith when driving oxen, use language of the greatest profanity." He heard Smith and Martin Harris say that "adultery was no crime." Levi Lewis heard Smith say that he was "as good as Jesus Christ; – that it was as bad to injure him as it was to injure Jesus Christ." "With regard to the plates, Smith said God had deceived him – which was the reason he (Smith) did not show the plates."[56] *Sophia Lewis,* Mrs. Levi Lewis, the wife of Emma's cousin, had "frequently heard Smith use profane language." "She states that she heard Smith say 'the Book of Plates could not be opened under penalty of death by any other person but his (Smith's) first-born, which was to be a male.' She says she 'was present at the birth of this child, and that it was still-born and very much deformed.'"[57] *Hezekiah M'Kune,* the husband of Emma's cousin, Elizabeth Lewis, reported that, "in conversation with Joseph Smith Jr., he (Smith) said he was nearly equal to Jesus Christ; that he was a prophet sent by God to bring in the Jews, and that he was the greatest prophet that had ever arisen."[58]

---

[53]Nathaniel Lewis Statement, 1834, Ibid., 4:294.
[54]Ibid.
[55]Ibid., 4:295.
[56]Levi Lewis Statement, 1834, Ibid., 4:296-97.
[57]Sophia Lewis Statement, on or before 20 March 1834, Ibid., 4:298.
[58]Hezekiah McKune Statement, 1834, Ibid., 4:327.

Other Principals

Charles Anthon, a Columbia University professor who met with Martin Harris at Harris' request, later described Harris' visit: "*The whole story about my having pronounced the Mormonite inscription to be 'reformed Egyptian hieroglyphics' is perfectly false.*"[59] "Some years ago, a plain, and apparently simple-hearted farmer, called upon me with a note from Dr. [Samuel L.] Mitchell[60] of our city, now deceased, requesting me to decypher, if possible, a paper, which the farmer would hand me, and which Dr. M[itchell]. confessed he had been unable to understand. Upon examining the paper in question, I soon came to the conclusion that it was all a trick, perhaps a *hoax.*"[61] Now the farmer further explained: "A 'gold book,' consisting of a number of plates of gold, fastened together in the shape of a book by wires of the same metal, had been dug up in the northern part of the state of New York, and along with the book an enormous pair of '*gold spectacles*'! ... Whoever examined the plates through the spectacles, was enabled not only to *read* them, but fully to *understand* their meaning."[62] "On hearing [the further details of] this odd story [gold plates, spectacles, translation], I changed my opinion about the paper, and, instead of viewing it any longer as a hoax upon the learned, I began to regard it as part of a scheme to cheat the farmer of his money . . . ." "The

---

[59]Charles Anthon to E.D. Howe, February 17, 1834, Ibid., 4:378, emphasis retained and added.

[60]Before Harris visited Anthon, he visited with Samuel L. Mitchell, the "vice president of Rutgers Medical College, . . . known the country over as a living encyclopedia. If Harris hoped to impress anyone with documentary proof that the Indians were brother to the Jews, he could scarcely have selected a less sympathetic scholar. For Mitchell was one of the few antiquarians of his day who believed the now established theory that the Indians had originated in eastern Asia. This theory already had a bulky though recondite literature supporting it. But even in the nineteenth century, Mongolian civilization was too remote to most Americans for the idea to be widely accepted." (Fawn M. Brodie, *No Man Knows My History: The Life of Joseph Smith the Mormon Prophet*, 2d ed., rev. and enl. [New York, NY: Alfred A. Knopf, 1972], 51).

[61]Charles Anthon to E.D. Howe, 17 February 1834, Vogel, ed., *Early Mormon Documents*, 4:378, emphasis retained.

[62]Ibid., emphasis retained.

paper was in fact a singular scrawl."[63] "I have frequently conversed with my friends on the subject, since the Mormonite excitement began, and well remember that the paper contained any thing else but *'Egyptian Hieroglyphics.'*"[64]

Jesse Townsend, a graduate of Yale University, the pastor of Palmyra's Western Presbyterian Church (the Smiths' future congregation) until about 1820, and the pastor in neighboring Sodus from 1827 to 1831, responded to a request for information about Joseph Smith by one Phineas Stiles, as follows:

> For the ten years I have known any thing of him, he has been a person of questionable character, of intemperate habits, and latterly a noted *money digger* . . . . He has had a stone, into which, when placed in a hat, he pretended to look and see chests of money buried in the earth. He was also a *fortune-teller*, and he claimed to know where stolen goods went – probably too well.[65]

> Joe Smith dare not come to Palmyra, from fear [p. 290] of his creditors; for he ran away to avoid their just demands.[66]

These excerpts (a sampling of many) give voice to the feelings of those who knew the Smiths in New York and Pennsylvania. "They are too numerous, too similar in content, and too diverse in origin to be dismissed as non-Mormon contrivances. The fact that the Smiths organized and participated in treasure digging expeditions indicates their belief in the physical reality of what they saw by second sight. Significantly, none of the Smiths' seeric adventures

---

[63]Ibid., 4:379-80.
[64]Ibid., 4:380, emphasis retained.
[65]Jesse Townsend to Phineas Stiles, 24 December 1833, Ibid., 3:21, emphasis retained.
[66]Ibid., 3:23.

yielded any real physical treasure."[67]

> *In later years Joseph found it expedient to ignore the tales by his old neighbors at Palmyra. His followers have improved upon his example. Their prophet gave them a sufficient history of his youth to run a church on, and they have never been willing to go back of that history. It has been easier to believe that there was no one of any integrity in the whole town of Palmyra than to open the door upon doubt . . . . But the picture of Joseph, his family, and their friends as indefatigable searchers after buried treasure, limned in contemporary newspapers and the recollections of their neighbors, stands forth clearly after every discount has been made for malice and dislike.[68]*

One thing is inexplicably missing from the 1830s testaments of those more than eighty neighbors and acquaintances in Palmyra and Manchester, New York, and Harmony, Pennsylvania – that is any mention of a great spiritual event supposed to have occurred in a sacred grove near Palmyra, New York, in the spring of 1820.

---

[67]Grant H. Palmer, *An Insider's View of Mormon Origins* (Salt Lake City: Signature Books, 2002), 189.

[68]Walker, ed., *Dale Morgan on Early Mormonism*, 238-39, emphasis added.

One God

For I know that God is not a partial God, neither a changeable being; but he is unchangeable from all eternity to all eternity.

Moroni 8:18

And this is Life Eternal, that they might know Thee the only true God, and Jesus Christ whom thou has sent.

John 17:3

INTRODUCTION

Joseph Smith's early complicated evangelical concept of deity is a dagger in the heart of the 1838-39 Pearl of Great Price Account of an 1820 Vision of the Father and the Son, the canonized founding story of the Church of Jesus Christ of Latter-day Saints. Until 1834 or so, Joseph Smith taught his followers that the Father and the Son were one indivisible God. This early Mormon teaching tracked nineteenth-century Protestant doctrine. Basing its modern theology on Joseph Smith's 1838-39 Pearl of Great Price Account, but ignoring Joseph Smith's 1832 one-hundred and thirty-three year suppressed one and only Holographic Account, the twenty-first century Church describes the Father and the Son as separate and distinct anthropomorphic beings, and the Holy Ghost as a personage of spirit. Joseph Smith described "two personages" in his 1838-39 Account of an 1820 vision. "*. . . I saw two Personages . . . standing above me in the air. One of them spake unto me . . . pointing to the other – This is My Beloved Son. Hear Him!*"[1] That is true or it is not.

---

[1] The Pearl of Great Price, Joseph Smith – History 1:17, emphasis retained and added.

Every Latter-day Saint is familiar with those words. This great story (only much later recognized to have been at least the fourth different account of Smith's vision) is the "hinge pin" upon which the whole cause turns. Joseph's masterpiece, the 1838-39 Account of an 1820 vision, is described verbally and distributed in pamphlet form to investigators of the Mormon Church in many different languages all over the world. It posits an event supposed to set the Mormon Church apart from all other Christian denominations. Until fairly recently relatively few Latter-day Saints, and probably none of Mormonism's investigators, ever became familiar with the details of three discrepant *1832* and *1835 Accounts* of the same event, accounts the contents of which were concealed and suppressed in the Mormon archives until the second half of the twentieth century. The implications of these late-to-the-table accounts unavailable to multigenerational Mormons until in and after 1965 are not easy to dismiss.

THE MODERN MORMON CONCEPT OF GOD

Joseph Smith's 1838-39 Pearl of Great Price Account of an 1820 Vision (the only account known to ordinary members of the Church until 1965) – first published in Edinburgh, Scotland, in 1840 by Orson Pratt, then modified and published in America in 1842 – is the canonized official account of the First Vision of the Father and the Son and sacred Mormon scripture.[2] The significance of this account of the First Vision to the Latter-day Saints can not be overstated. "Its importance," according to one prominent Mormon scholar, "is second only to belief in the divinity of Jesus of Nazareth. The story is an essential part of the first lesson given by Mormon missionaries to prospective converts, and its acceptance is necessary before baptism."[3] Another prominent Mormon scholar reports that, "[T]he First Vision of 1820 is of first importance in the history

---

[2]The Pearl of Great Price is one of the four standard works of the Church of Jesus Christ of Latter-day Saints. The others are the King James Bible ("as far as it is translated correctly"), the Book of Mormon, and the Doctrine and Covenants (which contains the published revelations of Joseph Smith, with but very few additions by some few of his successors).

[3]James B. Allen, "The Significance of Joseph Smith's 'First Vision' in Mormon Thought," *Dialogue: A Journal of Mormon Thought*, vol. 1 no. 3, (Autumn 1966): 29.

of Joseph Smith. Upon its reality rest the truth and value of his subsequent work."[4] Every Mormon missionary has recounted the details of Smith's 1820 vision repeatedly. In the late 1950s and the early 1960s, missionaries taught their investigators these particular concepts in this particular way:

Elder:	Mr. Brown . . . . In 1820 Joseph Smith . . . saw, standing above him in the air, *two personages* in the form of men . . . . Mr. Brown, who were these two personages?
Brown:	*God and Jesus Christ.*
Elder:	I know that Joseph Smith did see the Father and the Son . . . . He could see that his own body truly was created in the image and likeness of God . . . . *What do we learn about God from the experience of Joseph Smith?*
Brown:	*That he has a real body.*
Elder:	Yes, he does. The churches also taught that God the Father and Jesus Christ, his Son, were both the same person, but *what did Joseph Smith see?*
Brown:	*He saw two personages in the form of men.*[5]

From the moment Joseph Smith saw God and Jesus as a fourteen-year-old boy, he is supposed to have known that God had "a real body" and that the Father and the Son were separate. Mormon

---

[4]John A. Widtsoe, *Joseph Smith – Seeker After Truth* (Salt Lake City: Bookcraft, 1951), 19, cited by Jerald and Sandra Tanner, *The Changing World of Mormonism: "A condensation and revision of Mormonism: Shadow or Reality?"* rev. ed. (Chicago: Moody Press, 1981), 148.

[5]"A Uniform System For Teaching Investigators, Presented at Mission Presidents' School, August 1961, The Church of Jesus Christ of Latter-day Saints," 11-12, quoted in Tanner and Tanner, *Mormonism – Shadow or Reality?*, 5 ed. (Utah Lighthouse Ministry, 1987), 169, emphasis retained and added.

missionaries utilize the canonized 1838-39 Pearl of Great Price Account of Joseph Smith's Vision of the Father and the Son to enlighten investigators trapped in religions that teach false sectarian concepts of deity, doctrines attributable to "corrupt" professors, promoting abominable "creeds." "[T]hey draw near to me with their lips," Jesus told Joseph Smith, "but their hearts are far from me, they teach for doctrines the commandments of men . . . ."[6]

The Nicene Creed (or belief in one God), "followed in time by the Athanasian Creed," is singled out by the Latter-day Saints. It is, perhaps, of all of the creeds the one most particularly reviled by the missionaries. The belief that God the Father, Jesus Christ and the Holy Ghost are "one God" – that God, an unidentifiable entity "without body, parts, or passions" – is "at variance with the scriptures" and "contradicted by the revelations . . . ." "We affirm that to deny the materiality of God's person is to deny God; for a thing without parts has no whole, and an immaterial body cannot exist."[7] Those "declarations of sectarian faith" contained in the Nicene Creed exemplify for Latter-day Saints how far Christianity has fallen since the great apostasy destroyed the last vestiges of the primitive church. A church that doesn't understand the nature of God, or the characteristics of the Godhead, could only "teach for doctrines the commandments of men." The Nicene Creed, according to the Latter-day Saints, was the creation of the Roman Catholic Church (the "whore of all the earth" and the "mother of harlots"[8]). Mormons hold, whether publicly or privately, severely negative attitudes toward traditional Christianity.

"We believe in God, the Eternal Father, and in His Son Jesus Christ, and in the Holy Ghost."[9] That is the fact today, but wasn't always so. In the early Church, *and until at least 1834,* Joseph Smith and those who followed him then believed that the Father

---

[6]The Pearl of Great Price, Joseph Smith – History 1:19.

[7]James E. Talmage, *A Study of the Articles of Faith: Being a Consideration of the Principal Doctrines of The Church of Jesus Christ of Latter-day Saints*, 33rd ed. (Salt Lake City: The Church of Jesus Christ of Latter-day Saints, 1955), Article 1, 47-48.

[8]Book of Mormon, 1 Nephi 14:10, 13:34.

[9]Talmage, *A Study of the Articles of Faith*, 33rd ed., Article 1, 29.

was the Son and that the Father and the Son were one God, not so very unlike the trinitarian teachings of the Catholics and the Protestants. What had been a Protestant epiphany in Smith's one-hundred-and-thirty-three year suppressed 1832 first and only Holographic Account of a vision of Jesus Christ, a vision of but one God, what had first presented as an essentially Nicene vision of the Trinity, became in 1838-39 a great restoration event identifying two of what would only later become countless gods in modern Mormonism's evolutionary theology. The gods of this earth (one God in Joseph's first and only 1832 Holographic Account) became separate and distinct when the 1838-39 Pearl of Great Price Account of the Vision of the Father and the Son looked back to an 1820 event for redefinition. Joseph Smith's godhead gravitated from extreme monotheism in 1830 and beyond to extreme polytheism in and after 1839. The Mormon God, as history defiantly proves, is a "changeable being," endless but not eternal.[10]

Mormonism did not use the official 1838-39 Pearl of Great Price Account of the First Vision to support the modern Mormon concept of the Godhead – meaning three separate personages, two anthropomorphic beings and a personage of the spirit – for many years. Parley P. Pratt, for example, did not refer to the 1838-39 Pearl of Great Price Account in his book *A Voice of Warning*, which became the most important missionary tract of the nineteenth-century church. Pratt's book was originally published in 1854. The Protestant concept of God the Father and Jesus as spirits, and as one with the Holy Ghost (deity as a union of spirits), is no more unthinkable than the modern Mormon concept of the Holy Ghost as a personage of spirit, both material and omnipresent, or than the earlier Mormon concept that the Holy Ghost was the shared mind of God and Jesus.[11] Jesus said God is a Spirit, and who is man to say that he is not? "God *is* a Spirit: and they that worship him must worship *him* in spirit and in truth."[12]

---

[10]Book of Mormon, Moroni 8:18. "God . . . is unchangeable from all eternity to all eternity."

[11]Joseph Smith Jr., *Lectures on Faith: Prepared by the Prophet Joseph Smith, Delivered to the School of the Prophets in Kirtland, Ohio, 1834-35* (Salt Lake City: Deseret Book Company, 1985), Lecture Fifth, 60.

[12]The Holy Bible, John 4:24.

The Mormon Church stands or falls on Joseph Smith's First Vision claims. If Joseph Smith didn't see God the Father and Jesus Christ in 1820 (as he privately said in 1838-39 that he did, and as he publicly said in 1842 that he did), if God the Father and Jesus Christ were not standing above him in the air in 1820 (as he said that they were), if he did not see "*two personages* in the form of men," then the "truth and value of his subsequent work" is fatally flawed.

FROM TRINITY TO TRITHEISM

The Long After-the-Fact Vision

Joseph (and/or others) brilliantly described a glorious 1820 event in a history he is supposed to have dictated in 1838 and 1839 when he was thirty-two or -three years of age. By the time he dictated what later became the founding story of the Mormon Church, Joseph Smith had lived as long as Jesus. Having survived seismic adversity in Missouri, and faced with gathering threats to his spiritual authority, the prophet now described, albeit at first in private, the elaborate details of a stirring vision of his early youth. The 1838-39 Pearl of Great Price Account described God the Father and Jesus Christ as two separate and distinct personages. Those who drew near to Jesus with their lips – men and women who embraced the false sectarian notion that the Father and the Son were part of the same sacred trinity – had not known them up close and personal as Joseph had. In 1838-39, Joseph Smith, the prophet of the dispensation of the fullness of times, said that he had seen both God and Jesus *simultaneously*, learning first hand and for himself that the doctrine of the trinity was false. He then published the details of that transaction, for the first time in America, in the *Times and Seasons* in 1842, when he was thirty-six and twenty-two years after the alleged event.

Years passed before Joseph Smith taught his followers that God the Father, Jesus Christ and the Holy Ghost were separate – one, the Son, a physically finite personage of tabernacle; the second, the Father, a personage of spirit; the third, the Holy Spirit, not yet a personage but rather the common mind of the spirit Father and the anthropomorphic Son. Those teachings, described in the *Lectures on Faith* "Prepared by the Prophet Joseph Smith in 1834-35,"[13] became part of the Doctrine and Covenants in 1835 and remained there (and canonized) as the doctrine part of the Doctrine and Covenants for nearly ninety years. How did Joseph Smith come to know in 1834 or 1835 that the Father and the Son were two separate personages? How did Joseph Smith know the Son was anthropomorphic but that the Father was not? Joseph Smith said (but not publicly until 1842) that he saw the Father and the Son in the woods in 1820 when he was fourteen years of age, ten years before the Church was legally organized. The fact that Joseph Smith said that he had seen the Father did not deter him from distinguishing God the Father from Jesus in 1834-35, or from declaring that the Father, separate from and different than an anthropomorphic Jesus, was a personage of spirit. Nor either did it deter his successors from keeping that teaching, the doctrine part of the Doctrine and Covenants, in the Doctrine and Covenants with Joseph's other canonized revelations until 1921.

Modern missionaries tell Mormonism's investigators that as a result of the 1820 vision, Joseph knew in 1820 that the incomprehensible doctrine of the Trinity was incorrect. Joseph Smith's First Vision proved once and for all, they now say, that God the Father and Jesus Christ, *"two personages, whose brightness and glory defy all description,"* were both anthropomorphic, separate and distinct. But in that there is the germ of a problem. No one knew in 1830 that Joseph Smith had seen the Father and the Son in 1820. Furthermore, the *Lectures on Faith* prepared by Joseph Smith and Rigdon in 1834-35 described the Father as "a personage of spirit." "There are two personages who constitute the great, matchless, governing and supreme power over all things . . . . They are the Father and the Son – the Father being *a personage of spirit*, glory and power, possessing all perfection and fullness, the Son . . . *a personage of tabernacle*, made or fashioned like unto man . . . ."[14] The Holy Spirit is the "*mind*" of the spirit Father, and the mind of the anthropomorphic Son, but not a personage, "and these three are one . . . ."[15] These words, found in the Doctrine and Covenants until

---

[13]Joseph Smith, *Lectures on Faith*, Title, cover sheet.
[14]Joseph Smith, *Lectures on Faith*, Lecture Fifth, 59, emphasis added.
[15]Ibid., 60, emphasis added.

1921, were canonized. That did then later change. *Ramus, Illinois, April 2, 1843*: Changing his mind (and in defiance of the canonized *Lectures on Faith* which served to separate what until 1834-35 were indivisible deities), Joseph now reported that, "The Father has a body of flesh and bones as tangible as man's; the Son also, but the Holy Ghost has not a body of flesh and bones, but is a personage of Spirit."[16] Although the Holy Ghost wasn't a "personage" in the *Lectures on Faith* (there were only two), he is a "personage" now. "All spirit is matter," it came to be said, but "more fine and pure."[17] Thus a personage of the Spirit, by those changing standards, was thought to be plausible. This 1843 Holy Spirit, composed of "matter" but "more fine and pure," and by now a "personage," unlike those other anthropomorphic personages, is by modern Mormon reckoning omnipresent. He is in the form of a man. He is a personage. That is a bit of a stretch when one considers how the Holy Spirit is supposed to function, and that "all spirit is matter." What the Father had been in 1834-35 in the canonized *Lectures on Faith*, the Holy Ghost became in 1843. What the Son had been in the canonized *Lectures on Faith* in 1834-35, the Father became in 1843.

THE TESTIMONY OF THREE WITNESSES

The Three Witnesses to the Book of Mormon adopted Joseph's early essentially trinitarian view of the Godhead in 1830 in a highly visible statement that couldn't be changed. After they said that they saw an angel and heard the voice of God, and after they said that they saw the golden plates, they offered this generous benediction: *"And the honor be to the Father, and to the Son, and to the Holy Ghost, which is one God. Amen."*[18] What did the witnesses mean by that? The Three Witnesses to the Book of Mormon solemnly affirmed in 1830 in a statement they didn't sign that wasn't notarized – ten years after the supposed but then unknown 1820 vision of the Father and the Son, and twelve years before the 1842 first American publication of an account of it – that all honor was owed to the Father and to the Son and to the Holy Ghost,

---

[16]Doctrine and Covenants 130:22.
[17]Doctrine and Covenants 131:7.
[18]Book of Mormon, "The Testimony of Three Witnesses," emphasis added.

"which is one God."   The statement, which was singular and consistent with his other early teachings, was prepared by Joseph Smith. The declaration was not ambiguous, required no allegorical interpretation, and left no room for doubt.

After acting as witnesses, Smith's trusted relatives and allies described God in evangelical terms. Whatever Joseph is supposed to have known in consequence of some 1820 vision wasn't known to the Three Witnesses in 1830. They didn't know that Joseph had seen God and Jesus, who were not indivisible, and neither did anyone else. The lessons of 1820 were lost on them, and on the author of the highly visible, plain spoken unambiguous trinitarian document, the Testimony of Three Witnesses.

THE BOOK OF MORMON

The nature of God did not come to rest in the Book of Mormon, but rather evolved. Moroni knew that God was not "a changeable being,"[19] but Joseph Smith did not. The most correct of any book on earth and the prophet of the restoration, when those issues finally came to rest, told different stories about the nature of God. In the *first* edition of the Book of Mormon (published in 1830), the prophet Nephi, while conversing with an angel in a vision, described this heavenly message: "Knowest thou the condescension of God? ... *[T]he virgin which thou seest, is the mother of God, after the manner of the flesh.*"[20] "And I . . . beheld the virgin again, bearing a child in her arms. And the angel said unto me, behold the Lamb of God, yea, even the Eternal Father!"[21] "And I looked [again] and beheld the Lamb of God, that he was taken by the people; yea, the Everlasting God, was judged of the world; . . . . And I, Nephi, saw

---

[19]Book of Mormon, Moroni 8:18.

[20]Grant H. Palmer, *An Insider's View of Mormon Origins* (Salt Lake City: Signature Books, 2002), 121, citing Wilford C. Wood, *Joseph Smith Begins His Work, Volume I: Book of Mormon, 1830 First Edition: Reproduced from uncut sheets* (USA: Wilford C. Wood, 1962; lithographed, Salt Lake City: Publishers Press, 1995), 1:25.   This footnote, and the three footnotes that follow, are referenced at Palmer, *An Insider's View of Mormon Origins*, 121, where references to chapter and verse in Palmer's 1981 edition of the Book of Mormon are also found.

[21]Book of Mormon (1830), 25.

that he was lifted up upon the cross, and slain for the sins of the world."[22] *The "Eternal Father," the "Everlasting God," the child in the arms of the virgin – the mother of God in the flesh – was crucified.* "[T]he Lamb of God is the Eternal Father and the Saviour of the world."[23] The "Lamb of God is the Eternal Father"? Jesus is the "Eternal Father and the Saviour of the world"? The "Everlasting God"? God the Eternal Father "was lifted up upon the cross, and slain for the sins of the world"? Are Nephi (who "saw the Heavens open") and the angel ("who came down and stood before me"[24]) somehow dreadfully confused? The Book of Mormon crucified a trinitarian Father.

The prophet Abinadi taught "that Christ was *the* God, *the* Father of all things." And he said "that God should come down among the children of men, and take upon him flesh and blood,"[25] "and take upon him the form of man, ..."[26] "Christ was *the* God, *the* Father of all things"? This 1830 Book of Mormon God was not anthropomorphic. The Book of Mormon God wasn't "flesh and blood" in his preexistent state. Not until he came down among the children of men did he take upon himself flesh and blood and the form of man. The virgin Mary was the mother of God after the manner of the flesh. The Prophet Abinadi's Book of Mormon God was a preexistent spirit. The brother of Jared's Book of Mormon God was a preexistent spirit. Jared saw "the finger of the Lord" and "feared lest he should smite me." "I knew not," he said, "that the Lord had flesh and blood." The Lord responded and said, "Because of thy faith thou hast seen that *I shall take upon me flesh and blood . . . .*"[27] The God of the brother of Jared said that he was Jesus Christ ("Behold, I am Jesus Christ. *I am the Father and the Son.*") and that he had been "prepared from the foundation of the world to redeem my people." Jesus showed himself to the brother of Jared and shared this great secret: "*Behold, this body, which ye now behold, is the body of my spirit; and man have I created after the body of my spirit; and even as I appear unto thee to be in the spirit will*

---

[22]Ibid., 26.
[23]Ibid., 32.
[24]Ibid., 24.
[25]Book of Mormon, Mosiah 7:27, emphasis added.
[26]Ibid., Mosiah 13:34.
[27]Ibid., Ether 3:8-9, emphasis added.

I appear unto my people in the flesh."[28]   Moroni (while busy abridging the plates of Ether) said, "*Jesus showed himself to this man in the spirit . . . .*"[29]

Moroni's God was "unchangeable."   How shall the teachings of Nephi, the teachings of the angel who instructed Nephi, and those of Abinadi, the Brother of Jared and Moroni, treating the deity as a spirit, be distinguished from the teachings of evangelical Christians practicing nineteenth-century Christianity in and around Palmyra, New York? According to Abinadi, "God himself" will come. "And because he dwelleth in flesh he shall be called the Son of God, and having subjected the flesh to the will of the Father, being the Father and the Son. The Father, because he was conceived by the power of God, and the Son, because of the flesh; thus becoming the Father and the Son – *And they are one God, yea, the very Eternal Father of heaven and earth.*"[30]   This is not logic; this is revelation. Like Christ's even earlier representations to the Brother of Jared, it does not invite allegorical interpretation.

This God did not dwell in the flesh until he came down "among the children of men." And when he came to dwell in the flesh, because he was conceived by the power of God (both begetter and begotten), and because he subjected the flesh to the will of the Father, he was to "be called the Son of God," "being [then] the Father and the Son," "becoming [then] the Father and the Son." *And they*, God the Father and Jesus Christ, "becoming the Father and the Son," *are* "*one God, yea, the very Eternal Father of heaven and earth.*" This is not logic; this is Book of Mormon revelation. "*Teach them,*" Abinadi says, "*that redemption cometh through Christ the Lord, who is the very Eternal Father. Amen.*"[31]   Is Abinadi dreadfully confused? Has this Book of Mormon prophet fallen victim to sectarian double-talk?   Are Abinadi's words by any measure imprecise? Abinadi instructed them – before the coming of Christ – that the Father was the Son. The "one God" the first edition of the Book of Mormon and the Three Witnesses described in 1830 was a trinitarian (or "essentially Trinitarian") deity.

---

[28]Ibid., Ether 3:8, 9, 13, 14, 16, emphasis added.
[29]Ibid., Ether 3:17, emphasis added.
[30]Ibid., Mosiah 15:1-4, emphasis added.
[31]Ibid., Mosiah 16:15, emphasis added.

Amulek (another Nephite prophet) agrees with Nephi, the angel who instructed Nephi, Abinadi, the Brother of Jared and Moroni. "Now Zeezrom ["a man who was expert in the devices of the devil"] said [to Amulek]: *Is there more than one God? And he [Amulek] answered No. Now Zeezrom said unto him again: How knowest thou these things. And he [Amulek] said: An angel hath made them known unto me.*"[32] Then Zeezrom said again: "*Is the Son of God the very Eternal Father? And Amulek said unto him: 'Yea, he is the very Eternal Father of heaven and of earth, and all things which in them are; he is the beginning and the end, the first and the last.'*"[33] A firstborn Son in the Spirit is not the beginning or the end, the first or the last. An only begotten Son in the flesh is not the beginning or the end, the first or the last. Amulek then summarized and said that when "everything shall be restored to its perfect frame," all should be brought and "arraigned before the bar of *Christ the Son, and God the Father, and the Holy Spirit, which is one Eternal God,* to be judged according to their works."[34] The Trinity, singular ("*which is*"), shall judge.

The Book of Mormon, like Jesus in the meridian of time, described God as a Spirit. Ammon posed the spirit question to King Lamoni: "*Believest thou that there is a Great Spirit? And he said, Yea. And Ammon said: This is God.*"[35] The message of the Book of Mormon's prophets was: *God – in his heaven – is a Spirit.* In the book's most striking epiphany, the Brother of Jared learned and taught his people that *God – in his heaven – is a Spirit.* More than a century later, in the Gospel of John, Jesus would say to Israel what Ammon said to King Lamoni. "*God is a Spirit: and they that worship him must worship him in spirit and truth.*"[36] Why would Jesus intentionally mislead those who faithfully followed him? Why would Jesus seek to confuse them?

By 1843,[37] Joseph had changed his mind and his theology to say that

---

[32]Ibid., Alma 11:21, 28-31, emphasis added.
[33]Ibid., Alma 11:38-39, emphasis.
[34]Ibid., Alma 11:43-44, emphasis added.
[35]Ibid., Alma 18:26-28, emphasis added.
[36]The Holy Bible, John 4:24, emphasis added.
[37]"During the Nauvoo period of 1839 to 1844, Joseph began to teach the corporeality of the Father, the plurality of gods, and that humans can become gods." These teachings later caused "confusion . . . among members of the

God the Father, like God the Son, had a body of flesh and bones. The Book of Mormon identified the Father as a preexistent Spirit. It said the Father was the Son. It said that the Father and the Son were one God. Joseph's Ramus, Illinois, declaration (April 2, 1843) that the Father was corporeal[38] followed the 1820 vision by twenty-three years. Joseph's declaration that the Father and the Son were separate and distinct and that the Father was a spirit personage (in the canonized *Lectures on Faith*) followed the 1820 vision by fourteen or fifteen years.

How could Joseph Smith, who said in 1842 that he saw the Lamb of God and the Eternal Father in 1820, have made so many colossal mistakes after 1820? No amount of clever sophistry can change the fact that Book of Mormon prophets described the Son as *"the very Eternal Father of heaven and earth,"* the Eternal Father as a spirit, the Father as the Son, and the Father and the Son as *"one Eternal God."* Then *"the virgin"* as *"the mother of God, after the manner of the flesh."* Furthermore, the Book of Mormon crucified the Father. James E. Talmage, a respected Mormon scholar, famously criticized ancient creeds that promoted concepts confidently described by the prophets in the Book of Mormon. Talmage said this of the creeds: "It would be difficult to conceive of a greater number of inconsistencies and contradictions expressed in words as few."[39] Talmage had in mind the doctrine of the Trinity, the Nicene and Athanasian Creeds.[40] Unhampered by semantic distortion, the Book of Mormon promoted a form of the Trinity.

If the Book of Mormon is a divinely inspired history of the ancient inhabitants of North and South America, if it was translated by the gift and power of God, and if it contains the fullness of the everlasting Gospel, then the Father and the Son are not distinct physically finite beings. If Joseph Smith was right when he said – some time after the *Lectures on Faith* in 1834 – that the Father and the Son evolved to become two separate and distinct anthropo-

---

Church" who found them to conflict with the "teachings of the Book of Mormon." (Boyd Kirkland, quoted in Earl M. Wunderli, *An Imperfect Book: What the Book of Mormon Tells Us About Itself* [Salt Lake City: Signature Books, 2013], 292).

[38]Doctrine and Covenants 130:22.

[39]Talmage, *A Study of the Articles of Faith*, 33rd ed., Article 1, 48.

[40]Ibid., Article 1, 47.

morphic beings, then he was wrong when he said before 1834 that they were not, and when he said in 1832 that *the "crucifyed"* Lord who visited him on the occasion of his first encounter with deity was *"omnipotant and omnipreasant,"* by that to say a Spirit. The same kind of Spirit that had earlier revealed himself to the Brother of Jared. And if Joseph was ultimately right, then God, the prophet Nephi, the angel who instructed the prophet Nephi, the prophet Amulek, the angel who instructed the prophet Amulek, the prophet Abinadi, Ammon, the Brother of Jared, Moroni, the Book of Mormon and the Three Witnesses were all wrong. *Joseph Smith started his ministry (one may take this to the bank) as a committed monotheist who believed in one god.* When considered carefully against all early Mormon resources, that proposition is undeniable.

Before some of its provisions were secretly amended in 1837 to separate the Father from the Son, and even after those amendments, the Book of Mormon, assigned the very names, titles and glories of God to Jesus. *"JESUS is the CHRIST, the ETERNAL GOD . . . ."*[41] *Mary is called the "mother of God." Jesus is called "the Christ," "the Eternal God," "the Father," "the Father and the Son," "the Redeemer," "the Creator," "the Creator of all things from the beginning," "the Father of the heavens and of the earth, and all things that in them are," "the light, and the life, and the truth of the world," "Alpha and Omega," "the first and the last," "the beginning and the end," "the Lamb of God," "the Savior of the world," "the Eternal Father," "the very Eternal Father of heaven and earth," "Christ the Lord, who is the very Eternal Father," "the Eternal Ruler" and "the Father of Eternity." "Christ was God, the Father of all things," "the Everlasting God," "the King of all the earth," "the King of heaven," "the King of the Kingdom of Heaven," "the only Begotten," "the Lord your God," the "Lord God," "one God" ("thou shalt have no other God before me"), "the Lord Omnipotent," "Christ, the Lord God Omnipotent," "the author of everlasting salvation and eternal life," "the God of Abraham, and Isaac, and Jacob," and "that God who brought the children of Israel out of the land of Egypt, . . . and fed them . . . manna . . . in the wilderness." He was "the MOST HIGH GOD,"* the Son of God and a Spirit *("that Great Spirit [who] created all things both in heaven and in earth").* And in the first

---

[41]Book of Mormon, Title page.

(1832 Holographic and Suppressed) Account of the First Vision he is further described as "an omnipotant and omnipreasant power," meaning all powerful and present in all places at all times. Joseph's Book of Mormon Messiah was all powerful, everywhere present, infinite, underived, truly eternal, and a Spirit. Then, and finally, "GOD ABOVE ALL."

In the Book of Mormon, the Father Was the Son

If Joseph Smith authored the Book of Mormon, and if it is not a literal history of ancient civilizations rooted in antiquity (a faithful history of Hebrews), then Joseph Smith didn't know in 1829 and 1830 (when the Book was written and published and the Church was being formed) that God the Father and Jesus Christ were separate beings. "One would expect to find this foundational doctrine [separate and distinct beings] taught clearly and in 'plainness' in this important second 'witness for Christ.' Yet this is not the case. In 2 Nephi 31:21 and in the 'Testimony of Three Witnesses,' we read of 'the Father, and of the Son and of the Holy Ghost, *which is* one God.'"[42] "The LDS church today teaches that God the Father and Jesus Christ are two separate and distinct beings but the Book of Mormon does not."[43]

The 1830 first edition of the Book of Mormon reports that, "These last records, . . . shall make known to all kindreds, tongues and people, *that the Lamb of God is the Eternal Father and the Saviour of the world; . . . .*"[44] The Nephite records proclaim, as an eternal truth, that *"the Lamb of God is the Eternal Father."* In later editions of the Book of Mormon, those words – engraved on metal plates – were changed to read as follows: "These last records, . . . shall make known to all kindreds, tongues and people, *that the Lamb of God is the Son of the Eternal Father and the Savior of the world; . . . .*"[45] Mary then also became *"the mother of the Son of God,"* rather than *"the mother of God."* These changes and others

---

[42]Ibid., 2 Nephi 31:21, cited at Palmer, *An Insider's View of Mormon Origins*, 121, emphasis added.
[43]Ibid.
[44]Book of Mormon (1830), 32, emphasis added.
[45]Book of Mormon, 1 Nephi 13:40, emphasis added.

of the same or similar import were made in 1837 unannounced. The nature of the godhead described in the Book of Mormon, and other doctrinal restorations of the "fullness of the gospel" in the Book of Mormon, "are closer to evangelical Protestantism than either ancient Jewish or current LDS belief." The teachings of the Book of Mormon are compatible with the evangelical teachings of the nineteenth-century churches.[46] Until 1837, when the Book was surreptitiously amended, the Book taught for doctrine what Mormons later described as "the commandments of men, having a form of godliness." Even after those amendments, and still today, the Book reflects the views of those "corrupt" professors and their abominable creeds.

Until approximately 1834 – fourteen years after Joseph only very much later reported that he saw "two Personages, whose brightness and glory defy all description, standing above me in the air" – Joseph Smith – then a monotheist – taught his followers that the Lamb of God was the Eternal Father *and* the Savior of the world. The title page of the Book of Mormon tells its purpose. *It is "to the convincing of the Jew and Gentile that JESUS is the CHRIST, the ETERNAL GOD."*[47] *In Joseph Smith's Book of Mormon, the Father was the Son.*

THE BOOK OF COMMANDMENTS

The Book of Mormon essentially described the "traditional Christian God," a deity who was "unchangeable." How could Mormonism's founder, who was supposed to have seen the Father and the Son in 1820, describe just one indivisible deity in 1830, an unchangeable being supposed to be "the same yesterday, today and forever"?[48] A God who is "the same yesterday, today and forever" cannot be "a work in progress." The very presence of this passage borrowed from the Apostle "Paul's late first- or early second-century writings"[49] in the Book of Mormon in the reformed Egyptian before the Babylonian captivity, before there was a mortal

---

[46]Palmer, *An Insider's View of Mormon Origins*, 123.
[47]Book of Mormon, Title page, emphasis added.
[48]Ibid., 1 Nephi 10:18, quoted in Wunderli, *An Imperfect Book*, 290.
[49]The Holy Bible, Hebrews 13:8.

Messiah, a Paul or a passage, is a preposterous Book of Mormon anachronism.[50]

The Articles and Covenants published in the Book of Commandments in 1833 read as follows:

> *[W]e know that there is a God in heaven, who is infinite and eternal, from everlasting to everlasting, the same unchangeable God, the maker of heaven and earth and all things that in them is, and that he created man male and female, and after his own image, and in his own likeness created he them;*
>
> *And that he gave unto the children of men commandments, that they should love and serve him the only being whom they should worship, ...*
>
> Wherefore, the Almighty God gave his only begotton Son . . . .
>
> That he was crucified, died, and rose again the third day, and that he ascended into heaven to sit down on the right hand of the Father, to reign with Almighty power according to the will of the Father. ...
>
> *Yea . . . the Holy Ghost, which truly testified of him in all things . . . beareth record of the Father and of the Son,* <u>*which*</u> *Father and Son and Holy Ghost, is one God, infinite and eternal, without end. Amen.*[51]

This God ("one God") is the "*only* being" whom "the children of men" should worship. The worship of any God other than this "*only*" God, this "*one God*," was idolatry. Shall the Father not be the object of such worship? Is the Father not "the maker of heaven and earth"? Is man not made in the image of the Eternal Father? This Christ is not described as some "firstborn Son in the Spirit,"

---

[50]Wunderli, *An Imperfect Book*, 290.

[51]Articles and Covenants of the Church of Christ, June 1830, Book of Commandments, 24:13-18, emphasis added. Compare with Doctrine and Covenants 20:17-28.

finite, twice birthed, and less than eternal, but rather as the underived, "infinite," "unchangeable" and "only" evangelical God. For this "JESUS is the CHRIST, the ETERNAL GOD."[52]

The Holy Ghost "beareth record" of the Father and the Son, "which Father and Son and Holy Ghost, *is one God, infinite and eternal, without end.*" Is this not plain language? Isn't this revealed? The deities "*is*" singular, three "*is*" one, and Christ is "eternal." This is not about logic, but rather the revealed word of God.

If the Father literally begat the Son in the spirit and in the flesh in the way that parents beget their children, the Son is not eternal. Then he is not "from everlasting to everlasting, but rather finite, created, derived, subordinate to his creator. While such a creation – creations are creatures – was "endless," a created Christ was not "eternal," meaning without father, mother or descent, beginning of days or end of years. So the question became how could a finite "creature" affect an infinite atonement? The 1830 Articles and Covenants published in the Book of Commandments in 1833, "the Testimony of Three Witnesses," and the teachings of the Book of Mormon concur to conclude that there "*is one God, infinite and eternal, without end,*" and that that infinite and eternal God, the Book of Mormon's Messiah, is "*the only being whom they should worship.*" The Book of Commandments was a further reflection of Joseph Smith's early (and undeniable) monotheism.

THE DOCTRINE AND COVENANTS AND UNPUBLISHED REVELATIONS

In a revelation given to Oliver Cowdery, Hiram Page, Josiah Stowell and Joseph Knight at Manchester, New York, *Circa Early 1830 and unpublished*, Jesus ("Behold I the Lord am God") tells these prominent servants that "I Created the Heavens & the Earth & all things that in them is wherefore they are mine & I sway my scepter over all the Earth & ye are in my hands . . . ."[53] "Behold I

---

[52]Book of Mormon, Title page.
[53]"23 Commandment AD 1830, Revelation Book 1," *The Joseph Smith Papers: Revelations and Translations: Manuscript Revelation Books, Facsimile Edition*, ed.

am God," he says. "I have spoken it . . . ."[54] And in provisions stricken from the unpublished revelation by "An unidentified scribe," "Behold I Am God" also said this: "& I grant unto my servent a privelige that he may sell <a [Book of Mormon] copyright> through you speaking after the manner of men for the four Provinces [Canada] . . . ." "*Behold*," Jesus speaking says, "*I am the father & it is through mine o{◊\nly} begotten* which is Jesus Christ your Redeemer amen[.]"[55] Jesus is "the father" and "Jesus Christ your Redeemer" is Jesus the father's only begotten Son ("*mine o{◊\nly} begotten*").[56]   Jesus, who is the Father, is the Begetter and the Begotten. *Can that be denied?*

Jesus was assigned (by John Whitmer) the title "Lord God." "W{◊\herefore}," he said, "I <the Lord God> will send <forth> flies . . . ."[57] "Wherefore I the Lord God [now Jesus assigned to himself the title "Lord God"] caused that he should be cast out from the Garden of Edan from my presence because of his transgression . . . ."[58] "But Behold I [Jesus speaking] say unto you that I *the Lord God* gave unto Adam & unto his seed that they should not Die as to the temporal death untill *I the Lord God* should send forth Angels to declare unto them Repentance =ance & redemption through faith *on the name of mine only begotten Son* & thus did I *the Lord God* appoint unto man the days of his probation . . . ."[59] *The Lord God, Jesus speaking says, that redemption was contingent upon faith "on the name of mine only begotten Son." Jesus is the Lord God and the Redeemer is the Lord God's "only begotten Son."* The Lord God is

---

Robin Scott Jensen, Robert J. Woodford, and Steven C. Harper (Salt Lake City: The Church Historian's Press, 2009), 31.

[54]Ibid., 33. "Wherefore be diligent in Securing the Copy right of my ~~Servent~~ work upon all the face of the Earth . . . ."

[55]Ibid., emphasis added.

[56]Ibid., emphasis added.

[57]"29th Commandment AD, September 1830, Revelation Book 1," *The Joseph Smith Papers: Revelations and Translations: Manuscript Revelation Books, Facsimile Edition*, 45. Doctrine and Covenants 29:18.

[58]"29th Commandment AD, September 1830, Revelation Book 1," *The Joseph Smith Papers: Revelations and Translations: Manuscript Revelation Books, Facsimile Edition*, 49. Doctrine and Covenants 29:41.

[59]"29th Commandment AD, September 1830, Revelation Book 1," *The Joseph Smith Papers: Revelations and Translations: Manuscript Revelation Books, Facsimile Edition*, 49, 51, emphasis added. Doctrine and Covenants 29:42-43.

yet again the Begetter and the Begotten, because the Father is the Son. *Can that be denied?*

Here Jesus decides when Adam shall die and the conditions of his probation. Here Jesus assigns a Father's title ("Lord God") to himself and says that Jesus ("mine only begotten Son") is Jesus the Lord God's Son.[60] Jesus is Adam's God. Jesus is the Father and Jesus is his own "only begotten Son." Jesus "laid the foundation of the Earth." Jesus "made the Heavens" and "all the hosts" of the Heavens. By this Jesus "all things were made." Whatever lives and moves and has a being, Jesus made. He is mankind's "advocate with the Father." He is "Alpha & Omega," the "Begining & the end," the "light & life of the world," and "a light that shineth in darkness."[61] He "has all power" and is "from everlasting to everlasting."[62] *"[T]hus saith the Lord [Jesus] for I am God & have sent mine o{Ɐ\nly} begotten Son into the world for the redemption of the world & have decreed that he that receiveth him shall be saved & he that receiveth him not shall be damned . . . ."*[63] The Lord is God. Jesus, Joseph's revelator and God, the Lord God and the Father, is his own only Begotten. *Can that be denied?*

"Hear," Christ says, "O ye heavens, & give ear, O earth, & rejoice ye inhabitants thereof, *for the Lord he is God, & beside him there is none else*; & great is his wisdom; . . . ." "I the Lord am mercyful & gracious unto them who fear me . . . ."[64] The Lord is God and Jesus, and *"beside him there is none else."* Could Jesus say this if

---

[60]"29th Commandment AD, September 1830, Revelation Book 1," *The Joseph Smith Papers: Revelations and Translations: Manuscript Revelation Books, Facsimile Edition*, 49, 51.

[61]"47, A prophecy, March 7th 1831, Revelation Book 1," *The Joseph Smith Papers: Revelations and Translations: Manuscript Revelation Books, Facsimile Edition*, 115. Doctrine and Covenants 45:1, 3, 7.

[62]"64 Commandment given Aug 12th 1831, Revelation Book 1," *The Joseph Smith Papers: Revelations and Translations: Manuscript Revelation Books, Facsimile Edition*, 175 (August 12, 1831). Doctrine and Covenants 61:1.

[63]"51st Commandment, May 7th 1831, Revelation Book 1," *The Joseph Smith Papers: Revelations and Translations: Manuscript Revelation Books, Facsimile Edition*, 133, emphasis added. Doctrine and Covenants 49:5.

[64]"A Vision of Joseph and Sidney [Rigdon], Revelation Book 1," *The Joseph Smith Papers: Revelations and Translations: Manuscript Revelation Books, Facsimile Edition*, 243 (February 16, 1832), emphasis added. Doctrine and Covenants 76:1-2.

"beside him" there was another higher God? This is monotheism. The following words spoken by the Savior in 1832, when Joseph believed in one God, were changed in the 76th section of the Doctrine and Covenants published in 1835, when Joseph believed in two gods.

From: "*[F]or the Lord he is God, & beside him there is none else . . .*"[65]

To: "*[F]or the Lord is God, and beside him there is no Savior.*"[66]

The surreptitious revision, made by figures unknown, changes Jesus from the *only* God ("beside him there is none else") to the *only* Savior ("beside him there is no Savior").[67] But it is Jesus who will punish the wicked. "[S]aith the Lord Almighty I will rend their kingdoms I will not only shake the earth but the Starry <heavens> {. . . Shall tremble} . . . ."[68] And It Is Jesus whose kingdom is to come. "[K]now that I am and that I will come and reign with my people I am Alpha and Omega the begining and the end Amen."[69]

When the Church published James E. Talmage's *Jesus the Christ* in 1915, Jesus was identified as Jehovah, the God of the Old Testament. In 1916, the Church issued "A Doctrinal Exposition by the First Presidency and the Twelve" on the subject of the "Father and the Son." This directive is now "the official position of the

[65]"A Vision of Joseph and Sidney [Rigdon], Revelation Book 1," *The Joseph Smith Papers: Revelations and Translations: Manuscript Revelation Books, Facsimile Edition*, 243 (February 16, 1832), emphasis added.

[66]Doctrine and Covenants (1835 ed.), 76:1 (February 16, 1832), emphasis added.

[67]Another change made by Oliver Cowdery adds the words "For thus saith the Lord." From "I the Lord am mercyful and gracious unto them <those> who fear me . . ." ("The Vision, Revelation Book 2," *The Joseph Smith Papers: Revelations and Translations: Manuscript Revelation Books, Facsimile Edition*, 415 [February 16, 1832]) to "For thus saith the Lord, I, the Lord, am merciful and gracious unto <those> who fear me, ..." (Doctrine and Covenants 76:5).

[68]"A Revelation given at Kirtland, September 22 & 23, 1832, Revelation Book 1," *The Joseph Smith Papers: Revelations and Translations: Manuscript Revelation Books, Facsimile Edition*, 289. Doctrine and Covenants 84:118.

[69]"A Revelation given at Kirtland, September 22 & 23, 1832, Revelation Book 1," *The Joseph Smith Papers: Revelations and Translations: Manuscript Revelation Books, Facsimile Edition*, 289. Doctrine and Covenants 84:119-20.

church."[70]   "[W]hen Benjamin says that Christ (Jehovah) is 'the Lord Omnipotent' who reigns 'from all eternity to all eternity' and was the Creator of all things from the beginning (Mosiah 3:5, 8, 17, 18), it does not sound like there is any God prior to or greater than Jehovah."[71] By this reckoning Jehovah died on the cross.

THE BOOK OF MOSES

Jesus spoke to Moses and said: "Behold, I am the Lord God Almighty, and Endless is my name,[72] *for I am without beginning of days or end of years, and is not this endless."*[73] Modern Mormonism's "firstborn Son in the spirit" is not without "beginning of days." Modern Mormonism's "only begotten son" in the flesh is not without mother, father, descent or "beginning of days." *Jesus (Jehovah) spoke to Moses and said*: "And I have a work for thee, Moses, my son; and thou art in the similitude of mine Only Begotten [Jesus, the God of the Old Testament, is speaking to Moses]; and mine Only Begotten [Jesus, this God of the Old Testament in his human mode] is and shall be the Savior, for he is full of grace and truth; *but there is no God beside me* [Jesus speaking], and all things are present with me, for I know them all."[74]

Here Jesus speaks of himself, yet again, as both the Father *and* the Son, and as his own "mine Only Begotten," not as two but rather as one. Jesus in the flesh is Jesus the Spirit Revelator's "mine Only Begotten." And beside him, Jesus the Revelator, his own "mine Only Begotten" and soon to be Savior, there is no other God (*"but there is no God beside me"*). He is the Father, he is also the Son, and he is the only God. Could Jesus say that he is the Father *and* the Son *and* the only God in the face of another Father? If there was a higher god, and he was not the Father? Only the Father could say what Jesus said.

---

[70]Wunderli, *An Imperfect Book*, 292.
[71]Ibid., 298 fn 65.
[72]The God that spoke to Moses, "*the Lord God Almighty*," though Jesus, was literally the son of no one. He was without beginning of days or end of years.
[73]The Pearl of Great Price, Moses 1:3, emphasis added.
[74]Ibid., Moses 1:6, emphasis added.

"And it came to pass that the Lord [meaning Jesus] spake unto Moses, saying: Behold, I reveal unto you concerning this heaven, and this earth; write the words which I speak. *I am the Beginning and the End, the Almighty God; by mine Only Begotten I created these things; yea, in the beginning I created the heaven, and the earth upon which thou standest.*"[75] Moses is the revelator's son. The revelator is the Eternal Father,[76] the "*Lord God Almighty*," and "*Endless*" is his name. The revelator, the Father *and* Jesus, *is* "*mine* Only Begotten," meaning the Father in his human mode. He is the creator of *heaven* and earth. He is the beginning and the end and endless. Joseph's revelator is Jesus, God Almighty and God Almighty's "Only Begotten," and Moses is in the similitude of "mine Only Begotten; and mine Only Begotten is and shall be the Savior, for he is full of grace and truth."[77] Jesus is the Eternal Father, and Jesus is the Eternal Father's "Only Begotten," and beside him "*there is no God.*" The Book of Moses reports that the God of heaven, meaning Jesus, spoke to Moses and said, "*there is no God beside me.*"

In the Book of Moses, "*I, God*" said let there be light, divided the light from the darkness, called the dry land Earth, made the beasts of the earth after their kind, and planted a garden eastward in Eden.[78] That God was Jesus. After an I-ectomy, further consideration, and later in what came to be called the Book of Abraham, "*the Gods*" said let there be light, divided the light from the darkness, pronounced the dry land earth, organized the earth to bring forth the beasts after their kind and planted a garden eastward in Eden.[79] The "*I God*" who then became "*the Gods*" was not unchangeable. He became a work in process. Thus did the doctrine progress from one God – "the Lord he is God" and "beside him there is none else,"[80] from "And the honor be to the Father,

---

[75]Ibid., Moses 2:1, emphasis added.

[76]"JESUS is the CHRIST, the ETERNAL GOD." (Book of Mormon, Title page).

[77]The Pearl of Great Price, Moses 1:3, 6.

[78]Ibid., Moses 2:3, 4, 10, 25; 3:8.

[79]Ibid., Abraham 4:3, 4, 10, 25; 5:8. Tanner and Tanner, *Mormonism – Shadow or Reality?*, 163.

[80]*The Joseph Smith Papers: Revelations and Translations: Manuscript Revelation Books, Facsimile Edition*, 243 (February 16, 1832).

and to the Son, and to the Holy Ghost, which is one God"[81] – to two Gods – "the Father being a personage of spirit," the Son being "a personage of tabernacle," but "possessing the same mind with the Father, which mind is the Holy Spirit"[82]; from "I saw two Personages, whose brightness and glory defy all description, standing above me in the air"[83] – to three Gods and tritheism – "We believe in God, the Eternal Father, and in his Son, Jesus Christ, and in the Holy Ghost."[84]

THE JOSEPH SMITH TRANSLATION OF
THE KING JAMES BIBLE

The essentially trinitarian conceptions described in the "Testimony of Three Witnesses," in the Book of Mormon, the Book of Commandments and the Book of Moses are further perfected in Joseph Smith's "Inspired" translation of the King James Bible. In that translation he clarifies ambiguities in order to make his monotheism unequivocal. Grant H. Palmer describes those early inspirations.

> [S]ome of Joseph's doctrinal changes in the JST [Joseph Smith Translation] are at odds with current LDS beliefs. For example, [the] KJV [King James Version] Luke 10:22 reads: "[N]o man knoweth who the Son is, but the Father; and who the Father is, but the Son, and he to whom the Son will reveal him." The JST reads: "[N]o man knoweth that the Son is the Father, and the Father is the Son, but him to whom the Son will reveal it [as he did repeatedly in the passages we have seen]." In 1 Timothy 2:4, Joseph expands the verse to clarify that the Father and Son "is one God." This view is consistent with Joseph's

---

[81]Book of Mormon, The Testimony of Three Witnesses.
[82]*Lectures on Faith*, 59-60. "How many personages are there in the Godhead? Two: the Father and Son." (Ibid., Questions and Answers, Lecture Fifth, 61).
[83]The Pearl of Great Price, Joseph Smith – History 1:17.
[84]Talmage, *A Study of the Articles of Faith*, 33rd ed., Article 1, 29.

other scriptural writings of 1829-34 but not with his later thought.[85]

From 1829 to at least 1834, Joseph Smith was an unrepentant monotheist. In this corrected passage from the Inspired Translation, Joseph Smith goes beyond the teachings of the Christian Bible to flat out decide the trinity issue for his early followers: "*THE SON IS THE FATHER, AND THE FATHER IS THE SON.*" And in the Timothy passage, Joseph expands that declaration further to say that the Father and Son "*IS ONE GOD.*" In this interpretation Joseph alters the Christian Bible to further support his early monotheistic theology. *This transparent refinement dated 1832 posits a challenge to the 1838-39 Account of an 1820 vision of the Father and the Son (the vision "That becomes the hinge pin on which this whole cause turns."[86]).*

In the King James Version of the Bible, there is a controversial provision at 1 John 5:7 which reads as follows: "*For there are three that bear record in heaven, the Father, the Word, and the Holy Ghost: and these three are one.*" That passage, which was once considered authentic, now is not. Biblical scholars describe the passage as an interpolation added by trinitarians to later and less authentic texts. In various modern versions of the Christian Bible, 1 John 5:7-8 has been removed in order "to [more nearly] conform with the ancient Greek manuscripts." "The text is found in no Greek MSS, except a few of very late date in which it has been inserted from the Latin." The suspicious text found a place in the King James Bible (after it had spread over Europe) "as an unequivocal Scripture 'proof' of the doctrine of the Trinity."[87] Those who put that passage in the Bible in an auspicious place, and those who left it there after they should have known better, did what they did in support of the doctrine of the Trinity.[88]

---

[85]Palmer, *An Insider's View of Mormon Origins*, 11-12, emphasis added.

[86]Gordon B. Hinckley, "Messages of Inspiration from President Hinckley," *Church News* (1 Feb. 1997), 2.

[87]Tanner and Tanner, *Mormonism – Shadow or Reality?*, 389, citing *Our Bible and the Ancient Manuscripts*, 258, emphasis added.

[88]"Trinitarian theology permits such a paradox as having the Son on earth while the Father is in heaven as is depicted in the New Testament and in 3 Nephi, while at the same time proclaiming there is only one God." (Boyd Kirkland,

In the JST (Joseph Smith Translation) of the KJV (King James Bible), Joseph Smith left that "Trinitarian statement" called the "Comma Johanneum," 1 John 5:7, in its appointed place, unchanged and rendered verbatim. An "inspired" prophet of God who had seen in a vivid supernal display "two personages, whose brightness and glory defy all description," must be said to have known better. Smith left the controversial statement in its suspicious place unamended because it represented his then present "unequivocal" view. "Among the thousands of Greek manuscripts of the New Testament examined since the time of Erasmus, only three others [besides that of Erasmus whose use of the passage was reluctant] are known to contain this spurious passage."[89] Joseph Smith's "Inspired Revision," like the King James Bible (which Joseph so brazenly plagiarized), preserves "this spurious passage": *"For there are three that bear record in heaven, the Father, the Word, and the Holy Ghost; and these three are one."*[90] The passage is a trinitarian statement intended by its sponsors to afford "unequivocal Scripture 'proof' of the doctrine of the Trinity." Joseph Smith (in 1832) was good with that. His then present intent was to offer "unequivocal Scripture 'proof' of [his version of] the doctrine of the Trinity."

THE 1832 ACCOUNT OF THE FIRST VISION

Until 1834 or so, Joseph Smith taught his Church of Christ (early LDS) that *"the Lamb of God" <u>was</u> "the Eternal Father" <u>and</u> a "Spirit."*[91] In all of that, he promoted a sectarian notion that his followers later came to ridicule as incomprehensible. Smith could

---

"Jehovah As Father: The Development of the Mormon Jehovah Doctrine," *Sunstone* (1984), 37, 42 n 7, quoted in Wunderli, *An Imperfect Book*, 293-94].

[89] *The Text of the New Testament*, 101-102, Tanner and Tanner, *Mormonism – Shadow or Reality?*, 389. "The passage does not appear in manuscripts of the Latin Vulgate [it was "inserted from the Latin"] before about A.D. 800."

[90] Joseph Smith, Inspired Version, 1 John 5:7, emphasis added.

[91] "[W]hen I considered all these things [things that spoke for the existence of God] and that <that> being seeketh such to worship him as wor=ship him in spirit and in truth ["God is a Spirit: and they that worship him must worship him in spirit and in truth" {John 4:24}] . . . I cried unto the Lord . . . ." (*The Personal Writings of Joseph Smith*, ed. Dean C. Jessee [Salt Lake City: Deseret Book, 1984], 5-6).

not have written his 1838-39 Pearl of Great Price Account of the vision of the Father and the Son in the early years of his ministry, or until some time after he changed his mind about the nature and number of gods. When he first put his pen to paper in 1832 (twelve years after the alleged vision) to describe for the first time and in his own hand the most important event since the resurrection in an account the Church concealed and suppressed for one hundred and thirty years, *his "crucifyed" "Lamb of God," just as the 1830 edition of the Book of Mormon had previously reported, was still "the Eternal Father and the Savior of the world."* There was a persuasive affinity between the substance of Joseph's 1832 concept of the Godhead and those sectarian declarations Mormons later cynically chose to dismiss. When Joseph Smith prepared his *1832 First and Only Holographic Account of the First Vision* in his own hand, the first ever account of the First Vision, he described the experience in these terms:

> . . . I cried unto the Lord for mercy for there was none else to whom I could go and to obtain mercy and the Lord heard my cry in the wilderne=ss and while in <the> attitude of calling upon the Lord <in the 16th year of my age> a piller of fire light above the brightness of the sun at noon day come down from above and rested upon me and I was filled with the spirit of god and the <Lord> opened the heavens upon me and *I saw the Lord [like the brother of Jared saw the Lord] and he spake unto me saying Joseph* <my son> thy sins are forgiven thee. go thy <way> walk in my statutes and keep my commandments *behold I am the Lord of glory I was crucifyed for the world that all those who believe on my name may have Eternal life . . . .*[92]

The Book of Mormon and the 1832 Account of Joseph's first encounter with deity "crucifyed" the Father. This earliest known account of the First Vision, unequivocally describing only one Personage, recognized the godhead theology of the early Church. In the beginning, Joseph's Church of Christ taught its members

---

[92]Ibid., emphasis added.

that *the Father, Son* and *Holy Ghost "is one God,"* that Jesus was *"the Lamb of God . . . the Eternal Father and the Savior of the world"*; and that the virgin was *"the mother of God after the manner of the flesh."* Joseph could scarcely have forgotten in 1832 that the Father and the Son had appeared to him in 1820 – if they had – or that it was the Father who spoke to him and said, *"This is My Beloved Son. Hear Him!"* – if he did. Those recitals were towering features of the glorious 1838-39 Pearl of Great Price Account crafted by Smith with assistance from Sidney Rigdon, George W. Robinson and James Mulholland. But in 1832[93] Joseph believed the Father appeared because the Son appeared, because *"the Son is the Father, and the Father is the Son."*[94]

The unitary God (a more authentic Jewish and Book of Mormon concept), the God that Joseph described in 1832 in an account first published in 1965 was *"one God"*; the Father and the Son and the only God ("there is no God beside me"). He was *singular, "crucifyed," "omnipotant," and "omnipreasant."* There was no part of creation, however remote, into which this infinite and eternal spirit could not penetrate. This omnipresent God was present in all places at all times. *"[M]y heart exclaimed all these bear testimony and bespeak an omnipotant and omnipreasant power . . . who filleth Eternity who was and is and will be from all Eternity to Eternity . . . ."*[95] Christ, this Christ, because he was eternal, filled eternity. The *"crucifyed"* Lord that Joseph chose to describe in the concealed and suppressed 1832 Holographic Account of a vision of Jesus without the Father is not the modern Mormon God. The modern Mormon

---

[93]The Mormon Church concealed and suppressed Joseph's discordant holographic account of the First Vision – a Mormon historical document of supreme importance – in its manuscript archives for more than one hundred and thirty years. The 1832 Account describes an *1821* or *1822* occurrence, and contradicts the 1838-39 Account, which describes an *1820* occurrence. The 1832 Account – first published in 1965 – says that Joseph Smith was *in the 16th year of his age.* The 1838-39 Account – first published in its final form in 1842 – says that Joseph Smith was fourteen years old. The *1832 Account*, an evangelical vision of but a single personage, is primarily concerned with the forgiveness of sin.

[94]Joseph Smith Translation, Luke 10:22, 23.

[95]Joseph Smith's 1832 Account, Jessee, ed., *The Personal Writings of Joseph Smith*, 5, emphasis added.

God, a post-1834 creation, is not *"omnipreasant,"*[96] nor either eternal.

THE LECTURES ON FAITH

The *Lectures on Faith*, prepared (*and owned*) by Joseph Smith[97] and Sidney Rigdon (and canonized by the voice of the Church), were published in the 1835 edition of the Doctrine and Covenants. The members of the Church at Kirtland, Ohio, now suddenly learned from the *Lectures on Faith* that God the Father, the indivisible God, was a "personage of spirit," that Jesus, previously a spirit, was now a "personage of tabernacle," that there were two personages in the Godhead, and that the Holy Spirit was the mind of the spirit Father and the anthropomorphic Son. The Holy Ghost described in the Doctrine and Covenants (in the canonized doctrine part of the Doctrine and Covenants) by the *Lectures on Faith* was not a "personage." Although the Father, Son, and Holy Spirit constituted the *Lectures'* Godhead, the Holy Spirit was not a personage when this godhead theology was canonized, becoming an important part of the Doctrine and Covenants from 1835 to 1921.

In 1835, Smith (then in Michigan on business) directed Oliver Cowdery and Sidney Rigdon to preside over the General Assembly of the Church, the body that canonized the early revelations – including the *Lectures on Faith* – making the revelations, and the *Lectures*, divinely-approved Mormon scripture.

---

[96]"It has been said . . . that God is everywhere present ["through the medium of the Spirit"]; but this does not mean that the actual person of any one member of the Godhead can be physically present in more than one place at one time [as Joseph Smith's 1832 Holographic Account of the First Vision of the Son said that Jesus was]." (Talmage, *A Study of the Articles of Faith*, 33rd ed., Article 1, 42-43). When Apostle Talmage spoke those words, the 1832 Holographic Account of the First Vision of the ["omnipreasant"] Son was in the vault out of sight, unknown and unpublished. Unavailable, perhaps, even to him. We may suppose that that first account of the First Vision was not something with which that particular Mormon scholar needed to then contend.

[97]Joseph Smith, *Lectures on Faith*, Title page. *"Prepared by the Prophet Joseph Smith. Delivered to the School of the Prophets in Kirtland, Ohio, 1834-35."*

Prior to the publication of the *Lectures on Faith*, Joseph Smith was a monotheist and the Church's godhead theology was "essentially trinitarian." After 1835, and even though the *Lectures on Faith* appeared to separate the deities and to abandon "essentially trinitarian" theology, that effort did not fully succeed. Mormon scholar Thomas G. Alexander: "The Lectures on Faith differentiated between the father and the Son somewhat more explicitly, but even they did not define a materialistic, tritheistic Godhead."[98] The Holy Ghost, not yet a personage, was "an impersonal spiritual member of the godhead."[99] The doctrine of the Holy Ghost presented in the "Articles and Covenants of the Church of Christ" in the Book of Commandments in 1833, and in the *Lectures on Faith* in 1834 and 1835, is not the doctrine "defended" in the modern Church. "The Lectures on Faith defined the Holy Ghost as the mind of the Father and the Son, a member of the Godhead, but not a personage, who binds the Father and the Son together. This view of the Holy Ghost reinforced trinitarian doctrine by explaining how personal beings like the Father and Son become one God through the noncorporeal presence of a shared mind."[100] "The Articles and Covenants [of the Church of Christ (early Mormon)] called the Father, Son and Holy Ghost 'one God' rather than the Godhead, a term which Mormons generally use today to separate themselves from trinitarians."[101]

In the *Lectures on Faith*, the Son was anthropomorphic (physically finite) and the Father was a Spirit (infinite and eternal). The Holy Ghost (let it be emphasized) was not a personage (*"How many personages are there in the Godhead? Two: the Father and the Son"*[102]), but rather "the [shared] . . . mind" of the Father and the Son.[103] The Father, a Spirit, and the Son, who inhabited a "tabernacle of clay," now became more nearly separate and distinct, five years after the Church was organized and fifteen years after Smith's only later retroactively reported vision was supposed

[98]Thomas G. Alexander, "The Reconstruction of Mormon Doctrine: From Joseph Smith to Progressive Theology," *Sunstone*, vol. 5 no. 4 (July-August 1980): 25.

[99]Ibid.

[100]Ibid., 26.

[101]Ibid., 25.

[102]*Lectures on Faith*, Lecture 5:1, emphasis added.

[103]Ibid., 60-61.

to have occurred (in 1820). *"There are two personages who constitute the great, matchless, governing, and supreme power over all things,"* the canonized Lectures said.[104]   The Holy Ghost, as originally described in the *Lectures on Faith*, was a mysterious noncorporeal inexplicable essence of some undefinable sort.

As Joseph's Godhead theology evolved, as the Father and the Son became theoretically divisible, as the Son became endless but not eternal, and as God became a "changeable being,"[105] the *Lectures on Faith* defined God the Father in 1834-35 as "a personage of spirit, glory and power, possessing all perfection and fullness . . . ."[106]   They then redefined Jesus Christ, as "a personage of tabernacle, made or fashioned like unto man."[107]   The Father was "a personage of Spirit," the Son was "a personage of tabernacle,"[108] the Holy Spirit was "the noncorporeal presence" of the shared mind of the spirit Father and the anthropomorphic Son.   That is a complexity. "[H]e [the Son] is . . . called the Son because of the flesh . . . possessing the same mind with the Father, which mind is the Holy Spirit, that bears record of the Father and the Son, and these three are one."[109]   "Do the Father and the Son possess the same mind?   They do."[110]   This strange composition is said to have actually "reinforced trinitarian doctrine by explaining how personal beings like the Father and Son become one god through the noncorporeal presence of a shared mind."

Why do modern Mormons never speak of this? The Father a spirit; the Son a man; the Spirit a noncorporeal presence (a shared mind, but not a personage). The *Lectures on Faith*, as published in the 1835 edition of the Doctrine and Covenants, described the Father as *"omnipresent."*[111] The Father was a spirit, present at all times in all places. The Son was a man, not present at all times and all places. The spirit Son, Joseph's "Lord" and the subject of the first First

---

[104]Ibid., Lecture Fifth, 59.

[105]Book of Mormon, Moroni 8:18.

[106]*Lectures on Faith*, Lecture Fifth, 59.

[107]Ibid., Lecture Fifth, 59.

[108]Doctrine and Covenants 1835 ed., 53. *Lectures on Faith*, Lecture Fifth, 59.

[109]*Lectures on Faith*, Lecture Fifth, 59-60.

[110]Ibid., 65.

[111]Doctrine and Covenants 1835 ed., 12, 26, quoted in Jerald and Sandra Tanner, *The Changing World of Mormonism*, 185.

Vision, was, however, *"omnipreasant"* (and *"omnipotant"*) in the Holographic Account of the First Vision prepared by Joseph Smith (but not published) in 1832. Is it not perfectly apparent why the *1832 Holographic Account*, the only account written by Joseph Smith in his own hand, was concealed and suppressed in the archives of the Church for more than one hundred and thirty years? The *Lectures'* divinely approved (canonized) descriptions no longer apply to modern Mormonism's reconstituted anthropomorphic "changeable" Father.[112]   Or to Mormonism's reconstituted anthropomorphic "changeable" Son. Or to the spirit Son (1832) who became the anthropomorphic Son (1834-35). Or to the noncorporeal mind that later became a spirit personage in the form of a man.

The *Lectures on Faith* comprised the doctrinal part of the Doctrine and Covenants from 1835 to 1921, when they were rudely dismissed because of their incongruities.[113] When those previously canonized *Lectures* were abandoned in the twentieth century, their passing was insufficiently solemn. It was not attended by appropriate formal canonical solemnity. The *Lectures on Faith* did not describe two anthropomorphic deities, as Joseph only later did, or as the modern Church is seen to do today. How could a boy who had seen "two personages whose brightness and glory defy all description" in 1820, describe but "one God" until 1834, then the Father as "a personage of spirit," then the Son as "a personage of tabernacle" in 1834-35?

---

[112]"There is no part of creation, however remote, into which God cannot penetrate; through the medium of the Spirit [a Spirit that is more than a mind] the Godhead is in direct communication with all things at all times. It has been said, therefore, that God is everywhere present . . . . The senses of each of the Trinity are of infinite power; His mind is of unlimited capacity; His powers of transferring Himself from place to place are infinite; plainly, however, His person cannot be in more than one place at any one time. . . . If God possesses a form, that form is of necessity of definite proportions and therefore of limited extension in space." (Talmage, *A Study of the Articles of Faith*, 33rd ed., 42-43). Modern Mormonism's amended deities – Father and Son – are not "omnipreasant," nor either eternal. Those verities from the *Lectures on Faith* and the 1832 Account of Joseph's first encounter with deity – a single deity (only Jesus) and not the Father – are not those "defended in our time."

[113]Tanner and Tanner, *The Changing World of Mormonism*, 185-86.

WHEN JOSEPH CHANGED HIS MIND

Joseph's evolving theology came to rest, many years after Moroni and the Book of Mormon said God was not "a changeable being," in new (and peculiar) directions:

1. *The prophet divided his previously indivisible God and "eventually taught that God the Father, his Son Jesus, and the Holy Ghost" were separate.*

2. *The Father and the Son had bodies "of flesh and bones as tangible as man's . . . ." Having once been mortal, they had grown to perfection. Human beings could also "grow to perfection and become gods themselves."*

3. *Joseph "spoke of other gods" who were "higher in authority and glory" than the gods of this earth. The Holy Spirit, "unlike the other gods," now became "'a personage of Spirit,' which is 'matter' but 'more fine and pure.'"*[114]

Joseph Smith decided in and/or after 1834, when his "one God" theology changed and he abandoned monotheism – and not in 1820 as the result of a visionary experience – that the Father and the Son were separate identifiable entities. Sometime after the formulation of the *Lectures on Faith* in 1835, Smith further determined that the Father was not really "a personage of spirit," as the canonized *Lectures* reported, but rather a separate and second "personage of tabernacle."

> *Chapters 4 and 5 of [the Book of] Abraham reflect Joseph's changing theology on the godhead. From 1820 to 1834 he believed that there is one God, as seen in the Book of Mormon, the testimony of the three witnesses, the Book of Commandments 24:13-18, the Book of Moses, the JST [Joseph Smith translation], and the 1832 account of his first vision. By 1835 he had come to believe that two personages formed the godhead, as taught in the Doctrine and Covenants*

---

[114]Wunderli, *An Imperfect Book*, 290.

*20:28 (cf. Book of Commandments 24:18), the
Lectures on Faith (5), and the 1835 and 1838
accounts of his first vision. From 1839 on, he
preached a plurality of gods, as seen in Abraham 4
and 5 and the LDS temple ceremony.*[115]

"Joseph first clearly taught the plurality of gods in March 1839."[116]
"His evolving concept of God suggests that he imposed his own
changing view onto the Abrahamic period as well as onto other
periods of history." That overconfident assumption, at odds with
the theology of the Hebrews, shows the depth and breadth of a great
deceit. "The implication is that the material in these chapters is not
'[a] translation of some ancient Records,' as the heading of the
Book of Abraham claims, but rather [creations from] nineteenth-
century sources."[117] The Book of Abraham, which divided the
indivisible god, is one colossal fraud. In 1837 the words of the
ancient prophets in the Book of Mormon, a book "translated by the
gift and power of God," were changed to separate the indivisible
Father from the indivisible Son. The cynical revisions that
disfigured the 1830 first edition of the Book of Mormon in 1837
imposed new meanings on supposedly ancient text.

Comparison:[118]

1830 Edition	1837 Edition
1 Ne. 11-19 – *The virgin whom thou seest is the mother of God, after the manner of the flesh.*	1 Ne. 11:19 – *The virgin whom thou seest is the mother of the Son of God, after the manner of the flesh.*
1 Ne. 11:21 – *Behold the Lamb of God, yea, even the Eternal Father.*	1 Ne. 11:21 – *Behold the Lamb of God, yea, even the Son of the Eternal Father.*

---

[115]Palmer, *An Insider's View of Mormon Origins*, 19, 21, emphasis added.
[116]Ibid., 21 fn 49.
[117]Ibid., 21.
[118]From Melodie Moench Charles, "Book of Mormon Christology," in Brent
Lee Metcalfe, ed., *New Approaches to the Book of Mormon: Explorations in Critical
Methodology* (Salt Lake City: Signature Books, 1993), Chapter 4, emphasis added.

1 Ne. 11:32 – *[The Lamb of God] was taken by people; yea, the Everlasting God was judged of the world.*

1 Ne. 13:40 – *[These records] shall make known to all . . . that the Lamb of God is the Eternal Father, and the Savior of the world.*

1 Ne. 11:32 – *[The Lamb of God] was taken by people; yea, the Son of the everlasting God was judged of the world.*

1 Ne. 13:40 – *[These records] shall make known to all . . . that the Lamb of God is the Son of the Eternal Father, and the Savior of the world.*

In 1837 the Golden Bible was quietly altered by means of substantive revisions designed to separate the Father from the Son. Missionaries tell their investigators that Joseph Smith separated the Father from the Son in 1820. These revisions prove that he did not. One critic opines that had Joseph's doctrine not evolved, "defenders would surely accept that the Book of Mormon taught the doctrine of the Trinity, meaning that God the Father is a Spirit and the Son has a fleshly form."[119] A distinguished Mormon scholar adds this noteworthy insight: *"The Book of Mormon tended to define God as an absolute personage of spirit who, clothed in flesh, revealed himself in Jesus Christ."*[120] To this author's knowledge, no one has described the Book of Mormon God any better than that.

Because Joseph did the unconscionable – changed (and depreciated) the unchangeable God as his views on the Trinity evolved – "Defenders have tried . . . to harmonize the single God of the Book of Mormon with the plurality of Gods within and outside of the Godhead of his later thinking, despite his evolution of thought."[121] They have tried to say his view did not evolve, that the man at Nauvoo was the boy at Palmyra. That was far from the truth. Smith changed the meaning of those godhead passages in the Book of Mormon in order to support his changing theology. What had been one and trinitarian, then two and binitarian, then three and

---

[119]Book of Mormon, 1 Nephi 11:18; 2 Ne. 31:21; Mosiah 15:1-9; Alma 5:48, 7:10, 13; 11:38-39; Mormon 7:7; 9:12; 3 Nephi 1:13-14; all quoted in Wunderli, *An Imperfect Book*, 298-299.

[120]Alexander, "The Reconstruction of Mormon Doctrine," *Sunstone*, vol. 5 no. 4 (July-August 1980): 25, emphasis added.

[121]Wunderli, *An Imperfect Book*, 299.

tritheistic, became an undeniable plurality of gods in 1839 and on, as God became whatever Joseph thought that he should be at any given moment in time.

God Changes: Polytheism

"During the Nauvoo period of 1839 to 1844, Joseph *began to teach* the corporeality of the Father, the plurality of gods and that humans can become gods."[122] "[B]etween 1842 and 1844 Joseph Smith spoke on and published doctrines such as the plurality of Gods, *the tangibility of God's body, the distinct separation of God and Christ*, the potential of man to become and function as a god, the explicit rejection of *ex nihilo* creation, and the materiality of everything including spirit."[123] The sky was now the limit. The prophet opened Pandora's box.

From Enoch, December 1830:

> Jesus valued: *"And were it possible that man could number the particles of the earth, yea, millions of earths like this, it would not be a beginning to the number of thy creations; . . . ."*[124]

To Orson Pratt, February 1855:

> Jesus devalued: *"If we should take a million of worlds like this and number their particles, we should find that there are more god's than there are particles of matter in those worlds."*[125]

In 1832 Jesus, Joseph's indivisible god, the only deity to appear in the first and only *Holographic Account* of Joseph's first encounter with deity, was "a [powerful] being who makith Laws and decreeth

---

[122]Ibid., 292, emphasis added.

[123]Alexander, "The Reconstruction of Mormon Doctrine," *Sunstone*, vol. 5 no. 4 (July-August 1980): 27, emphasis added.

[124]The Pearl of Great Price, Moses 7:30, emphasis added.

[125]Orson Pratt (18 Feb. 1855), *Journal of Discourses*, 2:345, 346, emphasis added.

and bindeth all things in their bounds who filleth Eternity who was
and is and will be from all Eternity to Eternity . . . ."[126] In a few
short years that imposing 1832 *persona* will be seen to become
incredibly deflated. Joseph, who didn't really know God (else why
the mistakes), supervised the downgrade. His now new eclectic
godhead theology was hither and yon, monotheism, modalism,
trinitarianism, binitarianism, tritheism and polytheism, some of this
and some of that. Now he who "decreeth and bindeth all things in
their bounds," and "who filleth eternity," will change being to
become but one of a perfectly incomprehensible number of Gods, a
particle of matter in a super gargantuan cosmos.

When Joseph Smith proclaimed the "plurality of Gods" in 1839, God
gravitated from one *"crucifyed"* Lord in 1832 ("an *omnipotant* and
omnipreasant power") to "an astonishing assembly of *'crucifyed'*
lords," gods in prototype. In 1838-39, in a history published in
1842, Jesus became a "space-bound God in a grove."[127] In Orson
Pratt's plurality equation, there were more gods than all the
particles of matter to be found in "a million of worlds like this."
Pratt described modern Mormonism's polytheistic evolutionary
endpoint. Gods, including higher gods, are a dime a trillion dozen,
and anyone can become one. Jehovah is threatened and
inconsequential. In much of its nearly two-hundred-year history,
for most of this author's life and until recent times, Mormonism's
prophets and apostles have often been more highly valued than an
overlooked Messiah.[128] See evidence of this at Appendix B.

---

[126]Joseph Smith's 1832 Account, Jessee, ed., *The Personal Writings of Joseph Smith,* 5-6.

[127]Latayne C. Scott, *The Mormon Mirage* (Grand Rapids, MI: Zondervan, 2009), 283.

[128]Joseph Smith, May 1844 (one month before his death): "I have more to boast of than ever any man had. I am the only man that has ever been able to keep a whole church together since the days of Adam. A large majority of the whole have stood by me. Neither Paul, John, Peter, nor Jesus ever did it. I boast that no man ever did such a work as I. The followers of Jesus ran away from Him; but the Latter-day Saints never ran away from me yet." (Joseph Smith Jr., *History of The Church of Jesus Christ of Latter-day Saints*, B.H. Roberts, ed., 2d ed., rev., [Salt Lake City: The Deseret Book Company, 1978], 6:408-409], emphasis added).

REVISIONS TO THE WORD OF GOD – THE CRISIS OF THE OLD ORDER AND THE COMING OF THE NEW DEAL

The early Joseph Smith taught his followers that God the Father, Jesus Christ and the Holy Ghost were "one God," mimicking various sectarian creeds. In, and or shortly after 1834, Smith began to teach his followers that God the Father and Jesus Christ were separate and distinct, but not the same, while bidding an awkward farewell to the "Lamb of God" as "the very Eternal Father." It now became important to decide how to get to a new place from an old place. The Book of Mormon – that venerable record engraved on plates of gold and translated by the gift and power of God – would have to be revised, and what couldn't be revised would have to be ignored or weaseled around. The teachings of Nephi, Abinadi, Amulek and Ammon, and those of the angels who instructed them, would have to be abandoned. The teachings of those early prophets and messengers would be replaced by overblown allegorical sophistry. The word of God, spoken by the malleable Smith, would have to support this wonderfully creative new theology. Joseph Smith's after-the-fact revisions – supposed to change the nature of that supposedly "unchangeable" God – challenged the gift and power of God, the engravings on the plates, the method of translation and the integrity of the revelator.

Was God Confused?

"We believe the Bible to be the word of God as far as it is translated correctly; we also believe the Book of Mormon to be the word of God."[129] The Bible, according to Smith, was corrupted by awkward translation by fallible humans devoid of the spirit of God; but the Book of Mormon was translated *"by the gift and power of God."* "The book professes not to be dependent upon the wisdom or learning of man; its translator was not versed in linguistics; his qualifications were of a different and of a more efficient order."[130]

> *Although Joseph said he was a reader rather than a literal translator of the Book of Mormon, it has*

---

[129]The Pearl of Great Price, Articles of Faith 1:8, emphasis added.
[130]Talmage, *A Study of the Articles of Faith*, 33rd ed., 267.

*become clear that he was also a participant in the
book's creation. He made textual alterations in 1837,
changing passages that described the Father and the
Son as one God to a description of them as distinct
and separate beings. He did not view the original text
as inviolate, in other words. Otherwise the corrected
text would either reflect a previous error upon God or
upon the translator for changing God's words as read
from the stone.*[131]

If it was easy for Smith to change his mind, it would be more
difficult to change the Book of Mormon seven years after the first
edition had already been published. In the absence of the plates,
that would seem to require a refreshed composition. If Jesus told
those Book of Mormon prophets that he was the Almighty God, the
Eternal Father, Alpha and Omega, the Creator of Heaven and
Earth, then "God above all," he will now be construed to have
spoken allegorically. Those previously validated misconceptions
would have to be changed, notwithstanding the blessed translation
of the "most correct of any book on earth" by the "gift and power of
God." So what if God and Jesus had been "one God" (*"the Son is
the Father, and the Father is the Son"*), and what if Joseph Smith
had been a monotheist from 1828 to 1834, and/or perhaps even
beyond? Those theological perceptions described in all early sacred
important Mormon resources would have to be changed or ignored.
There would have to be *two* anthropomorphic persons (separate
and distinct) from here on out. The Father and the Son, whatever
anyone had earlier said, must now become separate and distinct.
The explicit descriptions of their literal oneness, changed only in
part by means of those awkward amendments, will survive to
confuse the members of the modern Church. For these doctrines
had been engraved on metal plates, fixed in brass and gold by
inspired prophets of God, then also inscribed by Christianity's
patriarchs on ancient papyri. Joseph's 1837 corrections were a
clumsy attempt to set his rapidly changing record straight. He will

---

[131]Palmer, *An Insider's View of Mormon Origins*, 9-10 (Cf. The Book of
Mormon [1982], 1 Nephi 11:16, 18, 21, 32; 13:40, with Wood, *Joseph Smith Begins
His Work, Volume I*, 1:25-26, 32. *"The godhead alterations were not continued
beyond 1 Nephi"*), emphasis added.

set the deity straight, correct the Book of Mormon and revisit the nature of God.

When Joseph Smith, who *"was not versed in linguistics,"* altered the contents of the Book of Mormon – seven years after the fact – to more nearly reflect his "post-1830 understanding of the godhead," "it can be demonstrated that theological considerations were operative."[132] The changes he then made were *"dependent upon the wisdom or learning of man."* The plates had disappeared. Joseph imposed his own changing theology on ancient records supposed to have been protected by North and South American prophets for several thousand years before they were perfectly translated to become the "most correct of any book on earth" by "the gift and power of God."

If Joseph could change the 1830 edition of the Book of Mormon in 1837 to more accurately reflect his "post-1830 understanding of the godhead," Joseph could have changed the 1830 edition of the Book of Mormon in 1830 to more accurately reflect his post-1820 understanding of the godhead, if there had actually been an 1820 understanding of the godhead. The nature of God could not have been an open question for Joseph Smith in 1830, or for his Lord, if what Joseph only later said was true. The nature of the godhead should have been meticulously documented on the Book of Mormon's carefully crafted industriously protected golden plates. The fact that Joseph Smith covertly changed the text of the 1830 edition of the Book of Mormon in 1837 to separate the Father from the Son, after he had come to believe that the Father and the Son were separate and distinct persons, leads to only one conclusion: Joseph Smith didn't see the Father and the Son, two persons separate and distinct, in some sacred grove in 1820.

So What? The Implications of Change

Before 1834, Joseph Smith and various early Mormon resources taught early Mormons that the Father and the Son were "one God."

---

[132]Richard P. Howard, RLDS Church Historian, *Restoration Scriptures: A Study of Their Textual Development*, 2nd ed. (Independence, MO: Herald Publishing House, 1995), 47-48.

God in his heaven was a spirit. In 1835 in the *Lectures on Faith*, Joseph broke ranks to describe the Father as "a personage of Spirit," not entirely separated from the Son, who was "a personage of tabernacle," because of the noncorporeal presence of a shared mind. There were, he now said, *two personages* in the godhead. Still later he reversed himself again to further say that the two separate deities described in the *Lectures* were both anthropomorphic. Still later he, and/or others, reversed his teachings to say that the "noncorporeal presence of a shared mind" was actually a personage of the spirit in the form of a man.

Joseph changed his mind about the godhead as his theology evolved, but not before he had first provided many incontrovertible evidences in support of his earlier discarded views. So what should it matter that Joseph Smith changed his mind about "one God"? It matters because the Book of Mormon God (Moroni's God) is not a changeable being. It matters because God is "the same yesterday, today and forever" and not a work in process. It matters because God is eternal without father, mother or descent, beginning of days or end of years, meaning he is uncreated and underived. It matters because gods are not a dime a trillion dozen, threatened and inconsequential. It finally matters because Smith's disingenuous reversal – *abandoning monotheism severe and extreme* – threatens the founding story of the Mormon Church. It suggests there was no great First Vision of the Father and the Son. For the Mormon founder Joseph Smith, there is no room for error here.

Joseph Smith retroactively said (privately in 1838 and 1839 and publicly in 1840 and 1842) that he saw God the Father and Jesus Christ, two glorious personages whose "brightness and glory" defied all description (in 1820), about ten years before he commenced his prophetic ministry. So what is so wrong with Smith changing his mind about the nature of God? He saw them or he didn't. If he saw them, and he said that he did, he knew they were not "one God." He knew that the Son was not the Father, and that the Father was not the Son.[133] Yet he taught unsuspecting disciples for a period of critical years that they were indivisible. He reinterpreted the King James Bible to be more firmly able to say

---

[133]Joseph Smith Inspired Translation, Luke 10:22, 23; 1 Timothy 2:4.

that, *"the Son is the Father, and the Father is the Son,"* and that the Father and the Son "is one God." When Joseph Smith embraced the notion that *". . . the Lamb of God is the Eternal Father and the Savior of the world"* as an adult, he in effect confessed that he had not seen the Father and the Son in 1820 as a child. The Book of Mormon, the Testimony of Three Witnesses, the Book of Commandments, the Doctrine and Covenants, the Book of Moses, the Inspired Translation of the King James Bible, the 1832 Holographic Account of the First Vision of Jesus Christ and the *Lectures on Faith* all challenge, in various powerful ways, the tenuous substance of the supposedly settled 1838-39 Official Canonized Account of an 1820 vision of the Father and the Son.

Joseph Smith didn't know that the Father and the Son were separate and distinct personages until 1834 or so. He didn't know that the Father was anthropomorphic, like the Son was anthropomorphic, until some time after 1835. A person who didn't know that the Father and the Son were separate beings, or that the Father wasn't a spirit, or that the Father and the Son didn't literally share the same mind, hadn't seen the Father and the Son in 1820, or ever at all. When Mormon missionaries tell investigators that Joseph Smith knew that God the Father and Jesus Christ were two separate and distinct anthropomorphic beings because he saw them in the flesh in 1820, they are kicking against the pricks. No missionary teaching an investigator about the godhead ever stops to say that there is an unresolved conflict between the teachings of the Book of Mormon and the teachings of the modern Church concerning God and Jesus. Ten years after his alleged vision, and for years yet to come, Joseph Smith taught his followers in all important early Mormon resources that the Father, Son and Holy Ghost *"is"* *"one* God."

How could Joseph Smith have promulgated by modern Mormon reckoning so many such obvious errors? In each of the following ways: (1) Joseph Smith didn't see the Father and the Son in 1820, or know that they were separate and distinct; (2) He published the Book of Mormon, the Testimony of the Three Witnesses, the Book of Commandments, the Doctrine and Covenants and the Book of Moses, revised the King James Version of the Christian Bible, and prepared the *Lectures on Faith* before he ever said, publicly or privately, that he had seen the Father and the Son in 1820; and (3) He revised his earlier teachings in order to finally publicly say, more than twenty years after the supposed and alleged fact, that he had seen the Father and the Son in 1820. Without explaining these unsettling contradictions, Latter-day Saints ridicule "sectarians" for teaching what Joseph Smith in all important early Mormon resources initially taught. "[T]he Book of Mormon and early revelations of Joseph Smith do indeed vividly portray a picture of the Father and the Son as the same God . . ."

> *This seems particularly ironic, since a major avowed purpose of the book was to restore lost truths and end doctrinal controversies caused by the "great and abominable church's" corruption of the Bible . . . In later years he reversed his earlier efforts to completely "monotheize" the godhead and instead "tritheised" it.*[134]

So What? Joseph Smith and Evolutionary Theology

While a desire to learn and the willingness to change are admirable traits, and while there may be nothing wrong with an evolving theology when God is at the helm, if he is a "changeable being" and "a work in process," these hopeful alternatives were not available to Joseph Smith after 1820. A person who hadn't been visited by the Father and the Son at the age of fourteen, someone who hadn't been carefully instructed by heavenly messengers on repeated occasions, might be heard to reason as follows: "When I was young I thought the Father and the Son were the same person, one God. That is what I was taught. As I have matured, after further study, and as my knowledge has deepened, I have prayerfully come to the conclusion that they are not the same person. In my view, my later

---

[134]Palmer, *An Insider's View of Mormon Origins*, 122-23 (citing "Boyd Kirkland, 'An Evolving God,' *Dialogue* 28 [Spring 1995]: v-vi). See also Melodie Moench Charles, 'Book of Mormon Christology,' in *New Approaches to the Book of Mormon: Explorations in Critical Methodology*, ed. Brent Lee Metcalfe [Salt Lake City: Signature Books, 1993], 81-114; and Dan Vogel, 'The Earliest Mormon Concept of God,' in *Line upon Line: Essays on Mormon Doctrine*, ed. Gary James Bergera [Salt Lake City: Signature Books, 1989], 17-33)," emphasis added.

conclusion is better supported and more tenable than my earlier one."

A Joseph Smith capable of candor might have said something like this: "In 1821, in my sixteenth year, I saw Jesus Christ in a 'piller of light above the brightness of the sun at noon day.' He spoke to me and said, 'Joseph [my son] thy sins are forgiven thee.' 'I am the Lord of glory,' he said. 'I was crucifyed for the world that all those who believe on my name [might] have Eternal life.' I wrote about this event in a history I prepared in my own hand in 1832, but didn't publish. I thought at that time (when I was in my sixteenth year), that the personage I saw was the Father and the Son, because the Father was the Son. That was what the churches said. And that is what I thought in 1832 when I first described my vision in the pages of a ledger book. And that is what I thought when I translated the Book of Mormon published in 1830, and when I prepared a statement to be signed by the Three Witnesses in 1830, when I received revelations in 1829, 1830 and after, when I had a vision of Moses in 1830, and when I revised the King James Bible.

I believed then that 'the Lamb of God' and 'the Eternal Father' were 'one God,' and that Mary was the mother of God after the manner of the flesh. I believed Jesus when he said, 'He who hath seen me, hath seen the father.' I believed that Jesus was '*omnipotant*' and '*omnipreasant*,' and that the Father was '*crucifyed*.' But then I remembered in 1838 or 1839 in a history I allowed to be published in Edinburgh, Scotland, in 1840, and in Nauvoo, Illinois, in 1842, that I had seen the Father and the Son, 'two Personages, whose brightness and glory defied all description, standing above me in the air' in 1820 in New York when I was fourteen and in my fifteenth year. I forgot to mention when I described that event in 1832, and again in several other unpublished 1835 accounts, and in the history I prepared with Oliver Cowdery in 1834-35, that 'One of them spake unto me, calling me by name and said, pointing to the other – *This is My Beloved Son. Hear Him!*' But I do now remember that there were two personages, two separate and distinct beings, anthropomorphic beings, both of whom spoke to me on that occasion. From now on I am going to say that – no matter what I said before."

Why can't Joseph Smith say: "I think my later conclusion is better supported and more tenable than my earlier one"? Or that "God clarified my earlier understanding"? Because this Joseph said – twenty years after the fact as a mature adult in the prime of his life in 1838-39 – that he saw the Father and the Son when he was fourteen years old in 1820, but not until after he wrote in the *1832 Account* of his vision, in the statement of Three Witnesses, in the Book of Mormon, in the Book of Commandments, in the Doctrine and Covenants, in the Book of Moses and in the Inspired Translation of the King James Bible, that the Father and the Son were "*one God*." There was no entirely satisfactory way out of this web of deceit. By the time Joseph decided there were two personages in the godhead, he had already prepared several contradictory accounts, the terms of which challenged the integrity of the vision, the credibility of the reporter and the limits of the prophet's considerable ingenuity. What Joseph Smith said about God until at least 1834 conflicted with what the founding story of the Church of Jesus Christ of Latter-day Saints said about God in 1842. His problem with an evolving godhead, as his theology changed, was the 1820 vision. Why would a boy who "saw two Personages, whose brightness and glory [defied] all description," and heard these words – "*This is My Beloved Son. Hear Him!*" – ever teach that "the Lamb of God was the very Eternal Father"? Or that "the Son is the Father, and the Father is the Son"? Or that Mary was the mother of the Everlasting God "after the manner of the flesh"? Or that the Father, Son and Holy Ghost "*is* one God"? And why would the earliest edition of the Book of Mormon crucify the Father?

CHAPTER TWO

First Vision Accounts: 1832 to 1842

. . . I cried unto the Lord for mercy . . . and the Lord heard my cry in the wilderne=ss . . . while . . . calling upon the Lord <in the 16ᵗʰ year of my age> a piller of f̶i̶r̶e̶ light above the brightness of the sun at noon day come down from above and rested upon me . . . . I saw the Lord and he spake unto me saying Joseph <my son> thy sins are forgiven thee. go thy <way> walk in my statutes and keep my commandments behold I am the Lord of glory I was crucifyed for the world that all those who believe on my name may have Eternal life . . . .

Joseph Smith,
1832 Account

The 1832 Account first published in 1965 was not used for any gospel purpose. It was rescued from historical purgatory out of regrettable necessity and reluctantly published at an inconspicuous place without institutional comment.

Joel M. Allred

FOUNDING STORIES

There are at least six versions of five presently known primary accounts of Joseph Smith's First Vision, the founding story of the Church of Jesus Christ of Latter-day Saints[1]: (1) Joseph Smith's 1832 Holographic (Handwritten) Account; (2) Joshua 1:1835; (3) Erastus Holmes:1835; (4) Joshua 2:1835; (5) The John

---

[1]The two Joshua versions are separated here. Joshua 1 (the third-person version) is so identified because it was the first of the two accounts to be disclosed in 1966. Joshua 2 (the first-person version) was not disclosed until 1971. These two versions of the same account are considered to be the second chronological account for the purpose of this analysis.

Wentworth:1842 Account[2]; and (6) The 1838-39 Pearl of Great Price Account. Joshua 1:1835 (found in the Manuscript History, Book A-1) is the same account in substance as Joshua 2:1835 (found in Joseph Smith's Personal Diary). Joshua 1:1835 is a third-person account and Joshua 2:1835 is a first-person account.

Of these five different accounts, only two – the 1838-39 Pearl of Great Price Account and John Wentworth:1842 – were known to the members of the Mormon Church until 1965. That historic betrayal tainted the teaching of every investigator asked to consider the First Vision prior to 1965. All First Vision scholarship is accordingly suspect. Latter-day Saints were not told about these alternative accounts until 1965 (Joseph Smith's 1832 Holographic Account), 1966 (Joshua 1:1835), 1969 (Erastus Holmes:1835) and 1971 (Joshua 2:1835). Until 1965, the 1838-39 Pearl of Great Price Account – Mormon scripture (summarized in Wentworth, an insufficiently detailed report of somewhat lesser consequence) – was the only known account. Until 1965, and for more than thirteen decades, the Church perpetuated the deception that Joseph Smith told his story only once.

When the Church informed its membership (by means of a major address from the First Presidency in 1907) that it had not been duplicitous in any of its dealings and that "[e]nlightened

---

[2]The Wentworth letter was published in the *Times and Seasons* 3, no. 9 (March 1, 1842) in Nauvoo, Illinois, before the 1838-1839 Pearl of Great Price Account, which was published in the *Times and Seasons* in Nauvoo, Illinois, on April 1, 1842. Chronologically, the John Wentworth Account:1842 – although published before the 1838-39 Pearl of Great Price Account – is the last of these six versions of five different accounts. John Wentworth:1842 (though published first) was composed several years after the 1838-39 Pearl of Great Price Account. The Pearl of Great Price Account was excerpted from a history started in April 1838 in Far West, Missouri, by Joseph Smith, Sidney Rigdon and George W. Robinson. That history continued to be composed in the handwriting of James Mulholland (one of Joseph's scribes) in 1839. In this chapter, Joseph Smith's 1832 Holographic Account will constitute the first chronological account; the two versions of the Joshua Account, Joshua 1:1835 and Joshua 2:1835, will jointly constitute the second chronological account; Erastus Holmes:1835 the third account; the 1838-39 Account, published in 1842 then later amended (probably in 1843 *and/or* 1844), will be considered the fourth chronological account; and John Wentworth:1842 ("a much less detailed account of the vision" [James B. Allen]) will be considered the fifth chronological report.

investigation" had always been its goal,[3] there lay concealed in its
highest value archives no less than three unfamiliar accounts of
Mormonism's founding story, the earliest accounts of the First
Vision of the Mormon Prophet Joseph Smith.   The first of those
suppressed accounts was "brought to light" nearly sixty years after
the First Presidency's "[e]nlightened investigation" pronouncement.
The 1832 Holographic Account of the vision of the Son – one God,
"omnipotant," "omnipreasant" and "crucifyed," the only presently
known account ever written in the hand of the prophet Joseph
Smith – was suppressed by the Church from 1832 to 1965.   And
when that unsettling account did awkwardly surface to be read by
twentieth-century saints, and to be explained by a cadre of
apologetic scholars, the disclosure was involuntary.

Tardy Visions

The three suppressed accounts of Joseph Smith's First Vision were
(1) Joseph Smith's 1832 Holographic (Handwritten) Account; (2)
Joshua 1 and 2: 1835, third and first-person accounts describing a
November 9, 1835, encounter of Joseph Smith with Robert
Matthews, or Matthias, *alias* Joshua the Jewish Minister; and (3)
Erastus Holmes: 1835, describing a November 14, 1835, encounter
with Erastus Holmes.

Mormon scholars cannot find *any* persuasive contemporaneous
historical resources to support Joseph's late-in-life claim that he
saw a vision in 1820 and was severely persecuted because of it by
"men of high standing".   They are forced to concede "that none of
the available contemporary writings about Joseph Smith in the
1830s, none of the publications of the church in that decade, and no
contemporary journal or correspondence yet discovered mentions
the story of the first vision . . . ."[4]   One Mormon scholar, James B.
Allen, admits that, "The earliest anti-Mormon literature attacked

---

[3]1907 Address (March 26, 1907), *Messages*, 4:145-46, B. Carmon Hardy,
Solemn Covenant: The Mormon Polygamous Passage (Urbana, Chicago: University
of Illinois Press, 1992), 363.
    [4]James B. Allen, "The Significance of Joseph Smith's 'First Vision' in
Mormon Thought," *Dialogue: A Journal of Mormon Thought*, vol. 1 no. 3, (Autumn
1966): 30.

the Book of Mormon and the character of Joseph Smith but never mentioned the first vision."[5]   Critics of the early Church – Alexander Campbell, E.D. Howe, Ezra Booth, Doctor Philastus Hurlbut, J.B. Turner, John Corrill, and others (very many others), including more than eighty-two Manchester and Palmyra (New York) and Harmony (Pennsylvania) neighbors of the Smiths, whose declarations and affidavits were published in *Mormonism Unvailed* in 1834 – were unaware of an 1820 vision first publicly described by Orson Pratt in a protected setting, Edinburgh, Scotland, in 1840.

Not until 1843 – one year before the death of Joseph Smith – did any *"non-Mormon* source publish any reference to the story of the first vision."[6]   Although the Articles and Covenants of the Church of Christ dated June 1830 said that "he had received a remission of his sins" (Book of Commandments 24:6; Doctrine and Covenants 20:5), they did not specifically mention a vision. The First Vision was not mentioned in the introductory material to the 1830 first edition of the Book of Mormon, in the 1832-33 Mormon publication known as *The Evening and the Morning Star,* or in Oliver and Joseph's 1834-35 History (offered as a "full history of the rise of the Church of the Latter Day Saints, and the most interesting parts of its progress, to the present time . . ."[7]). The First Vision was not mentioned in the 1833 Book of Commandments, in the 1835 Book of Doctrine and Covenants, or in the 1835 Lectures on Faith.[8] "As far as Mormon literature is concerned," yet again let it be repeated here, that "there was no reference to Joseph Smith's first vision in any published material in the 1830's."[9] Versions of that vision were, however, described in three unfamiliar 1830s accounts,

---

[5]Ibid.

[6]Ibid., 31, emphasis retained. "Apparently not until 1843, when the *New York Spectator* printed a reporter's account of an interview with Joseph Smith, did a *non-Mormon* source publish any reference to the story of the first vision."

[7]Oliver Cowdery (and Joseph Smith), "Letter to W.W. Phelps, Esq." (Oliver Cowdery and Joseph Smith's 1834-35 History), *Messenger and Advocate*, vol. 1 no. 1, October 1834, 13. The 1834-35 History, the first "authorized" history of the Mormon Church, was published in eight separate installments in the *Latter-day Saints' Messenger and Advocate*, a Mormon publication for a Mormon audience.

[8]Allen, "The Significance of Joseph Smith's 'First Vision' in Mormon Thought," *Dialogue*, vol. 1 no. 3 (Autumn 1966): 32. The Lectures on Faith were the doctrine part of the 1835 edition of the Doctrine and Covenants.

[9]Ibid., 31.

unseen by the members because they were concealed in the manuscript archives of the Mormon Church.

Staggering Bad News

Over the six-year period from 1965 to 1971, four versions of three previously unknown accounts of Joseph Smith's First Vision surfaced after one hundred and thirty years in lock-up. All of the documents were found in the highest value archives of the Mormon Church, where their existence could not have escaped detection. The contents of these forbidden documents were revealed in increments by Paul R. Cheesman in 1965, James B. Allen in 1966 and Dean C. Jessee in 1969 and 1971. In 1965, Latter-day Saints were gently apprised that there was an earlier and previously unknown *first* account of Joseph Smith's first encounter with deity, Joseph Smith's 1832 Holographic Account. In 1966, Latter-day Saints were apprised that there was an earlier and unknown *second* account of Joseph Smith's first encounter with Deity, Joshua 1:1835. In 1969 Latter-day Saints were apprised that there was an earlier and *third* account of Joseph Smith's first encounter with deity, Erastus Holmes:1835. In 1971 Latter-day Saints were apprised that there was a previously unknown *second* version of the *second* account of Joseph Smith's first encounter with deity, Joshua 2:1835.

The accounts known to the Latter-day Saints before 1965 – the 1838-39 Pearl of Great Price Account and John Wentworth: 1842, compatible narratives of the same vision – were published in the *Times and Seasons* (Wentworth first) in March and April 1842.[10] Each of the three *suppressed* accounts preceded in time the 1838-39 Pearl of Great Price Account. The "traditional," "canonized," "official" lionized 1838-39 Pearl of Great Price Account was actually the fourth of the five different accounts to be composed. By 1969, the 1838-39 Pearl of Great Price Account could be

---

[10]Orson Pratt published a version of the 1838-39 Pearl of Great Price Account in Scotland in 1840. Orson Hyde published "an elaborate account" of the 1838-39 Pearl of Great Price Account in Germany in 1842. (Allen, "The Significance of Joseph Smith's 'First Vision' in Mormon Thought," *Dialogue*, vol. 1 no. 3 [Autumn 1966]: 38).

correctly seen for what it then was, at least the fourth, next to last and next to least contemporaneous of what had by then become five presently known primary accounts.

1838-39: THE PEARL OF GREAT PRICE ACCOUNT – JOSEPH SMITH'S FOURTH ACCOUNT OF HIS FIRST ENCOUNTER WITH DEITY

Joseph Smith commenced to create his fourth chronological account of the First Vision in Missouri in 1838. The 1838-39 Pearl of Great Price Account was canonized (divinely sanctioned) and is (since 1965) the Church's "official" (as opposed to "only") account of the First Vision, the founding story of the Church of Jesus Christ of Latter-day Saints and modern Mormon scripture.

"The Prophet's journal containing the 1835 history was turned over and utilized as Book A-1 of the ensuing multivolume work. Evidence in the opening pages of the 'History' shows that Mulholland [Smith's clerk] began writing from a record that had been written the previous year [1838]."[11] Joseph started to compose the 1838-39 Pearl of Great Price Account in 1838; it was recopied and further composed in 1839. He then allowed Orson Pratt to publish an account of it in Scotland in 1840, and it was published by editor Joseph Smith in the *Times and Seasons* in Nauvoo, Illinois, on April 1, 1842. The *Times and Seasons* account was amended in December 1842 after it had already been published.[12] Smith died on June 27, 1844. From the time of its publication in Nauvoo in 1842 until 1965, the 1838-39 Pearl of Great Price Account of the First Vision of the Father and the Son stood supreme and uncontested in grand and glorious prose. "During the last four decades of the twentieth century, all missionaries in every mission, in every language, were required to present the official version of Joseph Smith's First Vision"[13] to their investigators. Joseph Smith,

---

[11]Dean C. Jessee, "The Early Accounts of Joseph Smith's First Vision," *BYU Studies* 9, no. 3 (Spring 1969): 286.

[12]Dean C. Jessee, "How Lovely was the Morning," *Dialogue: A Journal of Mormon Thought* 6, no. 1 (Spring 1971): 87-88.

[13]Stan Larson, "Another Look at Joseph Smith's First Vision," *Dialogue: A Journal of Mormon Thought*, vol. 47 no. 2 (Summer 2014), 55.

the Mormon prophet, had told his story only once.

Contents of the 1838-39 Pearl of Great Price Account

Surrounded by a great religious revival at the place where he lived, Joseph Smith questioned which of all of the sects was right. After reading the Epistle of James[14] (*"If any of you lack wisdom, let him ask of God, that giveth to all men liberally and upbraideth not; and it shall be given him"*[15]), Joseph approached the Lord in prayer in a grove on a "beautiful, clear day, early in the spring of eighteen hundred and twenty" at the age of fourteen and in the fifteenth year of his life. While praying, and preliminary to the vision, he was seized upon by a dark power, entirely overcome and on the verge of despair. At a "moment of great alarm," Joseph "saw a pillar of light" exactly over his head "above the brightness of the sun." "When the light rested upon me I saw two Personages, whose brightness and glory defy all description, standing above me in the air. One of them spake unto me, calling me by name and said, pointing to the other – *This is My Beloved Son. Hear Him!*"[16] Joseph, true to his intended purpose, asked the "Personages" "which of all the sects was right," that he might know which to join. "I was answered that I must join none of them, for they were all wrong; and the Personage who addressed me said that all their creeds were an abomination in his sight; that those professors were all corrupt; that: 'they draw near to me with their lips, but their hearts are far from me, they teach for doctrines the commandments of men, having a form of godliness, but they deny the power thereof.'"[17] God is supposed to have said that to Joseph Smith. With his mind now "satisfied so far as the sectarian world was concerned," Joseph was instructed "to continue as I was until further directed."[18]

---

[14]"Never did any passage of scripture come with more power to the heart of man than this did at this time to mine." (The Pearl of Great Price, Joseph Smith – History 1:12).

[15]Ibid., 1:11, emphasis retained.

[16]Ibid., 1:16-17, emphasis retained.

[17]The Pearl of Great Price, Joseph Smith – History 1:19.

[18]Ibid., 1:26.

Latter-day Saints date the commencement of the dispensation of the fullness of times and the restoration of Christ's original church from this 1820 event. Joseph Smith then grew in stature to become the prophet of the restoration. Upon his untimely death, it was said of him: *"Joseph Smith, the Prophet and Seer of the Lord, has done more, save Jesus only, for the salvation of men in this world, than any other man that ever lived."*[19] *"He holds . . . the keys to rule in the spirit-world; . . . . He reigns there as supreme a being in his sphere capacity, and calling, as God does in heaven."*[20] For members of the church he founded, Joseph Smith is the most important man who ever lived next only to Christ. Sometimes even that is not entirely certain. Everything that made Smith what his followers now say that he was started with that vision of the Father and the Son in the Sacred Grove on a "beautiful clear day, early in the spring of eighteen hundred and twenty."

In 1840, Apostle Orson Pratt market tested an account that tracked the 1838-39 Pearl of Great Price Account in Edinburgh, Scotland, a place far from early Mormonism's center of gravity.[21] Pratt's first publication of what essentially later became the canonized Pearl of Great Price Account was part of a collection entitled *"Remarkable Visions."* The notice of the first American publication of the First Vision in Nauvoo, Illinois, two years later was shockingly understated. When Joseph Smith announced the vision in the semi-monthly *Times and Seasons* on Friday, April 1, 1842, the "thunderbolt" laid "obscurely on page 748: God the Creator of the Universe, had visited the earth and in company with his Son, Jesus Christ, the Redeemer of the World!"[22] The stunning event – if true, the most important event since the resurrection – was not described on the cover page of the Mormon publication, honored with a headline, introduced in bold type or capitalized. "This plain

---

[19]Doctrine and Covenants 135:3, emphasis added.

[20]*The Essential Brigham Young*, with a foreword by Eugene E. Campbell (Salt Lake City: Signature Books, 1992), 130-31, emphasis added.

[21]References to unidentified dual beings who resembled each other and appeared to the boy Joseph were first published in Orson Pratt, *An Interesting Account of Several Remarkable Visions and of the Late Discovery of Ancient American Records* (Edinburgh: Ballantyne and Hughes, 1840) from LaMar Petersen, *The Creation of the Book of Mormon: A Historical Inquiry* (Salt Lake City: Freethinker Press, 2000), 6.

[22]Petersen, *The Creation of the Book of Mormon*, 1.

announcement, set in lower case, and without fanfare, was one of the most astounding items ever to appear in an American publication."[23]

1832: THE HOLOGRAPHIC ACCOUNT – JOSEPH SMITH'S FIRST ACCOUNT OF HIS FIRST ENCOUNTER WITH DEITY

"Sometime during 1831 or 1832 Joseph Smith began his first attempt at autobiography, dictating . . . to his secretary, Frederick T. [sic] Williams."[24] (When Fawn McKay Brodie wrote this in about 1972, she didn't know that the report of the First Vision in Joseph Smith's 1832 Account had been written in his own hand). The 1832 History containing the 1832 Holographic Account was written by Joseph Smith and Frederick G. Williams. It was composed in first person and created at the front of what survived to become the 1829-35 Kirtland Letterbook. The pages, which were subsequently cut from the document for reasons never explained, were obviously vintage, handwritten and autobiographical.

The 1832 Holographic Account was not the work of some disenchanted detractor, some hostile historical resource prepared by some angry critic. Joseph Smith's 1832 Holographic Account "is the earliest explicit mention of a vision."[25] It represents Joseph Smith's "initial personal attempt to record his experience" and is "a record of his own life and a history of 'the rise of the church.'"[26] If one were to disregard for a moment the details of the 1832 manuscript's contents in order to separately consider the manuscript's historical credentials, it is seen to have had an impeccable Mormon provenance. It is easy to see it is a manuscript

---

[23]Ibid.

[24]Fawn M. Brodie, *No Man Knows My History: The Life of Joseph Smith the Mormon Prophet*, 2d ed., rev. and enl. (New York, NY: Alfred A. Knopf, 1972), Supplement, 406. The time period surrounding Joseph's first attempt at autobiography has since been more accurately identified as having been "between 20 July and 27 November 1832" based on Frederick G. William's service to Joseph Smith as scribe. (Joseph Smith Jr., *The Personal Writings of Joseph Smith*, ed. Dean C. Jessee [Salt Lake City, UT: Deseret Book, 1984], 3-4 and fn 6, p. 640).

[25]Grant H. Palmer, *An Insider's View of Mormon Origins* (Salt Lake City: Signature Books, 2002), 236.

[26]Jessee ed., *The Personal Writings of Joseph Smith*, 3-4.

that should never have been ignored. The 1832 Holographic Account was the most important part of "A History of the life of Joseph Smith Jr. an account of his marvilous experience and of all the mighty acts which he doeth in the name of Jesus Ch[r]ist the son of the living God of whom he beareth record *and also an account of the rise of the church of Christ in the eve of time . . . ."*[27] It describes a visionary event supposed to have occurred "in the 16[th] year" of Joseph Smith's life ("<in the sixteenth year of my age>"[28]). The 1832 Account is a pristine foundational document of extraordinary significance.

Origins and Contents

This "earliest known attempt by Joseph Smith to record a history of his life" was handwritten on both sides of the first three leaves of a journal ledger that came to be known as the Kirtland Letter Book: 1829-35.[29] "The non-holograph portions of the document are in the handwriting of Frederick G. Williams."[30] The part written by Smith is a most uncommon rare example of the prophet describing his "marvilous experience" and "mighty acts" in his own hand. This three double-sided six-page history is the earliest known account of the First Vision, the first account of Joseph Smith's first encounter with deity. It is the *only* one of the five presently known primary accounts that was actually written by Joseph Smith. Joseph Smith's 1832 Holographic Account is the primordial telling of the founding story of the Mormon Church.

---

[27]1832 Holographic Account, reproduced at Jessee ed., *The Personal Writings of Joseph Smith*, 4, emphasis added.

[28]This phrase "<in the sixteenth year of my age>" was added above the line (Joseph Smith's line) in the handwriting of Frederick G. Williams.

[29]Dan Vogel, ed., *Early Mormon Documents* (Salt Lake City: Signature Books, 1996), 1:26. Williams began his clerical work for Joseph Smith on July 20, 1832. On November 27, the volume in which the history was written "was converted to a letterbook." (Jessee ed., *The Personal Writings of Joseph Smith*, 640 fn 6).

[30]Jessee ed., *The Personal Writings of Joseph Smith*, 639. In 1969 (and until 1971), Jessee failed to report that any part of the 1832 Account had been handwritten by Joseph Smith. *"An analysis of the handwriting,"* according to Jessee in 1969, *"shows that the narrative was penned by Frederick G. Williams, scribe to the Prophet and counselor in the First Presidency."* (Jessee, "The Early Accounts of Joseph Smith's First Vision," *BYU Studies* 9, no. 3 [Spring 1969]: 277, emphasis added). That is now known to have been incorrect.

Some time after the Mormon prophet wrote the 1832 Account of the First Vision in a journal ledger, *"the leaves [containing the account] were afterward cut from the volume."*[31]   The remainder of the volume survived – with or without those pages – to become the historically important "Kirtland Letter Book: 1829-1835." (*On November 27, 1832, the ledger book containing the 1832 History "was converted to a letter book for recording important historical Church documents"*).[32]   "This volume was listed in an inventory made in Nauvoo, came across the plains to Utah, and ended up in the LDS Church archives – with impeccable 'continuous institutional custody.'"[33]   This 1832 first chronological and only holographic account of Joseph Smith's First Vision was not seen by any general Mormon audience from the date of its drafting *in 1832* until *1965*. It is now known that "the missing pages were kept in the office safe of Joseph Fielding Smith . . ." (the Church Historian who later became the President of the Church).[34]

> At about the age of twelve years my mind become seriously imprest [p. 1] with regard to the all important concerns for the well=fare of my immortal Soul which led me to search=ing the scriptures believeing as I was taught, that they contained the word of God thus applying myself to them and my intimate acquaintance with those of

---

[31]Jessee ed., *The Personal Writings of Joseph Smith*, 639, emphasis added. The "Source Note" and the "Historical Introduction" in the *Joseph Smith Papers* omit "any discussion as to *why* the three leaves were cut out and *who* it was that cut this history out of the letterbook." (Larson, "Another Look at Joseph Smith's First Vision," *Dialogue*, vol. 47 no. 2 [Summer 2014], 41, emphasis retained). "The editors of the Histories volume of the *Joseph Smith Papers* do not discuss why the 1832 history was excised." (Ibid.). "[O]ne can actually date the time period when these [three double-sided] leaves were removed, because the tearing of the last of the three leaves was done with such little care that a small triangular fragment (containing four words of the text) was initially left in the gutter of the letterbook and then removed and taped back onto the last leaf. The clear cellophane tape that was used for this repair was not invented until 1930, which supplies a *terminis a quo*." (Ibid., 40).

[32]Dean C. Jessee, "The Early Accounts of Joseph Smith's First Vision," *BYU Studies* 9, no. 3 (Spring 1969): 277, emphasis added.

[33]Larson, "Another Look at Joseph Smith's First Vision," *Dialogue*, vol. 47 no. 2 (Summer 2014), 40.

[34]Ibid., 41.

different denominations led me to marvel excedingly
for I discovered that <they did not ~~adorn~~> ~~instead~~ of
adorn~~ing~~ their profession by a holy walk and
God=ly conversation agreeable to what I found
contain=ed in that sacred depository this was a grief
to my Soul thus from the age of twelve years to
fifteen I pondered many things in my heart
concerning the sittuation of the world of mankind
the contentions and divi[si]ons the wick[d]ness and
abominations and the darkness which pervaded the
~~of the~~ minds of mankind my mind become
excedingly distressed for I become convicted of my
sins and by searching the scriptures I found that
~~mand~~ <mankind> did not come unto the Lord but
that they had apostatised from the true and liveing
faith and there was no society or denomination that
built upon the gospel of Jesus Christ as recorded in
the new testament and I felt to mourn for my own
sins and for the sins of the world . . . .[35]

After then considering God's unchanging character and the
wonders of the universe, after reflecting upon "the sun the glorious
luminary of the earth," the "moon," the "stars," the "earth," "the
beast of the field and the fowls of heaven and the fish of the waters
and also man walking forth upon the face of the earth in magesty,"
Joseph's heart exclaimed "*well hath the wise man said ~~the~~ <it is a>
fool <that> saith in his heart there is no God.*"[36]

[M]y heart exclaimed all all these bear testimony
and bespeak an omnipotant and omnipreasant
power a being who makith Laws and decreeth and
bindeth all things in their bounds who filleth
Eternity who was and is and will be from all
Eternity to Eternity and when I considered all these
things and that <that> being seeketh such to
worship him as wors=hip him in spirit and in truth
therefore I cried unto the Lord for mercy for there

---

[35]Jessee ed., *The Personal Writings of Joseph Smith*, 4-5.
[36]Ibid., 5, emphasis added.

was none else to whom I could go and ~~to~~ obtain
mercy and the Lord heard my cry in the wilderne=ss
and while in <the> attitude of calling upon the Lord
<in the 16th year of my age> a piller of ~~fire~~ light
above the brightness of the sun at noon day come
down from above and rested upon me and I was
filled with the spirit of god, and the <Lord> opened
the heavens upon me and I saw the Lord and he
spake unto me saying Joseph <my son> thy sins are
forgiven thee. go thy <way> walk in my statutes and
keep my commandments behold I am the Lord of
glory I was crucifyed for the world that all those
who believe on my name may have Eternal life
<behold> the world lieth in sin ~~and~~ at this time and
none doeth good no not one they have turned asside
from the Gospel and keep not <my> commandments
they draw near to me with their lips while their
hearts are far from me and mine anger is kindling
against the inhabitants of the earth to visit them
acording to th[e]ir ungodliness and to bring to pass
that which <hath> been spoken by the mouth of the
prophe=ts and Ap[o]stles behold and lo I come
quickly as it [is] wr=itten of me in the cloud
<clothed> in the glory of my Father and my soul
was filled with love and for many days I could
rejoice with great Joy and the Lord was with me but
[I] could find none that would believe the hevnly
vision nevertheless I pondered these things in my
heart . . . .³⁷

This profoundly important 1832 epiphany was:

*An account of a vision that reflected Joseph's 1832 early
monotheistic belief in one God, and*

*An account of the First Vision that marked the visit of but a
single personage; only Jesus (the "crucifyed" Lord) appeared*

---

³⁷Jessee ed., *The Personal Writings of Joseph Smith*, 5-6.

> to Joseph Smith in this 1832 Account of an 1821 vision
> received "<in the 16th year of my age>."

The Suppression of the Holograph
1952: LaMar Petersen Interviews President Levi Edgar Young

LaMar Petersen, a young Mormon musician from a strong Mormon
family, gathered information over the years from more than half a
dozen important Mormon leaders.[38] In his book entitled *The
Creation of the Book of Mormon, A Historical Inquiry*, Petersen
described visits with President Levi Edgar Young, an academic and
one of the Seven Presidents of the Seventies from 1941-1963. In
1952 Petersen and his wife had six sessions with President Young,
who described Joseph Smith's 1832 account of the First Vision
twelve or thirteen years before a typescript mysteriously surfaced in
1965 and approximately seventeen years before the Church
acknowledged the authenticity of the 1832 account in 1969.

> He [President Levi Edgar Young] was forthright in
> discussing Mormon problems in history and theology,
> but always in loyal church terms. He told us that he
> had been defended before the First Presidency by his
> "buffers" – Apostles Merrill, Callis, and Widtsoe.
>
> He told us of a "strange account" (Young's own term)
> of the First Vision, which he thought was written in
> Joseph's own hand and which had been concealed for
> 120 years [in 1952] in a locked vault. He declined to
> tell us details, but stated that it did not agree entirely
> with the official version. Jesus was the center of the
> vision, but God was not mentioned. I respected
> Young's wish that the information be withheld until
> after his death.[39]

---

[38]George Albert Smith, David O. McKay, J. Reuben Clark, Jr., James E.
Talmage, John A. Widtsoe, Richard L. Evans, Joseph Wirthlin, Milton R. Hunter,
Hartman Rector, Jr., and Levi Edgar Young. (Petersen, *The Creation of the Book
of Mormon*, Foreword, xi-xii).

[39]Petersen, *The Creation of the Book of Mormon*, Foreword, xii, emphasis
added.

President Young thought the account had been "written in Joseph's own hand." While he did not wish to be identified with the disclosure of that information during his lifetime, he did not foreclose the possibility that the existence of the "strange account" might be declared sometime "after his death."[40] Notes prepared by LaMar Petersen after a February 3, 1953, interview, provided this further clarification.

> *His [Levi Edgar Young's] curiosity was excited when reading in Roberts' Doc. History reference to "documents from which these writings were compiled." Asked to see them. Told to get higher permission. Obtained that permission. Examined the documents. Written, he thought, about 1837 or 1838 [later determined to be 1832]. Was told not to copy or tell what they contained. Said it was a "strange" account of the First Vision. Was put back in vault. Remains unused, unknown.*[41]

A Secret That Couldn't Be Kept

Given that higher permission was required to see those severed double-sided leaves, given that those who were allowed to see them after first obtaining "higher permission" were not allowed to copy or discuss them, Levi Edgar Young defied convention and broke the rules. With the passage of time, it came to be suspected that the Mormon Church secretly possessed a previously unpublished account of Mormonism's greatest ever event – that there was an early and unpublished account of the founding story of the Mormon Church. The fact that the Church had suppressed an unfamiliar account of Joseph Smith's First Vision became known to some of Mormonism's detractors. In early 1964 LaMar Petersen told Jerald and Sandra Tanner about this "strange account" of the First

---

[40]Ibid.

[41]Jerald Tanner and Sandra Tanner, *Mormonism – Shadow or Reality?* (Salt Lake City: Utah Lighthouse Ministry, 1987), 145, citing notes from LaMar Petersen, author of *The Creation of the Book of Mormon*, emphasis added.

Vision.[42] Before the 1965 publication of the previously unpublished manuscript, Jerald and Sandra Tanner wrote a letter to the Church Historian, Joseph Fielding Smith, and requested a copy of the missing secret account.[43] Smith did not respond to the Tanners' request. The letter did, however, put the leaders of the Church on notice that the dissident historians had acquired confidential information concerning the concealed account. No outsider had written about the 1832 Account (or about the true contents of two other unpublished 1835 accounts), and Mormon scholars had not described them. The 1832 Account could not have escaped detection in the high value Kirtland Letter Book: 1829-35 for a hundred and thirty years.

Meeting the World as "Appendix D"

The allegedly innocent discovery of the first account of Joseph Smith's first encounter with deity, as improbable as it may seem, is supposed to have been made by a Brigham Young University graduate student, Paul R. Cheesman, one hundred and thirty-three years after the account was first composed. In 1965, Mr. Cheesman attached a typescript of Joseph Smith's 1832 Holographic Account to his Brigham Young University Master's Thesis, marking the profoundly important historic document "Appendix D." It was ultimately by means of this inconspicuous Appendix D that the members of the Mormon Church learned *in 1965* that Joseph Smith had told his story more than once.

Cheesman said that he found the previously unpublished "earliest written account of the first vision" lying loose in the same "journal ledger" from which the three double-sided leaves had been "cut." "This account was never published or referred to by any of the authorities of the church as far as the writer has been able to determine. From the lack of recognition and importance given this document, it seems evident that it was a draft which was started but

---

[42]Larson, "Another Look at Joseph Smith's First Vision," *Dialogue*, vol. 47 no. 2 (Summer 2014), 42.
    [43]Tanner and Tanner, *Mormonism – Shadow or Reality?*, 145.

never corrected or finished."[44] The graduate student suggested the document although known, was unimportant, incomplete and never published.

Mr. Cheesman then further reported that Joseph Smith had provided an account of the First Vision to a man by the name of Erastus Holmes. He included an incomplete description of that account in the text of his Thesis entitled, "An Analysis of the Accounts Relating Joseph Smith's Early Visions."[45] The graduate student's purpose had been to identify and describe early accounts of early visions and he had found the prize – Joseph Smith's 1832 first chronological and only holographic account of a vision of Jesus.

1832 to 1965: "What Once Was Lost Now Is Found"

The 1965 disclosure of the 1832 Account demonstrated that Joseph had described the First Vision in writing before he and Cowdery prepared the first authorized History of the Church of Latter Day Saints (a history that failed to describe the vision at all) in 1834-35. Smith knew in 1834-35 that he had already written an account of an encounter with the "crucifyed" Lord in 1832.

When Mr. Cheesman discovered that Joseph Smith had either written or dictated what was then an "undated" account of his first encounter with deity, he reported that, *"This account was found in a journal ledger in the Church Historian's office [in] Salt Lake City. The pages had been cut out but were matched with [the] edge of the journal to prove location."*[46] "This [ensuing authentication of the proof of location] was done in the presence and with agreement of Earl Olsen and Lauritz Peterson of the Church Historian's office." When the three double-sided pages containing the six-page history were examined, it was determined that "The first page of this ledger

---

[44]Paul R. Cheesman, "An Analysis of the Accounts Relating Joseph Smith's Early Visions" (Master of Religious Education Thesis, Brigham Young University, 1965), 64.

[45]Ibid., 23.

[46]Cheesman, "An Analysis of the Accounts Relating Joseph Smith's Early Visions," 126, emphasis added.

identified Frederick G. Williams as the scribe and bore the date of 1833."[47] Cheesman then referred to the attached Exhibit D as an "Undated Manuscript." A more precise date (1832) would be assigned sometime later based on the period of Williams' known service to Smith as scribe.[48] The "journal ledger" described by the graduate student was the prominent "Kirtland Letter Book: 1829-1835."[49] No Mormon leader, historian or scholar stepped forward to say that the account was authentic, and what the student said was this:

> There was not date nor indication of scribe of the account of the manuscript which follows [Appendix D]. The information provided in the above statements seem to suggest that this account was written near 1833. Since it is recorded in the first person this would also suggest either that Joseph Smith wrote it or he dictated it. From handwriting comparisons it would appear that the latter supposition is the more likely one.[50]

The graduate student had seen more than a typescript. President Levi Edgar Young thought (in 1952) that the "strange account" "was written in Joseph's own hand." The student who first produced the typescript (Appendix D) in 1965, who had examined the manuscript, said that it probably wasn't. That uncomplicated issue wouldn't be resolved for another six years, until 1971.

In order to credit Mr. Cheesman's allegedly innocent recounting, one must assume that no historian, archivist, librarian, scholar, clerk, member, secretary, student or future Church president identified (or appreciated the importance of) Joseph Smith's handwritten first account of his first encounter with deity. One

---

[47] Ibid.

[48] Jessee ed., *The Personal Writings of Joseph Smith*, 3 fn 6, 640.

[49] "Subsequent pages in the journal [Kirtland Letter Book: 1829-35] contained copies of letters of Oliver Cowdery, Joseph Smith, Hyrum Smith, William W. Phelps, Reynolds Cahoon, Jared Clark, Sidney Rigdon, and John Murdock. The earliest letter was dated June 14, 1829; the latest August 4, 1835." (Cheesman, "An Analysis of the Accounts Relating Joseph Smith's Early Visions," 126).

[50] Ibid.

must assume that no one ever before had thought to match the loose pages found in the important "journal ledger" against the "edge of the journal to prove location," and/or that no one read those materials and recognized the manuscript's remarkable contents. No matter who wrote them. Had anyone who was in and out of that important book placed those loose pages against "the terminal letters of words severed when the pages were removed," an obvious match was easily made. So why wasn't an obvious match easily made? (1) Because the cut and severed pages were not lying loose in the "journal ledger" for a hundred and thirty years; but were rather concealed – "unused, unknown" – available only to those who could be trusted not to tell the truth; and/or (2) because they couldn't be removed without "higher permission," or copied or described. If a Brigham Young University graduate student had access to the historic Kirtland Letter Book: 1829-35, others undoubtedly did. It would seem impossible to say that the undated account had been kept for a hundred and thirty years in that journal ledger at the place the graduate student said it was found. If that had been the case, then why were the pages cut?

Misgivings: Softening the Strange Disclosure

No Brigham Young University graduate student enjoyed privileged access to the materials in the Church Historian's locked vault,[51] and it is highly unlikely that a graduate student accidentally stumbled upon Joseph Smith's century-long highly restricted hidden holograph while doing research in the "manuscript archives of the Mormon Church in Salt Lake City." The three double-sided pages represented (in the Thesis) by the typescript, "Appendix D," hadn't spent one hundred and thirty-three years in the Kirtland Letter Book. The journey from locked vault, "do not copy or tell," to

---

[51]The graduate student's analysis of the accounts relating to Joseph Smith's early visions failed to describe the contents of two 1835 accounts Joseph gave to Joshua the Jewish Minister ("Joshua 1:1835" and "Joshua 2:1835"). No ordinary Latter-day Saint knew at the time that Joseph Smith had given an account of the First Vision to "the Jewish Minister." While the graduate student knew that Joseph Smith had given an account of the First Vision to a man by the name of Erastus Holmes (Erastus Holmes: 1835), he didn't know that the contents of that account had been falsified in the History of the Church (his research resource).

"Appendix D" ("it was a draft which was started but never corrected or finished") could not have been inadvertent. The publication of the first chronological account of the First Vision could not have occurred without the permission of the highest leaders of the Mormon Church, one of whom was Joseph Fielding Smith.

To present the missing materials in an innocuous way in an inconspicuous place was to minimize their importance and soften the impact of a thirteen-decade deception. What needed to be minimized and softened? *The fact that the earliest known and only handwritten account of the First Vision failed to mention God the Father. What it did mention was just "one God."*

"Strategery"

The Church allowed the publication of the controversial holographic document without institutional comment in the face of two equally unsuitable options: First, to say that there was no such document; second, to call it restricted and refuse to see it produced. There is a certain perverse logic to the Appendix D approach to the disclosure of the potentially explosive document. The leaders of the Mormon Church have *suppressed* the publication of Joseph Smith's first handwritten account of his first encounter with deity from 1832 to 1965. Can they simply say so? Can they say we cut those three double-sided leaves containing six pages of profoundly historic text out of the letter book and kept them concealed in a locked vault for a hundred and thirty years? Can they say that only the most highly trusted insiders knew anything about that strange and unfamiliar account? Or that "higher permission" was required to see the account? Or that those who got permission promised not to copy the contents, or say what the account contained? Can they say it wasn't something the members needed to know?[52] Could the Church step up and admit historical fraud? Or simply say that it was sorry?

---

[52]"There is a temptation for the writer or the teacher of church history," a modern Mormon leader says, "to want to tell everything whether it is worthy or faith promoting or not. Some things that are true are not very useful." (Apostle Boyd K. Packer, quoted in the *Salt Lake Tribune*, July 30, 2007).

How shall the Church begin to explain this problem in 1965 if its detractors know about this early and discordant account, and if disclosure has become an unfortunate imperative? Can it say that the leaves laid loose in the ledger from 1832 to 1965, somehow overlooked? Can it say that some of its scholars may have seen the manuscript without recognizing how important it was? That the document was fragmentary and incomplete? That Joseph's 1832 understanding of his 1821 vision wasn't all that someone might expect? And if it should decide to say those things, and/or some other things like them, who is equipped to discover and softly reveal what those leaders could only hope against hope to call an unintended mistake? How should the Church identify and softly describe that hundred-year hidden manuscript, an unforgivable deception?

A Brigham Young University graduate student reports that "this account was never published or referred to by any of the authorities of the church as far as the writer has been able to determine."[53] Could there be any more impressive proof of the manuscript's insignificance? It was known about, thought about, but never mentioned or published. *Enter then Brigham Young University graduate student Paul R. Cheesman and his inconspicuous Appendix D.*

Making the "It Is Only Fragmentary" Case

The graduate student did not describe his allegedly remarkable discovery with anything approaching elation. "It is also notable that Joseph Smith evidently attempted to dictate an account of these experiences as early as approximately 1833."[54] When Mr. Cheesman composed his thesis, he believed the 1832 Account had been written as early as 1833. Without hesitation the graduate student made the "it is only fragmentary" case. In that, the most contemporaneous and intimate account of Smith's First Vision – an account which substantively challenged all later accounts – was immediately depreciated. "From the lack of recognition and

---

[53]Cheesman, "An Analysis of the Accounts Relating Joseph Smith's Early Visions," 64.

[54]Ibid., 3.

importance given this document, it seems evident that it was a draft which was started but never corrected or finished."[55] Although no Mormon authority referred in print to the contents of this account, no authority familiar with the document could have failed to recognize its supreme historic importance. The first account of the First Vision, the first report of Joseph's first encounter with deity written by the prophet in his own hand, was a document no one could ever think to dismiss.

The contents of the hundred-year hidden manuscript had to be embarrassing to the leaders of the Church. The twentieth-century disclosure of this vitally important nineteenth-century document challenged the integrity of generations of leaders, historians and archivists. And Joseph Smith's handwritten 1832 Account, a monotheist's first account, challenged Joseph's masterpiece, the founding story of the Mormon Church, the 1838-39 Pearl of Great Price Account, which was the "hinge pin" upon which the whole cause turned. The 1832 first chronological and only holographic account of a vision of Jesus was part of a record kept according to commandment. ("Behold, there shall be a record kept among you . . ."[56]). Yet it was not used for any gospel purpose. It was rescued from historical purgatory out of regrettable necessity, because known to influential others, and reluctantly published at an inconspicuous place without institutional comment.

Minefields

The graduate student described the uncomfortable relationship between the 1832 Holographic Epiphany and the 1838-39 Pearl of Great Price Account in these terms: "Instead of going back over and revising, Joseph Smith evidently dictated the story later as we have it in Appendix A."[57] Appendix A to the student's Thesis was the manuscript history. What that meant was that it might still be said that Joseph Smith told his story only once. That the two

---

[55]Ibid., 64.

[56]Doctrine and Covenants 21:1.

[57]Cheesman, "An Analysis of the Accounts Relating Joseph Smith's Early Visions," 64. Appendix A is Joseph Smith's Original Manuscript History, and Appendix B is the 1838-39 Pearl of Great Price Account.

strikingly different tellings written six years apart had been reconciled. It meant that Smith ignored the early account and composed his elaborate 1838-39 Account of that 1820 event from scratch. It is immediately apparent that the 1838-39 Account, composed with the help of a committee, is better regarded than the 1832 Holographic Account handwritten by Smith. The 1838-39 Pearl of Great Price Account, composed for "institutional purposes" and "streamlined" for publication (by God knows whom), is anything but a restatement of Joseph Smith's 1832 Account. It is a new account several times the size of the earlier account, full of never-before mentioned events, asking a different question to different messengers, receiving a different answer and promoting a different purpose. The 1838-39 Pearl of Great Price Account, the _fourth_ chronological draft of Joseph Smith's 1820 vision, only barely resembles the 1832 Holographic Account, the _first_ chronological draft of Joseph Smith's 1821 vision. They are substantively different accounts. In 1832 the prophet Joseph Smith, a pronounced monotheist, believed in "one God." The first account of the First Vision described a trinitarian deity.

The awkward sequence of events and the manipulation of the various accounts reflecting the serial drafting of previously unreported enhancements was described by Richard L. Bushman: "In his first narrative [the 1832 Holographic Account], Joseph said only that he saw the Lord in the light and heard His words of forgiveness. In 1835, he said that first one personage appeared and then another [he said he saw "many angels" in this vision]. In 1838, he reported [that] the first [personage] pointed to the other [these persons appeared simultaneously] and said, 'This is my beloved Son, Hear him' [Smith's fourth narrative, was not publicly reported until 1842]."[58] In this vision (the 1838 vision), there is no reference to any "angels." Bushman states these controversial facts but doesn't try to explain them.

---

[58]Richard Lyman Bushman with the assistance of Jed Woodworth, *Joseph Smith: Rough Stone Rolling* (New York: Alfred A. Knopf, 2005), 40.

Joseph's Age

Joseph Smith's 1832 Holographic Account described the visit by Jesus as having occurred when Joseph Smith was fifteen years old ("<in the 16th year of my age>"). In the 1835 second and third chronological accounts of the First Vision (Joshua 1 and 2: 1835, and Erastus Holmes: 1835), Joseph is "about fourteen years old." In the 1838-39 Pearl of Great Price Account he is fourteen years old and in the fifteenth year of his age in the spring of 1820. Would Joseph Smith, who achieved his majority many years before he described any of these incredible encounters as a mature adult, forget the date he was visited by the "crucifyed" Lord, or his age at the time of the great event?

Jesus was the center of the vision, but God was not mentioned.

What was it that made the reluctant disclosure of this previously unknown 1832 Account so threatening? What caused the graduate student to immediately denigrate this allegedly remarkable discovery? The first great contradiction, as already expressed, is this: The most intimate and first contemporaneous account of the First Vision describes a visit by Jesus Christ to Joseph Smith no earlier than 1821. In this unfamiliar account, Smith describes the "crucifyed" Lord, meaning only Jesus; the Father isn't mentioned. Levi Edgar Young knew this about the "strange account" in 1952. Joseph Smith's 1832 Account was composed when Joseph Smith and all early sacred Mormon scriptural resources[59] still taught that there was only *one God*. It can not be said often enough that the Mormon prophet was a monotheist in 1832. He had not yet divided the Father from the Son. In 1832 he believed in an indivisible God and in a union of the deities. Prior to 1832, and even later, Joseph Smith embraced a peculiar nineteenth-century New England Alternative Trinitarian Godhead of Christ theology. During his early monotheistic (modalistic) period, he posited the Father as the Son and "one God," "omnipotant," "omnipreasant," "eternal," "crucifyed," a "spirit" and "supreme." The Book of Mormon's 1830 indivisible Messiah (until the second edition was amended in

---

[59]See Chapter 1.

1837) was "the Lamb of God, yea, even the Eternal Father." The Father was the begetter and the begotten. "[T]he Lord he is God, & beside him there is none else."[60] "And they [the Father and Son] are one God, yea, the very Eternal Father of heaven and of earth."[61] The 1832 Holographic Account of Joseph's earliest encounter with the "crucifyed" Lord is but further proof of those assertions.[62] The teachings of Joseph Smith in the early 1830s were "essentially trinitarian" and decidedly monotheistic. Smith's early teachings more closely resemble those of the nineteenth-century New England alternative Trinitarians than they do the teachings of the modern

---

[60]*The Joseph Smith Papers: Revelations and Translations: Manuscript Revelation Books*, ed. Robin Scott Jensen, Robert J. Woodford, Steven C. Harper, vol. 2, facsimile ed. (The Church Historian's Press, general editors: Dean C. Jessee, Ronald K. Esplin, Richard Lyman Bushman, 2009), Revelation Book 1, 243.

[61]Book of Mormon, Mosiah 15:4.

[62]When Joseph Smith thought that God the Father and Jesus Christ were *one* God in 1832, he described *one* God in 1832. When Joseph Smith thought that God the Father and Jesus Christ were *two* Gods in 1838-1839, he described *two* Gods in 1838-1839. The following revisions made by Joseph Smith in the 1837 second edition of the Book of Mormon (repeated here) reflect how Joseph Smith's conception of God and Jesus changed after 1832 and before 1838-39:

. . . Behold, *the virgin which thou seest, is the mother of God, after the manner of the flesh."* [Book of Mormon, 1830 edition, page 25, emphasis added].

. . . Behold, *the virgin which thou seest is the mother of the Son of God, after the manner of the flesh.* [Book of Mormon, current edition, 1 Nephi 11:18, emphasis added].

And the angel said unto me, *behold the Lamb of God, yea, even the Eternal Father!* [Book of Mormon, 1830 edition, 25, emphasis added].

And the angel said unto me, *Behold the Lamb of God, yea, even the Son of the Eternal Father!* [Book of Mormon, current edition, 1 Nephi 11:21, emphasis added].

. . . *[T]he Everlasting God, was judged of the world; and I saw and bear record.* [Book of Mormon, 1830 edition, page 26, emphasis added].

. . . *[T]he Son of the everlasting God was judged of the world; and I saw and bear record.* [Book of Mormon, current edition, 1 Nephi 11:32, emphasis added].

. . . [A]nd shall make known to all kindreds, tongues, and people, that the Lamb of God is the Eternal Father and the Saviour of the world [Book of Mormon, 1830 edition, 32].

. . . [A]nd shall make known to all kindreds, tongues, and people, that the Lamb of God is the *Son of the* Eternal Father and the Saviour of the world . . . . [Book of Mormon, current edition, 1 Nephi 13:40, emphasis added].

With these revisions, Joseph hoped to separate the Father from the Son.

Mormon Church.   When Joseph Smith abandoned his early
monotheistic views after the publication of the Book of Mormon,
which made that reordering very difficult, he changed his mind
about the Godhead of Christ and tried to separate the Father from
the Son (Smith did not take steps to separate the Father from the
Son until 1834-35).   That irreconcilable discrepancy (conflicting
teachings about the nature of God) threatened the philosophical
foundations of the Church and consigned Joseph Smith's 1832
Holographic Account – an account that reflected an earlier and
abandoned view – to the historical dustbin for more than one
hundred and thirty years.

From God to Gods: 1832 to 1838-39

Graduate Student Paul R. Cheesman: *"As he writes briefly of the
vision, he does not mention the Father as being present; however this
does not indicate that He was not present."*[63]   The thought, on its
face, given that this is 1832, is preposterous. President Levi Edgar
Young: ". . . *God was not mentioned.*"[64]   The 1832 Account
described but one God, the "*crucifyed*" Lord.   The 1832 and 1838
Accounts, supposed to describe the same event, involved different
messengers, messages, missions, ages and dates.   Student/scholar
Cheesman, at his core, shared the stated views of men like B.H.
Roberts, Gordon B. Hinckley, Joseph Fielding Smith, Hugh B.
Brown, Sterling McMurrin, and many others, to the effect that
Mormonism stands or falls with these visions.

> *Members of the Church of Jesus Christ of Latter-day
> Saints bear testimony that they have received a
> spiritual assurance of the actuality of Joseph Smith's
> first vision. The principle of revelation from heaven
> has become the rock upon which the organization has
> grown. Thus the Church of Jesus Christ of Latter-day
> Saints and the story of Joseph Smith must stand or*

---

[63]Cheesman, "An Analysis of the Accounts Relating Joseph Smith's Early
Visions," 63, emphasis added.

[64]Levi Edgar Young quoted in Petersen, *The Creation of the Book of Mormon*,
xii, emphasis added.

fail on the authenticity of the First Vision and the appearance of the Angel Moroni.[65]

Joseph Smith's 1832 Holographic Account, like the 1830 first edition of the Book of Mormon (before those 1837 amendments), challenges modern Mormon teachings about the nature of God. Some scholars say that until about 1834 Joseph Smith believed and taught "the [orthodox] Trinitarian concept of traditional Christianity."[66] Others describe his early teachings as "essentially Trinitarian." Some Latter-day Saints and some detractors have said that the godhead theology of the Book of Mormon promotes the Sabellian heresy, by that to say a peculiar (heterodox) doctrine called modalism.[67] The 1830 first edition of the Book of Mormon (before those 1837 second edition amendments) "crucifyed" the Father, like Tertullian said the Sabellians did. Mormonism's early sacred texts gave a Josephized kind of trinity a clean sweep. The plain language of those early resources, unhampered by semantic distortion, consistently supports the authenticity of the godhead theology described in the 1830 edition of the Book of Mormon and in the 1832 Holographic Account of the First Vision, and threatens the authenticity of the godhead theology described in the 1837 altered edition of the Book of Mormon and in the 1838-39 Pearl of Great Price Account of an 1820 vision of the Father *and* the Son. Until 1834 or so, Joseph Smith's godhead theology was uncommonly close to the "trinitarian" concepts advanced by various nineteenth-century New England Alternative Trinitarian reformers like Nathanael Emmons, Moses Stuart, Ethan Smith,

---

[65]Cheesman, "An Analysis of the Accounts Relating Joseph Smith's Early Visions," 75, emphasis added. Mr. Cheesman was predictably distressed by Joseph's use of the word "angel" to describe the visitation of deities. His laborious efforts to justify the awkward use of that particular term to describe the Father and the Son are discussed in his Thesis at pp. 66-67.

[66]*See* those assertions in the chapter entitled "One God."

[67]The Book of Mormon's teachings about the Father and the Son have caused confusion in the ranks. ("Behold, I am Jesus Christ. I am the Father and the Son. [Book of Mormon, Ether 3:14]). In 1916 the First Presidency and the Quorum of the Twelve Apostles issued "A Doctrinal Exposition" intended to clarify the meaning of certain scriptures that clearly designated Jesus Christ as the Father. It is a painful disquisition. ("Jesus Christ the 'Father' by Divine Investiture of Authority," "Jesus Christ the 'Father' of Those Who Abide in His Gospel," "Father as Creator"). (*Improvement Era* [August 1916], 934-42).

Jedidiah Morse and others.[68]

"[T]he four editors of this volume of the *Joseph Smith Papers* [the volume that printed the 1832 account in 2012 under the title 'History, Circa Summer 1832'] . . . leave the content of this significant 1832 narrative largely unaddressed." This is a clever stratagem. "They use generic terms in their 'Historical Intro- duction,' purposefully and carefully referring to it as a 'vision of Deity' and a 'theophany.' This allows them to legitimately refer to a vision of God, a vision of Jesus, or a vision of both the Father and the Son, without drawing attention to the fact that the 1832 account mentions only a vision of Jesus."[69]

> Later, in the reproduction of the actual text of the 1832 account of the First Vision, at the point where Joseph Smith states: "I saw the Lord," the editors add a footnote: "JS later recounted [years later] that he saw two 'personages,' that one appeared after the other, and that 'they did in reality speak unto me, or one of them did.'"[70]

After Joseph changed his mind about the trinity, and many years after his death, Mormon missionaries began to use what the Church had by then come to consider the discredited doctrine of the trinity to their proselytizing advantage. The missionaries routinely described a trinitarian strawman, informing other Christians what the Mormons said that they believed. "[You] [everyone but Mormons] 'worship one God in Trinity, and Trinity in Unity,

---

[68]The Community of Christ (formerly known as the Reorganized Church of Jesus Christ of Latter Day Saints and the church of Joseph Smith's namesake son (another prophet, Joseph Smith III), faithful to the doctrine enunciated in the Book of Mormon and in other early Mormon resources, "still interprets Book of Mormon godhead passages as trinitarian." (Anthony Chvala-Smith, "A Becoming Faith," *Saints Herald* 145 [April 1998]:17, quoted in Palmer, *An Insider's View of Mormon Origins*, 123).

[69]Karen Lynn Davidson, David J. Whittaker, Mark Ashurst-McGee, and Richard L. Jensen, eds., *Joseph Smith Histories, 1832-1844*, first volume of the Histories series of *The Joseph Smith Papers* (Salt Lake City: The Church Historian's Press, 2012), 11-13, quoted and clarified in Larson, "Another Look at Joseph Smith's First Vision," *Dialogue*, vol. 47 no. 2 (Summer 2014), 57 fn 3.

[70]Ibid, 40-41, 57 fn 6.

neither confounding the persons, nor dividing the substance . . . . So the Father is God, the Son is God, and the Holy Ghost is God, and yet there are not three Gods but one God.'" "You [everyone but Mormons] believe in a 'mystical union of substance' and in an 'unnatural and therefore impossible blending of personality.'" "It would be difficult," James E. Talmage says, "to conceive of a greater number of inconsistencies and contradictions expressed in words as few."[71]

The most sluggish missionary could use these arguments to good advantage. With the help of the 1838-39 Pearl of Great Price Account of an 1820 vision of the Father and the Son – by now two separate and distinct personages – the missionaries knocked that trinitarian strawman down by ignoring Smith's *early* conception of the Father and the Son as "one God," and emphasizing Smith's *later* conception of the Father and the Son as two Gods "in form and stature perfect men."[72] For more than a hundred years, Mormon missionaries have routinely disparaged a doctrine their founder *initially* taught with monotheistic exuberance. Modern Mormons see God the Father and Jesus Christ through the eyes of the *later* Smith. What Joseph described in 1832 – in his own hand – was exactly what one would have expected him to describe in 1832, given his then belief.

The 1838-39 Pearl of Great Price Account, describing "two Personages, whose brightness and glory" defied "all description," could not have been written in 1832, because in 1832 Joseph Smith believed the indivisible Father was the indivisible Son. The Book of Mormon said Jesus was the Eternal Father. Joseph Smith, who first believed in "one God," changed the Book of Mormon (in 1837), separating the Father from the Son, in order to reflect his then evolving view. The 1832 Account of the First Vision of the Son, describing the visit of a single personage – the "omnipotant," "omnipreasant," "crucifyed" Lord – in the sixteenth year of the prophet's age, cannot be reconciled with the 1838-39 Account of the

---

[71]James E. Talmage, *A Study of the Articles of Faith: Being a Consideration of the Principal Doctrines of The Church of Jesus Christ of Latter-day Saints*, 33rd ed. (Salt Lake City: The Church of Jesus Christ of Latter-day Saints, 1955), 48; *see*, e.g., 41, 47.
[72]Ibid., 42.

First Vision of the Father and the Son, describing the visit of two anthropomorphic personages (two gods in a grove) in the fifteenth year of the prophet's age. Or with the canonized Lectures on Faith, the doctrine part of the Doctrine and Covenants from 1835 to 1921, describing what was a spirit Father and an anthropomorphic Son.

1835: JOSHUA THE JEWISH MINISTER (JOSHUA 1 AND 2:1835): JOSEPH SMITH'S SECOND ACCOUNT OF HIS FIRST ENCOUNTER WITH DEITY

Joshua the Jewish Minister

He briefly walks into Mormon history on Monday morning, November 9, 1835. His beard is about three inches long and quite grey. "[H]is hair is long and considerably silvered with age." He appears to be "about 50 or 55 years old, tall and strait slender built of thin visage blue eyes, and fair com=plexion." He wears "a sea green frock coat" and "pantaloons of the same," and a "black fur hat" with a narrow brim. When he speaks, he "frequently shuts his eyes with a scowl on his countinance."[73] This unusual man will inform his fascinated host that he is "God the Father reincarnated in the body of Matthias the ancient apostle." In 1830, Joshua the Jewish Minister "prophesied the destruction of Albany." "He taught that no man who shaved could be a true Christian." He left his home and family in Albany "to embark on a grand apostolic preaching tour through the East and South." "Committed to the hospital for the insane at Bellevue for a time, he was brought to trial in April 1835 at White Plains, New York, on murder charges." A Mr. Pierson had died after eating blackberries he had prepared. "He was acquitted of the murder charge but was confined in jail three months for brutality,"[74] for "contempt of court," and for "whipping his daughter."[75] On November 9, 1835, when he introduced himself to Joseph Smith, he had only recently been released from prison.

---

[73]Roberts, ed., *History of The Church of Jesus Christ of Latter-day Saints*, 2:304, quoted in Jessee ed., *The Personal Writings of Joseph Smith*, 74-75.
[74]Jessee ed., *The Personal Writings of Joseph Smith*, 654 fn 57.
[75]Brodie, *No Man Knows My History*, Supplement, 407-08.

"[W]hile setting in my house between the hours of ten & 11 this morning a man came in, and introduced himself to me, calling <himself> by the name of Joshua the Jewish minister."[76]   Not entirely satisfied with half a name, that too exceedingly strange, Joseph Smith "made some [further] enquiry after his name but received no definite answer; we soon comm=enced talking upon the subject of religion . . . ."[77]   Joseph took this peculiar Joshua seriously.   The strange man was "Robert Matthews or Matthias, *alias* Joshua the Jewish Minister."[78]   Joseph "proposed that he should deliver a lecture" to a congregation of curious saints, who suspected that the "reputed" Jew was "the noted Matthias of New York," and he was.[79]   It is to Matthews, "God the Father reincarnated in the body of Matthias the ancient apostle," a "religious mystic" and an ex-convict, that Joseph Smith will provide an unusual *second* chronological account of the First Vision. Smith's first-person account, Joshua 2:1835, was recorded in Joseph's Personal Diary – although no ordinary Mormon will know that until 1971 – in the handwriting of Joseph's scribe, Warren Parrish.   It was also written in "third person singular," Joshua 1:1835, in Smith's Manuscript History, Book A-1 (the handwritten manuscript of the *History of the Church*) – although no ordinary Mormon will know that until 1966 – in the handwriting of yet another scribe, Warren A. Cowdery.[80] The "Manuscript" account appears to be a copy of the "Diary" account. Joshua 2:1835, the version of the account first written, was the second of the two accounts to be disclosed (that in 1971). The actual contents of both accounts were, for obvious reasons, long suppressed.

While informing the faithful and teaching investigators until 1965 that Joseph Smith told his story only once, the Church secretly retained in its highest value archives at least three other discrepant accounts of the now famous vision, one of them the handwritten

---

[76] Jessee ed., *The Personal Writings of Joseph Smith*, 74 (citing Joseph Smith's Diary for November 9, 1835).

[77] Ibid., 75.

[78] Ibid., 654 fn 57, emphasis added. Jessee recounts that, "He was described as 'one of the most striking figures in the New York of the early Thirties.'"

[79] Ibid., 79.

[80] Vogel, ed., *Early Mormon Documents* (Salt Lake City: Signature Books, 1996), 1:43. The two early Warrens, Warren Parrish and Warren Cowdery, both Smith scribes, later apostatized.

earliest autobiographical 1832 Account. The contents of two other accounts, both of them dated 1835, were also concealed and suppressed. One of those accounts, Joseph's report to the man who called himself Joshua the Jewish Minister, was penned in 1835 in two different versions. Joshua 1:1835 was written in third person in the handwritten Manuscript History, Book A-1 by one scribe, and in first person, Joshua 2:1835, in Joseph Smith's Personal Diary by another scribe. Both versions of the Joshua Account describe the First Vision event reported by Joseph to Joshua on November 9, 1835. The second suppressed 1835 Account, Erastus Holmes:1835, is dated November 14, 1835. Erastus Holmes:1835, like Joshua 1:1835, is found in the high value Manuscript History, Book A-1. Joseph Smith's November 9, 1835, diary, describing the bizarre details of his encounter with Joshua the Jewish Minister, provided materials used (and abused) in the History of the Church.[81] The First Vision discussion between Joseph Smith and Erastus Holmes was also used (and abused) in the History of the Church.[82] The true contents of those accounts, falsified in the *History of the Church* for more than a hundred years, were produced by Mormon scholars – after the disclosure of the 1832 Holographic Account in 1965 – in articles written in 1966 by James B. Allen, and in 1969 and 1971 by Dean C. Jessee.

"Brought to Light"

Fawn McKay Brodie, Joseph's brave and brilliant biographer, accepted the tardy disclosure of what were three *"newly released"* accounts graciously. "The texts of these three versions were published in full," she said, "with scrupulous regard to accuracy in both the reproduction and the dating by Mormon historian Dean C. Jessee in 'The Early Accounts of Joseph Smith's First Vision,' in

---

[81]Joseph Smith Jr., *History of The Church of Jesus Christ of Latter-day Saints*, B.H. Roberts, ed., 2d ed., rev., (Salt Lake City: The Deseret Book Company, 1978), 2:304-307. "What was not printed in the official *History of the Church* was the fact that Joseph Smith was sufficiently stimulated by Robert Matthias [Joshua] to tell him his own story of the 'first vision,' and that this account was faithfully recorded by his secretary, Warren A. Cowdery, [who prepared a third-person copy] as part of his [Smith's] daily journal." (Brodie, *No Man Knows My History*, 408).

[82]Roberts, ed., *History of The Church of Jesus Christ of Latter-day Saints*, 2:312.

the spring of 1969."[83] No one should accuse the many custodians of
those documents – suppressed from 1832 and 1835 to 1965, 1966,
1969 and 1971 – of historical integrity. "This document [the 1832
Account] was unknown save to Mormon archivists until it was
copied by Paul Cheesman for his Brigham Young University
Master's Thesis, 'An Analysis of the Accounts Relating to Joseph
Smith's Early Visions,' in 1965. This thesis apparently stimulated
the publication of Dean C. Jessee's authoritative account [in the
spring of 1969]."[84]

All of the discrepant accounts – all drafted years before the
canonized 1838-39 Pearl of Great Price Account – have been
conspicuously ignored for use as missionary tools. It is unlikely that
one in ten thousand Mormon converts is familiar with the details of
those aberrant accounts of Mormonism's founding event, or that
most of the members and missionaries are. The text of the 1832
Account should have been "[p]ublished in full, with scrupulous
regard to accuracy" in 1832, the year that James Allred, this
author's first Mormon ancestor, joined what was then the Church
of Christ. Mrs. Brodie's response to the newly released evidence
from the manuscript archives of the Salt Lake City Church was
uncharacteristically tepid. She praised Dean C. Jessee for reluctant
disclosures made many decades after the fact. Where was the
insightful historian's sense of outrage? Where are Mormon
historians, academics of character and conscience, men and women
of honor, moved to say that the thirteen-decade suppression of three
"strikingly" different accounts of Joseph Smith's first encounter

---

[83]Brodie, *No Man Knows My History*, Supplement, 406. The three accounts
described by Mrs. Brodie were not all released in 1965 as in the case of the 1832
Account. Joshua 2:1835 (the first-person account) and Joshua 1:1835 (the third-
person account) were not described in Paul Cheesman's 1965 thesis entitled, *"An
Analysis of the Accounts Relating Joseph Smith's Early Visions."* The Erastus
Holmes account (Erastus Holmes: 1835), although mentioned in Mr. Cheesman's
Thesis, was unfaithfully described in the *History of the Church*, Mr. Cheesman's
primary resource. The true contents of the third chronological account, Erastus
Holmes: 1835, remained concealed (until 1969) in the Manuscript History, Book A-
1.

[84]Brodie, *No Man Knows My History*, 407, fn*. When her book was
republished (as revised) in 1972, Mrs. Brodie apparently had not yet seen a second
article written by Dean C. Jessee, in which he admitted in 1971 that Joseph Smith's
1832 account had been written in Joseph's own hand. (Jessee, "How Lovely was
the Morning," *Dialogue* 6, no. 1 [Spring 1971]: 86-87).

with deity was unconscionable? The concealment of the discordant accounts was a crime against history committed by apostles and prophets.

Two Intermittent Personages and "Many Angels"

Smith told the notorious Matthias that he had been "about 14 years old" when he received "this *first* communication" with heavenly messengers. He had "retired," he said, "to the silent grove" "perplexed in mind." There, in the grove, he "called upon the Lord for the first time" "under a realising sense that he [the Lord] had said (if the bible be true) [an open question at the time[85]] ask and you shall receive knock and it shall be opened seek and you shall find . . . ." "*[I]nformation*," he said, "*was what I most desired.*" As he "made a fruitless attempt to p[r]ay," his "toung," at first seemed to be "swolen" in his mouth. He heard a noise behind, like someone walking toward him, then "strove again to pray, but could not." He quickly "sprung" to his feet and looked around, but saw "no person or thing." Now he "kneeled again" and "called on the Lord in mighty prayer." Now his mouth was opened and his "toung" was "liberated."[86] A "pillar of fire appeared" above his head. "*[A]* personage appeard in the midst of this pillar of flame which was spread all around, and yet nothing consumed, another *personage* soon appeard like unto the first.*" This second personage told him that his sins were forgiven, then "testifyed" that "Jesus Christ is the Son of God."

Would Jesus tell this youngster that "Jesus Christ is the son of God"? Wouldn't he say, in terms the boy would understand, "I am the son of God"? Joseph didn't say the two personages weren't angels and said that he saw "*many angels in this vision.*" He didn't

---

[85]The Joseph Smith described in the 1832 Holographic Account of the First Vision need not have had to wonder whether or not the Bible was true. "At about the age of twelve years," he said in that account, "my mind become seriously imprest [p. 1] with regard to the all importent concerns for the well=fare of my immortal Soul *which led me to search=ing the scriptures believeing as I was taught, that they contained the word of God . . . .*" (Jessee ed., *The Personal Writings of Joseph Smith*, 4-5, emphasis added).
[86]Ibid., 75.

say the first personage said, *"This is My Beloved Son, Hear Him!"* He didn't say the two personages "appeard" simultaneously. He didn't say the second personage said that *he* was Jesus Christ. And he didn't identify the two persons as the Father and the Son. Joseph didn't say the personages he said that he saw weren't the angels he said that he saw. He didn't attempt to identify any of the "many angels" he said that he saw "when [he] received this first communication" at about the age of fourteen.[87] He did then further say – in this same account and about the vision of Moroni – that when he was about seventeen years old he *"saw another vision of angels* in the night season" (that is a vision of Moroni) after he had retired to bed.[88] To say that the second vision (Moroni) was "another vision of angels" was supposed to mean that the First Vision was a "vision of angels." In another account of the visions which followed this account by less than one week, Erastus Holmes: 1835, Joseph simply described what he then called "the first vision of Angels."

Parts of the first-person account located in Joseph Smith's Diary, Joshua 2:1835, were used to prepare the *History of the Church*, but the contents of the account, as opposed to the fact of the strange encounter, were falsified. *It was not publicly known until 1966 (Joshua 1:1835) and 1971 (Joshua 2:1835) that Joseph had actually given an alternative account of the First Vision (as opposed to "a relation of the circumstances connected with the coming forth of the Book of Mormon")* to Robert Matthews or Matthias. What Joseph actually said to Joshua the Jewish Minister was yet another closely guarded more than hundred-year hidden secret. The *contents* of the Joshua disclosure were not *publicly* described to the members of the Church for the first time until 1966 (by James B. Allen) and were not *officially* authenticated by the Church until 1969 (by Dean C. Jessee).[89]

---

[87]Ibid., 75-76.

[88]Ibid., 76, emphasis added.

[89]Professor James B. Allen's 1966 article in *Dialogue: A Journal of Mormon Thought* was not official. Allen, who was destined to become a future Assistant Church Historian (a position of great importance), was the first to publicly disclose the true contents of the 1835 Joshua the Jewish Minister Account (Joshua 1:1835). *"Another document of almost equal importance [Joshua 1:1835] has recently been brought to light by a member of the staff at the Church Historian's office."* The document to which Joshua 1:1835 was compared was Joseph Smith's 1832

Falsification

The *History of the Church* falsified the contents of Joseph's Joshua account (Joshua 2:1835):

> ... *I commenced giving him [Joshua] a relation of the circumstances connected with the coming forth of the book of Mormon, <u>as recorded in the former part of this history</u>. While I was relating a brief history of the establishment of the Church of Christ in the last days, Joshua seemed to be highly entertained.*[90]

Although Joseph Smith's Personal Diary was the first-person source for the preceding first-person entry in the *History of the Church*, the actual contents of this *second* chronological account of the First Vision remained concealed and suppressed. Although the true contents of this Joshua account were "faithfully recorded by his secretary, Warren A. Cowdery, as part of the daily journal,"[91] they were not faithfully recorded in the *History of the Church*. In order to omit the contents, Joseph's words *"as follows"* (as found in the Diary), were changed to *"as recorded in the former part of this history"* (as found in the *History of the Church*).[92] About eight hundred words found in the Personal Diary of Joseph Smith, comprising all of Joshua 2:1835, were then concealed and suppressed from 1835 until 1971. The story that was related in the Diary (Joshua 2:1835) was not the story *"recorded in the former part of this history"* as stated in the *History of the Church*. This misrepresentation supported the 1842 to 1965 deception that Joseph

---

Holographic Account "<u>*brought to light*</u> in 1965 by Paul R. Cheesman, a graduate student at Brigham Young University." (Allen, "The Significance of Joseph Smith's 'First Vision' in Mormon Thought," *Dialogue*, vol. 1 no. 3 [Autumn 1966]: 35, emphasis added).

[90]Roberts, ed., *History of The Church of Jesus Christ of Latter-day Saints*, 2:304, emphasis added. What the *History of the Church* didn't say was that Joseph gave Joshua an account of the First Vision that had been faithfully recorded in the Manuscript History, Book A-1, and again in Smith's Personal Diary, by two different scribes, Warren Parrish and Warren A. Cowdery. The actual contents of the Joshua Accounts in those prominent repositories were then concealed.

[91]Brodie, *No Man Knows My History*, 408.

[92]November 9, 1835, Manuscript History Book B-1: 637, written in September 1843, emphasis added.

Smith told his story only once.[93] Until 1965 and prior to Appendix D in Mr. Cheesman's Thesis, no one had to differentiate the 1838-39 Pearl of Great Price Account from any other account by calling it "official" or "traditional." It was the only account. Because no one knew about Joseph's 1832 Holographic Account, Joshua 1:1835, Joshua 2:1835 or Erastus Holmes:1835.

> *Whenever new historical information is published, a host of questions demand answers, and the disclosure that Joseph Smith told his story more than once has been no exception.*[94]

We may assume that every conversion for over a hundred years was tainted by those unfortunate deceptions.

In 1984, after the dust surrounding the awkward disclosures of the concealed accounts had settled, Dean C. Jessee, modern Mormonism's Joseph scholar, compiled and edited *The Personal Writings of Joseph Smith*. There he recounted the words that the *History of the Church* had earlier omitted as they were actually found in the Personal Diary of Joseph Smith for Monday morning, November 9, 1835.

> *[A]f=ter I had made some remarks concerning the bible I commenced giving him a relation of the circum=stances connected with the coming forth of the book of Mormon, as follows –* [95]

> being wrought up in my mind respecting the subject of religion and looking at the different systems taught the children of men, I knew not who was right or who was wrong and I considered it of the first importance that I should be right, in matters that involve eternal consequ[e]nces; being thus

---

[93]The 1838-39 Pearl of Great Price Account "was the only one known to the general Mormon audience until 1965." (Brodie, *No Man Knows My History*, 409).

[94]James B. Allen, "Eight Contemporary Accounts of Joseph Smith's First Vision: What Do We Learn from Them?" *Improvement Era* (April 1970), 6, emphasis added.

[95]Jessee ed., *The Personal Writings of Joseph Smith*, 75, emphasis added.

perplexed in mind I retired to the silent grove and bow[e]d down before the Lord, under a realising sense that he had said (*if the Bible be true*) ask and you shall receive knock and it shall be opened seek and you shall find and again, if any man lack wisdom let him ask of God who giveth to all men libar=ally and upbradeth not; *information was what I most desired at this time*, and with a fixed determination to obtain it, I called upon the Lord for the first time, in the place above stated or in other words I made a fruitless attempt to p[r]ay. my toung seemed to be swolen in my mouth, so that I could not utter, I heard a noise behind me like someone walking towards me, I strove again to pray, but could not, the noise of walking seem=d to draw nearer, I sprong up on my feet ~~and~~ [p. 23] and looked around, but I saw no person, or thing that was calculated to produce the noise of wal=king. I kneeled again, my mouth was opened and my toung liberated, and I called on the Lord in mighty prayer. A pillar of fire appeared above my head, it presently rested down upon me ~~head~~, and filled me with Joy unspeakable, a *personage appeard in the midst of this pillar of flame* which was spread all around, and yet nothing consumed, *another personage soon appeard like unto the first, he said unto me thy sins are forgiven thee, he testifyed unto me that Jesus Christ is the son of God –* [96] *<and I saw many angels in this vision> I was about fourteen years old when I received this first communication; When I was about 17 years old I saw another vision of angels* in the night season after I had retired to bed . . . .[97]

---

[96]Jessee ed., *The Personal Writings of Joseph Smith*, 74-76, emphasis added. In the interest of accuracy, these recitals from the Personal Diary of Joseph Smith (Joshua 2:1835) are reproduced in their original form. In the disclosures of these two accounts by James B. Allen in 1966 (Joshua 1:1835) and Dean C. Jessee in 1971 (Joshua 2:1835), there are stylistic improvements. In making future references to those and other accounts in future chapters, the stylistically improved accounts will be preferred.

[97]Ibid., 75-76.

All of the above recitals – every unfamiliar word – were deleted from the *History of the Church's* description of Joseph's November 9, 1835, encounter with Joshua. The actual words Joseph Smith used in 1835 to describe his vision to Joshua the Jewish Minister would be concealed from everyone, members, missionaries, investigators and converts for one hundred and thirty-one years until 1966 (when James B. Allen disclosed the third-person version from the Manuscript History, Book A-1, Joshua 1:1835) and for one hundred and thirty-six years until 1971 (when Dean C. Jessee disclosed the first-person version from Joseph Smith's Personal Diary, Joshua 2:1835 as recounted above).

1969: THE ERASTUS HOLMES ACCOUNT (ERASTUS HOLMES: 1835) – JOSEPH SMITH'S <u>THIRD</u> ACCOUNT OF HIS FIRST ENCOUNTER WITH DEITY

On November 14, 1835, five days after being visited by Joshua the Jewish Minister, Joseph Smith was visited by a gentleman "by the name of Erastus Holmes of Newbury Clemon [Clermont] Co., Ohio, he called to make enquiry about the establish=ment of the church of the latter=day Saints to be instructed more perfectly in our doctrine . . . ."[98] To this man, who "listened verry attentively and seemed highly gratified," Joseph gave a second 1835 and *third* chronological account of the First Vision:

> *I commenced and gave him a brief relation of my experience while in my [p. 36] juvenile years, say from 6 years old <u>up to the time I received the first visitation of Angels</u> which was when I was about 14. years old and also the visitations that I received afterward, concerning the book of Mormon, and a short account of the rise and progress of the church, up to this, date . . . .*[99]

Mr. Holmes "intends to unite with the Church he is a verry candid man indeed and I am much pleased with him."[100] Holmes attended

---

[98]Ibid., 84.
[99]Jessee ed., *The Personal Writings of Joseph Smith*, 84, emphasis added.
[100]Ibid.

church with Joseph on Sunday November 15, where he listened to Sidney Rigdon preach, then came home with Joseph and dined. He had been a member of the Methodist Church before being "excommunicated for receiving the Elders of the church of the latter-day Saints into his house."[101] In his discussion with Erastus Holmes, Joseph did not mention one personage, the "crucifyed" Lord (1832), two unidentified personages and "many angels" (1835), or "two Personages" whose "brightness and glory" defied all description and no angels (1838-39). The *History of the Church* (published after Joseph's death) and Paul R. Cheesman's Master's Thesis (published in 1965) both described Joseph Smith's encounter with Erastus Holmes in exactly these words:

> *I gave him [Erastus Holmes] a brief relation of my experience while in my juvenile years, say from six years old up to the time I received my first vision, which was when I was about fourteen years old; . . .*[102]

Paul R. Cheesman said that was what Joseph had said "in a journal entry dated November 14, 1835," but it was not. The journal entry in the *History of the Church* had been falsified before Joseph's death and while he was still in charge. The History had been completed to August 1838 when Joseph died in 1844.

What Joseph Smith actually said to Erastus Holmes on November 14, 1835, was this:

> *I commenced and gave him [Erastus Holmes] a brief relation of my experience while in my [p. 36] juvenile years, say from 6 years old up to the time I received the first visitation of Angels which was when I was about 14 years old . . . .*[103]

---

[101]Ibid.

[102]Roberts, ed., *History of The Church of Jesus Christ of Latter-day Saints*, 2:312; Cheesman, "An Analysis of the Accounts Relating Joseph Smith's Early Visions," 23, emphasis added.

[103]Jessee ed., *The Personal Writings of Joseph Smith*, 84, emphasis added.

The graduate student inadvertently perpetuated the deception described in the *History of the Church*, 2:312 (published in 1904).[104] When the *History of the Church* reported after the death of Joseph Smith and when Paul R. Cheesman reported in 1965 that Joseph said, "*up to the time I received my first vision*," those resources conveyed the false impression that what Joseph told Erastus Holmes in 1835 was what Joseph told the Church in the Pearl of Great Price Account in 1838-39. That report by that means told the members yet once again that Joseph told his story only once. Joseph Smith did not describe a visitation of the "crucifyed" Lord (1832 Holographic Account), or a visit of the Father and the Son (1838-39 Pearl of Great Price Account), to Erastus Holmes. The vision related to Holmes is now (since 1969) known to have described "*the first visitation of Angels.*"

Why were the accounts in the *History of the Church* (Joshua 1:1835; Joshua 2:1835; Erastus Holmes:1835) suppressed and falsified? Because their contradictions threatened various recitals described in the 1838-39 Pearl of Great Price Account, then further exposed the changing doctrines of the early Church. Joseph Smith did not describe a vision of the Father _and_ the Son in his handwritten hundred-and-thirty-year-hidden 1832 Account, and he did not describe a vision of the Father _or_ the Son to Erastus Holmes in 1835. Erastus Holmes:1835 cannot be reconciled with the erroneous account described in the *History of the Church,* or with the 1832 Account, or with the 1838-39 Pearl of Great Price Account. Dean C. Jessee finally told the truth about the contents of the Account in 1969, while speaking for the Church in a Mormon publication, but he didn't say that his sponsor was sorry.

---

[104]The entries in the Manuscript History Book and in the Joseph Smith Journal were misrepresented in the *History of the Church* published in 1904.

CHAPTER THREE

The Evolution of First Vision Accounting

Belief in the vision is one of the fundamentals to which faithful members give assent. Its importance is second only to belief in the divinity of Jesus of Nazareth.

James B. Allen, 1966

[N]one of the available contemporary writings about Joseph Smith in the 1830's, none of the publications of the Church in that decade, and no contemporary journal or correspondence yet discovered mentions the story of the first vision . . . .

James B. Allen, 1966

BITING THE BULLET SLOWLY

1966: James B. Allen and the 1832 Account

Professor James B. Allen presented a more or less personal 1966 response to Paul R. Cheesman's 1965 disclosure of Joseph Smith's 1832 Account of an 1821 vision. Allen (unlike Cheesman) did not depreciate the newly released manuscript.[1] Professor Allen's 1966 article in *Dialogue: A Journal of Mormon Thought* provided early scholarly comment.

> One of the most significant documents of that period ["the formative decade of church history"] yet discovered was brought to light in 1965 by Paul R. Cheesman, a graduate student at Brigham Young

---

[1]James B. Allen, "The Significance of Joseph Smith's 'First Vision' in Mormon Thought," *Dialogue: A Journal of Mormon Thought*, 1 no. 3, (Autumn 1966): 35.

University.   This is a handwritten manuscript
apparently composed about 1833 and either written
or dictated by Joseph Smith. It contains an account
of the early experiences of the Mormon prophet and
includes the story of the first vision. While the story
varies in some details from the version presently
accepted, enough is there to indicate that at least as
early as 1833 Joseph Smith contemplated writing
and perhaps publishing it.   The manuscript has
apparently lain in the L.D.S. Church Historian's
office for many years, and yet few if any who saw it
realized its profound historical significance.[2]

For more than a hundred years Mormon scholars faced the claim
from detractors that there had been no 1820 First Vision because
Smith hadn't thought to compose an account of it until 1838-39, or
to publish that after-the-fact account until 1842.   Here in a
document prepared in 1832 is support for the proposition that
Smith had spoken of an encounter with deity.   How could any
historian fail to realize the "profound historical significance" of
Joseph Smith's early and only handwritten account of his first
encounter with deity?

Allen's explanation as to just how this one-of-a-kind priceless
original Mormon manuscript somehow escaped detection in the
"L.D.S. Church Historian's office" from 1832 to 1965 conflicts with
President Levi Edgar Young's 1952 representation that this
"strange account" of the vision had been kept in a locked vault for
one hundred and twenty years, that the leaders of the Church knew
exactly what it was and had taken strong steps to protect it from
disclosure. To say that the manuscript had "apparently lain in the
L.D.S. Church Historian's office for many years" in a high value
resource waiting to be discovered tests credulity. The manuscript
may have been seen, Allen admits. What of those who had seen or
known of it? What of those who controlled access to this early
account?   How could anyone who knew anything not have
recognized its "profound historical significance"?   The highest
leaders of the Church knew exactly what the document was.

---

[2]Ibid.

James B. Allen, to his credit, did not dismiss Joseph Smith's 1832 Holographic Account of the First Vision as fragmentary or denigrate the account by saying it had never been "referred to by any of the authorities of the church."[3] Allen would ultimately describe the manuscript as "a rough, unpolished [twelve year after-the-fact] effort to record the spiritual impact of the vision on him [Joseph Smith]." The experienced historian refused to accept the graduate student's apologetic description of the recovered manuscript's insignificance.

> **Another impressive fact is that the 1831-1832 version, which was the first to be recorded, is actually the most comprehensive of all. This early narrative includes all the essential elements of the more carefully prepared Manuscript History [the 1838-39 Pearl of Great Price Account] and contains more additional details than any other source.[4] [For a supportive view by yet another faithful scholar, the reader is referred to Appendix C].**

Allen identified the manuscript as *"One of the most significant documents of that ['formative'] period yet discovered . . . ."*[5] That narrative contained the first words the Lord is supposed to have spoken to the prophet Joseph Smith.

James B. Allen, Dean C. Jessee and Joshua 1 and 2:1835

In his 1966 article, James B. Allen – while responding to the publication of the 1832 Account – made his own remarkable disclosure. The Mormon scholar identified and described a second previously unknown account of Joseph Smith's First Vision, Joshua

---

[3]Paul R. Cheesman, "An Analysis of the Accounts Relating Joseph Smith's Early Visions" (Master of Religious Education Thesis, Brigham Young University, 1965), 64.

[4]James B. Allen, "Eight Contemporary Accounts of Joseph Smith's First Vision: What Do We Learn from Them?" *Improvement Era* (April 1970), 6. For corroboration of Professor Allen's conclusion, see Richard L. Bushman's analysis at Appendix C (Richard L. Bushman Statement, 16 December 2013).

[5]James B. Allen, "The Significance of Joseph Smith's 'First Vision' in Mormon Thought," *Dialogue* (Autumn 1966): 35, emphasis added.

1:1835, another document with an impeccable provenance. Although James B. Allen's article in *Dialogue: A Journal of Mormon Thought* did not rise to the level of institutional comment, it contained information acquired and published by a trusted Mormon insider who enjoyed privileged access to the LDS archives and archivists. In his article, Professor Allen presented members of the laity with yet another significant challenge. There was, he said, a *second* unknown account of the First Vision. The true contents of the Joshua 1:1835 Account were concealed and suppressed from 1835 until *Dialogue* published Professor Allen's article in 1966. This second chronological account of the First Vision was found, bound in place at the back of Book A-1 of the handwritten Manuscript History.[6]   Allen attempted to explain how another profoundly significant document managed to escape detection in another highly prominent resource for yet another hundred and thirty years.

The unusual story of Smith's encounter with Robert Matthews (or Matthias), *alias* Joshua the Jewish Minister, was described in the *History of the Church*. While historians could determine that Smith was supposed to have given "a relation of the circumstances connected with the coming forth of the Book of Mormon" to Joshua in 1835, they could not determine that what he actually provided to the peculiar Joshua had been a second chronological account of the First Vision. Nor could anyone hope to ascertain the true contents of that falsified account. Members were misled by the deceptive description of the contents of that account in the *History of the Church*. Mr. Cheesman did not include a report of the Joshua Account with the reports that he described in his controversial thesis because nothing about the strange encounter served to suggest it had anything to do with a vision of the Father or the Son. In the *History of the Church*, the Joshua Account had surfaced as just another recounting of the "circumstances connected with" Moroni and the plates. It was not stated (or even implied) that Joseph Smith had told the founding story twice.

The 1835 third-person version of Joseph Smith's First Vision – Joshua 1:1835 – was "brought to light by a member of the staff at

---

[6]Ibid.

the Church Historian's office."[7]   The publication of the true contents of Joshua 1:1835, as opposed to the falsified *History of the Church* report, occurred in Professor Allen's article one hundred and thirty-one years after the account was written, and one-hundred-and-forty-six years after the vision is supposed to have occurred.

James B. Allen, who personally acknowledged the authenticity of Joseph Smith's first 1832 Holographic Account of the First Vision, now personally acknowledged the authenticity of Joseph Smith's 1835 (third-person) version of the second account of the First Vision (Joshua 1:1835).   While Allen essentially acknowledged the authenticity of the two recently surfaced accounts, the leaders of the Church did not. After their prolonged incarcerations, both of the manuscripts were "brought to light" (rather than discovered) almost simultaneously, one by the graduate student in 1965, the other by James B. Allen in 1966.

Allen admitted that the printed *History of the Church* conveyed the impression that Joseph told Joshua "only the Book of Mormon story." He then guardedly described the newly released account, Joshua 1: 1835, as "a most curious and revealing document." It was "not written in the finished style that characterized the 'Manuscript History.'" From that he decided "that it was not intended for publication without some revision." In order to read this account located at the back of Book A-1 (the handwritten "Manuscript History"), "one must turn the book up-side down." That suggested to Professor Allen "that the manuscript certainly was not intended to be part of the finished history." It consisted of some "original notes" used to compile the "Manuscript History" and was "actually

---

[7]The *Deseret News* (a Mormon publication) described this allegedly remarkable discovery: "Dean C. Jessee, a staff member at the Church historian's office in Salt Lake City, searched through documents of the Church historian's library concerning events of the 1820's. *He located* and analyzed *three early accounts* of Joseph Smith's first vision *dictated by the Prophet himself.*" (*Deseret News*, Church Section [3 May 1969], 15, quoted by Jerald Tanner and Sandra Tanner, *Mormonism – Shadow or Reality?* [Salt Lake City: Utah Lighthouse Ministry, 1987], 152). The Mormon newspaper made it appear that the "strange" accounts were new discoveries. The publication of this report, the details uncovered described, tracked the 1969 article written by Jessee for a Brigham Young University resource.

a daily account of Joseph Smith's activities in 1835, as recorded by a scribe."

> The importance of the manuscript [Joshua 1:1835] here lies in the fact that the scribe wrote down what Joseph Smith said to his visitor, and he began not by telling the story of the Book of Mormon [as the History of the Church had misreported], but with an account of the first vision. Again the details of the story vary somewhat from the accepted version, but the manuscript, if authentic, at least demonstrates that by 1835 the story had been told to someone.[8]

This second remarkable release in the short span of two years (the 1966 release of Joshua 1:1835) was followed three years later by the 1969 release of Erastus Holmes:1835, then two years later by the 1971 release of Joshua 2:1835. We must presume that in 1966 James B. Allen was unaware, when trying to explain the suppression of Joshua 1:1835, an account "bound with" Mormonism's priceless Manuscript History Book A-1, that there was a Joshua 2:1835 recounted in Joseph Smith's Personal Diary. Allen's convoluted explanation for the 1966 release of Joshua 1:1835 didn't account for Joshua 2:1835, a second first-person Joshua narrative waiting to be found in Joseph Smith's Personal Diary:

> *The document [Joshua 1:1835] was brought to the attention of this writer in June, 1966, and he had the opportunity to examine it. Since the document is bound with the 'Manuscript History,' it is unusual that someone had not found it earlier and recognized its significance. It seems apparent, however, that, as in the case of Cheesman's document [Joseph Smith's 1832 Holographic Account], few if any people have been aware of it. The fact that the use of the 'Manuscript History' is highly restricted, due to its extremely high value, and that any research done in it is done through a microfilm copy could help account*

---

[8]Allen, "The Significance of Joseph Smith's 'First Vision' in Mormon Thought," *Dialogue,* 1 no. 3 (Autumn 1966): 36.

*for the fact that researchers generally had not
discovered what was in the back of the book.*[9]

Professor Allen tried to explain why no one seemed to have found
this *second* account of the First Vision in the "high value" "highly-
restricted" Manuscript History. His explanation presupposed that
the most contemporaneous accounts of the First Vision – Joseph
Smith's first 1832 Holographic Account and Joseph's second 1835
Joshua Account – had been preserved in the archives from 1832
and 1835 until 1965 and 1966, as parts of priceless collections
without scholarly detection.

A 1971 disclosure by Dean C. Jessee[10] made Allen's 1966
explanation of the suppression of *Joshua 1:1835* implausible.
"Although this [the 1966 release of Joshua 1:1835] was certainly an
important discovery, it was overshadowed in 1971 when Dean C.

---

[9]Allen, "The Significance of Joseph Smith's 'First Vision' in Mormon
Thought," *Dialogue,* 1 no. 3 (Autumn 1966): 35, fn 11, emphasis added.
[10]Dean C. Jessee is a "leading expert on the writings of Joseph Smith, Jr." "In
his career, Jessee was a respected archivist, editor and historian, as well as an
authority on early Mormon handwriting." ("Dean C. Jessee" [accessed 18 October
2013]; available from wiklpedia.com; Internet, 1). Jessee catalogued manuscripts
and produced "useful documents in the archive that historians had not yet
studied." He "published most of Smith's own writings and many of his dictations
in *The Personal Writings of Joseph Smith*." (Ibid., 2). "Jessee's efforts were
eventually made an official joint effort of BYU and the LDS Church in 2001, called
the Joseph Smith Papers Project." When Larry Miller began funding the venture
(in 2001), he "announced the goal of completing the project by 2015, 'while Dean
C. Jessee is still around,' since Jessee was then in his 70's." Leonard Arrington
said, "he [Jessee] knew more about the documents of LDS history than any other
person." (Ibid., 2-3). Jessee's career, despite the encomiums, was not an unbridled
success. "In the 1980's, Jessee was a major player in the Historical Department's
examinations of important historical documents produced by Mark Hofmann,
which were later found to be forgeries. Jessee was considered the preeminent
expert on early Mormon handwriting, especially Joseph Smith's . . . ." He
"authenticated and defended [in the 1980's] a number of Hofmann's forgeries,
including the famous 'Salamander Letter.'" "Texts from Hofmann's forgeries that
Jessee identified as Joseph Smith holographs made it into the 1984 first edition of
Jessee's *The Personal Writings of Joseph Smith*. A corrected second edition was
published in 2002." (Ibid., 9 fn 22). A few years earlier, "Jessee's 1974 *Letters of
Brigham Young to his Sons* caused Boyd K. Packer to bring concerns to the First
Presidency about the Historical Department's 'orientation toward scholarly work,'
an early sign of the tension that would eventually lead to the History Division's
disbandment." (Ibid., 2).

Jessee, of the Church Historian's Office, reported that this same story [Joshua 2:1835] (this time written in the first person) had been found in Joseph Smith's own diary."[11]   Five years after Professor Allen identified Joshua 1:1835 in 1966, Dean C. Jessee identified Joshua 2:1835 in 1971.[12] These century-late releases had reference to two versions of the same account given to "Joshua the Jewish Minister" by Joseph Smith in 1835. Now two versions of the 1835 Joshua Account – written by Warren Cowdery and Warren Parrish – have been located in separate prominent early Mormon repositories. How could the third-person version (Joshua 1:1835, located in Book A-1 of the Manuscript History of the Church) and the first-person version (Joshua 2:1835, found in Joseph Smith's Personal Diary) have escaped detection from 1835 to 1966 and 1971? It was, simply said, impossible.

In his 1966 article that introduced the true contents of Joshua 1:1835 for the first time to a Mormon audience, Allen earnestly attempted to protect the Church and explain why no one had discovered that errant account. It became impossible to say that the narrative had been innocently overlooked in the Manuscript History at the back of Book A-1 when Dean C. Jessee revealed that a second version of the same account "had been found in Joseph Smith's personal diary."[13]   Professor Allen disclosed the third-person version of Joseph Smith's second account of the First Vision, "Joshua 1:1835," in 1966. Dean C. Jessee disclosed the first-person version of Joseph Smith's second account of the First Vision, "Joshua 2:1835," in 1971. The failure to recognize and disclose the contents of these accounts can never be happily explained.[14] These suppressed accounts were "brought to light." They were not newly discovered; they were newly released.

---

[11]Tanner and Tanner, *Mormonism – Shadow or Reality?*, 147.

[12]Dean C. Jessee, "How Lovely was the Morning," *Dialogue: A Journal of Mormon Thought* 6, no. 1 (Spring 1971): 85-88.

[13]Ibid., 86-87.

[14]The Manuscript History version, Joshua 1:1835, was penned by Warren Cowdery. The Joseph Smith Diary version, Joshua 2:1835, "was recorded in the prophet's 1835-36 Diary by his scribe, Warren Parrish." [Jessee, "How Lovely was the Morning," *Dialogue* 6, no. 1 (Spring 1971): 87].

THE 1832 ACCOUNT: AUTHENTICITY AND DISCLOSURES

1971: Admitting the Holograph

When Paul R. Cheesman published his typescript copy of the 1832 Account in 1965,[15] he reflected as follows: "Since it is recorded in the first person this would also suggest either that Joseph Smith wrote it or he dictated it. From handwriting comparisons it would appear that the latter supposition is the more likely one."[16] Why didn't the Church permit the graduate student to publish a copy of Joseph Smith's holograph in 1965? When President Levi Edgar Young received "higher permission" to examine the 1832 Account in 1952, he was not permitted to copy the document or to discuss its contents. He could not have created or published a typescript. If the Church opened the locked vault, removed the manuscript, reversed the "don't copy/don't tell" policy, put the document back in the "journal ledger," then allowed a graduate student to create and publish a typescript, why didn't it allow him to copy the original? In the beginning? In 1965?

With nothing more than a typescript and in the absence of official authentication, no scholar could challenge the graduate student's conclusion that the text, like almost all of Smith's other texts, was probably dictated. In 1966, James B. Allen reported that "This is a handwritten manuscript apparently composed about 1833 and either written or dictated by Joseph Smith."[17] Allen remained uncertain after a year had passed without clarification. It is 1966 and the Church has not produced a copy of the original manuscript. This uncertainty, clearly intentional, denied to the strange new account its higher dignity as a holograph. Some Latter-day Saints, upon becoming familiar with the previously unfamiliar contents of the typescript, doubted its authenticity. No authorized leader of the

---

[15]After reading Cheesman's Thesis, Jerald and Sandra Tanner prepared a publication entitled "*Joseph Smith's Strange Account of the First Vision*" in which they published in 1965 a copy of Cheesman's typescript, all that anyone had at the time. (Tanner and Tanner, *Mormonism – Shadow or Reality?*, 145-46). "[T]housands of copies were distributed throughout the world."

[16]Appendix D to Cheesman, "An Analysis of the Accounts Relating Joseph Smith's Early Visions," 126.

[17]Allen, "The Significance of Joseph Smith's 'First Vision' in Mormon Thought," *Dialogue*, 1 no. 3 (Autumn 1966): 35.

Church stepped forward to say that the document was authentic, or to otherwise discuss its Mormon archival provenance.

The 1965 publication of Joseph Smith's handwritten 1832 Account presented a challenge to the preeminence of the canonized 1838-39 Pearl of Great Price Account. Smith's handwritten first 1832 Holographic Account, "artless and uncalculated,"[18] was more intimate, personal and workmanlike, more contemporaneous, more accurate and of a higher dignity than the greatly more glorious fourth 1838-39 Pearl of Great Price Account. Mormon historian Richard L. Bushman described the 1832 Account in these terms: "I think this account has the marks of an authentic visionary experience" ("more revealing than the official account . . . contained in the Pearl of Great Price").[19] (See Appendix C). To say no more than the graduate student said in his thesis, and to present the account in typescript, was to surround the potentially explosive disclosure with a protecting layer of calculated ambiguity. New details could surface, a few at a time (as happened in 1966, 1969 and 1971), softening the impact of the more than one hundred-year deception. The description of the vision reported in the 1832 Account was in fact written in the hand of Joseph Smith (as Levi Edgar Young said in 1952 he thought that it was), a fact that may have been recognized by historians and scholars had they been permitted to examine copies of the original document instead of a typescript.

In 1969 (when the Church finally checked in) Dean C. Jessee confidently reported – officially and in a Mormon publication – that "An analysis of the handwriting shows that the narrative was penned by Frederick G. Williams, scribe to the Prophet and counselor in the First Presidency." Then this master-of-all-things Joseph further reported that, "Both the history and the letter are in Williams's handwriting."[20] Four years have passed since the

---

[18]Richard L. Bushman, Statement ("Dear Forum Members"), 16 December 2013, "Ask Me Anything Series," Ex-Mormon Reddit Community Website (accessed 13 January 2014).

[19]Ibid.

[20]Dean C. Jessee, "The Early Accounts of Joseph Smith's First Vision," *BYU Studies* 9, no. 3 (Spring 1969): 277. "The pages of the history [the 1832 Holographic Account] were numbered one through six and the November 27, 1832, letter begins on page '1a.'"

Appendix D "disclosure" and the 1832 Account is still not given its due as the only account written in the prophet's own hand. Now that the handwriting issue is laid to rest, copies of the three double-sided previously excised pages (pages one through six) are finally produced – substituted for the typescript – in 1969, four years late. Dean C. Jessee reminds his audience that the Mormon prophet "did very little writing himself." "I was dictating history," Jessee quotes the prophet. "I say dictating, for I seldom use the pen myself. I always dictate all my communications, but employ a scribe to write them."[21] Relating that fact to the discrepant account described by him in 1969 (Erastus Holmes: 1835), and to the 1965 and 1966 disclosures attributed to Paul R. Cheesman and James B. Allen (Joseph Smith's 1832 Holographic Account, and Joshua 1:1835), Jessee then further supported his earlier conclusion: "The *extreme scarcity* of holographic material among the documents originated by Joseph Smith confirms this statement. Joseph Smith's authorship of the three historical accounts portrayed in these pages [Joseph Smith's 1832 Account, Joshua 1:1835 and Erastus Holmes: 1835] must be regarded within this [1969] framework."[22]   Jessee's representation – for the Church in a Mormon publication and official – was that each of those three separate accounts had been written by the scribes employed to write them.

In a short two years, the Church will be forced to recant. The leaders of the Church didn't admit the obvious until 1971. Given six years to consider the document and its contents, the Church reversed itself and said:

> *In the analysis of Joseph Smith's earliest account of his Vision written in 1832, Frederick G. Williams is listed as the scribe. (p. 155) A closer look at the original document has shown that while Williams wrote the beginning and end of the narrative, Joseph Smith wrote the remainder, including the portion containing the details of his First Vision. This is the only known account of the Vision in his own hand.*

---

[21]Ibid., 277 fn 10 (Joseph Smith Journal for 4-5 July 1839 has "dictating History," which was expanded after his death).

[22]Ibid., emphasis added.

> *Most of his writings were dictated, which is not to say that other accounts are less authentic.*[23]

Oops!

Scientific method?

Handwriting analysis?

"Gravitas": Measuring Dignities

Who would think to say that the 1832 Holographic Account is more authentic than other accounts? Why, anyone who knows the "extreme scarcity of holographic material" attributed to Joseph Smith. The scarcity of such material traceable to the Mormon prophet makes the 1832 First and Only Holographic Account a Pearl of Great Price:

> *Because it is the only presently known account of the First Vision ever written in Smith's own hand, untouched by scribes.*[24]

> *Because it is "the earliest known historical narrative of the prophet's life."*[25]

> *Because it is the first account of Smith's first encounter with deity.*

---

[23]Jessee, "How Lovely was the Morning," *Dialogue* 6, no. 1 (Spring 1971): 86, emphasis added. Jessee reviewed Dr. Milton V. Backman's book entitled, *"Joseph Smith's First Vision: The First Vision in Historical Context,"* published by Bookcraft, Inc., in 1971, in an article published in *Dialogue: A Journal of Mormon Thought,* also in 1971. (Ibid., 85-88).

[24]Richard L. Bushman: "We don't know who wrote the 1838 [official] Account. Joseph's journal indicates that he, Sidney Rigdon, and George Robinson collaborated on beginning the history in late April, but we don't know who actually drafted the history. It is a polished narrative but unlike anything Joseph ever wrote himself." (Bushman, Statement ["Dear Forum Members"], "Ask Me Anything Series." *See* Bushman's statement at Appendix C).

[25]Jessee, "The Early Accounts of Joseph Smith's First Vision," *BYU Studies* 9, no. 3 (Spring 1969): 278.

Because it is the earliest known history of the Mormon Church.

Because it is Joseph Smith's first attempt at autobiography.

Because it is the earliest explicit mention of a vision.

Why would the scholar say, "This is the only known account of the vision in his own hand. Most of his writings were dictated, which is not to say that other accounts are less authentic."[26] Why shouldn't he rather have said, "This is the primordial telling of the founding story of the Mormon Church"? How could the Church even think to say in 1969, four years after the publication of the typescript, that "handwriting analysis" had identified Frederick G. Williams as scribe? After "higher permission" had been required to see that "strange account"? After it had spent one hundred and twenty years in a "locked vault"? Laymen should have been able to see that the document was written in two distinctive hands if the Church had conscientiously furnished copies of the manuscript. The Church owed the members a true copy of the original document in 1965. The 1832 Account written by the hand of Joseph Smith had an impeccable provenance. President Levi Edgar Young identified the author of this narrative in 1952. So did those leaders whose "higher permission" was required before a President of the Seventies could examine the document if he promised not to speak of it.

Why would the historian/spokesman speaking for the Church say that other and later accounts are no less authentic than the only known account of the vision ever written in Joseph Smith's own hand?

Because a handwritten account has a higher dignity.

Because a more contemporaneous account has a higher dignity than a less contemporaneous account.

Because the leaders of the Church don't like Joseph Smith's

---

[26]Jessee, "How Lovely was the Morning," *Dialogue* 6, no. 1 (Spring 1971): 86.

1832 handwritten first and most contemporaneous account prepared by the prophet as much as they like the 1838-39 fourth and less contemporaneous account prepared by the prophet, George W. Robinson, Sidney Rigdon and James Mulholland, and do not think that others will.

Because the contents of Joseph's first account are strikingly different than the contents of Joseph's fourth account.

Because the 1832 Account is a message of forgiveness and a promise of grace.

Because the 1832 Account is an epiphany indistinguishable from thousands of other similar evangelical epiphanies.

Because the 1832 Account describes no deliberate mission.

Because faithful Mormons had been informed for more than one hundred and twenty years that Joseph Smith told his story only once.

Because this and other discrepant accounts – accounts that suggested that Joseph Smith's 1838-39 Pearl of Great Price Account was an evolutionary theological construct prepared in several successive drafts and streamlined for publication – posed a challenge to the official account's sacred place in Mormon scripture.

Because the handwritten first most workmanlike, intimate and contemporaneous account mentioned only Jesus, one God, "omnipotant," "omnipreasant," "crucifyed," a "spirit" and supreme, while failing to mention the Father.

The Church doesn't want this one-hundred and thirty-year suppressed first account of a monotheistic Joseph Smith's first encounter with a single deity to undermine the familiar faith-promoting canonized official fourth account of Joseph Smith's first encounter with multiple deities. If other accounts are no *"less authentic"* because they are not handwritten, or because they are later and less contemporaneous, why doesn't the 1832 Account find its own prominent place among the materials presented by the missionaries to their investigators?[27] Why isn't it, and why aren't those other early accounts, given their place as scripture, canonized and embraced? Why aren't every one of those early accounts published in the Doctrine and Covenants or the Pearl of Great Price? Why isn't the 1832 "artless and uncalculated" "flood of raw experience" account accorded a station appropriate to its intimate, more personal, most workmanlike, contemporaneous and historically dependable provenance?

Was Joseph Smith's 1832 Account Fragmentary?

In 1981 Brigham Young University Professor Marvin S. Hill challenged the assumption that Joseph Smith's 1832 Holographic Account was fragmentary, an assumption promulgated by the graduate student in 1965, and by Dean C. Jessee (for the Church) in 1969.[28] Professor Hill – a Mormon-friendly resource, an expert on the prophet Joseph Smith and the brother of one of Smith's prominent biographers[29] made two remarkable admissions in a speech to the Sunstone Theological Symposium in 1981: (1) that the Palmyra revival did not occur in 1820, and (2) that Joseph Smith "probably changed his view of the Godhead between 1832 and 1838."[30] Confirming everything that we have said. Speaking of the discrepant accounts of Joseph Smith's First Vision (which threatened Mormon chronology) and of the detractors and

---

[27]There is no mention of the 1832 account in "Preach My Gospel, A Guide to Missionary Service," a missionary manual published by The Church of Jesus Christ of Latter-day Saints in 2004. The only references to the First Vision in the manual as this is written are to the 1838-39 Pearl of Great Price Account.

[28]"The factors that retarded Joseph Smith's progress on his history ["Missouri grievances," James Mulholland's death, Robert B. Thompson's death, the "treachery" of some of his clerks, "long imprisonments," "vexations . . . lawsuits," "poverty" and "plunder"] did not prevent *periodic beginnings*." "On at least three occasions prior to 1839 Joseph Smith began writing his history." (Jessee, "The Early Accounts of Joseph Smith's First Vision," *BYU Studies* 9, no. 3 [Spring 1969]: 277).

[29]Donna Hill, *Joseph Smith: The First Mormon* (USA: Doubleday & Company, Inc., 1977; reprint, Salt Lake City: Signature Books, 1977, 1982, 1999).

[30]Tanner and Tanner, *Mormonism – Shadow or Reality?*, 162C (reproducing some of Hill's remarks to the Sunstone Theological Symposium, 1981).

apologists who advanced their various arguments, pro and con, Hill further reported as follows:

> It is my belief that both sides have overlooked some important points and that a plausible argument can be made for the basic church chronology despite some contradictions in some sources, provided that concessions be made with respect to some inaccuracies in the 1838 [Pearl of Great Price] account.

> It seems to me that everybody has approached the issue from the wrong end, by taking as the point of departure the 1838 official version when the account that they should be looking at is that of 1832. Merely on the face of it, the 1832 version stands a better chance to be accurate and unembelished [sic] than the 1838 account which was intended as a public statement streamlined for publication . . . .

> I am inclined to agree with him [Reverend Wesley P. Walters, the Palmyra revival and Bainbridge trial scholar] that the turmoil that Joseph describes that led to some family members joining the Presbyterians and that led to much sectarian bitterness, does not fit well into the 1820 context detailed by Bachman.

> An 1824 revival creates problems for the 1838 account, but not that of 1832. Walters overlooks the fact that Joseph said nothing in his 1832 account about a revival prompting his prayer . . . . Not only does this account ignore the revival, so, too, does the 1835 account . . . .

> The Walters/Tanner argument that Lucy's joining the Presbyterians, and Joseph the Methodists, destroys Joseph's credibility, fails to consider that unlike 1838, the 1832 version says nothing about Joseph's being forbidden to join a church . . . . there

is no great inconsistency as Walters and Tanners assume, when Lucy Mack Smith joins the Presbyterians, or Joseph tried to become a Methodist in 1828.[31]

1969 AND 1971: INSTITUTIONAL DISCLOSURES

Dean C. Jessee disclosed in 1971 – six years after Cheesman's disclosure of the 1832 Account, and five years after Allen's disclosure of Joshua 1:1835 – that another first-person version of the Joshua account, Joshua 2:1835, had been located in Joseph Smith's Personal Diary.

> There are *two* versions of the 1835 recital of the First Vision. That reproduced by Dr. Backman in Appendix B is recorded in Joseph Smith's 1835-36 effort to write a history which is found in the back of Volume A-1 of the 1838-39 Manuscript of Joseph's official History. *The second version was recorded in the Prophet's 1835-36 Diary by his scribe, Warren Parrish.* The existence of these two accounts are reflective of Joseph's effort to keep a personal record at that time.[32]

The introduction of this first-person version of the long-suppressed account is handled matter of factly. "The Diary account [Joshua 2: 1833] is given here for comparison: . . . ."[33] Why is that? Because the Manuscript History back of Book A-1 Account (Joshua 1:1835) had been reproduced as Appendix B in Dr. Milton V. Backman Jr.'s 1971 book, *"Joseph Smith's First Vision: The First Vision in its Historical Context."*[34] Dean C. Jessee's *Dialogue* article, where the comparison of the two accounts is made, was a review of Dr. Backman's book. Joshua 2:1835 was a comparison because the

---

[31]Tanner and Tanner, *Mormonism – Shadow or Reality?*, 162C.
[32]Jessee, "How Lovely was the Morning," *Dialogue* 6, no. 1 (Spring 1971): 86-87, emphasis added.
[33]Ibid., 87.
[34]Milton V. Backman, Jr., *Joseph Smith's First Vision: The First Vision in Its Historical Context* (Bookcraft, Inc., 1971), 209.

"Joseph Smith Diary Account" had never before been seen by the Mormon laity.

All four versions of the three early and suppressed accounts – Joseph Smith's 1832 First Holographic Account, Joshua 1:1835, Erastus Holmes:1835 and Joshua 2:1835 – were written or dictated before the "traditional" "canonized" "official" "fourth" 1838-39 Pearl of Great Price Account, the grand but less authentic narrative (the founding story of the Mormon Church).[35]

1965 to 1969: "There Is No Joy in Mudville"

The Brigham Young University graduate student's allegedly remarkable discovery is not heralded in the Mormon media, called to the attention of investigators or converts, or made the subject of a conference talk. The graduate student's stunning but obscure disclosure is followed by four years of official silence. Although James B. Allen addressed the subject in *Dialogue* in 1966, his voice was not official. The Church did not authenticate the 1832 Account "brought to light" in 1965 until 1969. A graduate student reports that he has found the first account of Joseph Smith's first encounter with deity in the manuscript archives of the Mormon Church, and the Church says nothing? Why should the Church not be thrilled to learn that a graduate student recognized a priceless historical document in a prominent historical ledger? A document with an impeccable provenance?

1969: Mormon Leaders React

In the spring of 1969, approximately four years after Paul R. Cheesman published his "Thesis" containing a typescript of Joseph Smith's 1832 Vision of the "crucifyed" Lord, and three years after James B. Allen published his 1966 article in *Dialogue*, Dean C. Jessee delivered an official response to Cheesman's disclosure of

---

[35]"The story is an essential part of the first lesson given by Mormon missionaries to prospective converts, and its acceptance is necessary before baptism." (Allen, "The Significance of Joseph Smith's 'First Vision' in Mormon Thought," *Dialogue*, 1 no. 3 [Autumn 1966]: 29).

Joseph Smith's 1832 Account, and to Allen's disclosure of Joshua 1:1835, in an article published by *Brigham Young University Studies*.[36] In the 1969 article, Jessee discussed the authenticity of the 1832 Account and provided a copy of the original manuscript. After years of awkward silence, the Church now finally admitted that the 1832 Account was authentic (but not that it was holographic).[37] We may surmise that the three double-sided leaves containing the history hadn't always been kept in the "journal ledger" (The Kirtland Letter Book, 1829-35, commencing at page 1a); that those leaves had been kept in a locked vault, or in some other seriously secluded place, while the "journal ledger" in which the account was later found had been somewhere else. If that hadn't been the case, how could there ever have been confusion on so simple a point? Dean C. Jessee reports: "On at least three occasions prior to 1839 Joseph Smith began writing his history.[38]

---

[36]Jessee, "The Early Accounts of Joseph Smith's First Vision," *BYU Studies* 9, no. 3 (Spring 1969): 275-94.

[37]Jessee described how the Church Historian's office was supposed to have determined the authenticity of the *1832 Account*:

> *First,* although they were later cut from the volume, the three leaves containing the history match the cut edges and quality and markings of the paper of the page ends. The terminal letters of words severed when the pages were removed also match. The cut page stubs immediately precede the November 27, 1832, letter entry on the first of the remaining pages.
>
> *Second,* the numbering sequences indicate this arrangement. The pages of the history were numbered one through six and the November 27 letter begins on page "1a." *Both the history and the letter are in Williams' handwriting.* He would not have needed to begin the letter page with "1a" had there not been other numbered pages preceding it . . . . [Jessee, "The Early Accounts of Joseph Smith's First Vision," *BYU Studies* 9, no. 3 (Spring 1969): 277-78, emphasis added.

This should have been an extraordinarily easy process *if* the account (meaning the three double-sided leaves containing the six-page history) had been kept in the Kirtland Letter Book: 1829-35, for one hundred and thirty years.

[38]Jessee explains how the date of the undated manuscript – which confused scholars like Paul R. Cheesman, Fawn McKay Brodie, James B. Allen and Levi Edgar Young – was finally determined.

> Inasmuch as Williams [Frederick G. Williams] was converted to Mormonism in the fall of 1830 and immediately left on a mission to Missouri, the writing of this history could not have preceded his meeting with Joseph Smith in mid-1831. Nor was the history written after November 27, 1832, since on that date the ledger book in which it was written was converted to a letter book for recording important historical Church documents. There are many evidences for this assertion. [Jessee,

The earliest of these is a six-page account recorded on three leaves of a ledger book, written between the summer of 1831 and November 1832 . . . ."[39]

The Kirtland Letter Book:1829-35

Joseph Smith started the Kirtland Letter Book and a daily journal on November 27, 1832. "On that day he records having purchased a book for the purpose of keeping 'a minute account of all things that come under my observation.'"[40] And on that day, he started both "a daily journal" and the (Kirtland) "letter book." Some time on or before November 27, 1832, Smith wrote his particular part of the First Vision account described in the leaves later cut from what then became the Kirtland Letter Book. The fact that the Kirtland Letter Book started on November 27, 1832, commencing at page "1a," does not necessarily mean that the excised pages 1 through 6, preceding the pages that started at "1a," were not composed at the same time. November 27, 1832, seems to have been a day when the Mormon prophet got serious about keeping a written history. "The beginning of the journal and letter book on the same day is of more than coincidental significance. It not only provides the terminal point in dating the earliest known historical narrative of the

---

"The Early Accounts of Joseph Smith's First Vision," *BYU Studies* 9, no. 3 (Spring 1969): 277].

Jessee admits that the Kirtland Letter Book: 1829-1835, a "ledger book," was a place for the "recording" of "important historical Church documents," and a prominent repository. While Paul R. Cheesman claimed to have discovered Joseph Smith's 1832 Account in the "journal ledger," President Levi Edgar Young told LaMar Petersen the "strange account" "had been concealed for 120 years in a locked vault." (LaMar Petersen, *The Creation of the Book of Mormon: A Historical Inquiry* [Salt Lake City: Freethinker Press, 2000], xii). Those conflicting claims allow for the possibilities (1) that the 1832 account remained in the "journal ledger" for 133 years until it was found by a graduate student who recognized its significance, when for 130 years other Mormon leaders, scholars, historians and archivists had not, or (2) that it was transferred back to the ledger, from whence it sprang, from some other secure and private place of safekeeping, when disclosure became an imperative. In the face of that much more likely scenario, it could be averred that the alleged discovery was a sham from start to finish, orchestrated by leaders and scholars in order to save face with the faith's detractors.

[39]Jessee, "The Early Accounts of Joseph Smith's First Vision," *BYU Studies* 9, no. 3 (Spring 1969): 277, emphasis added.
[40]Ibid., 278.

Prophet's life, but establishes the start of an important precedent in preserving the history of the Church."[41]

What does the Church spokesman say? That the 1832 History is the earliest of three histories started by Joseph Smith prior to 1839; that it was recorded on those three double-sided leaves of the "ledger book" that became the Kirtland Letter Book: 1829-1835 no later than November 27, 1832; and that the recently released accounts of the First Vision, representing Joseph's early attempts to write history, were fragmentary.[42] Jessee's 1969 article, written on behalf of the Church in a Mormon publication, treats Joseph's early efforts to write his history indulgently. Those early accounts were evidence of the Mormon prophet's historical good faith, but they were also but "fragmentary beginnings" superceded by later efforts greatly more complete. There were things that the Church's spokesman did not say or try to explain: Why this account, unknown to the membership, had not been published from 1832 to 1965; how it came to be overlooked in its prominent place of deposit; how the profound importance of the vintage document could have gone unrecognized; why the pages were cut from the journal ledger. After admitting the document's contemporaneity, and after presenting a copy of the undated manuscript (to replace the now four-year-old typescript in 1969), the Church's spokesman admitted that *"The 1831-32 history transliterated here contains the earliest known account of Joseph Smith's First Vision."*[43] And it is, the Mormon scholar admits, the *"earliest known historical narrative of the prophet's life."*[44]

---

[41]Ibid.

[42]Jessee, "The Early Accounts of Joseph Smith's First Vision," *BYU Studies* 9, no. 3 (Spring 1969): 294. It would be difficult to describe Oliver and Joseph's 1834-35 history (published in the *Messenger and Advocate* in eight successive installments) as fragmentary. But what other choice can there be? How else can you explain a "full history of the rise of the Church of the Latter Day Saints, and the most interesting parts of its progress to the present time" that contains no account of the First Vision? Fourteen or fifteen years after the alleged fact? While informing his readers that the earliest histories of the Church are but "fragmentary beginnings," Dean C. Jessee describes how the 1834-35 history, containing that unbelievable omission, was considered sufficiently important to be laboriously transcribed into the prophet's journal. ("A copy of the eight letters was transcribed into the Prophet's journal in 1835." [Ibid., 283]).

[43]Ibid., 278, emphasis added.

[44]Ibid., emphasis added.

Now finally, four years after the first account is first disclosed, the Church admits that that account of Joseph Smith's First Vision of the Son is authentic and officially (but only by implication) informs the Mormon people what the Church never before has said: Joseph Smith told his story more than once!

Joseph Smith's 1832 Account, Joshua 1:1835, Joshua 2:1835 and Erastus Holmes:1835 – four different versions of three different previously unknown accounts – speak with a single voice: Joseph Smith told his story more than once!

But never once the same.

There will be no apology.

1969 and 1971: "Love Means Never Having to Say You're Sorry"

In 1966, James B. Allen admitted something that no Latter-day Saint preaching to the uninformed about persecution should ever forget: "As far as Mormon literature is concerned, there was apparently no reference to Joseph Smith's first vision in any published material in the 1830's."[45] Early Mormon converts like Parley P. Pratt, Sidney Rigdon, Brigham Young, Heber C. Kimball, Peter Whitmer, Ziba Peterson, John Corrill, John Taylor and others were converted largely because of the Book of Mormon. None of the early writings and records of these prominent Mormon men seem "to indicate that an understanding or knowledge of the first vision was in any way" important to their conversion. Parley P. Pratt didn't even describe the first vision in his early influential missionary pamphlet, *Voice of Warning*. In the 1830s, "it was not considered necessary for prospective converts" to know about the vision. "The story of Joseph Smith's first vision was not given general circulation in the 1830's. Neither Mormon nor non-Mormon publications made reference to it, and it is evident that the general membership of the Church knew little, *if anything*, about it."[46] The persecution claims so prominent in the canonized account

---

[45]Allen, "The Significance of Joseph Smith's 'First Vision' in Mormon Thought," *Dialogue*, 1 no. 3 (Autumn 1966): 31.
[46]Ibid., 33-34, emphasis added.

of the vision, and so important to the missionaries, have no foundation in fact.

Dean C. Jessee does not begin to explain how generations of leaders and scholars managed to overlook four separate versions of three discrepant accounts of Mormonism's founding story for more than one hundred and thirty years. Ignoring the fact that the Church had concealed and suppressed the publication of those 1832 and 1835 Accounts of the First Vision, Jessee (like James D. Allen) chose rather instead to emphasize the fact that Joseph Smith had actually dictated accounts of the First Vision in 1832 and 1835. What they said that meant to them was that Smith had actually said something about Mormonism's founding event before 1838, 1839, 1840, 1842, 1843 and/or 1844 – years when what later became the 1838-39 Pearl of Great Price Account was composed, revised and composed, published in Scotland, published in Nauvoo, and then later amended. The First Vision, though described in the *Times and Seasons*, was not actually published in the Pearl of Great Price until 1851.

In his *Dialogue* article published in 1971, Dean C. Jessee – while failing to account for the historically reprehensible hundred-year-late disclosure of the suppressed accounts – made the best of a bad thing. *In the twentieth-century disclosure of those accounts, he said, was an answer of sorts to some of those "evolution theory" detractors who claimed "that the time-lag between the Vision and its official recording, plus the discrepancies between various accounts of the event, indicate that the story was born late and gradually evolved in complexity."*[47] The strange new renderings of the vision pushed the date of Joseph's first private report of his first encounter with deity back from 1838-39, eighteen or nineteen years after-the-alleged-fact, to 1832, approximately twelve years after-the-alleged-fact. The time-lag is shortened to about twelve years, from about eighteen or nineteen years (if one fails to consider that the 1832 Account was not reported at all, and that the 1838-39 Pearl of Great Price Account was not reported in Scotland until 1840, or in Nauvoo until 1842). The historian, blithely ignoring the deception, changes the emphasis, and the Church stands mute. He will instead

---

[47]Jessee, "How Lovely was the Morning," *Dialogue,* 6, no. 1 (Spring 1971): 88, emphasis added.

describe how the alleged discovery of the discrepant accounts narrows the time line.

Jessee informs Latter-day Saints in 1971 that the Joshua 1:1835 (Third-Person) Account, the account first described by Professor James B. Allen in 1966 as a document bound at the back of the *Manuscript History, Book A-1*, has also been found in *Joseph Smith's Personal Diary* where it is now described as the Joshua 2:1835 Account.   Jessee (and the Church) completely ignored the inconvenient fact that the contents of the Joshua 1 and 2:1835 and Erastus Holmes: 1835 Accounts had been falsified for more than one hundred years in Joseph Smith's *History of the Church*. The true importance of the true contents of those documents is only emphasized by the Church's more than century-long efforts to conceal them. It will not now do to say that they were fragmentary, incomplete or unimportant. The leaders of the Church recognized how important those discrepant accounts were when they falsified their contents in the *History of the Church*.

What is memorable about the Church's 1969 institutional response (by Dean C. Jessee) to Paul R. Cheesman's 1965 disclosure of Joseph Smith's 1832 Holographic Account of Smith's 1821 vision?

What is memorable about the Church's 1969 institutional response (by Dean C. Jessee) to James B. Allen's 1966 disclosure of Joseph Smith's 1835 Joshua 1 Account of Smith's 1820 vision?

> *The failure to admit the holograph; the failure to admit in 1969, four years after the 1965 and 1966 disclosures, or until 1971, six years after the 1965 disclosure, that Joseph Smith's 1832 Account was in a class by itself because it was written by the hand of Joseph Smith.*
>
> *The failure to admit in 1965, 1966 or 1969 that Joseph Smith's 1832 Account, a document with an impeccable provenance, was the only known account of the First Vision that was ever written by Joseph Smith in his own hand.*
>
> *The 1969 misrepresentation based on alleged handwriting analysis that the 1832 Account was written in its entirety by*

Frederick G. Williams.

The four-year failure to furnish historians and scholars with a copy of the original manuscript of the handwritten 1832 Account instead of a typescript.

The failure to disclose until 1971 that Joshua 1:1835, the third-person version bound in the back of Book A-1 of the Manuscript History, and published in 1966, was also written in a first-person version, Joshua 2:1835, in Joseph Smith's Personal Diary.

The failure to explain why the 1832 Account was not described in Joseph Smith's History of the Church, or in the 1834-35 History (the first authorized history of the Church), in the Book of Commandments, in the introductory material to the Book of Mormon, the Lectures on Faith, the Doctrine and Covenants, The Evening and the Morning Star, the Evening and Morning Star, the Latter-day Saints Messenger and Advocate, the Times and Seasons and the Pearl of Great Price.

The disclosure that there was a second 1835 and third chronological account of the First Vision (Erastus Holmes:1835), and the failure to admit that the true contents of that account had been falsified, concealed and suppressed from 1835 to 1969.

The failure to admit that the Church had misrepresented the contents of Joshua 1:1835, Joshua 2:1835 and Erastus Holmes:1835 in repeated publications of Joseph Smith's History for more than a hundred and thirty years.

The first disclosure of the hundred-year-hidden words that Joseph Smith actually spoke to Erastus Holmes.

The failure to explain how two versions of the 1835 Joshua the Jewish Minister account – one (Joshua 1:1835) in third-person found in the Manuscript History, Book A-1, the other (Joshua 2:1835) in first-person found in Joseph Smith's

Personal Diary – and their contents could have escaped detection by Mormon leaders, historians, scholars, archivists and staffers from 1835 until 1966 and 1969.

The failure to admit that the contents of the three earliest and most contemporaneous accounts of the most important event in the history of the Mormon Church had been concealed and suppressed for more than one hundred and thirty years.

The failure to explain why the handwritten pages of the 1832 Account were cut from the Kirtland Letter Book: 1829-35.

The failure to straightforwardly identify and honestly describe the contradictions that discouraged the publication of those discordant accounts and caused their twentieth-century disclosure to embarrass the Mormon Church.

The failure to apologize for a more than one hundred-year deception that involved the historic betrayal of scholars, members, missionaries, investigators and converts and tainted all First Vision scholarship.

CHAPTER FOUR

1971: Six Versions of Five
Discrepant Accounts

*. . . **I saw the Lord** and he spake unto me saying "Joseph <my son> thy sins are forgiven thee. go thy <way> walk in my statutes and keep my commandments . . . .*[1]

Joseph Smith

__I saw two personages__ . . . the Personage who addressed me said that all their Creeds were an abomination in his sight . . .[2]

Joseph Smith

Our whole strength rests on the validity of that vision. It either occurred or it did not occur. If it did not, then this work is a fraud. If it did, then it is the most important and wonderful work under the heavens.[3]

Gordon B. Hinckley

INVENTING THE VISION

Personages

In his 1832 Holographic Account, Jesus visited Joseph Smith. The only account of the First Vision written by Joseph Smith in his own hand (and the only presently known account of the vision prepared

---

[1] 1832 Holographic Account.

[2] 1838-39 Pearl of Great Price Account.

[3] General Conference Report, *Ensign* (November 2002), 32. "The visitation of God the Father and Jesus Christ to Joseph Smith . . . is fundamental to the theology of the Church. Upon the reality of the First Vision rests the Church's claim to divine authority." ("First Vision: 'Bedrock Theology,'" *Church News* [9 January 1993], 14).

before 1834) mentions only one personage, the "crucifyed" Lord. In two versions of a second suppressed account of the same vision, both composed in 1835 (Joshua 1:1835 and Joshua 2:1835), Joseph was visited by "two personages" one after the other. He said he saw "<. . . *many angels* in this vision>" consisting of two versions (third- and first-person versions) of a second chronological account. Smith told Joshua that "*a personage appeard*" in the midst of a "pillar of flame, which was spread all around, and yet nothing consumed, another personage soon appeard like unto the first."[4]   These unidentified personages were not together to start; their appearances were consecutive. The second unidentified personage spoke to Smith to say, "*thy sins are forgiven thee,*" after which he further spoke to him to say, "*Jesus Christ is the son of God.*"[5]   There is no assurance that Jesus was the second personage or personally present, or that the first personage was the Father. The text doesn't say that these visitors were the Father and the Son, or that they were anything other than two of the "many angels" Joseph said that he saw "in this vision." There is no "*This is My Beloved Son. Hear Him!*" in the Joshua versions of the second account. No one says that all of the sects were wrong, and there was no revival in the second account. The conversions of Joseph's mother and siblings were not described. This vision concerned "forgiveness" and "a promise of grace."

---

[4]Joseph Smith Jr., *The Personal Writings of Joseph Smith*, ed. Dean C. Jessee (Salt Lake City, UT: Deseret Book, 1984), 75-76, emphasis added. The Joshua versions described intermittently-appearing personages, but the 1838-39 Pearl of Great Price Account reported that, "When the light rested upon me I saw two Personages, whose brightness and glory defy all description, standing above me in the air. One of them spake unto me, calling me by name and said, pointing to the other – *This is My Beloved Son. Hear Him!*" (Joseph Smith Jr., *The Pearl of Great Price: Being a Choice Selection from the Revelations, Translations, and Narrations of Joseph Smith, First Prophet, Seer and Revelator to the Church of Jesus Christ of Latter Day Saints* [Liverpool, UK: F.D. Richards, 1851], Joseph Smith – History 1:17, emphasis retained).

[5]Why would Jesus say, "Jesus Christ is the Son of God"? Why wouldn't Jesus rather say, "I am the Son of God," or "I am Jesus Christ"? If this was the Father speaking, why didn't he say, "*This is My Beloved Son. Hear Him!*"? If these personages were the Father and the Son, and not two of the many angels Joseph said that he saw, and if the speaker wasn't Jesus, why was the Father speaking in Joshua 1 and 2: 1835, when the Son spoke in the 1832 Account, and when it was mostly the Son who spoke in the 1838-39 Account? Why, if the Father was speaking, didn't he say in the 1832 and 1835 Accounts what he is supposed to have said in the 1838-39 Account?

In Joshua 2:1835, Joseph saw "many angels" (and two intermittent unidentified personages).[6] In his handwritten 1832 Account he saw the "crucifyed" Lord, but not the Father and no angels. In his 1838-39 Pearl of Great Price Account he saw "two Personages," one a Father, the other a Son, but no angels. The appearances of these personages were not consecutive; they were simultaneous. In the Erastus Holmes:1835 Account, Smith received "the first visitation of Angels." Why did the second personage (in Joshua 1 and 2: 1835) say "Jesus Christ is the son of God"? Why didn't the first personage (in Joshua 1 and 2: 1835) say, "*This is My Beloved Son. Hear Him?*" Why didn't the 1838-39 Pearl of Great Price personages appear "in the midst" of a "piller of fire light"? Why didn't the brightness and glory of the Joshua personages "defy all description"? Why didn't those Joshua personages stand above the boy "in the air"? Why didn't the first personage call Joseph by name? Why did Joseph identify two personages in 1835, in his Joshua Accounts, but only one personage in 1832 in the 1832 Account? Why were there many angels in Joshua 1 and 2:1835, and only angels in the Erastus Holmes:1835 Account, when there were no angels in the 1832 Holographic Account, or in the 1838-39 Pearl of Great Price Account, or in the 1842 John Wentworth Account?

The 1842 Wentworth Account and the 1838-39 Pearl of Great Price Account both described two personages but no angels. The 1832 Account, Joshua 1 and 2:1835, Erastus Holmes:1835, the 1838-39 Pearl of Great Price Account and the 1842 Wentworth Account – six versions of five different accounts – describe different messengers, messages, missions and facts. These conflicting reports describe strikingly different circumstances prompted by strikingly different concerns. Grant H. Palmer recognized that each vision was amplified to become more grand with the passage of time. Smith followed what has proven to be a successful formula. His "foundational versions" (including gold plates, priesthood restoration, first vision) all became "more physical, impressive,

---

[6]Dean C. Jessee, "The Early Accounts of Joseph Smith's First Vision," *BYU Studies* 9, no. 3 (Spring 1969): 284.

unique, and miraculous" in the retelling.[7]

The discordant accounts were suppressed and concealed because the prophet undercounted the gods and overcounted the angels in multiple drafts, and then because of his changing views about the nature of God. Joseph believed one thing in 1832 (monotheism), another thing or things in 1838 (bitheism or tritheism) and something else in and after 1839 (the plurality of Gods). He imposed his own changing view of God upon each of several separate accounts.[8] Until at least 1834 Joseph Smith's godhead theology was decidedly monotheistic.[9] On the way to 1839, the year that his then exorbitant acceptance of polytheism (multiple gods) publicly surfaced, one God, the undivided, "crucifyed," "omnipotant," "omnipreasant" spirit personage of the first 1832 Account, became two separate unidentified personages and many angels in a second account, a first visitation of angels in a third account, and two personages without any angels in fourth and fifth accounts. The 1832 Holographic Account posits the visit of a single "omnipotant" (almighty), "omnipreasant" (present in all places at all times) "*crucifyed*" Lord. Why weren't there two personages in this vision? Because Joseph didn't believe that there were two personages in 1832. Grant H. Palmer described this foundational dilemma: "Since Joseph Smith believed God and Christ to be the same being . . . between 1829-1834 – how many Gods would you expect to appear in his 1832 First Vision account?; or find in the *Book of Moses*, in the *Joseph Smith Translation* of the Bible, in the *Book of Commandments*, and in the 1830 edition of the *Book of Mormon*?"[10] Those resources, in their times, were consistent with the early monotheistic views of Joseph Smith.

---

[7]Grant H. Palmer, "Joseph Smith's changing view of God as seen in his First Vision accounts," Outline of a Lecture given at the Salt Lake City Library (6 November 2013).

[8]Ibid.

[9]Smith's monotheism was powerfully reflected in the 1830 Articles and Covenants of the Church of Christ, called "The Mormon Creed," and in the 1830 First Edition of the Book of Mormon, the 1830 Testimony of the Three Witnesses, the 1830 Book of Moses, Joseph Smith's 1832 Holographic Account, the 1830-1833 Inspired Translation of the King James Bible and the 1833 Book of Commandments.

[10]Palmer, "Joseph Smith's changing view of God as seen in his First Vision accounts" (6 November 2013), emphasis retained.

Forgiveness

Joseph Smith told Robert Matthews – *alias* Matthias, *alias* Joshua *alias* God the Father – in Joshua 1 and 2:1835, that the second unidentified personage in his vision said "thy sins are forgiven thee." The 1838-39 canonized Pearl of Great Price Account, first composed in 1838 in the presence of Sidney Rigdon and George W. Robinson, then copied and further composed in 1839 by James Mulholland, failed to mention forgiveness. That was a dramatic revision, a major change and a stunning omission. It represented the substantive reformulation of the foundational narrative. This new First Vision was not a plea for forgiveness and a promise of grace. Why was such a revision thought to have been required? Because the 1832 vision was so "unremarkably similar to many other epiphanies of that era" that "no one took notice of it."[11] What Joseph publicly described as his objective in his 1838-39 History ("to know which of all the sects was right") was not what Joseph privately described as his objective in his hundred-year hidden 1832 Holographic Account (" . . . I cried unto the Lord for mercy for there was none else to whom I could go"), or in his hundred-year hidden Joshua 1 and 2: 1835 Accounts ("information was what I most desired . . ."). Joseph Smith described his 1832 objective in these following words unknown to the laity until 1965:

> [M]y mind become excedingly distressed for I become convicted of my sins and by searching the scriptures I found that ~~mand~~ <mankind> did not come unto the Lord but that they had apostatised from the true and liveing faith . . . ."[12]

> [A]nd when I considered all these things . . . I cried unto the Lord for mercy for there was none else to whom I could go and ~~to~~ obtain mercy . . . .[13]

The 1832 Account begged forgiveness, mercy, conversion, guidance and grace.

---

[11]Ibid.

[12]Jessee ed., *The Personal Writings of Joseph Smith*, 5, emphasis added.

[13]Ibid., 5-6, emphasis added.

> *[A]nd the Lord heard my cry in the wilderne=ss and while in <the> attitude of calling up the Lord <in the 16th year of my age> a piller of ~~fire~~ light above the brightness of the sun at noon day come down from above and rested upon me and I was filled with the spirit of god and the <Lord> opened the heavens upon me and I saw the Lord and he spake unto me saying Joseph <my son> thy sins are forgiven thee. go thy <way> walk in my statutes and keep my commandments . . . .*[14]

Joseph, who said he "felt to mourn for my own sins and for the sins of the world," was searching for "mercy."[15] The 1832 vision did not concern mission or power. There was no call to the work. The message was simple and direct: "thy sins are forgiven thee"; "walk in my statutes and keep my commandments."

Why didn't the deities forgive the young seeker's sins in the greatly more grand 1838-39 Account like the messengers in Joshua 1 and 2: 1835 specifically did in those earlier accounts? Because forgiveness from sin was not essential to the streamlined and embellished new and expanded final draft of the founding story's fourth revisionary retelling. The message and the mission, the scope of the operation, and the possibilities had by now evolved. Two sets of contradictory facts are now seen to support two separate contradictory objectives. The 1832 facts hadn't taken the young prophet in the direction he later determined to travel. The *fourth* canonized 1838-39 Pearl of Great Price Account of what is supposed to have been the First Vision of the Father and the Son, unlike the *first, second* and *third* hundred-year suppressed accounts of other messengers, was about "the beginning of the restoration of the Gospel and the commencement of a new dispensation."[16] With that in mind, the elaborate Pearl of Great Price Account sought to set itself apart from what were literally "thousands" of evangelical "forgiveness" and "promise of grace" epiphanies. The 1838-39 description of an 1820 Joseph was not the 1832 description of an 1821 Joseph, a

---

[14]Ibid., 6, emphasis added.

[15]Ibid., 5-6.

[16]Richard Lyman Bushman, with the assistance of Jed Woodworth, *Joseph Smith: Rough Stone Rolling* (New York: Alfred A. Knopf, 2005), 39.

simple youth seeking forgiveness, correction, guidance, mercy, acceptance and conversion. The 1838-39 fourth retelling of the foundational narrative described a glorious event calling a remarkable youth to an amazing work. Sin (and thus forgiveness) wasn't the item there. This prophet had by now become more than he had previously been. It had been up to her son Joseph, his mother reported, "to bring forth that light and intelligence which has been long lost in the Earth . . . ."[17]

There is one thing these two strikingly different accounts of the same supposed event had in common. Until 1840 and 1842 in the case of the 1838-39 Account, and until 1965 in the case of the 1832 Account, "the vision was not mentioned by friends, family, institutions, or enemies," whatever Joseph had said about persecution.[18]   Neither vision was published during the new church's "formative decade," and the 1832 Account wasn't published for one hundred and thirty-three years.

Sects

In his 1832 recounting Joseph Smith knew (and said) that all the churches were wrong before he retreated to the wilderness to seek the Lord in prayer. He prayed about the "wellfare" of his immortal soul. "[B]y searching the scriptures," he said, "I found that . . . there was no society or denomination that built upon the Gospel of Jesus Christ as recorded in the new testament . . . ."[19]   God didn't have to tell him that; his study of the scriptures and his "intimate acquaintance with those of different denominations"[20] told him that. He didn't pray to know which church to join. The 1838-39 Pearl of Great Price Account was an unrecognizable embellishment of his first and privately held epiphany. Grant H. Palmer compared Joseph's 1838-39 Account to Joseph's 1832 Account:

---

[17]Lucy Mack Smith, 1845 Manuscript History, Dan Vogel, ed., *Early Mormon Documents* (Salt Lake City: Signature Books, 1996), 1:290.

[18]Palmer, "Joseph Smith's changing view of God as seen in his First Vision accounts" (6 November 2013).

[19]Jessee ed., *The Personal Writings of Joseph Smith*, 5.

[20]Ibid., 4-5.

> *During the leadership crisis of April 1838, Joseph remembered a different purpose in going to pray. There is nothing about forgiveness of sins. His prayer occurs within the context of a major revival. Motivated by this setting, he now says, "My object in going to enquire of the Lord was to know which of all the sects was right." While it was unnecessary to even ask this question in his 1832 report, in 1838 the matter of importance was apostasy from the only true church.*[21]

In the 1838-39 Account, the Palmyra revival stirred Joseph's soul and prompted him to repair to the grove and pray. During "this time of great excitement" on the subject of religion "in the place where we lived," he reflected on the issues and felt "great uneasiness." During "this time of great excitement," he attended the "several meetings" of the contending sects "as often as occasion would permit."[22] In 1832 there was no revival, no persecution, no famous question and no famous answer. Joseph already knew that none of the sects were right; that wasn't the question then. In three versions of two other early accounts, Joshua 1 and 2: 1835 and Erastus Holmes: 1835, there were no revivals, no famous questions and no famous answers. In the 1838-39 Pearl of Great Price Account, the Palmyra revival called Joseph's mind "up to serious reflection."[23] During a revival Joseph hadn't mentioned in 1832, or to Joshua or Erastus Holmes in 1835, Lucy Mack Smith and three of Joseph's siblings (Hyrum, Samuel and Sophronia) joined the Presbyterian Church.[24] It was Joseph Smith's participation in those Palmyra revival events – his attendance at the meetings, the sermons, conflicts, divisions and a sense of unease – that caused Joseph to retire to the woods and ask the Lord which of all the sects was right. "My mind at times was greatly excited, *the cry and tumult were so great and incessant.*"[25] The 1838-39 Account of an 1820 revival-induced First Vision was by now all about the sects.

---

[21]Grant H. Palmer, *An Insider's View of Mormon Origins* (Salt Lake City: Signature Books, 2002), 252, emphasis added.
[22]The Pearl of Great Price, Joseph Smith – History 1:5, 8.
[23]Ibid., 1:8.
[24]Ibid., 1:7.
[25]Ibid., 1:9, emphasis added.

> *. . . I asked the Personages who stood above me in the light, which of all the sects was right[26] – and which I should join. I was answered that I must join none of them, for they were all wrong; and the Personage who addressed me said that all their creeds were an abomination in his sight; that those professors were all corrupt; . . . . He again forbade me to join with any of them . . . .[27]*

Of the five different primary accounts of Joseph's first encounter with deity, only the 1838-39 Pearl of Great Price Account is seen to have mentioned the Palmyra revival. In his 1832 forgiveness epiphany, Joseph knew before he kneeled to pray that none of the sects were right. Now (in 1838-39) Joseph changed his mind and said that his 1820 objective had been to "know which of all the sects was right, that I might know which to join."[28] He sought an answer to that question, he said, *while* the revival raged. The great First Vision event occurred in "the midst" of "this war of words and tumult of opinions."[29]

In his embellished 1838-39 Account, Joseph's reformulated "object in going to enquire of the Lord was to know which of all the sects was right? that I might know which to join . . . *(for at this time it had never entered into my heart that all were wrong . . .).*"[30] That parenthetical addendum was omitted and removed – then later admitted and included – in different editions of the Pearl of Great Price. Jerald and Sandra Tanner described the unannounced omission and the prodding that may have encouraged its reinstatement. "In the 1972 edition of this book[31] we pointed out

---

[26]The term "sect" has come to have an odious connotation to modern Mormons. Sects to Mormons are characterized as offshoots of the "abominable [Catholic] church" described in the Book of Mormon as the "mother of harlots." (Book of Mormon, 1 Nephi 13:34).

[27]The Pearl of Great Price, Joseph Smith – History (author's 1957 printing), 1:18-20, emphasis added.

[28]Ibid., 1:18.

[29]Ibid., 1:10.

[30]"History of Joseph Smith (Continued)," *Times and Seasons*, vol. 3 no. 11 (1 April 1842): 748, emphasis added.

[31]Jerald Tanner and Sandra Tanner, *Mormonism – Shadow or Reality?* (Salt Lake City: Utah Lighthouse Ministry, 1987).

that the clause, *'for at this time it had never entered into my heart that all were wrong,'* had been entirely deleted from the story as it appears in modern editions of the *Pearl of Great Price*" (that parenthetical addendum was omitted from this author's 1957 printing of the Pearl of Great Price). That particular omission concerned a matter of some importance. "Strange as it may seem, in the new printing of the *Pearl of Great Price* in the triple combination (*Joseph Smith — History 1:18*), the clause which was previously suppressed has been reinserted in its proper place."[32] The omission had to be reinstated because – as the 1832 Account which was not published until 1965 reflects – it had entered into his heart that "all" of the sects were wrong. He had known, as he had said in 1832, that all the sects were wrong even before he knelt to pray. After 1965 the 1832 Holographic Account of the vision of the Son had to be taken into account.

COMPARISONS

The 1832 Account

The boy described in Joseph's 1832 *first* chronological and *only* Holographic Account of the First Vision is not "laboring under . . . extreme difficulties" caused by "the contests" of "parties of religionists."[33] He was not victimized by some partisan "war of words" and didn't mention any "unusual excitement" on the subject of religion in "the place where he lived."[34] There was no dark force in this account. There were no "Personages" (plural), and there were no "angels" in this account. He didn't say that he saw God as a separate personage introducing his Son. And he wasn't ridiculed or mocked. There was no persecution described in this account. He knew before he "cried unto the lord for mercy"[35] that none of the churches were true. He had addressed his inquiry to "concerns" identified with the welfare of his "immortal Soul."

---

[32]Ibid., 146, emphasis retained.
[33]The Pearl of Great Price, Joseph Smith – History 1:11.
[34]Ibid., 1:10, 5.
[35]Jessee ed., *The Personal Writings of Joseph Smith*, 5-6.

The 1832 Holographic Account was not about Joseph's search for one true church. He pondered what he said he saw, but it was when he became convicted of his "sins," and when "his mind become excedingly distressed" because he "become convicted of his sins," that he "cried unto the Lord for mercy." He recognized contention, wickedness, darkness and division, but he was concerned with forgiveness, mercy, information, guidance and a promise of grace. He was not threatened by any "tumult of opinions" or disturbed by any "great and incessant" outcry. Jesus forgave Joseph Smith's sins in this account. Forgiveness and mercy were at the center of the 1832 encounter. Jesus didn't mention forgiveness in the 1838-39 Pearl of Great Price Account of the vision of the Father and the Son, or in the 1842 John Wentworth Account. In 1832 Joseph didn't ask "which of all the sects was right," and the Lord didn't say that all of them were wrong, or that he "must join none of them." The 1832 Account did not describe abominable creeds or corrupt professors, a great Palmyra revival, a dark power that bound his tongue, a Methodist minister or persecution. All of those things were subsequent additions to earlier narratives in later drafts.

In the one hundred and thirty-year suppressed 1832 Account Joseph was fifteen years old and "<in the 16th year of my age>"[36] in 1821, and he had already searched the "scriptures." He said that he was born "of goodly Parents who spared no pains to instructing me in <the> christian religion."[37] Surely a boy from such an environment and so instructed had to have prayed many times before the vision, both publicly and privately. From the age of twelve to fifteen years he said that he had "pondered many things" in his heart concerning "the sittuation of the world of mankind the contentions and divi[si]ons the wicke[d]ness and abominations and the darkness which pervaded the ~~of the~~ minds of mankind."[38] And he had concluded as early as 1818 that "no society or denomination" "built upon the gospel of Jesus Christ as recorded in the new testament."[39]

---

[36]Jessee ed., *The Personal Writings of Joseph Smith*, 6.
[37]Ibid., 4.
[38]Ibid., 5.
[39]Ibid.

In the 1832 Account he was not forbidden to join any of the churches, and no one instructed him to continue as he was "until further directed." He did not suffer severe persecution "at the hands of all classes of men," and he was not reviled by "the great ones of the most popular sects of the day." There was no Paul, no Agrippa and no persecution, and he left the vision happy: "[M]y soul was filled with love and for many days I could rejoice with great Joy and the Lord was with me but [I] could find none that would believe the hevnly vision nevertheless I pondered these things in my heart."[40]   Because there was no instruction not to join the churches in this account, no one should be surprised when "Smith family members join the Presbyterian Church, and Joseph tries to join the Methodists."[41]

The 1838-39 Account

The canonized account, modern Mormon scripture, had nothing to do with forgiveness, for by 1838-39 the equation had changed. It was the same event, but the facts were now reworked. The boy described in Joseph's 1838-39 fourth account of the First Vision was fourteen years old and in the fifteenth year of his age in 1820. There was a religious revival in Palmyra, New York, that awakened his mind to the subject of religion. This was the only one of the six versions of five different accounts (including Wentworth) supposed to have mentioned an "unusual excitement on the subject of religion" in "the place where we lived."[42]   This 1838-39 Account (and Wentworth, its theoretical sidekick) was the only account to mention the restoration of the gospel. There was, nevertheless, no dark force in Wentworth, or in the 1832 Account. The 1838-39 Account is the only account known to have mentioned Joseph's fabled encounter with a Methodist minister. In this account Joseph prayed to determine which of the sects was right, because "*at this time it had never entered into my heart that all were wrong.*" "Amidst" all of his anxieties he had "never before made the attempt to pray vocally." There was a dark power that bound his tongue so

---

[40]Ibid., 6.
[41]Palmer, "Joseph Smith's changing view of God as seen in his First Vision accounts" (6 November 2013).
[42]The Pearl of Great Price, Joseph Smith – History 1:5.

he could not speak. Two separate personages then appeared. He was twice forbidden to join any of the churches. His call to the work is now described by means of directions that were clear and precise.[43] He discussed the vision with the Methodist minister who treated his report "lightly" and with great contempt.[44] And he – like the Apostle Paul – then suffered severe and relentless persecution.[45]

> *I continued to pursue my common vocations in life until the twenty-first of September one thousand eight hundred and twenty three [over a period of about three-and-a-half years], all the time suffering severe persecution at the hands of all classes of men, both religious and irreligious, because I continued to affirm that I had seen a vision."*[46]

History doesn't support this claim. The 1838-39 Account "contains an extensive description of vision-related persecution that is totally unsupported by external evidence."[47] In the Joshua Accounts, while Joseph "looking at the different systems taught by the children of men" is now supposed not to have known "who was right or who was wrong," no one stepped forward to say that all of them were wrong. No one said that "their creeds were an abomination," that their "professors were all corrupt," that "they draw near to me with their lips," or "teach for doctrines the commandments of men."[48] Neither did anyone say the gospel was going to be restored. "There is no call from God to the work in these accounts."[49]

---

[43]Fawn M. Brodie, *No Man Knows My History: The Life of Joseph Smith the Mormon Prophet*, 2d ed., rev. and enl. (New York, NY: Alfred A. Knopf, 1972), 409 ("Their directions to him are clear and precise, and the nature of his mission is spelled out").

[44]The Pearl of Great Price, Joseph Smith – History 1:21.

[45]Ibid., 1:23-27.

[46]Ibid., 1:27, emphasis added.

[47]Gregory A. Prince, "Joseph Smith's First Vision in Historical Context: How a Historical Narrative Became Theological," *Journal of Mormon History*, vol. 41 no. 4 (October 2015), 79.

[48]The Pearl of Great Price, Joseph Smith – History 1:19.

[49]Palmer, "Joseph Smith's changing view of God as seen in his First Vision accounts" (6 November 2013).

The Palmyra revival described in the 1838-39 Pearl of Great Price Account as having occurred in 1820 actually occurred in 1824-25, after the death of Alvin Smith and during the ministries of the Reverends George Lane and Benjamin Stockton. When that revival occurred, Joseph Smith was eighteen or nineteen years old and in the nineteenth or twentieth years of his age. "Joseph appears to have combined these two incidents [the 1832 Account of an 1821 vision and an 1824-25 revival] into his 1838 version."[50]

> *All of these factors indicate that Joseph's 1832 narrative is more accurate than the 1838 version in not identifying a revival preceding his forgiveness epiphany.*[51]

> *When a crisis developed around the Book of Mormon in early 1838, he conflated several events into one. Now he was called by God the Father and Jesus Christ in 1820 during an extended revival, was forbidden to join any existing church, and was greatly persecuted by institutions and individuals for sharing his vision of God. This version is not supported by the historical evidence.*[52]

---

[50]Palmer, *An Insider's View of Mormon Origins*, 244. "Brigham Young University Professor Marvin S. Hill concurs that the revival occurred in 1824 rather than 1820." (Ibid). And in the first authorized 1834-35 History of the Church penned by Oliver Cowdery working under the direct personal supervision of Joseph Smith, Cowdery made this astounding admission: "*You will recollect that I mentioned the time of a religious excitement, in Palmyra and vicinity to have been in the 15th year of our brother J. Smith Jr.'s age – that was an error in the type – it should have been in the 17th – You will please remember this correction, as it will be necessary for the full understanding of what will follow in time. This would bring the date [of the revival] down to the year 1823.*" (Oliver Cowdery [and Joseph Smith], "Letter IV To W.W. Phelps, Esq." [Oliver Cowdery and Joseph Smith's 1834-35 History], *Messenger and Advocate*, vol. 1 no. 5 [February 1835]: 78, emphasis added). That is an admission by Oliver Cowdery and Joseph Smith that the revival didn't occur in 1820. The 1832 Account, which didn't describe a revival, describes Joseph as "in the 16th year of my age" when the vision occurred, which would place the event in 1821. The 1838-39 Account places the vision event and the revival in 1820, in Joseph's 15th year when he was fourteen years of age. The 1834-35 Account places the revival in 1823.

[51]Palmer, *An Insider's View of Mormon Origins*, 244, emphasis added.

[52]Ibid., 253-54, emphasis added.

The 1832 and 1835 messengers didn't tell Joseph Smith not to join any of the sects or say that all of them were wrong. They were concerned with forgiveness and conversion rather than issues of power or mission. They did not portend the restoration of the gospel or the commencement of a new dispensation. If the 1832 and 1838-39 accounts of Mormonism's founding event were presented side by side to disinterested and uninformed observers without identification or provenance, they would never be recognized as different accounts of the same event.

The 1838-39 Pearl of Great Price Account of the First Vision is the only one of the first four accounts of the First Vision to be faithfully published in the *History of the Church*. The contents of the earliest and most contemporaneous accounts of Joseph Smith's First Vision were either entirely omitted from the *History of the Church*, as in the case of the 1832 Account, or referenced and falsified, as in the cases of Joshua 1 and 2:1835 and Erastus Holmes. The true contents of Joshua 1 and 2:1835, and Erastus Holmes: 1835, and all of the contents of the 1832 Account were concealed and suppressed.

"Rational Argument Does Not Create Belief, But It Maintains a Climate in Which Belief May Flourish."[53]

Joseph did not live to explain the contradictions implicit in four early discrepant accounts of the same vision, of three that carried messages of personal forgiveness, against a fourth that indicted every Christian faith. Until 1965 members thought the story had been told but once. The 1838-39 Pearl of Great Price Account of the First Vision of the Father and the Son, a statement of mission and power, unlike Joseph's 1832 Holographic Account of the First Vision of the Son, a plea for forgiveness and a promise of grace, doesn't sweat the small stuff. Those that finished his history after

---

[53]Austin Farrer cited at Terryl L. Givens, *By the Hand of Mormon: The American Scripture that Launched a New World Religion* (*n.p.*: Oxford University Press, Inc., 2002; reprint, New York, NY: Oxford University Press paperback, 2003), 118.

his death ignored Smith's 1832 Account.[54] They rather favored his
fourth 1838-39 Account. Would Joseph Smith have forgotten the
day and year he saw and spoke to the deities? Would he have
forgotten to say that there was more than one? Could he have
forgotten the year of his age at the time? The Palmyra revival?
The Methodist minister? The dark "marvelous" "power of some
actual being from the unseen world"?[55] Would someone visited by
the Father and the Son refer to that event as a vision of angels? Is it
likely that someone describing the same event to different people
would remember the "crucifyed" Lord in a first account, two
unnamed personages and many angels in a second account, a first
visitation of angels in a third account, and two unnamed personages
and no angels in fourth and fifth accounts? Or create five different
accounts? Would a person actually visited by deity need to
compose six contradictory versions of five different accounts? Then
misrepresent their contents and keep some of them concealed?

Joseph's 1832 first and only handwritten account of his first
encounter with Deity did not concern the restoration of the gospel
or the commencement of a new dispensation. Joseph Smith's one-
hundred-and-thirty-three year suppressed 1832 Holographic
Account unequivocally describes a vision of the *"crucifyed"* Lord –
a vision of Christ, one Deity, one Personage – and of no one else.
Smith's 1838-39 Pearl of Great Price account describes an
embellished vision of two Personages and a different and
incompatible mission. The years of the visions conflict. The 1832
question is different, Jesus' answer is different, and the Father
doesn't appear. Joseph's first 1832 Holographic Account of a vision
no earlier than 1821 challenges Joseph's fourth 1838-39 Pearl of
Great Price Account of an 1820 vision because of what it doesn't
describe. The Holographic Account fails to describe guidance from
the Epistle of James, the Palmyra revival, a dark power, the
conversion of Joseph's mother and siblings, the minister's great
contempt for Joseph's communication, ridicule, prejudice,
persecution, multiple messengers, heavenly power, a call to the
work, a sense of the mission or a call to serve. It wasn't a "creation

---

[54]The men that completed the *History of the Church* after the death of Smith
cynically changed third-person documents into first-person recollections, as if
Joseph had spoken words that he had not.
[55]The Pearl of Great Price, Joseph Smith – History 1:16.

narrative" for a new society.   Orson Pratt's multigenerational grandson put these conflicts in this stark perspective: "His story of the visions is not a record of genuine event, objective or subjective, but a literary creation of which we have both the trial draft and the finished work, revealing Joseph's mind and personality only as any literary work reveals any writer."[56]   "By 1839, institutional prerogatives had transformed a historical narrative into a theological one . . . [including] a divinely uttered condemnation of all other churches."[57]

THE 1834-35 HISTORY – A SIXTH DISCREPANT ACCOUNT

There is another important history of the early Church meticulously prepared by Oliver Cowdery and Joseph Smith, the First and Second Elders of the Mormon movement. Their 1834-35 History – the first *authorized* history of the Mormon Church – was published in the *Messenger and Advocate* (a Mormon periodical) in eight consecutive installments in 1834 and 1835. This history took the form of eight detailed letters written by "one of the presidents of this church" (Oliver Cowdery) to an important early editor, W.W. Phelps. It is written in plain English and is difficult to describe as fragmentary, despite some few discernible shortcomings. Cowdery introduced the joint production:

> You will recollect that I informed you, in my letter published in the first No. of the Messenger and Advocate, that this history would necessarily embrace the life and character of our esteemed friend and brother, J. Smith, Jr. one of the presidents of this church . . . .[58]

---

[56]Dale Morgan, *Dale Morgan on Early Mormonism: Correspondence & A New History*, ed. John Phillip Walker, with a Biographical Introduction by John Phillip Walker and a Preface by William Mulder (Salt Lake City: Signature Books, 1986), 260.

[57]Prince, "Joseph Smith's First Vision in Historical Context," *Journal of Mormon History*, vol. 41 no. 4 (October 2015): 84.

[58]Oliver Cowdery (and Joseph Smith), "Letter III To W.W. Phelps, Esq." (Oliver Cowdery and Joseph Smith's 1834-35 History), *Messenger and Advocate*, vol. 1 no. 3 (December 1834): 42.

> [W]e have thought that a full history of the rise of the church of the Latter Day Saints, and the most interesting parts of its progress, to the present time, would be worthy the perusal of the Saints . . . .[59]

> That our narrative may be correct, and particularly the introduction, it is proper to inform our patrons, that our brother J. Smith jr. has offered to assist us. Indeed, there are many items connected with the fore part of this subject that render his labor indispensible.[60]

In their 1834-35 History, Oliver Cowdery and Joseph Smith didn't describe a great First Vision of the "crucifyed" Lord, a great First Vision of the Father and the Son, or the angelic restoration of the Melchizedek Priesthood by Peter, James, and John. In this account, Joseph wonders out loud and in despair in 1823 – during events supposed to have been associated with a great Palmyra revival (and at the age of seventeen) – if a Supreme Being does indeed exist. By way of contrast and conversely, in the 1832 Account describing an event supposed to have occurred in the "16th year" of his age, Joseph's heart had exclaimed "well hath the wise man said <it is a> fool <that> saith in his heart there is no God."[61]

Modern Mormon apologists find it convenient to explain the omissions and contradictions found in this first published account "of the rise of the church" by treating the 1834-35 History as the less than authoritative work of the later discredited Cowdery, Joseph's first and most important early colleague. They cite Cowdery as the uninspired source of the conceptual difficulties found in this early and incriminating history. Various other early Mormon stalwarts – who were not constrained by the 1965, 1966, 1969 and 1971 disclosures of four separate and previously unpublished versions of three discrepant accounts of Joseph' Smith's First Vision – made a substantially different case. Joseph

[59]Oliver Cowdery (and Joseph Smith), "Letter to W.W. Phelps, Esq." (Oliver Cowdery and Joseph Smith's 1834-35 History), *Messenger and Advocate*, vol. 1 no. 1 (October 1834): 13.
[60]Ibid.
[61]Jessee ed., *The Personal Writings of Joseph Smith*, 5.

Fielding Smith[62] – the bulldog guardian of the Mormon archives, the ultimate insider and a Mormon theologian of last resort, speaking with the liberty that the pre-1965 hundred and thirty-year suppression of Joseph Smith's 1832 Holographic Account of the First Vision allowed (that being a document he held in his office safe) – said this about the 1834-35 History:

> *The quibbler might say that this statement from Oliver Cowdery is merely the opinion of Oliver Cowdery and not the expression of the Prophet Joseph Smith. It should be remembered that these letters in which these statements are made were written at the Prophet's request and under his personal supervision. Surely under these circumstances, he would not have permitted an error of this kind to creep into the record without correction ....*

> *Later, during the Nauvoo period of the Church, and again under the direction of the Prophet Joseph Smith, these same letters by Oliver Cowdery, were published in the Times and Seasons, without any thought of correction ....*[63]

Joseph Fielding Smith accepted the letters of Cowdery to Phelps – first published in the *Messenger and Advocate*, and then later in the

---

[62]Joseph Fielding Smith, the Church Historian, later became the Tenth President ("Prophet, Seer and Revelator") of the Mormon Church. One cannot say that Joseph Fielding Smith, the son of Joseph F. Smith and grandson of Hyrum, did not know about Joseph Smith's 1832 Holographic Account, or about the restricted true contents of Joshua 1 and 2:1835 and Erastus Holmes:1835, about the omission of the first from, or about the misrepresentations of the second and third in, the *History of the Church*. Joseph Fielding Smith is the person supposed to have torn the 1832 Account out of the *Kirtland Letter Book: 1829-35*, and to have kept that account under his personal control in a safe in his office. (Palmer, "Joseph Smith's changing view of God as seen in his First Vision accounts" [6 November 2013]). The suppressed accounts were ultimately found in the Kirtland Letter Book: 1829-35, in the Manuscript History, Book A-1, and in Joseph Smith's Personal Diary, all high-value resources subject in that particular era to Joseph Fielding Smith's direct supervision and control.

[63]Joseph Fielding Smith, *Doctrines of Salvation*, vol. 3, p. 236, predating 1965, quoted in Tanner and Tanner, *Mormonism – Shadow or Reality?*, 152, emphasis added.

Times and Seasons – as having been "written at the Prophet's request and under his personal supervision," after which they were then republished under the Prophet's direction "without any thought of correction."

We must assume that the same Joseph Smith (who "would not have permitted an error" to creep into that record without correction) personally requested and supervised the production, publication and republication of a history that (1) identified the vision of the Angel Moroni with the Palmyra revival, (2) identified the vision of the Angel Moroni with the conversion of Joseph Smith's mother and siblings, (3) identified the vision of the Angel Moroni with Joseph Smith's first ever encounter with a heavenly messenger, (4) identified the vision of the Angel Moroni with forgiveness from sin, (5) failed to mention an 1821 vision of the Son of God, (6) failed to mention an 1820 vision of God the Father and Jesus Christ, (7) failed to mention the angelic restoration of the Melchizedek Priesthood by Peter, James and John, (8) assigned the date of the Palmyra revival as 1823 (in the eighteenth year of Joseph Smith's age), and (9) suggested that a seventeen year old Joseph didn't know in 1823 *"if a Supreme being did exist."*[64]

B.H. Roberts (twice selected by modern scholars as the preeminent intellectual in the history of the Mormon Church), the author and editor of the six volume *Comprehensive History of the Church*, stated that, *"Joseph Smith's association with Cowdery in the production of these letters make them, as to the facts involved, practically the personal narrative of Joseph Smith."*[65] Thus the first two histories of the Mormon Church – the 1832 Account that included the concealed first, most historically dependable, most contemporaneous, most workmanlike, least embellished and only holographic account of Joseph's first encounter with deity, and the 1834-35 first authorized history of the Church containing the first published account of the first vision of the Angel Moroni – contradict each

---

[64]"Letter IV" (Cowdery and Smith's 1834-35 History), *Messenger and Advocate*, vol. 1 no. 5 (February 1835), 78, emphasis added.

[65]B.H. Roberts, *A Comprehensive History of The Church of Jesus Christ of Latter-day Saints*, 6 vols. (Provo, Utah: Brigham Young University Press, 1965), 1:78, quoted in Tanner and Tanner, *Mormonism – Shadow or Reality?*, 152, emphasis added.

other in irreconcilable ways. For the better part of a decade, the vision of the Angel Moroni was the First Vision. It was the call to the work and the harbinger of the restoration. The 1832 Holographic Account fails to mention a vision of the Father. The 1834-35 History, the first authorized and published history of the Church, fails to mention a vision of the Father or the Son. Because the 1832 History mentioning only Christ had never been acknowledged or published and was unknown to the members of the Church until 1965, and because the 1834-35 History, which had been acknowledged and carefully published, didn't mention a vision of the Father or the Son, the Mormon laity didn't know about the First Vision until late in the life of the prophet, meaning late in the life of the early Church.

WHEN DISCLOSURES DISAPPOINT

How should the Church have responded to Brother Cheesman's 1965 disclosure? If an enterprising graduate student had really located a previously unknown first and only handwritten account of Joseph Smith's first encounter with deity? "[T]he earliest known historical narrative of the prophet's life,"[66] and his first effort at autobiography? How should Brigham Young University have chosen to respond if one of its students recognized the "profound historical significance" of a document, the importance of which had been overlooked by other students and scholars for more than one hundred and thirty years? Was that not cause for a celebration? Shouldn't the discussion of that remarkable discovery have taken center stage at the first following conference of the Mormon Church? Why shouldn't that manuscript have been thoroughly discussed in the Church's periodicals, at devotionals and firesides, in seminaries, religion classes and missionary lessons? Should the "earliest known account" of Mormonism's greatest ever event, a document of impeccable provenance fashioned by the hand of the prophet of the restoration, not be added to all of those other revelations in the Doctrine and Covenants? Or given some honored place in the Pearl of Great Price? In proselyting instructions and tracts? Should Joseph Smith's "comprehensive," innocently

---

[66]Jessee, "The Early Accounts of Joseph Smith's First Vision," (*BYU Studies*, 1969): 278.

"accurate," "handwritten," most contemporaneous account of the First Vision not be read and revered in all the world wherever the faith is practiced? Should it not be canonized? Is it anything less than divinely approved scripture for faithful true believing Latter-day Saints?

Is it not difficult to imagine that the Church would allow a profoundly important historical document to be revealed to the world as an inconspicuous Appendix D to some graduate student's Master's Thesis? Is it hard to think that the leaders of the Church would support that incredible disclosure with a typescript? Or fail to officially authenticate that profoundly important document with an impeccable Mormon provenance for a full four years? Or deny to the document its higher dignity as a holograph for six long years?

This previously unknown manuscript, the only account of the First Vision prepared by the hand of the prophet Joseph Smith, wasn't a *new* discovery; it was a *new* release. The concealed and suppressed account wasn't "*located*"; it was rather "*brought to light*." The controversial process involved the begrudging disclosure of a forbidden document, knowledge of the existence of which had leaked to some of the faith's most ardent detractors. The supposed discovery and the subsequent release of Joseph Smith's 1832 Handwritten Account, and the reluctant disclosures of the true contents of two other early accounts, was not met with the kind of excitement that people who value truth should have had reason to expect. If the Mormon leaders had not recognized the "*profound historical significance*" of the doubled-sided leaves cut from the pages of the Kirtland Letter Book – containing the first account of Joseph Smith's first encounter with deity – they would not have assigned them to historical purgatory for more than a hundred years. Or required "higher permission" for anyone to see them. If the leaders had not wanted the manuscript suppressed, they would not have instructed President Levi Edgar Young in 1952 not to copy the document, or say what the account contained? The leaders of the Mormon Church kept those materials under wraps in the belly of the beast, "*unused*" and "*unknown*," protecting them from the eyes, hearts and minds of the members for one hundred and thirty years. You may assume that no faith-promoting document would ever have languished in the archives for more than several lifetimes.

Every brother, sister, investigator and convert should be informed that Joseph Smith, the Mormon prophet, told his story more than once, but never once the same.

CHAPTER FIVE

Priesthood

Joseph Smith holds the keys of this last dispensation, ... no man or woman in this dispensation will ever enter into the celestial kingdom of God without the consent of Joseph Smith. From the day that the Priesthood was taken from the earth to the winding-up scene of all things, every man and woman must have the certificate of Joseph Smith, junior, as a passport to their entrance into the mansion where God and Christ are – I with you and you with me. I cannot go there without his consent. He holds the keys of that kingdom for the last dispensation – the keys to rule in the spirit world; He reigns there as supreme a being in his sphere capacity, and calling as God does in heaven.

Brigham Young[1]

I am [an] apostle of Joseph Smith, Jr., the prophet of God.

Brigham Young[2]

INTRODUCTION

Modern Mormons believe that Joseph Smith Jr. saw the Father and the Son as a fourteen year old boy, saw the Angel Moroni as a seventeen year old boy, then waited for and obtained the golden plates and translated the Book of Mormon through the gift and power of God. They believe that he received the Aaronic and Melchizedek Priesthoods from ancient patriarchs by the laying on

---

[1]Brigham Young, *Journal of Discourses*, 26 vols. (Liverpool, England: F.D. Richards, 1855-1866), 7:282-91, emphasis added. *See* also *The Essential Brigham Young*, with a foreword by Eugene E. Campbell (Salt Lake City: Signature Books, 1992), 130-31.
[2]John G. Turner, *Brigham Young: Pioneer Prophet* (Belknap Press of Harvard University Press, 2012), 108.

of hands.   They believe he conversed with the deities, angels, apostles, patriarchs and prophets, that he replicated Christ's one true church, described heaven and earth, built temples and cities and revealed the word of God.   To his faithful followers, Joseph Smith Jr. was the prophet of the restoration and the voice of God on earth.   "Joseph Smith, the Prophet and Seer of the Lord, has done more, save Jesus only, for the salvation of men in this world, than any other man that ever lived . . . ."[3]   The tenth President of the Mormon Church, Elder Joseph Fielding Smith, described his controversial grand-uncle in polarizing terms: "[Joseph Smith] was either a prophet of God, divinely called, properly appointed and commissioned, or he was one of the biggest frauds the world has ever seen; there is no middle ground."[4]

Priesthood, the power to act for God, is the ruling principle in the Church of Jesus Christ of Latter-day Saints. It permeates every Mormon nook and cranny. The Church's tenacious claim to linear hierarchical authority directly from God in heaven is the force supposed to set the faith apart. The entire superstructure of the Mormon Church is dependent upon the fragile assumptions that John the Baptist and Peter, James, and John visited Joseph Smith and Oliver Cowdery, put their resurrected hands upon their heads and conferred upon them two different orders of priesthood – the first the lesser or Aaronic Priesthood, a Levitical patriarchal inheritance (bestowed by John the Baptist); the second the greater "Holy Melchizedek Priesthood after the Order of the Son of God" (bestowed by Peter, James, and John).

"The earliest reference to priesthood authority appeared in the 1833 Book of Commandments, the earliest version of, and precursor to, the Doctrine and Covenants . . . ."[5]   That reference, dated June 1829, did not specifically mention the word "authority" (the term in use in the early Church) or "priesthood" (a term only

---

[3]Doctrine and Covenants (1957), 135:3.
    [4]Joseph Fielding Smith, *Doctrines of Salvation*, 3 vols. (Salt Lake City: Bookcraft, 1956), 1:188, quoted in Robert A. Rees, "Seeing Joseph Smith, The Changing Image of the Mormon Prophet," *Sunstone*, Issue 140 (December 2005): 25.
    [5]Grant H. Palmer, *An Insider's View of Mormon Origins* (Salt Lake City: Signature Books, 2002), 21f5.

later used). It referred, rather instead, to the fact of the baptism of Oliver Cowdery. "Wherefore as thou hast been baptized by the hand of my servant [Joseph], according to that which I have commanded him: Wherefore he hath fulfilled the thing which I commanded him."[6] Cowdery's baptism, supposed to have occurred on May 15, 1829, preceded the organization of the Church of Christ (early LDS) on April 6, 1830, by about one year. Joseph was first supposed to have baptized Oliver because God "commanded him." In this revelation – published in the Book of Commandments in 1833, three years after the Church was organized and four years after the date of the baptism – Joseph's revelator failed to describe John the Baptist, Levi, the Aaronic/Levitical Priesthood, Peter, James, and John, or the Melchizedek Priesthood. In the sixty-five revelations published in the Book of Commandments in 1833, four years after May 15, 1829, the first compilation of the revelations of Joseph Smith, John the Baptist and Peter, James, and John are not described. No ordinary Mormon knew in 1833 that John the Baptist had visited the earth on May 15, 1829, to confer what only later came to be called the Aaronic or Levitical Priesthood on Joseph Smith and Oliver Cowdery. And no one knew in 1833 that Joseph Smith had seen and visited with the "crucifyed" Lord in 1821.

Sterling M. McMurrin (the United States Commissioner of Education during the administration of President John F. Kennedy, a formidable intellectual and a cultural Latter-day Saint) provided this historical perspective:

> *In a unique way the Mormons even today have tied their faith to their historical roots [providing objective content for evaluation]. They insist that the truth of their religion, the authority of their priesthood, and the divine foundations of their Church depend entirely on the factual truth of certain of their historical claims.*
>
> *The truth of two of those claims is held to be absolutely crucial. If Joseph Smith's vision of the*

---

[6]Book of Commandments 15:6-7.

Father and the Son [a historical narrative] was not in fact an objective, veridical experience, and if the Book of Mormon [another historical narrative] was not brought forth, as Joseph Smith insisted, by the hand of God, in very fact an account of God's involvement with ancient Americans descended from the people of ancient Judah, then the Church and its priesthood and Mormonism as a religion are abject frauds.[7]

PRIESTHOOD IN THE EARLY CHURCH

The third son of Joseph Smith Sr. and Lucy Mack Smith was precocious, gifted, exceedingly clever, usually lucky and uncommonly resilient. Joseph Smith Jr. challenged the existing order. He was logical when logic worked, dogmatic when it did not. Smith did not surrender to the intellect what belonged to the emotions. His disciples, while frequently poor and unlearned, didn't suffer outsiders well. Fanatical early Mormons were terrible neighbors in Kirtland, Ohio, in Missouri, then later in Illinois. With the passage of time, they wore out their welcome with the locals every place they settled. The nineteenth-century Church was certain, aggressive and impolite. In Missouri, boastful Saints antagonized the "old settlers" by publishing revelations describing them as "enemies" and calling the state a Mormon "inheritance." They announced that when Jesus came again they would rule Missouri (and the world). They announced that when Jesus came again they would obtain the riches of the Gentiles (whatever belonged to anyone who wasn't a Mormon or a Jew, or an American Indian of Hebraic lineage). And they started down that prickly path (acquiring the riches of the Gentiles) in anticipation of his coming. They were the children of the kingdom, the chosen people, God's highly favored class. The rapid influx of Mormon emigrants to the tiny place first called Zion (the city of Independence in Jackson County, Missouri) caused some of the original settlers to speculate that the Mormons were destined to inherit Missouri even before the second coming.

---

[7]Sterling McMurrin, "Brigham H. Roberts: A Biographical Essay," in Brigham H. Roberts, *Studies of the Book of Mormon* (Urbana and Chicago: University of Illinois Press, 1985), xv, emphasis added.

Kirtland, Ohio; Independence, Missouri; Far West, Missouri; Nauvoo, Illinois, and the Utah Territory in the Rocky Mountains were nineteenth-century theocratic enclaves led by God through Joseph Smith and Brigham Young and spiritually exclusive. Ghettos for the faithful. The nineteenth-century Saints surrendered their temporal and spiritual governance to the arbitrary dictates of an infallible priesthood. Early Mormons voted *en bloc* for whomever their leaders decided they should, while shifting between the parties to gain political advantage.[8] These flimsy shifting allegiances, while temporarily efficacious, ultimately caused the political parties to abandon such self-serving allies. Ohio/Missouri/Iowa/Illinois/Utah Mormons were clannish and arrogant. The world turned on the controversial religion's truth claims. The Mormon Church was then and is now the only true and living church on the face of the earth. Joseph Smith *was* the prophet of God ("what this people receives through him is law"), and one of his successors *is* the prophet of God now (what this people receives through them is law). The prophets speak to God and hold the keys to the Kingdom of God on Earth and in the life to come. The truth is whatever the prophet currently says that it is. And what supports these extraordinary claims? The exclusive right to the linear hierarchical priesthood, the power to control, ordain, baptize, confirm, bind, loose, curse, bless and exalt.

Brigham Young

Brigham Young, Joseph Smith's durable successor, took the Mormon priesthood to new heights. "[I]f you what a wife you first

---

[8]In one election Mormon votes were delivered to every Whig but one, that being a then obscure Illinois politician by the name of Abraham Lincoln. Abraham Lincoln voted for the Nauvoo charter, which Smith used "to make the Mormon capital an independent theocracy," "even though Nauvoo's Mormons had voted as a bloc against him in the previous election." (D. Michael Quinn, *The Mormon Hierarchy: Origins of Power* [Salt Lake City: Signature Books in association with Smith Research Associates, 1994], 631). The Mormons scratched their ballots to vote for a Democrat, James H. Ralston, who had done some favors for Joseph Smith. (Fawn M. Brodie, *No Man Knows My History: The Life of Joseph Smith the Mormon Prophet*, 2d ed., rev. and enl. [New York, NY: Alfred A. Knopf, 1972], 267; see *e.g.*, Joseph Smith Jr., *History of The Church of Jesus Christ of Latter-day Saints*, B.H. Roberts, ed., 2d ed., rev., [Salt Lake City, UT: The Deseret Book Company, 1978], 6:248).

ask Brigham, then the Perrants & next the female."[9]   T.B.H.
Stenhouse (a Mormon dissenter and one of Brigham Young's most
literate nineteenth-century critics) equated the "Infallible
Priesthood" to the irrepressible will of Mormonism's second
infallible leader. To fail to follow the edicts of the priesthood in the
early days of the Church was to risk ridicule, disgrace, intimidation,
excommunication, bodily harm and even death. Lieutenant John
Gunnison (1852), an early and important non-Mormon observer,
described how Brigham Young used the priesthood to manage the
Church in Utah.[10]   "A High Council is selected out of the high-
priests, and consists of twelve members, which is in perpetual
session to advise the Presidency; in which each is free to give and
argue his opinion." The decision to act or not is not, however, made
by the Council. "The President sums up the matter and gives the
decision, perhaps in opposition to a great majority, but to which all
must yield implicit obedience; and probably there has never been
known, under the present head, a dissent when the 'awful nod' has
been given, for it is the 'stamp of fate and sanction of a god.'"[11]
Another prophet deity.

There were few brave enough to challenge the authoritarian
supremacy of the Mormon leader Brigham Young. When the
prophet Brigham Young revealed that Adam was God, the literal
father of Jesus Christ in the spirit and in the flesh, many important
Mormon men were soon on board. Wilford Woodruff, who became
the fourth Mormon prophet: "I believe that He preac[hed] the
greatest sermon that was ever delivered to the Latter Day Saints

---

[9]Albert P. Rockwood, quoted in Turner, *Brigham Young: Pioneer Prophet*,
240.

[10]Gunnison, a distinguished student at West Point, a friend of the American
President and a rising star in the United States Army, offered perceptive
commentary on the only recently established Great Basin Kingdom. He had been
stationed in the western regions. His analysis, although balanced and friendly, was
considered disrespectful.

[11]Lieut. John W. Gunnison, *The Mormons, or Latter-day Saints, in the Valley of
The Great Salt Lake: A history of their rise and progress, peculiar doctrines, present
condition, and prospects, derived from personal observation, during a residence
among them* (Freeport, NY: Books for Libraries Press, 1852, 1972), 58. Brutally
murdered with other members of his party in 1853 by the Pahvant band of the Ute
Indians, the tribe of Chief Kanosh (who became a Mormon in 1858), in a crime
that went unpunished, Gunnison may have surrendered his life for these words
and others like them.

since they have been a people." The speaker: Brigham Young. The subject: Adam is God.[12]

Orson Pratt, who tempted providence, didn't agree. According to Pratt, Adam had not walked and talked to himself in the Garden of Eden and wasn't exactly the spiritual and biological father of a less than eternal twice-created Christ. Pratt was severely punished for his unwelcome temerity. He was publicly criticized for his aberrant views, sent on many missions and demoted in the Quorum. The "Lion of the Lord" did not intend that the theoretical Pratt should someday lead his Church. ". . . I tell Brother Pratt," Brigham sermonized, that "if he goes on with his vain befogging speculations, there's not a saint in heaven nor a saint on earth . . . who will follow. And I warn him not to get up to talk more, unless he knows what he talks about . . . ."[13] The "awful nod" was given; it was the "stamp of fate and sanction of a god" and Pratt was forced to make a humiliating public confession of error.

John Gunnison (1852):

> *This council [the High Council] is eye, ear, and hand to the President – the members are the spies over all matters in the field or the temple, in the social party or the domestic circle. Is any novel opinion broached in conversation, it is brought before the council by any member cognizant of, or who has heard of it, and measures are taken to ferret it out, that the man who uttered it, if he is not sound to the core, may be marked and pounced upon before he is even aware that he is suspected.[14]*

Big brother ruled the roost in the Great Basin in 1852 ("I have to

---

[12]Wilford Woodruff, 8 October 1854.

[13]Bishop Daniel Sylvester Tuttle, *Missionary to the Mountain West: Reminiscences of Episcopal Bishop Daniel S. Tuttle, 1866-1886*, foreword by Brigham D. Madsen (Salt Lake City: University of Utah Press, 1987), 346 (quoting Brigham Young in a letter that the Bishop sent to Mrs. Tuttle dated 15 October 1867).

[14]Gunnison, *The Mormons, or Latter-day Saints, in the Valley of The Great Salt Lake*, 58.

think for the people Constantly"[15]). Those who failed to toe the
party line put themselves at terrible risk. Brigham Young's
powerful personality created a society of sycophants. Early
Mormons did what their leaders said that they should. The prophet
who spoke to God held democracy and the United States of America
in utter contempt. This Prophet, King and Priest of the Kingdom of
God on Earth defied the United States Government, despised
American Presidents, believed in and codified slavery in the Utah
Territory and was a racial bigot.[16] He favored the cause of
secession and the South in the Civil War. He predicted that the
government would fall and fervently prayed that it would. Until
February 15, 1927, Latter-day Saints took an oath of vengeance in
the endowment house and in their temples. "In that, they did
'covenant and promise' to 'pray and never cease to pray to
Almighty God to avenge the blood of the prophets upon this nation'
and to teach their 'children' and their 'children's children' to the
'third and fourth generation' to do the same."[17]

CHURCH AND STATE IN THE UTAH TERRITORY

Gunnison wrote that one of the accusations lodged against "the
early arrangement of the affairs of the Mormon church" was that it
was "raising up a society and people to be governed independent of
the state."[18] The Doctrine and Covenants came to include the
following item of belief: "We do not believe it just to mingle
religious influence with civil Government, whereby one religious

---

[15]Brigham Young quoted in Turner, *Brigham Young: Pioneer Prophet*, 289.

[16]"The story Turner tells in this elegantly written biography will startle and
shock many readers. He reveals a Brigham Young more violent and coarse than
the man Mormons have known. While lauding his achievements as pioneer,
politician, and church leader, the book will require a reassessment of Brigham
Young the man." (Richard L. Bushman in Turner, *Brigham Young: Pioneer
Prophet*, dust jacket). Every Utah Mormon's roots run through the prophet
Brigham Young.

[17]"*Proceedings Before the Committee on Privileges and Elections of the United
States Senate in the Matter of the Protests Against the Right of Hon. Reed Smoot, a
Senator from the State of Utah, to Hold His Seat*," 59th Congress, 1st Session, Senate
Document No. 486, 4 vols. (1 vol. index) (Washington; Government Printing Office,
1906). "Several former Mormons revealed the content of this oath."

[18]Gunnison, *The Mormons, or Latter-day Saints, in the Valley of The Great Salt
Lake*, 59.

society is fostered, and another proscribed in its spiritual privileges, and the individual rights of its members, as citizens, denied.'"[19] Anyone familiar with the history of the Mormon theocracy in the Utah Territory in the nineteenth century should recognize the hypocrisy of that particular declaration. Utah Mormons controlled every institution of civil government, justice and the courts, freedom of movement, the military and the police, the legislature, the distribution of property, the allocation of water rights and grazing privileges and the sale of goods. Nineteenth-century Utah Mormons didn't "mingle religious influence with civil Government," they dominated every aspect of civil and religious life – all things spiritual and temporal – suppressed thought and punished offenders. Gentiles, whether temporary or permanent, were oppressed, afraid and unsafe, and their rights were not recognized.

Early Utah Mormons didn't just foster one religion at the expense of the spiritual privileges of others. They allowed no meaningful spiritual privileges to others. A Mormon militia (a Utah territorial militia activated as a *posse comitatus*) under divided command obliterated the Morrisites, killing John Banks (formerly a distinguished leader of the Mormon London Conference), and Joseph Morris (a former Mormon and a prolific new prophet). Interested observers came from surrounding communities to watch Robert T. Burton and others allegedly mutilate or kill men, women and children, several of them (including Morris and Banks) under a flag of truce. In the Utah Territory the Morrisites were bluntly informed that there was no law for apostates.

In locations where they were in the minority, Mormons wanted no religious society favored over them and no interference with their spiritual privileges. In the Utah Territory, where they lived as an arrogant majority, they granted sparing privileges to others in communities where "this order of priests [called bishops] have charge of the temporal matters under the direction of the Presidency."[20] When Mormons were outnumbered, they claimed

---

[19]Doctrine and Covenants (1835), Of Governments and Laws in General, Section CII, verse 9, 253. *See* e.g., Doctrine and Covenants 134:9.

[20]Gunnison, *The Mormons, or Latter-day Saints, in the Valley of The Great Salt Lake*, 57.

persecution and wanted protection, a clear separation of church and state. They wanted to practice their religion in the havens of the Gentiles without interference in perfect safety. When they were in the majority, they favored the fusion of church and state and forged a connection with no plane of dissection. Gunnison described the governing principle:

> [I]t is taught that the priesthood is supreme in the state – not in the sense that all human law springs from the standard of right and wrong contained in the revealed word of God, but that this order has the control of the state, and ought to make the civil regulations, because it receives revelations from day to day, and can therefore keep both the temporal and spiritual from clashing, and fulfil the scripture that "the officers shall be peace and exactors righteousness." And in the selection of officers by ballot, the elective franchise[21] is made subservient to a vote for the nominee of the Presidency.[22]

The monolithic Mormon vote, the sword of the theocracy, was a tool of the priesthood. If Mormons voted as directed, they seemed to think that they were free. "They gloried in this *congé d' elire* [license from the crown] and it was averred by prominent men that to vote against any one proposed by the highest authority would be the height of folly. For the council knew what was wanted to be done, and of course what persons were the most suitable to accomplish the work."[23] Nineteenth-century Mormons did not exercise the franchise; they *ratified* what Brigham said that they should in the name of the priesthood.

---

[21]Latter-day Saints had an interesting concept of "the elective franchise." "It was related to us in conversation that a delegate was chosen and commissioned for Congress, at a time when it was desirable that he should start suddenly for the seat of government; and that the people were summoned to vote when he was far on the way to the states – his credentials either in his pocket, or sent to him by mail afterward." (Ibid., 59).

[22]Ibid., emphasis added.

[23]Ibid., 59, emphasis retained.

OBEDIENCE, DEVOTION AND SACRIFICE

One can only say tongue-in-cheek that "Priesthood would grow into one of the defining principles of Mormonism."[24]   Unquestioning obedience to the priesthood *was* the defining principle of nineteenth-century Mormonism, and not that much has changed. One prominent modern dissenter describes Mormonism's modern overreach. "It [the Church] claims to possess authority over every aspect of your life – who to marry, when to marry, how to love, where to marry, how to pray, how to worship, how to dress, how to speak, how to think, how to feel – everything . . . . It claims to hold the keys to seal someone up to damnation, or exalt them."[25]

The quality of life in Mormon Missouri in the 1830s was defined by blind obedience to the dictates of the priesthood. The Danite band (an oath-bound secret society, Mormon thugs, the very existence of which was denied by the leaders of the Church both early and late) was one of the instruments of the Missouri tyranny. Following the implosion at Kirtland, dissenters in Missouri, victims of authoritarian vulgarity, feared for their lives. They gathered their goods after dark to escape unseen. The fine line between obedience to the priesthood and devotion to God was unmistakably blurred.

Latter-day Saints have suffered incredible hardships to satisfy the demands of their priesthood. They have experienced years of privation and shortened and surrendered their lives. They have boarded boats to cross huge oceans. They have sold farms and crops and given the proceeds to their priesthood leaders. They have moved from New York to Ohio to Missouri to Iowa, to Illinois and Utah, to urgently gather at various times at several different promised lands. They have pushed handcarts thousands of miles in terrible weather poorly equipped with little or nothing to eat. They have delivered babies in rain and snow while living in wagons and tents. They have contracted cholera and watched their children die. Young Mormon women have been married to old Mormon men

---

[24]Richard Lyman Bushman, with the assistance of Jed Woodworth, *Joseph Smith: Rough Stone Rolling* (New York: Alfred A. Knopf, 2005), 159.

[25]Tal Bachman, "What kind of man are you, Epi? My Open Letter" (27 January 2014; accessed 1 February 2014), available from http://exmormon.org/ phorum/read.php?2,1149508,1151145; Internet.

who had other wives. Mormon children have grown up in families with many brothers and sisters and hundreds of cousins. Scores of nineteenth-century Mormon husbands left their families and went to jail as "prisoners of conscience," meaning as proponents of polygamy, a hateful practice perpetuated by the true followers of Joseph Smith even today.

Early Mormons demanded insularity, lived to their own light and ignored the nation's laws. They counterfeited money, stole their neighbors' cattle, burned houses and crops, lied for the Lord, walked away from contracts, filed for bankruptcy and ignored their debts. They milked the Gentiles (non-Mormons) and bled the beast (the Government), joined secret societies and took terrible oaths. They punished thought, brutalized dissenters, emasculated adulterers, whipped offenders, lynched lawbreakers and murdered Indians and innocent emigrants. Mormon men surrendered their manhood to follow their leaders right or wrong.

Early Mormons built homes, planted seeds and beautified thirsty deserts. They spread the Mormon gospel home and abroad without purse or script. They prepared for the apocalypse. They left everything and followed, often more than once. In all of this, and in everything else, Latter-day Saints have been obedient to the priesthood. In the final analysis, Mormonism is all about the priesthood. It is about authority to act for God and the control of a compliant people. The Latter-day Saints' primary allegiance is to the prophet and to a theocracy. A faithful Latter-day Saint may criticize the President of the United States with malicious intent, or any Gentile, and is in that sense liberated. The same person would never openly criticize the Mormon prophet, God's oracle on earth. Mormons can think whatever they like, a recent prophet reports, just as long as they keep their erring opinions between their own two ears[26]; but when they endeavor to influence others, the wrath of the Church can be terrible and swift. There are lines faithful Latter-day Saints simply dare not cross. Mormonism has

---

[26]Gordon B. Hinckley (1998), quoted in Simon G. Southerton, *Losing a Lost Tribe – Native Americans, DNA, and the Mormon Church* (Salt Lake City: Signature Books, 2004), 200. "They can carry all the opinion they wish within their heads . . . but if they begin to try to persuade others, then they may be called in to a disciplinary council."

demonstrated the willingness to destroy the families and relationships of those who fail to conform. Leaders may encourage divorce if husbands or wives leave the faith, and members who consort with apostates may fail a temple worthiness interview. Dissenters are forced to make new friends.

Mormonism is a theocracy, governed from heaven, and the priesthood rules. As this is written, fewer people able to vote are registered in Utah than in any other state. The secular governance of the citizens, although secure in Mormon Utah, isn't a matter of the highest priority. Utah leads the nation in the use of prescription drugs to combat an old and insidious Mormon enemy, depression. Finally, and as this is still written, Utah has the highest incidence of mental illness of any state in the union.

PRIESTHOOD RESTORATION

The Susquehanna and Aaronic Priesthood

In May 1829 while Joseph Smith and Oliver Cowdery were translating the Book of Mormon, they were supposed to have said that the "question of authority disturbed them." On May 15, 1829, they are supposed to have interrupted their translation of the Book of Mormon and traveled to the bank of the Susquehanna River to pray. That was nearly five-and-a-half years before they first described what prompted them to do what they only later said that they did in these terms:

> *No men in their sober senses, could translate and write the directions given to the Nephites, from the mouth of the Savior, of the precise manner in which men should build up his church, and especially, when corruption had spread an uncertainty over all forms and systems practiced among men, without desiring a privilege of showing the willingness of the heart by being buried in the liquid grave, to answer a "good*

conscience by the resurrection of Jesus Christ."[27]

Who says these men were unable to express themselves coherently? Richard L. Bushman, writing in the twenty-first century, described what happened next: "In the middle of the prayer, in the brightness of day, 'a messenger from heaven descended in a cloud of light.' As Joseph told the story in 1838 [about nine years later], the person said he was John the Baptist and that he had been 'sent by Peter, James, and John. Then he laid his hands upon their heads to ordain them . . . .'"[28]

Colesville and Melchizedek Priesthood

Joseph Smith, who had been arrested, tried and convicted on a charge of disorderly conduct in March of 1826, was arrested again in June of 1830,[29] when additional criminal charges were filed against him in South Bainbridge, Chenango County, New York.[30]

---

[27]Oliver Cowdery (and Joseph Smith), "Letter to W.W. Phelps, Esq." (Oliver Cowdery and Joseph Smith's 1834-35 History), *Messenger and Advocate*, vol. 1 no. 1 (*October 1834*), 15, emphasis added.

[28]Bushman, *Joseph Smith: Rough Stone Rolling*, 74. This early history, the story privately composed by Joseph and others "*in 1838*" (*and 1839*) was not published in America (*or then publicly "told"*) until 1842.

[29]When a former parishioner and several mentees of Sidney Rigdon – informed of Sidney's conversion to Mormonism – visited Rigdon and asked to be given "some reason for his present faith," Sidney presented "a transcript from the dockets of two [New York] magistrates" in support of the proposition that Smith was a man of good character. The transcript showed that Smith "had been tried as a disturber of the peace . . . ." But that he had been "honorably acquitted." (Eber D. Howe, *Mormonism Unvailed: Or, A Faithful Account of That Singular Imposition and Delusion* [Painesville, OH: E.D. Howe, 1834; reprint, New York: AMS Press Inc., 1977], 113). "'Even his enemies had nothing to say against his character,'" Rigdon reported. Rigdon did not describe the restoration of the Melchizedek Priesthood, that is now supposed to have been associated with those events, as might have been expected, nor did he associate that alleged restoration with Smith's journeys to and from South Bainbridge or Colesville.

[30]Joseph had been tried and convicted in Justice Neely's court in South Bainbridge in 1826. Because he was a minor in 1826, and because the authorities appeared to think he might reform, he was, according to one commentator (Benton), "designedly allowed to escape." Smith wasn't incarcerated in 1826. (Wesley P. Walters, "Joseph Smith's Bainbridge, N.Y., Court Trials," reprinted by permission from the *Westminster Theological Journal* 36, no. 2 [Winter 1974] [Salt Lake City: Utah Lighthouse Ministry, 1974 and 1977], 140).

His accusers could not but have remembered the 1826 offense brought against the young treasure-seeking seer by the relatives of Josiah Stowell. The nature of the charges in this second complaint, which may have been decided because of the statute of limitations, are not entirely clear. Tried yet again, this time Smith was acquitted. Before he could celebrate this success, he was arrested for a third time by a constable from Broome County, New York, on yet further charges. He was tried on this third offense and acquitted for a second time by a panel of judges. After the two acquittals on the 1830 charges, following a conviction in 1826, and after Joseph and Oliver had traveled safely back to Harmony, Pennsylvania (where both of them then lived), they returned to Broome County to confirm (confer the gift of the Holy Ghost upon) some Saints who had been baptized. Joseph had been arrested (and tried) after the baptisms but before the confirmations. Thus the confirmations represented unfinished business of the newly established church. Joseph and Oliver now returned, after Joseph's trials, to confirm those new Saints with such "authority" as they then thought that they had. In the face of the gathering of a hostile crowd, the two elders, threatened by angry citizens, were forced to retreat. "On Joseph's and Cowdery's return to Colesville, there was no time for a meeting or even a meal before they had to flee."[31] They traveled all night except for a short time during which they were forced to rest "under a large tree by the way side, sleeping and watching alternately." Richard L. Bushman described the events of that fitful evening further as follows:

> *It may have been on this occasion that Peter, James, and John appeared to Joseph and Cowdery and, as a later revelation [Section 27 of the Doctrine and Covenants] said, "ordained you and confirmed you to be apostles, and especial witnesses of my name, and bear the keys of your ministry: and of the same things which I revealed unto them."*[32]

---

[31]Bushman, *Joseph Smith: Rough Stone Rolling*, 118. Note that Bushman (Joseph's faithful biographer) describes the founders as *Joseph* and *Cowdery*, a distinction that may serve to reveal the author's opinion of their respective dignities.

[32]Ibid., emphasis added. The "later revelation," described by Mr. Bushman first published in the Doctrine and Covenants as Section 50 in 1835 (it is now

These events allegedly occurred "in early July 1830, probably the night of 5-6 July," after Joseph and Oliver "made an arduous nighttime escape."[33] If all of this really happened at the time and in the manner the biographer just described, it should have been remembered as one of the seminal events in all of human history. Latter-day Saints say that it happened, and it is a proposition upon which generations of believers have built a tradition of unshakeable faith. Yet Joseph's distinguished biographer is forced to say (for want of better proof), "*It may have been on this occasion that Peter, James and John appeared . . .*," and to cite by way of support the backdated falsified Section 50 of the 1835 edition of the Doctrine and Covenants.[34] Section 50, the first posting in 1835, was changed to become Section 27 in later editions. Importantly, the Mormon scholar places these events – as South Bainbridge and Broome County trials and later Mormon accounts appear to require – in June or July of 1830, *after* the Church was organized on April 6, 1830, *after* Joseph and Oliver had ordained themselves and others to the office of elder, *after* Oliver Cowdery had ordained Joseph Smith to be the "Prophet, Seer and Revelator" of the Church of Christ, and *after* various members of the early Church had been confirmed to receive the gift of the Holy Ghost by elders who didn't then hold what only sometime later came to be called the Melchizedek Priesthood.

UNITARY AUTHORITY AND DUAL ORDINATION

The first Mormons didn't look at issues of authority and priesthood the way that modern Mormons do, nor did the Book of Mormon,

---

Doctrine and Covenants 27), crudely altered a revelation first published in the Book of Commandments in 1833 (Book of Commandments 28). The first account of the revelation in the *Book of Commandments*, faithful to the text of the only manuscript, didn't mention Peter, James, and John, ordination, confirmation, "apostles," "keys," or "priesthood." The original manuscript failed to contain any reference to any of those later backdated additions. Those elements of Section 27, the revelation designed to disclose the restoration of the priesthood by Peter, James, and John in the Doctrine and Covenants, have no archival provenance.

[33]Quinn, *Origins of Power*, 24.

[34]*See* the history of the back-dated amendments to Chapter 28 of the 1833 Book of Commandments (now Section 27) in Section 50 of the 1835 edition of the Doctrine and Covenants located in this book in a chapter entitled, "History Is an Institution's Resumé."

nor did the Book of Commandments, the Old Testament, the New Testament, the Gospel Church, the Nephite Church or the early Joseph Smith. Smith didn't tell his early faithful followers that he had been invested with priesthood authority by the unprecedented intervention of resurrected messengers. The awkward, tardy retroactive disclosure of previously unreported supernatural events provides persuasive evidence of fabrication. Joseph Smith didn't mention John the Baptist, the Aaronic Priesthood, Peter, James, and John, the Melchizedek Priesthood, or separate orders of priesthood against the issue of authority on or at any time before April 6, 1830. Or until some time after he met Sidney Rigdon. Many years passed before Joseph Smith and Oliver Cowdery said that they received the "lower priesthood" from John the Baptist on May 15, 1829, followed by the "higher priesthood" from Peter, James, and John on a date, and at a time and following events they didn't ever describe. Angelic ordination and orders of authority, like the retroactively reported vision of the Father and the Son, do not seem to have initially been part of some great eternal plan. Or obvious elements of any kind of restoration.

Some of Smith's closest collaborators, those who knew him best, would find those clumsy priesthood tellings impossible to believe. Important founding faithful men, early Mormon insiders, left the Church citing issues with the new and unusual doctrines of the priesthood. Until Joseph Smith struck Aaronic and Melchizedek Priesthood paydirt, he floated traditional theories of empowerment having discretionary roots in scripture. The theoretical sources of early non-Melchizedek Mormonism's metaphysical authority included foreordination, commandments, revelations, dreams, visions and promptings. Charisma and the voice of God. In what was an essentially soft spiritual beginning lurked the possibility that the new society might politely take its place among believers in other Christian communities. That wasn't meant to be and wouldn't be long supposed.

In the early Church, baptisms, confirmations, ordinations, spiritual manifestations, glossolalia, healings and exorcisms were said to be effectuated under a relaxed concept of unitary "authority" having nothing to do with the divided "priesthood" structures seen to drive the twenty-first century Church. The office of elder during those early ministrations was not then associated with what only later came to be called the Melchizedek Priesthood. According to David Whitmer, a true insider,[35] about two thousand members were baptized before Joseph and Sidney abandoned the egalitarian concept of charismatic authority. Many members were confirmed and ordained before Mormonism's leaders began to articulate and apply the notion of "dual priesthoods of different ranks." D. Michael Quinn, a Mormon historian, seems to have coined that particularly insightful phrase. According to Quinn, early Mormons, *"Participants at the church's organization, had a unitary sense of authority rather than a belief in dual priesthoods of different ranks."*[36] Notions of authority in the Church of Christ (the Mormon name until 1834) were relaxed; "priesthood" was a nasty Catholic word ("an alien concept to Yankee Christians"[37]) and the instruments of empowerment in David Whitmer's cherished spiritual community were metaphysical and charismatic.

THE CONCEPT OF PRIESTHOOD IN THE EARLY CHURCH

In the modern LDS Church, the Aaronic (Levitical) or lower Priesthood, supposed to be John the Baptist's Priesthood, consists of three offices: deacon, teacher and priest. When the Mormon Church was organized on April 6, and for the rest of 1830 and beyond, the three offices (besides the office of prophet) were elder, teacher and priest. It is not absolutely certain that John the Baptist was a Levitical Priest, but it is certain that those three offices in the gospel church were not assigned to twelve-year-olds and teens, as in the Mormon Church today. Thus the concept of the restoration of the priesthood is conceptually flawed. In the gospel church, deacons (another early addition to the restoration) were adults

---

[35]Whitmer was "set apart in 1834 by Joseph Smith to preside over the Saints in Missouri; [then] 'blessed by the laying on of hands of the Presidency' (Joseph Smith, Sidney Rigdon and Frederick G. Williams), in connection with Oliver Cowdery and Martin Harris, Feb. 14, 1835, to choose the Twelve Apostles, in accordance with revelation (Doc. and Cov., 18:37); . . . ." (Andrew Jenson, comp., *Church Chronology: A Record of Important Events Pertaining to the History of the Church of Jesus Christ of Latter-day Saints*, 2d ed., rev. and enlarged [Salt Lake City: Deseret News, 1914], xxvii).

[36]Quinn, *Origins of Power*, 14-15, emphasis added.

[37]Bushman, *Joseph Smith: Rough Stone Rolling*, 157.

supposed to be the husbands of one wife.[38]

The Melchizedek or Higher Priesthood would now seem to consist of no less than six offices: elder, high priest, seventy, patriarch, apostle and prophet. Joseph Smith didn't restore the authority principle of the gospel church in the Eastern Hemisphere, or of the Nephite church in the Western Hemisphere, and the offices in the Mormon Church, both early and late, were not then and are not now the same. *In 1877, the year of his death, Brigham Young – the indispensable leader of the Utah branch of the Church, the largest schism of the Nauvoo church (there have been many schisms) – admitted, "That the office of elder was not originally included in the Melchizedek Priesthood . . . ."*[39]

The offices of deacon, teacher and priest were not assigned to twelve, fourteen and sixteen year-olds in the gospel church, where Peter, James, and John are supposed to have succeeded Jesus, or in the Nephite church, where there was no Aaronic Priesthood. There was no Aaronic Priesthood in the gospel church, and the Aaronic Priesthood played no part in the governance of the Nephites in the New World. But "there was a time when this Church [the nineteenth-century Mormon Church] was governed by the Lesser Priesthood."[40] Assistant, Associate or co-Presidents, formal First Presidencies, First Presidency Counselors, Assistant First Presidency Counselors, eleven-year-old Apostles (John Willard Young), fourteen-year-old Apostles (Joseph A. Young), nineteen-year-old apostles (Brigham Young Jr.), unquorumed Apostles (John Willard Young, Joseph A. Young, Heber C. Young), Counselors to the Quorum of the Twelve and Assistants to Apostles had no place in the gospel church, or in the Nephite church in the Book of Mormon. These offices and appointments can lay no claim to having been restored. They were "created" and have come and gone.[41] The "restoration" of the authority of the priesthood does

---

[38] "Let the deacons be the husbands of one wife, ruling their children and their own houses well." (1 Timothy 3:12).

[39]*Deseret News*, 6 June 1877 (sermon delivered on 21 May 1877), quoted in Richard S. Van Wagoner, *Sidney Rigdon: A Portrait of Religious Excess* (Salt Lake City: Signature Books, 1994; paperback 2006), 98, emphasis added.

[40]Ibid., quoting Orson Pratt.

[41]The previously distinguished office of Presiding Patriarch, an associate prophet position in the early Church – an office first held by Joseph Smith, Jr.,

not track the precepts of authority supposed to have characterized the gospel church in the east, or the Nephite church in the west. Those churches did not feature "dual priesthoods of different ranks." The Aaronic Priesthood, seen late in the life of the early Church to have disguised ancient Israel's opprobrious "law of a carnal commandment," an order of authority God nailed to the cross, can not be called "restored."

It has been difficult for the Latter-day Saints to frankly admit that the Church was organized without the Melchizedek Priesthood. Brigham Young, Orson Pratt, David Whitmer, Franklin D. Richards, then Richard L. Bushman, D. Michael Quinn, Dan Vogel and various important others have in one way or another admitted it was, and the facts are seen to support them.

PROPOSITIONS

The examination of Mormonism's priesthood roots, in this chapter and others, will *support* each of the following propositions:

- *"So far as can be told now, before 1831 men were called to church offices – elders, priests, and teachers – given authority and licensed without reference to a bestowal of priesthood."*[42] *The word "priesthood," although mentioned in the Book of Mormon, was not used in the early church until 1831. About two thousand members were baptized, confirmed and empowered under a license of authority regimen (meaning "without reference to a bestowal of priesthood"), and there were but three offices in the new church, namely "elders, priests, and teachers."*

---

then by Joseph Smith, Sr., Hyrum and William Smith (the father and brothers of the prophet), and even later by Uncle John – has been rudely abandoned by the modern Mormon Church. The office (and the authority) that recognized the primacy of the Smith family, a supreme Patriarch and a third and Patriarchal Priesthood, after years of indifference and neglect, was allowed to disappear. The descendants of the Smiths are no longer lineal presiding patriarchs in Joseph's previously patriarchal church. That historical development places at defiance the teachings of the prophet Joseph Smith.

[42]Bushman, *Joseph Smith: Rough Stone Rolling*, 157-58, emphasis added.

- *There was nothing called the "Aaronic Priesthood" in the newly established Church.*

- *There was nothing called the "Levitical Priesthood" in the newly established Church.*

- *At the time of the organization of the Church, before Joseph Smith met Sidney Rigdon, the members and leaders supported the notion that "authority" was unitary and seemed to think that what they had was all that they required.*

- *Joseph Smith and Oliver Cowdery were no more able to hold the Aaronic Priesthood (conferred by lineage) in the dispensation of the fullness of times than was the Savior who sprang from the tribe of Judah able to hold the Aaronic Priesthood (conferred by lineage) in the meridian of time.*

- *Lehi, Nephi, Jacob, Alma and various other Book of Mormon prophets and holy men were not Levites and did not hold the Levitical Priesthood. The Book of Mormon does not describe Aaron or Levi, or the Aaronic or Levitical Priesthood. The Hebrews in the Western Hemisphere, unlike the Hebrews in the Eastern Hemisphere, didn't hold, exercise or profess to confer the Aaronic/Levitical Priesthood, Israel's lesser law, a stringent written code, a lesser law and a lower authority designed to govern a lesser people at a time when God considered them "naught."*

- *There was no priesthood called after the name of the ancient patriarch "Melchizedek" when the Mormon Church was organized (meaning at any time on or before April 6, 1830).*

- *Joseph Smith and Oliver Cowdery didn't know there were "dual priesthoods of different ranks" when the Church was organized (on April 6, 1830), or at any time before, nor did they ever then say that they did.*

- *"The concept of higher or lower office did not exist until 1831."*[43]

- *There was no priesthood by the name of "Melchizedek" in the Book of Mormon, although there are references to a "high priest" by the name of Melchizedek. The Book of Mormon described "high priesthood." The Book of Mormon's Melchizedek was but one of "many" different priests. The New Testament reported that there was only one great High Priest in the gospel church, and that was Jesus Christ. The expansion of the office of high priest – conferred upon the multitudes in the Mormon Church both early and late – was not part of any kind of a restoration and did not follow and in fact violated New Testament precedent. It is also true that there was only one high priest at a time in ancient Judaism.*

- *The Book of Mormon, supposed to contain "the fulness of the everlasting gospel," and Nephite prophets, supposed to have been instructed by the Savior, did not acknowledge two separate orders of priesthood. The Book of Mormon, the Nephite prophets and Joseph Smith's early followers all treated their authority as unitary, and so did the Savior and the apostles in the gospel church.*

- *According to William E. McLellin, the words "high priest" and "priesthood" are not found in the Book of Mormon after Jesus personally ministered on this continent.*[44] *The word "Priesthood" and the words "Aaronic" or "Melchizedek Priesthood" are not found in any of the sixty-five revelations published in the Book of Commandments – after two supposed restorations (in 1829) – four years later in 1833.*

- *Neither Joseph Smith nor Oliver Cowdery held the Melchizedek Priesthood on April 6, 1830, when Oliver Cowdery ordained Joseph Smith to the highest office on earth,*

---

[43]Quinn, *Origins of Power*, 28, emphasis added.

[44]*The William E. McLellin Papers: 1854-1880*, eds. Stan Larson and Samuel J. Passey, foreword by George D. Smith (Salt Lake City: Signature Books, 2008), 473 fn.

"Prophet, Seer and Revelator" of what was then the Church of Christ.

- *Joseph Smith and Oliver Cowdery did not know on April 6, 1830, and wouldn't know until September 1832,[45] more than two years later, that, "The office of an elder comes under the Priesthood of Melchizedek."[46]*

- *On April 6, 1830, Joseph Smith and Oliver Cowdery didn't know there were offices other than elder, teacher, priest and prophet.*

- *Joseph and Oliver didn't know on April 6, 1830, that there would be other offices, high priest, seventy, apostle (ordained) and elder that were appendages of a higher order of priesthood. Joseph and Oliver did not appear to know until quite some time after September 1832 that what they called "authority" would still later be linked to John the Baptist and ancient Israel's law of a carnal commandment, and that authority would come to be called the Aaronic or Aaronic/Levitical Priesthood.[47]*

- *Mormon elders did not hold "the Holy Priesthood, after the Order of the Son of God" until the Fourth Conference of the Church on June 3-6, 1831.[48] There were forty-four men who*

---

[45]Doctrine and Covenants 84 (1832), emphasis added. "In September 1832, Smith received a revelation (Doctrine and Covenants 84) which added significant detail to the understanding of priesthood authority. The high priesthood introduced in June 1831 had been associated with Melchizedek. In the new revelation, the office of elder was linked for the first time with the high priesthood. A 'lesser priesthood' resembling that 'confirmed' on Aaron was mentioned (vv. 6-18). That the office of elder was not originally included in the Melchizedek Priesthood was pointed out by church president Brigham Young shortly before his death in 1877." (Van Wagoner, *Sidney Rigdon*, 98).

[46]Doctrine and Covenants 107:7, emphasis added.

[47]Ibid., 84:18, emphasis added. "And the Lord confirmed a priesthood also upon Aaron and his seed, throughout all their generations which priesthood also continueth and abideth forever with the priesthood which is after the holiest order of God."

[48]Bushman, *Joseph Smith: Rough Stone Rolling*, 158, emphasis added. Roberts, ed., *History of The Church of Jesus Christ of Latter-day Saints*, 1:175-76, quoted in Van Wagoner, *Sidney Rigdon*, 97 fn 23, emphasis added.

had previously been ordained to the office of elder present at the Fourth Conference of the Church of Christ held at Kirtland, Ohio, on June 3, 1831, when the "High Priesthood" was conferred for the first time on several of those previously ordained lower authority Elders. Prior to that Conference none of those forty-four elders held what didn't actually come to be called the "Melchizedek Priesthood" until very much later.[49] On that occasion, and at those proceedings, the "High Priesthood" made its Mormon debut more than one year after the Church was officially organized.

- *The Melchizedek or higher order of priesthood "holds authority over all the offices in the Church" – deacon, teacher, priest, elder, bishop, high priest, seventy, apostle, patriarch and prophet – "and includes [the] power to administer in spiritual things." It is said that "all the authorities and powers necessary to the establishment and development of the church" are vested in the higher or Melchizedek Priesthood.[50] Those powers and that authority did not exist when the Church was officially organized.*

This examination of Mormonism's "priesthood" claims will *challenge* each of the following twenty-first century assumptions:

- *That Peter, James, and John visited Joseph Smith and Oliver Cowdery in May or June of 1829.*

- *That the Aaronic and Melchizedek Priesthoods were restored and functioned in the Church "after the spring of 1829" and before April 6, 1830.*

- *That Joseph Smith and Oliver Cowdery ever held the lineage-dependent Aaronic/Levitical Priesthood that administered the*

---

[49]Doctrine and Covenants 107 cf., Quinn, *Origins of Power*, 29-30, emphasis added.

[50]James E. Talmage, *A Study of the Articles of Faith: Being a Consideration of the Principal Doctrines of The Church of Jesus Christ of Latter-day Saints*, 12th ed. (Salt Lake City: The Church of Jesus Christ of Latter-day Saints, 1943), 188, emphasis added.

law of a carnal commandment in ancient Judaism.[51]

- *That Joseph and Oliver were ordained to the Aaronic or Melchizedek Priesthoods by angelic visitors before or after the Church was officially formed.*

CHARISMA

"Since the 1840s every explanation of the church's claim to authority has included some mention of the angelic restorations by John the Baptist and by Peter, James, and John." The modern dependence upon linear hierarchical authority first conferred by heavenly messengers is complete and entire. *"Early converts heard no such claims, and therefore emphasized authority based on 'charismatic or spiritual power, not on priesthood ordination.'"*[52] "The Priesthood was first given to Joseph Smith by the Spirit, later by angels, and finally by John the Baptist, Peter, James and John."[53] The Church gravitated toward physical "priesthood ordination" because spiritual power wasn't exclusive. William E. McLellin didn't believe John the Baptist ordained Joseph Smith and Oliver Cowdery to the Levitical Priesthood, but did believe in the efficacy of charismatic authority, the kind of authority the Church has since dismissed.

> *An angel never ordained a man to any office since the world began. Then say you how did Joseph and Oliver get authority to start? I answer, that a revelation from the Lord gives a man both power and authority to do whatever it commands. The Lord commanded Joseph to baptize, confirm, and ordain Oliver, then Oliver to do the same for him. This was*

---

[51]God took that lower order authority and the written code and its orders "out of the way" ("He nailed it to the cross." [Colossians 2:14]).

[52]Quinn, *Origins of Power*, 20, emphasis added.

[53]livy (anonymous contributor), "My Personal Ninety-Five Thesis" posted on "Recovery from Mormonism discussion forum" (5 March 2014; accessed 6-7 March 2014), available from exmormon.org/phorum/read.php?2,1193668,1193668, quote=1; Internet, 1.

legal and valid.[54]

In the first reference to the exercise of divine authority in the Book of Commandments, the command of the Lord provided the pretext, and the ordination was earthbound. This non-exclusive authority soon became (and for a long time remained) the early Mormon model. The 1833 Book of Commandment's charismatic model did not survive to become the modern Mormon model. The Book of Mormon's 1830 charismatic model did not survive to become the modern Mormon model. "Alma received authority to baptize through the Spirit (Mosiah 18:13). Similarly, Alma II taught that holders of the high priesthood were preordained to their office (Alma 13:3), and Jesus' commission to Nephi and other disciples seems to have been conveyed verbally (3 Ne. 11:21)."[55]

Melchizedek's calling to the priesthood was charismatic or spiritual, and so was that of Jesus. The proselyting advantage of unprecedented angelic ordination, as opposed to more egalitarian concepts of authority – commands, dreams, visions, voices, promptings, preordination (which treated believers alike) – was that it allowed the brazen young prophet and his aggressive new Church to lay *exclusive* claim to priesthood authority, supported by another unprovable theory (angelic ordination) outing all other believers. By turning its back on democratic charisma, the Church changed course in order to claim a new source of authority by a more authoritative kind of supernatural process. If John the Baptist was nothing more than a fictional afterthought, any claim to exclusive authority was dead upon delivery (void *ab initio*). "[E]arly Mormons, including those who were the closest to Smith,

---

[54]*True L[atter] D[ay] Saints' Herald*, 19 (1 Aug. 1872): 472, quoted in Dan Vogel, *Joseph Smith: The Making of a Prophet* (Salt Lake City: Signature Books, 2004), 306-7. In 1834 and 1835, by altering this command of God equation, the remodeled Church changed grids. Now, by revelatory fiat, a command of God communicated by unprovable visions, promptings or feelings no longer provided the physical kind of authority required to do what God wanted to be done. By the mid-1840s, following a series of backdated revelations, the Church abandoned its "by the grace of God authority," a less-then-exclusive notion it shared with others, in favor of a more literal (and physical) kind of divine authority received under the hands of heavenly messengers.

[55]Book of Mormon passages, quoted in Vogel, *Joseph Smith: The Making of a Prophet*, 307, emphasis added.

were told nothing about an angelic bestowal of priesthood authority, nor did anyone, including Smith and Cowdery, claim that angelic ordinations would be essential for such a restoration."[56]

"At this early date [May 1829] the view was that the commandment received through the urim and thummim is what gave Joseph and Oliver the authority to baptize."[57] Baptism by commandment was metaphysical charisma. This authority was not *hierarchical*, meaning derived because of some linear person to person transfer by a heavenly messenger, but rather *charismatic*, derived because of a heavenly message – a message of a nature or kind that *any* person of faith might sincerely hope to receive. Mormons – burning their metaphysical bridges – turned their back on this equitable evangelical process. In that early and relaxed conception of non-exclusive authority, there was not the makings of the only true church on the face of the earth.

Beginnings

The *Painesville Telegraph* described in 1830 what had not yet come to be called priesthood: "Mr. Oliver Cowd[e]ry," the Telegraph said, "has his commission directly from the God of heaven, and [he says] that he has his credentials, written and signed by the hand of Jesus Christ, with whom he has personally conversed . . . ." That was a bold and extraordinary assertion. "[S]aid Cowd[e]ry claims that he and his associates are the only persons on earth who are qualified to administer in his name. By *this authority*, they proclaim to the world, that all who do not believe *their* testimony, and be baptised by them for the remission of their sins . . . must be forever miserable."[58] Cowdery didn't say that he had received that authority by the laying on of hands. He didn't mention John the Baptist, Peter, James, and John, angelic ordination, keys or "priesthood," and his curious claim to authority, *"this authority,"* was decidedly unitary. When all these things got sorted out four or five years later, by the expression of greater and grander more

---

[56]Vogel, *Joseph Smith: The Making of a Prophet*, 307.

[57]Palmer, *An Insider's View of Mormon Origins*, 216.

[58]*Painesville Telegraph*, 16 Nov., 7 Dec. 1830, quoted in Quinn, *Origins of Power*, 18-19 fn 90, emphasis retained and added.

physical theories, the "commission . . . from the God of heaven . . . written and signed by the hand of Jesus Christ" became unimportant and disappeared.

Cowdery's unitary authority claim was by no means defensibly exclusive. To prove that it was would have been next to impossible. Four years later (in October 1834), which was more than five years after the alleged event, Cowdery and Smith retroactively claimed literal hierarchical authority from John the Baptist by the laying on of hands. In that they did not continue to describe a commission "written and signed by the hand of Jesus Christ." The conferral of the authority of John the Baptist, an element in a new equation, was said to have come in a different more unique, impressive and physical way. These founding ordinations – none of which were reported in real time – were defended as having been kept secret for more than five years in order to protect Joseph Smith and Oliver Cowdery from persecution. That claim, on its face, was preposterous. When the story was finally told, it became apparent that what Cowdery told the *Painesville Telegraph* in 1830 had followed a series of supernal events supposed to have been associated with a celebrated but only later reported visit of John the Baptist in 1829. Was it any more difficult to say that a heavenly messenger came and ordained them than it was to say that they "personally conversed" with the Lord himself, who then furnished them with autographed credentials? Would one dismiss the first contention (John the Baptist) for fear of persecution, then embrace a second more tumultuous contention (that supposed visit with Jesus Christ)? This great belated five-and-a-half-year (May 1829 to October 1834) omission is impossible to explain.

Smith and Cowdery did not claim to have received the "priesthood" by angelic administration on April 6, 1830, or any time before, or for a long time after. In the beginning, before they changed their minds, various early revelations (and their theology), they claimed "*authority*" by special dispensation. Cowdery represented to the *Painesville Telegraph* that what was nothing more than yet another claim to charismatic authority, this time "*directly from the God of heaven,*" was by some unexplained stretch of the imagination unique and exclusive. Other Christians in other communities said that God directed them.

Confusion

A revelation received at Peter Whitmer Sr.'s house at Fayette, New York, *in June 1829* (found at Chapter 15 of the 1833 Book of Commandments) promised Joseph Smith, Oliver Cowdery and David Whitmer, the revelation's three recipients, that they might yet receive a gift they hadn't yet received, the gift of the Holy Ghost. It was *June*, the date of the revelation, not *May*, the date of the baptism, when this hopeful communication is said to have been received. Oliver and Joseph, who first said they baptized each other because of a message recovered from a fortune teller's stone concealed in Joseph's hat, hadn't yet received the gift of the Holy Ghost. In June 1829, before anyone ever described John the Baptist, Peter, James, and John, Aaron, Melchizedek, or even priesthood, this was the plan:

> *Ask the Father in my name in faith, believing that you shall receive, and you shall have the Holy Ghost which manifesteth all things, which is expedient unto the children of men.*[59]

This revelation, previously shown to contain the first reference to the exercise of authority in Joseph Smith's new society, lends support to the proposition that Joseph's God may confer the gift of the Holy Ghost upon request without hierarchical formality (meaning without linear person-to-person ordination by the laying on of hands). Is that not perfectly clear? The *Church Chronology* reported (long after the fact and in error) that Joseph and Oliver received the Holy Ghost when they were baptized *on May 15, 1829:* "*Fri. 15 [May 1829]* – . . . Immediately after being baptized, the Holy Ghost fell upon them in great measure and both prophesied."[60] Chapter 15 of the Book of Commandments, an important revelation received in June 1829 but not published until 1833, made it perfectly undeniably clear that wasn't true.

If Joseph and Oliver had just received the Aaronic Priesthood under the hands of John the Baptist on May 15, 1829 (*something they didn't claim until October 1834),* and if Joseph and Oliver had

---

[59]Book of Commandments 15:20 (June 1829), emphasis added.

[60]Jenson, comp., *Church Chronology*, 3, emphasis added.

already received the gift of the Holy Ghost on May 15, 1829, at the time of their baptisms (*as the Church Chronology claimed in 1914*), how strange is it that a revelation[61] received in June 1829 should fail to describe angelic ordination, orders of priesthood, the founders' previous reception of the gift of the Holy Ghost, Aaron, Levi, John the Baptist or Peter, James, and John? Is it not perfectly clear that Joseph Smith, Oliver Cowdery and David Whitmer hadn't received the gift of the Holy Ghost when they received that revelation, Chapter 15 of the Book of Commandments, in June of 1829? Not at the time of the baptism? Or ever yet at all? How could the description of the gift of the Holy Ghost fail to refer to the angelic restoration of the high priesthood in a revelation directed to the highest leaders of the Church in June of 1829? If John the Baptist had actually acted under the direction of the ancient apostles Peter, James, and John, as many years later in amendments to earlier revelations it was said that he did? Is it not undeniable that the gift of the Holy Ghost hadn't been conferred upon those founders by the time of this revelation, whatever the *Church Chronology* dishonestly said?

"Joseph, Oliver and David" were informed that Joseph baptized Oliver because he received, by way of the stone, a special command. *"Wherefore as thou hast been baptized by the hand of my servant [Joseph Smith], according to that which I have commanded him: Wherefore he hath fulfilled the thing which I commanded him."*[62] This was baptism by command. None of the sixty-five revelations described in the Book of Commandments published in 1833, four years after those supposed baptismal events, refer to the conferral of priesthood authority in 1829 by John the Baptist by the laying on of hands, or to the conferral of priesthood authority in 1829 by Peter, James, and John by the laying on of hands.

What Joseph's revelator (God himself) understood in June of 1829 is what David Whitmer understood in June of 1829:

> *. . . Oliver stated to me in Josephs presence that they had baptized each other seeking by that to fulfill the*

---

[61]Book of Commandments 15:20 (*June 1829*). No decision had been made to publish the revelations in 1829.

[62]Ibid., 15:6-7, emphasis added.

*command – And after our arrival at fathers sometime
in June 1829. Joseph ordained Oliver Cowdery to be
an Elder, and Oliver ordained Joseph to be an Elder
in the Church of Christ. <and during that year
Joseph both baptized and ordained me an elder in the
church of Christ.> Also, during this year the
translation of the Book of Mormon was finished, And
we preached ~~preached~~, baptized and ordained some as
Elders . . . I never heard that an Angel had ordained
Joseph and Oliver to the Aaronic priesthood until the
year 1834[,] [183]5. Or [183]6 – in Ohio . . . .*[63]

David Whitmer didn't describe angelic ordination by supernatural
process. David Whitmer moved Joseph and Oliver from Harmony,
Pennsylvania, to the house of David's father in Fayette, New York,
in June 1829. Whitmer was one of the three persons to whom the
June 1829 revelation (Chapter 15 of the Book of Commandments)
was specifically directed. He was one of the three witnesses to the
Book of Mormon, one of the first six elders, one of the three men
who selected and ordained the first Quorum of the Twelve Apostles,
the President of the Church at the place of the gathering (Zion in
the state of Missouri), and Joseph's first duly appointed successor
in the event of the prophet's death. This highly esteemed insider
later reported as follows:

> *I do not believe that John the Baptist ever ordained
> Joseph and Oliver . . . .*[64]

Revelations

If John the Baptist didn't ordain them – and for nearly five-and-
one-half years no one said that he did – then by what authority did
they say that they were authorized to act for God? Oliver and
Joseph's October 1834 disclosure, which identified a heavenly
messenger, didn't begin to explain how what couldn't be done in

---

[63]Dan Vogel, ed., *Early Mormon Documents*, (Salt Lake City: Signature Books, 2003), 5:137 (Whitmer interview with Zenas H. Gurley, 14 Jan. 1885), emphasis added.

[64]Ibid., emphasis added.

Israel for non-Levitical Hebrews (including Jesus) could be done in America for non-Levitical Gentiles (including Joseph and Oliver). Chapter 15 of the 1833 Book of Commandments supposed the conferral of spiritual power. "And behold, you are they which are ordained of me to ordain priests and teachers to declare my gospel, according to the power of the Holy Ghost which is in you, and according to the callings and gifts of God unto men: . . . ."[65] This may seem to have been the source of the authority Oliver Cowdery described to the *Painesville Telegraph* in 1830, authority he said that he received not from John, not from Peter, James, and John, nor by way of angelic ordination, but rather by way of a written commission "directly from the God of Heaven" with whom "he had personally conversed." The authority Cowdery described (*"this authority"*), please note yet again, was both spiritual and unitary.

Joseph's God didn't come down and ordain these disciples by the laying on of hands, thus empowering them "to ordain priests and teachers," nor did he say that he would be sending them anyone else. It was just then supposed that the Lord had granted them authority of a spiritual nature. "[Y]ou are they which are ordained of me" to ordain others, "to declare my gospel, according to the power of the Holy Ghost which is in you . . . ," not because you have been ordained in physical fact by supernatural messengers, but rather in spirit and by command "according to the callings and gifts of God unto men . . . ." That was the way that it was in the "full purpose of heart" church in the beginning. It was in this greatly more egalitarian atmosphere, with scant distinction between the authority exercised by elders, teachers and priests, that David Whitmer found his cherished "spiritual community." Life had been so simple to start. "Behold my grace is sufficient for you: You must walk uprightly before me and sin not."[66]

Mormons who hadn't been literally ordained by angels or deities, or by shepherds who said that they had been ordained by angels or deities, Mormons who didn't hold the high priesthood any earlier than June of 1831, took upon themselves the name of Christ, proceeded to bestow the gift of the Holy Ghost, ordained priests and teachers and elders, spoke in tongues, healed the sick, cast out evil

---

[65]Book of Commandments (1833), 15:35.
[66]Ibid., 15:34.

spirits, got married and preached to the pure in heart. At least they said that they did. The two thousand members who preceded the hierarchy were baptized and confirmed before there was a priesthood, a high priest, a high priesthood, or orders of priesthood. They took their places before what came to be called "priesthood" complicated the message. How were the members of the early Church called to the work? The revelation given to Oliver Cowdery and David Whitmer, who (together with Martin Harris) were given the task to select and empower the first twelve *ordained* apostles (an event delayed until 1835) was instructive:

> *And the twelve are they which shall desire to take upon them my name, with full purpose of heart: And if they desire to take upon them my name, with full purpose of heart, they are called to go into all the world to preach my gospel unto every creature: And they are they which are ordained of me to baptize in my name, according to that which is written; and you have that which is written before you: Wherefore you must perform it according to the words which are written.*[67]

"According to the words which are written."

What sincere Christian could not say as much? Who that desired to take upon themselves the name of Jesus "with full purpose of heart" could not lay claim to equivalent authority? What sincere Christian could not "go into all the world to preach my gospel unto every creature" metaphorically ordained of God, as these early Mormons said that they were, and baptize in the Lord's name, as these early Mormons said that they did, according to that "which is written"? In this June 1829 revelation published in the Book of Commandments in 1833 ("making known the calling of twelve disciples in these last days"[68]), there is no discussion of orders of priesthood, heavenly messengers, or angelic ordinations. The instruction to perform "according to the words which are written," when given in June 1829, included the words which were written on the gold plates, and in the revelations received by Smith prior to

---

[67]Ibid., 15:29-32, emphasis added.
[68]Book of Commandments 15, Introduction.

June 1829, none of which mentioned John the Baptist or Peter, James, and John in connection with angelic ordination or separate orders of priesthood.

Scriptural References to Priesthood

When there was a Book of Mormon in 1830, a few sparing references to a nearly invisible Melchizedek, high priests and high priesthood did not include a single reference to Aaron, or to Levi, or to the law of a carnal commandment, two different priesthoods or any kind of lower authority. No Nephite held the lineage-dependent Aaronic/Levitical priesthood (the lineal priesthood of the old law). Could those transplanted Hebrews, Levi, Ishmael and others have left the history of their centuries without ever mentioning Levi, Aaron, or the Aaronic/Levitical Priesthood? Why didn't the BCE (Before Common Era) church of the Nephites, Hebrews in the Western Hemisphere, resemble the BCE church of the Hebrews in the Eastern Hemisphere? Why didn't the gospel church, the church of Christ in the Eastern Hemisphere, why didn't the church of Christ in the Western Hemisphere resemble the church of Christ in Joseph Smith's nineteenth-century America? How did the gospel church and the Nephites manage their affairs without two different orders of the priesthood, both of them eternal? Without the priesthood that "the Lord [Joseph's Lord] confirmed . . . upon Aaron and his seed, throughout all their generations, which priesthood *also* continueth and abideth *forever* with the priesthood which is after the holiest order of God [Doctrine and Covenants 84:18]"? Where is evidence of this second so-called eternal priesthood found to exist in the gospel church? In the societies that followed the teachings of the apostles Peter, James, and John? Where is evidence of this so-called eternal priesthood found to exist in the Nephite church? This ancient discredited priesthood "is nowhere pretended to" in the societies supposed to have been associated with the Christian system in the meridian of time. There was nothing there to be restored.

Why was the Church restored by Smith so unlike the church established by Jesus in the Eastern Hemisphere, and so unlike the church established by Jesus in the Western Hemisphere, in regard to the vitally important issue of authority? Joseph's authority principle didn't begin to match the authority principles of his ecclesiastical models. The discredited Aaronic Priesthood wasn't something anyone should ever have sought to restore.

Furthermore, and as if in defiance of modern Mormon teachings, there is no indication in the New Testament that Paul or Barnabas were literally ordained to their offices by the laying on of hands. Paul, "because of his vision on the road to Damascus," was "an apostle not of man, neither by men, but by Jesus Christ' (Gal. 1:1) . . . . The New Testament portrayed Paul as a charismatic apostle and special witness, not an apostle through ordination by the laying on of hands."[69] When Lehi came to the New World, no one in his small colony is known to have held the high priesthood. The Hebrews in the Old World, bedeviled by authoritarian hyper-technicality, didn't hold the high priesthood. The distinction between high and low does not seem to have applied to them. While Lehi and his small colony multiplied in North and South America, spreading out over two vast continents, no Nephite is known to have ever held the Aaronic Priesthood.

Early Mormon leaders used the word "apostle" before 1835, the year apostles are first seen to have been ordained, "to designate unordained charisma."[70] In the beginning, visionaries, witnesses, missionaries and elders claimed the title "apostle." Their callings were charismatic rather than institutional. No apostle was ordained to the apostleship before 1835, but there were "apostles" before 1835.

In June 1829 Joseph Smith had no clear sense of what the structure of the priesthood was destined to become. The instructions he said that he received from the revelations in the Book of Commandments described a non-exclusive charismatic conferral of divine authority.[71] It was under the revelation's "full purpose of

---

[69]Quinn, *Origins of Power*, 10.

[70]Ibid.

[71]"Ask the Father in my name in faith, believing that you shall receive, and you shall have the Holy Ghost which manifesteth all things, which is expedient unto the children of men." (Book of Commandments [1833], 15:20).

heart" order of authority that the new Church ventured forth to declare the gospel and conquer the earth.

> *The distance between traditional accounts of LDS priesthood beginnings and the differing story of early documents points to retrospective changes made in the public record to create a story of logical and progressive development . . . .*

> *[A]s now published in D&C 68:15 a revelation of November 1831 referred to 'the Melchizedek Priesthood.' However the original text of the 1831 revelation did not contain that priesthood phrase which was a retroactive addition in 1835.*[72]

What is clearly seen in the clumsy dishonest historical revisions that betray every modern believer was a paradigm shift from Mormonism's early discarded *"charisma-based authority"* to Mormonism's present *"legalistic and hierarchical 'authority'"*[73] as the Latter-day Saints crossed the bar from David Whitmer's "full purpose of heart" spiritual community to Joseph and Brigham's physical, infallible, priesthood-promoting authoritarianism. It was not a pretty transition.

FOREORDINATION

Mormon theologian Bruce R. McConkie (in the some forty consecutive printings of his fifty year seminal text *Mormon Doctrine*) avers that Adam, the presiding high priest (under Christ), and others like him, "obtained the priesthood 'in the creation, before the world was formed.'" McConkie cites Joseph Smith and the Book of Mormon's Alma.[74] According to McConkie, Alma describes men ordained to the high priesthood of the holy order of

---

[72]Quinn, *Origins of Power*, 15, emphasis added.

[73]Vogel, *Joseph Smith: The Making of a Prophet*, 307, emphasis added.

[74]*Teachings of Presidents of the Church – Joseph Smith* (Salt Lake City: The Church of Jesus Christ of Latter-day Saints, 2007), 157, and Book of Mormon, Alma 13, quoted in Bruce R. McConkie, *Mormon Doctrine*, 2d ed. (Salt Lake City: Bookcraft, 1966), 477.

God in the preexistence because of their righteousness and exceeding faith exercised while in the presence of God. These worthy vessels, according to McConkie, are theoretically "'called and prepared from the foundation of the world according to the foreknowledge of God' to enjoy the blessings and powers of the priesthood." Faithful men who surfaced to obtain heavenly power in the preexistence came to hold heavenly power on earth. This proposition – emphasizing the foundation of the world and the foreknowledge of God – though less than exclusive was Joseph's earliest teaching. "Every man who has a calling to minister to the inhabitants of the world was ordained to that very purpose in the Grand Council of heaven before this world was."[75]

If that should happen to be true, if men were preordained, then literal ordination from person to person by the laying on of hands, the inflexible rule of the modern Church, is not exactly required. Preordination, a command of God, a spiritual prompting, a dream or vision as in the case of Lehi and others, under the parameters of McConkie's proposition, were considered to be predestined sources of power. An evangelical can claim the power to act for God on the basis of "the foreknowledge of God" just as easily as any Mormon elder can. Relaxed authority based on relaxed definitions of authority was the rule before David Whitmer's "spiritual community" surrendered to Joseph and Brigham's "infallible priesthood." Before Joseph promoted "dual priesthoods of different ranks," Mormons were baptized, confirmed and empowered under the relaxed concept of unitary "authority" without any reference to the bestowal of "priesthood."

McConkie explained how one thing led to another: "Through Moses the Lord attempted to set up the house of Israel as a kingdom of priests of the holy order, with each man and his family enjoying the full blessings of the patriarchal order and priesthood."[76] When in the history and tradition of the Hebrews, when in the history and tradition of the Christians, or in the Bible, was every man (and every boy) destined to hold the priesthood?

---

[75]*Teachings of the Prophet Joseph Smith*, 365, quoted in McConkie, *Mormon Doctrine*, 2d ed. (1966), 477.

[76]The modern Church abandoned "the patriarchal order" of the priesthood in 1979, after McConkie wrote these words in the early editions of his seminal work.

Israel rebelled, according to McConkie, and "Moses and the fulness of the priesthood" were taken away. From the time of Moses until the "personal ministry" of Jesus Christ, the "schooling ministry" (meaning the Aaronic/Levitical Priesthood) was "the most prevalent authority of God on earth." In order to explain how others – like the Book of Mormon prophets, who didn't hold and couldn't have held the Levitical Priesthood – obtained the power to act for God, it was reported that, "All the prophets had the Melchizedek Priesthood and were ordained by God himself."   The High Priesthood would have had to have come by special designation "for the general priesthood rule . . . was the Levitical order."[77]

If all visionaries, if all of those righteous and believing men who distinguished themselves by the exercise of great faith while in the presence (and/or foreknowledge) of God held the "high priesthood" because ordained "by God himself," the world can say goodbye to Mormon exclusivity.   Every decent man, every sincere and righteous man, every priest, every minister, every believing faithful Christian man, every Muslim man, every Evangelical man, can make a compelling case for preordination.

---

[77]"There were at many times, however, and may have been at all times, prophets and worthy men in Israel who held the Melchizedek Priesthood." (McConkie, *Mormon Doctrine*, 2d ed. [1966], 477-78 and authorities cited).

CHAPTER SIX

Messengers

I am the governor of the State of Deseret. I was elected for life, and no other person shall hold that office while I live.

Governor Brigham Young

The effect of the system . . . is to render the people in a high degree separate and peculiar; and to prevent, not only all amalgamation, but even any intimate association with other communities.

Major Howard Stansbury, 1852

The government of the United States founded upon a written constitution, finds within its jurisdiction another government – claiming to come from God – imperiam in imperio – whose policy and practice, in grave particulars, are at variance with its own . . . .

Justice James McKean, 1871

INTRODUCTION

D. Michael Quinn has studied Mormon power. "According to current tradition, both the Aaronic and Melchizedek priesthoods functioned in the church after the spring of 1829 when Smith and Cowdery were visited first by John the Baptist, who restored the lesser or Aaronic Priesthood, and then by Peter, James, and John,

who restored the higher or Melchizedek priesthood."[1]   Quinn
softens this foundational deception by equating modern doctrine[2] to
"current tradition." "[C]urrent tradition," something less dignified
than doctrine, may be subject to change, and may need to be
changed.   The 1829 priesthood restoration dates pronounced to
Mormonism's investigators over the years in more than one
hundred countries all over the world are not easy to change. They
are hard wired. The members of the Church are informed that the
"restorations" of each of two different priesthoods by separate sets
of heavenly messengers, despite the fact they were not reported in
real time, occurred before the Church was organized – *"1829, May
15"* for the Aaronic Priesthood, and *"1829, May-June"* for the
Melchizedek Priesthood.[3] That cannot be true for many different
reasons, not the least of which Quinn (a believer) then further
proceeded to describe.

> *A closer look at contemporary records indicates that*
> *men were first ordained to the higher priesthood over*
> *a year after the church's founding. No mention of*
> *angelic ordinations can be found in original*
> *documents [unaltered documents] until 1834-35.*
>
> *Thereafter accounts of the visit of Peter, James, and*
> *John by Cowdery and Smith remained vague and*
> *contradictory.*[4]

By that to say insufficiently explained, late to the table and difficult
to reconcile. The "higher or Melchizedek priesthood" was not
restored in the spring of 1829, whatever the modern Church has
carelessly chosen to say. Early Mormons knew absolutely nothing

---

[1]D. Michael Quinn, *The Mormon Hierarchy: Origins of Power* (Salt Lake City:
Signature Books in association with Smith Research Associates, 1994), 15,
emphasis added.
[2]See Bruce R. McConkie, *Mormon Doctrine*, 2d ed. (Salt Lake City: Bookcraft,
1966), 478.
[3]*Teachings of Presidents of the Church – Joseph Smith* (Salt Lake City: The
Church of Jesus Christ of Latter-day Saints, 2007), xv.
[4]Quinn, *Origins of Power*, 15, emphasis added.

about the alleged ordinations of Oliver Cowdery and Joseph Smith by John the Baptist and Peter, James, and John until some time after the humiliating events associated with the ignominious defeat of a Mormon militia called Zion's Camp, a military force under the command of Joseph Smith, in Missouri in 1834. After those early Missouri encounters involving many failed promises and prophecies, Smith desperately needed something to bolster his justifiably damaged reputation. Fresh reports of supposed past events, supernal events streamlined for publication, helped the depreciated prophet weather the embarrassing storm. The untimely reporting of crucial events facilitated by awkward amendments to previously published documents, original documents, puts the contents of those substantively embellished faith-promoting stories in doubt. The messengers came or they did not. Alternative theories of empowerment, although used and abused in the early days of the Church, are no longer available to Mormonism's indefatigable testators. For nearly two hundred years the leaders of the Church have attested to exclusive claims to linear hierarchical authority conferred by heavenly messengers (nothing else would do) with dogmatic certitude. Angelic ordination is the core principle of the modern Mormon claim to priesthood.

AARONIC PRIESTHOOD

The Church declared (*but not until 1834-35*) that Joseph Smith and Oliver Cowdery, Mormonism's First and Second Elders, received the Aaronic Priesthood under the hands of John the Baptist on May 15, 1829:

> *Fri. 15 [May 1829]. – While Joseph Smith, jun., and Oliver Cowdery were engaged in prayer in the woods, near Harmony [Pennsylvania], John the Baptist descended as a messenger from heaven in a cloud of light and ordained them to the Priesthood of Aaron and commanded them to baptize and ordain each*

other. This they did the same day.[5]

The Baptist, by this unprecedented accounting, ordained but didn't baptize. Smith and Cowdery were then retroactively supposed – five and a half years after that alleged baptismal event – to have received what came to be called the Aaronic Priesthood (even though they were not connected by lineage to Aaron or Levi). October 1834: *"On a sudden, as from the midst of eternity, the voice of the Redeemer spake peace to us."* **The** *"vail"* **was parted and** *"the angel of God came down clothed with glory and delivered the anxiously looked for message, and the keys of the gospel of repentance!"*[6] **In that first account, "the angel of God" was not specifically identified as John the Baptist. Not exactly then (in 1829), but with the passage of time, a lot of time, those keys would come to be publicly identified with ancient Israel's poorly respected less than eternal law of a carnal commandment.**[7]

Latter-day Saints are led to believe that the angel supposed to have appeared to Joseph Smith and Oliver Cowdery on the banks of the Susquehanna River on May 15, 1829, was John the Baptist (the same ancient holy man who baptized Jesus). As the story developed and settled during a period of angelic tumult, John the Baptist visited the earth while under the direction of Peter, James, and John (the leaders of the gospel church after the crucifixion), laid his

---

[5]Andrew Jenson, comp., *Church Chronology: A Record of Important Events Pertaining to the History of the Church of Jesus Christ of Latter-day Saints*, 2d ed., rev. and enlarged (Salt Lake City: Deseret News, 1914), 3.

[6]Oliver Cowdery (and Joseph Smith), "Letter to W.W. Phelps, Esq." (Oliver Cowdery and Joseph Smith's 1834-35 History), *Messenger and Advocate*, vol. 1 no. 1 (October 1834): 15, emphasis added.

[7]Doctrine and Covenants (1835), 107:6. "But there are two divisions or grand heads – one in the Melchizedek Priesthood, and the other in the Aaronic or Levitical Priesthood." *See, e.g.,* Doctrine and Covenants 84:26-27 (supposed to have been received in September 1832 but not published until 1835), where reference is made to Moses, the children of Israel in the wilderness, lesser priesthood, the ministering of angels, the preparatory gospel, repentance, baptism, the remission of sins and the law of a carnal commandment ("which the Lord in his wrath caused to continue with the house of Aaron among the children of Israel until John, whom God raised up, being filled with the Holy Ghost from his mother's womb").

hands on Joseph and Oliver's heads and conferred upon them the priesthood of Aaron, including the keys required to exercise all of its lower authority powers ("the keys of the ministering of angels, and of the gospel of repentance, and of baptism by immersion for the remission of sins . . . .").[8]   The Baptist didn't baptize and couldn't confirm.   Thus, an unbaptized Joseph baptized Oliver, after which Oliver baptized the unbaptized Joseph, after which Joseph and Oliver, though ordained by the messenger, followed his instructions and ordained each other again.[9]   Like the messenger, however, Joseph and Oliver didn't yet hold the power required to confer the gift of the Holy Ghost.

An Overview of "Authority"

Oliver and Joseph's first "authorized" 1834-35 History of the Church described the angelic conferral of "the holy priesthood" under the "hand" of "the angel of God."[10]   One "hand," one "angel," one "priesthood." It did not describe the conferral of any other order of priesthood under the hands of any other messengers, thus failing to mention those other patriarchs and priests, Abraham, Elias, Elijah, Melchizedek or Peter, James, and John. Oliver described his baptism "by the direction of the angel of God" at the hands of Joseph Smith, making him *"the first received into this church, in this day."*[11]   Why didn't the founders follow that up and say that in June 1829 (by "divine appointment") we saw Peter, James, and John and received additional authority?

What Joseph and Oliver did say in October 1834 (the date of the

---

[8]Doctrine and Covenants 13, Headnote and text.

[9]After the angel conferred the priesthood of Aaron (as described in a many years-after-the-fact amended prayer), he instructed them "to baptize one another and ordain each other again to the Priesthood of Aaron."   (Richard Lyman Bushman, with the assistance of Jed Woodworth, *Joseph Smith: Rough Stone Rolling* [New York: Alfred A. Knopf, 2005], 75).

[10]"Letter" (Cowdery and Smith's 1834-35 History), *Messenger and Advocate*, vol. 1 no. 1 (October 1834), 15-16.

[11]Ibid., 14, emphasis added.

first report of the visit of John the Baptist), about the visit of John the Baptist on May 15, 1829, was that before that visit and the ordination that followed, no one "had authority from God to administer the ordinances of the gospel."[12] By their reckoning (in October 1834), that meant that until John came (on May 15, 1829), the date assigned to the ordination, they didn't have authority "from God to administer the ordinances of the gospel," and no one else had authority "from God to administer the ordinances of the gospel." Those Mormon leaders retroactively rejected charisma and the voice of God as legitimate sources of divine authority.[13] The backdating of the Aaronic event thus became a matter of supreme importance.

For five-and-a-half years, from May 15, 1829, to October 1834, ordinary Mormons didn't know their leaders had been ordained to the priesthood, any priesthood, by John the Baptist, or Peter, James, and John. Nor did their leaders say, in person or by way of any original (unaltered) document, that they had been ordained by John the Baptist or Peter, James, and John. They did, notwithstanding, claim authority to administer the ordinances of the gospel. Those leaders baptized and confirmed each other and several thousand others, ordained lower authority elders, teachers and priests, and purported to confer the gift of the Holy Ghost. They said they translated ancient inscriptions from golden plates by the gift and power of God. They received revelations, gave blessings, healed the sick, spoke in tongues and cast out evil spirits.

---

[12]Ibid., 15. "After writing the account [meaning the Book of Mormon] given of the Savior's ministry to the remnant of the seed of Jacob [the Indians], upon this continent, it was easily to be seen, as the prophet said would be, that darkness covered the earth and . . . the minds of the people."

[13]Mormonism's founders reasoned as follows: Men who deny revelations upon which all true religion is based "in all ages of the world, when he has had a people on earth," are not authorized "to administer in the name of Christ." "If these facts were buried, and carefully concealed by men whose craft would have been in danger, if once permitted to shine in the faces of men, they were no longer to us; . . . ." On May 15, 1829, as first reported in October 1834, and until "we" (Oliver and Joseph) waited for the commandment to be given, "Arise and be baptized" on May 15, 1829, no one ("none") "had authority from God to administer the ordinances of the gospel." (Ibid.).

Then they organized and staffed the Church of Christ. In all of this, and for five-and-a-half years, no one mentioned angelic ordination by John the Baptist, or Peter, James, and John in person or in any revelation or manuscript that wasn't backdated or falsified. Angelic ordination is the core principle of the modern Mormon concept of the priesthood.

Joseph Smith and Oliver Cowdery did not publicly discuss angelic ordination against issues of authority after the supposed date of the baptism (May 15, 1829) for five-and-a-half years (until October 1834). During that lengthy interregnum, and despite Joseph and Oliver's retroactive repudiation of charisma and the voice of God as legitimate sources of authority, the society functioned under an egalitarian approach to the principles of power. Without much evidence of foresight, this relaxed approach was unsupported. The authority principles that guided the fortunes of the early Church, before the founders battened down the hatches in October 1834, mimicked authority principles more nearly associated with traditional Christianity. Early Mormons, without regard to more than one dozen backdated revelations, adopted metaphysical elements of authority, foreordination, dreams, visions and promptings, charisma, and the voice of God. History posits a system that was, in the beginning, nebulous, confused, fluid and non-specific. From May 15, 1829, to October 1834, angelic ordination, John the Baptist and Peter, James, and John played no part in the aggressive new society's more or less conventional authority equation. The authority principle that guided the affairs of the early Church was non-exclusive and not well suited to the particular needs of the only true church on the face of the earth. That would serve to suggest that the repudiation of charisma and the voice of God ("none had authority from God to administer the ordinances of the gospel"), a retroactive claim published in the first authorized history of the Church in 1834-35, was yet another part of a late design.

Joseph and Oliver described, but not until 1834, what they now said, but not until 1834, happened on May 15, 1829. After transcribing the Book of Mormon, and pondering the importance of baptism, and yearning for their own exposure to the "liquid grave," they waited "for the commandment to be given, 'Arise and be baptized.' This was not long desired before it was realized."[14]

> The assurance that we were in the presence of an angel; *the certainty that we heard the voice of Jesus*, and the truth unsullied as it flowed from a pure personage, dictated by the will of God, is to me, past description, and I shall ever look upon this expression of the Savior's goodness with wonder and thanksgiving . . . .[15]

Humbled, but not very, Joseph and Oliver remembered the date of this event, May 15, 1829, but didn't describe John the Baptist as having been a part of it until 1834-35. Until then and for no less than five-and-a-half years, it was said, by those who knew them best, that they baptized each other, not because of an instruction received from a heavenly messenger, but rather because of an instruction they received through Joseph's magical stone. The same stone he had previously used to tell fortunes and search for lost and hidden things. It was Oliver – apart from this new and surprising October 1834 account initially published without the messenger's name – who separately reported that the "angel of God" who conferred what the founders described as *"this priesthood and this authority,"* one priesthood and one authority, had actually been John the Baptist.

In the Bible, John the Baptist wore clothes made of camel hair and a leather belt (Matthew 3:4) (sans tunics, caps and sashes). He was not seen to have worn "the clothes required of a Levitical priest." He was not seen to have been closely aligned with Levitical priests in his ministry in what was a remote and isolated location. John's father, while filled with the Holy Spirit, failed to assign his son to the office of a lower authority less-than-eternal Levitical priest. "And thou child," Zechariah blessed him and said, "shalt be called

---

[14]Ibid.
[15]Ibid., 16, emphasis added.

the *prophet* of the Highest: . . . ." John "lived in the desert, away from other people, until the time when he came out to preach to Israel." (Luke 1:66-80). An Aaronic/Levitical priest could not have lived away from other people, or passed on priestly paraphernalia, and should have been ordained. The Holy Spirit identified John as a future prophet/preacher, and not as a Levitical priest. John the Baptist didn't give the outward appearance of having matriculated as a Levitical priest.[16] Section 84:28 of the Doctrine and Covenants claims that he was ordained by an angel of God when he was eight days old. The Bible does not assign his authority to an ordination by an angel of God.

Levites and Levitical Priesthood

"By what method or means were Oliver Cowdery and Joseph Smith (who were not sons of Aaron or Levi) qualified to receive the lineage-dependent Aaronic/Levitical Priesthood?" Such a result could simply not have occurred. In the Old Testament, God reminded the Israelites that "no stranger which is not of the seed of Aaron" should "come near to offer incense before the Lord, that he be not as Korah, and as his company . . ."[17] (by that to say swallowed by the earth for the abuse of Aaron's authority). In the Old Testament, it was not for Uzziah to burn incense unto the Lord, "but to the priests, the sons of Aaron, that are consecrated to burn incense . . . . (2 Chronicles 26:18)." Those who were not able to give evidence of their father's households, that is to say those unable to say "whether they were of Israel," and those who could not locate their ancestral registration, were considered unclean, "polluted, [and] put from the priesthood."[18] Most importantly, the original Christians firmly rejected ancient Israel's Aaronic/Levitical priests. "We have an altar," they said. The men who serve at the holy tent under the aegis of the Levitical order

---

[16]Sharon I. Banister, *For Any Latter-day Saint: One Investigator's Unanswered Questions* (Fort Worth, TX: Star Bible Publications, 1988), 43-44.

[17]Numbers 16:40.

[18]Numbers 16:40, 2 Chronicles 26:18, Ezra 2:59-62, referenced by Banister, *For Any Latter-day Saint*, 39. Bible version unknown.

"have *no* right to eat" at our altar. In other words, the descendants of Levi and Aaron had no lineal right "to partake of the Christian system."[19] Oliver Cowdery and Joseph Smith weren't sons of Levi in fact, nor either because of some perceived affinity, whether inherited or conferred.

Sharon I. Banister, a biblical scholar who has carefully studied the mysterious origins of the Mormon priesthood, carries that founding dilemma further to say: "Since God never made exceptions to the rule that only Aaron and his sons could be Levitical priests, how could Joseph Smith (a Gentile of English stock) qualify as a Levitical priest?"[20] In backdated entries to what some time later became Section 68 of the Doctrine and Covenants, entries added to the Mormon scripture in defiance of the uncorrupted text of the previously published original manuscript, an amended Lord is supposed to have said, "A literal descendant of Aaron 'may claim their anointing if at any time they can prove their lineage, or do ascertain it by revelation . . . .'"[21] Ms. Banister noted that, "Even if it were possible, what advantage would there be in tracing your lineage to a system of law (the Levitical Priesthood) which the Bible says 'was nailed to the cross?'"[22] Furthermore and importantly, no modern Jew "can trace his lineage back to Aaron" because the temple in Jerusalem and all of the records were destroyed in 70 A.D.[23] Joseph Smith claimed a mystical ancestral relationship with the Bible's patriarchal Joseph, the Son of Jacob, through Ephraim. But Joseph Smith was not a Levite, by either temporal or spiritual reckoning, or eligible by lineage to usurp the powers of those Levitical/Aaronic priests.

"Why would the Levitical priesthood be restored after Christ had 'become the guarantee of a better agreement?'"[24] Ms. Banister casts doubt upon the notion that the Levitical Priesthood was ever

---

[19]Banister, *For Any Latter-day Saint*, 42.
[20]Ibid., 39.
[21]Doctrine and Covenants 68:21.
[22]Banister, *For Any Latter-day Saint*, 39-40.
[23]Ibid., 40.
[24]Ibid.

restored: "If the Levitical Priesthood was brought back to this earth, why does the church not follow the priesthood rules: (1) the hereditary and physical qualifications (Leviticus 21), (2) the method for obtaining priests (Exodus 29, Leviticus 8), and (3) the age of priests (1 Chronicles 23)?"[25] Where is it said that "the Levitical priesthood was ever part of the first-century church"? It was not. When and where does the Bible say that John the Baptist was supposed to have been ordained? "The law appoints men as high priests . . . . But, *after* the law, God's vow came. It appointed the Son as High Priest."[26] "Thou art a priest for ever after the order of Melchisedec."[27] "By so much was Jesus made a surety of a better testament."[28]

Lucy Rocks the Boat

Lucy Mack Smith, Joseph Smith's mother, described the baptisms of Joseph and Oliver matter of factly, treating them as commanded but earthbound.

> *[O]ne morning . . . they sat down to their usual work when the first thing that presented itself to Joseph was a commandment from God that he and Oliver should repair to the water & each of them be baptized they immediately went down to the susquehana<h> river and obeyed the* comm[andment] *mandate given them through the urim and Thumim . . . .*[29]

By this time, after Oliver Cowdery came on board, what has been

---

[25]Ibid., 44.

[26]Ibid., 46-47, emphasis added.

[27]Hebrews 7:17.

[28]Ibid., 7:22.

[29]Lucy Smith's 1845 Manuscript History, Dan Vogel, ed., *Early Mormon Documents* (Salt Lake City: Signature Books, 1996), 1:381, emphasis added. "4 Nov. [1830]. Smith uses his white seer stone to dictate a revelation to Orson Pratt. This stone is often referred to as the 'Urim and Thummim.'" (Quinn, *Origins of Power*, 616).

called the Urim and Thummim was nothing more than Joseph's stone. Lucy's recitals were consistent with the first accepted non-angelic description of the baptism of Oliver Cowdery, the first exercise of authority described in the Book of Commandments four years later in 1833. Lucy's account, purporting to describe an 1829 event, was prepared in 1845 after the prophet's death in 1844. She didn't describe a heavenly messenger, angelic ordination by the laying on of hands, separate sets of messengers, or the hierarchical grant of authority.[30] Lucy's vision of Joseph and Oliver's authority was metaphysical. "They had now received authority to baptize . . . ."[31] They were instructed to proceed because of a command transmitted through Joseph's miraculous stone by means of the use of which it was said that he could see things invisible to the natural eye. Like a money digger or a fortune teller. Five (and-a-half) years after May 15, 1829, and in October 1834, "Smith and Cowdery would begin telling that their baptisms were preceded by the appearance of an angel who gave them authority. Even later, they [Cowdery first] would identify this angel as John the Baptist."[32] In Joseph's own particular case, he didn't specifically identify John the Baptist by name until 1838. Lucy Mack Smith reported that the two men found their "authority to baptize" in the "urim and Thumim," her name for the stone Joseph carried in his pocket.   Joseph and Oliver baptized each other in the "susquehana[h]," after which "they again went on with the translation as before . . . ."[33] "Smith's own mother made no

---

[30]Brigham Young, for obvious reasons, told the Latter-day Saints not to read Lucy Mack Smith's book. He encouraged the members of the Church to collect and destroy all of the copies of Joseph's mother's book.

[31]Lucy Mack Smith, *History,* 1845, Vogel, ed., *Early Mormon Documents,* 1:381.

[32]Dan Vogel, *Joseph Smith: The Making of a Prophet* (Salt Lake City: Signature Books, 2004), 306, emphasis added. "Smith's 1832 unpublished history mentioned 'the reception of the Holy Priesthood by the ministering of Angels.' However, one should not read a later understanding into what, at the time, meant authority generally derived from the appearances of various angels." (Ibid., 642 fn 9). This history failed to mention Melchizedek and was "a glancing reference at best." (Bushman, *Joseph Smith: Rough Stone Rolling,* 75).

[33]Vogel, ed., *Early Mormon Documents,* 1:381-82 (1845 Lucy Mack Smith Manuscript).

reference to [the] angelic restoration of authority in an 1831 letter she wrote to her brother about the new church."[34]

> *Until Cowdery's 1834 history [Oliver Cowdery and Joseph Smith's 1834-35 History] and retroactive [backdated] changes in the 1835 Doctrine and Covenants [Section 27], there was nothing in Mormonism to attract converts who expected a literal restoration of apostolic authority. Charisma and the voice of God were the only bases of authority that early Mormon converts knew until the publication of Cowdery's [Cowdery and Smith's] history in 1834.*[35]

"Charisma and the voice of God," the "only bases of authority" known to Mormon converts from 1829 until in or after 1834, kept the ship afloat but were far from exclusive. And in 1834 Joseph and Oliver retroactively dismissed those metaphysical concepts as having, or as ever having had, any efficacy, virtue or force. Why would converts have ever "expected a literal restoration of apostolic authority" by resurrected historical figures in any event? In the annals of the Hebrews, or of the Christians, when had there ever been a "literal restoration" of some previous but missing priesthood by some resurrected being? Where is any biblical precedent for some literal physical restoration of "apostolic authority" under the hands of heavenly messengers?

---

[34]Lucy Mack Smith to Solomon Mack, Jr., 6 Jan. 1831, quoted in Quinn, *Origins of Power*, 19.

[35]Quinn, *Origins of Power*, 32, emphasis added. The history described by Quinn and attributed by him to Cowdery, which is now recognized as the first "authorized" history of the Church of the Latter Day Saints, was prepared under the direct personal supervision of Joseph Smith, and at the Mormon prophet's request. It was recorded in Smith's journal and treated as Smith's work. Cowdery had no independent access (other than Smith) to that history's highly personal details. The participation of Smith in the preparation of this earliest commissioned account, as Cowdery faithfully reported, was "indispensible." Smith arranged to publish (and then to republish) this exceedingly important early account (without any thought of correction). The 1834 History (and its authors) dismissed charisma and the voice of God as less than legitimate subjective sources of divine authority.

David Whitmer, Joseph, Oliver, and Baptism

David Whitmer[36] corroborated the details of an unembellished baptism event when that event was first described in terms similar to those propounded by Joseph's mother after the prophet's death. Whitmer's account, like Lucy Mack Smith's account, didn't describe a heavenly messenger. The Book of Mormon witness contradicted those greatly more glorious accounts offered years after-the-fact in altered documents by Joseph Smith and Oliver Cowdery.[37] When David Whitmer moved Joseph Smith and Oliver Cowdery from Harmony, Pennsylvania, to the home of the Whitmers in Fayette, New York, in that particularly meaningful month of June 1829, Mormonism's founders didn't mention John the Baptist, Peter, James, and John, or call the society's authority "priesthood."

Having received his information directly from Joseph Smith and Oliver Cowdery, Whitmer repeated Lucy Mack Smith's assertion "that they were commanded" to baptize each other "by revealment through Joseph."[38] Such authority as they then had came by way of instructions received through the stone Joseph used to see things invisible to the natural eye. Thus charisma and the voice of God, resources Oliver Cowdery and Joseph Smith later impugned, were the only sources of authority known to David Whitmer until 1834 or 1835. Whitmer, like Joseph's mother, treated the baptismal event as commanded but earthbound. He didn't believe that Joseph and Oliver received the priesthood from heavenly messengers. He

---

[36]Whitmer was one of the Three Witnesses to the Book of Mormon. His brother, John Whitmer, another Book of Mormon witness but not one of the three, was the scribe for many of the early revelations and the Church's first historian. In 1834 David Whitmer was ordained to be a "seer and revelator," like Joseph Smith and in his own right. On July 8, 1834, Joseph Smith set David Whitmer apart as the President of the Church in the land of Zion, Mormonism's important Missouri.

[37]"David Whitmer told Zenas H. Gurley he had heard nothing of John the Baptist until four years after the Church's organization" (which was about five and one-half years after the alleged event). (Interview with Zenas H. Gurley, 14 Jan. 1885, Vogel, ed., *Early Mormon Documents*, 5:137).

[38]Ibid.

believed, because they said, that they received their authority through the spirit by way of command. According to a revelation "given to David" (one of the founding fathers) in June 1829, he had a gift and a calling to "*stand as a witness of the things of which you shall both hear and see . . . .*"[39] In his approach to these issues of authority, he said what he both heard and saw.

Other Accounts

Joseph Knight Sr., Joseph Smith's early dependable money-digging ally, is another insider who knew nothing about the heavenly messenger theory of priesthood. "About 1833 Knight wrote a history of important events of Mormonism up to that year. Knight's history made no reference to either John the Baptist or to Peter, James, and John. This omission is significant because Knight was eager to discuss angelic ministrations. His history is the only Mormon source for details of the angel Moroni's annual visits with Smith from 1823 to 1827."[40] Oliver and Joseph's disclosure of an 1829 ordination in the history they joined to prepare many years after the fact, "far from being a simple reminder of what had been related in the past, was surprising news to Missouri Mormons."[41] David Whitmer didn't know that any such events were supposed to

---

[39]David Whitmer's respected status as one of Mormonism's most important early stalwarts is reflected in a revelation received at Fayette, New York, in June 1829, one month after Oliver and Joseph baptized each other, but before the publication of the Book of Mormon. "And it shall come to pass, that if you [David Whitmer] shall ask the Father in my name, in faith believing, you shall receive the Holy Ghost, which giveth utterance, that you may stand as a witness of the things of which you shall both hear and see; and also, that you may declare repentance unto this generation." (Book of Commandments 12:4). The promise was that he could receive the gift of the Holy Ghost, and the power to stand as a witness, upon request without the laying on of hands.

[40]Quinn, *Origins of Power*, 20.   Knight's favored status as a friend of Mormonism's founder was further reflected in the fact that he was a houseguest of the Smiths on September 22, 1827, the day that Joseph Smith claimed to have obtained the golden plates.

[41]Vogel, *Joseph Smith: The Making of a Prophet*, 306.

have occurred; nor did Joseph Knight or William E. McLellin.[42] Whitmer and McLellin later left the Church, citing issues with priesthood. They were eyewitnesses to the alterations of the earlier published contents of no less than a dozen revelations published in the Book of Commandments in 1833 that came to rest as modified ("mutilated," "mixed-up," "bungled") in the first edition of the Doctrine and Covenants in 1835.

MELCHIZEDEK PRIESTHOOD

In the beginning, in its formative decade and/or later, the Church instructed its members that Joseph Smith and Oliver Cowdery were generally believed to have received the "Melchisedek Priesthood" in "June or July, 1829."[43] Apostle Bruce R. McConkie, the author of *Mormon Doctrine*, the man who grabbed the iron rod, was sure of it. "In June, 1829," he said, "by divine appointment, Peter, James, and John came to Joseph Smith and Oliver Cowdery and conferred upon them the Melchisedek Priesthood (D&C 27:12-13)."[44] The modern Church, like the theologian, ever more certain with the passage of time, now reports that the restoration of the Melchisedek Priesthood occurred in "*1829, May-June.*"[45] In the 1914 second edition of the *Church Chronology*, it was reported that, "Joseph Smith, jun., and Oliver Cowdery being desirous to obtain the Melchisedec Priesthood which had been promised them by John the Baptist, engaged in 'solemn and fervent prayer,' at Fayette, when 'the word of the Lord came,' commanding them to ordain each other. But they were to wait for this ordination till the others who had been baptized assembled together."[46] Joseph, the second elder to be ordained, became the "First Elder"; Oliver, the first elder to

---

[42]McLellin's ordination as a member and a secretary of the founding Quorum of the Twelve Apostles, and the cynical reworking of many of the revelations previously published in the (1833) Book of Commandments, were both 1835 events.

[43]Jenson, comp., *Church Chronology*, xxii.

[44]McConkie, *Mormon Doctrine*, 2d ed. (1966), 478.

[45]*Teachings of Presidents of The Church – Joseph Smith* (2007), xv (Historical Summary), emphasis added.

[46]Jenson, comp., *Church Chronology*, 4.

be ordained, became the "Second Elder."[47] They didn't wait. They ordained each other and others before the Church was officially formed.

Documentation of the Melchizedek Event

The events surrounding the alleged visit of Peter, James, and John are thinly documented. There is an Aaronic Priesthood restoration prayer,[48] and there is an altered Aaronic Priesthood restoration prayer,[49] but there is no Melchizedek Priesthood prayer, original or falsified. Furthermore, Joseph and Oliver didn't ever assign a specific date or time to an encounter with Peter, James, and John. In a controversial amendment to an altered revelation, Section 50 of the 1835 edition of the Doctrine and Covenants (later reordered to become Section 27) – an emendation that disfigured the previously published Chapter 28 of the 1833 Book of Commandments – there is a retroactive, backdated reference to a time when Peter, James, and John "ordained you and confirmed you to be apostles, and especial witnesses of my name . . . ."[50] This demonstrably altered revelation, principally cited by Bruce R. McConkie, Richard L. Bushman and the *Church Chronology*, a section now exposed for its duplicity, emphasized the apostleship.

Joseph Smith's *History of the Church*, six hefty volumes, contains thousands of pages of content and a voluminous index, much of it published in small print. Events of merely minor significance are described in extraordinary detail. But nowhere in those thousands of pages, the preparation of much of which was supposed to have been supervised by Joseph Smith prior to his death, and nowhere in that voluminous index does that massive history purport to say *when and just exactly where* the Melchizedek Priesthood was supposed to have been conferred upon Joseph Smith and Oliver

---

[47]Ibid., xxii.

[48]"Letter" (Cowdery and Smith's 1834-35 History), *Messenger and Advocate*, vol. 1 no. 1 (October 1834), 16.

[49]Doctrine and Covenants (1842), 13.

[50]Ibid., 27:12.

Cowdery by Peter, James, and John. And nowhere does that history, or any other history, purposefully describe the pertinent details of that "vague and contradictory" monumentally important encounter.

In the "Preface" to the 1830 first edition of the Book of Mormon, in the Articles and Covenants of the Church of Christ published in 1831, 1832 and 1833, and in the sixty-five revelations compiled and published in the *Book of Commandments* in 1833, nothing is found to describe John the Baptist or Peter, James, and John as figures important to the restoration of either of what only years later became two separate priesthoods. Those early resources do not differentiate between orders of priesthood each having different offices, powers and authorities. In consequence of such glaring omissions, Sharon I. Banister asks several important questions:

> *Can you explain why Doctrine and Covenants 13 (which tells of Joseph and Oliver's ordination to the Aaronic Priesthood in 1829) [the dramatically altered Aaronic Priesthood restoration prayer] was omitted from the 1833 Book of Commandments and not published [in the Doctrine and Covenants] until 1876? Since the date of the Book of Commandments [1833] encompassed the bestowals [restorations] of the two priesthoods [by modern Mormon reckoning "1829, May-June"], why are the notable revelations on the priesthood (Doctrine and Covenants 2 [1823], 13 [1829], and 68 [1831]) missing from the Book of Commandments?*
>
> *Can you explain why the Book of Commandments didn't tell of the restoration of the Priesthood which, if actual, had been known for four years at the time of publication?*[51]

---

[51]Banister, *For Any Latter-day Saint*, 51, emphasis retained.

The Night of the Revelation?

The details surrounding the supposed angelic restoration of the Melchizedek Priesthood are sparing, hard to find, easy to miss, awkward and unpersuasive. After Joseph Smith was acquitted in back-to-back South Bainbridge and Broome County (New York) trials, after the Book of Mormon was published, after the Church was organized and in July 1830, Joseph and Oliver traveled to Colesville, Broome County, New York, from their then home in Harmony, Pennsylvania, to confirm several new converts whose confirmations had been delayed by Joseph's Broome County legal proceedings.[52] At Colesville, when Joseph and Oliver found themselves confronted by a group of threatening detractors, they were forced to get away and travel all night "except [for] a short time, during which we were forced to rest . . . under a large tree by the way side, sleeping and watching alternately."[53] Joseph described a difficult trip without providing a date. Let it be repeated that Richard L. Bushman described that event in these terms:

> *It may have been on this occasion that Peter, James, and John appeared to Joseph and Cowdery and, as a later revelation said, "ordained you and confirmed you to be apostles, and especial witnesses of my name, and bear the keys of your ministry: and of the same things which I revealed unto them."*[54]

The way the sentence is phrased would seem to allow for some

---

[52]In the modern Church those able to confirm (meaning those able to confer the gift of the Holy Ghost by the laying on of hands) have first to hold the Melchizedek Priesthood.

[53]Joseph Smith, quoted in Bushman, *Joseph Smith: Rough Stone Rolling*, 118.

[54]Ibid., emphasis added. The revelation to which Bushman yet again refers when he says ("and, as a later revelation said") is the backdated Section 50 of the 1835 edition of the Doctrine and Covenants (now Section 27, the massively altered version of the previously published Chapter 28 of the 1833 Book of Commandments). Bushman doesn't attempt to explain the absence of any reference to Peter, James, and John in the original manuscript of this particularly troubled revelation. This convoluted 1835 passage has no archival provenance.

amendment if some resourceful scholar should ever be able to explain that Joseph and Oliver received the Melchizedek Priesthood at the hands of Peter, James, and John before the Church was officially organized. That, of course, is what the modern Church is forced to contend without support in the original manuscript of the biographer's "*later revelation*," and would, after the passage of much time and many efforts, appear to be quite impossible. Paraphrasing Christopher Hitchens, that which can be asserted without support can be dismissed without support. So it is with the Church's modern contention. In a 2007 study manual used by the Church all over the world, but in which the dates are fudged, there is no "*may have been*." With the passage of time, the deception has become expected and comfortable and settled in; every doubt has disappeared.

> *1829, May 15: With Oliver Cowdery [Joseph Smith] receives the Aaronic Priesthood from John the Baptist. Joseph and Oliver baptize one another in the Susquehanna River.*
>
> *1829, May-June: With Oliver Cowdery, [Joseph Smith] receives the Melchizedek Priesthood from the ancient Apostles Peter, James, and John near the Susquehanna River between Harmony, Pennsylvania, and Colesville, New York.*[55]

In the "Joseph Smith Chronology" at the front of his book, Bushman lists a visit by John the Baptist on May 15, 1829. He then further describes "Ordination to high priesthood" on *June 3, 1831*, but fails to mention "Peter, James and John."[56] It is immediately apparent that the scholar's chronology for the restoration of the "high priesthood" (*1831, June 3*) and the Church's chronology for the restoration of the "high priesthood" (*1829, May-June*) are seen to conflict. Bushman's chronology doesn't attempt to describe the

---

[55]*Teachings of Presidents of The Church – Joseph Smith* (2007), xv (Historical Summary), emphasis added.

[56]Bushman, *Joseph Smith: Rough Stone Rolling*, xiii, xiv, xv, emphasis added.

discrepancy, or the time and place of a visit from Peter, James, and John. On the basis of just such uncertainty, the Church is forced to make its less than impressive case for a before-the-Church-was-officially-formed restoration of the Holy Melchizedek priesthood.

> *Richard L. Bushman was the first Mormon historian to acknowledge these accounts [the South Bainbridge and Broome County trials ended on Thursday, 1 July 1830] suggesting a July 1830 date for the visitation of Peter, James, and John. Bushman's 1984 [first and earlier] biography of Smith concludes that the second priesthood restoration [by Peter, James, and John] occurred in the summer of 1830. He observes that a July 1830 appearance of Peter, James, and John is further supported by the first reference to their visit in the Doctrine and Covenants (D&C 27:12-13). In 1835 Smith chose to make this retroactive addition to the text of the [1830] revelation [previously published without that addition in "The Evening and the Morning Star" in 1833, and in the Book of Commandments in 1833] immediately following the revelation instructing him to travel to Colesville in July 1830. Bushman did not [then] discuss the significance of the date.*[57]

The revelations in the Book of Commandments, and in the original manuscripts found in facsimile form in the *Joseph Smith Papers*, are in chronological order. The "first reference" to the belated visit of Peter, James, and John was in the conspicuously altered Section 50 (now Section 27) of the 1835 edition of the Doctrine and Covenants. The retroactive 1835 amendment – the amendment that first mentioned Peter, James, and John restoring the priesthood – got (and to this day dishonestly retains) the benefit of the unamended original revelation's 1830 date.[58] Peter, James, and John were not

---

[57]Quinn, *Origins of Power*, 25-26, emphasis added.

[58]Doctrine and Covenants 27, dated August/September 1830. Chapter 28 (xxviii) of the Book of Commandments, which was altered by the inclusion of

mentioned in the original manuscript of the revelation when it was initially published in the Book of Commandments in 1833.[59] This deception, clearly known to scholars but used to the modern Church's advantage every day (consider its vitally important repeated use in the McConkie, Bushman and *Church Chronology* quotes), remains triumphant in its dishonest uncorrected place. It has been part of the Doctrine and Covenants, deceiving Latter-day Saints and their investigators every day all over the world, since 1835. The amendment has no archival provenance.

Blowing Smoke: Erastus Snow and Addison Everett

When Joseph Smith (Oliver Cowdery had been dismissed) revisited the restorations of the two priesthoods in 1838-39 and 1842 (privately in 1838-39, publicly in 1842), and when he personally assigned names to the messengers, he wasn't the same person he had been in 1829, and the Church was different. The 1842 public rendition of these significant events involved the yet further reconfiguration of the original documents.

Erastus Snow – who was baptized in 1833,[60] ordained an elder in 1835, made a high priest in 1839 and an apostle in 1849[61] – is a hearsay source for the dating and timing of the restoration of the Melchizedek Priesthood. Snow (although he was not an apostle during Joseph Smith's lifetime) described events supposed to have occurred in 1830 (after the Church was officially organized) and

---

unprovenanced amendments added to the Doctrine and Covenants in 1835, was first dated in the headnote as "September 4, 1830." Nevertheless, Bushman puts the date in August: "Joseph inserted the first reference to Peter, James, and John," he said, "in a revelation [Section 50, now Section 27] dated Aug. 1830." (Bushman, *Rough Stone Rolling*, 588). That doctored revelation ("the first reference to Peter, James, and John") is of first and primary importance to the case for the "restoration" of the Melchizedek Priesthood. It stands almost alone in support of the higher priesthood's thinly supported restoration claim.

[59]Book of Commandments 28.

[60]Snow was baptized about four years after the modern Church teaches that the Melchizedek priesthood was restored ("*1829, May-June*").

[61]Jenson, comp., *Church Chronology*, xxvii.

before June of 1831 (the date of the Fourth Conference in Kirtland, Ohio, when the authority of what still only later came to be called the Melchizedek Priesthood was conferred for the first time upon some of the elders). Erastus Snow was eleven years old in July 1830. Richard L. Bushman tells Snow's account:

> . . . *Peter, James, and John appeared to Joseph and Cowdery "at a period when they were being pursued by their enemies and they had to travel all night, and in the dawn of the coming day when they were weary and worn who should appear to them but Peter, James and John, for the purpose of conferring upon them the Apostleship, the keys of which they themselves had held while upon the earth, which had been bestowed, upon them by the Savior."*[62]

Erastus Snow was not a member of the Church in the summer of 1830, or any kind of a witness to anything just described. The Mormon historian appears to have permitted Erastus Snow to say what "Joseph and Cowdery" never publicly said to any known congregation of believers, or anywhere else in writing, without naming a source.

Addison Everett wrote a letter to Oliver B. Huntington in February of 1881, followed by another letter to Joseph F. Smith (a future President of the Mormon Church) in January of 1882, *in each case more than fifty years after the priesthood was supposed to have been restored.* Everett, an 1847 pioneer to the Great Basin, claimed to have *overheard* a conversation between Joseph Smith and his brother Hyrum. Everett "spoke of a trial involving Mr. Reed." "[T]he visit to Colesville, the trial, and the assistance of Mr. Reed are all well-attested occurrences in the summer of 1830."[63] In trying to escape a mob,

---

[62]Snow quoted in Bushman, *Joseph Smith: Rough Stone Rolling*, 118, emphasis added.
[63]Ibid.

Joseph & Oliver went to the woods in a few rods, it being night, and they traveled until Oliver was exhausted & Joseph almost Carried him through mud and water. They traveled all night and just at the break of day Olive[r] gave out entirely and exclaimed O! Lord! How long Brother Joseph have we got to endure this thing; Brother Joseph said that at that very time, Peter, James & John came to them and Ordained them to the Apostleship.[64]

The modern Church can not comfortably accept Addison Everett's fifty-year-after-the-fact reminiscence, the kind of a claim almost anyone could make, because it describes events supposed to have occurred after the Church was organized. The accounts of Snow and Everett, like the reports of the historians D. Michael Quinn and Richard L. Bushman, push the alleged visit of Peter, James, and John over to the summer months of 1830. Both of the witness accounts – unspecific as to Melchizedek and priesthood – describe the "Apostleship." We are left to infer that by that they may have meant by that some higher power. They seem to have taken their lead from similar representations found in the falsified Section 27, Section 50 of the first edition of the Doctrine and Covenants in 1835.

Time and Place Issues

While the Church cannot be certain in respect to its own unsupported calculation as to the precise time of the appearance of Peter, James, and John (beyond "*1829, May-June*"), it purports to be yet more certain that the great event occurred "near the Susquehanna River between Harmony, Pennsylvania, and Colesville, New York."[65] Late in his ministry (many years after the fact and in 1842), Smith publicly reported that he heard the "voice"

---

[64]Everett, quoted in Ibid., emphasis added.
[65]*Teachings of Presidents of The Church – Joseph Smith* (2007), xv (Historical Summary).

of Peter, James, and John "in the wilderness between Harmony, Susquehanna county, and Colesville, Broome county on the Susquehanna River."[66] He didn't say that he saw them or provide details. And he didn't mention a date or a prayer or describe an ordination.[67] On April 6, 1830 (the date of the founding), Joseph and Oliver, without mentioning the word ("priesthood"), *ordained* (in point of fact *reordained*) each other to office as elders. They were, as history soberly recounts, lower authority non-Melchizedek elders.

> *The "high priesthood" ([only later the] "order of Melchizedek") was introduced in June 1831, and it was not until September 1832 that the office of elder was linked to that priesthood. Rather, the restoration of the eldership was associated with the "word of the Lord" received in the chamber of Peter Whitmer Sr.'s house in Fayette, New York, in June, 1829.*[68]

In the beginning, Joseph and Oliver's non-exclusive authority was linked to charisma and the voice of God. Dan Vogel: "[T]here is good reason to date the origin of the angelic visitation to early July 1830, although the identities of the three angels and the purpose of their appearance would remain unclear until 1835."[69] High priesthood power assigned to non-Melchizedek elders is supposed to

---

[66]Joseph Smith to the Church of Jesus Christ of Latter Day Saints, 6 September 1842, *Times and Seasons* (Nauvoo, IL), 3 (1 Oct. 1842), 936, Vogel, ed., *Early Mormon Documents*, 1:177; cf. Doctrine and Covenants 128:20, quoted in Vogel, *Joseph Smith: The Making of a Prophet*, 520.

[67]" . . . And again, what do we hear? . . . The voice of Peter, James, and John, in the wilderness between Harmony, Susquehanna county and Colesville, Broom[e] county on the Susquehanna River, declaring themselves as possessing the keys of the kingdom, and of the dispensation of the fulness of times." (Joseph Smith, letter to the Church, 6 Sept. 1842, Vogel, ed., *Early Mormon Documents*, 1:177, canonized at Doctrine and Covenants 128:20-21).

[68]Vogel, *Joseph Smith: The Making of a Prophet*, 520. "If the office of an elder comes under the Melchizedek Priesthood and that priesthood was not given until June 1831 [or "linked to that priesthood" until September 1832], on what basis did elders exist in the church its first year [or years]?" (Banister, *For Any Latter-day Saint*, 50).

[69]Vogel, *Joseph Smith: The Making of a Prophet*, 520.

have first occurred at the Fourth Conference of the Church held at Kirtland, Ohio, in June 1831.[70] Joseph Smith was ordained to the high priesthood under the hands of Elder Lyman Wight on June 3, 1831. Addison Everett's reminiscence purports to provide perspective and texture to time and place.[71] Joseph and Oliver were said to have escaped from a mob with the help of attorney John Reed, who supposedly opened a window "in the back of the courthouse" after a trial, and directed them to flee into the woods. An account of their journey passed to posterity in Everett's 1882 letter to Joseph F. Smith as Mormonism struggled more than five decades later to provide evidence in support of the high priesthood restoration event. In his 1882 letter to Smith, Everett provided these additional details: That they were given "the keys of the dispensation of the fullness of times," that they were sixteen or seventeen miles from home (Harmony, Pennsylvania), that brother Oliver got his second wind after the "Endowment" ["Apostleship"], and that he (Everett) heard "the name of the banks of the Susquehanna river spoken of."[72] As to the time, a desperately obvious concern in 1882, Everett could not be "very exact."[73]

HOW MANY PRIESTHOODS DO THE SAINTS REQUIRE?

In their *1834-35 History* published in installments starting in October 1834, Oliver Cowdery and Joseph Smith opened the page on angelic ordination and the lineal priesthood of the old law. In that the founders (after December 1834 they were "the presidents of this church"[74]) first described the power and authority of only one heavenly messenger. "[W]hat joy filled our hearts . . . when we

---

[70]Bushman, *Joseph Smith: Rough Stone Rolling*, xiii (Chronology).

[71]Vogel, *Joseph Smith: The Making of a Prophet*, 520.

[72]Ibid., emphasis added.

[73]Addison Everett Accounts, 1881 & 1882, Vogel, ed., *Early Mormon Documents*, 1:196-203, quoted in Vogel, *Joseph Smith: The Making of a Prophet*, 520.

[74]Oliver Cowdery (and Joseph Smith), "Letter III To W.W. Phelps, Esq." (Oliver Cowdery and Joseph Smith's 1834-35 History), *Messenger and Advocate*, vol. 1 no. 3 (December 1834): 42.

received under *his* hand *the holy priesthood*, as *he* said, 'upon you my fellow servants, in the name of Messiah *I confer this priesthood and this authority*, which shall remain upon earth that the sons of Levi may yet offer an offering unto the Lord in righteousness.'"[75] The Sons of Levi were the failed executors of the less than eternal Aaronic/Levitical Priesthood known in its time, and in ancient Israel, as the law of a carnal commandment. The title suggests that law was not eternal.

There are in all of that lessons to be learned. *This history (the 1834-35 History) contains "[t]he first evidence of angelic restoration in public discussion . . . ."*[76] The founders' five-year-after-the-fact first report is nothing more than a tardy unsupported claim. This contention was not publicly described in any known sermon, periodical, prayer, meeting, revelation or scripture over the period from May 15, 1829, to in and after October 1834. That kind of silence in the private and public deliberations of the leaders and members would be exceedingly difficult to ever achieve.

"This [Oliver and Joseph's 1834-35 First Authorized History] was the first time the Mormons learned that a heavenly conferral of authority occurred before the church's organization." The 1834-35 History, the first "full history of the rise of the church of the Latter Day Saints," describes the "restoration of only one priesthood"[77] ("I confer *this* priesthood and *this* authority . . ."). It not only fails to mention "dual priesthoods of different ranks," it fails to mention Peter, James, and John, and more egregious yet, that great First Vision of the Father and the Son. The *1834-35 History* retroactively "confirms the idea of one priesthood at the church's organization and indirectly suggests that Smith and he [Cowdery] had not yet encountered, Peter, James, and John or the 'higher' priesthood in April 1830." Furthermore, the unitary priesthood the founders reportedly "received under his hands," the hands of a single

---

[75]"Letter" (Cowdery and Smith's 1834-35 History), *Messenger and Advocate*, vol. 1 no. 1 (October 1834), 15-16, emphasis added.

[76]Quinn, *Origins of Power*, 15, emphasis added.

[77]Ibid., emphasis added.

messenger, was called "the Holy Priesthood."[78]   "By later
definitions only the Melchizedek priesthood was 'the Holy
Priesthood' (DC 84:25-27)."[79]   That suggests (in addition to
confusion) that in October 1834 (nearly five-and-a-half years after
May 15, 1829), Joseph and Oliver appeared to have settled on but
one authoritative unitary high priesthood, everything they thought
they then required. Everything after that must seem to have been
the product of some *even later* design.

In and/or after 1834, when John the Baptist is first reported to have
conferred *"this priesthood and this authority"* upon Oliver and
Joseph, Mormonism's "authority-principle" became identified with
the lineal priesthood of the old law, meaning by that ancient Israel's
law of a carnal commandment, the Aaronic/Levitical priesthood.
What was supposed to have happened on May 15, 1829, was
explained one way, John the Baptist out of the loop, until October
1834, and another way, John the Baptist in the loop, after October
1834. Until October 1834, Mormonism's visible authority principle
was totally dependent upon charisma and the voice of God. After
October 1834, the society's retroactive reliance upon heavenly
messengers and angelic ordination was almost immediately seen to
become complete and entire. While early Mormonism's relaxed
egalitarian "authority" was initially recognized, the "impressive,
unique and physical" source of its literal lineage-based successor
was initially not. Who knew that John the Baptist had been
personally present when Joseph and Oliver baptized each other in
1829, until Joseph and Oliver either abandoned or altered earlier
narratives in and/or after October 1834 to say that he was. Oliver,
separately (meaning not in the published text of the *1834-35
History*), but later, specifically identified the heavenly messenger (in
1834-35) as John the Baptist. Not until 1838 did Joseph Smith
specifically say, outside of the earlier history and for himself, that
the heavenly messenger had actually been John the Baptist.

---

[78]Ibid.
[79]Ibid., 16.

Furthermore, no one is known to have known, even in October 1834, that there was supposed to have already been a second angelic ordination to yet another and higher priesthood, a mysterious kind of high authority first recognized in insufficient perplexing unprovenanced detail in June 1831, under the hands of the Savior's ancient apostles, Peter, James, and John. By 1835, after the publication of the October 1834 segment of the 1834-35 History and the separate identification of the messenger, accounts of a second priesthood restoration began to appear.[80] The evolution of the uneven process now began to assume a more definitive form. An apprehensive David Whitmer watched these belated disclosures begin to change the previously accepted charismatic principle. "This matter of the two orders of priesthood in the Church of Christ, and lineal priesthood of the old law being in the church, all originated," according to Whitmer, "in the mind of Sidney Rigdon."[81] *In the mind of Sidney Rigdon!* Whitmer had problems with the concept of simultaneous priesthoods, the ordination of high priests (Christ alone was worthy), and with the unfathomable restoration of the poorly regarded less-than-eternal unimportant "lineal priesthood of the old law."

"[W]hen Christ came into the world, he . . . claimed his own holy order of priesthood . . . doing away with all types and shadows under the old law . . . ." He then became "our great and last High Priest . . . ."[82] So thought David Whitmer, so thought the Apostle Paul, so thinks traditional Christianity. There was no Levitical Priesthood in the Christian system in the gospel church in the Old World, and there was no Levitical Priesthood in the Christian system in the Nephite church in the New World. Because Joseph and Oliver were not lineage-eligible sons of a lineage-dependent Levi by any genetic or other supernal reckoning, and because the early Christians thoughtfully dismissed the Levitical order, the law of a carnal commandment, the lineal priesthood of the old law, was

---

[80]Ibid.

[81]David Whitmer, *An Address to All Believers in Christ: by A Witness to the Divine Authenticity of The Book of Mormon* (Richmond, MO: n.p., 1887; photographic reprint, Concord, CA: Pacific Publishing Company, 1993), 64.

[82]Ibid., 67.

a pig in a Christian poke. What place does ancient Israel's written order – the preparatory gospel, the law of animal sacrifice, the tutorial authority (anticipating Christ), a lesser law for a lesser people – have in the Savior's new and enlightened, greater, kinder, gentler regime? That oppressive law, intended to govern a rebellious people at a time when God considered them "naught," was dead to Christians in Christ, nailed by God to the cross.[83] Not eternal, not valued, and nothing to be restored.

Jesus didn't appear to intend that the law of the Levitical Priesthood, the burdensome codification of ancient Jewish ritual, should continue to oppress those disciples who separated themselves from the old order and the Hebrews in order to follow "the holy order of the Son of God." That which Christ and his followers dismissed as tired, old and unworthy, Joseph Smith and Sidney Rigdon inexplicably chose to "restore." What Christ and Paul and Nephi were seen to reject, Smith and Rigdon were seen to embrace. It was never intended that the lineal priesthood of the less-than-eternal old law should somehow survive the emergence of "the holy order of the Son of God." *For Christ was not made "after the law of a carnal commandment, but after the power of an endless life."*[84] That alone should sink the Aaronic/Levitical ship. The Savior's system was without beginning or end eternal. The less than eternal law of a carnal commandment – administered by less than eternal priests (men defined by lineage, mother, father, death and descent) – did not become eternal by revelatory fiat in and/or after 1834. *"For there is verily a disannulling of the commandment going before for the weakness and unprofitableness thereof."*[85] Jesus oversaw "the bringing in of a better hope."[86]

What Christ and those who followed him dismissed, no one should have thought to "restore." The "schooling" ministry, a flawed and temporary response to an ancient problem, was a burr on the

---

[83]Colossians 2:14.
[84]Hebrews 7:16, emphasis added.
[85]Ibid., 7:18, emphasis added.
[86]Ibid., 7:19. "By so much was Jesus made a surety of a better testament." (Hebrews 7:22).

Messiah's saddle and a curse to the Apostle Paul. To represent that that ancient discredited order should be eternal in order that the unidentifiable descendants of the rigid ideologues of antiquity could yet make peace with their maker ("that the sons of Levi may yet offer an offering unto the Lord in righteousness!") is beyond preposterous. That postulate, which is canonized in the Doctrine and Covenants (D&C 84:18), is awkward and unconvincing. Given his New Testament feelings about the ancient priestly caste and its primitive authority principle, the Lord could not have entertained the perpetuation of the flawed and failing lineal priesthood of the old law. The concept of the restoration of that failed order was fatally flawed. Dead upon delivery.

THE "RESTORATION" OF THE LOWER PRIESTHOOD

The operative principle of the modern Mormon priesthood, quoting the Apostle Paul, is that, "No man taketh this honor unto himself, but he that is called of God, as was Aaron." "The remarks of Paul concerning high priests are applicable [by modern Mormon reckoning] to every office of the Priesthood."[87] The precise claim of the modern Church to an entry-level authority may be correctly stated as follows:

> On May 15, 1829, while Joseph Smith and Oliver Cowdery were engaged in earnest prayer for instruction concerning baptism for the remission of sins, mention of which Joseph Smith had found in the plates from which he was then engaged in translating the Book of Mormon, a messenger from heaven descended in a cloud of light. He announced himself as John, called of old the Baptist, and said he had

---

[87]James E. Talmage, *A Study of the Articles of Faith: Being a Consideration of the Principal Doctrines of The Church of Jesus Christ of Latter-day Saints*, 24th ed. (Salt Lake City: The Church of Jesus Christ of Latter-day Saints), 186 (citing Heb. 5:4).

come under the direction of Peter, James, and John,
who held the keys of the higher Priesthood.[88]

If this is true, as just stated by one of Mormonism's preeminent scholars, it may be said that on May 15, 1829, Joseph and Oliver knew (1) the identity of the "messenger from heaven" – John the Baptist; (2) that there were higher and lower priesthoods; (3) that John the Baptist held the lower priesthood; (4) that John the Baptist had come under the direction of Peter, James, and John; (5) that John the Baptist could baptize for the remission of sins; and (6) that Peter, James, and John held the keys of the higher priesthood.

More than five years after the alleged occurrence of this only later recorded event, and in Oliver and Joseph's "full" first "authorized" history of the "rise" of the Church (published as eight carefully drafted installments in the *Messenger and Advocate* in 1834 and 1835) – the history which first identified *a* heavenly messenger (priesthood restoration and angelic ordination) – the two elders failed to mention a vision of God the Father and Jesus, a visit by Peter, James, and John, or dual priesthoods of different ranks. They didn't say the messenger said that he had come under the direction of Peter, James, and John, or that Peter, James, and John held the keys of some second and higher priesthood. In the recently published *Joseph Smith Papers*, which contain the original manuscript for what has become Doctrine and Covenants Section 27 – a manuscript first published in 1833 as Chapter 28 of the Book

---

[88]Ibid., 188, emphasis added. Brigham Young taught the Latter-day Saints that: "You could not legally baptize a second person for the remission of sins until some person *first* baptized you and ordained you to this authority." (*Discourses of Brigham Young*, selected and arranged by John A. Widtsoe [Salt Lake City: Deseret Book Company, 1925], 160, quoted in Banister, *For Any Latter-day Saint*, 41). Thus in the Church, according to Young, an unbaptized person, even if ordained, couldn't baptize others. If that was so, as Joseph's successor reported, Oliver Cowdery's baptism at the hands of an unbaptized Joseph could not have been valid. (Banister, *For Any Latter-day Saint*, 41, 42). The heavenly messenger allegedly ordained (but did not baptize) Mormonism's founders. Young's order of events is seen to have been reversed.

of Commandments – there are no references to Peter, James, and John, or to any higher priesthood.[89]

Now Mormon scholar James E. Talmage describes the mechanics of the conferral of the priesthood upon Joseph Smith and Oliver Cowdery as supposed to have occurred on May 15, 1829.

> *The angel [John the Baptist] laid his hands upon the two young men and ordained them to authority, saying: "Upon you my fellow servants in the name of Messiah I confer the Priesthood of Aaron, which holds the keys of the ministering of angels, and of the gospel of repentance, and of baptism by immersion for the remission of sins; and this shall never be taken again from the earth, until the sons of Levi do offer again an offering unto the Lord in righteousness." (D&C 13).*[90]

If this had all happened exactly as the scholar said, then from that moment these two men knew (1) that they had the "Priesthood of Aaron" (the Aaronic Priesthood), (2) that the priesthood they had was the lower priesthood, (3) that the authority they had received allowed them to baptize by immersion for the remission of sins; (4) that they didn't have the higher priesthood held by Peter, James, and John, or the keys to the higher priesthood held by Peter, James, and John, and (5) that the Aaronic Priesthood, the law of a carnal commandment, the lineal priesthood of the old law, would never again be taken from the earth "until the sons of Levi" offered an offering unto the Lord in righteousness.[91] The priesthood of Aaron

---

[89] *The Joseph Smith Papers: Revelations and Translations: Manuscript Revelation Books, Facsimile Edition*, ed. Robin Scott Jensen, Robert J. Woodford, and Steven C. Harper (Salt Lake City: Church Historian's Press, 2009), 40-43.

[90] Talmage, *A Study of the Articles of Faith*, 24th ed., 188, emphasis added.

[91] The Aaronic Priesthood, administered by Levitical priests, found no place in the Christian system in the community of Christ. Brigham Young visited this incongruity: "Then why was the law of Moses given? In consequence of the disobedience of the children of Israel, the elect of God . . . This seed of Abraham so rebelled against him and his commands that the Lord said to Moses, 'I will give

("the law of carnal commandments"), the carnal law, was, in all of this, envisioned as eternal.

Despite Apostle Talmage's disingenuous description of the altered prayer (D&C 13), first published in a Mormon source in 1842, and his calculated avoidance of the original and unaltered prayer, first published in Joseph and Oliver's authorized history in 1834, it should be perfectly clear that Joseph Smith and Oliver Cowdery didn't know those things on May 15, 1829. For years after that alleged ordination, and until at least 1834, they treated "this authority" – not yet called "Aaronic" authority, and not yet identified with John the Baptist or the lineal priesthood of the old law – as unitary, as "*this* priesthood and *this* authority." Furthermore, they baptized and confirmed members of the Church, bestowed the gift of the Holy Ghost and ordained presiding officials without differentiation of priesthoods.

Not until 1835 does the "Distinction between the Aaronic and Melchizedek Priesthoods" appear to become firmly clarified in Mormon theology. "But there are two divisions or grand heads – one is the Melchizedek Priesthood and the other is the Aaronic or Levitical Priesthood."[92] Not until this revelation, first published as Section 107 of the Doctrine and Covenants in 1835, were the Latter Day Saints unmistakably apprised that what they had long called "authority," then only later called "priesthood" (generic unitary "priesthood"), was actually something called the "Aaronic Priesthood," an order of authority more precisely identified as ancient Israel's law of a carnal commandment. "The second priesthood is called the Priesthood of Aaron because it was conferred upon Aaron and his seed, throughout all their generations."[93] "So far as can be told now, before 1831, men were called to church offices – elders, priests, and teachers – given

---

you a law which shall be a schoolmaster to bring them to Christ. But this law is grievous; it is a law of carnal commandments.'" (*Discourses of Brigham Young*, 160). The law of carnal commandments, which Brigham labeled as "grievous," was superceded in Christ. It wasn't lost; it was dismissed.
[92]Doctrine and Covenants, 107:6.
[93]Ibid., 107:13.

authority and licensed without reference to a bestowal of priesthood."[94] And until 1831 the term "priesthood" (as opposed to the term "authority") wasn't used.

Documentation

Before several different committees bastardized the 1833 Book of Commandments – sixty-five revelations which said nothing about Aaron, Levi, John the Baptist, visions of the deities, angelic ordination or the restoration of the priesthood – before Joseph and his associates backdated and altered various previously published revelations and documents, and until October 1834, Mormonism's authority principle, charisma and the voice of God, was unexceptional. "[P]ublic claims for authority in the church were made largely on the basis of religious experience and charisma rather than priestly power through lineage and angelic ministration."[95] Apostles (there were apostles) weren't ordained until 1835. Until 1835 the word "apostle" was basically used to designate unordained charisma. Mormonism's opening case for power, whatever the founders said in 1834, was conventional, unitary and non-exclusive. The founders didn't act like men who secretly knew they had been ordained by angels and apostles.

The Book of Commandments (in press in July 1833),[96] meaning published four years after "*1829, May-June*" failed to describe the first "priesthood of Aaron." The authority principle the Book of Commandments did describe was charismatic and metaphysical. An early revelation (Book of Commandments 15, June 1829), described another path to power, a more conventional path to power that left John the Baptist out of the loop. In what was the

---

[94]Bushman, *Joseph Smith: Rough Stone Rolling*, 157-58.

[95]Quinn, *Origins of Power*, 7.

[96]"Behold, this is mine authority, and the authority of my servants, and my Preface unto the Book of my Commandments, which I have given them to publish unto you, O inhabitants of the earth: – Wherefore fear and tremble, O ye people for what I the Lord have decreed, in them, shall be fulfilled . . . ." (Book of Commandments, Chapter 1:2).

first Mormon reference to the subject of authority, Joseph's Lord recognized the verbal conferral of power by less than literal physical means. The revelation didn't describe the "priesthood," or even use the word. Joseph didn't, Oliver didn't, David Whitmer didn't, and neither did Joseph's mother. There was no "[i]n the middle of the prayer, in the brightness of day"[97] in this equation in the Book of Commandments in June 1829, and it was not so "easily" seen that no one "had authority from God to administer the ordinances of the gospel," a retroactive claim first made (then dutifully applied) in and after 1834.[98] At no time before 1834, a full five years after a revelation that praised Joseph (and not some heavenly messenger) for doing what God required (the baptism of Oliver Cowdery), did anyone see or say that they saw "a messenger from heaven descended in a cloud of light"[99] to deliver in some unprecedented way some heavenly-based authority.

When Joseph – who told a different story of the 1829 baptism in the 1834-35 History he worked with Oliver to prepare – told the story yet again in 1838-39, this time without the excommunicated counterfeiter's dependable assistance, he identified John the Baptist (for Joseph for the first time by name) as a messenger sent under the direction of Peter, James, and John, and provided the date of the visit (May 15, 1829). In the October 1834 installment of Oliver and Joseph's 1834-35 History, the heavenly messenger didn't mention Peter, James, and John, the "Priesthood of Aaron," "the keys of the ministring of angels," "the gospel of repentance," "baptism by immersion for the remission of sins,"[100] or two separate priesthoods. The 1834 Account mentioned only one priesthood (*"this priesthood and this authority"*) and only one messenger. In 1838-39, in materials that weren't published until 1842, the original message was altered to become "more impressive,

---

[97]Bushman, *Joseph Smith: Rough Stone Rolling*, 74.
[98]"Letter" (Cowdery and Smith's 1834-35 History), *Messenger and Advocate*, vol. 1 no. 1 (October 1834), 15.
[99]Bushman, *Joseph Smith: Rough Stone Rolling*, 74.
[100]Doctrine and Covenants 13 (canonized in 1876).

unique and physical."[101]

John the Baptist's Aaronic Priesthood restoration prayer was described one way in the history prepared by Cowdery and Smith in 1834-35, and another way in the history prepared by Joseph Smith, Sidney Rigdon, George W. Robinson and James Mulholland in 1838-39. The 1838-39 recklessly altered recounting of the Aaronic Priesthood prayer wasn't published in the *Times and Seasons* until 1842 or added to the Doctrine and Covenants until 1876. It took a long time to find a comfortable place in the scheme of things. The 1834-35 History's unamended prayer, Oliver and Joseph's first and most contemporaneous version of the restoration prayer – although published in the *Messenger and Advocate* in 1834, and in a note at the end of an excerpt of the Joseph Smith History in the Pearl of Great Price in 1851[102] – would never be faithfully recorded in the Doctrine and Covenants, or treated as the most contemporaneous foundational narrative it actually was.

The disingenuous 1838-39 amended prayer has graced the canonized pages of the Doctrine and Covenants as Section 13 since 1876. The substantive retroactive alterations of the "ministring" prayer concerned issues no less important than "greater" and "lesser" rather than "unitary" priesthood. The prayer reported in the *1834-35 History* spoke of "*this* priesthood and *this* authority"; the 1842 revision, although based upon the prayer in the *1834-35 History*, described the lesser "Priesthood of Aaron." The clumsy amendments made to the original Aaronic Priesthood restoration prayer, when added to the Doctrine and Covenants nearly fifty years after May 15, 1829, changed history in order to describe "dual priesthoods of different ranks." The 1838-39 altered backdated recounting, although seriously substantively amplified, was clearly based upon the founders' more sparing 1834-35 First Authorized History Account. The later account, when first

---

[101]Grant H. Palmer, *An Insider's View of Mormon Origins* (Salt Lake City: Signature Books, 2002), 232.
[102]The Pearl of Great Price, Joseph Smith – History, note 1-7.

published in 1842, was at odds with the manuscript, and the two disparate accounts are incompatible.

Joseph Smith publicly identified an angelic messenger and "an angelic conferral of authority" when the Kirtland High Council was organized in February 1834. In that particular account he "gave early Mormons no reason to look beyond the angel Moroni for that unnamed angel's identity. About eight months later Cowdery announced that the messenger had actually been John the Baptist."[103] That disclosure, which was separate from the 1834-35 History and attributable to Cowdery, could not have occurred without the consent of Joseph Smith. That notwithstanding, "There is no record of Smith giving further details about angelic ordinations [beyond the 1834-35 History, where the messenger wasn't specifically identified by name] until he began his expanded historical narrative in 1838."[104] Smith didn't specifically separately identify "John the Baptist" by name in 1834-35, or until 1838 or 1839, nine or ten years after "*1829, May-June.*"

In *1838-39* Joseph Smith changed the founders' earlier story to say that John the Baptist had "*acted under the direction of Peter, James and John who held the keys of the Priesthood of Melchizedek, which Priesthood he said would in due time be conferred upon us . . . .*"[105] Why would Joseph's Lord be reluctant to let it be known that two separate orders of priesthood had been restored to the earth if that had been the Master's original divine intent? In those discussions with the Kirtland High Council in February 1834, Smith described "the dignity of the office which has been conferred upon me by the ministring of the Angel of God by his own will and by the voice of this Church." In that he mentioned but one unidentified angel "as the agent of restoration."[106] The disclosure concerned "the dignity

---

[103]Quinn, *Origins of Power*, 21.

[104]Ibid.

[105]Joseph Smith Jr., *History of The Church of Jesus Christ of Latter-day Saints*, B.H. Roberts, ed., 2d ed., rev., (Salt Lake City: The Deseret Book Company, 1978), 1:40.

[106]In 1832 Smith mentioned (in an account he didn't publish) "the reception of the holy Priesthood by the ministring of _Aangels_ to administer the letter of the

of the office," not the nature of the priesthood or the restoration of the apostleship. When the two founders published their 1834-35 History in the *Messenger and Advocate* in October 1834, they described only one unidentified messenger and said nothing about Peter, James, and John.

The foundational narratives had a "ripe" form. "Joseph did not tell anyone about John the Baptist at first."[107] He didn't announce the miraculous version (the retroactive 1834 version) of the May 15, 1829, event to his family, to his friends, or to the members of the Church until October 1834. On April 6, 1830, the day the Church was organized, Smith didn't mention a vision of the deities, angelic ordination, John the Baptist, Peter, James, and John, "priesthood" or "priesthoods," and said nothing about the restoration of the lineal priesthood of the old law. From 1829 to 1831, about two thousand members were baptized and confirmed by men whose license of "authority" did not include any reference to the bestowal of "priesthood."

When Joseph Smith finally published a remodeled description of the priesthood restoration events in 1842, new and unfamiliar facts associated with a second unknown restoration of a different priesthood by Peter, James, and John were minimized. His tepid description of what should have been an utterly unforgettable event was uncharacteristically sparing. This was an amended Joseph and a vacillating Lord treading lightly after many events and much history on dicey revisions. In respect to the first priesthood, John the Baptist's lineage-driven inheritance, why wouldn't Cowdery and Smith mention long before 1834 an 1829 vision of a messenger from "the midst of eternity," the parting of "the vail," an "angel of God . . . clothed with glory,"[108] the receipt of "the keys of the ministering of angels," the keys "of the gospel of repentance," and

---

Gospel." (Joseph Smith's 1832 Holographic Account of a Vision of Christ, Joseph Smith Jr., *The Personal Writings of Joseph Smith*, ed. Dean C. Jessee [Salt Lake City: Deseret Book, 1984], 4).

[107]Bushman, *Joseph Smith: Rough Stone Rolling*, 75.

[108]"Letter" (Cowdery and Smith's 1834-35 History), *Messenger and Advocate*, vol. 1 no. 1 (October 1834), 15.

the keys "of baptism by immersion for the remission of sins"?[109] To hold all of those things in a state of lock-up for five-and-a-half years because of some only suspected threat of persecution was not prophet-like, or consistent with Smith's boastful self-pronounced persona. "The Lord," he said, "has constituted me so curiously that I glory in persecution . . . ."[110]

It is hard to imagine legitimate reasons for such striking omissions. These incomprehensible delays excused for inconsequential reasons, following alleged events of earth-shaking magnitude, allow us to conclude that they were unconscionable revisions to an earlier history made as knowledge deepened – stone-cold fabrications written after the fact. Legend rather than history; theological constructs.

Doctrine and Covenants Section 13 –
The Falsified Backdated Aaronic Priesthood Restoration Prayer

John the Baptist's altered Aaronic Priesthood ordination prayer, the text of which was not faithfully followed, and the facts of which are mostly lost to history, is found unfettered in Oliver and Joseph's 1834-35 First Authorized History of the Mormon Church.

> *The Mormon Church claims that on May 15, 1829, John the Baptist conferred the Aaronic Priesthood on Joseph Smith and Oliver Cowdery. Section 13 of the Doctrine and Covenants is cited as evidence that the Aaronic Priesthood was conferred on Joseph Smith and Oliver Cowdery. We must remember, however, that this section did NOT appear in the revelations as they were originally printed in the Book of Commandments [in 1833]. It was published in the Times and Seasons on August 1, 1842, but it was not*

---

[109]Doctrine and Covenants 13.
[110]Roberts, ed., *History of the Church*, 6:408-9 (May 1844).

added to the Doctrine and Covenants until 1876.[111]

The current heading of Section 13 of the Doctrine and Covenants, another retroactive headnote, has John the Baptist say on May 15, 1829, "that he was acting under the direction of Peter, James, and John, the ancient Apostles, who held the keys of the higher priesthood." It then further reports, God only knows when, that John the Baptist promised Joseph and Oliver "that in due time this higher priesthood would be conferred upon them."[112] Section 13 of the Doctrine and Covenants is supposed to contain John the Baptist's Aaronic Priesthood restoration prayer, by that to say the words pronounced over Joseph Smith and Oliver Cowdery by John the Baptist on May 15, 1829. The claim that John the Baptist actually said what Section 13 changed the story to say that he did made its first public appearance on August 1, 1842 (thirteen years after May 15, 1829), in the *Times and Seasons*, published in Nauvoo, Illinois. The editor of the *Times and Seasons* who published the revisions on August 1, 1842, was Joseph Smith. "An examination of the published prayer shows that Cowdery's [Cowdery and Smith's] 1834 prayer-text [found in the 1834-35 History published in the *Messenger and Advocate* in Kirtland, Ohio, in October 1834] was its source and that an entire central portion was retroactively added."[113] Those amendments forever changed the meaning of the text. Here is another vitally important unmistakably altered foundational document concerning the vital subject of the priesthood. The alterations, using time tested deceitful technique, received the benefit of the unamended account's eight-year earlier date.

The 1834-35 History's more sparing (and authentic) version read like this:

> *[U]pon you my fellow servants, in the name of*

[111]Jerald Tanner and Sandra Tanner, *Mormonism – Shadow or Reality?* (Salt Lake City: Utah Lighthouse Ministry, 1987), 180, emphasis retained and added.

[112]Doctrine and Covenants (2013), 13, Headnote.

[113]Quinn, *Origins of Power*, 15.

> *Messiah I confer <u>this priesthood and this authority</u>,*
> *which shall remain upon earth, that the sons of Levi*
> *may yet offer an offering unto the Lord in*
> *righteousness.*[114]

Section 13 of the Doctrine and Covenants published in the *Times and Seasons* in 1842, and added to the Doctrine and Covenants in 1876, which was substantively retroactively enhanced, was based upon the prayer-text described in the 1834-35 History published in the *Messenger and Advocate* in Kirtland, Ohio, in 1834-35. That extensively embellished canonized account now reads as follows:

> *Upon you my fellow servants, in the name of Messiah*
> *I confer <u>the Priesthood of Aaron</u>, which holds the*
> *keys of the ministering of angels, and of the gospel of*
> *repentance, and of baptism by immersion for the*
> *remission of sins; and this shall never be taken again*
> *from the earth, until the sons of Levi do offer again*
> *an offering unto the Lord in righteousness.*[115]

The amended 1842 prayer retroactively recognized different levels of priesthood power, then placed limits on John the Baptist's earlier unambiguous utterance. "I indeed baptize you with water unto repentance," the Gospel of Matthew reports, "but he that cometh after me is mightier than I, whose shoes I am not worthy to bear: he shall baptize you with the Holy Ghost, and with fire."[116] The Biblical power assigned to John the Baptist was not the power required to "baptize . . . with the Holy Ghost, and with fire." Note that *"this priesthood and this authority,"* the power described in the original 1834 *Messenger and Advocate* prayer text – a unitary and unlimited concept – has been changed to *"the Priesthood of Aaron"* in 1842 in the altered *Times and Seasons* (D&C 13) prayer – a dual and limited concept. *"This addition delimited the role of authority*

---

[114]"Letter" (Cowdery and Smith's 1834-35 History), *Messenger and Advocate*, vol. 1 no. 1 (October 1834), 16, emphasis added.

[115]Doctrine and Covenants 13:1, emphasis added.

[116]Matthew 3:11.

restored by John the Baptist and made the 1829 event appear to be a prelude to the later division of church authority into the lesser and the greater priesthoods."[117]

The priesthood-restoration-prayer alterations to the 1829 report, first put forward in 1842, when canonized in and/or after 1876, reflected a reconstituted understanding of what had miraculously divided to become two separate priesthoods instead of one, and of what then later became the final doctrine of the modern Church. The retroactive amendments to more than a dozen revelations when the Book of Commandments published in 1833 was superceded by the Doctrine and Covenants published in 1835 were made to suggest that Joseph *always understood what he later understood,* and then to show that the prophet's Lord wasn't confused.[118]

THE "RESTORATION" OF THE HIGHER PRIESTHOOD

The message of the Fourth Conference of the Church in June 1831 was that there was something greater and more important than anything ever before described. There was no high priesthood, in fact there was no "priesthood," and there were no dual priesthoods of different ranks before 1830. There was no high priesthood, and there were no dual priesthoods of different ranks, when the first forty-four non-Melchizedek lower authority elders were ordained sometime before the Fourth Conference of the Church in June 1831. At that Fourth Conference at Kirtland, Smith conferred the "high priesthood" on one of them, an interesting character by the name of Lyman Wight. Wight, a flame thrower on fire at that Conference, then returned the favor and "ordained" the prophet

---

[117]Quinn, *Origins of Power*, 15-16, emphasis added.

[118]It would seem safe to say that not one in a hundred Latter-day Saints knows that Section 13 of the 1876 edition of the Doctrine and Covenants, and of all editions since, is a substantively altered and incompatible version of a different prayer making a different case first published by Oliver Cowdery and Joseph Smith in 1834.

Joseph Smith.[119]   D. Michael Quinn noted this, and so did a respected Mormon scholar by the name of Greg Prince:

> *A recent interpreter [Prince] has noted that previously ordained elders [there were forty-four of them in attendance] received the "high priesthood" at the June 1831 conference but not the office of high priest. He suggests that the official history retroactively assigned the later office to 1831. In that respect it is true that until April 1832 [meaning for nearly one more year] the original minutes continued to list men as "elders" despite their ordination to the "high priesthood."[120]*

Quinn, taking issue with Prince, maintains that "The June 1831 conferral of 'high priesthood' clearly included ordination to the office of high priest" for several different reasons: (1) Because Mormons (since 1829) do not accept the Bible provisions that restricted the office of high priest to one man ("as in ancient Judaism") or to the Savior Jesus Christ alone ("as in traditional Christianity").[121]   (2) Because *"Book of Mormon* scribe Oliver Cowdery who recorded the minutes about the 'high priesthood' in 1831 did not use the terms 'high priest' or 'office of high priest' because he was following the *Book of Mormon's* equation of 'high priesthood' with the office of high priest."[122]   (3) Because Sidney Rigdon, while speaking to those "who were ordained to the Highpriesthood [sic] last evening," described "that office" and the "power of that office," thus meaning to say the office of a high

---

[119]Quinn, *Origins of Power*, Selected Chronology, 617.

[120]Ibid., 29.

[121]How unlike the gospel Church's precepts are these presently discernible abruptions? Things supposed to be restored? These disavowals pertaining to pivotal priesthood things ("as in ancient Judaism," and "as in traditional Christianity") put the Mormon concept of a "restoration" at risk. A "restoration" would not have included orders of priests or thousands of high priests. (As an aside, the Latter-day Saints also fail to accept traditional Christianity's pronounced dismissal of ancient Israel's primitive law of a carnal commandment with the coming of Christ.)

[122]Quinn, *Origins of Power*, Selected Chronology, 29.

priest. According to Quinn, "everyone in 1831" would have understood (because of the Book of Mormon) that when someone said "high priesthood" they were describing "the office of high priest."[123] That isn't the way it is today; why would it have been that way then?

Oliver Cowdery, "who recorded the minutes about the 'high priesthood' in 1831,"[124] referred to the "high priesthood," not to "high priest" or to the "office of high priest," or to an undeniably second separate "higher" priesthood. The message of 1831 may have sounded, at least at first, like the conferral of additional authority. In the Book of Mormon the Levitical Priesthood "is nowhere pretended to." The Book of Mormon didn't describe multiple overlapping orders of authority. The importance of that to this study, where that "carnal" order of authority is only now perceived to be eternal, can not be overstated. Until 1831 "the word 'priesthood' although it appeared in the *Book of Mormon*,[125] had not been used in sermonizing, or modern revelations. Later accounts [cynically amending earlier accounts] applied the term retroactively, but the June 1831 conference marked its first appearance in contemporary records." The word "authority" was initially used in a conventional way to describe the power to act for God.

On June 3, 1831, no one reported that Peter, James, and John had come to restore the "high priesthood" that twenty-three of the forty-four lower authority elders in attendance on that occasion had only just received. While one sophisticated dissenter (a former Protestant minister, Ezra Booth) later reported that "[m]any of them have been ordained to the High Priesthood, or the order of Melchisedec; and profess to be endowed with the same power as the

---

[123]Ibid.

[124]Ibid.

[125]The word "priesthood" did not appear in Moroni Chapter 3 (Book of Mormon) where the method of ordination among the Nephites at or about the time of the end of their era ("401-421" AD) is more specifically described.

ancient apostles were,"[126] he, like everyone else, including all of the newly empowered elders, knew nothing about angelic ordinations, John the Baptist, or Peter, James, and John. On June 3, 1831, no one knew that John the Baptist was supposed to have visited the earth in 1829 to restore the lineal priesthood of the old law. No one knew that the "authority" principle would be reconfigured to become "the lineal priesthood of the old law." Or that the office of an elder was an appendage of the "holy priesthood after the order of the son of God." Or that the Aaronic/Levitical Priesthood was an appendage of what would only some time very much later come to be called the Melchizedek Priesthood.

Apostle Talmage described the restoration of the Melchizedek Priesthood as having almost immediately followed the restoration of the Aaronic Priesthood:

> *A short time after this event [John the Baptist's May 15, 1829, appearance], Peter, James and John appeared to Joseph Smith and Oliver Cowdery, and ordained the two to the higher or Melchizedek Priesthood, bestowing upon them the keys of the apostleship, which these heavenly messengers had held and exercised in the former Gospel dispensation.*[127]

Joseph and Oliver didn't ever say when Peter, James, and John came to confer some new and higher priesthood. Can anyone imagine two history-conscious reporters unable to assign a date and time to such an important event? Who could forget (or fail to report) when they suddenly became the two most important men on earth?

---

[126]Eber D. Howe, *Mormonism Unvailed: Or, A Faithful Account of That Singular Imposition and Delusion* (Painesville, OH: E.D. Howe, 1834; reprint, New York: AMS Press Inc., 1977), Letter II, 180.

[127]Talmage, *A Study of the Articles of Faith*, 24th ed., 188, emphasis added.

CHAPTER SEVEN

Revisions

[T]here is no definite account of the event [the Melchizedek Priesthood restoration event] in the history of the Prophet Joseph, or for matter of that, in any of our annals . . . .

B.H. Roberts

The 1832 History, the thoroughly provenanced unamended first and only holographic account of Joseph Smith's first encounter with deity (a vision concealed and suppressed in the archives of the Church until 1965), while mentioning "the reception of the holy Priesthood by the ministering of Aangels," didn't mention Aaron, Levi, John the Baptist, the Aaronic/Levitical Priesthood, Melchizedek, Peter, James, and John, or the Melchizedek Priesthood, and treated "the high Priesthood after the holy order of the son of the living God" as unitary.

Joel M. Allred

"MOVING THE GOAL POSTS"

The modern Mormon concept of priesthood is the byproduct of extravagant alterations as the 1835 first edition of the Doctrine and Covenants introduced new and discordant elements into revelations previously published in their original form in *The Evening and the Morning Star*, the *Book of Commandments* and the *Messenger and Advocate*. The first documentary support for the tenuous proposition that the three apostles visited Smith and Cowdery is found in what were extensive 1835 alterations to a previously innocuous revelation concerning the sacrament and initially dated September 4, 1830. The unaltered revelation described in the communication's original manuscript, protected in the archives for about one hundred and eighty years, was faithfully published in the Book of Commandments in 1833.[1] The awkward amendments seen to have disfigured Chapter 28 of the Book of Commandments published in 1833 in the canonized Section 27 of the Doctrine and Covenants published in 1835 abruptly associated the previously unknown visitation of the three apostles, in a revelation that concerned the sacrament, with the restoration of the apostleship.[2] All of this meets the trusting public in a backdated unprovenanced revelation offered in the name of the Lord.

D&C Section 84, supposed to have been received in September 1832 (but not published until 1835), told the Latter Day Saints (when it surfaced in 1835) that "'elder and bishop are necessary appendages belonging unto the high priesthood.'" That would have been something important to know in 1829, *before* the Church was officially formed, or on April 6, 1830, *when* the Church was officially formed. Although this revelation associated the higher priesthood in a general way with Melchizedek, and the lesser priesthood in a general way with Aaron, "the actual terms 'Melchizedek Priesthood' and 'Aaronic Priesthood' first appeared in another 1835 revelation (now sec. 107)."[3] Section 107 (v. 7) of the Doctrine and Covenants was the first revelation to explicitly state that "the office of Elder comes under the Priesthood of Melchizedek."[4] That would have been something important to know at the Fourth Conference of the Church on June 3, 1831,

---

[1]Book of Commandments 28.

[2]Addison Everett Accounts, 1881 & 1882, Dan Vogel, ed., *Early Mormon Documents*, 5 vols. (Salt Lake City: Signature Books, 1996-2003), 1:202, quoted in Dan Vogel, *Joseph Smith: The Making of a Prophet* (Salt Lake City: Signature Books, 2004), 520-21. Until 1835 apostles, who weren't part of an organized quorum, were not ordained. (Book of Commandments 24:33. An apostle is an elder.) *"To the mid-nineteenth century Mormon leaders continued to use the word 'apostle' to designate unordained charisma."* (D. Michael Quinn, *The Mormon Hierarchy: Origins of Power* (Salt Lake City: Signature Books in association with Smith Research Associates, 1994), 10, emphasis added). Until the publication of the first edition of the Doctrine and Covenants in 1835, apostles purported to exercise unordained charismatic authority.

[3]Quinn, *Origins of Power*, 29-30.

[4]Ibid., 30.

when twenty-three of some forty-four *non-Melchizedek* (low authority) elders presented themselves to receive some poorly defined (and unprovenanced) kind of high authority. Section 84 was not published in the Book of Commandments in 1833 – even though it was "the first detailed explanation of priesthood" – most probably (according to Quinn) because "it also made it awkward to explain that Smith organized the church in April 1830 without Melchizedek Priesthood."[5]

If the restoration of the Melchizedek Priesthood had indeed occurred as Joseph Smith and Oliver Cowdery said that it did many years after the fact (by means of backdated alterations to earlier narratives), it would not have been necessary for Erastus Snow and Addison Everett to have offered uncorroborated hearsay to Latter-day Saints desperately seeking proof of their priesthood near the end of the nineteenth century. The time, place and paternity of an epic visitation from Peter, James, and John, come to confer "the Holy Priesthood after the Order of the Son of God" on men of faith, could not have been overlooked in the *Articles and Covenants* of *the Church of Christ* in 1830, in the Preface to the Book of Mormon in 1830, in the Holographic Account of Joseph Smith's first encounter with deity in 1832, in the sixty-five revelations published in The Book of Commandments in 1833, or in the first "authorized" history of the Church published by Oliver Cowdery and Joseph Smith in the *Messenger and Advocate* in 1834-35. "Though argument does not create conviction, lack of it destroys belief. What seems to be proved may not be embraced; but what no one shows the ability to defend, is quickly abandoned. Rational argument does not create belief, but it maintains a climate in which belief may flourish."[6] The falsification of foundational narratives, an epidemic in the early Church, uncorrected in the later Church, was then and is now indefensible.

---

[5]Ibid., 30-31.

[6]Austin Farrer, "Grete Clerk," in Jocelyn Gibb, comp., *Light on C.S. Lewis* (New York, Harcourt & Brace, 1965), 26, quoted in Terryl L. Givens, *By the Hand of Mormon: The American Scripture that Launched a New World Religion* (*n.p.*: Oxford University Press, Inc., 2002; reprint, New York, NY: Oxford University Press paperback, 2003), 118.

Joseph Smith's 1832 History

Following the twentieth-century exposure of his one hundred and thirty year suppressed 1832 Holographic Account of the visit of "the ['crucifyed'] Lord" (Jesus without the Father), Latter-day Saints learned *in 1965* that Joseph Smith had privately discussed "*the* holy Priesthood" as a unitary authority, yet again without mentioning Melchizedek, in 1832. In what was "an account of his marvilous experience and . . . mighty acts," and "an account of the rise of the church of Christ in the eve of time," Smith recounted a series of events starting with "testamony from on high" followed by the "min=istering of Angels," followed by "the reception of *the* holy Priesthood by the ministring of Aangels to administer the letter of the Gospel − < − the Law and commandments as they were given unto him − > and the ordinencs . . . ."[7]

After May 15, 1829, and at the age of twenty-six, Smith said that he received "a confirmation and reception of the high Priesthood after the holy order of the son of the living God pow=er and ordinence from on high to preach the Gospel in the administration and demonstra=tion of the spirit the Kees of the Kingdom of God confered upon him and the continuation of the blessings of God to him &c − . . . ."[8] These privately protected pristine recitals describing the status of the priesthood after the Fourth Conference of the Church in 1831, and late in the year 1832, did not associate the reception of "the holy Priesthood" with Melchizedek. Or with the office of a high priest. In 1832, Joseph Smith, an extreme monotheist, had yet to separate the Father from the Son.

This 1832 Account followed by more than one year the still to be described exorbitant behavior associated with the June 1831 ordinations of Lyman Wight, Joseph Smith and others to the high priesthood at the extraordinary Fourth Conference of the Church held at Kirtland, Ohio, on June 3, 1831. In these long suppressed

---

[7]*The Personal Writings of Joseph Smith*, ed. Dean C. Jessee (Salt Lake City: Deseret Book, 1984), 4, emphasis added.
[8]Ibid.

impeccably provenanced 1832 recitals associated with Smith's first encounter with a single deity, the "crucifyed" Lord, the Mormon leader doesn't mention deacons, teachers, elders, priests, high priests, bishops, seventies, apostles, pastors, patriarchs, evangelists, seers or prophets.[9] Then finally, June 3, 1831, Fourth Conference be damned, he described "*the* holy Priesthood," the only priesthood, as unitary. In these 1832 recitals, following those 1831 events, there were no "dual priesthoods of different ranks" and "*the* holy Priesthood" didn't have a nickname.

Oliver and Joseph Collaborate: The 1834-35 History

"The first published consecutive account of the origin of the Church began in the October 1834, issue of the Messenger and Advocate. It consists of eight letters written by Oliver Cowdery to W.W. Phelps."[10] From 1834 to 1837, Kirtland's *Messenger and Advocate* was an official publication of the Mormon Church. Cowdery penned this important history under the direct personal supervision of the prophet Joseph Smith. According to the "Defender of the Faith," B.H. Roberts, "Joseph Smith's association with Cowdery in the production of these *Letters* make them, as to the facts involved, practically the personal narrative of Joseph Smith."[11] The letters,

---

[9]Elders, teachers and priests, representing Mormonism's ungraded early authority principle, "had different functions but no discernible difference in status." (Quinn, *Origins of Power*, 28). This "aversion to ranking," an egalitarian approach prized by David Whitmer, was abruptly interrupted by seismic events that unsettled the Fourth Conference of the Church held at Kirtland, Ohio, in June of 1831. Whitmer's "spiritual community" ("We were an humble happy people, and loved each other as brethren should love" [David Whitmer, *An Address to All Believers in Christ: by A Witness to the Divine Authenticity of The Book of Mormon* (Richmond, MO: n.p., 1887; photographic reprint, Concord, CA: Pacific Publishing Company, 1993), 33]) was set to the side when that early and prized "aversion to ranking" ceased to be a governing principle.

[10]Francis Kirkham, *A New Witness for Christ*, vol. 1, 17, quoted in Jerald Tanner and Sandra Tanner, *The Changing World of Mormonism: A Behind-the-Scenes Look at Changes in Mormon Doctrine and Practice* (Moody Press, 1979), 160, emphasis added.

[11]Brigham H. Roberts, *A Comprehensive History of the Church of Jesus Christ of Latter-day Saints*, 6 vols. (Provo, UT: Brigham Young University Press, 1965),

published over a period of months in successive segments, covered a number of different subjects.[12]

The heavenly messenger described in the 1834-35 History as having visited Joseph and Oliver in 1829 made no claim to have acted under the direction of Peter, James, and John, priests of a higher order, as the deceptive headnote added to Section 13 of the 1876 edition of the Doctrine and Covenants said that he did. He didn't say that the "high Priesthood was called the Priesthood of Melchizedek."[13] The unamended messenger didn't describe two separate tiers of priesthood authority, neglected to promise an in-due-time conferral of some greater priesthood, and failed to identify Melchizedek (an obscure but respected biblical figure supposed to have received his own authority metaphysically). The 1834-35 History failed to describe the "Melchizedek" Priesthood, or "dual priesthoods of different ranks." It also failed to mention the Sacred Grove and a great First Vision of the Father and the Son.

In the theology of the modern Church, John the Baptist doesn't confer a generic *"this priesthood"* and a generic *"this authority"* (powers singular), as Oliver and Joseph said in 1834 that he did. An amended John the Baptist in an altered prayer (*Doctrine and*

1:77-78 fn 8.   "The *Letters* have several times been reproduced in L.D.S. periodicals, the latest of which is the *Improvement Era*, vol. ii, 1899." [Ibid.].

[12]Some modern historians ascribe the 1834-35 History to Cowdery – putting distance between Cowdery and the prophet – because the account contains harmful insights impervious to revision. Among other things, the History poses a threat to the canonized 1838-39 Pearl of Great Price Account of the First Vision, the founding story of the Mormon Church, describing an 1820 event not yet thought to have occurred, that Oliver and Joseph failed to describe in their first authorized history of the Church in 1834. Oliver Cowdery didn't know that Joseph Smith had been visited by the Father and the Son in 1820 when he and Joseph prepared the "first published consecutive account of the origin of the Church" in 1834. Oliver knew about the messenger with the plates, the first First Vision, but never said that he knew about the First Holographic Vision of the "crucifyed" Lord, or the Fourth First Vision of the Father and the Son. Smith did not create the Fourth (now "official") account of the vision of the Father and the Son until 1838-39, or publish that account until 1842. Oliver Cowdery, an excoriated deceiver, was excommunicated in 1838.

[13]Doctrine and Covenants 13, headnote.

Covenants 13, Headnote and Text) is now retroactively said to have conferred *"the Priesthood of Aaron"* in an altered document describing events resupposed to have occurred on May 15, 1829.

The headnote to Section 13 avers that John the Baptist told Joseph and Oliver on May 15, 1829, "that he was acting under the direction of Peter, James, and John, the ancient Apostles, who held the keys of the higher priesthood, which was called the Priesthood of Melchizedek."[14] The 1834-35 History didn't say so. It is easy to discredit these late-to-the-table claims. The Church didn't use the word "priesthood" in the revelations, or in its sermonizing, until 1831. The Lord didn't unequivocally identify "the higher Priesthood" as "the Priesthood of Melchizedek" until 1835.[15] Now, in 1842, in a falsified ordination prayer first published thirteen years after the alleged fact in a Mormon periodical, and forty-seven years after the alleged fact in the Doctrine and Covenants, the Priesthood of Aaron is correctly seen for what the modern Church (accepting the altered account) now says that it is, as the lower of two different orders of priesthood, and as authority to baptize "by immersion for the remission of sins." Now "the high Priesthood after the order of the Son of the living God" is seen for what Joseph many years after 1829 then *said that it was*, as the higher of two distinct and overlapping orders of priesthood, as an authority by means of which one can bestow the gift of the Holy Ghost, ordain elders, administer in spiritual things, supervise every priesthood office, then establish and develop a church.[16]

Cowdery and Smith: Priesthood Restoration Milestones

After declaring "with words of soberness, that an angel of God

---

[14]Doctrine and Covenants 13, headnote.

[15]Ibid., 107:1-7.

[16]Ibid., 84:29 (22 and 23 September *1832*, first published in the 1835 edition of the Doctrine and Covenants), cf. – "And again, the offices of elder and bishop are necessary appendages belonging unto the *high priesthood*" (emphasis added). Doctrine and Covenants 107:7 – "The office of an elder comes under the *priesthood of Melchizedek*." (March 28, 1835), emphasis added.

came down from heaven" and brought and laid the plates before his eyes, after saying that "the voice of the Lord commanded" him to "bear record of it"; after receiving the Aaronic Priesthood under the hands of John the Baptist, after "the voice of the Redeemer spake peace to us"; after receiving the Melchizedek Priesthood under the hands of Peter, James, and John; after being visited by Jesus Christ and Moses, Elias and Elijah behind the veil in the Kirtland temple on April 3, 1836, Apostle Oliver Cowdery ("one of the presidents of this church") fled Far West, Missouri, in 1838 with little but his life and joined the Methodist Church. After the death of Joseph Smith and a lengthy sabbatical (approximately ten years), he then briefly became some kind of a Mormon again. In all of that, the indefatigable Cowdery, like so many of Mormonism's other important early men, distanced himself from Joseph Smith.

Why would Mormonism's founders fail to mention in their October 1834 letter to W.W. Phelps, a segment of their 1834-35 History, the angelic restoration of the greater of what is now seen to have become two separate priesthoods? If they knew at the time of the publication of that report that there were two separate priesthoods? If they had known that John the Baptist had acted under the direction of Peter, James, and John, priests of a higher order? If they knew at the time that they had been ordained by Peter, James, and John? If these aggressive young militants were fearful of persecution, why were they free to say, "we heard the voice of Jesus"? Why would they identify John the Baptist but then ignore Peter, James, and John? If the revelations were somehow sacred, better kept to themselves, why did they describe the Aaronic event but then ignore the Melchizedek event? Or publish sixty-five revelations in the Book of Commandments? Why is there an Aaronic prayer, but not a Melchizedek prayer?

The claim to exclusive priesthood in the modern Church is clearly dependent upon the allegation that Peter, James, and John specifically visited Joseph Smith and Oliver Cowdery in "*1829, May-June*" before the Church was officially formed. Yet Oliver Cowdery and Joseph Smith themselves, as opposed to the Church, failed to ever assign a date to a visit from Peter, James, and John.

While Joseph Smith's 1832 Holographic Account ("an account of his marvelous experience and of all the mighty acts which he doeth in the name of Jesus Ch[r]ist the Son of the living God") mentioned "the reception of *the* holy Priesthood by the ministring of Aangels [sic]," it wasn't published, didn't identify the messengers, neglected Aaron, neglected Melchizedek, failed to assign a title to generic authority, and described a unitary priesthood.

In the Manuscript History, the drafting of which commenced at Far West, Missouri, in 1838, then continued to be composed in 1839, Smith (as opposed to Cowdery) finally (and for himself) specifically identified the priesthood-bearing messenger as John the Baptist. According to Smith, speaking nine or ten years after May 1829, John reported that he had acted under the authority of "Peter, James, and John, who held the keys of the Priesthood of Melchizedek," a priesthood which "would in due time be conferred on us."[17] "It seems extraordinary," Quinn reports, "that in his official history Smith would say that a crucial event was to occur 'in due time' and then drop the subject completely."[18] It seems extraordinary that what was promised to occur "in due time" would not be further explained in 1838-39, when the Manuscript History was prepared, or in 1842 when it was finally published. It is important to understand that these were risky revisions difficult to explain and not easy to implement. The description of a visit of Peter, James, and John remains dependent upon one more uncomfortable addition to yet another previously published account.[19] While Joseph Smith "gave at least season, month, and year for the first vision" and for the visions of Moroni, John the Baptist and the Three Witnesses, he repeatedly avoided "saying that Peter, James, and John restored this priesthood in 1829. . . ." "There is no evidence that a restoration of what was later called the Melchizedek priesthood happened in June 1829. But historical evidence indicates that the second priesthood restoration occurred more than a year later than assumed in traditional Mormon

---

[17]Doctrine and Covenants 13, headnote, quoted in Quinn, *Origins of Power*, 21.
[18]Quinn, *Origins of Power*, 21-22.
[19]Doctrine and Covenants 27.

histories."[20]   "Bushman," according to Quinn, agreed that "the second priesthood restoration occurred in the summer of 1830."[21]

D. Michael Quinn concludes that the restoration of the Melchizedek Priesthood occurred after the Church was formed on April 6, 1830: "[W]hen retroactive changes [textual alterations] are eliminated from original documents, evidence shows that the second angelic restoration of apostolic authority could not have occurred before the church's organization on 6 April 1830."[22]   In his personally prized "Selected Chronology," Quinn is carefully thoughtful.   "3 June [1831]," he says, "The Melchizedek Priesthood and the office of high priest [others might be heard to say "additional authority"] are conferred on previously ordained elders.   Lyman Wight, *the first ordained high priest*, ordains Smith to that office."[23]   The high priesthood, according to Quinn, was restored as follows: "6 July [1830].   Priesthood restoration by Peter, James and John occurs shortly after dawn near Harmony, Pennsylvania, as Smith and Cowdery are fleeing a mob at Colesville, New York."   Bushman's "Joseph Smith Chronology" reports that the "Ordination to [the] high priesthood" occurred on June 3, 1831, but doesn't mention Peter, James, and John.   Nor does he provide a date for their second supposed endeavor.

Onward, Ever Onward!

The incredible additions to Chapter 28 of the 1833 Book of Commandments – after it was reconfigured and republished in 1835 (found now as Section 27 of the Doctrine and Covenants) – substantive alterations apparent to anyone who has ever had access to the original manuscript or to a copy of the 1833 Book of Commandments, were noted by Dan Vogel, a distinguished (and honored) Smith biographer:

---

[20]Quinn, *Origins of Power*, 22.
[21]Ibid., 26.
[22]Ibid., 18.
[23]Ibid., Appendix 7, 617, emphasis added.

In this expansion [an 1835 addition made to a short revelation delivered to Smith at Harmony, Pennsylvania, on "September 4, 1830"[24]], Jesus declares that when he returns he will drink of the "fruit of the vine with . . . *John the son of Zacharias . . . Which John I have* sent to you, my servants, Joseph Smith, Jun., and Oliver Cowdery, to ordain you unto the first priesthood . . . And also with *Peter, and James, and John,* whom I have sent unto you, by whom I have ordained you and confirmed you to be apostles." (D&C 27:5, 8, 12-13).[25]

Two priesthoods and then apostles appear to be the principal focus of these cynical and unsupported amendments. "Prior to Smith's 1835 expansion, the identity of the angels and the purpose of their appearance had eluded Smith and Cowdery, which is why the earliest members, even those close to Smith, were unaware that these angelic ordinations had occurred."[26]   David Whitmer and William E. McLellin, leaders perfectly positioned to know, didn't know that Peter, James, and John visited Oliver and Joseph in 1829, or even later. The voice of McLellin is instructive:

"*I never heard of John the Baptist ordaining Joseph and Oliver. I heard not of James, Peter and John doing so.*"[27]

[Although McLellin said he heard Smith tell the story of the church's founding] "probably more than twenty times, I never heard of . . . John, or Peter, James and John."[28]

---

[24]Book of Commandments 28.

[25]Vogel, *Joseph Smith: The Making of a Prophet*, 521, emphasis added.

[26]Ibid.,

[27]William E. McLellin to J.L. Traughber, 25 Aug. 1877, *Salt Lake Tribune* (4 Dec. 1985), Vogel, ed., *Early Mormon Documents*, 5:329 n 9, emphasis added.

[28]William E. McLellin, *True L[atter] D[ay] Saints Herald*, 17 (15 Sept. 1870): 556, Ibid., Vogel, ed., *Early Mormon Documents*, 5:329 n 9, quoted in Vogel, *Joseph Smith: The Making of a Prophet*, 521, emphasis added.

> *But as to the story of John, the Baptist ordaining Joseph and Oliver on the day they were baptized: I never heard of it in the church for years, altho I carefully noticed things . . . .*[29]

McLellin joined the Church in 1831. He was a prominent apostle ("ordained [in 1835] under the hands of Oliver Cowdery, David Whitmer and Martin Harris"[30]), a founding member of the Quorum of the Twelve and a Secretary to the Quorum. An 1835 (backdated) addition to an 1830 revelation (Book of Commandments, Chapter 28) described Joseph and Oliver as having been ordained and confirmed "to be apostles," a title that began its modern tenure unordained. In 1830, when the original revelation (Book of Commandments, Chapter 28) was first received, and before it was massively remodeled (Doctrine and Covenants, Section 27) and until 1835, the leaders of the Church didn't ordain apostles.

That there was supposed to have been an angelic ordination of a literal physical nature was first publicly announced in or just before October 1834, after the humiliating failure that same year of the armed Mormon expedition known as Zion's Camp, after scores of failed prophecies, after the involuntary abandonment of Zion and at a time when Smith's prophetic *bona fides* were under rigorous scrutiny. On 7 September 1834, at a critical time and for self-serving reasons, in a letter to William W. Phelps, Cowdery wrote to say "that an angel had bestowed upon him and Smith the authority to baptize"[31] (bolstering the prophet's flagging fortunes at that particular time was a matter of high priority). Cowdery did not then describe a second ordination (Peter, James, and John) or another priesthood. How, if he had been ordained a second time to a high authority, could he have ever not?

---

[29]William E. McLellin to Joseph Smith III, July 1872, Community of Christ (RLDS) Archives; Vogel, ed., *Early Mormon Documents*, 5:329, emphasis added.

[30]Andrew Jenson, comp., *Church Chronology: A Record of Important Events Pertaining to the History of the Church of Jesus Christ of Latter-day Saints*, 2d ed., rev. and enlarged (Salt Lake City: Deseret News, 1914), xxv.

[31]Vogel, *Joseph Smith: The Making of a Prophet*, 521.

The event that paved the way for Smith's hierarchical innovations [the ordination of apostles] was Cowdery's ordination as co-president . . . [a December 1834 event]. In June 1829, Cowdery resisted Smith's attempt to organize twelve apostles. Now that his special status was recognized and his position in the hierarchy secured, Cowdery aided Smith in institutionalizing the apostleship.

Addressing the newly ordained apostles on 21 February [1835], Cowdery said: "You have been ordained to *this* holy priesthood, you have received it from those who have the power and authority from *an angel*." The context of the statement implies that the authority to "preach the gospel to every nation" came from the angel who appeared to the three witnesses in late June 1829, commanding them to bear witness to the world concerning the truth of the Book of Mormon. Thus, it would appear that as of 21 February 1835, neither Smith nor Cowdery had yet connected their July 1830 experience [everything associated with the flight from Colesville, New York, to Harmony, Pennsylvania] with an ordination to the apostleship.[32]

On this date in early 1835, Cowdery is again seen to have described but one angel and unitary priesthood ("*this* holy priesthood").

Revising Revelations

Various documents that refer to John the Baptist, Peter, James, and John and distinctive orders of priesthood were created and/or altered after-the-fact. Retroactive recitals positing new facts were inserted in previously existing documents, including previously

---

[32]Ibid., 522, emphasis added.

published revelations. Joseph's revelator's words were tortured to support the notion that the conferral of what subsequently became two distinct orders of priesthood had been *early not late, literal not charismatic, plural not singular*. Who knew that the "first and second elders" of what was then the Church of Christ claimed to have received priesthood authority at the hands of heavenly messengers a year before the Church was officially formed? No *unaltered* Mormon document prior to 1834-35 mentions John the Baptist or Peter, James, and John against the restoration of any order of priesthood.

The first public reference to angelic ordination in an unaltered document is found in the first of eight separate installments of Joseph and Oliver's "consecutive" 1834-35 History first published in the *Messenger and Advocate* in October 1834. The first public reference to Peter, James, and John having been associated with the restoration of the priesthood is found in the amendments made to the discredited Section 50 of the first edition (1835) of the Doctrine and Covenants (now Section 27). Joseph Smith mentioned in March 1844, very much later, the power/spirit of Elias and the Susquehannah River and an angel that laid hands upon him.[33]

CONFLICTING ACCOUNTS

Protecting the Improbable

In February 1831, the *Palmyra Reflector* reported that Mormon missionaries were preaching that "Joseph Smith had now received a commission from God." Smith "(they affirmed) had seen God frequently and personally . . . ." The newspaper went further to say that Oliver Cowdery and his friends had had "frequent interviews with angels." Newspapers citing Mormon sources suggested that

---

[33]"Sermon delivered at Nauvoo temple grounds on March 10, 1844 – Sources: Wilford Woodruff journal, James Burgess notebook, Franklin D. Richards 'Scriptural Items,' Joseph Smith diary (Willard Richards), Thomas Bullock diary and the John S. Fullmer papers" (accessed 26 January 2016), available from http://www.boap.org/LDS/Parallel/1844/10Mar44.html; Internet, 1.

while Smith and Cowdery had seen angels, they had obtained their "authority" directly from God (but not through angelic ministration).[34] The newspaper accounts thus contradicted what each of Mormonism's founders would later change their positions to say. "In August 1832 McLellin had written a long letter explaining and defending Mormonism to his family. McLellin's 1832 letter referred to the angel Moroni but showed no knowledge of other angelic ministrations."[35] William E. McLellin said that he heard Joseph talk about angel visits many times, "But I never heard one word of John the Baptist, or of Peter, James, and John's visit and ordination till I was told some year ~~or two~~ afterward in Ohio."[36]

If Joseph did not hesitate to describe his having seen Peter, James, and John in a sermon in 1833, why would he hesitate to say that they came to him and to Cowdery to deliver the "high priesthood"? Why didn't he name a time and a place, mention a restoration prayer and provide details? It must seem to have been because the conferral of this priesthood by supernatural ministrations, which wasn't first supposed, became part of a late design. Five-and-a-half years after May 15, 1829, after describing the wonderful event supposed to have effected the restoration of what came to be called the Aaronic Priesthood, the two presidents failed to describe the wonderful event supposed to have effected the restoration of what came to be called the Melchizedek Priesthood. The twenty-first century Church stubbornly maintains, with thin support and against all odds, that the priesthood restoration events occurred five or six years before the 1834-35 First Authorized History of the Church, which described one of those events for the first time, was ever published. Of this we may be certain: The first "*Authorized History*" of the Mormon Church[37] published in 1834 and 1835 by

---

[34]Quinn, *Origins of Power*, 19.

[35]Ibid.

[36]William E. McLellin statement 10, numbered item 28, photocopy at *Salt Lake Tribune* office (Salt Lake City, UT), as of 24 Dec. 1985, quoted in Quinn, *Origins of Power*, 19 fn 94.

[37]"[W]e [Oliver Cowdery and Joseph Smith] have thought that a full history of the rise of the Church of the Latter Day Saints, and the most interesting parts of

Joseph Smith and Oliver Cowdery for the members of the Church failed to mention Peter, James, and John, Melchizedek, the Melchizedek Priesthood, or a great First Vision of the Father and the Son, and treated the only authority those founders did then say that they received as unitary.

In 1835 in a statement that was reported in Joseph Smith Sr.'s Patriarchal Blessing Book in which the dates were fudged ("attributed erroneously to 18 Dec. 1833"), Cowdery said just this much about a second priesthood restoration: "'After this [after John the Baptist's visit on May 15, 1829] we received the high and holy priesthood' [the word "Melchizedek" doesn't appear] from 'others . . . those who received it under the hand of the Messiah.'"[38] Although Cowdery's backdated report identified John the Baptist, he "rarely identified [by name] the angelic ministers for the second priesthood restoration and never gave a time or place for the event."[39] When Joseph Smith told the High Council in 1834 that his office had been "conferred" upon him "by the ministring of the Angel of God, by his own will and by the voice of this Church," may it again be noted that he "mentioned only one angel as the agent of restoration."[40]

In 1846 – fully seventeen years after "*1829, May-June*," after the death of Joseph Smith and his own excommunication – Cowdery identified (now by name) an angel involved in the second priesthood restoration, mentioning Peter, but omitting James and John. He "stood in the presence of John [the Baptist]," Cowdery reported,

---

its progress, to the present time, would be worthy of the perusal of the Saints." ("Letter" [Cowdery and Smith's 1834-35 History], *Messenger and Advocate*, vol. 1 no. 1 [October 1834], 13).
    [38]Quinn, *Origins of Power*, 20. See also this: "[A]nd after receive the holy priesthood under the hands of they <those> who had been held in reserve for a long season, even those who received it under the hand of the Messiah." (Oliver Cowdery's transcription of a blessing signed, "Oliver Cowdery, 'Clerk and Recorder,' Given December 18th 1833 and recorded in this book October 2 1835," *Patriarchal Blessing Book 1* [LDS Church Archives], 12 [angle brackets [< >] represent material inserted above the line by the original author]).
    [39]Quinn, *Origins of Power*, 20.
    [40]Ibid., 21.

"with our departed Joseph, to receive the Lesser priesthood – and in the presence of Peter," he said, "to receive the Greater." In 1848, nineteen years after "*1829, May-June,*" and in the year Cowdery rejoined the Mormon Church after the death of Smith, he said in a sermon that "the higher or Melchizedek Priesthood was conferred by the holy angel[s] from on high." In 1849, twenty years after "*1829, May-June,*" and just before he died, Cowdery signed a statement that did identify James and John. "Peter, James, and John," he said, "holding the keys of the Melchizedek Priesthood have also ministered." Thus it was, even then – after taking twenty years to finally assign names to all of the messengers – that he did not describe a transfer of power or provide confirming details.[41] One can feel Cowdery's discomfort over space and time (as he briefly rejoined the Church in 1848 shortly before his 1850 death).

Discrepancies

The *Messenger and Advocate's* first authorized history of the Church in October 1834 contained, according to Quinn, "*The first evidence of angelic restoration in public discussion . . . .*" "Cowdery confirms the idea of one priesthood at the church's organization and indirectly suggests that Smith and he had not yet encountered Peter, James, and John or the 'higher' priesthood in April 1830. ... This was the first time Mormons learned that a heavenly conferral of authority occurred before the church's organization."[42] What is wrong with these elements of that disclosure?

- *Oliver and Joseph have finally described the restoration of the Aaronic Priesthood but they have ignored the restoration of the Melchizedek Priesthood.*

- *Oliver and Joseph do not say that this is about the restoration of the lesser priesthood, or that they had already also received*

---

[41]Ibid., 20-21.
[42]Ibid., 15.

the higher priesthood, or that there were two different priesthoods.

- *Oliver and Joseph do not say in 1834 what that altered revelation said in 1835, that God had sent "Peter, and James, and John . . . by whom I have ordained you and confirmed you to be apostles, and especial witnesses of my name, and bear the keys of your ministry . . . ."*[43]

- *Oliver and Joseph do not then say that John the Baptist told them that Peter, James, and John "held the keys of the higher priesthood, which was called the Priesthood of Melchizedek," or that that priesthood should in "due time" "be conferred upon them."*[44]

- *Joseph, who is now more than six years into his ministry, fails to describe Peter, James, and John (or a great first vision of the Father and the Son).*

- *B.H. Roberts: "[T]here is no definite account of the event [the Melchizedek Priesthood restoration event] in the history of the Prophet Joseph, or for matter of that, in any of our annals . . . ."*[45]

Imagine that disciples who have built their lives upon a series of suppositions are left to guess when and where Peter, James, and John are supposed to have appeared to deliver the "Holy Priesthood after the Order of the Son of God," an order which "'has power and authority over all the offices in the church in all ages of the world, to administer in spiritual things.'"[46] The high priesthood restoration event sightings are awkward, altered, tardy, indefinite, uncorroborated, backdated, "vague and contradictory." They are encircled with deception and hard to ingest.

---

[43]Doctrine and Covenants 27:12, emphasis added.
[44]Ibid., 13, headnote, emphasis added.
[45]Roberts, ed., *History of The Church of Jesus Christ of Latter-day Saints*, 1:40 fn, emphasis added.
[46]Doctrine and Covenants 107:8.

According to Richard L. Bushman, "Joseph did not tell anyone about John the Baptist at first." Joseph had not told his mother about the First Vision, and spoke to his father about Moroni only when commanded. "His reticence may have shown a fear of disbelief. Although obscure, Joseph was proud. He did not like to appear the fool. Or he may have felt the visions were too sacred to be discussed openly." One remarkable sentence from Smith's twenty-first century biographer may serve to explain what such posturing is really all about: "The late appearance of these accounts raises the possibility of later fabrication."[47] That thought might very well occur in a most natural way to almost anyone.

Random Points:

> *The 1832 History, the first and the only holographic account of Joseph Smith's first encounter with deity, not published until 1965 but created more than one year after the Fourth Conference of the Church held from June 3-6, 1831, didn't mention Aaron, Levi, John the Baptist, Melchizedek, Peter, James, and John, or two priesthoods, and treated generic priesthood as unitary.*

> *Joseph "said nothing about the restoration of priesthood or the visit of an angel" on or at any time before the day the Church was officially organized on April 6, 1830.*

> *Oliver didn't "tell anyone about John the Baptist"[48] for five-and-a-half years.*

> *Joseph didn't publicly identify John the Baptist, calling him by name, for thirteen years (until 1842).*

---

[47]Richard Lyman Bushman, with the assistance of Jed Woodworth, *Joseph Smith: Rough Stone Rolling* (New York: Alfred A. Knopf, 2005), 75.
[48]Ibid.

Joseph didn't tell his mother and/or father about Peter, James, and John.

Joseph did not hesitate to publish sixty-five revelations reflecting his various encounters with Jesus Christ in 1833.

Persecution didn't inhibit Joseph (according to Joseph) from reporting the events surrounding his vision of the Father and the Son. On one particularly memorable occasion, Smith boastfully reported that his backbone was one of his most endearing features: "I should be like a fish out of water, if I were out of persecutions . . . . I glory in persecution. I am not nearly so humble as if I were not persecuted . . . . If they want a beardless boy to whip all the world, I will get on the top of a mountain and crow like a rooster: I shall always beat them."[49] Smith could not have been deterred by the threat of persecution.

Oliver Cowdery and Joseph Smith collaborated in that first authorized 1834-35 History to open a page on the story of the angelic restoration of the Aaronic Priesthood in the narrative prepared by Cowdery at the request and under the close personal supervision of Smith. Smith published the account in the *Messenger and Advocate*, a Mormon publication, in October 1834. He republished the account in the *Times and Seasons* after Cowdery had been excommunicated "without any thought of correction." It was published in yet another Church publication in Utah in 1899.

In his *1838-39 History* first published in 1842, Joseph retroactively described John's 1829 visit once again, adding new and previously unreported details. Following their baptisms, Joseph Smith and Oliver Cowdery experienced "great and glorious blessings." Their "minds" were "enlightened," and the Scriptures were "laid open" to their "understandings." Now the meaning of some of the "more mysterious passages" was attained to a degree never before thought

---

[49]Roberts, ed., *History of The Church of Jesus Christ of Latter-day Saints,* 6:408.

possible.[50] Whatever that was supposed to mean, less than one year later Smith was more than a little confused. "Participants at the church's organization [on April 6, 1830] had a unitary sense of authority rather than a belief in dual priesthoods of different ranks."[51] The Aaronic and Melchizedek Priesthoods were not described on April 6, 1830, and men who had already been ordained to the office of elder – some even before the Church was officially formed – were first ordained to the high priesthood on June 3, 1831, more than a year after the Church's founding.

The Issue of the Patriarchal Blessings

In its defense of the founders, the Church is able to say that Joseph and Oliver were representing "two angelic ministrations" as early as 1833, just four years after "*1829, May-June.*" Narrowing the timeline for the disclosure of the First Vision of the Father and the Son and for the disclosure of the restoration of the Melchizedek Priesthood by Peter, James, and John are projects that have always had a high priority. When did Joseph and Oliver first publicly announce that angels conferred "dual priesthoods of different ranks"? D. Michael Quinn describes an erroneous 1833 supposition and corrects an unsustainable timeline.

> Cowdery was also writing about two angelic ministrations *by late 1835.* When introducing the church's first book of recorded patriarchal blessings on 28 September 1835, he referred to both angelic ministrations . . . .[52]
>
> Four days later in the same book, Cowdery recorded Smith's blessing to him which said that the two had been ordained "by the hand of the angel in the bush, unto the lesser priesthood and after received the

---

[50]Bushman, *Joseph Smith: Rough Stone Rolling*, 75-76.

[51]Quinn, *Origins of Power*, 14-15.

[52]Ibid., 16, emphasis added.

holy priesthood under the hands of they who had
been held in reserve for a long season, even those
who received it under the hand of the Messiah."

Cowdery's 1835 document [actually a blessing by
Smith] claimed this was a blessing Smith gave him
on 18 December 1833, but the blessing was received
almost two years later on 22 September 1835, which
John Whitmer's history verifies. In December 1833
the prophet had recorded on Cowdery's behalf a
prayer-blessing which warned him of "two evils in
him that he must needs forsake." No contemporary
details are available, but Brigham Young and others
later described Cowdery's "evils": In 1833 newly
married Cowdery had either committed adultery or
entered into an unauthorized plural marriage which
Smith defined as adulterous. *Cowdery's substitution
of the 1835 blessing for the 1833 document had two
benefits. It omitted the earlier document's allusion to
his misconduct and retroactively provided a pre-1835
reference to Peter, James, and John.* This was
consistent with the reference to three angels Smith
and Cowdery had already added to an 1830
revelation in the 1835 *Doctrine and Covenants*.[53]

A reference dishonestly added to Section 27 of the Doctrine and
Covenants. The issue with the Patriarchal blessings involved yet
another doctrinal deception surrounding the delicate subject of the
priesthood – the substitution of a later document (a patriarchal
blessing) for an earlier document (a different patriarchal blessing).
Both blessings came from Joseph Smith. Cowdery (a Book of
Mormon witness) assigned the earlier document's earlier date to the
altered substitute. When the deception is discovered, nothing is
changed. Cowdery proved here, as he did on other important
occasions, that he was comfortable with deception. And the Church

---

[53]Ibid., 16-17, emphasis added (Doctrine and Covenants 27).

proved here, as it has proved on other important occasions, that it didn't care.

Oversights

Is it not remarkably significant that the 1834-35 History of the rise of the Church, prepared five or six years after modern Mormon historians continue to awkwardly date the alleged restoration of the Melchizedek Priesthood (*1829, May-June*), should fail to mention the date, time, place or occurrence of that second priesthood restoration event? The importance of high priesthood power? The divided duties of "dual priesthoods of different ranks"? A description of the messengers? A Melchizedek Priesthood restoration prayer? Could any "consecutive" history of the "full rise" of the Church fail to document the existence of two separate orders of the priesthood and the details of the restoration of the greater of the two of them? Could any "consecutive" history simply ignore Joseph's 1821 vision of the "crucifyed" Lord, or Joseph's 1820 vision of the Father and the Son? Or suggest that the Palmyra revival actually occurred in conjunction with the vision of the Angel Moroni in 1823? Or suggest that Joseph didn't know in 1823 whether or not a Supreme Being did in fact exist?

Oliver and Joseph collaborated to create this important early history in 1834 and 1835. To see the Father and the Son in the spring of 1820 and then fail to publicly say so for more than twenty years; to see the "crucifyed" Lord in 1821 and then fail to publicly say so until 1965; to see John the Baptist and Peter, James, and John in 1829, May-June without reporting those events until October 1834 (John the Baptist), or until late 1835 (Peter, James, and John), showed the founders' pitiful regard for transparency and truth. They either knew these things and chose to keep them secret or didn't know them and falsified previously published records to make it seem as if they did. These awkward retroactive backdated revisions show Joseph's Lord to have been complicit. Various altered resources at odds with their original manuscripts and earlier publications, and without separate archival provenance could only be assigned to a vacillating Lord in their entirety.

What had been a long after-the-fact disclosure of the restoration of a single priesthood (*"this* priesthood and *this* authority") at the hands of John the Baptist, became the even longer after-the-fact disclosure of the restoration of yet a second priesthood at the hands of Peter, James, and John. As the intricacies of the doctrine (unprecedented angelic restoration) slowly evolved, history had to be rewritten and revelations had to be remodeled to accommodate Mormonism's previously unfamiliar priesthood imperatives.

Peter, James, and John

At the June 1831 conference in Kirtland, Ohio – *"where the authority of the Melchizedek priesthood was manifested and conferred for the first time"* – no one mentioned Peter, James, and John. Joseph's earliest and most faithful followers failed to mention those apostles (or angelic ordination) in any contemporaneous account of those undignified proceedings. No Mormon diarist is seen to have mentioned Peter, James, and John in support of the literal physical restoration of the high priesthood ("the Holy Order of the Son of God") in 1831, the year that the very word "priesthood" is supposed to have at first applied. Before that turbulent conference, when what was only later identified as the Melchizedek Priesthood became available to every faithful male member of the Church – reckoned by the hundreds of thousands with the passage of time – that priesthood had been conferred upon only two men, Melchizedek and Christ.[54] Joseph didn't actually say in 1838-39 (in

---

[54]Fawn M. Brodie, *No Man Knows My History: The Life of Joseph Smith the Mormon Prophet*, 2d ed., rev. and enl. (New York, NY: Alfred A. Knopf, 1972), 111. Mrs. Brodie assigned "Joseph's concept of dual priesthood" to James Gray. "It seems likely that Joseph's concept of dual priesthood came directly from James Gray's *Dissertation on the Coincidence between the Priesthoods of Jesus Christ and Melchisedec* (Philadelphia 1810)." Joseph was familiar with Gray's works. His own signed copy of Gray's *Mediatorial Reign of the Son of God* (Baltimore [1821]) was (in Mrs. Brodie's time) available to scholars in the library of the Reorganized Church. (Ibid.). In one now dated but important Mormon text, an apostle

a statement not published until 1842) that Peter, James, and John conferred the Melchizedek Priesthood. He said, rather instead, that he heard *"The voice of Peter, James and John in the wilderness between Harmony, Susquehanna county, and Colesville, Broome county, on the Susquehanna river, declaring themselves as possessing the keys of the kingdom, and of the Dispensation of the Fulness of times."*[55] This essentially meaningless recital, publicly floated no less than thirteen years after the supposed occurrence, described a voice, but not a vision, an event or a prayer. He described an utterance, but not an ordination, and provided but few details.

Joseph failed to then further say that Peter, James, and John appeared to him and Oliver and laid their hands upon their heads in order to ordain them to the high priesthood "after the Holy Order of the Son of God." That makes Mormonism's modern claims to exclusive authority exceedingly tenuous. Those claims were (and continue to be) deceptively supported. Smith died without further describing a time or a place when or where the promise (*"that in due time the priesthood of Melchizedek would be conferred on them"*) could then be said to have been fulfilled. Much like Joseph said that he heard an "audable voice" at Kirtland, Ohio, directing him to sponsor the "Kirtland Safety Society Anti-Banking Company" (a mighty bank that would swallow up all other banks on earth), Joseph now claimed to have heard audible voices say that "in due time" he would receive "the keys of the Priesthood of

---

(LeGrand Richards) reported, "Today approximately a million men hold the Melchizedek and the Aaronic Priesthoods ["there is the wide distribution of the powers and offices of the priesthood among men and boys of the church" (Contributions of Joseph Smith, 2)] . . . ." (LeGrand Richards, *A Marvelous Work and a Wonder* [Salt Lake City: Deseret Book Company, 1976], 90). In the New Testament there is no such diffusion of authority. In the Bible, there is only one priest "after the order of Melchizedek," and that is Christ. (Sharon I. Banister, *For Any Latter-day Saint: One Investigator's Unanswered Questions* [Fort Worth, TX: Star Bible Publications, 1988], 45-46). With that assertion, the Apostle Paul is seen to have agreed.

[55]Doctrine and Covenants Section 128:20, quoted in Roberts, ed., *History of The Church of Jesus Christ of Latter-day Saints*, 1:40 fn, emphasis retained.

Melchizedek" from Peter, James, and John.[56]   One of the great supposed events in all of human history, the restoration of the Melchizedek Priesthood, has no date, time, description, prayer or paternity.   On the basis of such foundational uncertainty, Latter-day Saints have built their gospel structures.

CHURCH TEACHINGS VS. HISTORY

The Church teaches:

- *That Joseph and Oliver received the Aaronic Priesthood from John the Baptist on May 15, 1829.*

History shows:

- *That "The office of elder was at first associated with what would [only later] come to be known as the lesser (or Aaronic) priesthood."*

- *That "no concept of higher priesthood" existed on April 6, 1830, the day the Church was formally organized.*[57]

- *That Joseph Smith and Oliver Cowdery first baptized and ordained each other on May 15, 1829, claiming authority they said that they received because of a command transmitted by means of a stone found deep in a well deposited in Joseph's hat.*

- *That some five-and-a-half years after May 15, 1829, and in October 1834, Mormonism's Lord reversed that story in order to say that Joseph and Oliver baptized and ordained each*

---

[56]It would be 1849, as we have already seen – eleven years after Smith's history, five years after the death of Smith, and twenty years after the alleged event – before Oliver Cowdery awkwardly identified all three of the Savior's apostles by name for the first time. That stale disclosure failed to describe an ordination, time, place or prayer, the conferral of authority, or the details of a supposed restoration.

[57]Quinn, *Origins of Power*, 27, emphasis added.

other after they received lineage dependent hierarchical authority from an angel of God.

- *That what became the lower priesthood was first given to Joseph Smith and Oliver Cowdery by the spirit, and then by an angel identified as John the Baptist.*

- *That Smith and Cowdery failed to publicly describe John the Baptist and angelic ordination on or before April 6, 1830 (and in fact any time before October of 1834).*

The Church teaches:

- *That Joseph Smith and Oliver Cowdery received the Melchizedek Priesthood from Peter, James, and John in "1829, May – June."*[58]

- *That Joseph Smith, jun., and Oliver Cowdery ordained each other elders on April 6, 1830, according to a commandment from God; that they then laid hands on all the baptized members present, "that they might receive the gift of the Holy Ghost and be confirmed members of the Church." The Holy Ghost was poured out upon them "to a very great degree." Some prophesied and "all praised the Lord and rejoiced exceedingly."*[59]

- *That other elders were ordained and received the Melchizedek Priesthood when the Church was organized on April 6, 1830.*[60]

History shows:

---

[58]"The exact date . . . is not stated, but it is generally believed to have taken place in June or July, 1829." (Jenson, comp., *Church Chronology*, xxii). More recently it is definitively stated as "*1829, May-June*." (*Teachings of Presidents of The Church – Joseph Smith* [2007], xv [Historical Summary]).

[59]Jenson, comp., *Church Chronology*, 4, emphasis added.

[60]Quinn, *Origins of Power*, 27.

- *That Joseph and Oliver had not received the power to confer the gift of the Holy Ghost by June of 1829.*[61]

- *That authority was supposedly first given to Joseph Smith and Oliver Cowdery metaphysically, and only then, and very much later by John the Baptist and Peter, James, and John.*

The *Church Chronology* supposed, as the modern Church supposes, that without higher priesthood elders there is no "gift of the Holy Ghost" when members are confirmed. Had John the Baptist and Peter, James, and John visited the earth, each to confer particular priesthood authority upon Joseph and Oliver in *"1829, May-June"* (as the modern Church now says that they did), Mormonism's founders would have described "dual priesthoods of different ranks" when the Church was organized on April 6, 1830. On April 6, 1830, the Church had three offices – elder, teacher and priest. On April 6, 1830, Joseph Smith didn't know that the offices of elder, high priest, seventy, apostle, patriarch and prophet were administered by the high priesthood; or that there were higher authority elders, high priests, seventies, ordained apostles or patriarchs; or that there was a higher priesthood; or that there were orders of priesthood.

---

[61]Book of Commandments 15.

CHAPTER EIGHT

Strange Happenings

Joseph received a revelation that he should be the leader; that he should be ordained by Oliver Cowdery as "Prophet, Seer and Revelator" to the church, and that the church should receive his words as if from God's own mouth. Satan surely rejoiced on that day [April 6, 1830] . . . .

David Whitmer

On the occasion of and at all times prior to that ordination on April 6, 1830, no one had preached John the Baptist, Levi, the Aaronic/Levitical Priesthood, Peter, James, and John, the Melchizedek Priesthood, Elias, Elijah, the Patriarchal Priesthood, angelic ordination, apostolic keys or "priesthood."

Joel M. Allred

A SPIRITUAL COMMUNITY

Mormon historian D. Michael Quinn, an excommunicated believer equipped with strong and powerful arguments adduced from scripture and reason, has repeatedly demonstrated that his personal faith is more than a match for the slings and arrows of outrageous fortune. Quinn describes the untold story of the evolution of the Mormon concept of church: "The passage of time and changes in the historical record have obscured the early Mormon concept of 'church.' Although inconceivable to modern Mormons, the concept of a latter-day 'church' existed at first without being linked to the need for a religious organization or for religious ordinances."[1]

---

[1] D. Michael Quinn, *The Mormon Hierarchy: Origins of Power* (Salt Lake City: Signature Books in association with Smith Research Associates, 1994), 5. "His vision [of the Father and the Son] implied no religious mission, no church, no community, and certainly no ecclesiastical hierarchy." (Ibid., 3). It was but one of thousands of such epiphanies. Furthermore, that vision wasn't discussed in 1829 and 1830.

Quinn points to two revelations received in 1828 and 1829 in support of that extraordinary claim:

> *[An] 1828 revelation offered no alternative church, no latter-day institution with God's approval, no religious ordinances required of converts to "my church." The document read: "Behold this is my doctrine – whosoever repenteth and cometh unto me, the same is my church." And to erase all doubt that God's latter-day "church" required no baptism, the 1828 revelation immediately stated: "Whosoever declareth more or less than this, the same is not of me, but is against me; therefore he is not of my church" (D&C 10:67-68). In 1828 Smith's followers were part of a gathering which lacked organized form and which required only professions of faith and repentance from its converts.[2]*

> *[A] February 1829 revelation (D&C 4) said nothing about ecclesiastical or priestly authority as a qualification for the ministry. Instead it specified requirements of "faith, hope, charity, and love, with an eye single to the glory of God" to be a minister....[3]*

Offices and Early Confusion

According to Quinn, the early Church did not require a religious organization, religious ordinances, priestly authority or baptism. According to Richard L. Bushman, the early Church gave men authority "without reference to a bestowal of priesthood." "Until . .

---

[2]Doctrine and Covenants, 10:67-68, quoted in Quinn, *Origins of Power*, 5-6, emphasis added.

[3]Book of Commandments, 9; Doctrine and Covenants 4:5, quoted in Quinn, *Origins of Power*, 6. One month later a revelation in the Book of Commandments said this: "I will establish my church like unto the church which was taught by my disciples in the days of old." This bold assertion by Joseph's Jesus "did not survive the editing process for the 1835 *Doctrine and Covenants*. In its place [in its altered place] was inserted the requirement of priestly 'power' and about the need to be 'ordained.'" (Book of Commandments, 10-13; compare Doctrine and Covenants 5:6, 13-14, 17, quoted in Quinn, *Origins of Power*, 6, emphasis added).

. [June 1831], the word 'priesthood,' although it appeared in the *Book of Mormon*, had not been used in Mormon sermonizing or modern revelations."[4]   In the beginning, after the Church reassessed informality, the Church had prophets, more than one, and unordained apostles. Joseph was *a* prophet and *an* apostle and *an* elder, a non-Melchizedek generic charismatic lower authority elder. "[T]hou shalt be called *a* seer, *a* translator, *a* prophet, *an* apostle[5] of Jesus Christ, *an* elder of the church through the will of God the Father, and the grace of your Lord Jesus Christ . . . ."[6] "[T]he will of God the Father," and "the grace of your Lord," served to describe non-exclusive metaphysical charisma, the lower "authority" principle that actually guided the society's affairs from May 15, 1829, to June 3, 1831. A principle the validity of which Smith and Cowdery rudely dismissed in their October 1834 account of a visit from John the Baptist (before the visit of John the Baptist on May 15, 1829, no one had "authority from God to administer the offices of the gospel"[7]). Following the proceedings at the Fourth Conference of the Church at Kirtland, Ohio, on June 3-6, 1831, and "Until the revelation dated September 1832 (which wasn't published until 1835 [*D&C* 84]), Joseph Smith and others [according to Quinn] saw the higher priesthood as encompassing one office [high priest] exclusively." That was an office traditional Christians thought to have been held by only two men, Melchizedek and Christ. During this period,

> *The lesser priesthood applied to the offices of deacon, teacher, priest, elder and bishop. The 1832 revelation for the first time specified that "elder and bishop are necessary appendages belonging unto the high*

---

[4]Richard Lyman Bushman, with the assistance of Jed Woodworth, *Joseph Smith: Rough Stone Rolling* (New York: Alfred A. Knopf, 2005), 157-58, emphasis added.

[5]Men loosely called apostles (including Joseph Smith and the witnesses to the Book of Mormon) were not assigned to the Quorum, when twelve carefully selected apostles first formed an ordained founding Quorum in 1835, although the designation as earlier applied without ordination to witnesses, visionaries, missionaries and elders didn't disappear in the blink of an eye. The apostolic ordinations in 1835 put a pound of flesh on a new soon-to-be-privileged class of missionary insiders.

[6]Book of Commandments 22:1 (6 April 1830), emphasis added.

[7]Letter (Cowdery and Smith's 1834-35 History), *Messenger and Advocate*, vol. 1 no. 1 (October 1834), 15.

> *priesthood." Further it associated higher priesthood*
> *in a general way with Melchizedek and lesser*
> *priesthood with Aaron, but the actual terms*
> *"Melchizedek Priesthood" and "Aaronic Priesthood"*
> *first appeared in an 1835 revelation (now sec. 107).*
> *This revelation also stated explicitly for the first time*
> *that "the office of Elder comes under the Priesthood*
> *of Melchizedek" (v. 7).*[8]

Joseph Smith and Sidney Rigdon made a mountain out of
Melchizedek. The name had been briefly described in the Book of
Mormon and in the Bible in Genesis, Psalms and Hebrews. In the
New Testament it is found only in Hebrews. A Book of Mormon
prophet set the stage: ". . . Alma . . . spoke of men 'ordained unto
the High Priesthood of the holy order of God . . . .'" Melchizedek
was but one of those "many" men. The Book of Mormon's
Melchizedek received "the office of the High Priesthood according
to the holy order of God."[9] The ancient patriarch's name also
appeared in "three brief verses" in Genesis 14, where it captured
the attention of Joseph Smith and Sidney Rigdon who were busy
revising the King James Bible without archival resources. Smith
and Rigdon "elaborately" "embellished" the verses assigned to
Melchizedek in Genesis.[10] After the passage of time, in what was a
shock to the Christian system, and as if by way of rebuttal to the
author of the Epistle to the Hebrews (supposed to be the Apostle
Paul), Smith and Rigdon concluded that the high priesthood,
contrary to Christian precedent, was to be bestowed on as many as
believed on his name.

This newly minted concept (the notion that many believers were to
be ordained high priests) had nothing to do with a faithful
"restoration" of the power of the patriarchs. It did not advance the
proposition that, "I will establish my church like unto the church
which was taught by my apostles in the days of old." It challenged

---

[8]Quinn, *Origins of Power*, 29-30, emphasis added.
[9]Bushman, *Joseph Smith: Rough Stone Rolling*, 159-60.
[10]Smith's "Book of Enoch" composed in 1830 and associated with the
translation of Genesis was canonized in the Book of Moses, which included two
chapters on Enoch, another obscure biblical figure. (*See* The Pearl of Great Price,
Moses 6 and 7).

the teachings of the Apostle Paul and the gospel church, and the provisions of the King James Version of the Christian Bible. It is antagonistic to the principles of traditional Christianity. In the larger Christian world, there is but one great High Priest, Jesus Christ, the Son of God.

The so-called Patriarchal order of the Priesthood and the missions of Elias and Elijah are discussed in this work in chapter 13 entitled "The Forgotten Order."

Missing Priesthood

The Church was organized on April 6, 1830, without the authority of the Melchizedek Priesthood. Peter, James, and John didn't visit Joseph Smith and Oliver Cowdery before April 6, 1830, whatever the Church now says, and what only later came to be called the "high priesthood" hadn't been "restored" when the Church was officially formed.

James E. Talmage, a Latter-day Saint leader, an apostle and a revered early Mormon scholar, operated under the comfortable assumption that the Melchizedek Priesthood had been "manifested and conferred" upon Joseph Smith and Oliver Cowdery by Peter, James, and John before the Church was officially formed. In confident terms, Talmage carefully described the foundational significance, the vitally important foundational significance of the (alleged) *restoration* of the power of the Holy (Melchizedek) Priesthood after the Order of the Son of God: "This order of Priesthood," he said, "holds authority over all the offices in the Church, and includes power to administer in spiritual things, consequently all the authorities and powers necessary to the establishment and development of the Church were by this visitation [Peter, James, and John's visitation] *restored* to earth."[11] And if there was no visitation, they weren't. And if there was no visitation until sometime after the Church was officially formed (on

---

[11]James E. Talmage, *A Study of the Articles of Faith: Being a Consideration of the Principal Doctrines of The Church of Jesus Christ of Latter-day Saints*, 33rd ed. (Salt Lake City: The Church of Jesus Christ of Latter-day Saints, 1955), 188, emphasis added.

April 6, 1830), they weren't.   Apostle Talmage's prescription tracked concepts described in an 1835 revelation that clarified the importance of the power and authority of the higher priesthood: "The Melchizedek Priesthood holds the right of presidency, and has power and authority over all the offices in the church in all ages of the world, to administer in spiritual things."[12]   In 1835, this particular revelation was the first to explicitly call the High Priesthood of the holy order of God the "Melchizedek Priesthood."

The Church and its non-Melchizedek elders didn't have Apostle Talmage's all-encompassing power during its important formative period.   On April 6, 1830, Mormons laid faint claim to some unspecified metaphysical kind of generic unitary, less than exclusive lower "authority."   On April 6, 1830, the members of the Church had no reason to identify that unitary "authority" with those "dual priesthoods of different ranks" that were later ("in an 1835 revelation") divided to become the Melchizedek and Aaronic Priesthoods.

In 1838-39 Joseph Smith and several of his trusted associates collaborated to compose what became the canonized official account of the visit of the Angel Moroni.   In that carefully drafted chronological account (first published at Nauvoo, Illinois, in 1842), which was not the first account, the Mormon prophet publicly described, nineteen or twenty years after the fact, an 1823 message supposed to have been conveyed to a seventeen-year-old Joseph by the Angel Moroni: *"Behold I will reveal unto you the Priesthood, by the hand of Elijah the prophet, before the coming of the great and dreadful day of the Lord."*[13]   In this account, it is to Elijah the prophet, and not to Peter, James, and John, to whom Joseph must look for the restoration of the Priesthood "before the coming of the great and dreadful day of the Lord."   In this, in a vision first described in 1838-39, in a History that wasn't made public until 1842, Joseph's Lord described the promise of a Priesthood to be delivered by the hand of Elijah before the Second Coming. Joseph later treated "Elijah" (Hebrew) and "Elias" (Greek), two different names for the same prophet, as two different prophets, and went further to say that both of those prophets appeared to him, and to

---

[12]Doctrine and Covenants 107:8.
[13]The Pearl of Great Price, Joseph Smith – History 1:38, emphasis retained.

Oliver Cowdery, one after the other, behind the veil in the Kirtland temple on April 3, 1836.

If Moroni had actually promised Joseph the "Priesthood" in 1823 – using a word Joseph, the Church of Christ and Jesus didn't use until 1831 in a prophecy Joseph didn't report until 1842 – and if Joseph had actually anticipated from as early as 1823 a revelation on the subject of "the Priesthood," the 1828-29 community could not have ignored the necessity for baptism, issues of priestly authority, angelic ordination and the need for religious ordinances and a religious organization. Smith's spiritual community, had he actually received that kind of an instruction, would not have first grown to become a thinly-based assembly of like-minded believers dependent upon charisma and the voice of God for its "authority." "[F]rom 1828 to May 1829 'my church' was an unorganized body of 'my people' who had no priestly 'authority' and which required no religious ordinances."[14]

Smith didn't mention Moroni's supposed 1838-39 report of an 1823 promise of priesthood ("*Behold I will reveal unto you the Priesthood by the hand of Elijah . . .* ") in his one-hundred-and-thirty-year suppressed 1832 Holographic Account, an account that included an even earlier report of the vision of Moroni. The 1832 History, which wasn't "*brought to light*" until *1965*, purported to describe the most important events in Joseph's early life.[15] Oliver Cowdery and Joseph Smith didn't mention Elijah's priesthood promise in their "detailed description" of Moroni's words in the History they prepared in 1834.[16] What could have been any more important? The claim that Moroni said in 1823, in a document that was composed in 1838-39 and published in 1842, that he would reveal the priesthood by the hand of Elijah was just one more retroactive amendment applied to the touchy issue of priesthood.

Once various deceitful passages known to have been added to earlier resources (visions, revelations, histories) by way of backdated revisions are removed, the evidence in support of the

---

[14]Quinn, *Origins of Power*, 6.
[15]Joseph Smith Jr., *The Personal Writings of Joseph Smith*, ed. Dean C. Jessee (Salt Lake City: Deseret Book, 1984), 4.
[16]Quinn, *Origins of Power*, 6.

claim that Joseph and Oliver received physical authority from any heavenly messengers in 1829 may be rudely dismissed. Amendments that altered earlier revelations, visions, manuscripts and documents, and changed the historical record to abruptly include accounts of previously unknown visits of ancient religious figures were added to the first edition of the Doctrine and Covenants in 1835. Those 1835 unprovenanced alterations, backdated new additions to older revelations, claimed the older revelations' earlier dates and falsified their contents without archival support in the original records. Important discrepancies, long known to scholars, have never been corrected. What was true of the Church in the past (listen to Ezra Booth writing in 1831) is true of the Church in the present. "Mormonism has in part changed its character, and assumed a different dress, from that under which it made its first appearance on the Western Reserve. Many extraordinary circumstances which then existed have vanished out of sight; and the Mormonites desire not only to forget them, but wish them blotted out of the memory of others."[17] Booth's comment is both telling and true.

THE ORDINATION OF ELDERS

While they pretended to baptize by immersion for the remission of sins, a revelation dated June 1829 said that they didn't yet have (thus couldn't yet confer) the gift of the Holy Ghost (Book of Commandments, 1833, 15:20). On May 15, 1829, in May-June of 1829, and on April 6, 1830, Joseph Smith and Oliver Cowdery couldn't ordain anyone to any office assigned to what later came to be called the Melchizedek Priesthood. Without the authority of the high priesthood (and without using the word "priesthood"), Joseph and Oliver *ordained* each other and others to office as elders. We now know how that worked out; they purported to create metaphysical elders. The first Mormon to be baptized and the first elder to be ordained (Oliver Cowdery) became the Second non-Melchizedek Elder. The second Mormon to be baptized and the second elder to be ordained (Joseph Smith) became the First non-

---

[17]Ezra Booth in Eber D. Howe, *Mormonism Unvailed: Or, A Faithful Account of That Singular Imposition and Delusion* (Painesville, OH: E.D. Howe, 1834; reprint, New York: AMS Press Inc., 1977), 183.

Melchizedek Elder.   By modern Mormon reckoning, John the Baptist lacked the power to ordain Joseph and Oliver to the office of elder and couldn't confer the gift of the Holy Ghost.   Without additional authority, they couldn't confirm each other, or ordain each other or others, to the office of elder.

Ordained and Reordained

Before the first generic lower authority elder was ordained to the high priesthood at Kirtland, Ohio, in June 1831, and before the high priesthood was "manifested and conferred for the first time upon several of the Elders" at Kirtland, Ohio, in June 1831, Oliver Cowdery, who didn't hold the Melchizedek Priesthood or say that he did, who wasn't a Melchizedek elder and didn't say that he was, ordained Joseph Smith (on April 6, 1830) to be the "Prophet, Seer and Revelator" of the newly established Church.   Cowdery ordained Smith to the highest office in the only true church on the face of the earth without the authority of what only later came to be called the Melchizedek Priesthood.   Mormonism's charisma, as the events in Kirtland, Ohio, in 1831 later proved, was a lesser lower kind of claim to non-Melchizedek authority.   The leaders later retroactively denied the efficacy of charismatic authority.

> *The traditional account of church origins, which assumes that Smith encountered Peter, James, and John sometime in 1829, also claims that at the church's organization in April 1830 those ordained "elders" were ordained on that date and received the Melchizedek priesthood. A closer look at the evidence demonstrates that they were in fact re-ordained and that no concept of higher priesthood existed. The office of elder was at first associated with what would come to be known as the lesser (or Aaronic) priesthood.*[18]

Many authorities present and past, faithful and not, say that on April 6, 1830, the office of elder was of necessity associated with

---

[18]Quinn, *Origins of Power*, 27, emphasis added.

nothing more than generic unitary nonexclusive metaphysical lower "authority." The authority principle in the early Church depended upon unverifiable charisma and the voice of God. That was admitted at the Fourth Conference of the Church at Kirtland, Ohio, on June 3, 1831. It would be years before the concept of generic authority would surrender its egalitarian place to become the lesser (Aaronic) priesthood, the lineage-dependent less-than-eternal roundly-disparaged non-restorable priesthood of the old law.

Before the high priesthood was "manifested and conferred for the first time upon several of the elders" at Kirtland, Ohio, in June 1831, more than a year after the Church was officially formed, forty-four men had been ordained to the office of elder by other unprovenanced men exercising something not yet called "lineal," "linear," "hierarchical," "Aaronic," "Levitical," "Melchizedek," "Patriarchal," or even "priesthood." These men did not know when they were ordained – and would not know until June 1831 – that they would come to hold something to be called "priesthood," on top of something called "authority." "The idea of priesthood descending in a line of authority was Roman, not Puritan."[19] It is important to yet again report that about two thousand members were baptized into the Church on the basis of an unembellished charismatic authority principle. Those early members knew little or nothing about a mysterious biblical figure by the name of Melchizedek and, even after some of the early elders were reordained to the office of elder and to the power of the high "priesthood," had no reason to associate the reception of such additional authority with Peter, James, and John.

No one knew or would know until 1834 and 1835 that Joseph and Oliver had ever encountered John the Baptist, or Peter, James, and John. In 1832 (in a revelation that wasn't published until 1835, quite some time after the Fourth Conference of the Church on June 3, 1831) the offices of elder and bishop were classified (for the first time) as "appendages belonging unto the high priesthood."[20] Not until 1835 could it actually be said in more than a general way that

---

[19]Bushman, *Joseph Smith: Rough Stone Rolling*, 157.
[20]Doctrine and Covenants 84:29, quoted in Quinn, *Origins of Power*, 29. This revelation, supposed to have been received in 1832, was not included with sixty-five other revelations published in the Book of Commandments in 1833.

Peter, James, and John brought the "Melchizedek Priesthood" to the service of the new society. On April 6, 1830, Oliver Cowdery ordained Joseph Smith to the highest office on earth.[21] On April 6, 1830, Oliver Cowdery didn't hold the high priesthood. And on April 6, 1830, Oliver Cowdery didn't hold and couldn't have held the lineage-dependent Aaronic Priesthood.

Sinful Ordinations

"Joseph may not have realized that elders were part of the Melchizedek Priesthood already and were being ordained to the office of high priest rather than receiving the powers of the high priesthood."[22] Whatever that is supposed to mean, it wasn't what the prophet said. Forty-four men had been ordained to the office of elder before Joseph Smith and about half of them were ordained to the high priesthood at the Fourth Conference of the Church held at Kirtland, Ohio, on June 3, 1831. The Mormon scholar James E. Talmage, who may have thought he was above this battle,[23] described the pristine nature of proper authority:

> *Unauthorized Ministrations in priestly functions are not alone invalid, but also grievously sinful. In His dealings with mankind God recognizes and honors the Priesthood established by His direction, and countenances no unauthorized assumption of authority. A lesson is taught by the case of Korah and his associates, in their rebellion against the authority of the Priesthood in that they falsely professed the right to minister in the priest's office. The Lord promptly visited them for their sins, causing the ground to cleave asunder and to swallow them up with*

---

[21]David Whitmer, *An Address to All Believers in Christ: by A Witness to the Divine Authenticity of The Book of Mormon* (Richmond, MO: n.p., 1887; photographic reprint, Concord, CA: Pacific Publishing Company, 1993), 33.

[22]Bushman, *Joseph Smith: Rough Stone Rolling*, 158.

[23]Talmage operated on the less-than-safe assumption that Peter, James, and John restored the Melchizedek Priesthood in 1829 before the Church was officially formed.

all their belongings.[24]

Talmage, emphasizing the supreme importance of the Mormon priesthood as a twentieth-century scholar, went further to say that: "[N]ot an instance is set down in Holy Writ of anyone taking to himself the authority to officiate in sacred ordinances and being acknowledged of the Lord in such administration."[25] Unfortunately for that unsupported assumption, two thousand early members of the Church were baptized and confirmed before being ordained teachers, deacons, priests, elders and bishops by men whose "authority" was uncertain, non-exclusive, under construction and insecure. In every case without the bestowal of priesthood. Prior to 1835, and until the Church was upwards of six years old, "the structure was fluid, and public claims for authority in the church were made largely on the basis of religious experience and charisma rather than priestly power through lineage and angelic ministration."[26] There was literally no "structured sense of authority or priesthood,"[27] and the issues were flexible. Mormonism's early baptisms, confirmations and licenses set at defiance the much later and powerfully heralded claim that no one shall take "to himself the authority to officiate in sacred ordinances." And then also the further claim that "a man must be called of God, by prophecy, and by the laying on of hands, by those who are in authority, to preach the Gospel and administer in the ordinances thereof."[28] Linear authority and angelic ordination were peculiar concepts unknown to the members of the early Church. Yet they managed to order their affairs and seemed to think they lacked for nothing.

---

[24]Talmage, *A Study of the Articles of Faith*, 33rd ed., 183-84, emphasis added. "God reminded 'the Israelites' that *no one* except a *descendant of Aaron* should come to burn incense before the Lord . . . ." (Numbers 16:40, quoted by Sharon I. Banister, *For Any Latter-day Saint: One Investigator's Unanswered Questions* [Fort Worth, TX: Star Bible Publications, 1988], 39, emphasis retained). Korah's crime? The "unauthorized assumption" of the authority of ancient Israel's lineage-dependent "Levitical Priesthood."
[25]Talmage, *A Study of the Articles of Faith*, 33rd ed., 179.
[26]Quinn, *Origins of Power*, 7.
[27]Ibid., 8.
[28]The Pearl of Great Price, Articles of Faith 5. *See also* Talmage, *A Study of the Articles of Faith*, 33rd ed., 179.

From its earliest authority-principle beginnings – from April 1830 until at least June 1831 – the Church did *many* things it later said could not be done without the authority of the high priesthood (think of Oliver Cowdery purporting to ordain Joseph Smith to the office of Prophet, Seer, and Revelator on April 6, 1830). According to Talmage, "The remarks of Paul concerning high priests are applicable to every office of the priesthood." Paul said, and Talmage repeated that, "No man taketh this honor unto himself, but he that is called of God, as was Aaron."[29] The Apostle Paul was not "called of God, as was Aaron," nor either Melchizedek, nor either Jesus, nor either very many other metaphysical priests, including Book of Mormon figures. Members of the early Church of Christ (Mormon) took Talmage's priesthood honor unto themselves. One can only surmise that they imagined the reception of the Holy Ghost under the hands of those generic unitary (non-Melchizedek) elders in a late-to-the-table process that required a power John the Baptist wasn't equipped to confer.

If John the Baptist didn't confer the Aaronic Priesthood upon Joseph and Oliver in 1829, as both of them (nearly five-and-a-half) years later said that he did; if Joseph and Oliver were not Hebrews able to hold an Aaronic/Levitical lineage-dependent inheritance; if Peter, James, and John didn't confer the Melchizedek Priesthood upon those founders in 1829, as the modern Church has stubbornly chosen to say that they did, then Mormonism's founders were guilty of "invalid," "grievously sinful" "unauthorized" ministrations of authority. If those founders were not ordained by heavenly messengers (Peter, James, and John), as they only later (nearly six years later) reconsidered to say, if the veil between heaven and earth didn't disappear, as they later claimed that it did, then they usurped priestly authority. By 1835 the Church was fully invested in some unprecedented kind of exclusive authority supposed to have been received by angelic ordinations under the hands of heavenly messengers. By then, by Mormon reckoning, nothing less would do. In that they turned their backs on the practices and procedures that kept the ship afloat during the society's formative period.

---

[29]Hebrews 5:4, quoted in Talmage, *A Study of the Articles of Faith*, 33rd ed., 186.

Ordination Claims Amplified: Before 1835

At the Peter Whitmer Sr. home in June 1829, Joseph Smith (who hadn't yet received the gift of the Holy Ghost) claimed charismatic authority by way of a heavenly message, as his mother (Lucy Mack Smith), David Whitmer, William E. McLellin and the Book of Commandments (published in 1833) all at first proclaimed. This procedure, involving a heavenly message instead of a heavenly messenger, was delivered to Joseph through that magical stone, the acorn of the Mormon oak. This non-Melchizedek supposed spiritual authority was, but not for years, awkwardly reconfigured to theoretically become the historically-disparaged Levitical Priesthood, the Old Testament's burdensome codification of ancient Jewish themes. There was no John the Baptist in the Church from May 1829 until October 1834, and there was no undeniable identifiable "Aaronic Priesthood" in what became the Church of the Latter Day Saints until 1835.[30]

Section 68 verse 21 of the current Doctrine and Covenants reports that, "[A] literal descendant of Aaron may claim their anointing if at any time they can prove their lineage, or do ascertain it by revelation . . . ."[31] The problem with that particular provision is that verse 21 (like verses 15 to 21 of Section 68, which are not found in the original manuscript) is falsified. This claim to authority is dependent upon backdated additions to an earlier revelation without archival support in the original transcript, or in the October 1832 issue of *The Evening and the Morning Star* where the original manuscript was initially published, or in the 1833 Book of Commandments, where it was published for a second time.

Jesus and his disciples didn't hold (or much admire) the Aaronic/Levitical Priesthood. It was "evident," according to the author of Hebrews, "that our Lord sprang out of Juda; of which tribe Moses spake nothing concerning priesthood."[32] Joseph Smith and Oliver Cowdery were not Levites or biological Hebrews. Like Jesus, they didn't hold and couldn't have held Levi's lineage-

---

[30]Doctrine and Covenants 107:1. Doctrine and Covenants Section 84 was not published until 1835.

[31]Ibid., citing Doctrine and Covenants 68:21.

[32]Hebrews 7:14.

dependent less-than-eternal priesthood. Joseph and Oliver, who would claim to be (affinity children) of Israel, even then sprang from tribes of which "Moses spake nothing concerning priesthood." What was true of Joseph Smith, Ephraim and Manasseh was true of Oliver Cowdery, Ephraim and Manasseh, whether they were of the blood of Israel (biological or affinity Hebrews) or not. Thus, the Church of Christ (early Mormon) laid *no* defensible claim to lineage-based Levitical authority on April 6, 1830.

When the story as it is was then supposed to have at first developed was finally told, and before it was revised, Joseph and Oliver said they were promised additional authority. Heavenly messengers, out of the loop, didn't fit that early equation. "Ask the Father in my name in faith believing that you shall receive," the Lord is supposed to have said – before the Church was officially formed and in that fateful month of June 1829 – "and you shall have the Holy Ghost which manifesteth all things, which is expedient unto the children of men."[33] When this revelation was reduced to writing in June 1829, Joseph, Oliver and David Whitmer, the three men to whom it was directed, hadn't yet received the gift of the Holy Ghost.

This revelation-tendered gift, in that month of June 1829, wasn't something to be physically conferred upon the Mormon leaders by the laying on of other worldly hands. It was dependent upon charisma and the voice of God. In this portended metaphysical conferral, there was no angelic ordination, there were no apostolic keys, there was no John the Baptist, no Aaronic Priesthood, no Peter, James, and John, no Melchizedek Priesthood, the authority was not exclusive and the ordination was earthbound. This egalitarian gift of a loving God was available to any worthy person, upon request or by command without the necessity for the interference of meddlesome ethnocentric intermediaries. The Church wasn't the "gospel" then, and "authority" wasn't the "priesthood" then. After what was innocently described as "diligent" and "anxious" inquiry, and long before Joseph much later settled on other out-of-this-world explanations, he described how this alleged metaphysical authority, and the supposed power of

---

[33]Book of Commandments 15:20.

the Holy Ghost, first came to be conferred.[34]

> We had for some time made this matter a subject of
> humble prayer, and at length we got together in the
> Chamber of Mr. Whitmer's house in order more
> particularly to seek of the Lord what we now so
> earnestly desired . . . . [W]e had not long been
> engaged in solemn and fervent prayer, when *the
> word of the Lord,* came unto us in the Chamber,
> *commanding us;* that I should ordain Oliver
> Cowdery to be an Elder in the Church of Jesus
> Christ, And that he also should ordain me to the
> same office, and then to ordain others . . . [W]e were
> however commanded to defer this our ordination
> untill, such times, as it should be practicable to have
> our brethren, who had been and who should be
> baptized, assembled together . . . .[35]

Peter, James, and John are not an element in this early equation. It
is more than six years too early for them. Apostolic keys and
angelic ordination had nothing to do with this first and early design.
The original authority to ordain and confirm was said to have been
derived from *commandments* given to Joseph and Oliver, who were
transcribing the Book of Mormon at Peter Whitmer Sr.'s house in
June of 1829. With the passage of time, the original records were
altered and ignored in order to suggest a different more glorious
supernal and physical process. Grant H. Palmer described this
deceptive transition:

> *As in his accounts of an angel and the gold plates,
> Joseph was willing to expand on another foundational
> narrative. The events surrounding priesthood
> restoration were reinterpreted, one detail emphasized
> over another. A spiritually charged moment when*

---

[34]Grant H. Palmer, *An Insider's View of Mormon Origins* (Salt Lake City:
Signature Books, 2002), 218.

[35]Joseph Smith Jr., *The Papers of Joseph Smith: Autobiographical and
Historical Writings*, Dean C. Jessee ed. (Salt Lake City: Deseret Book Co., 1989),
1:299, quoted in Palmer, *An Insider's View of Mormon Origins*, 218, emphasis
added.

*participants felt that the veil between heaven and
earth was thin became, in the retelling, an event with
no veil at all.   The first stories about how Joseph
received his authority show that, like other prophets
and religious founders throughout history, he and
Oliver first received their callings in a metaphysical
way.   Within a few years, their accounts became more
impressive, unique, and physical.*[36]

1831 CONFERENCE (FOURTH CONFERENCE)

The Fourth General Conference of the Church of Christ (the first to
be held in Ohio) convened in Kirtland, Ohio, on June 3-6, 1831.
That particularly memorable convocation held in a log schoolhouse
close to the farm of Isaac Morley (an early follower of Rigdon) saw
some dramatic changes made in the organizational structure of the
Church.   The Fourth Conference was supposed to be "the time
specified" for a great and mighty work to commence, nothing less
than "the work of miracles."   God was finally going to show his
great power at that Conference on those days.   "With such strong
assurance, and with the most elevated expectations, the conference
assembled at the time appointed."[37]

The congregation at Sidney Rigdon's Ohio included forty-four non-
Melchizedek elders, four priests and fifteen teachers.   Elders,
teachers and priests held three offices in the early Church.   Not
many Latter-day Saints are familiar with the sobering events
associated with those particular meetings.   Although June 3, 1831,
was more than two years after Joseph and Oliver said they were
commanded to baptize each other on May 15, 1829, Mormonism's
authority-principle was still fluid, undefined and overlooked.
"Authority" wasn't called "restored," or "Aaronic," or "Levitical,"
or "Patriarchal," or even "Priesthood," and it wasn't associated
with John the Baptist, Peter, James, and John, Elias, Elijah,
Nephites or the gospel church.   After other allegedly monumental
events supposed to have occurred on May 15, 1829 (as only later
described in a second unfamiliar scenario not actually reported

---

[36]Palmer, *An Insider's View of Mormon Origins*, 232, emphasis added.
[37]Ezra Booth in Howe, *Mormonism Unvailed*, 188.

until in and after October 1834), how could "authority" not have been identified by the use of the words "Priesthood," "Levi," "Aaron" or "John the Baptist" if what the founders chose to say in 1834 had in fact occurred? How could the Book of Mormon or the Preface to the Book of Mormon and other early important Mormon resources, under construction at or about that same time, have neglected to describe the lineal priesthood of the old law? Ancient Israel's primitive tutorial code? The shadow of heavenly things? Or Moroni's 1823 promise of priesthood?

Until this day (June 3, 1831), more than a year after the Church was organized, and more than two years after *May 15, 1829*, and/or *May-June 1829*, Mormonism's authority principle was still decidedly unitary. You may take that to the bank. In Joseph Smith's one hundred and thirty year suppressed first and only 1832 Holographic Account of his first encounter with deity, authority was unitary, not yet Aaronic, not yet Melchizedek, not yet Patriarchal. On June 3, 1831, before the Conference, no none knew that there were high priests, seventies, presiding patriarchs, higher authority elders, apostolic keys, angelic ordinations or three different priesthoods and apostles weren't ordained.   No one seemed to know that the offices of elders and bishops were appendages of some higher priesthood, or that some lower order of priesthood was an appendage of some higher order of priesthood, or that there were higher and lower orders of priesthood, multiple overlapping priesthoods, authorities and offices organized according to rank. No one knew that Mormonism's generic unitary "authority" had anything to do with ancient Israel's ossified law of a carnal commandment; or that "authority" would later be reconfigured to become something called the Aaronic/ Levitical Priesthood. "Prior to 1831 the only major division of authority was between elders and all others . . . members did not recognize two priesthoods within the church,"[38] or even use the controversial Catholic word as a vehicle designed to more accurately describe spiritual power. Considered against everything supposed to have happened in May and June of 1829, that is a bit of a problem.

---

[38]Richard S. Van Wagoner, *Sidney Rigdon: A Portrait of Religious Excess* (Salt Lake City: Signature Books, 1994; paperback 2006), 96.

Sidney and Melchizedek

When Joseph and Emma Smith moved to Ohio in 1831, it was to be close to an impressive new convert by the name of Sidney Rigdon. God is supposed to have told Joseph and Sidney in a revelation jointly given to both of them shortly after they met that the Saints were supposed to gather in Ohio. Rigdon had a communitarian society there. David Whitmer, a Book of Mormon witness and an important early Mormon leader, described Joseph's new best forever friend:

> *Rigdon was a thorough Bible scholar, a man of fine education, and a powerful orator. He soon worked his way deep into Brother Joseph's affections, and had more influence over him than any other man living. He was Brother Joseph's private counsellor, and his most intimate friend and brother for some time after they met. Brother Joseph rejoiced, believing that the Lord had sent to him this great and mighty man Sidney Rigdon, to help him in the work. Poor Brother Joseph! ... Sidney Rigdon was the cause of almost all the errors which were introduced while he was in the church.*[39]

During the winter of 1831, while they were jointly preparing their "Inspired Translation" of the King James Version of the Christian Bible (KJV), Smith and Rigdon expanded "three brief verses" in Genesis[40] to bolster the stature of an ancient patriarch named Melchizedek, a mysterious figure mentioned in the Bible, and by Alma, one of the prophets in the Book of Mormon. The winter of 1831 followed the extraordinary events known to have occurred at the Fourth Conference of the Church held in Kirtland, Ohio, in June of 1831. Melchizedek's emerging stature as a prominent patriarchal figure in the Church followed the conferral of "the high

---

[39]Whitmer, *An Address to All Believers in Christ*, 35, emphasis added. David Whitmer claimed that Rigdon was "the instigator of the secret organization known as the 'Danites,'" a violent society founded upon violent covenants "formed in Far West, Missouri, in June 1838." (Whitmer had been the well-positioned President of the Missouri Church).

[40]Bushman, *Joseph Smith: Rough Stone Rolling*, 159-60.

priesthood of the holy order of God" upon several of the elders, including Joseph Smith.

Melchizedek is said to have been one of a number of priests, none of whom were equal to or greater than him. The priesthood that arrived shortly after Rigdon did was initially called "the High Priesthood of the holy order of God" (and sometimes of "the Son of God"). Melchizedek was identified as one of the many high priests in God's "holy order." While Melchizedek was prominently mentioned by the author of the Epistle to the Hebrews, Sidney and Joseph made more of his calling and importance than the Bible or the Book of Mormon did. They embellished Melchizedek's biblical credentials – as an element of their King James Version translation – after that Fourth Conference of the Church, and during the winter of 1831. His name later became closely identified with an ancient order of authority. It is said that his name was assigned to that ancient order, which wasn't his order, so as to avoid the too frequent use of the sacred name of deity. Melchizedek became a dynamic factor in the Mormon equation after the biblically conversant Rigdon's ascension to his confident status as Joseph Smith's "most intimate friend and brother."

Strange Happenings

"During the three-day gathering (3-6 June 1831) a profound change was inaugurated in the church's organization."[41] The events at the meetings took an unexpected turn. The first day of the Fourth Conference started in *promising* fashion. The Mormon prophet laid the foundation for "a day of Pentecost," something extraordinary to be long remembered. "Joseph said that Christ's kingdom, like a grain of mustard seed, 'was now before him and some should see it put forth its branches and the angels of heaven would some day come like birds to its branches.'"[42] According to Smith, "not three days should pass away, before some should see their Savior, face to face."[43] Levi Hancock later reported that, "Joseph *promised* Lyman Wight he would see Christ that day. Wight soon turned stiff and

---

[41]Van Wagoner, *Sidney Rigdon*, 96.
[42]Smith, quoted in Bushman, *Joseph Smith: Rough Stone Rolling*, 156.
[43]Ezra Booth in Howe, *Mormonism Unvailed*, 188.

white, exclaiming that he had indeed viewed the Savior. According to Hancock, Joseph himself said, 'I now see God, and Jesus Christ at his right hand.'"[44]   Ezra Booth, a good man in a bad place, described Smith's ordination of Wight: "He then laid his hands on the head of Elder Wight, who had participated largely in the warm feeling of his leader, and ordained him to the High Priesthood."[45] Other ordinations followed.

Richard L. Bushman described the unsettling ordination of a disciple by the name of Harvey Whitlock:

> *[T]he meeting unraveled. Joseph ordained Harvey Whitlock to the high priesthood, the most important business of the meeting, and Whitlock reacted badly. "He turned as black as Lyman was white," Hancock reported. "His fingers were set like claws. He went around the room and showed his hands and tried to speak, his eyes were in the shape of oval O's." Astonished at the turn of events, Hyrum [Joseph's older brother] exclaimed, "Joseph, that is not of God." Joseph, unwilling to cut the phenomenon short, told Hyrum to wait, but Hyrum insisted: "I will not believe . . . unless you inquire of God and he ownes it." Hancock said, "Joseph bowed his head, and in a short time got up and commanded satan to leave Harvey, laying his hands upon his head at the same time." Then, Hancock said, Leman Copley, who weighed over two hundred pounds, somersaulted in the air and fell on his back over a bench. Wight cast Satan out of Copley and Copley was calmed.   The evil spirit,*

---

[44]Hancock Diary, 48 in Howe, *Mormonism Unvailed*, 188-89, quoted in Bushman, *Joseph Smith: Rough Stone Rolling*, 156, emphasis added. This author has never heard the grim details of this memorable occasion described in a conference talk, or at any other Mormon meeting, and until Bushman's biography published in 2005 had never heard the strange and turbulent story of such events. It is highly probable that most Latter-day Saints, including leaders and missionaries, don't know that Lyman Wight, "the first ordained high priest," ordained Joseph Smith to the high priesthood after the Holy Order of God more than one year after the Church was officially formed, and in the midst of unforgettable turmoil.

[45]Ezra Booth in Howe, *Mormonism Unvailed*, 188.

according to Hancock, was in and out of people all day and the greater part of the night. Joseph who was ordaining men to the high priesthood, came eventually to Hancock and assured him he had a calling "as high as any man in the house." The words brought Hancock relief: "I was glad for that for I was so scared I would not stir without his liberty for all the world."[46]

Ezra Booth, one of the men ordained to the high priesthood by Lyman Wight on June 3, 1831, was an eyewitness to those Fourth Conference proceedings. Booth was perhaps the first person known to have described the ordination of Harvey Whitlock:

Another Elder, who had been ordained to the same office as Wight, at the bidding of Smith, stepped upon the floor. Then ensued a scene, of which you can form no adequate conception; and which I would forebear relating, did not the truth require it. The Elder moved upon the floor, his legs inclining to a bend; one shoulder elevated above the other, upon which the head seemed disposed to recline, his arms partly extended; his hands partly clenched; his mouth partly open, and contracted in the shape of an italic O; his eyes assumed a wild ferocious cast, and his whole appearance presented a frightful object to the view of the beholder. – "Speak, Brother Harvey," said Smith.[47]

Unfortunately Brother Harvey, in a "state of suspense," "was unable to speak." Of those who were present, "some conjectured that Harvey was possessed of the devil, but Smith in a moment of profound reflection said, 'the Lord binds in order to set at liberty.'" After some discussion and "much confusion, Smith learnt by the spirit, that Harvey was under a diabolical influence," bound by Satan and in need of release. Thus enlightened, Smith then commanded "the unclean spirit to come out of him." Telling the elders that "the man of sin was revealed," telling them they "should

---

[46]Bushman, *Joseph Smith: Rough Stone Rolling*, 156-57, emphasis added.
[47]Ezra Booth in Howe, *Mormonism Unvailed*, 189, emphasis added.

become acquainted with the devices of Satan" and possess the knowledge required to manage him, Smith declared the episode to be a miracle.[48]

Intent upon working other miracles, Smith then commanded "Brother Murdock" to straighten a hand that "had been rendered defective" ("I command you in the name of Jesus Christ to straighten your hand . . ."). The prophet's command was wasted on this insufficiently faithful brother. "[A]fter the exertion of his power, both natural and supernatural, the deficient hand returned to its former position, where it still remains." Another elder "decriped in one of his legs was set upon the floor, and commanded, in the name of Jesus Christ to walk." He walked a step or two before his faith failed. "A dead body, which had been retained above ground two or three days, under the expectation that the dead would be raised, was insensible to the voice of those who commanded it to wake into life, and is destined to sleep in the grave till the last trump shall sound . . . ." Under these misapprehensions, and others, "the gloom of disappointed expectation, overspread the countenance of many . . . ."[49]

Welcome to the mostly unspoken details surrounding the supposed "restoration" of what, after further definition, later became (in about 1835) the "Holy Melchizedek Priesthood after the order of the Son of God." The accounts of this meeting described the "diabolical influence" of Satan and men possessed "in need of release." It would be no small miracle to find an investigator apprised of these details before he or she decided to join the Mormon Church. This history is swept under the rug; it is one of the skeletons in the Mormon closet.

John Whitmer, who was the duly authorized Church Historian in 1831, who would later leave the Church with his brothers, David, Jacob, Christian and Peter, and with his brothers-in-law Hiram Page and Oliver Cowdery (seven of the eleven witnesses to the Book of Mormon), cut the prophet some slack in the minutes of the

---

[48]Ibid.
[49]Ibid., 180.

"turbulent meeting."[50] "[T]he Lord showed to Joseph the Seer the design of this thing, he commanded the devil in the name of Christ and he departed to our joy and comfort." Future events conspired to create in the early and important John Whitmer (and his family) an increasingly dim view of "Joseph the Seer."

Ordinations

"The ordinations to the high priesthood [on June 3, 1831] marked a milestone in Mormon ecclesiology. Until that time, the word 'priesthood,' although it appeared in the *Book of Mormon*, had not been used in Mormon sermonizing or modern revelations. Later accounts applied the term retroactively [meaning later accounts were backdated], but the June 1831 Conference marked its first appearance in contemporary records."[51] Its first honest albeit misunderstood appearance in real time. This foundational insight begs to be remembered. The "high priesthood" made its first supposed appearance on June 3, 1831, more than one year after the Church was officially formed, after the conversion of Rigdon and in an intensely disturbing environment.

The Church Chronology offered this sparing description of the turbulent events known to have occurred at the Fourth Conference of the Church held in Kirtland, Ohio, in June 1831:

> *[S]everal brethren were called by revelation to the office of High Priests. This was the first occasion in which this office in the Priesthood was fully revealed and conferred upon any of the Elders in this dispensation.*[52]

The contemporaneous records promoted this different view:

---

[50]The seven Whitmers, five biological brothers and two brothers-in-law, were all apostles (unordained) in the pre-1835 Church. "[T]hese apostles . . . received their callings charismatically [through vision] rather than institutionally [through ordination to office]." (Quinn, *Origins of Power*, 10-11).

[51]Bushman, *Joseph Smith: Rough Stone Rolling*, 157.

[52]Jenson, comp., *Church Chronology*, 6, emphasis added.

*The official history compiled under Smith's direction
until his 1844 death records that on this date [June 3,
1831] "the authority of the Melchisedek Priesthood
was manifested and conferred for the first time" on
twenty-three elders.*[53]

On June 3, 1831, twenty-three of the forty-four non-Melchizedek
elders present at the Conference proceedings received the High
Priesthood after the Holy Order of God "for the first time." That
meant that two years after *May 15, 1829,* and two years after
May/June 1829, Joseph Smith himself admitted that the Church
was organized before April 6, 1830, without "the authority of the
Melchisedek Priesthood." Latter-day Saints may take that to the
bank.

Getting to Melchizedek

In their 1834-35 History, Oliver Cowdery and Joseph Smith said
that they received under the "hands" of one then unnamed angelic
visitor – separately determined in Section 50 (later Section 27) of
the 1835 edition of the Doctrine and Covenants to be John the
Baptist – "the Holy Priesthood." "By later definitions only the
Melchizedek priesthood was 'the Holy Priesthood' (D&C 84:25-
27)."[54] D. Michael Quinn refers to the 1834-35 History describing
this conferral of authority as *"Cowdery's 1834 history."* This author
(supported by Joseph Smith's Diary, the *Messenger and Advocate,*
the *Times and Seasons,* the *Improvement Era,* then Mormon scholars
B.H. Roberts and Joseph Fielding Smith) refers to the *1834-35
History* as *"Oliver and Joseph's 1834[-35] History."*

> Cowdery's 1834 history [*Oliver and Joseph's 1834
> history*] puzzles modern Mormons for two reasons.
> First, he says [first, they say] [that] John the Baptist
> restored "the Holy Priesthood," when modern

---

[53] Joseph Smith Jr., *History of The Church of Jesus Christ of Latter-day Saints,*
B.H. Roberts, ed., 7 vols., 2d ed., rev., (Salt Lake City: The Deseret Book
Company, 1978), 1:175-76, quoted by Van Wagoner, *Sidney Rigdon,* 97 fn 23,
emphasis added.

[54] Quinn, *Origins of Power,* 15-16.

Mormons have been taught that he conferred the Aaronic priesthood, not the "Holy Priesthood" of Melchizedek. Second Cowdery in 1834 does not refer to restoration of a second priesthood [a telling omission]. All official church histories after 1834 refer to a visitation of the ancient apostles Peter, James, and John, who gave the holy Melchizedek priesthood to Smith and Cowdery "shortly after" the visit by John the Baptist in 1829.[55]

Quinn uses the definition of "the Holy Priesthood" – a later definition of higher (ultimately construed to mean Melchizedek) authority – to differentiate the priesthoods, lesser (Aaronic) and greater (Melchizedek). Thus, the 1834 History, Joseph's Diary, then Oliver (by Michael Quinn's reckoning), misuse the term in 1834, yet further evidence of confusion. The capable historian then makes another important point. After noting that current Mormons (no doubt because of the backdated and falsified alterations of foundational narratives) "perceive all religious history" from a "dual priesthood perspective," he says:

> [I]t is anachronistic to apply the terms Melchizedek and Aaronic to Mormon concepts of authority before 1832 and even up to 1835. It is difficult to avoid all anachronisms in a situation where virtually every standard and familiar published text has been filled with statements introduced after the dates of the original events and manuscript texts.[56]

So do the winds blow; so is Mormon history, smoke and mirrors, created, altered and revised.

---

[55]Ibid., 281 fn 73.

[56]Quinn, *Origins of Power*, 282 fn 75, emphasis added. "An effort to avoid such anachronism is Prince, *Having Authority*, which analyzes the evolution of Mormon authority concepts in chronological order of their documentary formulation." (Gregory A. Prince, *Having Authority: The Origins and Development of Priesthood during the Ministry of Joseph Smith*, John Whitmer Historical Association Monograph Series [Independence, MO: Independence Press, 1993], statement from Quinn, *Origins of Power*, 282 fn 75).

"[I]F YOU WANT TO SEE A SIGN, LOOK AT ME . . . ."

Joseph Smith was but one of the twenty-three elders ordained at the Fourth Conference of the Church at Kirtland, Ohio, on June 3, 1831. A disappointed David Whitmer described what he perceived to have been the Lord's displeasure with those chaotic proceedings.

> *In Kirtland, Ohio, in June, 1831, at a conference of the church, the first High Priests were ordained into the church. Brother Joseph ordained Lyman Wight, John Murdock, Harvey Whitlock, Hyrum Smith, Reynolds Cahoon and others to the office of a High Priest. When they were ordained, right there at the time, the devil caught and bound Harvey Whitlock so he could not speak, his face being twisted into demon-like shape. Also John Murdock and others were caught by the devil in a similar manner. Now brethren, do you not see that the displeasure of the Lord was upon their proceedings in ordaining High Priests [an office for which only Christ was worthy]? Of course it was. These facts are recorded in the History of the Church – written by my brother, John Whitmer, who was the regularly appointed church historian.[57]*

It was not a pretty sight. Men were falling down as if possessed. Brethren acted crazy and out of control. Lyman Wight, who was exceedingly fierce, looked exceedingly fierce. Rigdon's biographer described those events with Wight front and center. "On Friday, 3 June 1831, the first day of the convocation, while Joseph Smith was prophesying to the congregation, 'The Lord made manifest to Joseph that it was necessary that such of the elders as were considered worthy, should be ordained to the high priesthood.' He then laid his hands on Lyman Wight and ordained him to the 'High Priesthood after the Holy Order of God.'"[58] Lyman Wight may have been early Mormonism's most martial spirit. What followed wasn't calming. "Wight . . . arose and according to one account 'presented a pale countenance, a fierce look, with his arms

---

[57]Whitmer, *An Address to All Believers in Christ*, 64-65, emphasis added.
[58]Van Wagoner, *Sidney Rigdon*, 96.

extended, and his hands cramped back, the whole system agitated, and a very unpleasant object to look upon.'"[59]   Then, as if in a perfect frenzy, the Wild Ram of the Mountains (as this particularly violent man came to be called) was heard to say:

> "[I]f you want to see a sign, look at me," and then [he] climbed up on a bench and pronounced in a loud voice that he saw the Savior. Waxing prophetic, he pronounced "there were some in the congregation that should live until the Savior should descend from heaven, with a Shout, with all the holy angels with him."[60]

These manifestations both preceded and followed what should have been a sublime and calming event.

> Wight, still enraptured in vision, then ordained Rigdon, John Whitmer, and Joseph Smith to the High Priesthood even though Smith had previously ordained him.[61]

"During the turbulent meeting, Joseph ordained five men to the high priesthood, and Lyman Wight ordained eighteen others, including Joseph."[62]   The occasion was marred by the erratic behavior of Lyman Wight, John Murdock, Harvey Whitlock,

---

[59]Booth, an eyewitness, in Howe, *Mormonism Unvailed*, 188, quoted in Van Wagoner, *Sidney Rigdon*, 96-97. Wight "exhibited himself as an instance of the great power of God, and called upon those around him, '*if you want to see a sign, look at me.*' He then stepped upon a bench, and declared with a loud voice, he saw the Savior: and thereby, for the time being, rescued Smith's prophecy [that Wight would see the Savior] from merited contempt. – It, however, procured Wight the authority to ordain to the rest. So said the spirit, and so said Smith. The spirit in Smith selected those to be ordained, and the spirit in Wight ordained them." (Ezra Booth in Howe, *Mormonism Unvailed*, 188-89, emphasis added).

[60]F. Mark McKiernan and Roger D. Launius, ed., *An Early Latter Day Saint History: The Book of John Whitmer – Kept by Commandment* (Independence, MO: Herald House, 1980), 66, quoted in Van Wagoner, *Sidney Rigdon*, 97, emphasis added. *See also*, Whitmer, *An Address to All Believers in Christ*, 65.

[61]"Minutes of a General Conference held in Geauga County, Ohio, June 3, 1831," in Cannon and Cook, eds., *The Far West Record*, 6-7, quoted in Van Wagoner, *Sidney Rigdon*, 97, emphasis added.

[62]Bushman, *Joseph Smith: Rough Stone Rolling*, 157.

Leman Copley and others.[63] David Whitmer, though not personally present, received an eyewitness account from his brother John, the Church Historian who was both personally and officially present. What was supposed to have been a spiritual feast proved to be a disquieting threat to the safety of terrorized participants. In Levi Hancock's thoroughly apprehensive report, crisis ruled the room. In Ezra Booth's report, craziness ruled the room. Joseph had "hoped for an endowment of power" at this June 1831 Conference. What it seemed that he had gotten was evil spirits inhabiting the bodies of stricken elders in public proceedings. The fanatical events that surfaced at this turbulent convocation were not intended for those faint of heart or faith. A disappointed Ezra Booth saw this in that: "Under these discouraging circumstances, the horizon of Mormonism gathered darkness . . . ."[64] Smith's modern biographer softened the ugly scene. "He had tolerated exorbitant behavior in hopes of receiving a pentecostal manifestation."[65]

HIGH PRIESTHOOD ISSUES

High Priesthood "for the first time"

Joseph confirmed many years after the fact, and after ample time to reflect, that "the authority of the Melchizedek priesthood was manifested and conferred for the first time upon several of the Elders" at the Fourth Conference of the Church in June, 1831.[66] With that confirmation Joseph Smith joined Brigham Young, Orson Pratt and David Whitmer, Franklin D. Richards, Richard L. Bushman, D. Michael Quinn and Dan Vogel as leaders and scholars, all of whom said or implied at one time or another that the Church was initially formed without the authority of the Melchizedek Priesthood. "Traditional Mormon history holds that Smith and Cowdery had been ordained to the Higher Priesthood in May 1829 under the direction of ancient apostles Peter, James, and John, though like

---

[63]Ibid., 156-57.

[64]Ezra Booth in Howe, *Mormonism Unvailed*, 191.

[65]Bushman, *Joseph Smith: Rough Stone Rolling*, 159.

[66]Roberts, ed., *History of The Church of Jesus Christ of Latter-day Saints*, 1:175-76.

other supernal events this detail was added later."[67] Some Mormon scholars, including B.H. Roberts, thought that Joseph Smith misspoke when he said that "the authority of the Melchizedek priesthood was manifested and conferred for the first time" at the Fourth Conference of the Church in Kirtland, Ohio, in June, 1831.

The uncomfortable, disruptive, belated, first bestowal of this supposed high priesthood power more than a year after the Church was organized, after many important early events, and after forty-four men had already been ordained to the office of elder, is distressing to the modern Church, and to its scholars. Apologists have been unable to change this history to their revisionary liking partly because Joseph stated to the congregation at the conference *"that it was necessary that such of the elders as were considered worthy, should be ordained to the high priesthood."*[68] Then further because of numerous contemporaneous accounts, including the history of the conference prepared by John Whitmer.[69] "John Whitmer," according to his brother David, "wrote this [his account of the facts] in the church history when he was in full fellowship with the church."[70] John Whitmer, who gave the prophet a pass, was personally present; B.H. Roberts, who thought the prophet was wrong, was not.[71] On June 3, 1831, "elders" who were "considered worthy" were "ordained to the high priesthood." How is that to be denied? Until then, elders, even "worthy" ones, didn't hold "the high priesthood," though they had already been "ordained."

"An array of Smith's close associates testified that the Higher or Melchizedek Priesthood was not conferred until 3 June 1831. These include brothers Parley P.[72] and Orson Pratt, Book of Mormon

---

[67]Van Wagoner, *Sidney Rigdon*, 97.

[68]McKiernan and Launius, 66, quoted in Van Wagoner, *Sidney Rigdon*, 96 fn 19, emphasis added.

[69]Whitmer, *An Address to All Believers in Christ*, 65.

[70]Ibid.

[71]B.H. Roberts, 25 (Smith, Roberts, ed., *History of The Church of Jesus Christ of Latter-day Saints*, 1:176).

[72]"This is the first occasion in which this priesthood had been revealed and conferred upon the Elders in this dispensation, although the office of an Elder is the same in a certain degree, but not in the fullness." (Parley P. Pratt, Jr., ed., *The Autobiography of Parley Packer Pratt* [Chicago: Law, King & Law, 1888], 72, quoted in Van Wagoner, *Sidney Rigdon*, 97).

witnesses David and John Whitmer, plus Lyman Wight, William E. McLellin, John Corrill, J.C. Brewster, and William Smith, the prophet's younger brother."[73] In the face of that formidable group of testators, the modern Church – by ignoring their words, and those of Joseph Smith – continues to deny that the high priesthood was *"manifested and conferred for the first time"* on twenty-three previously ordained generic lower authority elders on June 3, 1831. The unforgettable occasion concerned the authority of the "high priesthood." The Fourth Conference of the Church of Christ (early Mormon) saw about half of the men who had previously been ordained to the office of elder receive the "Holy Priesthood after the Order of the Son of God" *"for the first time."* Before those ordinations, and until June 1831, the Church of Christ was governed by metaphysical claims to unitary charisma,[74] not even Aaronic, not even Melchizedek, not even "priesthood," and not yet "high."

What the leaders of the Church said that they did before they received what later came to be called the Melchizedek Priesthood is reflected in a "High Priesthood Timeline: The Path to June 3, 1831" found at Appendix D.

The War of Chronologies – Conflicting Views

Richard L. Bushman prepared a "Joseph Smith Chronology" in which he reported a "Visit of John the Baptist" to Joseph Smith and Oliver Cowdery on May 15, 1829.[75] That claim, which went unreported by Joseph Smith and Oliver Cowdery for five-and-one-half years until October 1834, was dismissed by David Whitmer and William E. McLellin and threatened by incompatible reports posted

---

[73]Van Wagoner, *Sidney Rigdon*, 97, citing fn 26. *See* R. Kent Fielding, "The Growth of the Mormon Church in Kirtland, Ohio," Ph.D. Diss., University of Indiana (1957), 111-13. Marvin S. Hill, *Quest for Refuge: The Mormon Flight from American Pluralism* (Salt Lake City: Signature Books, 1989), 25.

[74]The priesthood of Aaron played no part in the organizational structure of the church of the Nephites in the Western Hemisphere, or in the organization of the gospel church. Those facts are consistent with the dismissive description of the less-than-eternal Levitical/Aaronic Priesthood described in the Bible at Hebrews and Colossians.

[75]Bushman, *Joseph Smith: Rough Stone Rolling*, xiii.

at various times by Smith, his mother, brother William and others. Bushman's Chronology failed to describe a "Visit of Peter, James, and John" and didn't assign a date (or probable date) to that vitally important visit.[76] It does, however, report "Ordination to high priesthood," June 3, 1831, at the Conference and by no one greater than Lyman Wight. Thus Bushman's "Joseph Smith Chronology" contradicts the fixed theology of the twenty-first century Church. On the issue of the appearance of the three apostles, Bushman punts. The Chronology's omission would seem to confirm that Smith didn't hold the "high priesthood" on April 6, 1830, when the "Church of Christ [was] organized,"[77] when Joseph and Oliver ordained each other elders, and when Oliver Cowdery, who didn't hold the Melchizedek Priesthood and couldn't hold the Aaronic Priesthood, ordained Joseph Smith "Prophet, Seer and Revelator" of the Church of Christ. While Bushman's "Chronology" fails to identify Peter, James, and John, or assign a date to their visit, or say that the 1831 ordinations had anything to do with them, it didn't forget the turbulent events that occurred at the Fourth Conference of the Church in Kirtland, Ohio, in June of 1831, more than a year after the Church was organized, and more than two years after Oliver Cowdery and Joseph Smith were resupposed to have received the high priesthood from Peter, James, and John (in *"1829, May-June"*).

Bushman's "Joseph Smith Chronology" recognizes that on June 3, 1831, when the *"Ordination to high priesthood"* is supposed to have first occurred, no one knew (or said) that the high priesthood had anything to do with Peter, James, and John. Bushman's entry doesn't mention "Melchizedek."

If there had been such a visitation and an earlier ordination, and if anyone at that Fourth Conference had known of it, and if Joseph had indeed received high authority from heavenly messengers (without ever saying so), then by what logical process did Lyman Wight, "the first ordained high priest" (D. Michael Quinn), ordain Joseph Smith to "the High Priesthood"? Oliver Cowdery was the first person ordained to the office of elder. Lyman Wight was the first person ordained to the office of high priest. Why did the

---

[76]Ibid.
[77]Ibid.

peculiar Wight ordain Joseph Smith to the high priesthood if Peter, James, and John ordained Joseph Smith to the high priesthood? Why didn't anyone say anything about Peter, James, and John in 1831, in 1834, or until 1835?

For about four years after those most unusual proceedings in 1831, the angelic ordination record is inexplicably silent. For reasons that are not exactly clear, Smith ordained Wight, who then said that he saw Jesus as Smith promised he would. Then Wight ordained Smith, who then said, "I now see God, and Jesus Christ at his right hand." The highly agitated Wight then proceeded to ordain seventeen other previously ordained elders (while Smith ordained four other previously ordained elders) to "the High Priesthood" in what became a Pentecostal melee. Wight reported that he had not held the high priesthood before that day. "I was ordained," he said, "by the hand of Joseph to the Melchisedic Priesthood."[78] Wight, like Smith and others, had already been ordained to the office of elder. But he, like all of those other elders, was not a Melchizedek elder. Elder Lyman Wight didn't hold the high priesthood, only later associated with Melchizedek, until June 3, 1831. *Charismatic authority, and the voice of God, by this unmistakable early Mormon reckoning, didn't include the higher authority of the high priesthood.*

None of the leaders who kept the several presently known contemporaneous accounts of those 1831 proceedings, or the minutes, or the records of the Conference, openly entertained the thought that Joseph Smith had somehow been reordained to "the High Priesthood." And none of those same resources suggest that the 1831 conference proceedings had anything to do with Peter, James, and John. In June 1831 no one knew that the office of elder was an appendage of the Melchisedek Priesthood, or that early Mormonism's generic unitary "authority" was associated with ancient Israel's less-than-eternal law of a carnal commandment.

The Church's high priesthood chronology, "*1829, May-June,*" is at odds with Bushman's "Joseph Smith Chronology," D. Michael Quinn's "Selected Chronology," and Franklin D. Richards' Chronology ("*1831 'June 6; the Melchisedek Priesthood was first*

---

[78]Wight, quoted in Quinn, *Origins of Power,* 30.

given'"[79]). Nor is it supported by the statements of Brigham Young, Orson Pratt and David Whitmer. Or the reckonings of those most distinguished twenty-first century scholars.   The Church's Chronology depends on unsustainable facts. The modern Church stubbornly continues to contend that Joseph Smith, "With Oliver Cowdery, receives the Melchizedek Priesthood from the ancient Apostles Peter, James, and John near the Susquehanna River between Harmony Pennsylvania, and Colesville, New York" in May or June of 1829.[80]

Smith made that trip between Harmony, Pennsylvania, and Colesville, New York, in June or July of 1830, after the Church was organized, to stand trial. He determined to return after the trial to confirm some newly invested Saints. The Church's Chronology doesn't begin to describe the grim events that attended the Fourth Conference of the Church at Kirtland, Ohio, on June 3, 1831. Every investigator trying to decide whether or not to join the Church should be fully informed about the turbulent origins of the ubiquitous priesthood.

THE CHURCH WAS ORGANIZED BEFORE JOSEPH AND OLIVER HELD THE HIGH PRIESTHOOD

A prominent Mormon theologian (by now a deceased apostle) reported in a seminal resource that when Israel first lived under "the law of carnal commandments" – a law for interns intended to tutor the Hebrews until they could enjoy the fulness of the gospel – "of necessity, a lesser order of priesthood was conferred to administer the lesser law." That lesser order of priesthood intended to govern a lesser people destined to live a lesser law was the Aaronic or Levitical Priesthood conferred by lineage upon Aaron by Levi and his sons, and upon most of "the whole house of Levi who were between 30 and 50 years of age."[81]

---

[79]Richards, quoted in Quinn, *Origins of Power*, 30, emphasis added.

[80]*Teachings of Presidents of The Church – Joseph Smith* (2007), xv (Historical Summary), emphasis added.

[81]Bruce R. McConkie, *Mormon Doctrine*, 2d ed. (Salt Lake City: Bookcraft, 1966), 9, 10.

The Hebrew tribal priests who held the fulness of the Aaronic or Levitical Priesthood, but not the "keys" of the Aaronic or Levitical Priesthood, according to Apostle Bruce R. McConkie, "participated in the offering of sacrifices" and performed functions "comparable to those of teachers and deacons in this dispensation."[82] Deacons and teachers in this dispensation are mostly twelve to fourteen years old (deacons), and fourteen to sixteen years old (teachers), or undistinguished adults. Those who held the *"keys"* of the Aaronic Priesthood, according to McConkie, like "Aaron and his sons," "acted in the full majesty and power" of the Levitical order. "[M]any of their functions were comparable to those of bishops and priests in this dispensation."[83] Priests in this dispensation are mostly sixteen to eighteen years of age; bishops are minor functionaries in charge of small and manageable congregations of Mormon members.

The Aaronic Priesthood was time bound and temporal, hereditary and tribal, passed by way of descent. It was the lineal priesthood of the old law. The Melchizedek Priesthood was "without father, without mother, without descent" – not time bound and temporal, hereditary or tribal – but rather without-beginning-or-end eternal. The Apostle Paul described Melchizedek as one who has become a priest not on the basis of a regulation as to his ancestry but on the basis of the power of an indestructible life.[84]   According to McConkie, "John the Baptist 'was a descendant of Aaron' and held the keys of the Aaronic Priesthood,"[85] an entry-level tutorial power that was deacon, teacher, priest or bishop friendly. The hereditary order (for priests unlike Melchizedek who were appointed on the basis of their "ancestry") was devised for errant followers in days of distress when God considered them "naught." In Mormon theology the "laying on of hands for the gift of the Holy Ghost" is not now, and was not then, an Aaronic Priesthood "prerogative."[86] Perfection did not attend this lesser order of priesthood, which did not have the power to offer its worthy and faithful ministers "the

---

[82]Ibid., 10.
[83]Ibid.
[84]Hebrews 7:15-16.
[85]McConkie, *Mormon Doctrine*, 2d ed., 10.
[86]Ibid., 11.

oath and covenant and perfection that appertain to the Melchizedek order."[87]

Why would anyone even think to restore the Aaronic/Levitical Priesthood after Christ became the "surety of a better testament?"[88] The law of a carnal commandment was superceded for Christians by the coming of Christ, by the establishment of a higher law administered by "a great high priest that is passed into the heavens."[89] The traditional primitive offering of animal sacrifice was no longer required. The tutorial power that foreshadowed the incarnation ran its course and served no discernible purpose for Hebrews becoming Christians by following Christ. God swiped that written less-than-eternal carnal code. He "took it out of the way, nailing it to his cross."[90] Why would anyone want to restore a dead and disrespected order, the codification of presently meaningless ancient Jewish ritual? The Church of Christ (early Mormon) was organized without the ministration of the Aaronic/Levitical order of the priesthood. The Church of Christ (early Mormon) was organized without the ministration of the Melchizedek order of the priesthood.

---

[87]Ibid.
[88]Hebrews 7:18, 22.
[89]Hebrews 4:14.
[90]Colossians 2:14, emphasis added.

CHAPTER NINE

Kirtland

Many extraordinary experiences which then existed, have vanished out of sight; and the Mormonites desire, not only to forget them, but wish them blotted out of the memory of others.[1]

Ezra Booth

They can at any time obtain a commandment suited to their desire, and as their desires fluctuate and become reversed, they get a new one to supercede the other . . . .[2]

Ezra Booth

GATHERING TROOPS

In December 1830 Sidney Rigdon and Edward Partridge (converts from Ohio) visited Joseph Smith at Fayette, New York. At the time of this extraordinary visitation, nine months after the Church was organized, "priesthood" wasn't a term anyone used. Smith had yet to describe one "crucifyed," "omnipotant," "omnipreasant Lord," two personages and many angels, "a first visitation of angels" or "two Personages whose brightness and glory defy all description."

---

[1]Ezra Booth, Letter VII, Eber D. Howe, *Mormonism Unvailed: Or, A Faithful Account of That Singular Imposition and Delusion* (Painesville, OH: E.D. Howe, 1834; reprint, New York: AMS Press Inc., 1977), 207, emphasis added.

[2]Ibid., emphasis added.

In the Book of Mormon, published earlier that year, there was no Aaronic/Levitical Priesthood, heaven and hell were undifferentiated, the begetter was the begotten and crucified. The Father was the Son and underived, from eternity to eternity eternal. He was without beginning of days or end of years, father, mother or descent. The "natural man" was corrupt, inclined to evil, incapable of doing good, "carnal, sensual, devilish,"[3] "worthless and fallen."[4] There were no degrees of glory, there was no spirit world, the Saints hadn't begun to gather, the dead weren't baptized and Adam wasn't God.

Sidney On Site

When Sidney Rigdon arrived, Mormonism was monotheistic. "JESUS is the CHRIST, the ETERNAL GOD."[5] "And the Honor be to the Father, and to the Son, and to the Holy Ghost, which is one God."[6] The Book of Mormon Messiah was "the very Eternal Father of Heaven and earth." Mary was "the mother of God after the manner of the flesh." Something called "authority" wasn't anything called "Aaronic." Something called "authority" wasn't anything called "Priesthood." There were no high priests. There was no temple marriage, no sealing for eternity, no plurality of gods, and no limitation on punishment.[7] Damnation was for the life of the soul.

Before Sidney Rigdon visited Joseph Smith at Fayette, New York, in December 1830, less than a year after the Church became official, that impressive new convert had been baptized by Oliver

---

[3]Book of Mormon, Mosiah 16:3.

[4]King Benjamin contrasted "the goodness of God . . . [with] your worthless and fallen state[,] . . . the greatness of God . . . [with] your own nothingness." (Ibid., Mosiah 4:5, 11).

[5]Ibid., Title Page, "An Account Written by the Hand of Mormon upon plates taken from the plates of Nephi."

[6]Ibid., The Testimony of Three Witnesses.

[7]Grant H. Palmer, *An Insider's View of Mormon Origins* (Salt Lake City: Signature Books, 2002), 124.

Cowdery. Parley P. Pratt, Oliver Cowdery, Peter Whitmer Jr. and
Ziba Peterson were the first missionaries to the book of Mormon's
Lamanites (Native American Hebrews), whose conversion was at
the top of formative Mormonism's excitable early agenda. The
Book of Mormon was "Written to the Lamanites, who are a
remnant of the house of Israel; and also to Jew and Gentile – ...."[8]
These North American Hebrews were supposed to be converted to
become Christian allies in the Mormonite quest for theocratic
supremacy. On their journey to Missouri to preach the gospel to
"Lamanites" who had been resettled on the edges there, these
missionaries established a branch of the Church at Kirtland, Ohio,[9]
where Pratt, like Sidney Rigdon, and with Sidney Rigdon, had been
a Campbellite Disciple of Christ (a Reformed Baptist). Before Pratt
(by now a Mormon) and his Mormon colleagues arrived in
Kirtland, Rigdon had argued with Alexander Campbell. The
relationship between the two men was fractious. Parley P. Pratt
recruited Rigdon, whose Campbellite fervor had waned. Pratt and
others convinced Rigdon, who was between things and unsettled, to
bring his considerable talents (and his followers) to the service of
the Mormons and a young new prophet by the name of Joseph
Smith. Rigdon had constituents (besides the departed Pratt) –
Edward Partridge, Sampson Avard, Zebedee Coltrin, Isaac Morley
and others – men who after joining him as Mormons molded and
shaped the early Church. These men were advocates, with Rigdon,
of a communitarian faction that would come to be called the United
Order.

When Rigdon arrived for his visit in December, the Church of
Christ was a loosely based spiritual community of like-minded
believers exercising charismatic authority as elders, teachers and
priests with no discernible divinely ordained authority and but little
separation between the different offices. David Whitmer, an early
favorite of Smith – before he was marginalized by the ascendant

---

[8]Book of Mormon, Title Page.
[9]Andrew Jenson, comp., *Church Chronology: A Record of Important Events
Pertaining to the History of the Church of Jesus Christ of Latter-day Saints*, 2d ed.,
rev. and enlarged (Salt Lake City: Deseret News, 1914), 5.

Rigdon – would later lament Rigdon's influence. "The office of high priests," Whitmer said, "was never spoken of, and never thought of being established . . . until Rigdon came in."[10] According to Whitmer, Rigdon was "a thorough Bible scholar," well educated and articulate. Rigdon remodeled the Church. Joseph invented a people; Sidney remodeled the Church.

E.D. Howe described Mormonism's new recruit in these terms:

> This Rigdon was a man of great eloquence, belonging to a denomination of Christians, who style themselves, "Disciples," or "Reformers," and who are also, by their opponents, in derision, called "Campbellites." ... He was a very popular preacher and had large congregations in different parts of the country. If there was a man in the world that could successfully spread and give name to the vagaries of the Smiths, it was Rigdon . . . . We may here stop to remark that an opinion has prevailed, to a considerable extent, that Rigdon has been the *Iago*, the prime mover, of the whole conspiracy.[11]

Rigdon's Influence

Rigdon quickly became "Brother Joseph's private counsellor, and his most intimate friend and brother . . . ." "He soon worked himself deep into Brother Joseph's affections, and had more influence over him than any other man living."[12] Whitmer said Rigdon manipulated the revelations. Rigdon persuaded Smith to ordain high priests because high priests exercised "great power in ancient times." Whitmer thought the ordination of high priests had been a colossal mistake. "[I]f God did not mean for this order of

---

[10]David Whitmer, *An Address to All Believers in Christ: by A Witness to the Divine Authenticity of The Book of Mormon* (Richmond, MO: n.p., 1887; photographic reprint, Concord, CA: Pacific Publishing Company, 1993), 35.

[11]Howe, *Mormonism Unvailed*, 107.

[12]Whitmer, *An Address to All Believers in Christ*, 35.

high priests to be ordained in the Church of Christ, it is a serious error to have added that office . . . ." Christ alone was worthy. Whitmer said Brother Joseph made another mistake when he had himself ordained "Prophet, Seer and Revelator" of the Church of Christ, the only man to speak for God. God, according to Whitmer, needed *voices* to carry the message around. Whitmer thought Joseph and Sidney had been mistaken about "the gathering of Israel and [the] building [of] the city [of the] New Jerusalem . . . ,"[13] projects Joseph had contemplated even before Rigdon joined the Church. As the leader of the Church in Missouri, Whitmer also believed that Rigdon instigated the formation of "the secret organization known as the 'Danites,'" a controversial assembly of violent men sworn to obey the strongest loyalty oaths language could invent. That still notorious society was first formed at Far West, Missouri, under Smith and Rigdon's watch, in June 1838.

Mormonism's important new convert was committed to the restoration of all things. He was a revivalist, like the Reverend George Lane, the Methodist preacher who "wakened" Joseph's mind to things of a spiritual nature in 1824. A complex melancholy man, Rigdon clashed with Campbell, a formidable figure in his own right, "over the question of re-establishing the ancient communism of the primitive Christian Church."

As the most fanatical and literal minded leader of the Disciples of Christ, Rigdon had "so zealously espoused the principle of holding things in common that he had set up a small communistic colony in Kirtland, a thriving town next door to Cleveland."[14] Rigdon explained some of his core beliefs (quite some time after he joined the Church) in a famous oration delivered at Far West, Missouri, on the fourth of July in 1838. "Many of us in times past were rich," he said, "but for Jesus sake and at the command of our God we have become poor, because he became poor for our sakes; so in like manner, we follow his example, and become poor for his sake . . . so

---

[13]Ibid., 35-36.
[14]Fawn M. Brodie, *No Man Knows My History: The Life of Joseph Smith the Mormon Prophet*, 2d ed., rev. and enl. (New York, NY: Alfred A. Knopf, 1972), 94.

do we choose to suffer with the people of God, rather than enjoy the flatteries of the world for a season." Rigdon, a notoriously poor financial manager (the failed President of the Kirtland Safety Society), was fiercely devoted to the "idea of equality." "It is not because we cannot, if we were so disposed, enjoy the honors and flatteries of the world, but we have voluntarily offered them in sacrifice, and the riches of the world also, for a more durable substance. Our God has promised us a reward of eternal inheritance . . . . The promise is sure, and the reward is certain."[15]

The contributions of Rigdon, a clever but credulous visionary, to Joseph Smith and Mormonism, many of which have been erased from history (literally) by his hard-bitten nemesis, Brigham Young, should never be underestimated. Had there been no Rigdon, the Church of Jesus Christ of Latter-day Saints would be very different today. He was, for most of nearly fourteen years, Joseph Smith's most important adviser, a man who had the prophet's ear. Mormonism is heavily indebted to this proletarian founder. Rigdon was sour, dour, straitlaced, sectarian, violent, a humorless ideologue, smart and seldom in doubt. He was "nursing his grievance" with Alexander Campbell when the Mormon missionaries directed by Parley P. Pratt arrived to facilitate his conversion. "In less than three weeks" the Mormons baptized "the whole of his communistic colony."

For most of those fourteen years, Rigdon was a vastly influential figure situated at the center of all things Mormon. Rigdon knew Joseph better than Brigham Young and had a far greater impact on the early eastern Church. In the month of their meeting, Joseph and Sidney shared a vision that directed the Church to gather from the state of New York to Sidney Rigdon's Ohio. Not long after that Joseph had visions that redirected the gathering to a place the center of which was near to the city of Independence in Jackson

---

[15]"Sidney Rigdon's Ultimatum," oration delivered at Far West, Missouri, reproduced at William Mulder and A. Russell Mortensen, eds., *Among the Mormons: Historic Accounts by Contemporary Observers* (New York, NY: Alfred A. Knopf, 1958), 94.

County, Missouri. As Joseph found the power in Sidney, Sidney found the power in Joseph. They complemented each other. Fawn McKay Brodie famously described a formidable Joseph's particular genius.

> *Liberally paraphrasing Isaiah and the revelation of St. John, he seized upon the most provocative of religious symbols – the chosen people, the gathering of Israel, the end of the world, eternal damnation, the second coming of Christ, [the return of the ten lost tribes], the resurrection – and exploited all the rich and moving irrationalism inherent in them.*
>
> *For centuries these symbols had been threaded into the patterns of Christian thinking. They were the stock in trade of every frontier preacher. But Joseph used them as no one had before him. Instead of retelling the legends of the ancient chosen people, he created a new chosen people. Instead of arguing about the ambiguities of St. John, he transformed the apocalypse into terse, naive prophecy and dispatched the most sophisticated metaphysical problems with dexterous oversimplifications.[16]*

Less than five months after the official organization of his Church, and even before the arrival of Rigdon, Joseph Smith had begun "to lay concrete plans for the building of the New Jerusalem."[17] Joseph, like Rigdon, was a primitivist, and his hindsight was not confined to the New Testament.

KIRTLAND MARKERS

In December 1830, the month that they met, the Lord gave a revelation to Joseph and Sidney, not to Joseph, the Seer, but to

---

[16]Brodie, *No Man Knows My History*, 93, emphasis added.
[17]Ibid.

Joseph and Sidney simultaneously. Sidney, like Joseph, was a revelator. That was an incredible accolade for Mormonism's surprising new convert. Joseph and Sidney together received "the first commandment concerning a gathering in this dispensation." It wouldn't be the last. "Behold, I say unto you," the Lord supposedly said, "that *it is not expedient* in me that ye should translate any more until ye shall go to the Ohio, . . . a commandment I give unto the church, that *it is expedient* in me that they should assemble together at the Ohio . . . . Behold, here is wisdom, and let every man choose for himself until I come."[18] The Saints in Joseph Smith's New York are abruptly instructed to leave everything and follow.

Mormonism's missionaries to the Lamanites first converted Rigdon and other like-minded members of his Kirtland colony. Kirtland, the place of the first gathering, then became the headquarters of the Church until 1838. Following Rigdon's importunements, Joseph's God came on board. The revelation's direction was not at first well received, but Joseph and Sidney convinced a reluctant majority to make the promising move. After Rigdon visited Joseph at Fayette in December 1830, Joseph, Emma, Sidney Rigdon and Edward Partridge (Rigdon's sidekick) left together in January 1831, Emma and Joseph to settle in Kirtland.

Joseph Consolidates His Authority

The earliest Ohio converts were recklessly Pentecostal. With the passage of time, Joseph came to denounce their religious excess, calling them to attention with a revelation in which the Lord described false spirits.[19] There are, it seems, false spirits, and they sometimes fool the faithful, as they did early on in Kirtland. Joseph's initial appeal, as Mrs. Brodie later perceived, was "as much to reason as to emotion." His logical approach to issues of faith, as contrasted to the notions of some of his early constituents,

---

[18]Doctrine and Covenants 37 and headnote, emphasis added.
[19]Doctrine and Covenants 50.

served the new Church well by bringing into the ranks "many able men who had turned in disgust from the excesses of the local cults." "The intellectual appeal of Mormonism, which eventually became its greatest weakness as the historical and 'scientific' aspects of Mormon dogma were cruelly disemboweled by twentieth century scholarship, was in the beginning its greatest strength."[20]   Mrs. Brodie, who wrote and revised her biography in 1945 and 1972, a book giving voice to dissent from an unexpected source, had no idea just how cruel that dismemberment was destined to become.

In Kirtland Joseph consolidated his authority, emphasized his leadership and controlled the laity. With the assistance of Rigdon, he introduced multiple priesthoods of different ranks.   While maintaining supreme authority, Joseph created a place in those orders of priesthood for every faithful male member. "The result was a pyramidal church structure resting on the broadest possible base and possessing astonishing strength."[21]   One man made the rules and decided everything of importance.   Other men implemented the strong man's rules.   All of the leaders were accountable to him (everyone was accountable to him), but others were also accountable to them. There was under the shadow of the fig tree a variegated chain of command. The implementation of edicts required discretion to be exercised by those in the under authority.   Men could be made to feel important administering rules made for them by others.   Many leaders shared in the interpretation and enforcement of the law of the Lord. They, like their prophets, were treated as royalty, but not quite to the same degree.

At Kirtland Joseph articulated new doctrines and embellished old ones – Zion, the further Gathering, the city of the New Jerusalem, the Temple, Temple Covenants, the Second Coming, the return of the Ten Lost Tribes and the Millennium. In 1832 Joseph and Sidney simultaneously shared the vision of the three degrees of

---

[20]Brodie, *No Man Knows My History*, 99.
[21]Ibid., 100.

glory.[22] At his Kirtland headquarters (which supervised the affairs of the Church in Missouri, when there came to be a Church in Missouri, the place described as "Zion," the place to build a city to be called the "New Jerusalem"), the prophet redefined God, redefined authority, differentiated heaven and hell, described a spirit world and speculated in business, banking and real estate. "The cornerstone of his metaphysics was that virile concept which pervaded the whole American spirit and which was indeed the noblest ideal of Jesus and Buddha, that man is capable of eternal progress toward perfection."[23]

At Kirtland Joseph received many of his revelations, mountains many more than those received by all of the mostly silent prophets since. At Kirtland Joseph revised the King James Bible, directed the publication of the Book of Commandments (in Missouri in 1833) and the publication of the Doctrine and Covenants (in Ohio in 1835), built the first temple and published the *Lectures on Faith*. At Kirtland he purchased and translated ancient Egyptian papyri. There he established the framework of the United Order, then located the place and planned the construction of the city of the New Jerusalem.   There he came to control the temporal and spiritual affairs of a compliant people. And it was from Kirtland that apostles were first ordained and sent to spread the faith in what has been generously described as the dispensation of the fullness of times.

Lessons from Priceless Papyri

The Book of Mormon's monotheistic Messiah was the "Creator of Heaven and Earth."   In 1835 a man by the name of Michael Chandler brought four Egyptian mummies and accompanying papyri to Kirtland.   One of those manuscripts, according to the

---

[22]This was a concept of a differentiated afterlife first promoted by Emanuel Swedenborg, a Swedish mystic who lived and died before Joseph and Sidney were born.
[23]Brodie, *No Man Knows My History*, ix (Preface).

prophet, was the work of Abraham, the father of the faithful. Another was that of Joseph, the ancient Jewish/Egyptian refugee. Moses and Aaron made cameo appearances in these priceless papyri, which – *if Joseph was right* – were by all reckoning the most important manuscript discoveries in the history of the Christian world.

Now, without the stone or the spectacles, but with a manuscript rooted in an ancient world, Joseph produced a true "translation" of the papyri at Kirtland, Ohio, which he then later published at Nauvoo, Illinois, in 1842. Now, after the passage of time (quite a lot of time), the monotheistic deity of Joseph's early theology became the polytheistic deity of Joseph's later theology. Now the "one God" didn't create the earth, as the Book of Mormon said that he did. Now the earth wasn't created *ex nihilo*, but was rather more nearly organized. Now *"the Gods"* *"organized"* heaven and earth using eternal materials already on hand.[24]

This represented a serious new change for what came to be called the Church of the Latter Day Saints. Now Elohim – a name Joseph had used as an "interchangeable epithet" to designate Jehovah, the God of the Old Testament – became abruptly plural. The *"God"* became *"the Gods"* when Joseph, after studying Hebrew, learned that *Elohim*, "one of the Hebrew words for God," was actually plural.[25] Now Joseph's metaphysics embraced the "idea of the plurality of Gods." So what if the Book of Mormon did repeatedly describe God as the monotheistic deity who created heaven and earth. From now on, whatever the Mormon scriptures previously said, there will be many Gods; an incomprehensible number of Gods will be seen to have organized an infinite number of heavens and earths. As Joseph studied Hebrew, as Elohim became something plural, Joseph concluded that the Bible, speaking of God in the singular, "had been carelessly translated." Parley P. Pratt, acting to support the prophet's challenging new doctrine, a doctrine

---

[24]Ibid., 171.
[25]Ibid.

that changed the nature of God, pointed that out in the *Millennial Star* in 1842.[26]

Thomas Dick

Mormonism, when clinically dissected, as Mrs. Brodie and various others have opined, owes much of its metaphysics to the errant speculations of a forgettable scholar by the name of Thomas Dick. Joseph Smith's rejection of *ex nihilo* creation, his adoption of the theory that the earth was organized out of materials God "had on hand," and his notion that "there is no such thing as immaterial matter" ("All spirit is matter, but is more fine or pure, and can only be discerned by purer eyes") followed his study of Thomas Dick's *Philosophy of a Future State*, a tome Mrs. Brodie dismissed as "a long winded dissertation on astronomy and metaphysics." Thomas Dick opined, then Joseph Smith opined, that matter is "eternal and indestructible."[27]   That didn't happen, at least for Joseph, until after the publications of the Articles and Covenants of the Church of Christ, the Book of Mormon, the Book of Commandments, the Doctrine and Covenants, the Book of Moses and the *Lectures on Faith*.   There was water under the bridge before Joseph and his Lord started to think like Thomas Dick.

"Sidney Rigdon quoted openly from Dick in an article called 'The Saints and the World,' [published in the] *Latter-Day Saints Messenger and Advocate*, November 1836, pp. 422-3."[28]   The Book of Abraham (the alleged contents of the transcription of the Egyptian papyri and a colossal deception), was the lengthened shadow of Thomas Dick. It was Dick who introduced Joseph Smith to "the mathematics of the heavens," to time, space and quantity, to an infinity of stars and distances. Now Joseph wedded his enhanced view of astronomy "to his own special structures of Jewish and

---

[26]*Millennial Star*, vol. III (Liverpool, England, August 1842), 71, quoted in Brodie, *No Man Knows My History*, 171.
[27]Ibid.
[28]Ibid.

Christian mysticism. He was groping for a new metaphysics that would somehow take account of the new world of science."[29] From this maelstrom Joseph created the story that modern scholarship has turned inside out and upside down for its unconscionable duplicity – the Book of Abraham.

Abraham, according to Joseph, is now quite suddenly seen as an eminent astronomer who penetrated the mysteries of the universe with his extraordinary intellect. Here is Kolob, the greatest of all of the stars, lying near the throne of God, revolving once in a thousand years, from which "God Himself reckons time." Here are countless lesser orbs inhabited by spirits which after 1835, but not before, are as eternal as matter. "These spirits are not cast in the same mold, but differ among themselves in quality of intelligence as the stars differ in magnitude." "These concepts, which developed peculiar ramifications in Joseph's later teachings, came directly from Dick, who had speculated that the stars were peopled by 'various orders of intelligences,' and that these intelligences were *progressive beings' in various stages of evolution toward perfection."[30] How Mormon can you get? To the Mormons from Thomas Dick, from Abraham, from Joseph. Thomas Dick was *an* author of the vaunted "plan of salvation."

The place of refuge, "a land of promise"

At the last conference to be held in New York and on January 2, 1831, the Lord remembers Zion and the Saints are sternly advised to prepare. The wicked "have I kept in chains of darkness until the judgment of the great day, which shall come at the end of the earth."[31] Now hear this: They "that will not hear my voice," the wicked "will I cause . . . to be kept." ("Wo, wo, wo is their doom."[32]) But to those who do not harden their hearts, "I say . . .

---

[29]Ibid., 172.
[30]Ibid.
[31]Doctrine and Covenants 38:5.
[32]Ibid., 38:6.

that mine eyes are upon you. I am in your midst, and ye cannot see me; But the day soon cometh that ye shall see me . . . and he that is not purified shall not abide the day."[33]   And the day against which the pure shall be measured, the great day, "shall come at the end of the earth." We are talking here about "the judgment of the great day, which shall come at the end of the earth."[34]

"[Y]e are clean, but not all; and there is none else with whom I am well pleased." "I will be merciful unto your weakness. Therefore, be ye strong from henceforth; fear not for the kingdom is yours." Now the promise is offered. "I . . . deign to give unto you . . . a land of promise, a land flowing with milk and honey, upon which there shall be no curse when the Lord cometh . . ." on the great day, when the wicked are kept, at the end of the earth. "And I will give it unto you for the land of your inheritance, if you seek it with all your hearts." The pure shall not be forced to abide the great and terrible day in strange and unfamiliar places with wicked people ("for all flesh is corrupted"). "And this shall be my covenant with you, ye shall have it for the land of your inheritance, and for the inheritance of your children forever, while the earth shall stand, and ye shall possess it again in eternity, no more to pass away."[35]

"Wherefore, hear my voice and follow me . . . ." "I say unto you, be one; and if ye are not one ye are not mine." "I tell you these things . . . that ye might escape the power of the enemy, and be gathered unto me a righteous people, without spot and blameless . . . ." "And let your preaching be the warning voice, every man to his neighbor, ... And go ye out from among the wicked. Save yourselves. Be ye clean that bear the vessels of the Lord. Even so. Amen."[36]   For now, the place of this gathering is Kirtland, Ohio. "Wherefore, for this cause [that ye should "be gathered unto me a righteous people, without spot and blameless"], I gave unto you the commandment that ye should go to the Ohio; and there I will give unto you my law;

---

[33]Ibid., 38:7-8.
[34]Ibid., 38:5.
[35]Ibid., 38:10-20.
[36]Ibid., 38:22-42.

and there you shall be endowed with power from on high."[37]
Rigdon, a millennialist, believed in the gathering of Israel, the great
and dreadful day of the Lord was just around the bend.

CRAZINESS IN KIRTLAND

There was a powerful strain of pentecostal fury in the early
Church. *Mormonism Unvailed* described the Ohio beginnings of the
nineteenth-century Church. From these unusual early beginnings,
Mormonism started on a long and fitful journey toward greater
respectability. Nevertheless, and not to be forgotten, it was in this
seething cauldron that the movement took some of its first breaths.
As a sophisticated early 1830s observer, at first a Mormon and a
believer, Ezra Booth, who had been a minister, observed that
"Mormonism has in part changed its character, and assumed a
different dress, from that under which it made its first appearance
on the Western Reserve." It was the kind of thing that could be
explained by saying that Joseph Smith was making it up as he went
along. And that those who followed him as leaders in the Church
were making it up as they went along. Booth, who became a
dissenter, had made a life-changing mistake.

These "vanished" wonders, according to Booth, "stand as the
principal foundation of the faith of several hundred of the members
of their church." Booth averred that his recounting was supported
by evidence "derived from my own experience and observation, or
from [the] testimony of persons" who still adhere to the Mormon
faith. A deeply religious man troubled by the thought that he had
made a wrong turn, and ashamed of having encouraged others to
do the same, Booth reported as follows: "I hold myself responsible
to any tribunal, whether on earth or in heaven, for the truth of what
I write, or at least for an intention to write the truth, and nothing
but the truth."[38]

---

[37]Ibid., 38:32.
[38]Ezra Booth, Letter III, Howe, *Mormonism Unvailed*, 183.

The Gift of Tongues

The exponents of this early practice in the similitude of the Bible (including Brigham Young) left something to be desired. When carried away by the spirit, these excitable patrons "were apparently lost to all surrounding circumstances wrapt up in the contemplation of things, and in communication with persons not present.–" As described by Booth, "They articulated sounds, which but few present professed to understand; and those few disclosed them to be the Indian language."[39] The preoccupation of the early members of the Mormon Church with the American Indians (meaning with the Book of Mormon's Lamanites) is in stark contrast to the indifference of twenty-first century Mormons to their Native American brothers and sisters. One nineteenth-century observer, who reported that he had traded with the Indians, reported that what he heard at those services was an Indian dialect. Another person, who offered himself as an interpreter to Booth, translated sounds "which were unintelligible, into the English language." "One individual could read any chapter of the Old or New Testament, in several different languages." This was made known to be the case by a second person who purported to be the speakers' inspired interpreter.

> In the midst of this delirium they would, at times, fancy themselves addressing a congregation of their red brethren; mounted on a stump, or the fence, or from some elevated siuation [sic], would harangue their assembly until they had convinced or converted them. They would then lead them into the water, and baptize them, and pronounce their sins forgiven. In this exercise, some of them actually went into the water; and in the water, performed the ceremony used in baptizing. These actors assumed the visage of the savage, and so nearly imitated him, not only in language, but in gestures and actions, that it seemed the soul and body were completely

---

[39]Ibid., 184.

metamorphosed into the Indian. No doubt was then entertained but that was an extraordinary work of the Lord, designed to prepare those young men for the Indian mission; and many who are still leaders of the church, could say, "we knew by the spirit that it is the work of the Lord." And now they can say, "they know it is the work of the devil." Most of those who were the principal actors, have since apostatized, and the work is unanimously discarded by the church.[40]

E.D. Howe, the intrepid journalist from Painesville, Ohio, and the father of much good reporting, described these and other "peculiarities":

On the conversion of Rigdon, a most successful starting point was thought to have been obtained. Cowdery and his associates then began to develope the peculiarities of the new imposition. Scenes of the most wild, frantic and horrible fanaticism ensued. They pretended that the power of miracles was about to be given to all those who embraced the new faith, and commenced communicating the Holy Spirit, by laying their hands upon the heads of the converts, which operation, at first, produced an instantaneous prostration of body and mind. Many would fall upon the floor, where they would lie for a long time, apparently lifeless. They thus continued these enthusiastic exhibits for several weeks. The fits usually came on, during or after their prayer-meetings, which were held nearly every evening. – The *young* men and women were more particularly subject to this delirium. They would exhibit all the apish actions imaginable, making the most ridiculous grimaces, creeping upon their hands and feet, rolling upon the frozen ground, go through

---

[40]Ibid., 184-85.

with all the Indian modes of warfare, such as knocking down, scalping, ripping open and tearing out the bowels. At other times, they would run through the fields, get upon stumps, preach to imaginary congregations, enter the water and perform all the ceremony of baptizing, &c. Many would have fits of speaking all the different Indian dialects, which none could understand. Again, at the dead hour of night, the young men might be seen running over the fields and hills in pursuit, as they said, of the balls of fire, lights, &c., which they saw moving through the atmosphere.

These were, according to Howe, the earliest Mormons.

Before these scenes fully commenced, however, Cowdery had departed for the country inhabited by the Indians, with the expectation of converting them to Christianity, by means of his new bible, and miracles which he was to perform among them. These pretensions appeared to have taken possession of the minds of the young men in their aspirations. Three of them pretended to have received commissions to preach, from the skies, after having jumped into the air as high as they could. All these transactions were believed to be the *Spirit of God*, by the whole congregation, *which now numbered more than one hundred.*–[41]

Smith himself applied the corrective. "All these things were afterwards pronounced by Smith to be the work of the Devil, although more than one hundred had been converted to Mormonism by merely witnessing the exhibitions."[42] The German Reformed minister of Fayette, New York, Diedrich Willers, offered "the earliest description" of the new church in the German

---

[41]Howe, *Mormonism Unvailed*, 104-5, emphasis retained.
[42]Ibid., 107.

language. "He writes that 'Mormonites' call themselves Die wahre Nach folger Cristi ('the True Disciples of Christ'). Concerning six *Book of Mormon* witnesses who had been his parishioners, Willers writes that the Whitmers 'even believe in witches. Hiram Page is likewise full of superstition.'" Reverend Willers predicted that Mormonism would soon be "given the stamp of oblivion."[43]

TIMELINES

From Ohio to Missouri

At the Fourth Conference of the Church, the first in Ohio, in June 1831, the "high priesthood" was initially introduced to twenty-three of some forty-four elders who were then in attendance there. Until that Conference those previously ordained elders didn't hold and hadn't held the high priesthood after the holy order of God. The Fifth Conference of the Church, and the first to be held in the Lord's only recently designated Zion, was "at the house of brother Joshua Lewis" in Jackson County, Missouri.[44]

In July 1831, the Lord revealed the location of the New Jerusalem – at and around the city of Independence in Jackson County, Missouri – and identified the spot upon which the temple was to be built[45] in "this generation." The first log houses, including the house of Brother Joshua Lewis, were "laid in Kaw Township, twelve miles southwest of Independence." In August, the "land of Zion was consecrated and dedicated by Elder Rigdon for the gathering of the Saints." On August 3, 1831, the place for the temple was dedicated in the presence of eight brethren at a spot lying a short distance west of Independence.[46] In September 1831,

---

[43]Diedrich Willers, Letter, June 18, 1830, in D. Michael Quinn, trans. and ed., "The First Months of Mormonism: A Contemporaneous View by Rev. Diedrich Willers," *New York History* 54 (July 1973): 331, quoted in Quinn, *Origins of Power*, 80 and 322 fn 7.

[44]Jenson, comp., *Church Chronology*, 6.

[45]Doctrine and Covenants 57.

[46]Jenson, comp., *Church Chronology*, 6.

Joseph Smith and his family moved from Kirtland to Hiram, Ohio, a distance of about thirty miles. At Hiram he continued to work (with Sidney Rigdon) on what came to be called the Inspired Translation of the King James Bible. The elders approved the publication of the Book of Commandments, a compilation of sixty-five of Smith's revelations in 1833.

In 1832, Smith made his second visit to Missouri.[47] During these early years, after missionaries were sent to convert the Lamanites (Indians) assembled on the Missouri frontier, missionaries were assigned to preach the gospel in various other locations, proceeding to their destinations and pursuing their missionary tasks, two by two. In December 1831, Joseph Smith and Sidney Rigdon were summoned "to go out and preach the gospel."[48] "[I]t is . . . expedient in me," the Lord had said, "that you should open your mouths in proclaiming my gospel." "[C]onfound your enemies; call upon them to meet you both in public and in private; and inasmuch as ye are faithful their shame shall be made manifest."[49] It is just beginning, but there are already "enemies." They are traditional Christians whose practices are to be seen to "their shame."

From 1831 to 1833 Joseph and Sidney collaborate, the Bible-savvy Sidney as scribe, to translate the scriptures, revising, by inspiration and without the support of earlier manuscripts, the English version of the King James Bible. On February 16, 1832, at Hiram, Ohio, Joseph Smith Jr. and Sidney Rigdon jointly receive the vision of the three degrees of glory (which has since become Section 76 of the Doctrine and Covenants). "Hear, O ye heavens, & give ear, O earth, & rejoice ye inhabitants thereof," the Lord initially said, "for the Lord he is God, & beside him there is none else . . . ."[50] In the modern version of this verse in the Doctrine and Covenants, those "one God" words are changed to: "Hear, O ye heavens, and give

---

[47]Ibid., 8.
[48]Ibid., 7.
[49]Doctrine and Covenants 71.
[50]*The Joseph Smith Papers: Revelations and Translations: Manuscript Revelation Books, Facsimile Edition*, ed. Robin Scott Jensen, Robert J. Woodford, and Steven C. Harper (Salt Lake City: Church Historian's Press, 2009), 242-43.

ear, O earth, and rejoice Ye inhabitants thereof, for the Lord is God, and beside him there is no Savior."[51] (Some time after 1832, and in 1839 and 1842, monotheistic Mormonism became polytheistic Mormonism blessed with gods galore). In this vision Joseph and Sidney "saw him, even at the right hand of God," and "heard the voice bearing record that he is the Only Begotten of the Father."[52] The vision tracked the writings of Emanuel Swedenborg – like the Book of Abraham tracked the writings of Thomas Dick, like the Book of Mormon tracked the writings of Ethan Smith – and it differentiated the Book of Mormon's previously undifferentiated heaven and hell. In March 1832, Joseph and Sidney were tarred and feathered at Hiram, Ohio. In that same year it was decided to print three thousand copies of the Book of Commandments. The Saints were commanded to build a temple at Kirtland and opened the School of the Prophets "for the benefit of the Elders."[53]

In 1833 the Ohio Saints laid the cornerstone for the temple at headquarters in Kirtland and the Missouri Saints at Zion in Jackson County, Missouri, were roughly expelled. In January, Joseph Smith Jr., Zebedee Coltrin and William Smith, followed by Sidney Rigdon, Frederick G. Williams, Newel K. Whitney, Hyrum Smith, Joseph Smith Sr., Samuel H. Smith, John Murdock, Lyman E. Johnson, Ezra Thayer, Levi Hancock and other members, both male and female, spoke in tongues. "Praises were sung to God and the Lamb, and speaking and praying in tongues occupied the conference until a late hour at night." The following day, when the conference recommenced, the "singing, praying and praising God" was "all in tongues."[54] On March 18, 1833, Sidney Rigdon and Frederick G. Williams were set apart by Joseph Smith as "Counselors in the Presidency." Associated with those events, "many of the brethren saw a heavenly vision of the Savior and concourses of angels."

---

[51]Doctrine and Covenants 76:1.
[52]Ibid., 76:23.
[53]Jenson, comp., *Church Chronology*, 8.
[54]Ibid., 8.

In October 1833, Joseph and Sidney "were commanded to continue their missionary labors in the East."[55] "And it is expedient in me that you, my servant Sidney, should be a spokesman unto this people; yea, verily, I will ordain you unto this calling, even to be a spokesman unto my servant Joseph . . . I will give unto thee power to be mighty in expounding all scriptures, that thou mayest be a spokesman unto him, and he shall be a revelator unto thee . . . ."[56] In 1834 Joseph organized a Mormon militia, Zion's Camp, to march from Kirtland, Ohio, to Missouri to reinstate Saints who had been evicted from their earthly and eternal inheritances. This reordering was to be accomplished by the "arm of flesh." In 1835 the Three Witnesses to the Book of Mormon were directed to select and organize the Quorum of the Twelve, Joseph received a revelation concerning the priesthood, and the Church effectuated the purchase of Egyptian mummies and papyri. In that same year, the Church approved the Doctrine and Covenants to replace the Book of Commandments, most copies of which were destroyed by Missouri vigilantes when the Saints were evicted from Jackson County, Missouri.[57]

Eighteen thirty-six became the year of the temple. Washings and anointings commenced, the Kirtland temple was dedicated, and everything miraculous became commonplace. On January 21 in connection with anointings with oil and blessings, "The visions of heaven were opened, angels administered to them, and the house was filled with the glory of God. The prophet 'beheld the celestial kingdom of God and the glory thereof . . . .'" He saw "the gate through which the heirs of that kingdom will enter," the throne of God where the Father and Son were seated and the streets of the kingdom. He saw Adam and Abraham; he saw his deceased brother Alvin, who had never been baptized or endowed, and heard the voice of the Lord. On January 28, angels again appeared to the authorities "in the Lord's House at Kirtland." On April 3, a

---

[55]Ibid., 8-9.
[56]Doctrine and Covenants 100:9-11.
[57]Richard Lyman Bushman, with the assistance of Jed Woodworth, *Joseph Smith: Rough Stone Rolling* (New York: Alfred A. Knopf, 2005), xiii, xiv.

Sunday, Joseph Smith and Oliver Cowdery said they "saw and heard the Savior in the Kirtland Temple." After they saw the Savior, Moses appeared and "committed unto them 'the keys of the gathering of Israel from the four parts of the earth, and the leading of the Ten Tribes from the land of the north.'"[58] Joseph saw Jesus with the Father in the spring of 1820, or Jesus by himself in 1821, then at the Fourth Conference of the Church on June 3, 1831, and then again in the Kirtland Temple on April 3, 1836.

After "the spirit of tongues came upon them [the congregation] 'like the rushing of a mighty wind,'" after angels administered to them and filled the house with the glory of God, after Joseph the Prophet beheld the celestial kingdom of God and all of its associated splendors, including the throne of God "whereon was seated the Father and Son," after Joseph saw Adam and Abraham, Michael, his unbaptized brother Alvin and Moses, after the voice of the Lord spoke to him concerning the condition of those who had died without knowledge of the gospel, after Joseph and Oliver saw and heard the Savior in the Kirtland temple, Elias, then Elijah then also now appeared.[59]

> *[Elias] appeared and committed the dispensation of the gospel of Abraham, saying that in us and our seed all generations after us should be blessed.*[60]

After the vision of Elias had closed, another great and glorious vision burst upon us; for Elijah the prophet, taken to heaven without tasting death, stood before us and said:

> *Behold, the time has fully come, which was spoken of by the mouth of Malachi – testifying that he [Elijah] should be sent, before the great and dreadful day of the Lord come –*

---

[58] Jenson, comp., *Church Chronology*, 12.
[59] Ibid.
[60] Doctrine and Covenants 110:12.

*To turn the hearts of the fathers to the children, and
the children to the fathers, lest the whole earth be
smitten with a curse –*

*Therefore, the keys of this dispensation are committed
into your hands; and by this you may know that the
great and dreadful day of the Lord is near, even at the
doors.*[61]

In all of this, certain disconcerting discrepancies are seen to occur.
Elias and Elijah are not two persons and prophets plural, but
rather one person. Elias is the Greek New Testament name for
Elijah, the Hebraic Old Testament prophet. Surely that colossal
mistake must cast doubt upon other visions of the Father and the
Son, Adam, Abraham, Michael, Alvin, Moses and concourses of
angels. "[T]he great and terrible day of the Lord" was not even
close to "near," nor "even at the doors." The urgent gathering was
in every respect misconceived, and the dedication of the Temple was
not "the beginning of . . . blessings which shall be poured out upon
the heads of my people."[62]

---

[61]Ibid., 110:13-16, emphasis added.
[62]Ibid., 110:10.

CHAPTER TEN

True Zion

For behold, I say unto you that Zion shall flourish, and the glory of the Lord shall be upon her . . . .

Doctrine and Covenants

The Lord has set us our stint; no matter how soon we perform it – for when this is done, he will make his second appearance.[1]

**Sidney Rigdon
by Ezra Booth**

Never do another day's work to build up a Gentile city, never lay out another dollar while you live, to advance the world in its present state.

**Joseph Smith by
Brigham Young**[2]

MISSOURI

In July 1831 Joseph's God identified the place of the gathering for the Church of Christ.[3] Missouri, he said, "is the land which I have appointed and consecrated for the gathering of the saints."[4] "[T]his," he said, "is the land of promise, and the place for the city

---

[1]Sidney Rigdon, quoted by Ezra Booth, Letter I, Eber D. Howe, *Mormonism Unvailed: Or, A Faithful Account of That Singular Imposition and Delusion* (Painesville, OH: E.D. Howe, 1834; reprint, New York: AMS Press Inc., 1977), 178.

[2]Brigham Young, "Sermon," February 3, 1867, *JD* 11:294-95, quoted in Stephen C. LeSueur, *The 1838 Mormon War in Missouri* (Columbia: University of Missouri, 1987), 32.

[3]While Smith identified Jackson County, Missouri, as the location of Zion in July 1831, Kirtland, Ohio, remained as headquarters of the Church from 1831 to 1838. (LeSueur, *The 1838 Mormon War in Missouri*, 15).

[4]Doctrine and Covenants 57:1.

of Zion,"[5] the capital of the Kingdom. "[T]he place which is now called Independence is the center place; and a spot for the temple is lying westward, upon a lot which is not far from the court-house."[6] This was the place Mormons died to come, the centerpiece of the "grand design." At that Zion of the Lord of Hosts, Mormonism's apocalyptic millennnarianism was intended to find firm footing. "The Saints were to prepare a holy city, like Enoch's of old, where they were to gather to await the Second Coming; then 'for the space of a thousand years shall the earth rest.'"[7] The promise of Zion was sure.

> *And, behold, there is none other place appointed than that which I have appointed; neither shall there be any other place appointed than that which I have appointed, for the work of the gathering of my saints.*[8]

In 1831, Joseph and a few of his favored followers looked out upon "beautiful rolling prairies . . . spread . . . like a sea of meadows" for "[a]s far [as] the eye can reach . . . ." A place where horses and cattle and hogs "seem nearly to raise themselves." A land "decorated with a growth of flowers so gorgeous and grand as to exceed description . . . ." "The soil is rich and fertile . . . ." The seasons are mild, the prairies and meadows well situated and central. There is wheat and corn, sweet potatoes and cotton. Luxuriant forests – oak and hickory and walnut, elm and ash and cherry, bass wood, cottonwood, butterwood, pecan and maple – faithfully mark "the meanderings of the streams." There are plums and grapes, apples and persimmons; buffalo and elk, deer and bears and wolves and beavers, turkeys and geese and swans and ducks.[9]

Here is the land of milk and honey marred in but one important respect. Those present Gentile inhabitants, "old settlers" and "Missourians," cast a pall upon this place of particular charm.

---

[5]Ibid., 57:2.
[6]Ibid., 57:3.
[7]William Mulder and A. Russell Mortensen, eds., *Among the Mormons: Historic Accounts by Contemporary Observers* (New York, NY: Alfred A. Knopf, 1958), editorial introduction to "Land of Promise," 68.
[8]Doctrine and Covenants 101:20, emphasis added.
[9]Joseph Smith, *History of the Church* (Salt Lake City, 1902), passage I, reproduced in Mulder and Mortensen, eds., *Among the Mormons*, 70.

They sit "in darkness," William W. Phelps noted. "[H]ow natural it was to observe the degradation, leanness of intellect, ferocity, and jealousy of a people that were nearly a century behind [the] times, and to feel for those who roamed about without the benefit of civilization, refinement, or religion . . . ."[10] Beyond that minor first impression distraction there is nothing, no privation or inconvenience, no self-evident disadvantage, "which the hand of industry, the refinement of society, and the polish of science" at the hands of the heavenly-blessed members of this Church of Christ cannot "overcome."[11] "[I]t bids fair – when the curse is taken from the land – to become one of the most blessed places on the globe."[12] May we recollect:

> *[H]ow the glory of Lebanon is to come upon her; the fir tree, the pine tree, and the box tree together, to beautify the place of His sanctuary, that he may make the place of His feet glorious. Where for brass, he will bring gold; and for iron, He will bring silver; and for wood, brass; and for stones, iron; and where the feast of the fat things will be given to the just; yea, when the splendor of the Lord is brought to our consideration for the good of His people, the calculations of men and the vain glory of the world vanish, and we exclaim, "Out of Zion, the perfection of beauty, God hath shined."[13]*

> Joseph Smith

THIS IS THE PLACE

A Place of Refuge

> *For, behold, I say unto you that Zion shall flourish, and the glory of the Lord shall be upon her;*

---

[10]Ibid., 69.
[11]Ibid., 70-71.
[12]Ibid., 70.
[13]Joseph Smith, *History of the Church* (Salt Lake City, 1902), passage I, reproduced in Mulder and Mortensen, eds., *Among the Mormons*, 71, emphasis added.

And she shall be an ensign unto the people, and there shall come unto her out of every nation under heaven.

And the day shall come when the nations of the earth shall tremble because of her, and shall fear because of her terrible ones. The Lord hath spoken it. Amen.[14]

Lyman, New Hampshire, April 28, 1832:

There has been in this town, and vicinity, for about a week, two young men from the westward . . . Mormonites . . . giving to the people lectures on the subject of their religion . . . .

They say they are commanded by God to preach to this generation, and say to them, that all who do not embrace their faith and mode of worship, forsake their friends, houses, and lands, and go with them to a place of safety, which is in the state of Missouri, where they are about building a city, will be destroyed by the sword, famine, pestilence, earthquakes, &c., and that reformation, repentance, and faith, unless it be accompanied with a speedy removal to their city of refuge, will be of no avail.

They state that they do not guess at this, but they absolutely know it, by a revelation from Heaven, through the immediate ministrations of Angels.[15]

Mormon Rage

The story of the conflict between the Mormons and Missouri is a more complex narrative than that described to Mormons by what are often poorly informed apologetic teachers in Mormon churches, seminaries, schools and publications. It is not suitably explained by the persecution-driven narrative written and spoken by apostles

---

[14]Doctrine and Covenants 64:41-43, emphasis added.
[15]*Independent Messenger* (Boston), June 7, 1832, reproduced in Mulder and Mortensen, eds., *Among the Mormons*, 72.

and prophets both early and late. The Missouri frontier in the 1830s was not ground zero for democracy, but it grasped the concept and celebrated the nation and democratic values. The Mormon community as established in Missouri was an unfamiliar unfriendly theocracy testing peculiar theological insights against the ideals of a flawed but civilizing frontier republic. This was at bottom a conflict between a theocracy guided from heaven above and republican principles, the providence of the people and a parliament. It was, like it or not, a struggle for sovereignty.

George Orwell would have understood Mormonism's early totalitarian mindset. Ezra Booth described the clever interplay between edicts and agency. "Every thing in the church is done by commandment: and yet it is said to be done by the voice of the church." Booth described this self-perpetuating process. "For instance," he reports, "Smith gets a commandment that he shall be 'head of the church' ["For his word ye shall receive, as if from mine own mouth, in all patience and faith"[16]], or that 'he shall rule the Conference,' or that the Church shall build him an elegant house, and give him 1,000 dollars. For this the members of the church must vote, or they will be cast off for rebelling against the commandments of the Lord."[17]

Mormons embraced the proposition (not unique to the Mormons) that unwelcome citizens might be warned out of unwelcoming communities. Frontier pariahs were not forever. Several notorious examples show that Mormons did (or tried to do) to others what others did (or tried to do) to them. "[A]n extraordinary effort at intimidation by LDS leaders" occurred at Kirtland, Ohio, in 1836. Twelve then current Mormon general authorities, including the entire First Presidency, "joined fifty-nine other Mormons in signing a warning to the non-Mormon justice of the peace to 'depart forthwith out of Kirtland.'"[18] Although that particular effort failed, it wasn't because the Mormons chose to abandon the extralegal proposition upon which the warning was based. Could they have forced the departure, had they had the power to do what

---

[16]Book of Commandments 22:5.

[17]Ezra Booth, Letter II, Howe, *Mormonism Unvailed*, 181-82.

[18]D. Michael Quinn, *The Mormon Hierarchy: Origins of Power* (Salt Lake City: Signature Books in association with Smith Research Associates, 1994), 91.

they wanted to do, they would have sent the Justice packing without regard for his constitutional rights. He was an unpopular man in Mormon Kirtland. Those early Mormons found the justice of the larger community too confining. For them the voice of their prophet and the law of their Lord applied. This early event identified a conflict between the law of God, interpreted by Joseph Smith, and the law of the land interpreted by the justice of the peace. In 1838 at Far West, Missouri, eighty-four Mormons, most if not all of them covenant members of a violent new secret society, demanded that five of their former leaders and their families leave Caldwell County in seventy-two hours at the risk of the loss of their lives. That particular effort was seen to have been a great success.

Changing Traditional Christianity

The "commandments" of the Church, meaning the law of the Lord, governed Joseph's most faithful followers. In 1831, God's revelations, most of which were still "concealed from the world," guided the new society. "These commandments come from Smith, at such times and on such occasions as he feels disposed to speak, and Rigdon or Cowdery to write them." Ezra Booth presumed that "there are betwixt fifty and a hundred" –including five or six crafted while he was with the prophet and carefully selected others in Missouri – the reception of some of which Booth was allowed to observe. Only those who are "strong in the faith," he said, "are permitted to witness their origin." "I had an opportunity," he said, to witness "this wonderful exhibition of the wisdom and power of God, at three different times . . . ." Booth hadn't been impressed. Those occasions, he said, "bore striking marks of human weakness and wickedness." The edicts were "received in the church as divinely inspired, and the name of the Lord is substituted for that of Smith."[19]

The early revelations were called "The Commandments of the Lord." They were "mysteries of the Kingdom" not then yet intended for the great unwashed. "When they [the "command-ments"] and the Scriptures are at variance, the Scriptures are

---

[19]Ezra Booth, Letter II, Howe, *Mormonism Unvailed*, 181.

wrongly translated; and Smith, though totally ignorant of the original, being a translator or an alterator, can easily harmonize them." Noting that Smith's revelations were more important than the Bible, Ezra Booth explained – to those who read his letters in the *Ohio Star* (a newspaper published in Ravenna, Ohio) – that: "*[T]he Bible is declared too defective to be trusted, in its present form; and it is designed that it shall undergo a thorough alteration, or as they say translation. This work is now in operation.*"[20] Joseph Smith prepared for that work as if the endeavor was urgent, but then failed to publish his own Inspired Translation of the Bible. The subordination of the uncorrected imperfect Bible to the Book of Mormon, "the most correct of any book on earth," is described in Mormon theology as an Article of the Faith. Joseph and Sidney, or Sidney and Joseph, corrected the King James Bible without the benefit of any ancient manuscript. If these brazen reformers were out of line, the faith they formed was out of line. If they were not inspired, if God was not their friend, the new faith's footings were never firm. The issue was divinity.

INVENTING POLYGAMY

These early Mormons, Pentecostal people unrestrained in their exuberance, embraced strange beliefs that aroused suspicion. "*The doctrines and principles relating to plural marriage were revealed to Joseph Smith as early as 1831.*"[21] Many Latter-day Saints don't know that even today, or didn't know that until comparatively recently. Mormon polygamy came just as early, and perhaps even earlier than the identification of true Zion. An unpublished revelation dated July 17, 1831, described the practice to some few carefully selected disciples. In a defense of Joseph Smith and his polygamy published in 1905, Joseph Fielding Smith, the son of Joseph F. Smith, the son of Joseph's brother Hyrum, acknowledged as much in a footnote in a tract that has long been out of print.

> *[A]s early as 1831 the Lord revealed the principle of celestial and plural marriage to him [Joseph Smith]*

[20]Ibid., 181-82, emphasis added.

[21]*Teachings of Presidents of the Church – Joseph Smith* (Salt Lake City: The Church of Jesus Christ of Latter-day Saints, 2007), xii, emphasis added.

and he taught it to others.[22]

To whom was the principle taught? According to Brigham Young, an expert on polygamy and a man Utah Mormons just have to trust, the principle was revealed to Joseph Smith and Oliver Cowdery, who were translating the Book of Mormon in 1829.[23] Who would know that any better than Brigham Young, the polygamous insider who said he knew Joseph Smith as well as any man on earth? The new doctrine was first taught in 1831 to W.W. Phelps "and five others" who "had gathered in Jackson County, Missouri," to teach the gospel to the Lamanites (Indians). Lamanites, according to Smith and as many as a dozen revelations, were the literal descendants of Abraham and Western Hemisphere Hebrews. The missionaries had been assigned to minister to the Indians who were living close to the Missouri border. Many early Indians, impoverished people theoretically intended to become a cherished early Mormon constituency (the battle ax of the Lord), had been relocated by the Federal Government to territories bordering the state of Missouri. These dispossessed early inhabitants, supposed

---

[22]*Blood Atonement and the Origin of Plural Marriage – A Discussion*, correspondence between Elder Joseph F. Smith, Jr., of the Church of Jesus Christ of Latter-day Saints, and Mr. Richard C. Evans, Second Counselor in the Presidency of the "Reorganized" Church (Salt Lake City: The Deseret News Press, 1905), 77, emphasis added. Joseph Fielding Smith (Joseph F. Smith, Jr.), like his father, later became the President of the Mormon Church. Fawn McKay Brodie, Joseph Smith's biographer and David O. McKay's niece, discussed the unpublished revelation with Joseph Fielding Smith in 1943. (David O. McKay became the prophet of the Church in 1951).

> Joseph F. Smith, Jr., the present historian of the Utah Church, asserted to me in 1943 that a revelation foreshadowing polygamy had been written in 1831, but that it had never been published. In conformity with the church policy, however, he would not permit the manuscript, which he acknowledged to be in the possession of the church library, to be examined. [Fawn M. Brodie, *No Man Knows My History: The Life of Joseph Smith the Mormon Prophet*, 2d ed., rev. and enl. (New York, NY: Alfred A. Knopf, 1972), 184].

Orson Pratt reported "in a speech at Plano, Illinois, on September 12, 1878," that apostle Lyman Johnson had told him that "Joseph had made known to him as early as 1831 that plural marriage was a correct principle." (*Historical Record*, vol. VI, 230, quoted in Brodie, *No Man Knows My History*, 184 fn).

[23]Brigham Young, quoted in Charles L. Walker, "Diary" (Harold B. Lee Library, BYU, 1855-1902), 25-26.

potential allies seething with rage, were objects of pronounced emphasis in the early Church.

The early Mormons believed that the Native Americans, who were the blood of Israel, were going to have a vitally important role to play in the restored Kingdom of Israel on Earth, where, according to prophecy, they were going to recover their past Hebraic glory. It was supposed that they would join the leading councils of the newly established Church, after which they would then become warriors with the Saints in the battle for Christian (meaning Mormon) spiritual/temporal/theocratic supremacy. In nearly two hundred years nothing of enduring consequence has come out of these mostly forgotten early revelations.[24] Many hopes have been dashed.

Smith revealed God's will to Phelps and his colleagues. "It is my will, that in time, ye should take unto you wives of the Lamanites and Nephites, that their posterity may become white, delightsome and just." *Following that, Phelps "asked brother Joseph privately, how 'we,' that were mentioned in the revelation could take wives of the 'natives' as we were all married men?" The prophet had been quick to reply, like Abraham took Hagar and Keturah, like Jacob took Rachel, Bilhah and Zilpha, "by Revelation."*[25]

Ezra Booth had been with Joseph and early prominent others in Missouri as an eyewitness in 1831. On December 8, 1831, at the very early stages of Mormonism's Missouri misadventure, Booth "published an account of the revelation" in the *Ohio Star*. The *Star*

---

[24]Native Americans are without influence in the leading councils of the modern Church. Simon Southerton, the DNA expert, in discussing what Mormons must now believe about the composition of "the former inhabitants of this continent," created a short list that included these formidable items: (1) anything Joseph Smith said that connects North America with the Book of Mormon civilizations is just his opinion; (2) when God refers to Indians in the Western United States as Lamanites in the Doctrine and Covenants, it is Joseph Smith's personal opinion influencing scripture; (3) anything any prophet said that implies that there are millions of Lamanites across North and South America is personal opinion and not doctrine. (Simon G. Southerton, "A House Divided – Book of Mormon Apologetics in the 21st Century," 17 May 2013 [accessed January 26, 2016], available from http://simonsoutherton.blogspot.com/2013/05/a-house-divided-book-of-mormon.html; Internet, 5).

[25]Richard S. Van Wagoner, *Mormon Polygamy: A History* (Salt Lake City: Signature Books, 1986), 3-4, emphasis added.

reported, on the authority of Booth, that "'*it has been made known by revelation*' that it would be 'pleasing to the Lord if the elders formed a matrimonial alliance with the natives,' whereby Mormons might 'gain a residence' in Indian territory, despite the opposition of government agents."[26]   Phelps and his associates "were soon ordered out of the Indian country as disturbers of the peace."[27]   But over time "intermarriage between Mormon males and Indian women became an accepted Mormon custom . . . ."[28]

INDEPENDENCE, MISSOURI, 1831
INDIAN OUTREACH

In 1831 Independence, Missouri, was a new town "containing a court-house built of brick, two or three merchant's stores, and 15 or 20 dwelling houses." The houses were mostly built of logs hewed on both sides. The new city is "situated on a handsome rise of ground about three miles south of the Missouri River, and about 12 miles east of the dividing line between the United States and the Indian Reserve, and is the county seat of Jackson County."[29]   The proximity of the city to the Indian Reserve was not inconsequential by early Mormon reckoning. Although outreach to the Indians, like the nineteenth century's frenetic gathering to places of peace and refuge, is on the back burner now, the issue was one of critical importance to the early Church for reasons related to "the commandments of the Lord." "It is well known," said Ezra Booth, "that the ostensible design of the Mormonites in settling in the western part of Missouri, is to convert the Indians . . . ." The Indians were part and parcel of the nineteenth-century Church's improbable dream of the theocracy, by that to say of world domination during the leaders' lifetimes. The Indians were intended to be numbered among the soldiers of the theocracy. Booth likened the intent of the Mormons to the intentions of the Jesuits. In the sixteenth century, the Jesuits established themselves in South America, where they gained complete control over "the

---

[26]Ibid., 223.
[27]Orson Pratt, Autobiography (1874), 57, quoted in Van Wagoner, *Mormon Polygamy: A History*, 223.
[28]Van Wagoner, *Mormon Polygamy: A History*, 223.
[29]Ezra Booth, Letter VI, Howe, *Mormonism Unvailed*, 196.

hearts and consciences of the natives and thereby became their masters."[30] By various modern means, the Mormons hoped to achieve with their Native Americans what the Jesuits had achieved with their Native Americans. The Lord's printing press, under the control of W.W. Phelps and Oliver Cowdery (conceived at Independence in 1831 and established at Independence in 1832), and the Lord's storehouse "committed" to the charge of S. Gilbert, were "two grand engines" calculated "to make the wicked feel the weight of their tremendous power."[31]

West of the dividing line between the United States and the Indian Reserve was "the territory, selected by the government of the United States, for the future residence of the Indians; to which place a number of tribes have recently emigrated." Booth lost his Mormon faith, on and after his trip to Missouri, where he and a number of others who walked to the sacred place had been joined by Joseph Smith, Sidney Rigdon, Martin Harris and Edward Partridge (distinguished men who had traveled more nearly first class).

Booth quickly recognized the futility of the conversion exercise at the center of Mormonism's Missouri expansion. "The question is frequently asked," he said, "do the Indians seem disposed to receive Mormonism; or have any of them as yet embraced it? To which question I have heard some of the leaders reply, 'O yes,' when the truth is, not an individual had embraced it when I left that place. Nor is there any prospect they will embrace it."[32]

Booth – who did acknowledge "that some of the Indians appear to listen with a degree of attention" – described the proffered conversion model. One detects in this what the old settlers and the government's Indian agents found reprehensible about Mormonism's Indian outreach. The Mormon teachers, according to Booth, pretended to disclose to their Indian students, "the source from whence they sprang,"[33] "the secrets of their origin," and "the history of their ancestors," all as described in the Book of Mormon.

---

[30]Ibid.

[31]Ibid., 196-97.

[32]Ibid., 197.

[33]The Pearl of Great Price, Joseph Smith – History 1:34.

They were, they were told, Lamanites and Hebrews. That was the missionary message. The missionaries told the Indians that the great Spirit was determined "in this generation, to restore them to the possession of their lands, now occupied by the whites . . . ." By the arm of flesh, by the power of their warriors, should these Lamanites arise and throw off the shackles of their servitude with the help of their non-Hebrew mentors (hopeful future Mormon co-religionists).

The Indians were told by their Mormon instructors that in time they should go forth among the white people "as a lion among the beasts of the forests, and as a young lion among the flocks of sheep, who, if he goeth through, both treadeth down and teareth to pieces, and no man can deliver." This, according to Ezra Booth, was a "fair specimen of the method adopted in the Book of Mormon and preached by the Mormonite teachers . . . ." It was a clear cut call to violence and rebellion. The teachers told these Indians (Lamanites) that, "Thy hand shall be lifted up against thy adversaries (the whites) and all their enemies (the whites) shall be cut off." In this way did those early Mormon missionaries seek to ingratiate themselves with putative Indian allies. In this way the Mormons encouraged the Indians to "regain the possession of the lands occupied by their forefathers."[34] Lamanites! The children of Lehi! Literal descendants of Abraham! Hebrews! That was the message then.

That message was threatening to the citizens of Jackson County, Missouri, living just miles east of the dividing line between the United States and the Indian Reserve. Indian agents in Kansas and Missouri, responsive to the feelings of the people, created obstacles to the missionary work. They believed the Mormons were "disturbers of the peace" and ordered them out of the Indian Country. Mormon initiatives directed at the "Lamanites" (Indians) alarmed the Missourians, who were fearful that Mormons, Indians and freed slaves might coalesce in such a way as to unsettle Missouri's southern slave-holding citizenry.

---

[34]Ezra Booth, Letter VI, Howe, *Mormonism Unvailed*, 196-97.

URGENT ZION

Missouri, more specifically Independence in Jackson County, was the center place of Zion, the heralded place of refuge for the hordes of uprooted Saints commanded by their God (and his prophet) to gather there. Come out of Babylon to the place of the city of the New Jerusalem that the day of desolation may pass you by. We are God's people; this is God's place; all that God has promised shall come to pass. Christ is coming to the temple we are going to build here; the hour of our deliverance is near; gather with the Saints to this sacred place of peace and safety. So it was that they did gather to the land of their eternal inheritance, to a place that should belong to them and to their posterity not just now, but also forever, while the earth shall stand and in the life to come. When God told Joseph that Independence, Missouri, was Zion, the great migration commenced. The center of spiritual gravity for Mormon converts began to shift from the headquarters of the Church in Kirtland, Ohio, to the Zion of the Lord of Hosts, to the place of the New Jerusalem, Independence, Jackson County, Missouri.

The Mormon presence at the place called Zion had 1831 beginnings. The new Saints organized experimental communities, sharing the products of their labor, erasing the distinction between the spiritual and the secular and alienating their new but earlier neighbors. The Mormons were insular, exclusive, patronizing, even then, though themselves common, often badly educated and desperately poor. They were aggressive in their religious outreach and foolishly oblivious to the sensitivities of the older inhabitants. Mormonism's frontier communism ("the idea of equality") created conflicts between the Mormons, settled on theocracy, and the old settlers, slave-holding democrats.

THE "VORTEX OF DELUSION"

Ezra Booth, whose journey to Missouri started on June 15, 1831[35] (within days of the conference at which what came to be called the

---

[35]The elders directed by commandment to take their journey to the "promised land," including Ezra Booth, were required to proceed "two by two," "with the exception of Rigdon, Smith, Harris, and Partridge." Those last elders traveled

Melchizedek Priesthood was first introduced to some of the Elders), described his discomfiture. "The plan is so ingeniously contrived, having for its aim one principal point, viz: the establishment of a society in Missouri, over which the contrivers of this delusive system, are to possess unlimited and despotic sway."[36] By means of a commandment given in Missouri as to which Booth "was both an ear and eye witness," the elders of the Church "are to go forth to preach Mormonism to *every creature*."[37]

Those who "embrace" the system are supposed to be selected to fulfill great promises, gifts, signs and wonders, "such as healing the sick, the blind made to see, the lame to walk." But saying so wasn't the same as doing so. It proved impossible to find persons with faith "sufficient to become the subjects of their miracles." They were not yet endowed "with the same power . . . the ancient apostles were." Thus, it came to be said that the performance of those "signs and wonders" would be deferred until the disciples had gathered in Missouri. The Lord, it came to be said, would refuse to "show those signs to this wicked and adulterous generation." Booth recalled another broken promise of the same or similar stripe. "In the commandment given to the churches in the State of New York, to remove to the State of Ohio, they were assured that these miracles should be wrought in the State of Ohio, but now they must be deferred until they are settled in Missouri."[38] In that, the Saints (and Ezra Booth) were met by an "old companion" (disappointment). "We would gladly have avoided here an interview with this, our old companion; but this was impossible, she met us, and stared us in the face which way soever we turned, nor was it possible to look her out of countenance, or put the blush upon her pallid features, or expel her from our society."[39]

---

more comfortably and not on foot, that "they might carry the appearance of gentlemen filling some important station in life . . . ." (Booth, Letter V, Howe, *Mormonism Unvailed*, 192).

[36]Ezra Booth, Letter I, Howe, *Mormonism Unvailed*, 178.

[37]Ibid., emphasis retained.

[38]Ezra Booth, Letter II, Howe, *Mormonism Unvailed*, 180-81.

[39]Ibid., 193.

The Law of Consecration

Pixley, a Baptist clergyman who lived in Independence in 1831, and John D. Lee, a Mormon zealot who lived at Adam-ondi-Ahman in 1838, saw the "law of consecration and stewardship" from opposing perspectives. Pixley reasoned that if their leaders forced the Mormons to live the "law of consecration and stewardship" ("the idea of equality"), the Mormon Church must at length implode like various other failed experiments of a similar nature. Lee, on the other hand, reasoned that if the Latter-day Saints didn't live the "law of consecration and stewardship" ("the idea of equality"), the Lord would not protect them.

> *In Kirtland early in 1831 Joseph Smith [Rigdon and Rigdon's Communitarian colleagues] had proposed that his ideal community practice the consecration of property and a system of stewardships which put the management of the temporal affairs of the church in the hands of a presiding bishop. Every man was to give his property unreservedly to the bishop with a binding covenant and to receive in return a deeded inheritance according to his need which became his stewardship to manage independently. Surpluses from his management were to go into the bishop's storehouse for obtaining inheritances for the poor. It was an ideal intended to make the Saints equal in temporal as in spiritual matters. Only on these terms could Zion be sanctified.*[40]

John D. Lee considered the "idea of equality" an unqualified blessing and posited harsh consequences in the event it should fail. "It was . . . revealed that unless this was done . . . as required . . . in the Revelation, . . . the Saints would be driven from State to State, from city to city, from one abiding place to another, until the

---

[40]Mulder and Mortensen, eds., *Among the Mormons*, editorial introduction to "New Jerusalem: Letter from Independence," 72-73, emphasis added. Sidney Rigdon, a recent convert and a person who greatly influenced events "in 1831," was a powerful advocate of "the idea of equality."

members would die and waste away . . . ."[41]

Each family, Pixley notes, gets twenty acres of land "to use and improve" for so long as they are members of the society. If they leave they "go out empty." People who have surrendered their wealth to the society "now find themselves in no very enviable circumstances." They look for work and their women wash for their non-member neighbors.[42] Pixley conjectured that a condition of equality was nothing but a distant dream. Time would show that some of those who are "most zealous and forward in the cause and prosperity of the society"[43] take deeds to the common property in their own names. Pixley speculated that there would be murmurings, pitting one faction against another, and that such contentions would result in feelings and defections. "There is much reason to believe they cannot hold together long. . . . [I]t is more than probable they will soon be scattered and brought to nought." The doctrine of inheritances and the "idea of equality," he thought, "[t]he very materials of which the society is composed must at length produce an explosion."[44]

Would the Latter-day Saints "consecrate their wealth to the Church"? That, both then and later, was a difficult question. When a vote was taken in 1838, the members unanimously said that they would. Lee reported that they voted "to please the priesthood" but acted "to suit themselves." There was a show of hands, he said, "but not a show of hearts."[45] When some of the leaders took large tracts of property in their own names, they became "the worst kinds of extortionists."[46] When some of the Saints defied the revelations because they thought they "could manage their worldly effects"

---

[41]John D. Lee, *Mormonism Unveiled; Or, The Life and Confessions of the Late Mormon Bishop, John D. Lee* (St. Louis, MO: Bryan, Brand & Company; New York, NY: W.H. Stelle & Co., 1877; photomechanical reprint of the original 1877 edition, Salt Lake City: Modern Microfilm Co.), 61.

[42]B. Pixley, 12 October 1832 letter to the editor of the *Christian Watchman*, reproduced from the *Independent Messenger* (Boston, MA: 29 November 1832), reproduced in Mulder and Mortensen, eds., *Among the Mormons*, 75.

[43]Ibid.

[44]Ibid.

[45]Lee, *Life and Confessions*, 62.

[46]Ibid., 64.

"better than any one of the apostles," Lee feared that all would be lost.

Spreading the Word

By July 1833, there were twelve hundred Mormons located in new settlements in Jackson County, Missouri. The leaders of this new colony founded a publication they called *The Evening and the Morning Star.*[47] That Mormon periodical greatly offended the old settlers. In July 1832, the *Star* "published a . . . revelation in which the Lord declared that 'I will consecrate the riches of the Gentiles, unto my people which are of the house of Israel.'" This contention followed by "[s]imilar claims regarding the role of the Indians (who were not Gentiles) in building the Kingdom and punishing God's enemies stimulated rumors that the Mormons were exhorting the Indians to drive the non-Mormon settlers from their land."[48] The Indians, according to the Mormon's early theology, were "of the house of Israel." The old settlers, in fact anyone who was not Mormon (Lamanite or Hebrew), were "the Gentiles."

Jackson County continued to fill with poor northern emigrants. The Missourians, faced with the prospect of Mormon hegemony, first offered to sell their land to their new neighbors. The Mormons, while "crazy to go up to Zion," didn't have the resources required to purchase the land. Furthermore, Mormons who were able to purchase property, those who gave money to their leaders in Ohio to purchase property in Missouri before they got there, were sometimes disappointed. The money sent to Missouri by the leaders of the Church wasn't enough to purchase the tracts the emigrants who provided the funds were told to expect. The Ohio leaders, under enormous pressure from their Ohio creditors, applied what should have been segregated funds to other imperatives. In the years that followed, the Ohio congregation came under attack because of its management, because of its doctrine, and for other reasons, often economic.

---

[47]Mulder and Mortensen, eds., *Among the Mormons*, editorial introduction to "Trouble in Jackson County," 76.

[48]Book of Commandments 44:32, quoted in LeSueur, *The 1838 Mormon War in Missouri*, 18.

The problems confronted by the new settlers were within and without, both early and late. "A dissenter sued the bishop for fifty dollars. As a member, he had sent the money from Ohio 'to purchase an inheritance for himself and the saints of God in Zion in these last days.'" He arrived to find that "the bishop had drawn the deed in his own name." Whether he was a dissenter when he arrived to find that there was no land, or became a dissenter because he arrived to find that there was no land, this much was true: Those who left the society had no recourse in a theocratic forum. There was no law for apostates and members couldn't resign. "The *Star* explained this as common procedure; the bishop held the property for the church. The fifty dollars had been a consecration [a term early Mormons often misused], a deed of gift no more returnable than donations to missionary societies or colleges in other churches." The curious application of the funds by the nominee fooled the dissenter, but then also faithful Mormons like John D. Lee, who called the offenders – leaders who held property in their own names – "extortionists" and described the practice as unconscionable. According to Lee (speaking after 1833), the Missouri leaders cheated well intended Saints. *"[T]he Missouri court found for the plaintiff, who 'shortly after denied the faith and ran away on Sunday,' to spread a further bad opinion about the Mormons. Other dissenters withdrew, vexing the church with lawsuits."*[49] As the Mormon presence exploded, as hordes of poor emigrants put strains on the local economy and threatened the peace, agitators caught the attention of the old settlers, the founders of the little village that had only recently become the Mormon colony's gathering place.

CONFLICT

What the Mormons Thought of the Old Settlers

William W. Phelps described the old settlers as dark and degraded. He said that society east and west defied comparison. One class was "highly cultivated"; the other was "without the benefit of

---

[49]Mulder and Mortensen, eds., *Among the Mormons*, editorial introduction to "Trouble in Jackson County," 76-77, emphasis retained.

civilization, refinement, or religion . . . ."[50] The land was blessed, but the occupants were blighted. "[M]any Mormons regarded the Missourians as ignorant, backward, and wicked people."[51] The place of the New Jerusalem lacked "mills and schools." The curse upon the land, by that to say those benighted ones, would have in time to be removed.

What the Old Settlers Thought of the Mormons

Pixley now (1832) further reports that "four or five hundred Mormonites" are living in Jackson County, "men, women and children."[52] "[T]here is no appearance here different from that of other wicked places. The people eat and drink, and some get drunk, suffer pain and disease, live and die like other people . . . ." These newly settled Mormons "declare that there can be no true church" without the gift of miracles, the gift of tongues, the healing of the sick, the raising of the dead, and other similar manifestations of Pentecostal grace. "Several of them, however, have died, yet none have been raised from the dead. And the sick, unhappily, seem not to have faith to be healed of their diseases. One woman, I am told, declared in her sickness, with much confidence, that she should not die, but here live and reign with Christ a thousand years; but unfortunately she died, like other people, three days after."[53] While the Mormons describe the existence of miracles, "these things, . . . are not *seen* to be done, but only *said* to be done."[54]

This "Mount Zion of the West," according to Pixley, is located "on a site of ground not much elevated." Those who come here "must calculate on being disappointed, if they believe all that is said of the place, or expect much above what is common in any new country of the West." These Mormons "seem to be made up of people of every

---

[50]Joseph Smith, *History of the Church* (Salt Lake City, 1902), passage I, reproduced in Mulder and Mortensen, eds., *Among the Mormons*, 69.

[51]LeSueur, *The 1838 Mormon War in Missouri*, 18.

[52]B. Pixley, 12 October 1832 letter to the editor of the *Christian Watchman*, reproduced in Mulder and Mortensen, eds., *Among the Mormons*, 73.

[53]Ibid.

[54]Ibid., 73-74, emphasis retained.

sect and kind, Shakers, Methodists, Baptists, Presbyterians and Campbellites, and some have been two or three of these different sects before they became Mormonites."[55]

Missouri in 1830 is temperamentally south, and 1830 Missourians are temperamentally southerners, many are owners of slaves. Those who spoke for "free people of color" in Missouri and in the south were under siege and often mistreated. Furthermore, these early Mormons were not only poor, but insular. "Their best requisite for the reception of their expected Saviour, it should seem . . . is their poverty. There is no doubt but that some suffer for want of the necessaries of life . . . . But they have no fellowship for Temperance societies, Bible societies, Tract societies or Sunday school societies."[56] The Mormon faith embraced a covenantal rather than a transactional language and approach to civic life. It lacked the grace to embrace the notion that it was part of something bigger, better, kinder, gentler than itself (*e pluribus unum*). It was characterized at its core by an angry ethnocentricity.

What Were the Old Settlers' Grievances?

Jackson County Missourians came to perceive, as the Indian agents did, that the Mormons were "disturbers of the peace." The Mormons purchased land. The Missourians suspected that they tampered with the slaves and agitated the Indians.[57] Claiming Missouri as the land of their inheritance, they said that they would rule and reign. The riches of the "Gentiles" in "*the land of their enemies,*" they said, would soon belong to them. They purchased a printing press, started *The Evening and the Morning Star* and published some of the prophet's "revelations," statutes to the unwary. They are disrespectful of other Christians, insular and

---

[55]Ibid., 74.

[56]Ibid.

[57]"William Phelps published an article in the *Evening and Morning Star* [in July 1833] about the legal requirements for bringing free negroes into the state, and locals interpreted the description as an invitation. Phelps quickly disavowed any such intention, insisting he was actually warning future immigrants against importing free blacks, but the damage had been done." (Richard Lyman Bushman, with the assistance of Jed Woodworth, *Joseph Smith: Rough Stone Rolling* [New York: Alfred A. Knopf, 2005], 223).

impolite. They gather together, pool their resources and practice the idea of equality. They claim to heal the sick, speak in tongues, seal, confirm, curse and bless and say that the Lord reveals himself to them. They are northerners. They claim that they are God's chosen people.

The old settlers "distrusted the Saints communitarian economic system. In Jackson County, the Mormons bought land and started businesses with Church funds, presenting their neighbors with what seemed to be unfair business competition."[58] In the eyes of the old settlers they are deluded, obnoxious fanatics. They speak for the law when it operates to their advantage, but their system is otherwise oppressively theocratic. The words of the prophet are more important than the laws of the commonwealth. They could be depended upon to do what their prophet said that they should. The "[f]ear of being overwhelmed politically, socially, culturally, economically by Mormon immigration was what fueled anti-Mormonism wherever the Latter-day Saints settled during Joseph Smith's lifetime."[59]

"BY THE ARM OF FLESH"

The missionaries who traveled to Missouri in 1831, on foot and devoid of much that travel then required, met with disappointment. It was thought "that those who were ordained to the gift of tongues, would have an opportunity to display their supernatural talent, in communicating to the Indians, in their own dialect." It didn't work for them, or for Oliver Cowdery who preceded them. "We expected to find a large church, which Smith said, was revealed to him in a vision, Oliver had raised up there. This large church was found to consist of four families." The missionaries expected to witness "the exercise" of "those miraculous gifts to which some were ordained while in the state of Ohio." That, most unfortunately, did not occur. "[T]he same difficulty, the same want of faith among the people, which counteracted them here [in Ohio], prevailed there [in Missouri]; consequently no miracles could be wrought."[60]

---

[58]LeSueur, *The 1838 Mormon War in Missouri*, 17.
[59]Quinn, *Origins of Power*, 91.
[60]Ezra Booth, Letter V, Howe, *Mormonism Unvailed*, 194.

Now the Lord spoke to his servant Sidney Rigdon by way of command ("Let my servant Sidney consecrate and dedicate the land"). Sidney was told to write a description of the land of Zion, "a statement of the will of God, as it shall be made to him by the spirit . . . ." Then, in a subscription to be presented to the Churches, he should "obtain money to purchase lands, for the inheritance of the children of God, for behold the Lord willeth that his Disciples, and the children of men, should open their hearts to purchase the whole region of country, lest they receive none inheritance, *save it be by the shedding of blood* . . . ."[61] So "the shedding of blood" in support of "the inheritance of the children of God" – this Zion of the Lord of Hosts – was one of several available options. For whether purchased with money or acquired by means of the shedding of blood, "this whole region of country is ours." With one last salvo, Booth described his own dim view of the threat that the Mormons would take the land by means of force and violence. The people of Missouri, he said, need not fear that the Mormonites, "were they so disposed, will obtain the possession of their lands 'by shedding of blood,' until the spirit selects more courageous leaders than *Smith or Rigdon*."[62] As Mormonism was seen to unfold, there were those who might have chosen to differ. The Mormon prophet was no shrinking violet. He challenged his detractors with pugnacious intensity.

The Evening and the Morning Star, Mormonism's Jackson County, Missouri, newspaper, "wrote matter of factly about tak[ing] possession of this country." Josiah Gregg, a merchant living in Independence, reported that "the Mormons grew bolder in their predictions as their numbers increased."[63] This Mormon arrogance was no small factor in helping turn Missouri against the members of the Church. "At last they became so emboldened by impunity, as openly to boast of their determination to be the sole proprietors of the 'Land of Zion.' By summer of 1833, the Saints held over 2,400 acres of land in and around Independence and threatened a

---

[61]Revelation, quoted by Ezra Booth, Letter V, Howe, *Mormonism Unvailed*, 195, emphasis added.
[62]Ezra Booth, Letter V, Howe, *Mormonism Unvailed*, 195-196, emphasis retained and added.
[63]Bushman, *Joseph Smith: Rough Stone Rolling*, 223.

complete takeover."[64]

"Gathering" Momentum

The old settlers, offended by the Mormons' economic solidarity, and their old world ways, characterized their new neighbors as a "singular sect of pretended christians." As time passed, the "Mormonite" threat was seen to become increasingly dire.

> *But little more than two years ago, some two or three of these people made their appearance on the Upper Missouri and they now number some 1,200 souls in this county, and each successive autumn and spring pours forth its swarm upon us, with a gradual falling off in the character of those who compose it; until it seems that those communities from which they come, were flooding us with the very dregs of their composition.*

> *Elevated as they mostly are but little above the condition of our blacks, whether in regard to property or education, they have become a subject of much anxiety on that part, serious and well grounded complaints having been already made of their corrupting influence on our slaves.[65]*

> *The evil [of this Mormon collection] is one that no one could have foreseen, and is therefore unprovided for by the laws, and the delay incident to legislation would put the mischief beyond remedy.[66]*

---

[64]Joseph Gregg, quoted in Bushman, *Joseph Smith: Rough Stone Rolling*, 223.

[65]Account of the minutes and resolutions of the Missouri settlers' 20 July 1833 meeting, taken from the *Missouri Intelligencer and Boon's Lick Advertiser* (Columbia) (10 August 1833), reproduced in Mulder and Mortensen, eds., *Among the Mormons*, 78, emphasis added. "One of the means resorted to by them, in order to drive us to emigrate, is an indirect invitation to the free brethren of color in Illinois, to come up, like the rest, to the land of Zion . . . ." (Ibid., 79).

[66]Missouri settlers' 20 July 1833 meeting, reproduced in Mulder and Mortensen, eds., *Among the Mormons*, 78, emphasis added.

"Gathering" Land

The gathering is urgent or the expulsion is urgent, depending upon one's point of view. The old settlers are told, "not by the ignorant alone, but by all classes of them, that we . . . are to be cut off, and our lands appropriated by them for inheritances." How that was supposed to occur had not been completely determined. It may be at the hand of "our destroying Angel," by means of "the judgements of God," or by "the arm of power."[67] They will say (but not until after 1833) that when the Kingdom of God is established in Jackson County that they will "literally tread upon the ashes of the wicked [presumably us] after they [we] are destroyed from off the face of the earth."[68] According to the Mormons, the land of Missouri is the land of their enemies. "[T]he vexation that would attend the civil rule of these fanatics . . . ," according to their detractors, "would require neither a visit from the destroying angel, nor the judgements of an offended God, to render our situation here, insupportable."[69]

There is thus an apprehension that the Mormons plan to take the established settlers' properties by force. That is to say, if necessary, by the shedding of blood. "[T]heir numbers are increasing beyond every rational calculation" and all of them are required, "as soon as convenient, to come up to Zion, [the] name they have thought proper to confer upon our little village. Most of those who have already come, are characterized by the profoundest ignorance, the grossest superstitions, [and] the most abject poverty."[70] They do not have the means to purchase our land for their inheritance here. They cannot procure food enough for themselves to eat. Yet the day is not "far distant when the government of the county will be in their hands."

What would be the fate of our lives and property, in the hands of jurors and witnesses who do not blush to declare and would not upon occasion hesitate to swear

---

[67]Ibid.

[68]LeSueur, *The 1838 Mormon War in Missouri*, 18.

[69]Missouri settlers' 20 July 1833 meeting, reproduced in Mulder and Mortensen, eds., *Among the Mormons*, 79.

[70]Ibid., 78-79.

that they have wrought miracles and supernatural cures; have converse with God and His angels; and possess and exercise the gift of Divination and of unknown tongues and fired with the prospect of obtaining inheritances without money and without price, may be better imagined than described.[71]

For now they buy the land when they can. They say that the land assigned to the Kingdom of God to be established in Jackson County belongs to them for as long as the earth shall stand. They inform the original settlers that they need not further improve their lands, for they will not live to enjoy the fruits of their labor.

Ezra Booth understood the system. "The system," he said, ". . . claims the Bible for its patron and proffers the restoration of the apostolic church, with all the gifts and graces with which the primitive saints were endowed." Sinners were "denounced." Those "who reject the Book of Mormon are threatened with eternal damnation." Those who "embrace" the system were promised the "signs and wonders" of "the primitive saints." Booth understood the significance of Zion in Missouri. "[T]hey are to receive," he said, "an everlasting inheritance in 'the land of Missouri,' where the Savior will make his second appearance; at which place the foundation of the temple of God, and the City of Zion, have recently been laid, and are soon to be built." This city to be built on consecrated ground will be a place of refuge and asylum "when the storms of vengeance shall pour upon the earth."

In 1831, when Ezra Booth visited Missouri at the beginning of the great apocalyptic exercise, in company with Joseph Smith and others, he was given to understand that "those who reject the Book of Mormon, shall be swept off as with the besom [broom] of destruction. Then shall the riches of the Gentile be consecrated to the Mormonites; . . . lands and cattle in abundance . . . the gold and silver, and all the treasures of their *enemies.*"[72] The old settlers are "*enemies*"; Missouri is Mormon by the gift of God.[73]

---

[71]Ibid., emphasis added.

[72]Ezra Booth, Letter 2, Howe, *Mormonism Unvailed*, 179-80, emphasis added.

[73]Doctrine and Covenants 52:42. *"[I]f ye are faithful ye shall assemble yourselves together to rejoice upon the land of Missouri, which is the land of your*

"Gathering" Allies

They indirectly invite free brethren of color to join them here.[74] Indians may be expected to join them here. They will have a corrupting influence on our slaves. We shall be subject to the civil rule of these fanatics. "True, it may be said, and truly no doubt that the fate that has marked the rise and fall of Joanna Southcote and Ann Lee will also attend the progress of Jo. Smith; but this is not copiate to our fears, for when the fabric falls the *rubbish* will remain."[75]   The Missourians thought (clearly in error) that the Mormonites (racists themselves) somehow threatened their slaves. "The Missourians suspected that the Saints were tampering with their slaves and stirring up the Indians with their preaching."[76]

"Gathering" Power

The migration had proved unsettling. The *Star* itself lamented that these new emigrants didn't have the wherewithal to purchase even small tracts of "wild land," and noted that they were "destitute." "Religious prejudice stimulated much of the opposition to the Mormons, but the Missourians' antipathy was also sustained by the social, economic, and political threat the Mormons posed to their communities."[77] The concerns of the old settlers raised an issue no less important than sovereignty. "When we reflect on the extensive field in which this sect is operating . . . it requires no gift of prophecy to tell that the day is not far distant, when the government of the county will be in their hands," or in the hands of "persons willing to court their favor from motives of interest or ambition."[78] The "idea of equality" that motivated these early emigrants

---

inheritance, which is now the land of your enemies . . . ." "Behold, I am Jesus Christ, the Son of God . . . ." (Doctrine and Covenants 52:43, emphasis added). Christianity's Messiah, we may suppose, has helped to prepare an enemies' list for the Church of Christ.

[74]Missouri settlers' 20 July 1833 meeting, reproduced in Mulder and Mortensen, eds., *Among the Mormons*, 79.

[75]Ibid., emphasis retained.

[76]LeSueur, *The 1838 Mormon War in Missouri*, 17.

[77]Ibid.

[78]Missouri settlers' 20 July 1833 meeting, reproduced in Mulder and Mortensen, eds., *Among the Mormons*, 79.

required the fusion of secular and spiritual forces. Mormon sovereignty was a prospect to be feared. Will they not soon be judges, justices, sheriffs, mayors and clerks? Missouri will be subject to the control of a Mormon theocracy with Joseph Smith in charge.

FRICTIONS AND FRUITION

If they refuse to leave us in peace, as they found us –
we agree to use such means as may be sufficient to
remove them.

Disappointed Mormons, Zion backouts, did their part to spread the word. Their complaints further inflamed the volatile Gentiles. Certain of their spiritual superiority, faithful Mormons also spread the word. They openly continued to describe the old settlers as "enemies" and depreciated their less than acceptable leaders. "[T]here were incidents between Mormons and Missourians. As early as 1832 houses had been stoned and shot at, a haystack burned, families insulted."[79] In April 1833, old settler concerns took center stage. Some three hundred Missourians gathered at Independence "to decide on a course of action." That particular early meeting "ended in drunken disagreement," but "On July 4th they circulated a set of resolutions called the 'Secret Constitution' setting forth their grievances against the Mormons."[80] On July 20 the old settlers, meeting at the courthouse in Independence, issued this ultimatum:

> 1. That no Mormon shall in future move and settle in this county.

> 2. That those now here, who shall give a definite pledge of their intention within a reasonable time to remove out of the county, shall be allowed to remain unmolested until they have sufficient time to sell

---

[79]Mulder and Mortensen, eds., *Among the Mormons*, editorial introduction to "Trouble in Jackson County," 77.
[80]Ibid.

their property and close their business without any
material sacrifice.

3. That the editor of the "Star" be required
forthwith to close his office, and discontinue the
business of printing of this county; and as to all
other stores and shops belonging to the sect their
owners must in every case strictly comply with the
terms of the second article of this declaration, and
upon failure, prompt and efficient measures will be
taken to close the same.

4. That the Mormon leaders here, are requested
to use their influence in preventing any further
emigration of their distant brethren to this county,
and to counsel and advise their brethren here to
comply with the above requisition.

5. That those who fail to comply with the above
requisitions, be referred to those of their brethren
who have the gift of divination, and of unknown
tongues to inform them of the lot that awaits them.

Which address being read and considered was
unanimously adopted. And thereupon it was
resolved that a committee of twelve be appointed
forthwith to wait on the Mormon leaders, and see
that the foregoing requisitions are complied with by
them; and upon their refusal, that said committee
do, as the organ of the county, inform them that it is
our unwavering purpose and fixed determination,
after the fullest consideration of all consequences
and responsibilities under which we act, to use such
means as shall insure their full and complete
adoption.[81]

The committee then marched to the Mormon quarter west of town
and presented their demands to the Mormon leaders.   The

---

[81]Missouri settlers' 20 July 1833 meeting, reproduced in Mulder and
Mortensen, eds., *Among the Mormons*, 80.

Mormons were to shut up all their workshops, their store, and their printing office, and then agree to leave the county.[82] The demand to decide, presented to Rigdon's friend Bishop Edward Partridge, quickly became immediate. The Mormon leaders were told that they should *agree to comply* within fifteen minutes. When they could not *agree to comply* in fifteen minutes, the old settlers (who were still in session) *voted* to demolish the printing office.[83] The Mormon publication had been a particular object of the old settlers' anger. This they then proceeded to do with some dispatch. They first demolished the office, then tarred and feathered Edward Partridge and Charles Allen. Three days later the vigilantes returned, determined "to continue the work of destruction." "Under this pressure the nine leading Mormon men promised they would leave the county with half the colony by January 1, the remainder to follow before spring."[84] With this concession, the Mormon leaders purchased a period of relative peace.[85]

MISSOURI DEMOCRACY

What the Missourians first did to the Mormons at Independence in 1833 was what the Mormons would try to do to a Justice of the Peace at Kirtland, Ohio, in 1836, and what the Mormons actually did to four or five prominent dissenters at Far West, Missouri, in 1838. And what the old settlers did to *The Evening and the Morning Star* in 1833 was what Mayor Joseph Smith and a Mormon mob did to the *Nauvoo Expositor* at Nauvoo, Illinois, in 1844. The Mormons later accepted in their other communities those Missouri populist precedents. The volatile Rigdon wanted to hang Mormonism's Missouri dissenters, those who had become disenchanted, and offered his assistance to construct a scaffold. He threatened his

---

[82]Mulder and Mortensen, eds., *Among the Mormons*, editorial introduction to "Trouble in Jackson County," 77.

[83]"When he [Edward Partridge] pleaded for more time, the men marched to the *Star* office, where they wrecked the press, smashed the furniture, and then razed the two story building. They carried off or destroyed all of the copies of the *Book of Commandments* [Joseph's revelations] that they could find." (Brodie, *No Man Knows My History*, 133).

[84]Ibid., 134.

[85]Mulder and Mortensen, eds., *Among the Mormons*, editorial introduction to "Trouble in Jackson County," 77.

formerly beloved colleagues with the same extralegal punishment that an enraged group of Mississippi vigilantes had administered to some unfortunate gamblers at Vicksburg, Mississippi. They had lynched them in front of a crowd.[86] The Mormons were capable of doing everything to others that the people of Missouri did to them as they then (and later) proved. The "shedding of blood" was always an option. Had the Mormons been the larger force, the outcome (and the process) could have been reversed.

The minutes of one of the meetings called to rid Jackson County "of the set of fanatics called Mormons" said that the assembly included "gentlemen from every part of the country." Four or five hundred persons met to deliberate the Mormon question. The Mormons had descended upon that pastoral place of a sudden in ways that defied all earlier experience. The Assembly resolved to evict the Mormons not for their spiritual but rather temporal pretensions:

> *Of their pretended revelations from Heaven – their personal intercourse with God and his Angels – the maladies they pretend to heal by the laying on of hands – and the contemptible gibberish with which they habitually profane the Sabbath and which they dignify with the appellation of unknown tongues, we have nothing to say. ... But as to the other matters set forth in this paper, we feel called on by every consideration of self-preservation, good society, public morals, and the fair prospects, that if not blasted in the germ, await this young and beautiful country, at once to declare . . . That no Mormon shall in future move and settle in this county.*[87]

---

[86]Brigham Young also accepted the principle that nothing could be done if a vast assembly of citizens exercising the supreme will of the people wanted someone lynched (and there were lynchings and executions in Brigham Young's Utah Territory). There were, in fact, said to have been as many lynchings as there were legal executions during the Utah Territory reign of Brigham Young. Dr. Martin Luther King, Jr., was heard to say that while a society can't legislate how one feels, it can write a law against lynching.

[87]Missouri settlers' 20 July 1833 meeting, reproduced in Mulder and Mortensen, eds., *Among the Mormons*, 79-80.

The issue was sovereignty. Would Jackson County be subject to the rule of a Mormon theocracy? Like the Utah Territory in the Great Basin later was?

Breaking the Camel's Back

The Mormons considered the July 1833 agreement to be illegal, and it was illegal because induced by force and duress. Now, in contradiction to the terms of the illegal agreement, and "after two or three months of quiet, they petitioned the state government to prevent their forced evacuation of Jackson County . . . ." Then Governor Dunklin referred them to the courts. That was "an empty comfort" because "the civil officers and influential citizens of Jackson," including the judiciary, had all signed "the agreement seeking to drive the Mormons out."[88] The Mormon leaders' attempt to circumvent the terms of the illegal agreement and prevent a forced evacuation caused consternation in the ranks of the old settlers, the more violent of whom then proceeded to pull down some Mormon houses (often at night) and whip some of the Mormon men. On October 31, 1833, fifty men "unroofed and partly demolished" ten Mormon cabins, "whipped and stoned the men, and drove the women and children shrieking into the woods." Other similar nights were said to have followed. Now the Mormons, turning their backs on capitulation, "began to organize for defense."[89] On November 4, 1833, the conflict escalated, taking an ominous turn. On that day Book of Mormon witness David Whitmer, soon to be ordained as Joseph Smith's probable successor and at the time a highly favored disciple, led a force of Mormon men against some Missouri marauders assaulting some Mormon settlements near the Blue River. In that encounter, the violence, never previously fatal, reached a new level. Now Missourians and at least one of the Mormons were killed.

That Independence, Missouri, observer, Minister Pixley described

---

[88]Mulder and Mortensen, eds., *Among the Mormons*, editorial introduction to "Excitement, Anxiety and Alarm," 80-81.

[89]Brodie, *No Man Knows My History*, 136.

the unsavory escalation.[90] According to Pixley, the Mormons had emigrated and settled at Independence, Missouri, under the pretense that Independence was "the Mount Zion spoken of in Scripture." Among their many offenses, Pixley recounted these: The "present inhabitants [were told they] would be driven off unless they sold to the Mormons and went off peaceably." "[T]he Mormons should possess the county," and invite "free negroes from all parts of the country to come and join them . . . ." They "pretended power to work miracles and speak with tongues."

> [A]ll these things taken together, aroused so much indignation in the minds of the inhabitants, that they assembled last summer, according to appointment, without noise or riot, or drunkenness, but with deliberate purpose, and pulled down the printing office (a brick building), and drew the roof into the highway. They were about to proceed to the same act of violence against the store, when a parley took place, and the parties came to terms of accommodation. The Mormons were to close up their business, and were all to move away before another summer; while the other party bound themselves to pay all damages done to the printing office, &c.[91]

> Thus peace was made, and so the matter stood until a few days since, when it was found not only that the Mormons did not intend to move according to agreement, but that they were arming themselves, and threatened to kill if they should be molested. This provoked some of the more wild and ungovernable among us to improper acts of violence, such as breaking in upon the Mormon houses, tearing off the covering &c. On this the Mormons began to muster, and exhibit military preparations. Two gentlemen, passing peaceably through the settlement on Saturday evening, were hailed, and

---

[90]B. Pixley, 7 November 1833 letter to the editors of the New York *Observer*, reproduced in Mulder and Mortensen, eds., *Among the Mormons*, 81.
    [91]Ibid., 82.

commanded to advance and give the countersign. But as they could not do this, they were put under arrest in what was called the guard house, and kept prisoners until morning.[92]

Now the violence became bilateral. Pixley describes events and reports the Mormon response:

On Sunday, I believe some shots were exchanged, the Mormons having given the first fire and wounded one man. On Monday a party of the inhabitants, some of them armed, went toward the Mormon settlement, mostly for the purpose of inquiry, and to learn whether the Mormons would attempt to attack them. These were led into ambuscade and fired upon by the Mormons before they arrived at their settlement, and two men were killed on the spot. This little party of inhabitants, said to be eleven in number, retreated before about fifty or sixty Mormons but, after the Indian mode, from tree to tree fired back upon the pursuers, till the Mormons had three killed (among whom was one of their elders) and several wounded. This was about sunset.[93]

One of the Missourians killed in Jackson County, Missouri, during the course of the hostilities there was the brother-in-law of Judge Austin King, a man who figured prominently in future Missouri events. (Judge King later became the tenth Governor of the State of Missouri). Following those events, according to the Reverend Mr. Pixley, a revelation directed the Mormons *"to arise and pursue and destroy their enemies."* God now entered the fray.

In obedience to the mandate . . . they were discovered under arms to the number of about one hundred and fifty advancing on Tuesday morning to the town of Independence. The alarm was given, and mounted horsemen, from all quarters, flew to

---

[92]Ibid., 82.
[93]Ibid., 82-83.

> the place of conflict, and advanced to meet the
> Mormons half a mile out of town. It was a serious
> moment; . . . . But happily the Mormon courage
> failed under a view of superior numbers, and they
> were induced to deliver up their arms and retire . . .
> [94]

Among those who convinced the Mormons to surrender their
weapons on that occasion, and then to retire, were Lieutenant
Governor Lilburn W. Boggs and Colonel Thomas Pitcher, Pitcher
being one of the many men who had signed the citizens' manifesto.
If the Mormons disarmed, according to Boggs, he would order
Pitcher to disarm as well. The Mormons disarmed, but Colonel
Pitcher's Missouri militia did not.[95]

> That night the mob systematically sacked every
> Mormon community, beat and whipped the men,
> and drove the women and children out like cattle.
> Before morning twelve hundred people had been
> herded forth in the teeth of a November gale. A few
> fled to Clay County where they were received with
> sympathy; the majority huddled for days among the
> cottonwoods lining the Missouri River, hungry,
> weaponless, and leaderless, praying passionately for
> a miracle.[96]

How could the failure of this great God-directed Missouri gathering
ever be explained? On December 16, 1833, Joseph's Lord decided
to try. "I, the Lord, have suffered the affliction to come upon them,
wherewith they have been afflicted, in consequence of their
transgressions . . . ." Mormon leaders never fail; only faithless
followers fail. "Behold, I say unto you, there were jarrings, and
contentions, and envyings, and strifes, and lustful and covetous
desires among them; therefore by these things they polluted their
inheritances."[97] The defeat was laid squarely on the backs of the

---

[94]Ibid., 83.
[95]Brodie, *No Man Knows My History*, 136-37.
[96]Ibid., 137.
[97]Ibid., 139, citing Doctrine and Covenants 101.

suffering Saints. Joseph, the prophet of broken promises, avoided censure.

By December 16, most of the Mormons had resettled in Clay County, a place that wasn't Zion. The Lord ordered the evicted colony to remain as near Jackson County as possible, and emphatically forbade them to sell their property. Pixley humanely lamented the plight of the evicted and suffering Saints.

> I am sorry to add that such was the ungovernable and unmanly conduct of some in our community, that it was with the utmost difficulty that the civil authorities could protect their prisoners from being massacred on the spot. Even now the Mormons who are peaceably moving off, are under the necessity of being guarded by the civil authorities to protect them from the violence which otherwise they would have the greatest reason to fear. In justice, however, to a goodly number of the community, I must remark that the sufferings of the Mormons, and especially the women and children, in being obliged to move off so suddenly at this season of the year, has excited much lively sympathy and humane feeling, and some have made very liberal contributions for their relief.[98]

Lyman Wight, the Wild Ram of the Mountains and a fierce militant disciple, had been in charge of the troops who marched on Independence before they then delivered up their arms and surrendered. In what the Missourians called an "ambuscade," and what the Mormons called a "depredation," three or four men were killed (accounts vary) and others were wounded. The news of that deadly violence reached Independence after dark on a day when several Mormons were in the middle of a "sham trial." The intensity of those events, when reported, so inflamed the citizenry "that the court had to shut the prisoners up in jail for their own protection. Lyman Wight, supposing them unjustly imprisoned and

---

[98]B. Pixley, 7 November 1833 letter to the editors of the New York *Observer*, reproduced in Mulder and Mortensen, eds., *Among the Mormons*, 83.

about to be shot, marched into Independence with 150 Mormons, only to give up their arms when they learned the situation."[99]

Until then, it was what they said, not so much what they did, that put the Mormons at risk. The men who signed the Independence manifesto (requiring the Mormons to leave Jackson County) were not exactly border ruffians. They "listed themselves as jailor, county clerk, Indian agent, postmaster, judge, attorney at law, justice of the peace – the most respectable characters in the county. They met on the courthouse steps to make their plans." "[T]he Jackson County citizens believed they could act legally against the Mormons. They were not a mob but the people in action."[100] They met on the fourth of July. In their Manifesto they pledged "our lives, fortunes and sacred honors" to the cause. And the cause? To shut down the hated Mormon press. To require every Mormon man, woman or child to leave the county. To see that no one else came.

The Mormon hegira from Independence was sad and appalling, and many suffered terribly.

> *The Mormons all left Jackson County during the winter. Some went briefly to Van Buren County; some backtrailed east. Most of them crowded the Missouri bottoms in wretched privation and crossed the Missouri River north into Clay County, where they were hospitably received. They were not permitted to return to Jackson County, even to settle up their business. The old settlers burned down over two hundred empty Mormon houses in the spring to finish their winter's work.*[101]

---

[99]Mulder and Mortensen, eds., *Among the Mormons*, editorial introduction to "Excitement, Anxiety and Alarm," 81.

[100]Bushman, *Joseph Smith: Rough Stone Rolling*, 223.

[101]Mulder and Mortensen, eds., *Among the Mormons*, editorial introduction to "Excitement, Anxiety and Alarm," 81, emphasis added.

ONE GOD

King James Bible: *"[N]o man knoweth who the son is, but the Father; and who the Father is, but the Son, and he to whom the Son will reveal him." (Luke 10:22).* **Joseph Smith Inspired Translation:** *"[N]o man knoweth that the Son is the Father, and the Father is the Son, but him to whom the Son will reveal it." (Luke 10:23).*

BOOK OF MORMON

Abinadi: *"I would that ye should understand that God himself shall come down among the children of men, and shall redeem his people. And because he dwelleth in flesh he shall be called the Son of God, and having subjected the flesh to the will of the Father, being the Father and the Son – The Father because he was conceived by the power of God; and the Son, because of the flesh, thus becoming the Father and the Son – And they are one God, yea, the very Eternal Father of heaven and earth." (Book of Mormon, Mosiah 15:1-4).*

Amulek: *"Now Zeezrom saith again unto him: Is the Son of God the very Eternal Father? And Amulek said unto him: Yea, he is the very Eternal Father of heaven and of earth, and all things which in them are; he is the beginning and the end, the first and the last; . . . ." (Book of Mormon, Alma 11:38-39)*

SCHOLARS

Thomas Alexander: *"The Book of Mormon tended to define God as an absolute personage of spirit who, clothed in flesh, revealed himself in Jesus Christ."*

Boyd Kirkland: *"The Book of Mormon speaks of only one God who could manifest himself either as the Father or the Son."*

JEHOVAH WASN'T JESUS IN 1842

In the modern Church, "*Christ in His preexistent, antemortal, or unembodied state . . . was known as Jehovah . . . .*" *In the early Church,* Jehovah and Elohim were sometimes used as interchangeable epithets for the same spirit person, Jehovah/Elohim, the Father of Jesus. "*O Thou, who seest and Knowest the hearts of all men – Thou eternal, omnipotent, omniscient, and omnipresent Jehovah – God – Thou Eloheim, that sittest, as saith the Psalmist, 'enthroned in heaven,' look down upon Thy servant Joseph at this time; and let faith on the name of Thy Son Jesus Christ, to a greater degree than Thy servant ever yet has enjoyed, be conferred upon him . . . .*" (Joseph Smith, History of the Church, 5:127-28)

POLYTHEISM

From Enoch, December 1830:

> *Jesus valued:* "*And were it possible that man could number the particles of the earth, yea, millions of earths like this, it would not be a beginning to the number of thy creations . . . .*"

To Orson Pratt, February 1855:

> *Jesus devalued:* "*If we should take a million of worlds like this and number their particles, we should find that there are more gods than there are particles of matter in those worlds.*"

GORDON B. HINCKLEY

Joseph Smith: "*God Himself was once as we are now, and is an exalted man, and sits enthroned in yonder heavens! ... It is the first principle of the gospel to know for a certainty the character of God, and to know that we may converse with him as one man converses with another, and that He was once a man like us . . . .*" *Lorenzo Snow:* "*As man now is, God once was; as God now is, man may be.*" *Joseph Smith:* "*Brother Snow, that is true gospel doctrine, and it is a revelation from God to you.*"

Image source: https://www.youtube.com/watch?v=UigmAkziKMY

Question to Gordon B. Hinckley: [D]on't Mormons believe that God was once a man?"

Gordon B. Hinckley: "*I wouldn't say that. There was a little couplet coined, 'As man is, God once was. As God is, man may become.' Now that's more of a couplet than anything else. That gets into some pretty deep theology that we don't know very much about.*"

BRIGHAM YOUNG

The Importance of Polygamy: *"Young . . . connected plural marriage [polygamy] with exaltation into the celestial kingdom. 'The Lord Almighty created you and me . . . to become a God like himself.' Each resurrected and exalted Saint would, like Adam had once done, 'organize an Earth, people it, redeem it, and sanctify it.'" A member's "future glory" depended upon "the embrace of plurality . . . . Young emphasized that without Joseph Smith's revelation on celestial marriage [Section 132 of the Doctrine and Covenants] 'there is not a man ([who]) can be a God.'" (John G. Turner)*

Image Source: Assumption College,
https://www.assumption.edu /news/renowned-historian-early-america-richard-bushman-deliver-assumption%E2%80%99s-history-honor-society

STATEMENT: RICHARD L. BUSHMAN
DECEMBER 16, 2013

"I am very much impressed by Joseph Smith's 1832 History account of his early visions. This is the one partially written in his own hand and the rest dictated to Frederick G. Williams. I think it is more revealing than the official account presumably written in 1838 and contained in the Pearl of Great Price. ... I think this account has the marks of an authentic visionary experience. ... It is a classic announcement of a prophet's call, and I find it entirely believable."

The 1832 account, partially written by Joseph Smith in his own hand, then dictated to Frederick G. Williams, is "more revealing" than the official account "contained in the Pearl of Great Price," which was "presumably written in 1838."

There are no persecution claims in Joseph Smith's 1832 Holographic Account, the first and most contemporaneous account of his first encounter with Deity. Joseph didn't ask the Lord "which of all the sects was right," and the Lord didn't answer him and say "that they were all wrong." Joseph was not "seized upon by some dark power," and God didn't say, "This is My Beloved Son. Hear Him!" Joseph's mother, two of his brothers and one of his sisters did not join the Presbyterian Church; there was no Methodist minister; there was no great Palmyra Revival; Joseph wasn't told not to join any of the sects. Joseph was a monotheist in 1832. "The Book of Mormon tended to define God as an absolute personage of spirit who, clothed in flesh, revealed himself in Jesus Christ." That was the God who appeared to Joseph Smith in this encounter. In that first First Vision account, the Father appeared because the Son appeared. Only one personage appeared to Joseph Smith in the first First Vision in 1832. That particular Father was an "omnipotant," "omnipreasant" spirit.

THE APOSTLE PAUL

"The New Testament portrayed Paul as a charismatic apostle and special witness, not an apostle through ordination by the laying on of hands."

"[B]ecause of his vision on the road to Damascus," he was "an apostle not of men, neither by men, but by Jesus Christ. (Galatians 1:1)."

APOSTLE JOSEPH SMITH

"I have more to boast of than ever any man had. I am the only man that has ever been able to keep a whole church together since the days of Adam. A large majority of the whole have stood by me. Neither Paul, John, Peter, nor Jesus ever did it. I boast that no man ever did such a work as I. The followers of Jesus ran away from Him, but the Latter-day Saints never ran away from me yet."

The Apostle Paul in Prison, Image source: https://bradstrait.com/2014/04/15/the-gift-of-friends/

APOSTLE GEORGE Q. CANNON

Cannon was a businessman smartly connected to more than fifty different businesses. He was a spiritually adopted son of the third prophet, John Taylor, under the now abandoned doctrine then known as the law of adoption, and the biological nephew of Taylor's first wife. Cannon's Religious Life: "[D]ream vision of Joseph Smith 1849; mission and vision of Christ (1849-54) . . . ." While Cannon was speaking at the dedication of the Salt Lake Temple in 1893, some were said to have seen a "halo of light around his head." Cannon later reported that he had seen and talked with Jesus Christ. In 1898 he said that he had seen God and Jesus and heard their voices. In 1899 he said that he heard the audible voice of the Holy Ghost as a separate personage. (cf., D. Michael Quinn). Apostle, mission president, secretary to Brigham Young and to the School of the Prophets, a "prophet, seer and revelator," Cannon twice became a counselor in First Presidencies. Behind Joseph Smith and Brigham Young, George Q. Cannon was arguably the most important leader of the nineteenth-century Church.

In December 1869, fully twelve years after the murders at Mountain Meadows, Cannon, who "had known the truth for more than a decade," continued to blame the Mountain Meadows Massacre on the Indians ("he claimed the citizens from Cedar City heard rumors of a battle but arrived too late to help"). (Will Bagley)

"Those trafficking in deceit . . . ," Cannon warned the people who followed him, "lost the spirit of God as well as the trust of man."

JOSEPH SMITH

Joseph Fielding Smith: *"Mormonism, as it is called, must stand or fall on the story of Joseph Smith. He was either a prophet of God, divinely called, properly appointed and commissioned, or he was one of the biggest frauds this world has ever seen. There is no middle ground."*

Last public address of Lieutenant-General Joseph Smith, John Hafen, 1888. Image source: https://history.lds.org/exhibit/early-images-of-historic-nauvoo?lang=eng

SIDNEY RIGDON

Life sketch of Sidney Rigdon made for Moore's New Yorker, January 23, 1869

The Fate of Dissenters: *"Regarding this Danite expulsion of prominent Mormon dissenters [in Missouri], Sidney Rigdon told Apostle Orson Hyde at Far West that 'it was the imperative duty of the Church to obey the word of Joseph Smith, or the presidency, without question or inquiry, and that if there were any that would not, they should have their throats cut from ear [to] ear.'"* This verification of *"the First Presidency's 1838 authorization for theocratic killings"* was published in 1844 in an official LDS newspaper, *"The Nauvoo Neighbor,"* by Apostle John Taylor, Editor. (D. Michael Quinn)

The Violent Rigdon: *"While the last expedition was going on in Daviess [Daviess County, Missouri, 1838, during the Mormon/Missouri War], there was a meeting in Far West, in which Mr. Sidney Rigdon presided. There were present about 60 or 100 men; a guard was put around the house, and one was placed at the door. Mr. Rigdon said that the last man had run away from Far West that was going to; that the next man who started, he should be pursued and brought back, dead or alive. This was put to vote, and agreed to, without any one objecting to it. He further said, that one man had slipped his wind yesterday, and had been thrown aside into the brush for the buzzards to pick, and the first man who lisped it should die."* (Testimony, Burr Riggs, Richmond, Missouri, 1838)

"He [Joseph] looked over the crowd as if searching for a familiar face. 'Some of the brethren aren't here today,' he said. 'Some of those that Brother Sidney likes to call "Oh, don't! men." In time of war we have no need for such. A man must declare himself friend or enemy. I move a resolution that the property of all "Oh, don't men" be taken over to maintain the war.' As the crowd laughed and applauded, Rigdon started up, his eyes blazing. 'And I move,' he shouted, 'that the blood of the backward be spilled in the streets of Far West!' But Joseph silenced him." (Fawn M. Brodie)

1844, Rigdon Unleashed: *"I guided the prophet's tottering steps till he could walk alone . . . ."*

LUCY MACK SMITH

In Lucy Mack Smith's 1845 Manuscript History (prepared after the death of Joseph Smith and the excommunication of Oliver Cowdery), Lucy described their May 15, 1829, baptisms matter of factly, treating them as mandated but earthbound. The prophet's mother didn't mention John the Baptist.

> *[O]ne morning . . . they sat down to their usual work when the first thing that presented itself to Joseph was a commandment from God that he and Oliver should repair to the water & each of them be baptized they immediately went down to the susquehana<h> river and obeyed the* ~~*commandment*~~ *mandate given them through the urim and Thumim . . . .*

Lucy Mack Smith, by Sutcliffe Maudsley

The baptisms of Joseph and Oliver were said to have happened one way in 1829 (because of an instruction given through the stone Joseph carried in his pocket and used to see things invisible to the natural eye) and another way in the founders' 1834-35 history (angelic ordinations under the hands of a heavenly messenger separately identified as John the Baptist).

THE FIRST REFERENCE TO AUTHORITY: BOOK OF COMMANDMENTS, CHAPTER 15:6-7 (1833)

"Wherefore as thou hast been baptized by the hand of my servant, according to that which I have commanded him:

"Wherefore he hath fulfilled the thing which I commanded him."

1833: *No heavenly messenger.*

BOOK OF MORMON, 1830 EDITION

When it was published in 1830, the Book of Mormon did not include a single reference to Aaron, or to Levi, or to the law of a carnal commandment (the lineal priesthood of the old law). The Book did not describe "The Melchizedek Priesthood," "The Patriarchal Priesthood," or any kind of lower authority.

THE CHURCH ASSIGNS PRIESTHOOD
RESTORATION DATES

"**1829, May 15:** *With Oliver Cowdery [Joseph Smith], receives the Aaronic Priesthood from John the Baptist. Joseph and Oliver baptize one another in the Susquehanna River.*"

"**1829, May-June:** *With Oliver Cowdery, [Joseph Smith], receives the Melchizedek Priesthood from the ancient Apostles Peter, James, and John near the Susquehanna River between Harmony, Pennsylvania, and Colesville, New York.*"

S.I. BANISTER

"Can you explain why the Book of Commandments didn't tell of the restoration of the Priesthood which, if actual, had been known for four years at the time of publication [in 1833]?"

TWO DIFFERENT AARONIC PRIESTHOOD
RESTORATION PRAYERS

1834-35, *Messenger and Advocate***, Aaronic Priesthood Restoration Prayer (supposed date: May 15, 1829), first reported in October 1834 by Oliver Cowdery and Joseph Smith:**

> *[U]pon you my fellow servants, in the name of Messiah I confer this priesthood and this authority, which shall remain upon earth, that the sons of Levi may yet offer an offering unto the Lord in righteousness!*

1842 *Times and Seasons,* **Aaronic Priesthood Restoration Prayer (supposed date: May 15, 1829) later revised and reported in August 1842 by Joseph Smith:**

> *Upon you my fellow servants, in the name of Messiah I confer the Priesthood of Aaron, which holds the keys of the ministering of angels, and of the gospel of repentance, and of baptism by immersion for the remission of sins; and this shall never be taken again from the earth, until the sons of Levi do offer again an offering unto the Lord in righteousness.*

PARLEY P. PRATT

Parley P. Pratt: "*Members of the early Christian Church were not ordained to the Aaronic Priesthood, neither is there any mention of the Aaronic Priesthood in the Book of Mormon.*"

Author's Note: "*The Melchizedek Priesthood*" isn't mentioned in the sixteen-hundred year history of the Jaredites, people the Book of Mormon supposed to have come to the Western Hemisphere from the Tower of Babel, people supposed to have perished before the birth of Christ. The Melchizedek Priesthood is not pretended to in the history of the Jaredites.

The important words "The Melchizedek Priesthood" are not used by any of the ancient authors known to have described the authority principles that guided the affairs of the Book of Mormon's Nephites, a second civilization that is supposed to have followed the Jaredites and inhabited the Western Hemisphere for a thousand years.

The Three Witnesses to the Book of Mormon: Oliver Cowdery, David Whitmer and Martin Harris
Image Source: http://www.pbs.org/americanprophet/18300406.html

THE THREE WITNESSES

The excommunications of Oliver Cowdery and David Whitmer (brothers-in-law) in Missouri in 1838, which followed the excommunication of Martin Harris in Ohio in 1837, "completed the work of apostasy among those who had seen the angel and heard the testimony about 'the plates,' and their translation into English. From the beginning, the devil had desired that he might possess these 'witnesses,' and at last 'the Lord' made the transfer . . . . From this time Oliver Cowdery and David Whitmer are handed down to posterity in Mormon Church history charged with being 'connected with a gang of counterfeiters, thieves, liars and blacklegs of the deepest dye,' and with 'cheating and defrauding the Saints.'" (T.B.H. Stenhouse, The Rocky Mountain Saints, 75-76). Joseph Smith called the three witnesses "too mean to mention; and we had liked to have forgotten them." (B.H. Roberts, History of the Church 3:232).

DAVID WHITMER

David Whitmer was one of the Three Witnesses to the Book of Mormon, one of the first six elders, one of the three men who selected and ordained the founding Quorum of the Twelve Apostles, the President of the Church at the place of the gathering in Missouri and Joseph's earliest duly appointed successor in the event of the prophet's death. With Joseph Smith and Oliver Cowdery, he was one of the three men to whom the revelation concerning the gift of the Holy Ghost (Book of Commandments, Chapter 15) was directed. Whitmer stated his authority-principle conviction in these terms: "I never heard that an Angel had ordained Joseph and Oliver to the Aaronic priesthood until the year 1834[,] [183]5, or [183]6 – in Ohio. my information upon this matter being . . . that they were commanded to do so by revealment through Joseph [as explained by Joseph's mother]. I do not believe that John the Baptist ever ordained Joseph and Oliver . . . ."

David Whitmer, photo by Jacob T. Hicks. Original photograph. Clay County Museum, Liberty, Missouri. From http://www.mormoninterpreter.com/david-whitmer-photograph-retouched-and-colorized/

RICHARD LYMAN BUSHMAN

Image Source: https://news.virginia.edu/content/uva-creates-richard-lyman-bushman-chair-mormon-studies

"So far as can be told now, before 1831, men were called to church offices – elders, priests, and teachers – given authority and licensed without reference to a bestowal of priesthood."

"[Fanny] Alger was fourteen when her family joined the Church in Mayfield, near Kirtland, in 1830. In 1836, after a time as a serving girl in the Smith household, she left Kirtland . . . . Between those two dates, perhaps as early as 1831 [she was fourteen until September 30, 1831], she and Joseph were reportedly involved, but conflicting accounts make it difficult to establish the facts . . . . Was he a blackguard covering his lusts with religious pretensions, or a prophet doggedly adhering to instructions from heaven, or something in between?"

ORSON PRATT

"Any people attempting to govern themselves by laws of their own making, and by officers of their own appointment, are in direct rebellion against the kingdom of God."

"All the modern Christian churches have no more authority to preach, baptize, or administer any other ordinance of the gospel than the idolatrous Hindoos have."

"A true servant of God will never teach a false doctrine. He will never deny new revelation. He will never tell you that the canon of scripture is full, or that the New Testament is the last revelation ever intended to be given to man."

JOHN W. GUNNISON

"The President [of the High Council] sums up the matter [every matter] and gives the decision, perhaps in opposition to a great majority, but to which all must yield implicit obedience, and probably there has never been known, under the present head [Brigham Young], a dissent when the 'awful nod' has been given, for it is the 'stamp of fate and sanction of a god.'"

BRIGHAM YOUNG

Speech: *". . . I tell Brother Pratt if he goes on with his vain befogging speculations, there's not a saint in heaven nor a saint on earth . . . who will follow. And I warn him not to get up to talk more, unless he knows what he talks about . . . ."*

Council of Fifty Minutes: *"He dont care about preaching to the gentiles any longer . . . he feels as Lyman Wight said let the damned scoundrels be killed, let them be swept off from the earth, and then we can go and be baptized for them, easier than we can convert them.*

Richard Lyman Bushman: *"The story Turner tells in this elegantly written biography [Brigham Young: Pioneer Prophet by John G. Turner] will startle and shock many readers. He reveals a Brigham Young more violent and coarse than the man Mormons have known. While lauding his achievements as pioneer, politician, and church leader, the book will require a reassessment of Brigham Young the man."*

Brigham Young and Almon Babbitt: *Young had a quarrel with Almon Babbitt. According to Thomas Kane, a man who had the prophet's ear, "Babbitt ["who had been representing the Church's interests in Washington"] had antagonized members of both [political] parties . . . over the issue of slavery, obstructed the nomination of additional*

*Mormons to federal offices, and had spoken in derogatory terms of his own religion."
When Young got to Babbitt alone, he threatened his delegate; "he would rather 'stand
here and cut throats than suffer lawsuits and technicalities.' 'If you interfere with any
of my dictation in the elections,' he warned, 'it will be the last.'" "You are shitting in
my dish and I will lick it out and you too...." Babbitt took Young's threats seriously. "I
am exceedingly fearful this will not work for good to me...." (John G. Turner). "Upon
hearing of his death [on Babbitt's "twenty-second trip on government business from
Utah to the capital"], he was murdered on the trail, Brigham Young commented that
Babbitt had 'lived like a fool and died like a fool'...." (Almon Babbitt, Wikipedia).*

Brigham Young and Ira West: *Young termed West, a young man accused of fraud and
failure to pay his debts, a "thief and a swindler." In a meeting attended by both,
Brigham bellowed, "I want his head cut off right before this people, and they to say
Amen . . . ." After further deliberations, and with the passage of time ("Ira E. West be
miss[ing] . . ."), Young motioned "that 'we forgive him the debt.' Young's final
statement encouraged West's extralegal demise." Young explained that because of his
conduct that West had "incurred a worse curse than the negro," that "there is no sin in
killing him – the people may do with him as they please." Shortly thereafter, West and
Thomas Burns, another offender, disappear from Mormon history. (John G. Turner)*

Image source: http://www.eugeneenglan
org/ a-professor-and-apostle-correspond
eugene-england-and-bruce-r-mcconkie-
on-the-nature-of-god

APOSTLE BRUCE R. McCONKIE

To Parishioner Eugene England (1981): *"It is my
province to teach to the Church what the doctrine is. It is
your province to echo what I say or to remain silent."*

Then: *"There are those [Brigham Young] who say God is
progressing in knowledge and is learning new truths. This
is false – . . . . There is not one sliver of truth in it."*

Then: *"There are those who believe or say they believe
that Adam is our father and our God [Brigham Young],
that he is the father of our spirits and our bodies and that
he is the one we worship."* McConkie *"indicated the utter
absurdity of this doctrine and said it was totally false."*

To Parishioner Eugene England (1981): *"True religion is found only where men
worship the true and living God. False religion always results from the worship of false
gods. Eternal life itself, which is the greatest of all the gifts of God is available to those
and those only who know God and Jesus Christ whom he hath sent."*

*"It is the first principle of revealed religion to know the nature and kind of being that
God is."*

IMPROVEMENT ERA 1945

*"When our leaders speak, the thinking has been done. When they propose a plan – it is
God's plan. When they point the way, there is no other which is safe. When they give
directions, it should mark the end of controversy." (Improvement Era, June 1945, p.
354)*

MARTIN HARRIS (TESTATOR),
"BOOK OF MORMON SCRIBE, BOOK OF MORMON WITNESS"

"Even before he had become a Mormon, Harris [". . . a great man for seeing spooks"] had changed his religion at least five times." "Harris had been a Quaker, a Universalist, a Restorationist, a Baptist, a Presbyterian, and perhaps a Methodist." (Walker, 1986, p. 30-33, cited at wikipedia. com). In 1836, "Harris married Caroline Young, the 22 year old daughter of Brigham Young's brother, John. Harris was thirty-one years older than his new wife; they had seven children together." His first wife, his first cousin, Lucy Harris, claimed that he abused her, and that he had committed adultery with a neighbor, "Mrs. Haggart." "Whether the Mormon religion be true or false, I leave the world to judge, for its effects upon Martin Harris have been to make him more cross, turbulent and abusive to me." (Vogel, Early Mormon Documents, Lucy Harris Statement, 2:34-36). In March 1830, he who is eternal, Christ the Lord, the Redeemer of the world, commanded Harris not to covet "thy neighbor's wife; nor seek thy neighbor's life" (D&C 19:25). Following Joseph Smith's unexpected death, Harris accepted James J. Strang as Mormonism's new prophet. He served a mission to England for Strang, then later became a Whitmerite (in a society organized by William E. McClellin). He then joined Gladden Bishop in a congregation based in Kirtland, Ohio. "In 1855, Harris joined with the last surviving brother of Joseph Smith, William Smith, and declared that William was Joseph's true successor." In 1844, the year that Joseph Smith was murdered, Phineas H. Young, Brigham Young's brother, reported in a letter to Brigham that Harris's testimony of Shakerism was "greater than it was of the Book of Mormon." Late in life, Harris became a Strangite, a Whitmerite, a Gladdenite, a Williamite and a Shaker. After the decline of other societies, Harris was rebaptized into the Mormon faith in 1870 at the age of 87. Harris was an early Mormon Apostle, a charismatic Apostle (by that to say unordained).

D. MICHAEL QUINN

"Scholars have long recognized that the first vision account was not published or used in any proselytizing tract until the 1840's and that it was not used regularly as a Mormon proselytizing tool until fifty years after Smith's theophany."

"A closer look at contemporary records indicates that men were first ordained to the higher priesthood over a year after the church's founding [April 6, 1830]. No mention of angelic ordinations can be found in original documents until 1834-35. Thereafter accounts of the visit of Peter, James, and John by Cowdery and Smith remained vague and contradictory."

"Before then [1835] the [priesthood] structure was fluid, and public claims for authority in the church were made largely on the basis of religious experience and charisma rather than priestly power through lineage and angelic ministration."

LYMAN WIGHT, THE FIRST HIGH PRIEST, JUNE 3, 1831

Lyman Wight Ordained Joseph Smith. *Joseph had hoped for an endowment of power at the Fourth Conference of the Church on June 3, 1831, the first Conference to be held at Rigdon's venue in the state of Ohio. What was supposed to have been a pentecostal feast proved to be a disquieting threat to the safety of terrorized participants. "He had tolerated exorbitant behavior in hopes of receiving a pentecostal manifestation." (Richard L. Bushman)*

Ezra Booth: *"Under these discouraging circumstances [the Fourth Conference of the Church in Kirtland, Ohio], the horizon of Mormonism gathered darkness . . . ."*

THE OATH OF VENGEANCE

Endowment House, Image source: Charles Roscoe Savage [Public domain], via Wikimedia Commons

Until February 15, 1927, during a long run in the Endowment House, and later in their temples, Latter-day Saints took an oath of vengeance against the United States of America. "You and each of you do covenant and promise that you will pray and never cease to pray to Almighty God to avenge the blood of the prophets upon this nation, and that you will teach the same to your children and to your children's children unto the third and fourth generation."

GEORGE ORWELL

"The past is whatever the records and memories agree upon. And since the Party is in full control of all records, and in equally full control of the minds of its members, it follows that the past is whatever the Party chooses to make of it."

"It also follows that though the past is alterable, it never has been altered in any specific instance. For when it has been recreated in whatever shape is needed at the moment, then this new version is the past, and no different past can ever have existed."

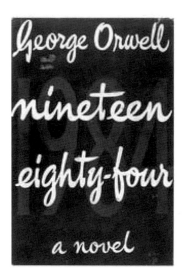

HISTORY OF THE CHURCH
by Joseph Smith

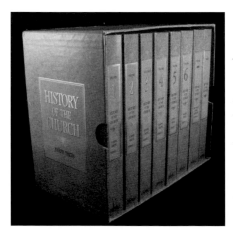

Joseph Smith's "History of the Church," six hefty volumes, contains thousands of pages of contents, and it is supported by a voluminous index. Events of merely minor significance are explained in extraordinary detail. Nowhere in those thousands of pages, and nowhere in that voluminous index, does Smith's massive history purport to say when or where the Melchizedek Priesthood is supposed to have been conferred upon Joseph Smith and Oliver Cowdery by Peter, James, and John.

Joseph's Chocolate-Colored Seerstone

EMMA'S FATHER, ISAAC HALE

Isaac Hale: *". . . I conscientiously believe . . . that the whole 'Book of Mormon' (so called) is a silly fabrication of falsehood and wickedness, got up for speculation, and with a design to dupe the credulous and unwary – . . . in order that its fabricators may live upon the spoils of those who swallow the deception."*

Fawn McKay Brodie: *"With every new success of his son-in-law, Isaac Hale's tongue grew more acid, for he never lost his conviction that the youth was a barefaced imposter."*

"MINERAL RODS AND SEEING STONES," KIRTLAND TEMPLE, 1836

"For behold, I have accepted this house and my name shall be here . . . ." (Doctrine and Covenants 110:7). On March 20, 1843, James C. Brewster published "his claim that as part of an 1836 Ohio treasure-quest, Presiding Patriarch Joseph Smith, Sr., 'anointed the mineral rods and seeing stones with consecrated oil, and prayed over them in the house of the Lord in Kirtland.'"

Kirtland Temple,
By Jack E. Boucher, HABS photographer
[Public domain], via Wikimedia Commons

Nauvoo Temple, Image source: http://
/www.historicnauvoo.net/nauvoo-temple-2017

REINVENTING ZION

"On 8 April [1844], JS [Joseph Smith] announced having received a 'great grand & glorious rev[elatio]n' that all of North and South America was Zion and that after the [Nauvoo] temple had been dedicated, the Saints would spread throughout the two continents building up churches wherever they went." (D. Michael Quinn)

The St. George Utah Temple of The Church of Jesus Christ of Latter-day Saints, in St. George, Utah, United States Photo by Ricardo630 Ricardo630 04:43, 9 August 2006 (UTC), from https://commons.wikimedia.org/wiki/File:St._George_Temple.jpg.

Brigham Young and the Demise of the United Order ("The Idea of Equality"): *The annual conference of the Church, and the formal dedication of the St. George Temple, simultaneous events, commenced on April 6, 1877, in St. George, Utah. The conference occurred after John D. Lee, Brigham Young's second adopted son, faced justice all by himself for the atrocities committed against a company of Arkansas pioneers – about one hundred and twenty men, women and children – by faithful Latter-day Saints at Mountain Meadows. "Young had been apprehensive [about this conference] since John D. Lee's execution two weeks earlier, worried that U.S. Marshalls might seek his arrest after Lee's insinuation of his guilt."*

"At the conference and dedication, there was no outpouring of Pentecostal blessings as had been the case in Kirtland." There had been no "ritual stampede" in the less exuberant church of Brigham Young in this last year of the Lion's life, when he was seen to become "more cantankerous than fearsome." "On April 8, Young delivered his final discourse in the St. George Temple [Utah's first] . . . . Instead of reflecting on the import of the temple's completion or on its sacred rites, Young used the occasion to bitterly lament the United Order's demise."

The Mormon prophet complained that "the First Presidency and the Twelve" had stood against his communitarian vision. The order's failure, he opined, rested squarely on the shoulders of the church's highest leaders, Erastus Snow being "singled out" for particular "condemnation." "In Young's mind, the temple and the United Order [Mormonism's "Idea of Equality"] were interconnected efforts to build up God's kingdom . . . . Thus Young could not celebrate the temple's completion without contemplating the United Order's failure." (John G. Turner)

Of this the world may be certain: "[T]he idea of equality," with all of its charm, was toast, a failed experiment assigned to God, the Presidency, the Twelve and the Saints, but not to Brigham Young!

CHAPTER ELEVEN

Promises and Prophecies

And now I am prepared to say by the authority of Jesus Christ, that not many years shall pass away before the United States shall present such a scene of bloodshed as has not parallel in the history of our nation; pestilence, hail, famine and earthquake shall sweep the wicked of this generation from off the face of the land, to open the way for the return of the lost tribes of Israel from the north country. The people of the Lord, those who have complied with the requirements of the new covenant, have already commenced gathering together to Zion, which is in the state of Missouri; therefore I declare unto you the warning which the Lord has commanded to declare unto this generation, remembering that the eyes of my Maker are upon me, and that to him I am accountable for every word I say . . . flee to Zion, before the over-flowing scourge overtake you, for there are those now living upon the earth whose eyes shall not be closed in death until they see all of these things which I have spoken, fulfilled . . . .

Joseph Smith

Joseph Smith described in more revelations than Latter-day Saints are allowed to read promises God didn't make and hasn't kept. Because God didn't say what Joseph said that he did, God didn't do what Joseph said that he would.

Joel M. Allred

It is the strongest proof of the firm hold of a party, whether religious or political, upon the public mind, when it may offend with impunity against its own primary principles.

Henry Hart Milman

PREFACE, "DOCTRINE AND COVENANTS"

PROMISE: The Doctrine and Covenants is the Lord's book of commandments. What Jesus has decreed in the commandments published in that book, by his servants and with his permission, "shall be fulfilled."[1]

The sweeping vision of the 1835 first edition of the Book of Doctrine and Covenants was undeniably apocalyptic, as were the only slightly less authoritative other teachings of the Mormon prophet. The identification of the site of the city of the New Jerusalem, of the spot for the temple and of the regions round about, as well as the stirrings of what quickly became a great migration, were warnings to the vigilant. The great and terrible day of the Lord was "nigh at hand." Under circumstances of great supposed urgency, and in response to the unflinching counsel of their leaders, obedient Saints left everything and followed. They put their affairs in order, departed the havens of the wicked and proceeded to gather at sacred places on consecrated ground. These faithful "Latter Day Saints" sought, thought they had found and were quick to occupy lands upon which there would be no curse when the Lord came.

The early members of the Mormon Church thought the day of tribulation and desolation was connected to the second coming of Christ and the return of the Ten Lost Tribes. On that day the graves of the Saints "shall be opened." On that day, the wicked would burn as stubble. The Lord's elect, the children of Israel who had wisely gathered in their places of refuge, would escape that horrific carnage. Early Mormons were commanded to leave Babylon and gather for safety with Saints. For the faithful, the promise was that the righteous indignation of an angry God would pass them by, like the destroying angels passed Israel by, leaving them and those they loved in peace.

The great and terrible day did not visit that generation of gathering Saints, as the prophet and various leaders solemnly prophesied, nor did it visit the days of their children, grandchildren, great-grandchildren, or those of any of the other generations that

---

[1]Part Second, Covenants and Commandments of the Lord to his servants of the Church of the Latter Day Saints, Section 1 (1835), 75, emphasis added.

followed.   The day of desolation has yet to visit the "Latter Day Saints," who are now a more scattered people feeling secure in the havens of the wicked.   The gathering ("the eyes of my Maker are upon me, and . . . I am accountable for every word I say . . .") has been abandoned as times have changed.   To modern Mormons, Zion is no longer "one place" – a literal location where Saints assemble hoping to avoid the towering judgments of an angry God – but rather many places.   Independence, Missouri, the place of the gathering, is no longer the center place of Zion.   Now the hearts and minds of believers are the center places of Zion.   Zion has evolved to become any place faithful Saints are found.

The fraudulent doctrine of the gathering, promoted unceasingly in Mormon scripture and acted upon under circumstances of great supposed urgency by nineteenth-century Latter-day Saints, has been repealed, superceded by double talk.   The millennial expectations of those early Saints are now dismissed.   The solemn promises described in the pages of the Doctrine and Covenants, commandments published by the Lord's servants with his permission, have not been kept.   Most of the promises, covenants, predictions and prophesies described in the Doctrine and Covenants and seen to pertain to the gathering of Zion can now be viewed – in perspective and with the passage of time – as unconscionable failures.   Scores of broken prophecies and promises outlined in the revelations litter the landscape and mock the notion that they were ever worthy of trust.   The early Mormon emigrants, men and women who shared the now discredited apocalyptic vision of an apocalyptic prophet, read those first person revelations and rushed to Zion under what was then believed to be circumstances of great urgency.   And at great cost.   There was, looking back, no reason for haste.

In 1835 Joseph represented to his only recently renamed Church of the Latter Day Saints that Jesus was the author of the Preface to the Doctrine and Covenants:

> *Behold, this is mine authority, and the authority of my servants, and my preface unto the book of my commandments, which I have given them to publish unto you, O inhabitants of the earth.*

Wherefore, fear and tremble, O ye people, for what I
the Lord have decreed in them shall be fulfilled.[2]

"Wherefore, fear and tremble." God has once again communicated with man on earth. The heavens have opened after centuries of apostasy and the Savior is speaking to his disciples. Now, the Savior says, "[W]hat I the Lord have decreed in them [the commandments contained in this book] shall be fulfilled." That is the unequivocal promise Joseph said Jesus made to the "inhabitants of the earth." The promises, prophecies, predictions and covenants pertaining to Zion and the city of the New Jerusalem, the Temple and the Second Coming, the return of the Ten Lost Tribes and the great and terrible day of vengeance have not come to pass. None of them have come to pass at such times, in such ways, or close to the place the Lord said that they would. Joseph's words ("I declare unto you the warning which the Lord has commanded to declare unto this generation, remembering that the eyes of my Maker are upon me, and that to him I am accountable for every word I say . . .") are seen for what they are – unforgivable bluster ("for there are those now living upon the earth whose eyes shall not be closed in death until they see all of these things which I have spoken, fulfilled . . .").

APOCALYPSE NOW: ZION DESPAIR

A Place of Safety for Saints

COMMAND: The Father commands that the elect shall be gathered "in unto one place upon the face of this land" to prepare their hearts "against the day when tribulation and desolation are sent forth upon the wicked"[3] *("before the over flowing scourge overtake you").*

In a revelation given in the presence of six elders at Fayette, New York, the Lord tells the twenty-four year old Joseph – and Joseph then tells the early members of the Church in a conference that convened on September 26, 1830 – that they "are called to bring to pass the gathering of mine elect; for mine elect hear my voice and

---

[2]Doctrine and Covenants (1957), 1:6-7, emphasis added.
[3]Ibid., 29:8, emphasis added.

harden not their hearts."[4] The sheep will recognize the shepherd's voice. "[T]hough the heavens and the earth pass away, my word shall not pass away, but shall all be fulfilled . . . ."[5] The righteous will be separated from the wicked before the wicked are punished.

The Saints will hear the word and gather together *"in unto one place."* Where they go to prepare their hearts against the day of desolation, the Lord will protect them. In that special place, the elect will find their safety. Those who are left behind have no such promise ("they that do wickedly shall be as stubble; and I will burn them up, saith the Lord of Hosts, that wickedness shall not be upon the earth"[6]). God's wrath shall be visited upon those wicked ones who do not hear his voice and continue to live in sin. The threat is imminent, and the need to gather is urgent. (" . . . *I will take vengeance upon the wicked, for they will not repent; for the cup of mine indignation is full; for behold, my blood shall not cleanse them if they hear me not").*[7] For such unrepentant souls, the atonement has not been efficacious. So spoke Joseph's Redeemer to nineteenth-century Saints. So spoke Brigham Young when he also articulated the doctrine of blood atonement in the Salt Lake Valley after the exodus of the Mormons from Nauvoo, Illinois. Joseph's Redeemer, like Joseph himself, and probably because he was Joseph himself, was the author of the underlying principle used in support of this hateful doctrine.

> *. . . I the Lord God will send forth flies upon the face of the earth, which shall take hold of the inhabitants thereof, and shall eat their flesh, and shall cause maggots to come in upon them;*
>
> *And their tongues shall be stayed that they shall not utter against me; and their flesh shall fall from off their bones, and their eyes from their sockets;*

---

[4]Ibid., 29:7.
[5]Ibid., 1:38.
[6]Ibid., 29:9.
[7]Ibid., 29:17, emphasis added.

> *And it shall come to pass that the beasts of the forest*
> *and the fowls of the air shall devour them up.*[8]

This is the unflattering view of the "Savior" and his punishments presented by Joseph Smith to his 1830 followers.[9] Joseph sold his vision with terrible threats.

> *[B]efore that great day shall come, the sun shall be*
> *darkened, and the moon be turned into blood; and the*
> *stars shall refuse their shining, and some shall fall,*
> *and great destructions await the wicked.*[10]

A Land of Promise

PROMISE: I shall give you a land of promise, a land flowing with milk and honey, a land upon which there shall be no curse when I come.

He who has heard his followers' prayers now grants unto them a precious gift.

> *And I hold forth and deign to give unto you greater*
> *riches, even a land of promise, a land flowing with*
> *milk and honey, upon which there shall be no curse*
> *when the Lord cometh;*

> *And I will give it unto you for the land of your*
> *inheritance, if you seek it with all your hearts.*

> *And this shall be my covenant with you, ye shall have*
> *it for the land of your inheritance, and for the*
> *inheritance of your children forever, while the earth*

---

[8] Ibid., 29:18-20, emphasis added.

[9] "And the righteous shall be gathered on my right hand unto eternal life; and the wicked on my left hand will I be ashamed to own before the Father; Wherefore I will say unto them – Depart from me, ye cursed, into everlasting fire, prepared for the devil and his angels. And now, behold, I say unto you, never at any time have I declared from mine own mouth that they should return, for where I am they cannot come, for they have no power." (Ibid., 29:27-29).

[10] Ibid., 34:9, emphasis added.

shall stand, and ye shall possess it again in eternity, no more to pass away.[11]

The earth is the Lord's footstool, and he has made it "rich." He will yet again stand on that footstool. He will provide a blessed land for a blessed people in perpetuity. It shall be a promised land for his soon-to-be-gathering Saints. Here will be a place of refuge for those who hearken to their Savior's voice. This will be a crossing to safety for those who are earnestly faithful – a place where "there shall be no curse" when the Savior comes. Here the honest in heart can congregate, escape the fate of the wicked, look for and find their peace. Here those who know their shepherd will find others who also do. For it is the Lord's holy will, "*[T]hat ye might escape the power of the enemy, and be gathered unto me a righteous people, without spot and blameless.*"[12]

Jerusalem and Inheritance

PROMISE: *Those Saints then presently emigrating to Ohio would be redirected to the place of the city of the New Jerusalem when land had been purchased and the foundation of the city had been laid.*

"[G]ather up your riches," the Savior said, that ye may be prepared to purchase your inheritance. The site of the place to be called Zion remains "to be revealed." After your brethren come from the east, certain men will be appointed, *"and to them it shall be given to know the place,* or to them it shall be revealed."[13] "And they shall be appointed to purchase the lands, and to make a commencement to lay the foundation of the city; and then shall ye begin to be gathered with your families, ..."[14] The settlement of the emigrating Saints in Ohio was to be temporary. "And I consecrate unto them this land for a little season, until I, the Lord, shall provide for them otherwise, and command them to go hence."[15] In 1831, Joseph Smith, Sidney Rigdon and others traveled to the land of Missouri.

---

[11]Ibid., 38:18-20, emphasis added.
[12]Ibid., 38:31, emphasis added.
[13]Ibid., 48:5, emphasis added.
[14]Ibid., 48:6.
[15]Ibid., 51:16.

If they are faithful, those early Saints were told, the land of their inheritance would be made known to them.[16] In anticipation of the gathering, the Lord told them something about their projected prosperity.

PROMISE: The Lord, whose words are sure and shall not fail, declares that his Saints shall obtain an inheritance in the land of Zion in these last days ("the willing and obedient shall eat the good of the land of Zion in these last days"[17]). The rebellious shall be expelled from Zion and shall not inherit the land.

"And he [the Lord] hath set you to provide for his saints in these last days, that they may obtain an inheritance in the land of Zion. *And behold, I, the Lord, declare unto you, and my words are sure and shall not fail, that they shall obtain it."*[18]   "Behold, the Lord requireth the heart and a willing mind; and the willing and obedient *shall eat the good of the land of Zion in these last days.* And the rebellious shall be cut off out of the land of Zion, and shall be sent away, and shall not inherit the land."[19]

PROMISE: The rising generations shall grow up on the land of Zion. They shall possess the land from generation to generation, forever and ever.

In a revelation dated November 1831, John Whitmer was instructed to preach and expound, write, copy, select and obtain all things "which shall be for the good of the church, and for the rising generations that shall grow up on the land of Zion, to possess it from generation to generation, forever and ever. Amen."[20]

---

[16]Ibid., 52:4-5.
[17]Ibid., 64:34, emphasis added.
[18]Ibid., 64:30-31, emphasis added.
[19]Ibid., 64:34, 35.
[20]Ibid., 69:8, emphasis added.

"A PROCLAMATION TO THE PEOPLE OF THE CHURCH TO GATHER TO ZION"

Gathering

In a revelation given to the prophet Joseph Smith at Hiram, Ohio, on November 3, 1831, the Lord called his disciples and the Church to attention:

> *HEARKEN, O ye people of my church, saith the Lord your God, and hear the word of the Lord concerning you –*

> *The Lord who shall suddenly come to his temple; the Lord who shall come down upon the world with a curse to judgment; yea, upon all the nations that forget God, and upon all the ungodly among you.*[21]

That "saith the Lord" prologue was followed by this "saith the Lord" proclamation:

> *Wherefore, prepare ye, prepare ye, O my people; sanctify yourselves; gather ye together, O ye people of my church, upon the land of Zion, all you that have not been commanded to tarry.*

> *Go ye out from Babylon. Be ye clean that bear the vessels of the Lord.*[22]

The gathering of the children of Israel, their flight from Babylon and their sanctification in Zion, were commandments to Joseph for the children of Israel, he said, straight from the mouth of Jesus Christ.

> *[T]he voice of the Lord is unto you: Go ye out of Babylon; gather ye out from among the nations, from the four winds, from one end of heaven to the other.*[23]

---

[21]Ibid., 133:1-2, emphasis added.
[22]Ibid., 133:4-5, emphasis added.
[23]Ibid., 133:7, emphasis added.

COMMAND: The Father commands that the elect shall be gathered "in unto one place" in the land of America to prepare their hearts against the day when tribulation and desolation are sent forth upon the wicked.[24]

No one knows the exact day and hour of the second coming. "Let them, therefore, who are among the Gentiles flee unto Zion." "[L]et them who be of Judah flee unto Jerusalem." Leave these "spiritual Babylon[s]" where those who are wicked dwell.[25] Let not your flight be in haste, "let all things be prepared." But when you take your flight do not look back "lest sudden destruction shall come upon [you]."[26] The message to repent and gather together at Zion was unequivocal. "For behold, the Lord God hath sent forth the angel crying through the midst of heaven, saying":

> *Prepare ye the way of the Lord, and make his paths straight, for the hour of his coming is nigh —* [27]

When he does suddenly come, the Bridegroom will stand upon the Mount of Olivet, and "upon the mighty ocean"; "upon the islands of the sea, and upon *the land of Zion.*"[28] On that great and terrible day, *"he shall utter his voice out of Zion,* and he shall speak from Jerusalem, and his voice shall be heard among all people."[29] On that day of tribulation, the Lord "shall stand in the midst of his people, and shall reign over all flesh."[30] Then shall he receive those who were lost, and those his servants have found.

> *And they who are in the north countries [the ten lost tribes] shall come in remembrance before the Lord; and their prophets shall hear his voice, and shall no longer stay themselves; . . .*[31]

---

[24]Ibid., 29:7-8, emphasis added.
[25]Ibid., 133:12-14.
[26]Ibid., 133:15.
[27]Ibid., 133:17, emphasis added.
[28]Ibid., 133:20, emphasis added.
[29]Ibid., 133:21, emphasis added.
[30]Ibid., 133:25.
[31]Ibid., 133:26, emphasis added.

And so great shall be the glory of his presence that the sun shall hide his face in shame, and the moon shall withhold its light, and the stars shall be hurled from their places.[32]

How important was this gathering of the children of Israel? It was critical. The Lord's elect, those who recognized the voice of their shepherd, were to order their affairs, leave everything and follow. "And they that have farms that cannot be sold, let them be left or rented as seemeth them good." Preserve everything that can be preserved. Endeavor to gather not only yourselves, but "all these [other] things" "unto the bosom of the church."[33]

PROMISE: The Lord will tell you when the city of the New Jerusalem shall be prepared. When it is prepared you shall gather there, where you shall be my people and I shall be your God.

PROMISE: The Lord promises the faithful that they shall be preserved and rejoice, and says he cannot lie. "Behold, I, the Lord, have brought you together that the promise might be fulfilled, that the faithful among you should be preserved and rejoice together . . . . I, the Lord, promise the faithful and cannot lie."[34]

PROMISE: The Lord holds Zion in his own hands. "And now, behold, this is the will of the Lord your God concerning his saints, that they should assemble themselves together unto the land of Zion, not in haste, lest there should be confusion, which bringeth pestilence. Behold, the land of Zion – I, the Lord, hold it in mine own hands."[35]

PROMISE: Zion shall flourish, and the glory of the Lord shall be upon her. The Lord hath spoken it.

PROMISE: Zion shall be an ensign unto the people, who shall flock to her out of every nation under heaven. The Lord hath spoken it.

---

[32]Ibid., 133:49, emphasis added.
[33]Ibid., 38:37-38.
[34]Ibid., 62:6, emphasis added.
[35]Ibid., 63:24-25, emphasis added.

PROMISE: The Saints shall gather and stand upon Mount Zion, the city of the New Jerusalem. The Lord hath spoken it.

Protection

PROMISE: The Lord will gather them "as a hen gathereth her chickens under her wings, if they will not harden their hearts." Those who come may partake of the waters of life freely. Whosoever "repenteth and cometh unto me, the same is my church."[36]

The graves of the Saints "shall be opened," and they shall "come forth and stand on the right hand of the Lamb, *when he shall stand upon Mount Zion, and upon the holy city, the New Jerusalem;* and they shall sing the song of the Lamb, day and night forever and ever."[37] Those who are not sanctified, those who do not repent and heed the Lord's call to gather to Zion, must expect suffering and punishment.

> *And upon them that hearken not to the voice of the Lord shall be fulfilled that which was written by the prophet Moses, that they should be cut off from among the people.*
>
> *And also that which was written by the prophet Malachi: For, behold, the day cometh that shall burn as an oven, and all the proud, yea, and all that do wickedly, shall be stubble; and the day that cometh shall burn them up, saith the Lord of hosts, that it shall leave them neither root nor branch.*[38]

Those who do not repent and gather, those who "obeyed not my voice when I called to you out of the heavens," those who "believed not my servants" and who "received them not" shall be "delivered over unto darkness." Of them it was said, "[Y]e shall lie down in

---

[36]Ibid., 10:65-67, emphasis added.
[37]Ibid., 133:56, emphasis added.
[38]Ibid., 133:63-64, emphasis added.

sorrow."[39]   Their lot was intended to be a difficult and unhappy one.

> *These shall go away into outer darkness, where there*
> *is weeping, and wailing, and gnashing of teeth.*
> *Behold the Lord your God hath spoken it. Amen.*[40]

To gather or not to gather, that is not the question; not to gather was not an option. Those looking for protection against the Lord's wrath (" . . . I have trampled them in my fury, and I did tread upon them in mine anger, and their blood have I sprinkled upon my garments, and stained all my raiment; for this was the day of vengeance which was in my heart"[41]) will repent and be sanctified. They will gather at holy and consecrated places, places that are not under a curse when the Lord "cometh." There to find peace and refuge. They will gather at the center place of Zion, at the place of the temple in the city of the New Jerusalem. There, their risen Lord will come to redeem those who heard their shepherd, left everything and followed.

The Importance of Place

The very place of the gathering, not at first determined, had been an important early issue. The missionaries, sent to prune the lord's vineyard for the last time, were instructed to go forth two by two, "declaring my word like unto angels of God," saying "Repent ye, repent ye, for the kingdom of heaven is at hand."[42] But what does it mean to say the kingdom of heaven is at hand?   Where is the kingdom of heaven at hand? Where is the land upon which there shall be no curse when the Lord comes? For a time before the Lord designated the place, the answer was to go "westward" and "build up my church in every region. . . ."[43] *"Until the time shall come when it shall be revealed unto you from on high, when the city of the New Jerusalem shall be prepared, that ye may be gathered in one, that*

---

[39]Ibid., 133:70.
[40]Ibid., 133:71-74, emphasis added.
[41]Ibid., 133:51.
[42]Ibid., 42:6-7.
[43]Ibid., 42:8.

ye may be my people and I will be your God. "[44]   There shall be a New Jerusalem, a place of gathering for the Lord's elect.   When the Lord has told them where that sacred place shall be, then shall they be gathered as one where "ye may be my people and I will be your God."   Where will this New Jerusalem be, and how will that be known?   That will be revealed to the Saints of the Most High God when the city of the New Jerusalem has been prepared.

> *Wherefore I, the Lord, have said, gather ye out from the eastern lands, assemble ye yourselves together ye elders of my church; go ye forth into the western countries, call upon the inhabitants to repent, and inasmuch as they do repent, build up churches unto me.*

> *And with one heart and with one mind, gather up your riches that ye may purchase an inheritance which shall hereafter be appointed unto you.*

> *And it shall be called the New Jerusalem, a land of peace, a city of refuge, a place of safety for the saints of the Most High God;*

> *And the glory of the Lord shall be there, and the terror of the Lord also shall be there, insomuch that the wicked will not come unto it, and it shall be called Zion.*[45]

> *And there shall be gathered unto it out of every nation under heaven; and it shall be the only people that shall not be at war one with another.*[46]

> *And it shall come to pass that the righteous shall be gathered out from among all nations, and shall come to Zion, singing with songs of everlasting joy.*[47]

---

[44]Ibid., 42:9, emphasis added.
[45]Ibid., 45:64-67, emphasis added.
[46]Ibid., 45:69, emphasis added.
[47]Ibid., 45:71, emphasis added.

The Saints will fly to Zion to escape the righteous indignation of an angry God. In Section 97 of the Doctrine and Covenants, the Lord describes the pruning of the sacred place, revealing his "will concerning your brethren in the land of Zion." Some of the brethren have pleased the Lord (one, brother Parley P. Pratt, by name). Others "must needs be chastened, and their works shall be made known." The solution is a drastic one. "The ax is laid at the root of the trees; and every tree that bringeth not forth good fruit shall be hewn down and cast into the fire. I, the Lord, have spoken it."[48]

This Is the Place

PROMISE: *Missouri, now the land of your enemies, is the land of promise, the land of your inheritance, and the place where the city of Zion will be built. God has appointed and consecrated the land of Missouri as the place for the gathering of the Saints.*

Now the place of the gathering has finally been revealed. Now the promises the Lord has made to his people in only general terms are rendered more specific.

> *Hearken, O ye elders of my church, saith the Lord your God, who have assembled yourselves together, according to my commandments, in this land, which is the land of Missouri, which is the land which I have appointed and consecrated for the gathering of the saints.*
>
> *Wherefore, this is the land of promise, and the place for the city of Zion.*[49]

Here the Lord's most solemn promises to a faithful and obedient people have come to rest.

> *Missouri is the land of promise, the land of their inheritance.*

---

[48]Ibid., 97:1, 3, 6-7.
[49]Ibid., 57:1-2, emphasis added.

Missouri is the place for the city of Zion.

PROMISE: The place now called Independence is selected by God to be the center place of Zion and the site for the city of Zion, to be called the New Jerusalem.

The Lord has now revealed that the center place of Zion, the gathering place for the faithful and obedient, and the land "upon which there shall be no curse when the Lord cometh,"[50] is the city of Independence in Jackson County, Missouri.[51]

THE HOUR IS "NIGH AT HAND"

PROMISE: The day "speedily cometh" when peace shall be taken from the earth, and the devil shall have power over his own dominion. The hour is not yet, but, is "nigh at hand." Though the heavens and the earth pass away, the Lord's word "shall not pass away," but shall rather be fulfilled by his voice or the voice of his servants. "What I the Lord have spoken, I have spoken, and I excuse not myself; and though the heavens and the earth pass away, my word shall not pass away, but shall all be fulfilled, whether by mine own voice or by the voice of my servants, it is the same."[52]

This became the superstructure of the "Gathering." There is time, but not much time. Here is the great and terrible voice ("Wherefore, fear and tremble . . .") that will help the humble navigate rough seas ahead. Whether the instruction comes to the Saints "by mine own voice," or "by the voice of my servants, it is the same."

PROMISE: The kingdom of heaven is at hand and the Lord is coming quickly. The Saints are instructed to gird up their loins because when they do, he will suddenly come to his temple.

The message is urgent and action is imperative. "For behold, verily, verily, I say unto you, that I come quickly. Even so.

---

[50]Ibid., 38:18.
[51]Ibid., 57:3.
[52]Ibid., 1:35, 38, emphasis added.

Amen."[53] "And verily, verily, I say unto you, I come quickly. I am your Lord and your Redeemer. Even so. Amen."[54] "And the poor and the meek shall have the gospel preached unto them, and they shall be looking forth for the time of my coming, for it is nigh at hand –."[55] "I am Jesus Christ, the Son of God; wherefore, gird up your loins and I will suddenly come to my temple. Even so. Amen."[56]

CALLING LABORERS FOR THE LAST TIME

PROMISE: October 1830 is the eleventh hour and the last time that the Lord shall call laborers into his vineyard.

The vineyard has been corrupted, *"and there is none which doeth good save it be a few;* and they err in many instances because of priestcrafts, all having corrupt minds."[57] The traditional Christian churches, exposed by poorly-intended priests to the devil and his dominion, had corrupted the minds and practices of their members. Nine or ten years earlier, in Joseph Smith's "16th year," Jesus told Joseph, when he visited him in person, that "the world lieth in sin at this time and none doeth good no not one."[58] So far, Smith taught, had priests and priestcraft corrupted the Christian world.

PROMISE: October 1830 is the last time that the Lord shall call laborers into his vineyard. Those laborers shall lift their voices and cry repentance, preparing "a crooked and perverse generation" for the second coming of Jesus Christ.[59]

The Church of Christ is called forth from out of the wilderness to gather the elect "from the four quarters of the earth, even as many as will believe in me, and hearken unto my voice."[60] "[Y]ou [Jesus

---

[53]Ibid., 33:18.
[54]Ibid., 34:12.
[55]Ibid., 35:15.
[56]Ibid., 36:8.
[57]Ibid., 33:4, emphasis added.
[58]Joseph Smith Jr., *The Personal Writings of Joseph Smith*, ed. Dean C. Jessee (Salt Lake City: Deseret Book, 1984), 6.
[59]Doctrine and Covenants (1957), 33:2-3, emphasis added.
[60]Ibid., 33:6.

said to Orson Pratt] are called of me to preach my gospel –To lift up your voice as with the sound of a trump, both long and loud, and cry repentance unto a crooked and perverse generation, preparing the way of the Lord for his second coming."[61] This is 1830, and that is what the Savior meant by the "eleventh hour."[62] What shall the shepherds say? *"Repent, repent, and prepare ye the way of the Lord, and make his paths straight; for the kingdom of heaven is at hand;"*[63] The elect – those who have repented, who are preparing the way for the Lord, and making his path's straight – are instructed to be "faithful, praying always, having your lamps trimmed and burning, and oil with you, that you may be ready at the coming of the Bridegroom."[64]

Joining the Church and gaining the wealth of the spirit was good. Joining the Church, gaining the wealth of the spirit and bringing the wealth of the world with you was better. "[I]f ye seek the riches which it is the will of the Father to give unto you, ye shall be the richest of all people, for ye shall have the riches of eternity; . . . ." But not only the riches of eternity, for "the riches of the earth are mine to give."[65] "[G]o ye out from among the wicked. Save yourselves. Be ye clean that bear the vessels of the Lord."[66] It is given to the Lord's "faithful laborers" to prune the vineyard "for the last time."[67]

The Message

PROMISE: The sound must go forth from Zion in the land of Missouri to the uttermost parts of the earth. *The message of the Lord will now go forth from the land of the Saints' inheritance, the "city of Zion": "For, verily, the sound must go forth from this place into all the world, and unto the uttermost parts of the earth – the gospel must*

---

[61]Ibid., 34:5-6.
[62]Ibid., 33:3.
[63]Ibid., 33:10, emphasis added.
[64]Ibid., 33:17.
[65]Ibid., 38:39.
[66]Ibid., 38:42.
[67]Ibid., 39:17.

be preached unto every creature, with signs following them that believe."[68]

Great numbers of converts will hear those promises and make extraordinary sacrifices to abandon the "congregations of the wicked," everywhere the gospel was taught, and join the Saints in Zion. The Lord made his will known to his Saints, "not by the way of commandment, for there are many who observe not to keep my commandments."[69] The elders of the Church were instructed to carry this message to the nations of the earth and to the islands of the sea, first to the Gentiles and then to the Jews:

> *Prepare "to meet the Bridegroom."*
>
> *Behold "the Bridegroom cometh, go ye out to meet him."*
>
> *Then too, "Prepare yourselves for the great day of the Lord."*[70]
>
> *Go ye forth unto the land of Zion, that the borders of my people may be enlarged, and that her stakes may be strengthened, and that Zion may go forth unto the regions round about.*[71]

THE TEMPLE

PROMISE: A place lying westward upon a lot not far from the courthouse is the spot selected by God for the construction of a temple to be built in the city of Zion to be called the New Jerusalem.

Independence is the divinely designated center place, the place where the New Jerusalem and the temple of the New Jerusalem, the crowning edifice of the Holy City, are going to be built. "And thus saith the Lord your God, if you will receive wisdom here is wisdom.

---

[68]Ibid., 58:64, emphasis added.
[69]Ibid., 63:22.
[70]Ibid., 133:10, emphasis added.
[71]Ibid., 133:9, emphasis added.

Behold, the place which is now called Independence is the center place; and a spot for the temple is lying westward, upon a lot which is not far from the courthouse."[72]

PROMISE: The Saints will build a temple at a spot consecrated and dedicated unto the Lord by Sidney Rigdon.

The Lord instructed Sidney Rigdon to dedicate the spot for the temple: "And let my servant Sidney Rigdon consecrate and dedicate this land, and the spot for the temple, unto the Lord."[73]

PROMISE: The temple shall be reared in this generation. This generation shall not pass away until the house of the Lord is built. A cloud shall rest upon the temple and the glory of the Lord shall fill the house.

In September of 1832, the Lord again described the gathering with "the word of the Lord concerning his church, established in the last days for the restoration of his people, . . . , *and for the gathering of his saints to stand upon Mount Zion, which shall be the city of New Jerusalem."*[74]

> *Which city shall be built, beginning at the temple lot, which is appointed by the finger of the Lord, in the western boundaries of the State of Missouri, and dedicated by the hand of Joseph Smith, Jun., and others with whom the Lord was well pleased.*
>
> *Verily this is the word of the Lord, that the city New Jerusalem shall be built by the gathering of the saints, beginning at this place, even the place of the temple, which temple shall be reared in this generation.*
>
> *For verily this generation shall not all pass away until an house shall be built unto the Lord, and a cloud*

---

[72]Ibid., 57:3.
[73]Ibid., 58:57.
[74]Ibid., 84:2, emphasis added.

*shall rest upon it, which cloud shall be even the glory
of the Lord, which shall fill the house.*[75]

The Lord discusses the land and the temple: "For I, the Lord, will
cause them to bring forth as a very fruitful tree which is planted in
a goodly land, by a pure stream, that yieldeth much precious
fruit."[76] *"Verily I say unto you, that it is my will that a house should
be built unto me in the land of Zion, like unto the pattern which I
have given you."*[77] The temple will be "a house built unto me for the
salvation of Zion," "a place of thanksgiving for all saints," "a place
of instruction for all those who are called to the work of the
ministry."[78] If the great work is done correctly, if no "unclean
thing" comes into the sacred temple, *"my glory shall rest upon it."*[79]
"[A]ll the pure in heart that shall come into it shall see God."[80]

> *And now, behold, if Zion do these things she shall
> prosper, and spread herself and become very glorious,
> very great, and very terrible.*
>
> *And the nations of the earth shall honor her, and
> shall say: Surely Zion is the city of our God, and
> surely Zion cannot fall, neither be moved out of her
> place, for God is there, and the hand of the Lord is
> there;*
>
> *And he hath sworn by the power of his might to be her
> salvation and her high tower.*[81]

Then shall Zion rejoice "while . . . the wicked . . . mourn," as
"vengeance cometh speedily upon the ungodly . . . ." The "Lord's
scourge" shall be utterly unrelenting. It shall "vex all people,"
night and day, and not be stayed "until the Lord come."[82] "For the
indignation of the Lord is kindled against their abominations and

---

[75]Ibid., 84:3-5, emphasis added.
[76]Ibid., 97:9.
[77]Ibid., 97:10, emphasis added.
[78]Ibid., 97:12-13.
[79]Ibid., 97:15, emphasis added.
[80]Ibid., 97:16.
[81]Ibid., 97:18-20, emphasis added.
[82]Ibid., 97:21-23.

all their wicked works."[83] Rejoice again in this, "Zion shall escape if she observe to do all things whatsoever I have commanded her." But if she does not observe to do "all things whatsoever I have commanded her," even she shall not escape. Success is measured by obedience to counsel. If Zion is disobedient, Jesus "will visit her according to all her works, with sore affliction, with pestilence, with plague, with sword, with vengeance, with devouring fire."[84] If Zion meets her great promise and sins no more, "none of these things shall come upon her." In such event, Jesus *will bless her with blessings, . . . upon her, and upon her generations forever and ever, saith the Lord your God. Amen.*"[85]

ENEMIES

The Great and Abominable Church

PROMISE: *"And the great and abominable church, which is the whore of all the earth, shall be cast down by devouring fire, . . . as it is spoken by the mouth of Ezekiel the prophet, who spoke of these things, which have not come to pass but surely must, as I live, for abominations shall not reign."*[86]

But it is not only the wicked and their havens that will suffer. Their institutions will suffer – those evil organizations that insidiously contributed to their corruption. Joseph's revelator had harsh words for the Holy Roman Catholic Church. The Lord's vineyard had been exposed to evil by contagious priests. Benighted so-called Christians, blind leaders of the blind, had caused a pandemic that affected the church that Christ established from top to bottom – from the highest reaches of the papacy of the mother of harlots to the archbishops, deacons and priests of her pernicious offspring. If the Lord and his laborers did nothing to change that ugly equation, no one would survive the terrible day.

---

[83]Ibid., 98:24.
[84]Ibid., 98:25-26.
[85]Ibid., 97:27-28, emphasis added.
[86]Ibid., 29:21, emphasis added.

The Wicked Will Be Destroyed

PROMISE: The day of wrath shall come upon the wicked, the rebellious and the unbelieving as a whirlwind. Let the wicked take heed, let the rebellious fear and tremble, let the unbelieving hold their lips, for on the day of wrath all flesh shall know that he is God.

Speaking to the Saints, and of discretion, Joseph's revelator promoted his vision.

> *[H]ear the word of him whose anger is kindled against the wicked and rebellious;*
>
> *Who willeth to take even them whom he will take, and preserveth in life them whom he will preserve;*
>
> *Who buildeth up at his own will and pleasure; and destroyeth when he pleases, and is able to cast the soul down to hell.*
>
> *Behold, I, the Lord, utter my voice, and it shall be obeyed.*
>
> *Wherefore, verily I say, let the wicked take heed, and let the rebellious fear and tremble; and let the unbelieving hold their lips, for the day of wrath shall come upon them as a whirlwind, and all flesh shall know that I am God.*[87]

PROMISE: The day shall come when the nations of the earth shall tremble, because of Zion, and shall fear because of her terrible ones. The Lord hath spoken it.

"For it shall come to pass that the inhabitants of Zion shall judge all things pertaining to Zion."[88] "For, behold, I say unto you that Zion shall flourish, and the glory of the Lord shall be upon her."[89] "And she shall be an ensign unto the people, and there shall come unto

---

[87]Ibid., 63:2-6, emphasis added.
[88]Ibid., 64:38.
[89]Ibid., 64:41.

her out of every nation under heaven."[90] *"And the day shall come when the nations of the earth shall tremble because of her, and shall fear because of her terrible ones. The Lord hath spoken it. Amen."*[91]

God's Army

In December of 1833, these visions of Zion are in turmoil. The "enemies" of the Church in Missouri have victimized the gathering Saints. After a series of skirmishes that increased in their ferocity, the brethren "have been afflicted, and persecuted, and cast out from the land of their inheritance."[92] And what they have gotten, the Savior suddenly says, was in consequence of their transgressions. The transgressions of the erring Saints who had gathered in Zion before they were dispossessed were then described:

> *Behold, I say unto you, there were jarrings, and contentions, and envyings, and strifes, and lustful and covetous desires among them; therefore by these things they polluted their inheritances.*
>
> *They were slow to hearken unto the voice of the Lord their God; therefore, the Lord their God is slow to hearken unto their prayers, to answer them in the day of their trouble.*[93]

"I, the Lord, have suffered the affliction to come upon them, wherewith they have been afflicted, in consequence of their transgressions."[94] The Lord allowed the Missouri Saints to be "afflicted" and "persecuted" because they were slow to hearken to the "voice" of "the Lord their God." Although they were chastised, they were not entirely forgotten. "Yet I will own them," the Lord is

---

[90]Ibid., 64:42.
[91]Ibid., 64:43, emphasis added.
[92]Ibid., 101:1.
[93]Ibid., 101:6-7, emphasis added.
[94]Ibid., 101:2.

heard to say, "and they shall be mine in that day when I shall come to make up my jewels."[95]

COMMAND: *The Lord's faithful followers, even those "who have been afflicted, and persecuted, and cast out of the land of their inheritance [Jackson County, Missouri]," shall gather together, and stand in holy places to worship him. "Behold, it is my will, that all they who call on my name, and worship me according to mine everlasting gospel, should gather together, and stand in holy places."*[96]

> *Therefore, let your hearts be comforted concerning Zion; for all flesh is in mine hands; be still and know that I am God.*[97]

PROMISE: *The gathering of the children of Israel, despite their privations, shall still occur in the land of Missouri, and only in Missouri.*

> *And, behold, there is none other place appointed than that which I have appointed; neither shall there be any other place appointed than that which I have appointed, for the work of the gathering of my saints* — [98]

Missouri Zion shall fill until there is no more room there. When Zion is full,"then I have other places which I will appoint unto them [the gathering Saints], and they shall be called stakes, for the curtains or the strength of Zion."[99] The Saints shall gather at the place "which I have appointed" until "there is found no more room for them."[100]

PROMISE: *The sword of the Lord's indignation shall fall in behalf of his people — without measure and upon all nations when the cup of*

---

[95]Ibid., 101:3.
[96]Ibid., 101:22, emphasis added.
[97]Ibid., 101:16, emphasis added.
[98]Ibid., 101:20, emphasis added.
[99]Ibid., 101:21.
[100]Ibid., 101:21.

their iniquity is full. In that day all Israel shall be saved; those that have been scattered shall be gathered; those who have mourned shall be comforted, and those who have given their lives for Jesus shall be crowned.

The Lord loves his people, but not the things they do. His "bowels are filled with compassion towards them," and he "will not utterly cast them off." And in the day of his wrath he will "remember mercy." For had he not said that he "would let fall the sword of mine indignation in behalf of my people; *and even as I have said, it shall come to pass.*"[101] *The problem, the transgressions of the people, was unacceptable, but not necessarily permanent.*

"Mine indignation is soon to be poured out without measure upon all nations; and this will I do when the cup of their iniquity is full."[102] I am angry and I will take vengeance upon those who practice iniquity. And "in that day" all who are found upon the watchtower, "all mine Israel, shall be saved." They "that have been scattered shall be gathered." They "who have mourned shall be comforted." They "who have given their lives for my name shall be crowned."[103] The early gathering Missouri Zion Mormons desperately wanted to be found upon the watchtower. They wanted to be gathered and comforted, and if they made the supreme sacrifice for their Savior, and for their comforting faith, they wanted to claim their crowns.

PROMISE:

> *Therefore, let your hearts be comforted concerning Zion; for all flesh is in mine hands; be still and know that I am God.*
>
> *Zion shall not be moved out of her place, notwithstanding her children are scattered.*
>
> *They that remain, and are pure in heart, shall return, and come to their inheritances, they and their*

---

[101]Ibid., 101:9-10, emphasis added.
[102]Ibid., 101:11, emphasis added.
[103]Ibid., 101:12-15.

*children, with songs of everlasting joy, to build up the
waste places of Zion –*

*And all these things that the prophets might be
fulfilled.*[104]

PROMISE:

*The Lord (Jesus Christ) will gather as many as will
hearken to his voice and humble themselves before
him, and call upon him in mighty prayer.*[105]

FAILED PROPHECIES

The city of Independence in Jackson County, Missouri, supposed to
be the center place of Zion, the site of the city of Zion, and the
gathering place, did not become the center place of Zion, the city of
Zion, or the gathering place. The Independence Saints, who were
evicted, did not stand upon Mount Zion there. The city of the New
Jerusalem, beginning at the temple lot appointed by the finger of
the Lord, wasn't built, and the temple was not erected. A cloud did
not come to rest on a temple that was never erected and the glory of
God did not fill the house. The foundation of the New Jerusalem
was never laid. The settlers did not become his people, and he was
not their God there. The land where the city was supposed to stand,
the land where the temple was supposed to be built, and the land of
the Saints' supposed inheritance, was taken from them.

This New Jerusalem became a place of persecution, not a place of
peace. It was not a city of refuge or a place of safety for the people
of God. The glory and terror of the Lord was not found there. The
wicked came and went at will, and the people did not come from
every nation under heaven to gather there. They did not become
the only people not at war one with another, and they didn't come
to Zion singing songs of everlasting joy. The Saints left their
consecrated land purchased with consecrated funds involuntarily.
The kingdom of God was not at hand and the Lord didn't come.

---

[104]Ibid., 101:16-19, emphasis added.
[105]Ibid., 29:1-2, emphasis added.

The Saints girded up their loins, but the Lord did not suddenly come to a temple that couldn't be built in that generation as the Lord said that it would be. The place called Independence did not come to be called the New Jerusalem. The Lord did not provide the Saints with a land of promise flowing with milk and honey. Or a land upon which there should be no curse when he returned. The Saints who gathered at consecrated places, according to their instructions, were brutally treated and God did not protect them. The Saints did not have the land of their inheritance for themselves or for their children "while the earth shall stand." The faithful did not eat of the good of that land. The rebellious were not expelled from Zion – or punished for their wickedness – and they survived to become Zion's inheritors.

The gathering of the children of Israel did not occur in Independence, Missouri, and could not occur at any other place. The time for the harvest had not come. The Lord did not build up his Saints at various appointed places and his word was not fulfilled. The Saints did not gather, were not preserved, and failed to rejoice. The Lord did not hold Zion in his hands. Zion did not flourish and the glory of God was not upon her. She did not become an ensign unto the people and the people did not flock to her out of every nation under heaven. The nations of the earth did not tremble because of Zion, or fear because of her terrible ones, and the Saints did not grow up there, or possess the land. Christ didn't come, the graves of the Saints were not opened, and the ten tribes didn't return. The Lord's words were not sure and did indeed fail. What the Lord had spoken did not come to pass.

October 1830 was not the last time the Lord called laborers into his vineyard, and the servants he called did not prune the vineyard for the last time. The sound did not go forth from Zion in the land of Missouri to the uttermost parts of the earth. What the Saints had built did not belong to them. They did not plant vineyards and eat the fruit. The kingdoms of the world were not subdued under the Lord's feet. The consecrated earth was not given to the faithful from generation to generation. They were not gathered at their sacred place or blessed in their possession. What the Lord decreed through his servant Joseph never came to pass. Nothing of anything promised ever came to pass.

CHAPTER TWELVE

The Redemption of Zion

[T]he time is near when the sun will be darkened, and the moon turn to blood, and the stars fall from heaven, and the earth reel to and fro . . . if we are not sanctified and gathered to the places God has appointed . . . we must fall.

Joseph Smith

These faithful "Latter Day Saints" sought, thought they had found and were quick to occupy lands upon which there would be no curse when the Lord came.

Joel M. Allred

I can see nothing that convinces me that God has been our leader; calculation after calculation has failed, and plan after plan has been overthrown . . . .

John Corrill

THE KINGDOM OR NOTHING

The Saints gathering in Missouri were suffering greatly. Nothing was working as promised. The fabric of Zion was unraveling. The old Missouri settlers had driven the Mormons from their homes in Jackson County, Missouri. Independence, according to Joseph, was more than merely the divinely selected location of Zion, the temple and the city of the New Jerusalem. Jackson County, Missouri, he said, and "not Mesopotamia or the Great Rift Valley of Africa –

had been old Eden, the cradle of humanity."[1] Adam and Eve lived
at the place that came to be called Jackson County before the fall.
Adam, mankind's first progenitor, had walked and talked with
God, as one man walks and talks to another, at Jackson County,
Missouri.   Thus, this was not the first expulsion from the sacred
place. Attempts to reestablish "some of the Saints" in Van Buren
County had been frustrated by the old settlers. Many of the Saints
evicted from the "New Jerusalem" ultimately relocated in Clay
County, Missouri, with the help of other old settlers who recognized
the Mormons' plight when their heralded Zion suddenly became
unsafe. The promise that the Saints should separate themselves
from the wicked in "a land flowing with milk and honey, upon
which there shall be no curse when the Lord cometh"[2] now became
ashes in Joseph's faithful followers' mouths. "Missouri mobs
annulled desultory Mormon plans to build utopia in Jackson
County and evoke the second advent of Jesus Christ"[3] and the
return of the Ten Lost Tribes. Something would need to be done.

**PROPHECY: *Joseph Smith emphasized the incredible importance of
the New Jerusalem on April 21, 1834.***

"During a conference at Norton [Ohio] . . . Smith prophesied that
'the time is near when desolation is to cover the earth.' Without the
redemption of Zion 'we must fall.'" [4]   Richard S. Van Wagoner,
Rigdon's biographer, described the causes of the frictions in
Missouri. Mormon isolation, he said, was a precipitating factor.
"To validate their uniqueness they minimized socialization with
outsiders and emphasized their differences." What was "solidarity"
to the new settlers was "insularity" to the earlier inhabitants.
Mormonism's vaunted "exclusivity . . . would provoke tragic
misunderstandings" followed by "persecution and bloodshed."[5]
Mormons "pressed their opinions on outsiders through newspapers

---

[1]Scott G. Kenney, ed., *Wilford Woodruff: Journal-Typescript*, 9 vol. (Signature
Books, 1983), 30 March 1873, 7:129, quoted in Richard S. Van Wagoner, *Sidney
Rigdon: A Portrait of Religious Excess* (Salt Lake City: Signature Books, 1994;
paperback 2006), 142 fn 1, 155-56.
[2]Doctrine and Covenants (1957), 38:18.
[3]Van Wagoner, *Sidney Rigdon*, 143.
[4]Journal History, 21 Apr. 1834, 1-2, quoted in Ibid., 149.
[5]Van Wagoner, *Sidney Rigdon*, 143.

or proselyting."[6]   The Latter-day Saints were beholden to the Kingdom of God, and to the commandments of God, and not so much to the laws and statutes of the United States of America.

The temperament of the Missouri populace has been described as another factor in a volatile mix. Missourians could be "'emotional, quick-tempered, quarrelsome and ruthless . . . . Rugged individualism and ill-temper were problems . . . .'"[7] Many of the old settlers, Jacksonians, were hunters, people who preferred life at the fringes of civilization – "Missouri flotsam." "Missouri Mormons," on the other hand, "were arrogant and self-righteous. Their zeal was viewed as presumptuous and contemptuous by local non-Mormons."[8]   The old settlers were determined to "rid the country of 'this tribe of locusts that . . . threaten to scorch and wither the herbage of a fair and good portion of Missouri.'" "[T]hey charged Mormons with a multitude of offenses, including religious fanaticism." The Mormons were "the 'dregs of that society from which they came, lazy [i]dle and vicious,' tampering with slaves, and 'enviting free negroes and mulatoes from other States to become Mormons, and remove and settle among us.'"[9] Mormons treated this "Promised Land" as their own "God-given entitlement," and said so openly.[10] The old Missouri settlers with earlier claims were not amused.

> Oliver Cowdery went to Kirtland to inform Smith
> and Rigdon of the turn of events in Missouri.
> Shortly after Cowdery's arrival, Smith issued a
> revelation.   In omniscient-sounding language the
> revelation (now D&C 101) explained why the
> promised Mormon plans of a just and stable society
> in the New Jerusalem ended so disastrously. Even
> though Missouri Saints had given up prior lives,
> profitable ventures, families, and friends, the
> revelation proclaimed their sacrifices inadequate,
> their efforts to seek a renewed sense of community

---

[6]Ibid.
[7]Ibid., 144.
[8]Ibid.
[9]Ibid.
[10]Ibid., 145.

and spiritual nourishment not enough.   The
manifestation criticized the Saints for their
"jarrings, and contentions, and envyings, and
strifes, and lustful and covetous desires." They had
been "slow to hearken unto the voice of the Lord,"
and in their sins had "polluted their inheritances."[11]

*PROMISE: The sword of the Lord's indignation will fall on behalf of
his people in Missouri. What the Lord has said shall come to pass.*

On December 16, 1833, Joseph's God addressed the plight of his
then evicted and suffering Saints. "'I have sworn, and the decree
hath gone forth by a former commandment which I have given unto
you, that I would let fall the sword of mine indignation in behalf of
my people; and even as I have said, it shall come to pass.'"[12] Now,
by means of a parable, the Lord describes a plan the purpose of
which is to "redeem" Zion.

ZION'S CAMP

The Parable of the Nobleman

There was a certain nobleman who owned a "spot of land"
considered very choice. While contemplating his good fortune, he
said to his servants: "Go ye unto my vineyard, even upon this very
choice piece of land, and plant twelve olive-trees." Set watchmen
"round about" and "build a tower" so that one of them, upon the
tower, "may overlook the land," "that mine olive-trees may not be
broken down when the enemy shall come to spoil and take upon
themselves the fruit of my vineyard." "Now, the servants of the
nobleman went and did as their lord commanded them, and planted
the olive-trees, and built a hedge round about, and set watchmen,
and began to build a tower."[13] While they were yet laying the
foundation, they began to murmur "among themselves." "What
need hath my lord of this tower, seeing this is a time of peace?"
And they reasoned thus, "Might not this money be given to the

---

[11]Ibid., 146.
[12]Doctrine and Covenants (1957), 101:10.
[13]Ibid., 101:44-46.

exchangers?" for there is no need for a tower. And as they discussed these priorities, "at variance one with another," they "became very slothful, and they hearkened not unto the commandments of their lord." "And the enemy came by night, and broke down the hedge; and the servants of the nobleman arose and were affrighted, and fled; and the enemy destroyed their works, and broke down the olive-trees."[14]

Now the nobleman, "the lord of the vineyard," called his servants to account. "Why! what is the cause of this great evil?" "Ought ye not have done even as I commanded you"? Should you not have planted the vineyard, and built the hedge round about, "and set watchmen upon the walls"? "Ought ye not" have built the tower, "and set a watchman upon the tower, and watched for my vineyard, and not have fallen asleep, lest the enemy should come upon you?" Would the watchman upon the tower not have seen the enemy "while he was yet afar"? And could you not have "made ready and kept the enemy from breaking down the hedge"? Could you not have "saved my vineyard from the hands of the destroyer"?[15]

Now the lord of the vineyard, taking these events into consideration, said to one of his servants: "Go and gather together the residue of my servants, and take all the strength of mine house, which are my warriors, my young men, and they that are of middle age also among all my servants, who are the strength of mine house, save those only whom I have appointed to tarry; . . . ."[16] So was Zion's Camp then at first envisioned. That notwithstanding, the original plan to arm a Mormon militia did not originate in the Book of Revelations with the lord of the vineyard. The plan to raise a Mormon army originated in the fertile minds of Parley P. Pratt and Lyman Wight. Wight, a ferocious disciple, thought to say that "two [Mormon warriors] shall put" tens of thousands to flight.[17] These early Mormon leaders proposed to raise a contingent of trained military men which would march to Missouri, look like a group of settlers, restore the Saints to their lands and guard them until "the

---

[14]Ibid., 101:47-51.
[15]Ibid., 101:52-54.
[16]Ibid., 101:55.
[17]A thought supported by Mormon scripture. *See* Ibid., 133:58.

church was wealthy enough to buy out the property of the mob's leaders."[18]

The plan was enthusiastically endorsed by many. The Lord was late coming on board, but the parable of the nobleman, the Lord's response to Pratt and Wight, did soon follow. In that the Lord endorsed the plan with a revelation. "Quick-springing visions of an army of liberation marching triumphantly into the promised land betrayed his [Joseph's] sounder judgment."[19] It was a comfortable assumption when considered in those rarefied confines at headquarters at Kirtland. When the Lord did finally choose to intervene, he did so decisively. "Behold I say unto you," he said, "the redemption of Zion must needs come by power; . . ."[20] "[G]o ye straightway unto the land of my vineyard, and redeem my vineyard; for it is mine; I have bought it with money. Therefore, get ye straightway unto my land; break down the walls of mine enemies; throw down their tower, and scatter their watchmen."[21] Through the efforts of his servants, the lord would recover the land. "And inasmuch as they gather together against you, avenge me of mine enemies, that by and by I may come with the residue of mine house and possess the land."[22]

The good news was that Zion, that abandoned enclave, was still in play. The lord's trusted servant and the lord's "warriors," those who were the "residue" of the lord's house, would evict the enemy, repossess the land and redeem the vineyard. So would it be at Zion and its center place, at the site of the city of the "New Jerusalem," and at the temple lot. The Lord's "warriors" were the members of the Mormon militia, a military force that came to be called Zion's Camp. In the parable, the servant and his corps went and did all the things his lord commanded him to do. For that he received the nobleman's seal and blessing. He had proven himself to be "a

---

[18]Fawn M. Brodie, *No Man Knows My History: The Life of Joseph Smith the Mormon Prophet*, 2d ed., rev. and enl. (New York, NY: Alfred A. Knopf, 1972), 146.
[19]Ibid.
[20]Doctrine and Covenants (1957), 103:15, as cited by Brodie, *No Man Knows My History*, 146.
[21]Doctrine and Covenants (1957), 101:56-57.
[22]Ibid., 101:58.

faithful and wise steward in the midst of mine house, a ruler in my kingdom."[23]

PROMISE: The time for the harvest is come. The gathering of the Saints will continue; the Lord will build up his Saints at holy places, and his word will be fulfilled.

The Lord now described what the work of redemption required. ". . . I will show unto you wisdom in me concerning all the churches, inasmuch as they are willing to be guided in a right and proper way for their salvation – That the work of the gathering together of my saints may continue, that I may build them up unto my name upon holy places; *for the time of harvest is come*, and my word must needs be fulfilled."[24] While the army of God continued to assemble and prepared to march, the civilian Saints were instructed to continue to gather in the state of Missouri. "Therefore, a commandment I give unto all the churches, that they shall continue to gather together unto the places which I have appointed."[25] Like the parable of the wheat and the tares, they should gather. The wheat to be "secured in the garners to possess eternal life, and be crowned with celestial glory"; the tares to "be bound in bundles, . . . that they may be burned with unquenchable fire."[26] The Lord continues to adjure his followers "to [also] purchase all the lands with money, which can be purchased for money, in the region round about the land which I have appointed to be the land of Zion, for the beginning of the gathering of my saints; . . . ."[27] The initiative to recover an elusive Zion is on a double track.

PROMISE: The evicted Saints will return and Zion will be redeemed. The Saints shall build, and what they build shall belong to them. They shall plant vineyards and they shall eat the fruit.

No one should sell or surrender the land they had already purchased. "[I]t is my will that my people should . . . hold claim upon that which I have appointed unto them, though they should

---

[23]Ibid., 101:61.
[24]Ibid., 101:63-64, emphasis added.
[25]Ibid., 101:67.
[26]Ibid., 101:65-66.
[27]Ibid., 101:70.

not be permitted to dwell thereon."[28]   "They shall build, and
another shall not inherit it; they shall plant vineyards, and they
shall eat the fruit thereof."[29]

*PROMISE: The Lord will pour out his wrath without measure upon
the enemies of the Saints in his own time. The oppressors will not be
punished until the measure of their iniquities fills their cups.*

It is February 1834. The status of Zion remains unsettled. The
Lord by revelation now tells his faithful followers "how to act in the
discharge of your duties concerning the salvation and redemption of
your brethren, who have been scattered on the land of Zion"
("[D]riven and smitten" by the hands of mine enemies "on whom I
will pour out my wrath without measure in mine own time").[30]
Their oppressors have not been punished, he says, "that they might
fill up the measure of their iniquities, that their cup might be full; . .
. ."[31]

*PROMISE: The season of their chastening (the chastening of the
faithful Saints), although necessary, shall be brief. Their oppressors
are enemies of God. The Lord has decreed, if they do what he asks
them to do, that they shall begin to prevail against his enemies from
this very hour.*

The Saints have been chastened "for a little season" because they
did not "hearken altogether unto the precepts and commandments
which I gave unto them."[32] "But verily I say unto you, that I have
decreed a decree which my people shall realize, inasmuch as they
hearken from this very hour unto the counsel which I, the Lord
their God, shall give unto them. *Behold they shall, for I have
decreed it, begin to prevail against mine enemies from this very
hour.*"[33]

---

[28]Ibid., 101:99.
[29]Ibid., 101:101.
[30]Ibid., 103:1-2.
[31]Ibid., 103:3.
[32]Ibid., 103:4.
[33]Ibid., 103:5-6, emphasis added.

PROMISE: If the Saints do all that the Lord says that they shall do, they shall never cease to prevail until the kingdoms of the world are subdued under the Lord's feet. Then the earth shall be given to the Lord's Saints, as their possession, forever and ever.

These early Mormons will listen. Their faith causes them to believe that if they do what God requires these promises will be fulfilled. This is his great promise to them: "And by hearkening to observe all the words which I, the Lord their God, shall speak unto them, they shall never cease to prevail until the kingdoms of the world are subdued under my feet, and the earth is given unto the saints, to possess it forever and ever."[34]

PROMISE: The Lord has decreed that those who have been scattered shall return to the lands of their inheritances and build up the waste places of Zion. After much tribulation, the scattered brethren shall be gathered and blessed.

But if they do not so hearken and observe, "the kingdoms of the world shall prevail against them."[35] "*But verily I say unto you, I have decreed that your brethren which have been scattered shall return to the lands of their inheritances, and shall build up the waste places of Zion. For after much tribulation, as I have said unto you in a former commandment, cometh the blessing.*"[36]

PROMISE: The Lord promises that Zion – the land of Missouri, the center place of which is the place called Independence, and the spot for the temple, a lot lying westward of the court house – shall be redeemed and restored and never again thrown down. "Behold, this is the blessing which I have promised after your tribulations, and the tribulations of your brethren – your redemption, and the redemption of your brethren, even their restoration to the land of Zion, to be established, no more to be thrown down."[37]

PROMISE: The redemption of Zion must come by power – by the arm of flesh. If the Saints "pollute their inheritances" they shall be

---

[34]Ibid., 103:7.
[35]Ibid., 103:8.
[36]Ibid., 103:11-12, emphasis added.
[37]Ibid., 103:13, emphasis added.

thrown down.[38] *God's power will be manifest in the redemption and restoration of Zion.*

> *Behold, I say unto you, the redemption of Zion must needs come by power.*[39]

BY THE ARM OF FLESH ALLIES:
"WHOMSOEVER YE CURSE, I WILL CURSE"

PROMISE: God's angels and God's sacred (and military) presence shall precede the Mormon force to the battlefield. The Saints are promised that in time they shall possess the goodly land or Zion.

And who shall lead the counterattack on behalf of the scattered Saints? Who shall redeem and restore those scattered Saints to their great Missouri inheritance? "I will raise up unto my people a man, who shall lead them like as Moses led the children of Israel."[40] That divinely appointed leader would be the prophet Joseph Smith. This is a military Joseph. In this great and dangerous undertaking, the Mormon warriors and the Mormon Moses will not be asked to stand alone.

> *Therefore, let not your hearts faint, for I say not unto you as I said unto your fathers: Mine angel shall go up before you, but not my presence.*

> *But I say unto you: Mine angels shall go up before you, and also my presence, and in time ye shall possess <u>the</u> goodly land.*[41]

The Mormon militia called Zion's Camp was told that angels would attend them and fight at their sides, and that one or two faithful Saints attended by God and angels could put tens of thousands to flight.[42] The prophet will lead them like Moses led the children of

---

[38]Ibid., 103:14, emphasis added.
[39]Ibid., 103:15, emphasis added.
[40]Ibid., 103:16.
[41]Ibid., 103:19-20, emphasis added.
[42]Ibid., 133:58.

Israel, and the presence of God and angels will attend them. How could such an army ever be defeated? The Mormon soldiers expected to fight and defeat their enemies, whatever their numbers and no matter their armaments, with a leader like Moses, then God and angels at their sides.

Joseph Smith, who had gathered the residue of the servants of the lord of the vineyard to do his master's bidding, was now prepared to "redeem" the vineyard. The parable of the nobleman and the vineyard is now unencoded for "the residue" of the Lord's servants and "the strength" of the Lord's house. "Verily, verily I say unto you, that my servant Joseph Smith, Jun. is the man to whom I likened the servant to whom the Lord of the vineyard spake in the parable which I have given unto you."[43] What then is the vineyard? It is Zion, the place of gathering in the "land of Missouri." It is the center place, the place called Independence, and the spot for the temple (a lot lying westward not far from the courthouse), and the regions round about. And who is the nobleman? The lord of the vineyard is Jesus Christ. And who is the servant directed to go "straightway unto the land of my vineyard" and "redeem my vineyard"? That is Joseph Smith. And who are the soldiers directed to assist him? They are those that Joseph has gathered from the strength of the residue of the lord of the vineyard's servants – from his younger men and those of middle age.[44] And what are the lord of the vineyard's instructions? "Gather yourselves together unto the land of Zion, upon the land which I have bought with money that has been consecrated unto me."[45] Far from abandoning Zion in the face of provocations, the Lord commands that it shall be enlarged. "And let all the churches send up wise men with their moneys, and purchase lands [in the regions round about] even as I have commanded them."[46] The Mormon army knows that the lord of the vineyard is going to follow them there.

---

[43]Ibid., 103:21. In this author's 1957 printing of the Doctrine and Covenants, the name Baurak Ale ("my servant Baurak Ale") is assigned as code to protect the identity of Joseph Smith, Jun.

[44]This author's third great-grandfather, James Allred, then close to fifty years of age, was one of them.

[45]Ibid., 103:22.

[46]Ibid., 103:23.

And inasmuch as mine enemies come against you to drive you from my goodly land, which I have consecrated to be the land of Zion, even from your own lands after these testimonies, which ye have brought before me against them, ye shall curse them;

And whomsoever ye curse, I will curse, and ye shall avenge me of mine enemies.

And my presence[47] shall be with you even in avenging me of mine enemies, unto the third and fourth generation of them that hate me.[48]

Joseph Smith will lead the redeemers in this great heavenly-directed, divinely inspired martial enterprise. Joseph and the Mormon troops, fortified by angels and by the "presence" of the Lord, will by force of arms "redeem" the vineyard. The Mormons will engage their enemies on different fronts, for this will be a dual assault. "[W]ise men" from all the churches will go up to the land of Missouri to purchase yet more property in the regions round about pursuant to the Lord's command. For the Lord has repeatedly promised these faithful inheritors that they will hold this property in perpetuity. Other men, "warriors" comprising the "strength" of the residue of the lord of the vineyard's servants, will march to Missouri, evict the usurpers and redeem Zion by force. By the arm of flesh will Zion be redeemed. They will fight this epic battle for the Lord in his name with his help. They will curse the usurpers, and they will avenge their war-like Savior of his enemies.

---

[47]The Lord does not say to Joseph Smith and Zion's Camp that "*I* shall be with you," or that "*I* shall precede you with my angels," because when these revelations were given to Joseph Smith, Joseph did not believe that God was anthropomorphic, an exalted man with body parts and passions, or that God and Jesus Christ were separate beings. God's "presence," and not God's "person," shall precede the Mormon force to the battlefield, because God was a "presence" and not a "person" when Joseph provided these early revelations to his faithful and scattered Saints. Joseph Smith believed in the trinitarian conception of God promoted by the Nicene Creed, or in something like it, until 1834 or so. The hundred-year hidden 1832 Account of the First Vision, describing only Jesus Christ, provides yet further support for that proposition. The Jesus of the *1832 Account* was "omnipotant" and "omnipreasant," a spirit.

[48]Ibid., 103:24-26, emphasis added.

The law and the militia, they must have thought, would ultimately protect the institution of private property – that property still to be purchased by wise men from the churches, and that property to be reclaimed by the Mormon army. Here is "the goodly land" the Saints were promised, the land the Lord has consecrated to Zion. Here "my presence shall be with you even in avenging me of mine enemies."[49] The Lord has promised their success. When the Lord is with them, who can be against them? His angels shall precede them into battle. His presence shall precede them into battle. "[F]or the redemption of Zion must needs come by power." Zion will be redeemed by the "arm of flesh" represented by Mormon militia force.

PROMISE: *Those who stood against the gathering and Zion were enemies of God and would be punished in their persons and in their posterity.*

PROMISE: The Mormon army would follow the commandments the Lord had given them "concerning the restoration and redemption of Zion."[50]

PROMISE: The lord of the vineyard's servants would go up unto the land of Zion; "break down the walls of mine enemies; throw down their tower, and scatter their watchmen."[51]

And this, according to Joseph's Lord, is how victory is defined:

> *[P]ray earnestly that peradventure my servant Joseph Smith, Jun., may go with you, and preside in the midst of my people, and organize my kingdom upon the consecrated land, and establish the children of Zion upon the laws and commandments which have been and which shall be given unto you.[52]*

---

[49]Ibid., 103:26.

[50]Ibid., 103:29, emphasis added.

[51]Ibid., 101:57, emphasis added. "And inasmuch as they gather together against you, avenge me of mine enemies, that by and by I may come with the residue of mine house and possess the land." (Ibid., 101:58).

[52]Ibid., 103:35, emphasis added.

FAILURE, SURRENDER AND DEFEAT

In Independence, Missouri, following the expulsion of the Mormons, and before the militia's arduous march, old settlers ruled. No Mormon was welcome there or safe. Those foolish enough to tempt providence risked punishment. Those humiliations were to be redressed.

PROPHECY: The Mormon troops, assembled in Kirtland and ready to march to Independence, would enjoy the glory of the Christian martyrs and the victories of the ancient Hebrew legions. (Rigdon).

"On Sunday, May 4, 1834, the army met in Kirtland to hear an address by Rigdon. With a full and measured eloquence he urged them to deeds of valor and promised them the glory of the Christian martyrs and the victories of the ancient Hebrew legions."[53] On that occasion it was announced that the name of the Church had been changed. The Church of Christ had now become the Church of the Latter Day Saints.[54] The Savior's name had been a casualty of this revision to the aggravation of several of the founders. The new name better described the millennial aspirations of the warriors prepared to redeem Zion – according to the Lord's instructions and by the arm of flesh – and those of the Church as a whole.

When the old Missouri settlers heard that a Mormon army was marching to Missouri – and even before – they acted decisively. They "stormed the Independence jail and seized the Mormon arms sequestered there." After that, "they methodically ravaged all the remaining Mormon property. Between April 24 and 30 they burned [at least] one hundred and fifty houses."[55] When the Governor of Missouri, who had first cautiously attempted to assist the beleaguered Mormons, heard there was a Mormon force *en route*, he informed "Joseph's emissaries" that the restoration of Mormon property, at that particular time, "was completely impracticable."[56] "Zions Camp was not a band of colonists, arriving in cumbrous wagons piled high with bedding and new seed.

---

[53]Brodie, *No Man Knows My History*, 147.
[54]Ibid.
[55]Ibid., 151.
[56]Ibid., 151-52.

It was an army, however ill-trained and badly armed. It was almost exclusively male, militarily organized, and secretive in its intentions."[57] Joseph Smith was the commanding officer.

In response to this provocation, news of which had "leaked," the Missourians cooperated by counties to form armies of their own. The Missouri River became the Mormons' Rubicon. Harsh circumstances beyond the power of warriors to control would soon derail the divinely appointed enterprise. Faced with implacable resistance by angry Missouri settlers who had earlier proved themselves capable of brutality, and by an organized resistance that greatly outnumbered Zion's army, the most holy and solemn promises "concerning the restoration and redemption of Zion" now suddenly seemed misguided. This was a war the Mormons could not hope to win. The Mormon prophet, theoretically a proud conqueror, had misgaged the cost of success. Now, as the supreme leader stuttered, the misadventure stalled. If Zion's Camp crossed the Missouri River, Joseph was given to understand, the battle was joined. Joseph's willing warriors, bolstered by the bravado of the Wild Ram of the Mountains, General Lyman Wight – the bellicose future apostle and Joseph's second in command – were undeterred. The Mormon infantry, spurred on by Wight, the leader who had earlier surrendered the Mormon arms at Independence, were spoiling for a fight.[58] Bolstered by their faith, believing that God's angels had preceded them and were prepared to fight at their sides, that God's presence had preceded them, and that God always did what he said that he would, the troops could hardly be restrained.

The saga of the prophet Joseph Smith might easily have ended in Missouri in 1834. Zion's Camp wasn't a German army marching into the Rhineland, where a superior force lacked the will to respond. The Missourians, who were angry and menacing, did not lack the will to respond. After this long and difficult march, Joseph Smith now found himself "in a hopeless quandary." If he engaged the Missourians in an epic battle, the kind of battle Rigdon had blessed them to fight, they would surely be slaughtered. "[S]couts kept him informed of the forces rising against him."[59] He may also

---

[57]Ibid., 152.
[58]Ibid.
[59]Ibid., 152.

have known something his troops did not. Joseph may have known that it was he, and not the Prince of Peace, who said, "The redemption of Zion must needs come by power." He may have known that he, and not the Lord, had ratified a plan first suggested by Lyman Wight and Parley P. Pratt. For the plan described in the parable of the noble man resembled the plan first designed by Wight and Pratt. Joseph may have known that he, and not the Savior, had said that angels and the presence of the Lord should precede them there.

Now, while the Mormons camped on Fishing River, there were negotiations between the potential combatants, then offers back and forth, concerning the possible purchase of the various lands in question. The Mormon commander did not choose to provoke the Missourians by attempting to cross the river of no return. Several incursions by the Missouri forces, on the other hand – one intended to involve as many as two hundred men – were seen to fail because of the river and because of the weather. These threats, although mostly aborted, were shots across the bow. A larger conflict, if nothing was done, seemed inevitable.

PROMISE: God's angels and God's presence would precede the Mormon army in battle. The Mormon troops shall in time possess the goodly land.

What had seemed so entirely logical in the safety of the Mormon enclave at Kirtland in Ohio – "If God be with us, who can be against us?" – must have seemed less promising in Missouri in the face of a larger army, better equipped and very determined. Yet still in all there was this: *"Mine angels shall go up before you, and also my presence, and in time ye shall possess the goodly land."*[60] In Missouri in 1834, while acting as the supreme commander of Zion's Camp, and as the Mormons' Moses, and despite all of those promises and prophecies, Joseph Smith quietly surrendered. He avoided a terrible carnage, but set the Savior's words at naught. *"The redemption of Zion must needs come by power."* The Savior's confident words, words that put the Mormon army on the march,

---

[60]Doctrine and Covenants 103:20, emphasis added.

would have to be reconsidered.   The great divine martial plan
would need to be revamped.

On this particular occasion, the Mormon prophet did not "go and
do the things which the Lord hath commanded," recognizing that
"the Lord giveth no commandments unto the children of men, save
he shall prepare a way for them that they may accomplish the thing
which he commandeth them."[61]   Joseph and his legion did not do
what he said Jesus commanded him to do. He made but feeble
attempts to validate that most Mormon of propositions, despite the
fact the Lord had solemnly promised success. (*"Mine angels shall
go up before you . . ."*). Joseph didn't choose to test his Lord's firm
resolve. What was good enough for Nephi, while fetching those
brass plates from Laban, was not good enough for Joseph, while
seeking the redemption of Zion. The Mormon prophet had less will
to engage in what promised to be a deadly encounter than did many
of his disappointed troops.   Joseph decided that his military
contingent, though supposedly fortified by the extraordinary
"presence" of God, and of angels, would simply be no match for an
organized and militarily superior force of determined Missouri
"mobbers." Joseph betrayed his troops at Fishing River, Missouri.

> Two days after . . . [an aborted attack on the
> Mormon troops] Cornelius Gilliam, sheriff of Clay
> County, came to Zion's Camp. Gilliam, who had
> campaigned for sheriff with the slogan that he had
> shot more wolves than any other man in Missouri,
> minced no words. To enter Jackson County with
> arms would be an act of insurrection. The Governor
> had said explicitly that it would bring the state
> militia down upon the heads of the invaders. To
> remain camped near the border was to invite
> bloodshed. The Mormons had only two alternatives
> – to sell their lands, disperse their army, and return
> to Kirtland, or to purchase the land of the old
> settlers at double its value [a proposition the settlers
> endorsed].[62]

---

[61]Book of Mormon, 1 Nephi 3:7.
[62]Brodie, *No Man Knows My History*, 155.

The Mormons would not sell their own land, for Jesus said that they should not. And they had not the means to purchase the land of the old settlers at double its value. What they could do, and what they did, was to disperse their army and return to Kirtland. Although there were some further negotiations intended to put a slightly more courageous face on capitulation, Joseph left the land unreclaimed, dispersed the army of Israel and returned disgraced to Kirtland. So much for Joseph, and so much for the optimistic but discredited notion that, "The redemption of Zion must needs come by power." Lyman Wight, Smith's belligerent deputy, raged at any disposition that cancelled an epic battle where he and others had hoped to demonstrate their reckless courage in support of the great redemption errand. Wight was pacified by the reading of a revelation. The "Wild Ram of the Mountains" would have other Missouri battles to fight, and then and at last another church to found.

REDEMPTION DEFERRED

Joseph told the troops with yet another revelation that the redemption of Zion had been deferred.

> *Behold, I say unto you, were it not for the transgressions of my people, speaking concerning the church and not individuals, they might have been redeemed even now.*[63]

There is a preposterous new element added to the redemption equation. The redemption of Zion is said to have been deferred because the people "have not learned to be obedient to the things which I required at their hands"; because they "are full of all manner of evil"; and because they "do not impart of their substance, as becometh Saints, to the poor and afflicted among them."[64] This is the lame excuse offered for the failure of the ill-advised expedition. The Latter Day Saints are not "united according to the union required by the law of the celestial

---

[63]Doctrine and Covenants (1957), 105: 2, emphasis added.
[64]Ibid., 105:3.

kingdom," and they must "be chastened until they learn obedience."[65]

> *I speak not concerning those who are appointed to lead my people, who are the first elders of my church, for they are not all under this condemnation;*
>
> *But I speak concerning my churches abroad — there are many who will say: Where is their God? Behold, he will deliver them in time of trouble, otherwise we will not go up unto Zion, and will keep our moneys.*[66]

The issue in Missouri is stalled because of some less than valiant Saints "abroad." The great redemption errand, according to this deflated Joseph, would be delayed but not abandoned. In consequence of the "transgressions" of the people, an abrupt new element in a suddenly strange equation at an odd place and time, the new revelation now declared that, *"[I]t is expedient in me that mine elders should wait for a little season for the redemption of Zion."*[67]

PROPHECY: Within three years, and on September 11, 1836, Zion shall be redeemed. The Saints shall then again march to Jackson County and there shall not be a dog to open his mouth against them.

"The prophet tried to soften his men's disappointment by an unofficial promise that 'within three years they should march to Jackson County and there should not be a dog to open his mouth against them.' Very shortly thereafter he set the official date for the redemption of Zion as September 11, 1836."[68] That date would quietly pass. There would be no second expedition.

How shall the Mormon leader explain this shocking humiliation to men who had marched a thousand miles to reclaim the nobleman's

---

[65]Ibid., 105:4-6.

[66]Ibid., 105:7-8, emphasis added.

[67]Ibid., 105:9, emphasis added.

[68]Brodie, *No Man Knows My History*, 157, citing the Reed Peck manuscript, and a letter from Joseph Smith to the High Council of Zion, dated August 16, 1834, Roberts, ed., *History of The Church of Jesus Christ of Latter-day Saints*, vol. 2, 145.

vineyard by the arm of flesh? To men who expected to break down the walls of their enemies, throw down their tower and scatter their watchmen? To men supposed to be preceded in their march and joined in their battles by the presence of God and angels? How shall the Mormon leader explain the ignominious defeat of good and faithful men by their "enemies"? To Christian warriors who represented the strength of the Lord's house? To obedient disciples who put their lives at risk? How shall the Mormon leader explain a hundred broken promises made to Latter Day Saints by an undependable, poorly predictive Savior? Awkward emendations to a divinely appointed plan? The failure of the faithful to "possess the goodly land"?

Excuses and Apology; Death by Disease

The residue of the lord of the vineyard's servants, comprising the strength of the lord of the vineyard's house, made an investment in redemption that failed to produce a return. Sixty- eight members of Zion's Camp, slightly more than thirty percent of the two hundred and five men who participated in those redemption events, men who didn't know how important it was to boil their water (the Lord didn't tell them), contracted cholera. The disease proved to be no respecter of persons and fourteen members of the militia died. The most fervent priesthood blessings did not protect those faithful and obedient men from becoming founding martyrs to the newly minted faith. Boiling the water would have protected them. Heber C. Kimball, who observed the terrible cholera convulsions suffered by his friends, resolved never to sin again. Sin was the cause of this cholera. The Lord imposed cholera on sinners who had marched a thousand miles on sore and bleeding feet to reclaim his stolen vineyard. Such sacrifices were all for the good, for had the Lord not said this to his faithful Saints:

> *Therefore, be not afraid of your enemies, for I have decreed in my heart, saith the Lord, that I will prove you in all things, whether you will abide in my covenant, even unto death, that you may be found worthy.*

For if ye will not abide in my covenant ye are not worthy of me.[69]

Had the Lord not told them also this:

And all they who suffer persecution for my name, and endure in faith, though they are called to lay down their lives for my sake yet shall they partake of all this glory.

Wherefore, fear not even unto death; for in this world your joy is not full, but in me your joy is full.

Therefore, care not for the body, neither the life of the body; but care for the soul, and for the life of the soul.[70]

And this:

Let no man be afraid to lay down his life for my sake; for whoso layeth down his life for my sake shall find it again.

And whoso is not willing to lay down his life for my sake is not my disciple.[71]

The troops, although willing to fight and die in battle, now learned that their further sacrifice was not required. Modern Mormons – in recognition of this colossal failure – have described their 1834 militia in peculiar terms. *"The Prophet had come from Kirtland, at the head of a party known as Zion's Camp, bringing clothing and provisions."*[72] Zion's Camp was not for resupply, nor was it an assembly of innocent emigrants traversing unfamiliar prairies in a

---

[69]Doctrine and Covenants (1957), 98:14-15, emphasis added.

[70]Ibid., 101:35-37, emphasis added.

[71]Ibid., 103:27-28, emphasis added.

[72]Ibid., 105, headnote, author's 1957 printing of the Doctrine and Covenants, emphasis added. In the headnote to the 2013 edition of the Doctrine and Covenants, their amended objective is described in different terms: "Their purpose was to escort the expelled Missouri Saints back to their lands in Jackson County."

wagon train. It was a paramilitary force. Sidney Rigdon didn't bless the bedding. He spoke of "deeds of valor" and invoked memories of "Christian martyrs" and "the victories of the ancient Hebrew legions."[73] Zion's Camp was not about "bringing clothing and provisions" from Kirtland to the Saints evicted from Independence, a journey of a thousand miles. Nor was it in any way initially supposed to be a training school for future leaders, hard-bitten militia types. This Mormon expeditionary force was all about unlawful detainer, throwing down towers, scattering watchmen and reclaiming the lord of the vineyard's vineyard.[74] It was about breaking heads and kicking ass.

Joseph Negotiates Defeat

Zion's Camp was Mormonism's first organized militia. It was a faint preview of much that was yet to come. These redeemers were concerned with eviction and reclamation. The Mormon legion would "redeem" the vineyard, restore the previously evicted Saints to the land of their inheritance and protect them in their possession. It would reclaim consecrated land promised to the Saints in perpetuity – while the earth should stand, and then forever. No other land anywhere on earth could take the sacred place of Jackson County, Missouri. Jackson County Zion was the place where Satan tempted Eve. It was the place where Adam walked. It was the land called Missouri, the place called Independence, and a spot for a temple on a lot lying westward not far from the court house.

> *And, behold, there is none other place appointed than that which I have appointed; neither shall there be any other place appointed than that which I have appointed, for the work of the gathering of my saints –*
> *."[75]*

---

[73]Brodie, *No Man Knows My History*, 147.
[74]Doctrine and Covenants (1957), 105:16, *see also* 101:56-57.
[75]Ibid., 101:20, emphasis added.

There, in Zion, they shall build, and "another shall not inherit"'; there, in Zion, they shall plant vineyards and "they shall eat the fruit thereof."[76]

PROMISE: The Lord – changing his mind – does not now require these Mormon soldiers to fight the battles the redemption of Zion requires. God will fight the battles the redemption of Zion requires.

This divinely inspired expeditionary force marched toward the great battlefield and to the Missouri River barrier, but did not cross or fight. How did Joseph explain this humiliation to his faithful and obedient troops other than to say that Zion would not be redeemed, because of transgression, and that the time of redemption "should wait for a little season"? Joseph told his troops Jesus told him this:

> *For behold, I do not require at their hands to fight the battles of Zion; for, as I said in a former commandment, even so will I fulfil – I will fight your battles.*[77]

How unusual is the sound of that uncertain trumpet? A trumpet with a litany of broken promises in trail. How contradictory must that have seemed? "[B]ehold," the troops are told, "'the destroyer I have sent forth to destroy and lay waste mine enemies; and not many years hence they shall not be left to pollute mine heritage . . . . For it is my will that these lands should be purchased . . . . And again I say unto you, sue for peace not only to the people that have smitten you, but also to all people . . . .'"[78] The destroyer will shoulder this burden. You may leave the sensitive issue of the redemption of Zion and the issues involved with the destruction of my enemies in the hands of the destroyer. But does Joseph's revelator really mean that? By suing for peace and gathering cautiously together, by being careful not to boast of faith or mighty works, the Mormon emigrants are now encouraged to find "favor and grace" in their enemies' eyes. Then may the Saints rest "in peace and safety," while saying words like these: "Execute

---

[76]Ibid., 101:101.
[77]Ibid., 105:14, emphasis added.
[78]Ibid., 105, cited by Brodie, *No Man Knows My History*, 156.

judgment and justice for us according to law, and redress us of our wrongs."[79]

> *Now, behold, I say unto you, my friends, in this way*
> *you may find favor in the eyes of the people, until the*
> *army of Israel becomes very great.*[80]

The army of Israel, Zion's Camp, had been outnumbered ("the strength of mine house have not hearkened unto my words"[81]). That had been a mistake the Saints did not want to repeat. The volunteer army had fallen short of its recruiting goals.

> *. . . I will soften the hearts of the people, as I did the*
> *heart of Pharaoh, from time to time, until my servant*
> *Baurak Ale [Joseph Smith, Jr.] and Baneemy [code*
> *for mine elders], whom I have appointed, shall have*
> *time to gather up the strength of my house . . . .*[82]

And when the wise men from all the churches have purchased all of the lands that can be purchased in Jackson County, "and in the adjoining counties round about," and when the Saints have possessed them "according to the laws of consecration,"[83] then,

> *I will hold the armies of Israel guiltless in taking*
> *possession of their own lands, which they have*
> *previously purchased with their moneys, and of*
> *throwing down the towers of mine enemies that may*
> *be upon them, and scattering their watchmen, and*
> *avenging me of mine enemies unto the third and*
> *fourth generation of them that hate me.*[84]

After further preparations, and when the armies of Israel are sufficiently strong, then you may strike. Does it not sound as if the Lord will indeed again require the Saints, and not the unseen and

---

[79]Doctrine and Covenants (1957), 105:23-25.
[80]Ibid., 105:26, emphasis added.
[81]Ibid., 105:17.
[82]Ibid., (1957) 105:27, emphasis added.
[83]Ibid., 105:28-29.
[84]Ibid., 105:30, emphasis added.

poorly understood destroyer, "to fight the battles of Zion"? But only when they are better prepared? Fool me once.

> *But first let my army become very great, and let it be sanctified before me, that it may become fair as the sun, and clear as the moon, and that her banners may be terrible unto all nations* . . . .[85]

PROMISE: *"Behold, the destroyer I have sent forth to destroy and lay waste mine enemies; and not many years hence they shall not be left to pollute mine heritage, and to blaspheme my name upon the lands which I have consecrated for the gathering together of my saints."*[86]

For now, the Lord, who has unleashed the destroyer, says that he no longer requires the services of Zion's Camp. The Mormon army, a force that traversed the vast expanses of Ohio, Illinois, Indiana and Missouri in order to fight this holy war, is now ordered to disband, having scarcely fired a shot in anger. The sacred redemption errand is now trivialized. ("[A]s many as have come up hither, that can stay in the region round about, let them stay; And those that cannot stay, who have families in the east, let them tarry for a little season, inasmuch as my servant Joseph shall appoint unto them"[87]). Their service was their offering. God has heard their prayers and accepted their service. But why did he bring them here? Why have they suffered so? And what have they accomplished?

> *I have heard their prayers, and will accept their offering; and it is expedient in me that they should be brought thus far for a trial of their faith.*[88]

What Joseph intended for them was what he later claimed that he intended for Miss Rigdon. When Joseph made a plural marriage proposal to Nancy Rigdon, at a time when the practice of polygamy was roundly condemned (even by Mormons), and when he was then trapped in a striking deception, saying he had not, he would reverse himself, admit the truth of her claims and say that *"He wished to*

---

[85]Ibid., 105:31, emphasis added.
[86]Ibid., 105:15, emphasis added.
[87]Ibid., 105:20-21.
[88]Ibid., 105:19, emphasis added.

ascertain whether she was virtuous or not, and took that course to learn the facts!!"[89] When Joseph surrendered his troops without evicting the usurpers or reclaiming the sacred ground, he said he had brought them there "for a trial of their faith." It was a test of their virtue. It had all been a trivial exercise to determine the faith of various previously tested trusted men. For the fourteen men who died of cholera – and because of sin – the test had been severe.

On June 22, 1834, with Mormon soldiers stalled at Fishing River, Missouri, their leader – reluctant to proceed because any further incursion might be perceived as provocative – tells the troops that Jesus told him this: *But for their transgressions, and those of Saints "abroad," the people might have been redeemed from their enemies.*[90] After mud, miles, beatings, burnings, hunger and cold, after service, sacrifice and devotion, violence and death by disease, this is the message? This is how Joseph's Lord explains defeat by broken promise? The redemption of the New Jerusalem is seen to turn on an unforseeable technicality? So ends the march of a thousand miles? Zion will not be redeemed by power? The destroyer will not lay waste the enemies of Zion? The walls and towers of the lord's enemies will not be broken down, and their watchmen will not be scattered?   Angry ungovernable men will expropriate the possessions of obedient men with impunity, and the lord of the vineyard's servants, the strength of the lord of the vineyard's house, will be put to flight?

> *"Mine angels shall go up before you, and also my presence, and in time ye shall possess the goodly land"?*[91]

The Mormon army, called Zion's Camp, will not set foot in Jackson County, Missouri, and the "presence" of God and "angels" will not precede them there. Zion will not be led out of bondage or redeemed by power,[92] and the "arm of flesh" will fail. The

---

[89]John C. Bennett, *The History of the Saints: Or, an Expose of Joe Smith and Mormonism* (Boston: Leland & Whiting, 1842; photomechanical reprint of 1842 original, Salt Lake City: Modern Microfilm Company), 246, emphasis added.

[90]Doctrine and Covenants (1957), 105:2, emphasis added.

[91]Ibid., 103:20, emphasis added.

[92]Ibid., 103:17.

suffering Saints will not be restored to consecrated lands purchased with consecrated money, and there will be no holy cities or temples built in the land of their inheritance in "this generation" or any other. Remember these words: " . . . *ye shall curse them; And whomsover ye curse, I will curse, and ye shall avenge me of mine enemies.* "[93] Remember these words: *"And my presence shall be with you even in avenging me of mine enemies, unto the third and fourth generation of them that hate me."*[94] Joseph's Lord will now awkwardly declare his amended will:

> *The redemption of Zion is deferred.*[95]

The great march was but a test.

> *[T]he strength of mine house have not hearkened unto my words.*

> *But inasmuch as there are those who have hearkened unto my words, I have prepared a blessing and an endowment for them, if they continue faithful.*

> *I have heard their prayers, and will accept their offering; and it is expedient in me that they should be brought thus far for a trial of their faith.*[96]

It was not about the redemption of the vineyard, walls, towers and watchman, but rather an experiment. God has brought them from Ohio, Illinois and Indiana to Missouri *"for a trial of their faith."* There will be no epic battle because the Mormon commander negotiated defeat.

Redemption Woes

The evicted Saints did not return. They did not build the waste places of true Zion. They did not gather there and were not blessed.

---

[93]Ibid., 103:24-25, emphasis added.
[94]Ibid., 103:26, emphasis added.
[95]Ibid., 105, Summary, verses 6-13.
[96]Ibid., 105:17-19, emphasis added.

The Lord did not pour out his wrath upon their enemies when the measure of their iniquities filled their cups. The Saints did not avenge the Lord of his enemies to the third or fourth generation of those who hated him, and he did not assist them. Nor did he curse those his servants cursed. The Mormon troops did not achieve the glory of the Christian martyrs or the victories of the ancient Hebrew legions. Or march to Jackson County on September 11, 1836, to test the proposition that there should not be so much as a dog to open his mouth against them. God did not fight the battles redemption required. The destroyer didn't show. Those who were scattered were not gathered. Those who mourned were not comforted. The fate of Zion was not in God's hands.

ZION IS LOST! PROMISES ARE BROKEN! PROPHECIES FAIL!

What Joseph said God promised the Zion's Camp militia didn't come to pass. Prophecies about the redemption of Zion, about the urgent gathering of Israel in the State of Missouri, about the return of the Ten Lost Tribes and the Second Coming didn't come to pass. Mormons couldn't hold title to their properties in Missouri because the old settlers resisted their efforts to settle there. The gathering of the Saints wasn't really as urgent as Joseph said that it was, and the Savior didn't come as Joseph said that he would. Joseph didn't live to see him come, and the Mormons never returned to Jackson County, Missouri. The Saints couldn't gather "to the places" God had "appointed." The sun wasn't "darkened." The moon didn't "turn to blood." The stars didn't "fall from heaven," and the earth didn't "reel to and fro."

The great promise of early Mormonism – that the Saints must urgently gather at Zion in the State of Missouri, and build a temple there, because the Savior's second coming was destined to occur in that generation during the lives of some of them – proved to be utterly false. Those uncompromising revelations and prophecies utterly failed. It isn't enough to say that this is not yet "the last syllable of recorded time." The "revelations" Joseph Smith delivered to nineteenth-century Saints in the name of the Savior with apocalyptic urgency were not the word of God.

When Joseph Smith died with Nauvoo looking more and more like Kirtland, and when the Church abandoned all hope of creating its promised sanctuary in the State of Missouri, and when the Latter-day Saints were forced to leave Nauvoo, approximately fifty percent of the people followed Brigham Young to a remote place in the American west. Many of the Mormons followed other schismatic leaders, most of whom, like Joseph, had revelations. Brigham Young, a spiritually barren revelator, need not have kept a carriage in his barn, ready at a moment's notice to take him back to the state of Missouri, for he would never return. Nor would ordinary Mormons – whatever Joseph had said. Nor would any of the Mormon prophets who succeeded him. Nor will they! Nor will the Mormons! Ever! Jesus didn't come when Joseph Smith said that he would, and Joseph wasn't there to meet him as he said that he would be.

Independence, Missouri, was not Christianity's Garden of Eden. Daviess County, Missouri, was not Adam-ondi-Ahman, the place where Adam and Eve lived after the fall in exile. Adam didn't leave the remains of one of his altars close to Lyman Wight's house on Tower Hill, and those of another a mile to the north on top of Spring Hill. Abraham didn't write on the Egyptian papyri, nor did Moses, Aaron or Joseph. The Greek Psalter was not an Egyptian dictionary. The Kinderhook plates did not contain the history of a descendant of Ham through the loins of Pharaoh. Joseph did not translate a fragment of St. John's manuscript. There was no Tower of Babel, no Brother of Jared and Zelph was not a Hebrew.

The very term "Latter Day Saints," a term cheapened by the passage of time and threatened by all of those broken promises, describes a failed apocalyptic vision. The covenants God supposedly made to the Latter Day Saints nearly two hundred years ago have all been broken in time. Heaven forbid that anyone should ever say, "God didn't make that promise!" Or "I did everything the Lord required!" Or, "Our leaders failed us!"

Joseph Smith described in more revelations than Latter-day Saints are allowed to read, promises God didn't make and hasn't kept. Because God didn't say what Joseph said that he did, God didn't do

what Joseph said that he would.   See "Failed Prophecies and Promises" at Appendix E.

CHAPTER THIRTEEN

The Forgotten Order

I will drink of the fruit of the vine with you on the earth . . . And also with Elias, to whom I have committed the keys of bringing to pass the restoration of all things spoken by the mouth of all the holy prophets, since the world began, concerning the last days.

Jesus Christ[1]

[T]he "second Priesthood [is] Abrahamic Patriarchal power which is the greatest yet experienced in this Church."[2] "The patriarchal office is the highest office in the church . . . ."[3]

Joseph Smith

In the presentation of officers he stood next to the First Presidency. Until his death in 1854, every general conference sustained the patriarch ahead of the Twelve . . . .[4]

D. Michael Quinn

---

[1]Doctrine and Covenants (2013), 27:5-6, amending and backdating Chapter 28 of the Book of Commandments (as seen in Section 50 of the 1835 [first] edition of the Doctrine and Covenants). "After this [after the appearance of Jesus Christ and Moses to Joseph Smith and Oliver Cowdery in the Kirtland Temple on April 3, 1836] Elias appeared and committed the dispensation of the gospel of Abraham, saying that *in us and our seed* all generations after us should be blessed." (Ibid., 110:12, emphasis added).

[2]Andrew F. Ehat and Lyndon W. Cook, *The Words of Joseph Smith: The Contemporary Accounts of the Nauvoo Discourses of the Prophet Joseph Smith* (Provo, UT: Religious Studies Center, Brigham Young University, 1980), 245; *see, e.g.*, D. Michael Quinn, *The Mormon Hierarchy: Origins of Power* (Salt Lake City: Signature Books in association with Smith Research Associates, 1994), 34.

[3]Minutes of the meeting of Joseph Smith, Hyrum Smith, James Adams, Newel K. Whitney, et al., 27 March 1843, LDS Archives (cf. Quinn, *Origins of Power*, 213, 425 n 144).

[4]Quinn, *Origins of Power*, 117.

THE PATRIARCHAL PRIESTHOOD

A revelation dated 1835 described *two* priesthoods, "namely, the Melchizedek and Aaronic, including the Levitical Priesthood."[5] "No form of the word 'patriarch' appears in the published version or available manuscripts of the revelations on priesthood received in 1832 and 1835."[6] Eight years later, in 1843, Smith explained that two had really meant *three*. The "great revelation on the priesthood" had been "incomplete" when it said there were "two priesthoods" in the Church. That happened because the 1835 revelation (D&C 107) had actually described a third kind of authority to which it hadn't assigned a proper name. Thus in August 1843, Joseph Smith awkwardly changed the authority principles to more completely describe *"three grand orders of priesthood,"* assigning them this revisionary priority: *Melchizedek first, Patriarchal second, Aaronic/Levitical third.* In August 1843, Joseph Smith – by clarifying a revelation first published in the Doctrine and Covenants in 1835 –described "three grand orders of priesthood" and ranked them. The Patriarchal (or second "grand") "order" of the priesthood, according to Smith, was accorded a higher dignity than the Aaronic/Levitical (or third "grand") order of the priesthood.[7]

---

[5]Doctrine and Covenants (1957), 107:1.

[6]Quinn, *Origins of Power*, 33, emphasis added.

[7]One hundred and fifty years later (and in 1993), LDS Apostle Boyd K. Packer reported that *three* meant *two* (yet again) when he instructed every "Elder" and "Sister" that, *"The patriarchal order is not a third separate priesthood. Whatever relates to the patriarchal order is embraced in the Melchizedek Priesthood."* (Boyd K. Packer, "What Every Elder Should Know – and Every Sister as Well: A Primer on Principles of Priesthood Government," *Ensign* [February 1993], 3, emphasis added). Packer's particular confusion (he is obviously at odds with Joseph Smith) is consistent with the twentieth-century demise of the Patriarchal order of the Priesthood. "[T]he existence and meaning of the Patriarchal Priesthood is controversial and uncertain." ("Presiding Patriarch" [accessed 16 July 2014], available from wikipedia.com; Internet, 1). "In the Church of Jesus Christ of Latter-day Saints . . . the patriarchal priesthood (or Abrahamic priesthood) is sometimes understood as one of types or 'orders' of priesthood [Packer admits "there are references to a patriarchal priesthood"]. The two more commonly known orders are the Aaronic Priesthood and the Melchizedek Priesthood. The Patriarchal Priesthood [this phantom order of priesthood] should not be confused with the calling of patriarch." ("Patriarchal Priesthood" [accessed 20 November 2014], available from wikipedia.com; Internet, 1). Why shouldn't everyone confuse the Patriarchal (or Abrahamic) order of the Priesthood with the office or

"The order of this [undenominated but Patriarchal] priesthood was confirmed to be handed down from father to son, and rightly belongs to the literal descendants of the chosen seed, to whom the promises were made."[8] This "grand" new lineal "order" was a priesthood for the Smiths, the spiritual successors to the patriarchs and high priests known to students of the Bible in Old Testament times. The Patriarchal (or Abrahamic) Priesthood – which was "restored" by the prophet "Elias" – as this authority came to be known, was about lineage, privilege and hereditary power. "Lineal priesthood was a concept in Mormon theology as early as 1832.[9] However, the office of patriarch and the term Patriarchal Priesthood did not exist until December 1834."[10] In December 1834 the First Presidency "formalized through ordination the patriarchal office which Joseph Sr. possessed by lineage and birthright."[11]

In 1835 Oliver Cowdery described Joseph Smith Jr. (and not Joseph Smith Sr.) as the "first patriarch of the church." In 1835, by way of an amendment that altered an earlier revelation, the Lord is supposed to have said that he had informed Joseph Jr. in 1830 to expect a visitation from a messenger by the name of Elias, "to whom I have committed the keys of bringing to pass the restoration of all things spoken by the mouth of all the holy prophets, since the world began, concerning the last days."[12] This important "Elias," the Restorationer – since supposed by some to be an Old Testament prophet at or about the time of Abraham – didn't have an Old Testament provenance or a Hebrew name. He was nevertheless a messenger assigned a name in a revelation from

---

calling of the Patriarch? Why shouldn't everyone who is familiar with the teachings of the prophet Joseph Smith understand that the Patriarchal Priesthood, whatever Elder Packer said and whatever Wikipedia says, was a third type or order of the priesthood, something supposed to be eternal and treated as important? The 1979 dismissal of the third order of the priesthood without appropriate formality begs to be further explained.

[8]Doctrine and Covenants (1957), 107:40, emphasis added.

[9]"Therefore, thus saith the Lord unto you, with whom the priesthood hath continued through the lineage of your fathers – For ye are lawful heirs, according to the flesh, and have been hid from the world with Christ in God – ." (Ibid., 86:8-9, December 6, 1832).

[10]Quinn, *Origins of Power*, 33.

[11]Ibid., 49. Ordination by the laying on of hands was seen as "visibly impressive and symbolically important."

[12]Doctrine and Covenants (1957), 27:6.

Joseph's God, not a theory or a code or a concept. Jesus told Joseph in a backdated Section 50 of the 1835 first edition of the Doctrine and Covenants, then Section 27 of the modern Doctrine and Covenants, "that the hour cometh that I will drink of the fruit of the vine with you" and with Moroni and John the Baptist (messengers supposed to have already visited Smith), and with others yet to come, a list that included both "Elias" and "Elijah." In this revelation, Joseph's Lord referred to "Elias" and "Elijah" as separate entities.

In October 1834 Oliver Cowdery and Joseph Smith first told their followers they had received what came to be called the Aaronic Priesthood in 1829 from a heavenly messenger. In September 1835, Joseph Smith and Oliver Cowdery told their followers they had received the Melchizedek Priesthood, without assigning a date, from some other heavenly messengers. In 1836 Joseph Smith and Oliver Cowdery said that they received the "keys" to the Patriarchal "order" of the "Priesthood," a third and separate order of the priesthood, from yet another heavenly messenger. Angelic ordination did thus then later become the order of the restored church. In 1836, following a vision of "the Lord standing upon the breastwork of the pulpit" in the newly constructed Kirtland temple, followed by a vision of Moses, who then appeared "and committed unto us the keys of the gathering of Israel from the four parts of the earth, and the leading of the ten tribes from the land to the north," "Elias appeared and committed the dispensation of the gospel of Abraham." This ancient Elias was then followed by "Elijah the prophet, who was taken to heaven without tasting death." Elijah came "[t]o turn the hearts of the fathers to the children, and the children to the fathers, lest the whole earth be smitten with a curse –."[13] In these epochal visions, Joseph Smith "revealed Elias and

---

[13]Doctrine and Covenants (1957), 110. These sealing conferrals made it possible for Smith to say, ". . . I have the keys of the kingdom, and whatever I bind on earth is bound in heaven, and whatever I loose on earth is loosed in heaven . . . ." (Joseph Smith to Martha Brotherton, Brotherton letter, 13 July 1842, reproduced at John C. Bennett, *The History of the Saints: Or, an Expose of Joe Smith and Mormonism* [Boston: Leland & Whiting, 1842; photomechanical reprint of 1842 original, Salt Lake City: Modern Microfilm Company], 239). Brother Joseph, who received that sealing power, was already the voice of God on earth. ("For his word ye shall receive, as if from mine own mouth, in all patience and faith." [Book of Commandments 22:5]).

Elijah to his followers as separate entities."[14] He described them as separate messengers differently tasked.

In his remarkable analysis of the origins of the Mormon priesthood, D. Michael Quinn uncharacteristically fails to properly credit the prophet "Elias" for the bestowal of the keys of "the dispensation of the gospel of Abraham," an extraordinary patriarchal power supposed by Smith to have been associated with antiquity's high priests and patriarchs.   The name of the messenger who "committed" this patriarchal priesthood power to Joseph Smith and Oliver Cowdery in what was a flurry of supernatural activity supposed to involve the literal presence of multiple patriarchs at the Kirtland, Ohio, Temple on April 3, 1836, was "Elias." The name "Elias," coincidentally, is the Greek transliteration of the name "Elijah," an Old Testament prophet and a separate messenger who, following Elias, then also later appeared. Smith received the "keys" to the dispensation of the gospel of Abraham from "Elias" in 1836, "more than one year after he formally established patriarchal authority as an ordained office in the new church." The ministration of Elias was to some extent symbolic because the Smiths, lineal heirs "hid from the world with Christ in God," spiritual high priests and patriarchs for their time, were supposed to have "inherited lineal priesthood without ordination." For more than a century (circa 1835 to 1979), Mormon doctrine presumed that the Smiths "possessed the priesthood at birth."[15]

According to one contemporary account in a sermon delivered in 1843, Smith described the prerogatives of "the second [or Patriarchal] Priesthood" as "the greatest yet experienced in this

---

[14]Samuel Brown, "The Prophet Elias Puzzle," *Dialogue,* vol. 39 no. 3 (Fall 2006), 3.

[15]Quinn, *Origins of Power*, 32-33. Doctrine and Covenants 86 made it clear that the lineal priesthood "was not of church but of family. According to that revelation, Smith had *lineal authority* before his first vision, before visits of angels, before the restorations of Aaronic priesthood, of apostolic authority, or of the high priesthood. Smith was never ordained to the lineal priesthood by the laying on of hands. Later called the Patriarchal priesthood, this authority existed in him from birth." (Ibid., 33, emphasis added). The keys to the Patriarchal Priesthood power ("the dispensation of the gospel of Abraham") were provided to Joseph Smith in 1836 by Elias, a person with no Old Testament provenance and a Greek name.

Church."[16]   That unconditional recital describing the "second
Priesthood, Abraham's Patriarchal power," was later and
posthumously altered.   Those extraordinary words, defining the
rank of that authority, were omitted from the contents of the
sermon when it was reported in the History of the Church after the
death of Joseph Smith.[17] The Patriarchal Priesthood was ancient,
lineal, monarchical and undemocratic.   The existence of such
power, a priesthood for the Smiths, posed a threat to the outsized
ambitions of Joseph's successor, a man by the name of Brigham
Young, who ordained one of his sons to the office of apostle at the
age of eleven.

Inherited Lineal Priesthood

Brigham Young detached the "sealing powers" from the office of
the Patriarch and slowly "diminished" the Patriarch's "prestige,"
finding support in a Quorum that knew the Patriarch outranked
them.   Before the office of the Presiding Patriarch was allowed to
expire in 1979, the hereditary occupants, relatives of Mormonism's
founder, suffered many humiliations both large and small.   There
was in all of this and over time a political struggle for spiritual
power.   The twentieth-century demise of the office of the Presiding
Patriarch, and of the separate order of the Patriarchal Priesthood,
was a disrespectful process, death by a thousand cuts.   The concerns
of the more recent patriarchal descendants of the Smiths, lesser
figures than their progenitors, were often ignored.

The Smith family's most prominent modern theologian, Joseph
Fielding Smith (who later became the tenth President of the
Mormon Church), buttressed the Smith family's legacy claims in
his multi-volume anthology, *Doctrines of Salvation*.   He was
speaking of something supposed to be eternal and unchangeable

---

[16]Joseph Smith Jr., *History of The Church of Jesus Christ of Latter-day Saints*,
B.H. Roberts, ed., 2d ed., rev., (Salt Lake City: The Deseret Book Company, 1978),
5:554-55; Ehat and Cook, *The Words of Joseph Smith: The Contemporary Accounts
of the Nauvoo Discourses of the Prophet Joseph*, 245, quoted in Quinn, *Origins of
Power*, 34.
        [17]Roberts, ed., *History of The Church of Jesus Christ of Latter-day Saints*,
5:554-55.

(that proved to be less than eternal and thoroughly changeable) as the Smith family's fortunes declined with the passage of time and the emergence of new priestly priorities. *"Down through time there has been a gradual development in the offices in the priesthood. Adam held the Melchizedek Priesthood,"* wrote Apostle Joseph Fielding Smith. *"Yet from Adam to Moses the order of the priesthood was that of the Patriarchal order. These men were high priests and patriarchs."*[18] Joseph Fielding Smith did not accept, in his time, Boyd K. Packer's 1993 refinement. There was a "Patriarchal order," and it wasn't a part of the Melchizedek Priesthood. The expectations of Joseph Fielding Smith's father, President Joseph F. Smith, for the future of the Patriarchal Priesthood and the office of the Presiding Patriarch were dashed by leaders less bound to the doctrine of an inherited lineal monarchical patriarchy. The un-Smiths had selfish reasons to downsize the office of the patriarch.

Today the Church reports that Joseph Smith Jr., the "first patriarch of the Church," ordained his father, Joseph Smith Sr., the patriarch of the family, to the office of Presiding Patriarch on December 18, 1833. Because of the confusion engendered by the many changes made to foundational documents, this dating – like so much else pertaining to the priesthood – is now seen to have been "incorrect." Quinn's historical analysis concludes that "[t]he prophet's words on this [1833] occasion were a prayer-blessing of encouragement, not of ordination, for his father was not even present on 18 December 1833." On December 6, 1834, Joseph Smith Sr. was ordained to the office of patriarch by Oliver Cowdery, Joseph Smith Jr., Sidney Rigdon and Frederick G. Williams.[19] Quinn wonders, "Why did Cowdery obscure the date?" before he then concludes, because "[t]here was no concept of an ordained patriarchal office in December 1833. His manuscript history tried to obscure this fact." In late 1834 Smith and Cowdery "redefined the notion of an unordained lineal priesthood (which existed early in the Mormon movement) into an ordained 'patriarchal priesthood.' The idea of an ordained patriarch thus emerged late." Cowdery revised "the historical record to suggest

---

[18]Joseph Fielding Smith, *Doctrines of Salvation*, ed. Bruce R. McConkie (Bookcraft, 1956), 3:83, quoted in Quinn, *Origins of Power*, 34, emphasis retained.

[19]Quinn, *Origins of Power*, 46-47.

[the] orderly evolution of Church priesthood and hierarchy."[20] *During his tenure, and before he was excommunicated, the Book of Mormon witness made other dishonest revisions.*

In May 1843 Joseph Smith – who would later be ordained King, Priest and Ruler of the Kingdom of Israel on Earth – said that, "The patriarchal office is the highest office in the church . . . ." In that same year he further reported that the power of the second Patriarchal order of the Priesthood, the keys to which had been bestowed upon the Presiding Patriarch, is "the greatest yet experienced in this Church," and the Patriarchal office is the "highest office in the [restored] church." The "second [Patriarchal] Priesthood, Abraham's patriarchal power . . ." is "the greatest yet experienced in this Church." After describing the majesty of the lineal pricsthood and the importance of the office of the Presiding Patriarch, Joseph reminded his followers that Hyrum Smith had been ordained to that office by Hyrum and Joseph's father, Joseph Sr., on Joseph Sr.'s deathbed.[21] On June 15, 1844, only days before he died, Hyrum Smith "signed an announcement as 'HYRUM SMITH, President of the Church.'"[22] That is seen to show just how important the Patriarchal Priesthood had by then become. Joseph Smith had "publicly designated his brother as his successor,"[23] about one year earlier, in July 1843. In 1844 the Apostles were forced to acknowledge that the Patriarch outranked them.[24] "Rank-and-file Mormons understood that Hyrum Smith, as patriarch, presided over the church with his brother."[25] The *Times and Seasons* reported in October 1843 "that Joseph and Hyrum Smith acted jointly as 'Presidents of the Church of Jesus Christ of Latter Day Saints.'"[26]

---

[20]Ibid., 48.

[21]Minutes of the meeting of Joseph Smith, Hyrum Smith, James Adams, Newel K. Whitney, et al., 27 March 1843, LDS Archives. The *History of the Church* (5:411), prepared after the prophet's death and during the reign of Brigham Young "omits the statement about Hyrum's patriarchal office." (*cf* Quinn, *Origins of Power*, 213, 425 n 144).

[22]Quinn, *Origins of Power*, 213.

[23]Ibid., 55.

[24]D. Michael Quinn, *The Mormon Hierarchy: Extensions of Power* (Salt Lake City: Signature Books in association with Smith Research Associates, 1997), 116.

[25]Quinn, *Origins of Power*, 53.

[26]Ibid., 56.

Joseph Sr.'s brother, "Uncle" John Smith, Brigham's patriarch after the death of Joseph and the excommunication of Joseph Smith's brother William Smith (another Smith patriarch), was a favored and dependable figure in Brigham's eyes. "Uncle" John was sustained as the "Patriarch over the whole Church of Jesus Christ of Latter Day Saints" at a general conference in October 1848. In that he held the keys to the patriarchal (Abrahamic) second order of the priesthood. "In the presentation of officers he stood next to the First Presidency. Until his death in 1854, every general conference sustained the Patriarch ahead of the Twelve, which was consistent with the patriarchal ranking before Joseph Smith's death."[27] On January 1, 1849, Uncle John was actually ordained to the office he had filled (since 1845) and to which he was sustained in 1848. Joseph Jr.'s uncle was the Patriarch. He held the "keys" to the office in much the same way that Joseph Jr., Joseph Sr., and Hyrum had previously done, each in his time; he was a "Presiding officer over this [the Patriarchal] Priesthood." He was ordained by Brigham Young – who trusted him to be "a Counsilor to thy Brethren" – before the office started its prolonged descent in the hands of less respected successors. *Uncle John was a member of the First Presidency* like Joseph Sr. and Hyrum, "who served simultaneously as church patriarchs and members of the First Presidency."[28]

The Reign of "Uncle" John

Although he didn't rock the boat like his nephew William Smith, Uncle John understood that he enjoyed a powerful lineage-based authority, like Joseph Jr., Joseph Sr., Hyrum (and William). "On 20 September 1853 John Smith [without first seeking permission] laid his hands on the head of his son, Apostle George A. Smith: 'I also seal upon you,' he said, all the Keys of the Patriarchal Priesthood that ever was sealed upon any man on Earth. In John's view, George A. Smith was now his ordained successor as Presiding Patriarch." He reasoned there was no plane of dissection between *his* patriarchal office and *the* Patriarchal Priesthood. By this

---

[27]Quinn, *Extensions of Power*, 117.
[28]Ibid.

independent exercise of patriarchal power, Uncle John understood:
1) that he held "all the Keys of the Patriarchal Priesthood that ever
was sealed upon any man on Earth"; 2) that the Presiding Patriarch
was "the Presiding officer over this [Patriarchal] Priesthood"; and
3) that there were "three grand orders of priesthood." Uncle John
supposed that he was acting within his lineage-based separate
authority, according to the keys he had received, when he ordained
George A. Smith to be his successor as the Presiding Patriarch.

Brigham Young didn't accept the otherwise dependable Uncle
John's death-bed request (although he much later named Apostle
George A. Smith to be one of his counselors in the First Presidency).
Young perceived that by allowing the Patriarch to name his
successor "independent of the First Presidency and Quorum of the
Twelve Apostles," he put the authority of his own office at risk. He
now decreed that the patriarchal order (whether ordained or not)
was subordinate to the Melchizedek order of the apostolate. Not
part of (as Boyd K. Packer later opined) but subordinate to "the
Melchizedek order of the apostolate." William Smith, who briefly
held the Grand Office (after the violent death of his brothers, and
before he was excommunicated), and before the reign of "Uncle"
John, was the first Presiding Patriarch to be ordained by apostolic
authority.

Despite his fondness for Uncle John (he of the noble birthright),
Brigham Young, himself a usurper, worried about the patriarchal
precedent. "Since Patriarch John Smith had been sustained ahead
of the apostles at general conferences since 1847, Young and others
feared that his patrilineally-ordained son or grandson might
someday claim an unbroken chain of authority back to Joseph
Smith that would bypass and conceivably supersede the Twelve's
own authority." That seemed to be a faithful interpretation of
Joseph's own stated understanding of the Patriarch's hereditary
entitlement. In order to protect the Presidency and most of the
Apostles (who were un-Smiths) from the lineal authority of the
heirs of Joseph Smith, "Young ignored George A. Smith's
patrilineal ordination and instead selected John Smith, oldest son of
the martyred Hyrum,"[29] to fill the patriarchal office.

---

[29]Ibid., 118.

The Reign of "Second" John

In the twentieth century and on October 17, 1901, Joseph F. Smith had John Smith, the second John Smith and the then Presiding Patriarch, set him apart as Church president. In November 1901, before a special conference voted for him as Church president, Joseph F. Smith "proposed that ["Uncle" John's successor, Joseph Smith Jr.'s nephew, Hyrum Smith's oldest son and Joseph F. Smith's half-brother] John [who served in the office of Patriarch from 1855 until 1911] be presented before the Twelve in the listing of officers." In support of that long forgotten precedent (which had been the established rule until 1855), and in further support of the preeminence of the office of the Patriarch and his Patriarchal Priesthood, President Joseph F. Smith counseled the congregation "that the correct procedure was to sustain the Presiding Patriarch ahead of the church president." Although "Second" John was awkward and undistinguished, his benefactor, Joseph F. Smith, sought in various ways through him "to reassert the administrative power of the patriarch"[30] – in this case the authority of his own half-brother. "President Smith let the public know he regarded the patriarch as higher in authority than the counselors in the First Presidency." And in 1902 he had the Presiding Patriarch sustained as a "prophet, seer, and revelator."[31] This was all about the Smiths, their sons and their power. Joseph F. Smith had forty-five children (plus five he adopted), including many sons. This was about them.

Despite his misuse of alcohol and tobacco, in the face of an unremarkable career, and although he was a reluctant polygamist, "Second" John was allowed to preside as the Presiding Patriarch over the quorum of patriarchs "of the whole church."[32] Joseph F. Smith was determined "to sustain the patriarch before the Twelve." "Thus Joseph F. Smith encouraged patriarchal views once promoted by William Smith and repudiated by Brigham Young."

---

[30]Ibid., 122.

[31]Ibid., 123.

[32]In that office, in addition to presiding over the Quorum of the Patriarchs, he sometimes appointed local patriarchs and gave patriarchal blessings. "[T]hough having two wives, he lived entirely with one." (Quinn, *Extensions of Power*, 123, 121). In 1886, John Smith had asked permission "to divorce his plural wife" in consequence of which he (the patriarch) was "debared the privileges of the Temple." (Ibid., 121).

This twentieth-century Joseph put the monarchical order (the divine rights of the Smiths) above the interests of the Twelve and the First Presidency. Because of opposition, including the humble Patriarch's own "anxiety" over the restoration of that earlier precedent, in the end it didn't occur.[33]

The Decline of the Patriarch and his Priesthood

The Presiding Patriarch enjoyed a prominent if contentious place in the restored Church most of the time for more than a hundred years. The preservation of the Smiths' hereditary entitlements caused friction between the Patriarchs, the First Presidency and the Quorum of the Twelve. The Smiths' lineal priesthood had no counterpart in the gospel church, or in the Nephite church in the Book of Mormon.[34] The relationship of the Patriarchs with the hierarchy was complicated and fractious. The children of the noble birthright had sometimes been so bold (consider the ordination of George A. Smith, then the claims of William Smith) as to contend that their power was independent of that of the First Presidency and the Quorum of the Twelve. They held what Joseph Jr. termed the "highest office in the Church" and the second grand "order" of the priesthood, "Abraham's Patriarchal power." Under Brigham and some of his successors, the "greatest [power] yet experienced in this Church" came under attack.

President Heber J. Grant (although sealed to Joseph Smith Jr., his mother's eternal consort) depreciated the duties and powers of the Presiding Patriarch ("second John's" successors), which included a claim to patrilineal succession. On President Grant's twentieth-century watch, the office went vacant for more than a decade. After fits and starts, Grant changed the patriarchal line in 1942, directing it now to the descendants of President Joseph F. Smith, its faithful and ardent advocate. Grant installed President Joseph F.

---

[33]Ibid., 122, 123.
[34]RLDS Apostle Jason Briggs rudely dismissed the Patriarchal Priesthood. The office of Patriarch was "a wart upon the ecclesiastical tree," he said, "unknown in the Bible, or Book of Mormon." (Doug Gibson, "The last years of William B. Smith, a mix of persistent hope and pity," *Standard Examiner* [Ogden, Utah, 21 May 2014]).

Smith's namesake grandson (the son of another Hyrum, Apostle Hyrum M. Smith) and a nephew of Joseph Fielding Smith in the patriarchal office.

The new Patriarch started with a flurry. After receiving the treasured second anointing with his wife in 1943 (a coveted blessing and a high point in what became a rather short career), his initial good fortune was followed by a nasty reversal in the form of a period of incapacitation because of an injury, the consequences of which continued into the summer of 1946. In July of 1946, "the hierarchy was stunned to learn that Patriarch Joseph F. Smith was homosexual." It was discovered that the Patriarch was having a homosexual relationship with another Latter-day Saint man. Those whose genders were considered to be confused were objects of derision in the kingdom of God in the 1940s, and still today. At conference in October 1946, Joseph F. Smith was released from his position as Patriarch on the pretext of "ill health."[35] What followed was the continued multiyear descent of the office of the Presiding Patriarch and the power of the Patriarchal Priesthood. The office of the Presiding Patriarch was vacated ("discontinued") in 1979. Abraham's Patriarchal Priesthood, the second grand supposed eternal "order" of the priesthood, and the office of the Presiding Patriarch, the "greatest" office in the "restored" Church, bought the farm in 1979.

"A GLARING ERROR OF TRANSLITERATION MADE CORPOREAL"[36]

Elias and Elijah

"The name 'Elijah' occurs in its Hebrew form (in the King James translation) only in the Old Testament, over sixty times." The name Elias, "Elijah" in its Greek form, "occurs thirty times in the King James New Testament," but not once in the Old Testament. Old Testament Elijah (Hebrew) is New Testament Elias (Greek). "At Romans 11:2-3, Paul quotes 'Elias' with the words of Elijah from 1

---

[35]Quinn, *Extensions of Power*, 127-28.
[36]Brown, "The Prophet Elias Puzzle," *Dialogue,* vol. 39 no. 3 (Fall 2006), 1.

Kings 19:14."[37]   The Apostle Paul's innocent clarification unencumbered by any desperate agenda is definitive. There is no prophet by the Greek name of Elias associated with Abraham or any other patriarch in the Old Testament. The name does not appear there. The King James Bible and mainstream Christianity do not recognize an Old Testament "Elias" and do not bifurcate Elijah (Hebrew) from Elias (Greek). This foundational error is not to be dismissed by imaginative sophistry and bombast. Joseph Smith, while making a big mistake, decided that Christianity's Old Testament Elijah and the King James Bible's New Testament Elias were two different identifiable entities.

"Most modern translations of the New Testament use the Hebrew version of the name ('Elijah') instead of the Greek 'Elias' in order to avoid confusion and to emphasize that these two names refer to the same Old Testament prophet." For a blind-sided Joseph Smith, who wasn't the philologist he thought that he was, "the Greek name referred to one prophet and the Hebrew name referred to another."[38] The issue is just that simple. All the preposterous apologia that has grown up around this stunning discrepancy is intended to protect the uninspired prophet, and his thoroughly confused Lord, from the consequences of a colossal shared mistake. "This seemingly pluripotent Elijah is shadowed by a doppelganger in the angelic tumult of early Mormonism named Elias, the King James rendering of the Greek transliteration of the prophet's Hebrew name."[39] The name was never supposed to have given rise to complicated theology. The case unfolds as follows: "Joseph Smith was simply ignorant of the fact that the King James New Testament uses the Greek version of Old Testament names." That was an exceedingly meaningful mistake, a blow sufficient to sink any ship. The true message of the canonized bifurcation of Elijah, a glaring foundational error impervious to revision and at odds with traditional Christianity and biblical scholarship, may be simply

---

[37]Richard Packham, "Elijah and Elias" in "A Linguist Looks at Mormonism: Notes on linguistics problems in Mormonism" (first published April 20, 2003; last revised March 2, 2011; accessed 15 January 2014), available from http://packham. n4m.org/linguist.htm; Internet, p. 10 of 36.

[38]Ibid., emphasis retained.

[39]Brown, "The Prophet Elias Puzzle," *Dialogue*, vol. 39 no. 3 (Fall 2006), 1.

stated: "Joseph made up shit."[40] Occam's razor applies.[41]

The Mission of Elijah

In and after 1835 Joseph Smith and his equally bewildered Lord introduced a sixth and then a seventh heavenly messenger to the dicey subject of priesthood.   In addition to Moroni, John the Baptist, then Peter, James, and John, Smith now identified two additional messengers, Elias and Elijah.   Among the many backdated (falsified) alterations to Section 27 of the Doctrine and Covenants – "[t]he prior ordination of Joseph Smith, Jun., and Oliver Cowdery to the Apostleship avowed . . ."[42] – Joseph's Lord reports that Elias and Elijah, two separate persons, will soon join other earlier visitors with other important "keys" essential to the restoration. This demonstrably altered revision of Chapter 28 of the 1833 Book of Commandments, which didn't mention Elias or Elijah in the Book or in the manuscript, fails to account for the fact that "Elijah" and "Elias" are different names for the same prophet. Smith and Cowdery now claim two different visitations from Elias and Elijah – two separate identifiable entities, one after the other – behind the veil in the Kirtland temple. Joseph's Lord anticipated this monumental error in Section 50 of the 1835 edition of the Doctrine and Covenants. In Section 27, the successor to Section 50, the Lord (who thinks just like Joseph) changed course to confidently report that he had previously "committed the keys of bringing to pass the restoration of all things spoken by the mouth of all the holy prophets since the world began, concerning the last days" to the prophet Elias.[43]   Joseph's Lord then proceeds to further say that he has "committed the keys of the power of turning the hearts of the fathers to the children, and the hearts of the children to the fathers" to Elijah (a second and separate messenger), "that the whole earth may not be smitten with a

---

[40]Anonymous Informant (Internet).
[41]A scientific and philosophic rule that requires "that the simplest of competing theories be preferred . . . ."
[42]Doctrine and Covenants (1957), Section 27, Headnote.
[43]Ibid., 27:6.

curse."[44] This is difficult subject matter and these are stupendous mistakes. Foundational mistakes impervious to facile revision.

The unsettling provisions, like so much else, do not appear in the only manuscript of the revelation (Chapter 28 of the 1833 Book of Commandments) and were not published until they found a place in the first edition of the Doctrine and Covenants in 1835. "Not until 1835 did original Mormon documents describe a role of Elijah [or Elias] in the restoration of authority. The Book of Commandments referred only once to Elijah 'which should come' and made no connection to priesthood restoration (BofC 76; D&C 35:4)."[45] The last verse of a less than chronological Old Testament did not refer to some impersonal "which" ("which should come"). "Behold, I will send you Elijah the prophet," it said, "before the coming of the great and dreadful day of the Lord. And *he* shall turn the heart of the fathers to the children, and the heart of the children to their fathers, lest I come and smite the earth with a curse."[46]

Elias is separated from Elijah in Mormonism, but not in traditional Christianity. Efforts by apologists to ameliorate the harmful effects of the prophet's catastrophic transliteration mistake are awkward and complicated. In the Doctrine and Covenants, Smith presented Elijah and Elias as separate identifiable persons (D&C 27, D&C 110). Doctrine and Covenants 110:12-13 has become, for Latter-day Saints, an epic account of monumental events. It is a foundational narrative. *"After this [a vision of Moses which followed a vision of Christ], Elias appeared and committed the dispensation of the gospel of Abraham . . . ."* [47] *"After this vision [the vision of Elias] had closed . . . Elijah the prophet . . . stood before us . . . ."*[48]

---

[44]Ibid., 27:9.

[45]Quinn, *Origins of Power*, 35.

[46]Malachi 4:5-6, emphasis added.

[47]Ibid., 110:12, emphasis added. In 1832 Joseph Smith committed another monumental error when he also referred to Isaiah and Esaias, Hebrew and Greek names for Isaiah, "separately." (Brown, "The Prophet Elias Puzzle," *Dialogue*, vol. 39 no. 3 [Fall 2006], 3). Joseph's Isaiah error, and another reference to Elias as a separate person, is found uncorrected in the 76th Section of the Doctrine and Covenants. B.H. Roberts (the "Defender of the Faith") saw this error (in the days of his faith) and tried to correct the problem (two Isaiahs identified like the two Elijahs as separate persons with different names) "in his redaction of the revelation . . . ." (Ibid.). Speaking of the glory of the telestial world, Smith and Rigdon simultaneously reported that "these are they who are of David, and of Apollos, and

Joseph's Mistakes

"For early Mormons, Elijah shouldered a burdensome mission . . . ."   He oversaw "LDS temple rites."   Elijah is the messenger supposed to have integrated "the human family into an organic whole, sealing up personal relationships against death."[49]   Smith and Jesus are supposed to have told those interested in the Mormon world that Elias *and* Elijah, two entirely different persons, visited the earth for disparate reasons at different times.   Joseph Smith perpetuated this mistake on yet another occasion in yet a different way: "[I] preached," he said, "on the subject of the spirit of Elias/Elijah, and Mesiah clearly defining the offices of the 3 personages."[50]

D. Michael Quinn appears to ignore the separate "Elias" (and Joseph's colossal mistake) in his thoughtful discussion of the origins of the three different orders of the priesthood. In a book of nearly seven hundred pages (according to the index, "Elias, 625"), there is but one sparing reference to the Lord's important "Elias." In a single sentence on page 625, that only-indexed but unavoidable reference simply says, "*3 Apr. [1836] Smith and Cowdery see Jesus and receive priesthood keys from Moses, Elias, and Elijah in the Kirtland temple.*"[51] What Quinn may have seemed to ignore, Joseph at least at first seemed keen to report: ". . . I retired to the pulpit [in the Kirtland Temple], the veils being dropped, and bowed myself, with Oliver Cowdery, in solemn and silent prayer."[52] "After this

---

of Cephas." In that, Mormonism's founders now proceeded to bifurcate Isaiah. The erroneous provisions in this important revelation read as follows:

> *These are they who say they are some of one and some of another – some of Christ and some of John, and some of Moses, and some of Elias [the Greek name for Elijah], and some of Esaias [the Greek name for Isaiah], and some of Isaiah [the Hebrew name for Isaiah], and some of Enoch.* [Doctrine and Covenants 76:100, emphasis added].

[48]Doctrine and Covenants, 110:13, emphasis added.

[49]Brown, "The Prophet Elias Puzzle," *Dialogue*, vol. 39 no. 3 (Fall 2006), 1.

[50]Scott Faulring, *An American Prophet's Record: The Diaries and Journals of Joseph Smith* (Salt Lake City: Signature Books and Smith Research Associates, 1987), 458, quoted in Brown, "The Prophet Elias Puzzle," *Dialogue*, vol. 39 no. 3 (Fall 2006), 1.

[51]Quinn, *Origins of Power*, 625, emphasis added.

[52]Doctrine and Covenants 110, Headnote.

[Moses had just appeared "and committed unto us the keys of the gathering of Israel . . ."], Elias appeared and committed the dispensation of the gospel of Abraham ["Abraham's Patriarchal power"] . . . . After this vision [of Elias] had closed, another great and glorious vision burst upon us; for Elijah the prophet, who was taken to heaven without tasting death, stood before us, and said: 'Behold, the time has fully come, which was spoken of by the mouth of Malachi – testifying that he [Elijah] should be sent, before the great and dreadful day of the Lord come – To turn the hearts of the fathers to the children, and the children to the fathers, lest the whole earth be smitten with a curse –.'"[53] Elias brought the keys to the Abrahamic Priesthood to the service of the Smiths. Elijah brought the sealing power to oversee the temple rites.

D. Michael Quinn:

> In 1836 the ancient prophet Elijah [Elias isn't separately mentioned] appeared to Smith and Cowdery, by which angelic ministration "the keys of this dispensation are committed into your hands" (D&C 110:13-16) [the separate vision of Elias is described a verse away in Doctrine and Covenants 110:12: "After this {after their vision of the Lord and Moses}, Elias appeared, and committed the dispensation of the gospel of Abraham . . ."]. Two years later [in a history that wasn't publicly reported until six years later] Smith dictated an official history which for the first time revealed what the angel Moroni had told him about Elijah in 1823: "Behold I will reveal unto you the Priesthood, by the hand of Elijah the prophet, before the coming of the great and dreadful day of the Lord."[54]

It would seem that by 1842 (the year the "official history" was finally published), it had occurred to Smith that he had made a mistake by bifurcating Elijah. Now Smith would like to make it appear that but one messenger, not two, restored but one authority,

---

[53]Ibid., 110:11-15.
[54]Roberts, ed., *History of The Church of Jesus Christ of Latter-day Saints*, 1:12, quoted by Quinn, *Origins of Power*, 35.

not two very different authorities, as the earlier revelation dated 1836 led everyone who read it to suppose. Quinn correctly perceives that the very use of the word "Priesthood" in "Moroni's promise" dates Joseph's questionable correction (the expectation of "*the* Priesthood," a unitary authority), "by the hand of Elijah" (a promise supposedly made in 1823 but not publicly reported until 1842) to sometime after 1830. "The Book of Mormon used only the phrase 'the High Priesthood,' whereas 'the priesthood' as a generic phrase did not enter Mormon use until 1831."[55] Quinn now further described Moroni's previously unreported assertion as evidence of a new process invented to create the more convenient assimilation of anachronisms. "Without finances to produce a new edition [of the Doctrine and Covenants], Smith added to his 1838 history [first published in 1842] a previously unknown 1823 revelation about Elijah and the priesthood, thereby simplifying the process of retroactive additions to previous revelations."[56] Joseph had the "finances to produce" an 1835 edition of the Doctrine and Covenants. This revelation supposed to have been received in 1823 was clearly not included there. Nor either in the Book of Commandments published in 1833.

The Significance of Elias and Elijah

With the passage of time, an unbifurcated Elijah, fortified by the consolidation of functions (Elias' and Elijah's functions), temporarily supplanted Peter, James, and John as one questionable assumption surrendered to another. "From 1839 to his death in 1844 Smith's sermons [taking a different tack] emphasized Elijah as restorer of supreme priesthood authority." This may serve to explain the disconcerting ambiguity that still today surrounds the "vague and contradictory" account of the underreported mission of Peter, James, and John. Elijah held "the keys of the authority to administer in all the ordinances of the Priesthood . . . . During these last five years Smith invoked Elijah's restoration of priesthood keys as the authority for essential ordinances for the living and the

---

[55]George Reynolds, *A Complete Concordance of the Book of Mormon*, 565, and Gregory A. Prince, *Having Authority*, 27-28, quoted in Quinn, *Origins of Power*, 35, 292 fn 169.

[56]Quinn, *Origins of Power*, 35.

dead." By that to say "baptism, the 'Holy Order,' preliminary anointing and endowment, the sealing of marriage for eternity, and the second anointing."[57] In the face of this now unbifurcated Elijah's awkward emergence, "Peter, James and John had disappeared from Smith's emphasis on priesthood restoration."[58] And the Lord's important Elias now also disappeared from this now reconstituted equation. Gregory A. Prince, a distinguished Mormon scholar, reported that, "By the time of Smith's death, Elijah's position in Restoration theology [Elias is the forgotten messenger] was second only to that of Jesus Christ."[59] Quinn, while accepting Prince's insight, added this: "That assessment [Prince's assessment] needs to be qualified only with respect to the corresponding elevation of Adam during the same period."[60]

Joseph Smith taught his followers that, "The Priesthood was first given to Adam . . . ." According to Smith, "whenever the Gospel is sent," the keys had to come from heaven. Thus the "keys" to the Patriarchal Priesthood (assigned to Smith and Cowdery by Elias) had needed to come from heaven. Conversely, the authority to "discontinue" the Patriarchal Priesthood couldn't come from earth. When the priesthood keys are revealed because the gospel is sent, it is by Adam's authority.[61] Joseph's Lord credits a literal Adam as the source of the power to act for God. "After presenting this expanded understanding of the role of Adam, Smith announced that Adam [like Nephi, Moroni, John the Baptist, Peter, James, and John, Moses, Elias, Elijah, Jesus, "many angels" and others] had appeared to him as one of the divine messengers of the restoration." Quinn concluded that Michael (meaning Adam) "probably appeared to Smith in June 1830 [after the Church has officially

---

[57]Roberts, ed., *History of The Church of Jesus Christ of Latter-day Saints*, 6:183-84, 249-52, quoted in Quinn, *Origins of Power*, 35-36.

[58]Quinn, *Origins of Power*, 35-36.

[59]Gregory A. Prince, *Having Authority*, 81 and 65-76, quoted in Quinn, *Origins of Power*, 36. Quinn has called Prince "[t]he most incisive interpreter of Elijah's significance . . . ." Prince noted that "this Old Testament prophet [Elijah] 'eclipsed' the importance of Peter, James, and John."

[60]Quinn, *Origins of Power*, 36.

[61]Joseph Fielding Smith, comp., *Teachings of the Prophet Joseph Smith* (Salt Lake City: Deseret News Press, 1938), 157; Ehat and Cook, *Words of Joseph Smith*, 8, quoted in Quinn, *Origins of Power*, 36.

formed and], just before the priesthood restoration by Peter, James, and John."[62]

"After Smith's death, Brigham Young spent thirty years elaborating the role of Adam in what is commonly known as the Adam-God doctrine."[63] Adam, "the only God with whom we have to do," was, according to Brigham Young, the ultimate source of the power to act for God on this particular earth. After Smith's death, Peter, James, and John resurged. They re-eclipsed Elijah (and the increasingly forgettable Elias) as actors in the authority-principle equation, probably because of the great transliteration discrepancy. Peter, James, and John were not as threatening to Brigham Young and his successors as Elias and Elijah, and "the dispensation of Abraham." Mormon leaders ignored Elias and Elijah, separate identifiable figures, and the revelatory origins of hereditary entitlement.

The Prophet Elias Puzzle

The persona of the prophet formerly known as Elias, a person somehow said to have been associated with Abraham and the Patriarchs, now became almost mystical, a little of this and a little of that, almost everything to nearly everyone. Defenders of the faith have come to call that resurrected heavenly messenger "The Spirit and Doctrine of Elias" come to prepare the world for some greater work, or the "Elias of the Restoration" "come to restore all things," or just another name for Jesus or John the Baptist. The name of Elias has come to denote some kind of code word for a messenger as perplexed apologists desperately attempting to ameliorate Joseph's phenomenal error have allowed themselves to suppose. In early Mormon theology, Elias was a patriarch, an ancient personage who had deep Old Testament roots and a Greek name.

In a society uncommonly "notable for a proliferation of angels," one historian reports that perhaps the most important is Elijah, "the biblical patriarch who ascended living to heaven . . . as a reward for

---

[62]Quinn, *Origins of Power*, 36.
[63]Ibid.

exemplary faithfulness."[64] Elijah was a man of his Old Testament time. He was also Elias. Old Testament Elijah and New Testament Elias were the same person. Without Elijah, Elias had no separate biblical provenance. Elias wasn't a second Moses, or a "Wandering Jew," or "the harbinger of the coming Messiah." He didn't raise the dead. He wasn't with Adam in "the Garden of Eden . . . ." He didn't visit Zacharias and wasn't present at the transfiguration of Christ. He wasn't "an Elias" or "a term for Christianity," or another name for "Moroni," or one of "the founding fathers." He wasn't a power or a concept or a code; he was a person. He wasn't a "which"; he was a whom. By the misuse of preposterous insinuations, Mormonism and its scholars have probed the limits of ingenuity in their efforts to identify "a mysterious Elias" with every one and every thing but a bifurcated "Elijah."

"Writers from within Mormonism have historically focused, with precedent in the Prophet's teachings, on a 'Spirit of Elias' borne by various angelic ministrants while positing the [separate] existence of a minor but essentially unknown prophet actually named Elias who stays away from center stage."[65] Bruce R. McConkie, the author of *Mormon Doctrine*, described Elias as a "composite personage" having both a name and a title, and compared him to John the Baptist. McConkie ignored almost everything obvious in a futile effort to try and explain Joseph and Oliver's unprovenanced patriarchal personage. Perhaps he was a prophet of Abraham's time. Perhaps he was the "spirit" or "doctrine" of that undocumented Old Testament prophet (a Hebrew with a Greek name). Maybe he was "Abraham." Maybe he was "Melchizedek." Maybe he was "The Greek form of Elijah." And maybe he was just some one or some thing preparing for some one or some thing to come, say "The Elias of the Restoration," or the angel Gabriel. And maybe he was just a mistake, Joseph Smith's colossal mistake, a prophet defeating foundational error repeatedly referenced in sacred texts that cannot be changed.

Richard Packham puts McConkie's far from persuasive wide-ranging perplexities in context. Which explanation, he wonders, "makes sense and is more likely the case?" McConkie's Elias "is a

---

[64]Brown, "The Prophet Elias Puzzle," *Dialogue,* vol. 39 no. 3 (Fall 2006), 1.
[65]Ibid.

hitherto unknown prophet of Abraham's time, with a Greek name, or maybe Abraham himself, or Melchizedek, or Gabriel – who is also Noah – and Christ, and Elijah, and John the Baptist, and John the Revelator, and a 'spirit or doctrine.'" Is that what scholars must now purport to present, or is "the more obvious conclusion that Joseph Smith was simply ignorant of the fact that the King James New Testament uses the Greek version of Old Testament names"?[66] "These creative solutions have been a response to incredulous critics who see . . . a chink in the armor of Joseph Smith's seerhood."[67] Is it to be wondered in the face of such a stunning array of less than impressive possibilities that one modern scholar "has identified Elias as a spirit not unlike the Holy Ghost rather than simply a prophetic aegis"?[68] Critics have seen the "Elijah-Elias bifurcation" as "emblematic of Smith's imaginative if inaccurate appropriation of the biblical lexicon."[69] There can be no debate over whether or not this Mormon "Elias" is a separate personage; he is. There can be no debate over whether or not "Elias" is the Greek name for "Elijah"; it is. "The Prophet Elias Puzzle" is nothing more than "a glaring error of transliteration made corporeal."[70]

SUMMARY

The twenty-first century Church has reversed course, *two* no longer equals *three*. In this twenty-first century, *three* now equals *two* yet once again. Although there are local patriarchs, the modern Church has closed the door on "three grand orders of the priesthood," on the "greatest office in the Church," and on "the greatest [power] yet experienced." Abraham's Patriarchal Priesthood, Mormonism's "second" priesthood, Joseph Jr., Joseph Sr., Hyrum, William, "Uncle" John and "Second" John's supposed hereditary entitlement, has simply disappeared. It was abandoned

---

[66]Packham, "Elijah and Elias" in "A Linguist Looks at Mormonism" (last revised 2 March 2011), 10-11 of 37.

[67]Brown, "The Prophet Elias Puzzle," *Dialogue,* vol. 39 no. 3 (Fall 2006), 2.

[68]Steven Davis, "But I Say unto You, Who Is Elias?" paper in the electronic possession of Samuel Brown, described in "The Prophet Elias Puzzle," *Dialogue,* vol. 39 no. 3 (Fall 2006), 6 fn 40.

[69]Brown, "The Prophet Elias Puzzle," *Dialogue,* vol. 39 no. 3 (Fall 2006), 1.

[70]Ibid., 2.

and is dismissed. There is no eternal lineal authority left to be passed from father to son, from Adam to Abraham to Moses to Noah, and then to the Smiths. There is no mystical priesthood said to belong "to the literal descendants of the chosen seed." To those who "have been hid from the world with Christ in God."

No Smith descendant continues to serve as the "first patriarch of the church," or to preside over the other patriarchs, as one of them did most of the time from the early 1830s until 1979. "Abraham's Patriarchal power" was supposed to have been conferred upon Joseph Smith and Oliver Cowdery behind the veil in the Kirtland Temple on April 3, 1836, as part of a series of events that mimicked the Transfiguration of Christ. The keys to the Patriarchal Priesthood are not often mentioned now. Most Latter-day Saints know next to nothing about the Patriarchal Priesthood. The use of the personal name "Elias" is not an object of modern emphasis. Who presumes to inherit "lineal priesthood [with or] without ordination"? Who is supposed to possess "the priesthood at birth"? The Patriarchal Priesthood, the once presumed historical authority of the patriarchs and high priests, has been jettisoned by the modern Church without the consent of the members, or the explicit approval of the modern Mormon God.

No Presiding Patriarch is a member of the First Presidency. No Presiding Patriarch is sustained before the Quorum of the Twelve, or given the title "Prophet, Seer and Revelator," or asked to ordain the President of the Church. Hyrum Smith, who succeeded Joseph Sr. as the Patriarch, was able to say that he was the President of the Church. No modern patriarch is given a chair between the prophet and the First Presidency and the Quorum of the Twelve Apostles. There is no Presiding Patriarch, and no patriarch outranks the Quorum. Jesus did not establish a lineal monarch-like inherited authority contingent upon some predestined notion of royal birth. Not on April 3, 1836, or any time later. Mormonism's Patriarchal Priesthood was part of a late design. It was created, not restored. It wasn't eternal, could be changed and hasn't survived.

"Elias," a prophet with a Greek name, wasn't an Old Testament prophet at or about the time of Abraham and didn't appear to Joseph Smith and Oliver Cowdery in the Kirtland temple before

Elijah did to present the keys of "Abraham's Patriarchal power." Because "Elias" was "Elijah." "Elias" was the Greek name given to "Elijah" by the translators of the Greek manuscripts that became the New Testament part of the King James Bible. The New Testament translation of the King James version of the English Bible involved the interpretation of Greek manuscripts. Joseph Smith, and the Lord for whom he said he spoke, declared that "Elijah" was "Elijah" and "Elias" was "Elias," describing just one prophet as two separate identifiable entities, and then said that both of them appeared to him, after Jesus and Moses appeared to him, as separate persons in the Kirtland Temple. That humiliating mistake has caused smart men defending deceit to promote foolish and dishonest arguments in defense of the faith.

CHAPTER FOURTEEN

Insights

Upon you my fellow servants, in the name of Messiah, I confer this priesthood and this authority, which shall remain upon earth that the sons of Levi may yet offer an offering unto the Lord in righteousness.

John the Baptist to Oliver Cowdery and Joseph
Smith (Cowdery and Smith reporting), 1834

Upon you my fellow servants, in the name of Messiah, I confer the Priesthood of Aaron which holds the keys of the ministering of angels, and of the gospel of repentance, and of baptism by immersion for the remission of sins; and this shall never be taken again from the earth, until the sons of Levi do offer again an offering unto the Lord in righteousness.

John the Baptist to Oliver Cowdery and
Joseph Smith (Smith reporting), 1842

DISCREPANCIES

Joseph described "the reception of *the* holy Priesthood by the ministring of Aangels" in his controversial 1832 History (uncovered in 1965). That early History "of his marvilous experience and of all the mighty acts which he doeth in the name of Jesus Christ" didn't mention John the Baptist, Peter, James, and John, Elijah, Elias, Aaron, Melchizedek, Abraham or separate orders of priesthood. What Joseph said that he received in an account prepared more than three years after "1829 – May, June" was "*the* high Priesthood after *the* holy order of the son of the living God" and "the Kees of the Kingdom of God . . ."[1]. Joseph Smith was still talking about *the* unitary priesthood in 1832, long after John the Baptist and Peter, James, and John were supposed to have separately conferred dual priesthoods of different ranks upon the society's founders before the Church was officially formed.

In Smith's one hundred-and-thirty-three-year suppressed 1832 History (the earliest known and only holographic account of the First Vision of the "crucifyed" Lord), Smith reported that he received "*the* holy Priesthood by the ministring of Aangels." This "strange account" was prepared nearly a year-and-a-half after the Fourth Conference of the Church at Kirtland, Ohio, in June 1831, that unruly assembly where several of the elders, including Smith, were said to have received "the authority of the Melchizedek Priesthood" for the "first time."[2] "At the June conference, the word 'priesthood' was used and priesthood was bestowed as if in addition to previous authority."[3] By that perhaps it is meant to say unitary higher authority added to unitary lower authority, but still and all but one undivided authority. "By later definitions only the Melchizedek priesthood was 'the Holy Priesthood.' (D&C 84:25-27)."[4] Those "later definitions," seen to have separated a generic unitary lower order of authority from some kind of separate higher authority, didn't seem to apply before September 1832 (when Doctrine and Covenants 84 – which was not made public until 1835 – is supposed to have been received). Joseph Smith's 1832 History, which described unitary "Priesthood" and which was concealed and suppressed in the archives of the Church for several lifetimes, was not made public ("brought to light") until 1965.

---

[1]Joseph Smith Jr., *The Personal Writings of Joseph Smith*, ed. Dean C. Jessee (Salt Lake City: Deseret Book, 1984), 4, emphasis added.

[2]Richard Lyman Bushman, with the assistance of Jed Woodworth, *Joseph Smith: Rough Stone Rolling* (New York: Alfred A. Knopf, 2005), 158.

[3]Ibid.

[4]D. Michael Quinn, *The Mormon Hierarchy: Origins of Power* (Salt Lake City: Signature Books in association with Smith Research Associates, 1994), 16. Doctrine and Covenants section 84, verses 25 to 27, were not published until 1835.

According to D. Michael Quinn, "[I]t is anachronistic to apply the terms Melchizedek and Aaronic to Mormon concepts of authority before 1832 and even up to 1835." Joseph's 1832 History (circa November 1832), a report which postdates the (September 1832) revelation on the Priesthood (D&C 84), fails to apply "the terms Melchizedek and Aaronic" to "the holy Priesthood," which in 1832 is a term still used to describe but one unitary authority. The 1832 Holographic Account didn't identify separate orders of priesthood, but rather once again described "*the* high Priesthood after *the* holy order of the Son of the living God . . . ."[5] In 1832, as in October 1834 ("*this* priesthood and *this* authority"), Smith identified but one "holy Priesthood" (in 1832 it was "*the* high Priesthood"). It would thus seem to appear that what he and several of the elders thought that they received at Kirtland in 1831 was additional unitary authority, not yet two separate priesthoods. Not yet something that could be said to have been identified with Melchizedek or Peter, James, and John. This sets at defiance the notion promulgated by the modern Church that Joseph Smith and Oliver Cowdery received "the Melchizedek Priesthood," the second of two separate orders of priesthood, somewhere between Harmony, Pennsylvania, and Colesville, New York, in "*1829, May-June.*"[6]

The pristine recitals protected in the unvarnished 1832 Account, untouched by revisionists until 1965 (unlike other known important early and altered documents) were not "filled with statements introduced after the dates of the original events and manuscript texts,"[7] falsified statements that retroactively identified separate priesthoods by two separate names brought by different messengers out of order and before their time. The Book of Commandments, sixty-five revelations published in 1833, did not describe "priesthood," "priesthoods," angelic ordinations, a heavenly messenger, or heavenly messengers. It associated unitary authority with ordinances that were commanded but earthbound.

---

[5]Jessee, ed., *The Personal Writings of Joseph Smith*, 4, emphasis added.

[6]*Teachings of Presidents of the Church – Joseph Smith* (Salt Lake City: The Church of Jesus Christ of Latter-day Saints, 2007), xv, emphasis added.

[7]Quinn, *Origins of Power*, 282 fn 75.

The words "Aaronic" and "Melchizedek," titles now used to differentiate multiple overlapping priesthoods, are not found in the minutes, notes or accounts of the Fourth Conference of the Church in June of 1831, or in the 1832 History in November of 1832, in the 1830 *Articles and Covenants of the Church of Christ*, in the Preface to the 1830 Book of Mormon, in the 1833 Book of Commandments, or in Oliver and Joseph's First Authorized History of the Church published in October 1834. From 1829 to 1834, then to and until 1835 (a period of about five-and-a-half to six years), the different orders of the modern Mormon priesthood were never publicly traced to angelic ordinations, John the Baptist, Peter, James, and John, Elias and Elijah. None of those alleged angelic ordination events are presently known to have been described any earlier than September or October of 1834 in any early meeting, note or journal, or in any unaltered contemporaneous account, sermon, prayer, ceremony, ordinance, blessing, diary, confirmation, history or revelation. "The *Book of Mormon* used only the phrase 'The High Priesthood,' whereas 'the Priesthood' as a generic phrase did not enter Mormon use until 1831."[8]

The 1834-35 History prepared and published by Joseph Smith and Oliver Cowdery (because it didn't mention Peter, James, and John, or Melchizedek, or John the Baptist by name, and because it did mention "*this* priesthood and *this* authority") did yet once again confirm "the idea of one priesthood [actually one "authority"] at the church's organization." When Oliver and Joseph came together to say that "we received . . . the holy priesthood" under the hands of an angel (separately identified as John the Baptist), they were talking about what no earlier than 1832, but more probably not until 1835, came to be called "the Aaronic Priesthood" while using the language ("the holy priesthood") of what even later came to be called "the Melchizedek Priesthood." There is evidence of confusion in those captions. When the angel says to Joseph and Oliver that, "I confer *this* priesthood ["we received under *his* hands *the holy priesthood*"] and *this* authority" in materials published in

---

[8]Ibid., 35.

October 1834, he is talking about unitary authority.[9] It is 1834
(long after that Fourth Conference of the Church on June 3, 1831),
and he is still talking about unitary authority. And when Joseph
talks about "the reception of *the* holy Priesthood by the ministring
of Aangels" in 1832, still and yet after that Fourth Conference of
the Church on June 3, 1831, he is still talking about unitary
authority. In that "strange account" that came to light in 1965,
Joseph reported that multiple messengers delivered one authority
at a time and place he then further failed to describe. That he then
said (in 1832) that multiple messengers delivered but one unitary
authority provides yet even further evidence of confusion. In
October 1834 Oliver and Joseph publicly retroactively altered
earlier accounts (a page of history is worth a volume of logic) in
order to say that a messenger, one messenger, delivered one
authority by means of an angelic ordination, the first angelic
ordination to be reported, in 1829. Additional messengers, as in
1832, and a second and higher authority, as in 1835, weren't then
described. In 1829 and 1830 the Mormons didn't refer to their
"authority-principle" as "priesthood," nor either as "priesthoods."
And in 1829 and 1830 they had no concept of what has since come
to be called "angelic ordination." The core principle of the modern
Church was invisible in 1829 and 1830.

Where at any time before 1834 or 1835 shall anyone find *unaltered*
contemporaneous evidence, direct or circumstantial, for the
proposition that two separate sets of messengers came at two
different times to confer two separate orders of priesthood upon
Joseph Smith and Oliver Cowdery in the spring of 1829? Where at
any time prior to 1831 (and more probably until 1834, 1835) shall a
student of the faith begin to see evidence of the distinctions between
the duties and responsibilities of two different orders of priesthood?
Where are the kinds of instructions that might be expected to
attend the divine conferral of unequal orders of authority by
heavenly messengers? Did John the Baptist say here is the lower

---

[9]Oliver Cowdery (and Joseph Smith), "Letter to W.W. Phelps, Esq." (Oliver
Cowdery and Joseph Smith's 1834-35 History), *Messenger and Advocate*, vol. 1 no.
1 (October 1834): 16, emphasis added.

"lineal priesthood of the old law," call it Aaronic, collect yourselves some tithes, ordain yourselves some elders, restore the offices of the primitive church, heal the sick, speak in tongues, cast out devils, baptize by immersion, bestow the gift of the Holy Ghost and ordain yourselves a prophet? Could any lower authority non-Melchizedek disciple – operating within the constraints of ancient Israel's law of a carnal commandment – so have said? Consider this: That is what John the Baptist had to say, if he really appeared to say anything at all, because the Church was literally organized without the power of the higher priesthood as Brigham Young, Orson Pratt and David Whitmer, undeniable insiders at the center of events, all reported at different times.

How were the differences between the Aaronic Priesthood (supposedly conferred upon Joseph and Oliver by John the Baptist) and the Melchizedek Priesthood (supposedly conferred upon Joseph and Oliver by Peter, James, and John) reflected in the administration and management of the early Church? What if anything changed in 1829 and 1830 because of the supposed occurrence of those only years later reported allegedly divine events? Or in the three or four years that followed? What if anything is seen to support the proposition that Joseph and Oliver received one authority from John the Baptist and another authority from Peter, James, and John in the spring of 1829? Or that the founders understood in 1829 that there actually were "dual priesthoods of different ranks"? Or that the founders understood on April 6, 1830, that there were "dual priesthoods of different ranks"? The after-the-fact separation of the comfortable concept of charismatic "authority" into two separate theoretically incompatible priesthoods was the awkward byproduct of falsified amendments to previously published documents, including revelations (more than a dozen of them), altered after the fact. Did Joseph and Oliver demonstrate, early on and in any meaningful way, that they understood the nature and uses of the separated powers they waited years to say that they received?

About two thousand converts had been baptized and confirmed by June of 1831 under an old and now thoroughly discredited regimen, without any subsequent effort at correction. Some of those members (including but not limited to Newel Knight, Joseph Smith, Oliver Cowdery, Lyman Wight and Sidney Rigdon) claimed that they saw or heard the Savior. Missionaries were called and blessed and sent. The early pre-priesthood power authority record purports to describe healings, the gift of tongues and interpretations, baptisms, confirmations, ordinations, blessings, visions, prophecies, dreams, revelations, exorcisms and the conferral of the gift of the Holy Ghost. While nothing seemed to be lacking before those other worldly endowments were said to have surfaced late in the life of the early Church, no one appeared to appreciate the emphatic distinctions so markedly evident and jealously guarded in the modern Church. Early Mormons, including Joseph's mother, father and siblings, most particularly Joseph's mother, father and siblings, knew nothing about those 1829 ordinations, angels and authorities. There was in respect to the authority-principle that preceded the advent of the "priesthood" in the early Church an "aversion to ranking."[10]

UNITARY PRIESTHOOD

"The first evidence [claim] of angelic restoration in public discussion comes from Cowdery [and Smith] in [about October] 1834," a mind-numbing five-and-a-half years after the great Aaronic event is now supposed to have occurred on May 15, 1829. "No mention of angelic ordinations can be found in original [unaltered] documents until 1834-35."[11] Cowdery (and Smith) described but one authority in their first "authorized" history of the Church in 1834.[12]

---

[10]Quinn, *Origins of Power*, 28.

[11]Ibid., 15, emphasis added. "Joseph Smith's 1832 history mentioned 'the reception of the holy Priesthood by the ministring of Aangels.' But he did not publish or circulate this history and gave no further details until he began an expanded narrative in 1838." (Ibid., 281 fn 71).

[12]"Letter" (Cowdery and Smith's 1834-35 History), *Messenger and Advocate*, vol. 1 no. 1 (October 1834): 15-16, emphasis added. The "holy priesthood," in modern Mormon parlance, refers to the "Holy Melchizedek Priesthood," an order

The message of the 1834 History (the Aaronic Priesthood restoration prayer) delivered by the angel and published in the "Latter Day Saints Messenger and Advocate" in October 1834 was:

> *[U]pon you my fellow servants, in the name of Messiah, I confer this priesthood and this authority, which shall remain upon earth, that the sons of Levi may yet offer an offering unto the Lord in righteousness!*[13]

The message of the 1838-39 History (the Aaronic Priesthood restoration prayer) delivered by the angel and published in the "Times and Seasons" in 1842, then added to the Doctrine and Covenants in 1876, was changed to say:

> *Upon you my fellow servants, in the name of Messiah I confer the Priesthood of Aaron which holds the keys of the ministering of angels, and of the gospel of repentance, and of baptism by immersion for the remission of sins; and this shall never be taken again from the earth, until the sons of Levi do offer again an offering unto the Lord in righteousness.*[14]

This substituted now canonized quote, describing events supposed to have occurred in 1829, was first published in the *Times and Seasons* in 1842. Joseph Smith was the editor of the *Times and Seasons* in 1842. The altered prayer only very much later became Section 13 of the 1876 edition of the Doctrine and Covenants. The unitary priesthood provision ("*this* priesthood and *this* authority") was ignored and dismissed in 1842, irrevocably changing the meaning of the Aaronic priesthood restoration prayer, the prayer first described in Oliver and Joseph's first authorized (and most contemporaneous) history of the Church in 1834. Section 13, which

---

of authority John the Baptist (by modern Mormon reckoning) lacked power to confer.

[13]Ibid., 16, emphasis added.

[14]Doctrine and Covenants 13, emphasis added.

was backdated to May 1829, as altered and falsified, is seen to have substantively reformulated John the Baptist's words to Joseph and Oliver on the occasion of their ordination to the Aaronic Priesthood on May 15, 1829, words they themselves didn't report until 1834. Section 13, which concerned events supposed to have occurred on May 15, 1829, "was omitted from" the Book of Commandments (meaning not included when sixty-five other revelations were published there four years later in 1833), and from the Doctrine and Covenants (when more than one hundred revelations were published there in 1835). The failure to include the 1842 amendments in those resources is inexplicable.

With the publication of one of the eight installments of the 1834-35 History in October 1834, Mormons learned for the first time "that a heavenly conferral of unitary authority [*this* priesthood and *this* authority"| |was supposed to have| occurred before the church's organization."[15] Before that publication, and until that History, and for five-and-a-half years, there was no heavenly messenger, and there was no angelic ordination to bolster Mormonism's authority principle. Section 13, a late concoction first composed in 1838-39 but not made public until 1842, wasn't published in the Doctrine and Covenants until 1876, forty-seven years after the events it purported to describe were supposed to have occurred. Although "the date of the Book of Commandments [1833] encompassed the bestowals of the two priesthoods," the "notable revelations on the priesthood (Doctrine and Covenants 2 [1823], 13 [1829], and 68 [1831]) are missing from the Book of Commandments."[16] What could possibly have been any more important to have been included there?

D. Michael Quinn discussed the staggering implications of these particular revisions:

---

[15]Quinn, *Origins of Power*, 15, emphasis added.

[16]The revelations in the Book of Commandments covered a period that ended in September 1831. That period embraces those events only later said to have occurred in "1829, May-June."

Cowdery's words [before they were altered in the
Times and Seasons in 1842] indicate a restoration of
only one priesthood ["*this* priesthood and *this*
authority"]. The version of this priesthood prayer
familiar to Mormons today was first published in
1842 (now [since 1876] D&C 13). An examination of
the published prayer shows that Cowdery's 1834
prayer-text [text from Oliver Cowdery and Joseph
Smith's 1834-35 History] was its source and that an
entire central portion was retroactively added. This
addition delimited the role of authority restored by
John the Baptist and made the 1829 event appear to
be a prelude to the later division of church authority
into the lesser and the greater priesthoods. By later
definitions only the Melchizedek priesthood was
"the Holy Priesthood." (D&C 84:25-27).[17]

Joseph Smith's *1838-39 History* had the angel alter and amend in
1838-39 (the draft) and 1842 (the publication) the words Cowdery
and Smith first said in 1834 that the angel had actually spoken in
1829. The deceptive headnote to Section 13 of the Doctrine and
Covenants, first published thirteen years after the fact, reported
that "[t]he angel explained that he was acting under the direction of
Peter, James, and John, the ancient Apostles, who held the keys of
the higher priesthood," which would "in due time" "be conferred
upon them [Joseph and Oliver]."[18] That unforgettable less-than-
contemporaneous recital isn't found in Joseph and Oliver's 1834
History.

"Accounts of a second priesthood restoration began appearing the
year after Cowdery's [Cowdery and Smith's] 1834 history [which
was more than six years after "*1829: May-June*"]. In August 1835
the church published the first edition of the *Doctrine and Covenants,*
which added passages to some previously published revelations."[19]

---

[17]Quinn, *Origins of Power*, 15-16.
[18]Doctrine and Covenants 13 (1957), headnote.
[19]Quinn, *Origins of Power*, 16.

Those passages received the benefit of the original (but then altered) revelations' earlier dates. The priesthood restoration events are riddled with clumsy deceptive manipulations. Those manipulations were not described in real time or until years after the fact.

CONFUSING NOTIONS OF PRIESTHOOD

The notion of "authority" in the early Church was put in place before the revelations were backdated and falsified. *"Participants at the church's organization had a unitary sense of authority rather than a belief in dual priesthoods of different ranks."*[20] The distinctions between the Aaronic and Melchizedek Priesthoods (jealously prominent in the modern Church) were not initially recognized. Not on *"1829, May 15;"* not in *"1829, May-June."* At the First Conference of the Church on June 9, 1830, more than one year after those unreported angelic ordinations were only later (in 1834 and 1835) supposed to have occurred, there were only twelve officers. Joseph and Oliver were elders (non-Melchizedek elders), and so were three Whitmers (David, John and Peter), Ziba Peterson and Samuel H. Smith. Joseph Smith, as the duly ordained (non-Melchizedek) prophet in charge, did take center stage. Smith and Cowdery "were the first and second elders." "Martin Harris, Hyrum Smith, and Joseph Smith Sr. were priests. Hiram Page and Christian Whitmer were teachers."[21] None of these early leaders, including teachers and priests, were preteens or teens, like those deacons, teachers and priests who often hold the lower priesthood, an entry level authority, in the modern Church.

After Joseph and Oliver, everyone seems to have been essentially equal. Power called "authority," not yet "Aaronic," not yet "Melchizedek" or even "priesthood," was unitary. On April 6, 1830, Joseph and his followers didn't preach "dual priesthoods of different ranks." Furthermore, until 1831 "priesthood" wasn't a

---

[20]Quinn, *Origins of Power*, 14-15, emphasis added.
[21]Ibid., 11.

term anyone used.[22]   The word wasn't yet recognized in the deliberations of the Church of Christ. On April 6, 1830, there was no "authority" called "priesthood." There was no "authority" called "Aaronic Priesthood."   There was no "authority" called "Melchizedek Priesthood."   There was only something called "authority."   Although they had different duties, priests and teachers and elders, representing the offices in the early Church, were essentially equals.   That benign but insidious scenario is dramatically inconsistent with the years later now familiar but retroactive accounts of the remarkable events resupposed to have occurred on and immediately after May 15, 1829.

Among the Nephites – in a Book of Mormon where the concept of priesthood is rudimentary – there are no Levites and there is no Aaronic Priesthood. Furthermore and importantly, the members of the gospel church were not ordained to the Aaronic/Levitical Priesthood after the coming of Christ.   In the Book of Mormon, pre-Christianity Christians are seen to worship an unborn Christ. With the passage of time, Joseph Smith and Sidney Rigdon purported to *restore* (and to make eternal) a discredited less-than-eternal priesthood identified with ancient Jewish ritual.   There was no Aaronic/Levitical Priesthood in the church of Christ in the Book of Mormon in the Western Hemisphere, and there was no Aaronic/Levitical Priesthood in the church of Christ in the Christian Bible in the Eastern Hemisphere. The gospel church did not pretend to perpetuate the Aaronic/Levitical Priesthood, an unsparing time-bound codification of ancient Jewish themes.

What was there then to be restored?   The Apostle Paul didn't describe Aaronic/Levitical priests as officers of the Christian church,[23] nor did he relate ancient Israel's law of a carnal commandment to the Messiah's new and better covenant. Or to the Christian system. There is no historical evidence to suggest that

---

[22]"Universalists like Joseph's grandfather linked priesthood with priestcraft and preaching the gospel for hire." (Bushman, *Joseph Smith: Rough Stone Rolling*, 157).
       [23]Hebrews 5-10.

"the Levitical Priesthood was part of the first-century church."[24] When Cowdery, a lower authority non-Melchizedek elder, pretended to ordain Joseph Smith to the highest office on earth on April 6, 1830, he didn't understand, and Smith didn't understand, that there were or would ever be "dual priesthoods of different ranks." Or that the offices of a Melchizedek elder and of a Melchizedek prophet were appendages of a second and higher authority. They failed to understand that some additional but necessary authority had not yet been "manifested and conferred" upon any of what were then only generic unitary lower authority non-Melchizedek elders, including elders ordained by Joseph and Oliver, and Joseph and Oliver. No one then knew that the Mormonites' charismatic authority didn't embrace the high priesthood. Or that elders, teachers and priests were not equal. Or that there were higher authority offices to be serviced by higher authority officers, elders, high priests, seventies, ordained apostles and patriarchs, stations divided by rank. Or that there was a third and powerful Patriarchal Priesthood, lineage based, deemed important, powerfully supported and not to be dismissed.[25] Furthermore, no one knew that "authority" had anything to do with the lineal priesthood of the old law, ancient Israel's ritual-ridden law of a carnal commandment. Temporary by definition. The Aaronic Priesthood is the lineal priesthood of the old law, ancient Israel's lineage-based ancient law of a *carnal* commandment.

When Oliver Cowdery ordained Joseph Smith to the office of prophet, the two of them didn't yet understand that there would be offices under each of two separate orders of priesthood. Or that those offices (and those who held them) would not be equal as they and those that they had already ordained had first supposed. Had the concept of greater and lesser priesthoods been understood, and

---

[24]*See*, e.g., Sharon I. Banister, *For Any Latter-day Saint: One Investigator's Unanswered Questions* (Fort Worth, TX: Star Bible Publications, 1988), 46-47.

[25]"The second (of "three grand orders of priesthood") [ranking ahead of the Levitical priesthood] is Abraham's Patriarchal power which is the greatest yet experienced in this Church." (Quinn, *Origins of Power*, 34). *See* Chapter 10, "The Forgotten Order."

had both of two separate priesthoods been conferred on Joseph and Oliver by "*1829, May–June*," there would have been a different and more proprietary order directing operations. *That there was not shows that the authority principle on April 6, 1830, if there was an authority principle on April 6, 1830, was egalitarian, metaphysical, unitary, lower than high, other than lineal and non-exclusive.*

If the members of the Church had known on April 6, 1830, that there were two distinct orders of priesthood (as the members of the modern Church now report), they would have known at the First Conference of the Church on June 9, 1830, that elders, teachers and priests were not equal in authority; that the offices of elders and bishops were appendages of the Melchizedek Priesthood; that the offices of deacons,[26] teachers and priests were appendages of the Aaronic Priesthood; that the Aaronic Priesthood was an appendage of the Melchizedek Priesthood; that apostles and high priests were elders; that there were high priests, seventies, apostles, and patriarchs, all of them ordained, and all of them elders; that a person holding the Aaronic Priesthood could not ordain an elder, a high priest, seventy, apostle, pastor, patriarch or *prophet*; that a person holding only the Aaronic Priesthood could not bestow the gift of the Holy Ghost; and that the high or holy priesthood after the order of the Son of God was the power required to minister in spiritual things – the power required to organize, establish, develop and restore the primitive "Church of Christ."

Modern Mormons claim to have had proper authority:

> *This order of Priesthood [Melchizedek] holds authority over all the offices in the Church, and includes power to administer in spiritual things; consequently all the authorities and powers necessary to the establishment and development of the Church*

---

[26]The New Testament said that deacons should be the husband of one wife. "Let the deacons be the husbands of one wife, ruling their children and their own houses well." (1 Timothy 3:10). In the modern Mormon Church, deacons are mostly twelve and thirteen years old.

> were by this visitation ["1829, May-June"] [Peter, James, and John] restored to earth.[27]

Careful scholarship states the case in different terms:

> [M]en were first ordained to the higher priesthood over a year after the church's founding. No mention of angelic ordinations can be found in original documents until 1834-35. Thereafter accounts of the visit of Peter, James, and John by Cowdery and Smith remained vague and contradictory.[28]

Because this is true, the chronology described in the *Teachings of Presidents of the Church* – published by the Church, translated in dozens of languages, and distributed all over the world – is not. That global teaching manual says: *"1829, May-June:* With Oliver Cowdery, [Joseph] receives the Melchizedek Priesthood from the ancient Apostles Peter, James, and John near the Susquehanna River between Harmony, Pennsylvania, and Colesville, New York."[29]

Because what the manual says isn't true, Joseph and Oliver assumed the titles and offices of "First and Second Elder[s]," ordained elders, teachers and priests, bestowed the gift of the Holy Ghost, administered in spiritual things, then further established and developed the Church without the necessary authority. For all of this, early administration is seen to have been accomplished before the High Priesthood was "manifested and conferred" for the first time upon several of the elders at the Fourth Conference of the Church on June 3, 1831. Brigham Young concluded that Joseph Smith didn't receive the Melchizedek Priesthood until after the

---

[27]James E. Talmage, *A Study of the Articles of Faith: Being a Consideration of the Principal Doctrines of The Church of Jesus Christ of Latter-day Saints*, 33rd ed. (Salt Lake City: The Church of Jesus Christ of Latter-day Saints, 1955), 188, emphasis added.

[28]Quinn, *Origins of Power*, 15, emphasis added.

[29]*Teachings of Presidents of The Church – Joseph Smith* (2007), xv (Historical Summary), emphasis added.

Church was organized,[30] and so did Orson Pratt.[31] Young believed that Peter, James, and John came to Smith in Kirtland, Ohio (meaning sometime after February 1831) and "as long as two years after the organization of the church."[32] Young went even further to say that when Joseph Smith had his vision of the "three degrees of glory" (a vision Smith shared with Rigdon) in February 1832 (Doctrine and Covenants 76) that he had only held "the aronic priesthood."[33] According to Brigham Young, Joseph Smith was an "aronic" elder in February 1832, more than eight months after the Fourth Conference of the Church held at Kirtland, Ohio, in June, 1831. Latter-day Saints, heavily invested in Brigham's schism, should take those representations directly to the bank. What Joseph had, after that Fourth Conference of the Church on June 3,

---

[30]Mormon historians "have been unwilling . . . to admit that Smith organized the LDS church in April 1830 without the Melchizedek priesthood." In April 1834 Smith provided this basic chronology "of significant events in church history: 'The President then gave a relation of obtaining and translating the Book of Mormon, the revelation of the Priesthood of Aaron, the organization of the Church in 1830, the revelation of the High Priesthood, and the gift of the Holy Ghost poured out upon the Church.'" (Joseph Smith Jr., *History of The Church of Jesus Christ of Latter-day Saints*, B.H. Roberts, ed., 7 vols., 2d ed., rev., [Salt Lake City: The Deseret Book Company, 1978], 2:52). Brigham Young "affirmed" this important sequence when he "stated publicly that Smith 'organized the Church for the Lord had revealed to him, the Aaronic priesthood upon which the Church was organized.'" Young went further to say that Smith "received the Melchisedic priesthood" after the Church was organized. (Brigham Young [1864], *Journal of Discourses* [Liverpool, England: F.D. Richards, 1855-1886], 10:303, quoted in Quinn, *Origins of Power*, 26). "This was also the position of the RLDS Church at the same time." (Quinn, *Origins of Power*, 287-88 fn 125).

[31]On Friday, December 24, 1847, at a General Conference held "in a very large log house" at Miller's Point, Orson Pratt, told his audience (Hosea Stout reporting) that, "There was a time when this Church was governed by the Lesser Priesthood." According to Pratt's reporter, "His discourse was very interresting and was recieved with breathless silence. The Spirit rested down upon the whole congregation." (Hosea Stout, *On the Mormon Frontier: The Diary of Hosea Stout, 1844-1861*, ed. Juanita Brooks, vol. 2 [Salt Lake City: University of Utah Press and Utah State Historical Society, 1964, 1982], 291-92).

[32]Quinn, *Origins of Power*, 26.

[33]Statement of Brigham Young, Salt Lake City Municipal High Council Minutes, 8 October 1848 (Young Papers, LDS Archives); Young (1861), *Journal of Discourses* 9:89; *History of the Church*, 1:145, 245, quoted in Quinn, *Origins of Power*, 26, 288 fn 126.

1831, according to Young, wasn't called "the Melchizedek priesthood" in February 1832. Young recognized that the angelic ordinations were part of a late design, and so did Orson Pratt and David Whitmer.

Because what the global teaching manual says isn't true, Oliver Cowdery ordained Joseph Smith to the position of "Prophet, Seer and Revelator" to the Church of Christ on April 6, 1830, without the necessary authority. Only very much later, after being starkly reconfigured, was Cowdery's alleged charismatic "authority" retroactively supposed to have been associated with John the Baptist and the Aaronic Priesthood, meaning more specifically with the lineage-dependent tutorial power supposed to have administered ancient Israel's less-than-eternal law of a carnal commandment. It wasn't until long after April 6, 1830, and even longer after "*1829, May-June,*" that Smith and Cowdery recognized that the office of elder was going to be associated with some higher order of the priesthood. An order of priesthood Cowdery didn't hold on April 6, 1830.

> *[T]he association of the office of elder with a higher order known as the Melchizedek priesthood was a later development. The "high priesthood" ([which later became the] "order of Melchizedek") was introduced in June 1831, and it was not until September 1832 that the office of elder was linked to that priesthood. Rather, the restoration of the eldership was associated with the "word of the Lord" received in the chamber of Peter Whitmer Sr.'s house in Fayette, New York, in June 1829.*[34]

According to the Book of Commandments, in that scripture's description of the earliest manifestation of the authority principle, Joseph became a seer, a translator, a prophet, an apostle and "*an*

---

[34]Dan Vogel, *Joseph Smith: The Making of a Prophet* (Salt Lake City: Signature Books, 2004), 520, and cites at fn 87 at 686; cf, Doctrine and Covenants 84:14, 29, emphasis added.

elder of the church through the will of God the Father, and the grace of our Lord Jesus Christ."[35] That may only be seen to suppose unordained charisma (the "will" of the Father, "the grace of our Lord").   In 1829 and 1830, Joseph Smith saw himself as a metaphysical priest.   "[W]hen retroactive changes [meaning doctrinal deceptions] are eliminated from original documents, evidence shows that the second angelic restoration of apostolic authority [meaning the "high priesthood"] could not have occurred before the church's organization on 6 April 1830."[36] Furthermore, Smith's early supposed non-exclusive charismatic authority was not identified with or treated as equal to "the high priesthood." The supposed charismatic elders didn't hold "the high priesthood" any earlier than June 3, 1831. The ordination of Joseph Smith (on April 6, 1830) to the office of Prophet, Seer and Revelator to the only true church on the face of the earth was a pretended act undertaken without the authority of the high priesthood.

---

[35]Book of Commandments 22:1, emphasis added.
[36]Quinn, *Origins of Power*, 18, emphasis added.

CHAPTER FIFTEEN

Authority Theory

In a single stroke the new accounts ["detailed accounts of physical appearances by . . . impressive biblical figures"] legitimized the leadership's religious authority, giving them exclusive rights and setting them apart from: anyone who claimed a non-literal or metaphysical reception of authority.

Grant H. Palmer

BIBLICAL AND MODERN PRIESTHOODS

Latter-day Saints maintain that the gospel church was lost to apostasy. They then aver that the church restored by the prophet Joseph Smith will never be lost to apostasy. The Mormon "Restoration" anticipated the Gathering of Zion at Jackson County, Missouri, the building of the city of the New Jerusalem at Jackson County, Missouri, the construction of a Temple at the city of the New Jerusalem, the return of the Ten Lost Tribes[1] and the Second Coming of Christ. The restored Church would stand until the Millennium, an event supposed to occur before the end of the

---

[1] At the first general conference of the Church to be held at Kirtland, Ohio, Joseph Smith unriddled a mystery that had perplexed religious scholars for years. He told his faithful followers what happened to the Ten Lost Tribes. They had settled, he said, in a land "contiguous to the north pole; separated from the rest of the world by impassable mountains of ice and snow." "In this sequestered residence, they enjoy the society of Elijah the Prophet, and John the Revelator, and perhaps the three immortalized Nephites. – By and by, the mountains of ice and snow are to give way, and open a passage for the return of these tribes, to the land of Palestine." (Ezra Booth, Letter III, Eber D. Howe, *Mormonism Unvailed: Or, A Faithful Account of That Singular Imposition and Delusion* [Painesville, OH: E.D. Howe, 1834; reprint, New York: AMS Press Inc., 1977], 186).

nineteenth century. If Jesus didn't teach his disciples in either of two different hemispheres about the Aaronic Priesthood, if he didn't ordain Aaronic priests or provide his followers with instructions concerning the joint priesthood governance of the gospel church, what was there about that Priesthood that stood to be restored? Priesthood is the centerpiece of the restoration. Joseph's Lord didn't know, in the beginning, and didn't tell the chosen people, that there were overlapping priesthoods of different ranks. Sidney Rigdon thought that he knew that there were. Alexander Crawford, Alexander Campbell and the Disciples of Christ thought that they knew that there were, but the Book of Mormon's Messiah, "God himself" and "the Eternal Father of Heaven and Earth," clearly did not.

The Articles of Faith crafted by Joseph Smith, when refined and further described in exquisite detail by the Mormon scholar James E. Talmage, confidently reported that the Holy Priesthood "descended from [Mormonism's literal] Adam to [Mormonism's literal] Noah under the [literal] hands of the fathers . . . Melchizedek, who conferred this authority upon Abraham, received his own [authority] through the direct lineage of his fathers from Noah."[2] So said Joseph Smith; so said Apostle Talmage; so say some Mormon scholars. The Apostle Paul described Melchizedek as one who has become a priest not on the basis of a regulation as to his ancestry, but on the basis of the power of an indestructible life.[3] Sharon I. Banister put Mormonism's late-to-the-table lineage-dependent high priesthood claim in this undeniable perspective: "The Old Testament gives much detail about the Levitical Priesthood. If all the leaders from Adam through Abraham belonged to another greater priesthood, can you explain why it is

---

[2]James E. Talmage, *A Study of the Articles of Faith: Being a Consideration of the Principal Doctrines of The Church of Jesus Christ of Latter-day Saints*, 33rd ed. (Salt Lake City: The Church of Jesus Christ of Latter-day Saints, 1955), 182.

[3]Sharon I. Banister, *For Any Latter-day Saint: One Investigator's Unanswered Questions* (Fort Worth, TX: Star Bible Publications, 1988), 45 *cf*, Hebrews 7:15-16. "[A]fter the similitude of Melchizedek there ariseth another priest, Who is made, not after the law of a carnal commandment [meaning by some undemocratic lineal concept of ancestral privilege], but after the power of an endless life."

nowhere described in the Old Testament?"[4]

In modern Mormonism the previously urgent doctrine of the gathering is smoke and mirrors. The return of the Ten Lost Tribes is far less important today. The magic of Missouri has passed and the great apostasy, an angry and controversial concept, is taking a less conspicuous place at the back of the modern bus. Did the Savior predict the failure of the gospel church?[5] Was that dismal spiritual drought, something Smith and others almost gleefully described, followed by Smith's supposed restoration, part of some great eternal plan? Why would the incomparable Christ design his Kingdom to fail? How could Joseph Smith, secretly crowned by his followers to be the King, Priest and Prophet of the Kingdom of Israel on Earth, design his Kingdom never to fail? And why would the architects of the earth ever consider the failure of the gospel church, the loss of legitimacy or the success of the Mormon Church to be a predicted part of some grand design?

Why Joseph and Oliver Could Not Have Been Aaronic Priests

In their "Inspired Translation" of the King James Bible, Smith (and Rigdon) tightened the connection between Jesus and Melchizedek, a connection made only in Hebrews.[6] The Epistle to the Hebrews describes "Christ Jesus" as "*the* Apostle and High Priest of our profession," as "faithful to him that appointed him" and as "worthy of more glory than Moses."[7] "*[W]e have a great high priest that is passed into the heavens, Jesus the Son of God, let us hold fast our profession.*"[8] Paul distinguished an exceptional Jesus, infinite and underived, from those less than eternal Levitical priests whose days were always numbered; from those lineage-dependent inheritors

---

[4]Banister, *For Any Latter-day Saint*, 45.

[5]"[U]pon this rock I will build my church; and *the gates of hell shall not prevail against it.*" (Matthew 16:18, emphasis added).

[6]Dan Vogel, *Joseph Smith: The Making of a Prophet* (Salt Lake City: Signature Books, 2004), 217.

[7]Hebrews 3:1-3, emphasis added.

[8]Ibid., 4:14, emphasis added.

supposed to administer a less than eternal priesthood; from Levitical priests who "were not suffered to continue by reason of death."[9]

After describing his Master as "holy, harmless, undefiled, separate from sinners, and made higher than the heavens," Paul pronounced a benediction upon the Levitical Priesthood and its oppressive written code. This Christ "needeth not daily, as those high priests, to offer up sacrifice, first for his own sins, and then for his people's: for this he did once, when he offered up himself."[10] This expression recognized the preparatory nature of that less than eternal Levitical power. While Jesus was not from the priestly tribe of Levi, according to Paul, or "called after the order of Aaron" and so a Levitical priest,[11] he was a priest, forever a priest, but "after the order of Melchisedec."[12]

Jesus did not simultaneously hold two overlapping priesthoods. Furthermore, "Hebrews does not assert that Jesus held the same priesthood as Melchizedek but that he held a priesthood that was similar to the ancient king-priest's: one that was neither lineal nor responsible for administering the law of Moses."[13] The Aaronic order, "the covenant I made with their fathers in the day when I took them by the hand to lead them out of the land of Egypt, because they continued not in my covenant, and I regarded them not . . . ,"[14] was not an entry level authority for Jesus or Paul, or for the apostles during the Messiah's ministry. Jesus was not "called after the order of Aaron," nor either the Apostle Paul, nor either Peter, James, and John.

The "Melchisedec" order of the priesthood was not designed to be a temporary tutorial arrangement for the training of poorly regarded interns, or a vehicle for the effectuation of ritualistic animal

---

[9]Ibid., 7:23.
[10]Ibid., 7:26-27.
[11]Ibid., 7:11.
[12]Ibid., 5:6.
[13]Vogel, *Joseph Smith: The Making of a Prophet*, 215.
[14]Hebrews 8:9, headnote: "The new and better covenant supersedes the old."

sacrifice. It was an eternal order of a kind better suited to the higher uses of an exceptional Christ. Christ "glorified not himself to be made an high priest . . . ," but rather to be one with him who said, "Thou art my Son, to day have I begotten thee."[15] The biblical Melchizedek was not a "high" priest.[16] Christ's priestly office was "Without father, without mother, without descent, having neither beginning of days, nor end of life . . . "; thus, it was not lineage based or Levitical. Melchizedek's priestly calling "made like unto the Son of God" "abideth a priest continually."[17] Neither the Savior nor his followers administered the ephemeral law of a carnal commandment.

Levite priests – transient, tribal, finite and lineal, creatures and derived – take tithes from the people "according to the law" and from their brethren "though they come out of the loins of Abraham."[18] But Melchizedek "whose descent is not counted from them received tithes of Abraham and blessed him that had the promises."[19] Melchizedek "whose descent is not counted from them," and whose power was infinitely greater than theirs, "received tithes of Abraham."[20] Levi "payed tithes in Abraham"[21] as "the less is blessed of the better."[22]

The Savior was not descended from the tribe of Levi, but rather from another tribe "of which no man gave attendance at the altar." He did not hold an order of authority the limited powers of which were reserved to time-bound creatures defined by their Levitical lineage. For such creatures were not without father, without

---

[15]Ibid., 5:5.

[16]"Another title that Smith creatively applies to Melchizedek is that of 'high priest' ([Inspired Translation] 13:14, 18). Neither Genesis 14 nor Hebrews 7 refers to Melchizedek as a 'high priest' . . . . Instead, Melchizedek is called simply 'priest' (Genesis 14:18; Hebrews 7:1)." (Vogel, *Joseph Smith: The Making of a Prophet*, 217).

[17]Hebrews 7:1-3.

[18]Ibid., 7:5.

[19]Ibid., 7:6.

[20]Ibid., 7:6.

[21]Ibid., 7:9.

[22]Ibid., 7:7.

mother, without descent, having neither beginning of days nor end of life. No one from the tribe of Judah, held the Aaronic Priesthood. *"For it is evident that our Lord sprang out of Juda; of which tribe Moses spake nothing concerning Priesthood."*[23] Christ Jesus from Judah became *"the* Apostle and High Priest of our profession . . . ,"[24] a priest "after the similitude of Melchisedec,"[25] independent of lineage[26] and free from the limitations of mother, father, life, death or descent. "JESUS is the CHRIST, the ETERNAL GOD."[27] The "ETERNAL GOD" was not subject to some finite lineal legacy. Since 1829, Mormon theology has resisted the notion that the office of high priest was "restricted to one man (as in ancient Judaism) or to Jesus Christ alone (as in traditional Christianity)."[28] The indiscriminate proliferation of the priesthood to the multitudes (not something that can be thought to have been restored) was neither Christian nor biblical.

If Jesus, "God himself" from "Juda" and a Jew, couldn't be "called after the order of Aaron" because he wasn't a Levite, how could Joseph Smith, who wasn't God, a Levite or a biological Jew, be "called after the order of Aaron"? No Gentile could have qualified to hold the Levitical Priesthood, the lineage-dependent priesthood of the old law. No lineal descendant of Ephraim or Manasseh could have qualified to hold the Aaronic Priesthood, the lineage-dependent priesthood of the old law. And if Jesus could not, and if Judah, Ephraim and Manasseh could not, and if Lehi and Nephi could not, then how could Joseph Smith, Oliver Cowdery, Hyrum Smith, Samuel H. Smith, Ziba Peterson or any of the several Whitmers? Or any of the forty-four non-Melchizedek elders who attended the Fourth Conference of the Church at Kirtland, Ohio, in

---

[23]Ibid., 7:14, emphasis added.

[24]Ibid., 3:1, emphasis added.

[25]Ibid., 7:15.

[26]Ibid., 7:3.

[27]Joseph Smith, trans., *The Book of Mormon: An Account Written by the Hand of Mormon, Upon Plates Taken from the Plates of Nephi* (Salt Lake City: The Church of Jesus Christ of Latter-day Saints, 1957), Title page.

[28]D. Michael Quinn, *The Mormon Hierarchy: Origins of Power* (Salt Lake City: Signature Books in association with Smith Research Associates, 1994), 29.

June of 1831? Or any of some hundreds of thousands of Latter-day Saints who claim to hold the lineage-dependent priesthood of the old law in this, the dispensation of the fulness of times? None of them Levites, none of them descendants of Aaron, few of them Jews? None of them able even if Jews to give evidence of their ancestral registration? It may also be quite certainly said that no descendant of Aaron had any right, then or now – based on lineage – "to partake of the Christian system."[29] Those early Hebrews becoming Christians in Christ had their own altar. Those who established the Christian system in the gospel church didn't ordain Levitical priests. There was thus nothing in the gospel church in the meridian of time to be restored by Smith and Rigdon in modern Mormonism's dispensation of the fullness of times.

The lineage-based Aaronic Priesthood had no place in the havens of the Nephites in the Western Hemisphere, and it had no place among the Christians in the gospel church in the Eastern Hemisphere. "For the priesthood [of Levi] [the "shadow of heavenly things"] being changed [superceded by the "substance of heavenly things"], there is made of necessity a change also of the law [Jesus was the guarantor of a better testament]."[30] If "perfection" was to be achieved "by the Levitical priesthood [for under it the people received the law]," by that to say by the "law of a carnal commandment," if "perfection" was to be achieved by the dictates of that "preparatory," "tutorial," "schooling," ritualistic order of authority, *what further need was there that another priest should arise after the order of Melchisedec and not be called after the order of Aaron?*[31] Is that not clear? Christ ("God himself") was not called after the order of Aaron. Who was *that another priest* not to be *"called after the order of Aaron"*? It was Jesus, the Everlasting God, the Book of Mormon's Father of Heaven and Earth. The law of a carnal commandment was consigned to oblivion when Christ became *"the* Apostle and High Priest of our profession." No longer was Levi's lower law of a carnal commandment (a less than eternal

---

[29]Hebrews 13:10; see, *e.g.*, Banister, *For Any Latter-day Saint*, 42.
[30]Ibid., 7:12.
[31]Ibid., 7:11, emphasis added.

law ministering to the needs of the insufficiently faithful) the basis of priesthood, nor was it the order of a new and better ministry, the foundation of Christ's new and better agreement. No longer would some lower law be administered by some lower priesthood for some lesser people. There came with the incarnation of Christ a new and higher order of things, a higher law to be administered for the benefit of a chosen people.

> *And it is yet far more evident: for that after the similitude of Melchisedec there ariseth another priest, Who is made, not after the law of carnal commandment, but after the power of an endless life. For he testifieth, Thou art a priest forever after the order of Melchisedec.* [32]

Joseph Smith and Oliver Cowdery did not hold and could never have held the Aaronic Priesthood (conferred by lineage) in the dispensation of the fullness of times; the Savior did not hold and could not have held the Aaronic Priesthood (conferred by lineage) in the meridian of time.   The old law (the law of a carnal commandment) and the lower priesthood (the preparatory order of authority) disappeared in the meridian of time in the community of Christ. [33]   Joseph and Oliver didn't hold (and couldn't have held) the Aaronic/Levitical Priesthood on April 6, 1830, the day the Church of Christ was officially formed.

A New Covenant – The Law of a New Order Fulfilled

Melchizedek's eternal inheritance would seem to have been vastly superior to the temporary and imperfect power exercised in

---

[32]Ibid., 7:15-17, emphasis added.

[33]The Christian Bible doesn't call Melchizedek a "high priest," like Joseph Smith (Inspired Translation) and the Book of Mormon. "[T]his designation was unnecessary until Aaron and his successors were appointed to preside over the Levite priests." (Vogel, *Joseph Smith: The Making of a Prophet*, 217). Before his attributes were upgraded and aggrandized by Smith and Rigdon, Melchizedek was only a "priest."

difficult times by Levi and Aaron. The Aaronic Priesthood was not for Christ because perfection, found in Christ, wasn't found in the less than eternal much disparaged order of Aaron. The Aaronic Priesthood was for people who had hardened their hearts "as in the provocation, in the day of temptation in the wilderness."[34] Traditional Christianity's Jesus was imbued with "the power of an endless life."[35] He dismissed the Levitical Priesthood, by means of which the law of a carnal commandment was administered to recalcitrants. The new order was introduced in these terms: "For the priesthood being changed, there is made of necessity a change also of the law."[36] For verily there is "a disannulling of the [Aaronic/Levitical] commandment going before for the weakness and unprofitableness thereof."[37] "For the law made nothing perfect but the bringing in of a better hope *did*; by the which we draw nigh unto God."[38]

It was not without an oath that Jesus was made a priest.[39] The Levitical Priesthood's monarchical priests were made without an oath. "The Lord sware and will not repent, Thou *art* a priest forever after the order of Melchisedec. By so much was Jesus made a surety of a better testament."[40] "And they [those Aaronic/Levitical priests] truly were many priests because they were not suffered to continue by reason of death."[41] "But this *man* [Jesus from Judah] . . . hath an unchangeable priesthood."[42] "For the law maketh men high priests which have infirmity; but the word of the oath, which was since the law, maketh the Son, who is consecrated for evermore."[43] The lower lesser lineal order of Levi, Aaron and the old law, a finite construct supervised by finite

---

[34]Hebrews 3:8.
[35]Ibid., 7:16.
[36]Ibid., 7:12.
[37]Ibid., 7:18.
[38]Ibid., 7:19, emphasis added.
[39]Ibid., 7:20.
[40]Ibid., 7:21-22, emphasis added.
[41]Ibid., 7:23.
[42]Ibid., 7:24, emphasis added.
[43]Ibid., 7:28.

priests, was not for Christians following Christ.

> *Now of the things which we have spoken this is the
> sum: We have such an high priest, who is set on the
> right hand of the throne of the Majesty in the
> heavens; . . . .*[44]

Christ is traditional Christianity's High Priest beside whom there is
none other. The lower authority Levitical priests were disannulled
and not replaced. When the Aaronic Priesthood and the carnal
elements of the lower law met the Messiah, they were done, wiped
away. When Christ came, the lineal law of ancient Israel ended its
earthly tutorial and completed its preparatory course. Its limited
objectives were met. Christ brought a new "more excellent
ministry" and "a better covenant."[45] The Aaronic Priesthood, the
"shadow of heavenly things,"[46] was replaced by a "new [and better]
covenant," the substance of heavenly things. ("For if that first
covenant had been faultless, then should no place have been sought
for the second."[47]) The coming of Christ's kinder, gentler less
burdensome agenda was "Not according to the covenant that I
made with their fathers in the day when I took them by the hand to
lead them out of the land of Egypt; because they continued not in
my covenant, and I regarded them not, saith the Lord."[48]

> *For this is the covenant that I will make with the
> house of Israel after those days, saith the Lord; I will
> put my laws into their mind, and write them in their
> hearts: and I will be to them a God, and they shall be
> to me a people . . . . And they shall not teach every
> man his neighbor, and every man his brother, saying
> Know the Lord: for all shall know me, from the least
> to the greatest.*[49]

---

[44]Ibid., 8:1, emphasis supplied.
[45]Ibid., 8:6.
[46]Ibid., 8:5.
[47]Ibid., 8:5, 7, 8.
[48]Ibid., 8:9.
[49]Ibid., 8:10, 11, emphasis added.

*For I will be merciful . . . . In that he saith, A new
covenant, he hath made the first [Aaronic/Levitical]
old. Now that which decayeth and waxeth old is ready
to vanish away.*[50]

And what was it that decayed, that waxeth old and vanished away
in the face of a new and better covenant? The first covenant, the
finite covenant, the old covenant, the carnal covenant, the
"ineffective" "tutorial" "bloody" covenant, the covenant God made
with their fathers when he "regarded them not." Before he put his
laws into their minds and wrote them in their hearts. Before he was
to them a God, and they were to him a people. Before all should
know him "from the least to the greatest." Before he was "merciful
to their unrighteousness, and their sins and their iniquities," and
promised to remember them no more. Before a new and better
covenant "hath made the first old."[51]

The Aaronic/Levitical Priesthood did not survive the coming of
Christ for Hebrews becoming Christians. Joseph Smith and Oliver
Cowdery, Mormonism's lineage ineligible founders, didn't hold
(and couldn't have held) the Aaronic Priesthood, an order of
authority God could not have chosen to restore. *Smith's original
nineteenth-century Church was organized without the authority of the
Aaronic Priesthood, ancient Israel's less than eternal law of a carnal
commandment.*[52]

How the Book of Mormon Managed Authority

"When Joseph receives a spiritual prompting to begin to baptize and

---

[50]Ibid., 8:12, 13, emphasis added.

[51]Ibid., 8:9-13.

[52]By definition "carnal" means "temporal." It is a "manifestation of a
person's lower nature." It implies appetites (often sexual), and it stresses the
physical "as distinguished from the rational nature of a person." It is a term seen
as relating to "crude bodily pleasures and appetites."

ordain others, he is following the pattern in the Book of Mormon."[53] The confident promise that the Book of Mormon contained "the fulness of the everlasting Gospel" didn't begin to stand the test of time. In respect to the concepts of priesthood developed and promoted by the modern Mormon Church, the Book of Mormon's authority principles are inexplicably obscure, both ignored and dismissed. The instructions found in the Golden Bible quickly proved to be less than one might have hoped. A Community of Christ (RLDS) scholar described the Mormon prophet's attention span:

> *Joseph Smith dictated the Book of Mormon to scribes and it was thereafter printed by E.B. Grandin in March 1830 at Palmyra, New York. Through the remaining fourteen years and three months of his life, Joseph Smith paid relatively little attention to the Book of Mormon as he moved far beyond its theology . . . . The Book of Mormon presented a conservative Protestant version of Christianity that fit well within the religious environment of the United States in 1830.*[54]

Issues of authority only sparingly described in the Book of Mormon would ultimately capture the attention of what became a more experienced prophet. Other doctrines completely overlooked by the keystone of the faith would rise to the fore, to use but several of a great many examples, baptism for the dead, differentiated heavens,

---

[53]Grant H. Palmer, *An Insider's View of Mormon Origins* (Salt Lake City: Signature Books, 2002), 223, emphasis added.

[54]William D. Russell, "Portrait of a 'True Believer' in Original Mormonism," in *The William E. McLellin Papers: 1854-1880*, eds. Stan Larson and Samuel J. Passey, foreword by George D. Smith (Salt Lake City: Signature Books, 2008), 111. Smith's faithful biographer admitted as much: "*. . . I am . . . impressed by the Book of Mormon. It is riddled with nineteenth-century Protestant theology and phrasing, but still is an incredible narrative of a civilization's rise and fall . . . .*" (Richard L. Bushman, "Dear Forum Members" statement, "Richard Bushman – Reddit – Ask Me Anything" [16 December 2013, accessed 13 January 2014], available from www.mormonthink.com/glossary/richard-bushman-ama.htm; Internet, emphasis added).

a more generous view of the nature of man, temple marriage and the plurality of gods. The Book of Mormon, whatever the Lord is supposed to have said, was an insufficient guide for the founders to follow in respect to the issues of priesthood. It was just as confused about the authority principles presently promulgated by the modern Church as Joseph Smith and Oliver Cowdery initially were. In nineteenth-century America, the milieu of the Mormon bible, the word "priesthood" was identified with the Roman Catholic Church, an institution the Book of Mormon not so generously described as "the great and abominable church," as "the mother of abominations," as "the church of the devil" and "the whore of all the earth."[55] The authority exercised by the Nephites was undeniably unitary; poorly defined, high not low, not Aaronic or Levitic or Melchizedek, but nebulous. There were no "dual priesthoods of different ranks" in the Book of Mormon, or in the New Testament, or in the Old Testament, or in any of the sixty-five revelations contained in the Book of Commandments in 1833. The seed of some simultaneous fusion of competing dualities made its first tenuous appearance at that Fourth Conference of the Church of Christ (Mormon) in 1831 (the first conference to be held in Sidney Rigdon's Ohio). The development of the authority principle remained, even then, under construction.

Nephites and the Aaronic Priesthood

None of the Hebrew men in the small colony of Lehi supposed to have inhabited the Americas in about 600 B.C. held the Aaronic Priesthood. The Mormon theologian Bruce R. McConkie reports that, "*There was no Aaronic Priesthood among the Nephites prior to the ministry of the resurrected Lord among them, for none of the tribe of Levi accompanied the Nephite peoples to their promised land.*"[56]

---

[55]Book of Mormon, 1 Nephi, 14:9-10.

[56]Bruce R. McConkie, *Mormon Doctrine*, 2d ed. (Salt Lake City: Bookcraft, 1966), 10, emphasis added. What McConkie said about the Nephites – that they didn't have the Aaronic Priesthood "because none of the tribe of Levi accompanied the Nephite peoples to their promised land" – applied with equal force to the groundless claims of Joseph Smith and Oliver Cowdery, Gentiles rather than Jews.

Isn't that apparent? He might also have said that there was no Aaronic Priesthood among the Nephites *after* the ministry of the resurrected Lord, a descendant of "Juda," "of which tribe Moses spake nothing concerning priesthood."   Jesus didn't hold and couldn't have held the Aaronic Priesthood, and there is nothing to suggest that he brought it with him. The Savior was "another priest" from "another tribe" and wasn't "called after the order of Aaron."[57] That the Aaronic Priesthood was nowhere pretended to in the Book of Mormon didn't change because of "the ministry of the resurrected Lord." The Mortal Messiah didn't hold and refused to promote the rule-constricted lineage-dependent less than eternal earthly order of the Levitical Priesthood. No one from the tribe of Levi accompanied the resurrected Savior to the Western Hemisphere. The Book of Mormon doesn't mention, before or after the visit of Christ, the biblical "Aaron," or "Levi," or the "Aaronic" or "Levitical" Priesthood. These omissions are telling because all that the Eastern Hemisphere Hebrews knew of the shadow of heavenly things prior to their journey to the new world concerned those words and others like them. Then further consider also this: They were supposed to have brought the brass plates of the murdered Laban with them.

When the Book of Mormon was translated and published in 1830, Joseph Smith (then presumed to have been unconnected to Rigdon) wasn't thinking about issues of authority in all the ways he only later would, or as the modern Church currently does. His undeniable confusion about the orders and issues of priesthood, and the Book of Mormon's confusion about the orders and issues of priesthood, and the Book of Commandments' confusion about the orders and issues of priesthood set at defiance the notion that John the Baptist, followed by Peter, James, and John, visited Smith and Cowdery in the spring of 1829, ordained them to two different orders of the priesthood and provided them with operating instructions. "The Nephite model is a consistent one in that 'the Spirit of the Lord' authorizes men to baptize and ordain each other and to organize a church. This [non-literal model] corresponds

---

[57]Hebrews 7:14, 11.

exactly to the Book of Commandments pattern for receiving authority . . . ."[58] Yet it is decidedly out of synch with the unprecedented authority principles that govern the affairs of the modern Mormon Church.

> *Joseph Smith was commanded to search the Book of Mormon . . . for instructions on how to receive and dispense priesthood authority. A revelation . . . given June 1829 instructed him: "I give unto you a commandment, that you rely upon the things which are written [on the gold plates, or in the Book of Mormon]; For in them are all things written concerning the foundation of my church, my gospel and my rock."[59]*

In the revelation (Book of Commandments 15:3, 1833) before the word of the Lord was revised (Doctrine and Covenants 18:3-4, 1835), the words *"the foundation of"* do not appear. In the Book of Commandments, the "pattern" was more faithfully (and contemporaneously) described as follows: *"For in them are all things written concerning my church, my gospel and my rock."*

If the Book of Mormon isn't historical, these following words were meant to deceive: *"The Book of Mormon is a volume of holy scripture comparable to the Bible. It is a record of God's dealings with ancient inhabitants of the Americas and contains the fulness of the everlasting gospel."[60]* The golden bible is described as complete, and it concerns the continents; the Book of Mormon is supposed to be scripture for the Western Hemisphere. For all of that, it doesn't begin to describe the orders of priesthood that replaced the less oppressive more informal non-literal charismatic authority David Whitmer admired before anyone knew anything about John the Baptist, Peter, James, and John, Elias and Elijah, the Aaronic or

---

[58]Palmer, *An Insider's View of Mormon Origins*, 222.

[59]Doctrine and Covenants 18:3-4, cf. Book of Commandments 15:3, quoted in Palmer, *An Insider's View of Mormon Origins*, 223, emphasis added.

[60]Book of Mormon, 1st ed. (Doubleday, 2004), Introduction, ix, emphasis added.

Levitical Priesthood, the Melchizedek Priesthood, the Patriarchal Priesthood, angelic ordination or transcendental gifts.

The Nephites Didn't Hold the Aaronic Priesthood

The general priesthood rule in Israel – a place more or less defined by intermittent episodes of piety and wickedness – was to be found in the Aaronic Priesthood.[61] A luke-warm Israel lived under a stringent lower law administered by a lesser lower priesthood. This lower priesthood, according to McConkie, was a tool designed to prepare the best and brightest of the Hebrew disciples "for the oath and covenant and perfection that appertain to the Melchizedek order" to which the lower priesthood, by modern Mormon reckoning, is undeniably appendant.[62]

Perhaps these fractious early American Hebrews, the surviving branch of two divisions of which became the "principal ancestors" of the American Indians (whatever the Church has presently ignored its history to say), divisions perpetually at war, did not require a "schooling ministry" to prepare them for the coming of Christ, for the fullness of a greater gospel and the blessings of a higher law. Perhaps they didn't require a preparatory gospel administered by a lesser law like unto that which applied to those they left behind. But then perhaps they did. Lehi's colonists, divided and divisive, often brutal and depraved, were not subjected to the same lineage-dependent tutorial that their brothers and sisters in the old world were. The Nephites had no concept of greater and lesser priesthoods and considered their authority, whatever its nature or source, as both high and unitary. In the Book of Mormon, there is no Aaronic Priesthood and the name Melchizedek is mentioned sparingly. The unique term "The Melchizedek Priesthood" wasn't used to describe the authority-principle ("the high priesthood") supposed to have applied to the Book of Mormon's Nephites. Though there are six references to

---

[61]McConkie, *Mormon Doctrine*, 2d ed. (1966), 9-10.
[62]Ibid.

Melchizedek in the Book of Mormon, none of them refer to the priesthood. It is said of the patriarch, in a phrase the Bible doesn't support, that Melchizedek was a "high priest" (Alma 13:14). One might be so bold as to say that the Melchizedek Priesthood, like the Aaronic Priesthood, is not really "pretended to" in the Book of Mormon.

The Hebrews in the Western Hemisphere managed their complicated affairs without the benefit of the Aaronic/Levitical Priesthood, and with but scant reference to some mystical Melchizedek. Why were the Hebrews in the old world governed by the Aaronic Priesthood when the Hebrews in the new world were not? Why didn't the Hebrews in the old world have "the high priesthood after the holy order of the Son of God" like the Hebrews in the new world supposedly did? Why did the Hebrews in the new world know Christ by name hundreds of years before he was born and call themselves Christians? Why didn't the Hebrews in the old world know Christ by name hundreds of years before he was born and call themselves Christians? How did the North and South American Hebrews know the Greek name for the Messiah ("Christ") before there was a Messiah, a New Testament or a Greek translation? Why didn't the Hebrews in the old world know the Greek name for the Messiah ("Christ") before there was a Messiah, a New Testament or a Greek translation?

Alma (a Book of Mormon figure) held the "high priesthood of the holy order of God."[63] Levi and Aaron, old world Hebrews, held a lower order of authority that administered ancient Israel's law of a carnal commandment. Alma explained the Nephite authority principle by making reference to non-literal metaphysical authority. The disciples in the Western Hemisphere were supposed to have received their special dispensation as "the result of

---

[63]Vogel, *Joseph Smith: The Making of a Prophet*, 214, citing Book of Mormon, Alma 4:20, *see also* Alma 5:49, 54; 6:1, 8; 7:22. "[T]he Book of Mormon," according to one scholar, "connects this priesthood (the "high priesthood of the holy order of God") with Jesus and Melchizedek, the latter a contemporary of Abraham who is mentioned in Genesis 14, rather than with Aaron." [Ibid.].

charismatic experience rather than physical ordination."[64]
"Neither the Nephites nor Joseph Smith could legally claim
Levitical priesthood. To resolve this difficulty, Smith draws on
Hebrews 7."[65]

The Church established by Joseph Smith in the state of New York
on April 6, 1830, didn't exercise the kind of authority established by
the Messiah in the gospel church in the Eastern Hemisphere, or by
the Messiah in the Nephite church in the Western Hemisphere.
When he "translated" the Book of Mormon in 1829, when he
published the Book of Mormon and organized the Church in 1830,
on April 6, 1830, and at that First Conference of the Church of
Christ on June 9, 1830, Smith didn't identify two separate orders of
priesthood,[66] each having different durations, offices, powers and
functions. The Hebrews in the old world held the lower Levitical
priesthood. The Hebrews in the new world held the high priesthood
of the holy order of God. Melchizedek was identified as a high
priest (one high priest among other high priests) of that particular
high priesthood of the holy order of God. The gospel church and
the Christian system, the historical Jesus and the author of
Hebrews, rudely dismissed the Levitical Priesthood. Joseph Smith,
Oliver Cowdery, Sidney Rigdon, Joseph's Lord and the Mormon
Church are seen to have warmly embraced the Levitical Priesthood.
With the passage of time, Mormonism's founders and Joseph's
revelatory Jesus settled upon multiple priesthoods of different
ranks, like Sidney Rigdon's *Disciples of Christ* (Rigdon's earlier
society) prior to Rigdon's departure, had already also done. Thus
the first Mormon prophet, Joseph Smith, is now supposed to have
held the Aaronic Priesthood of Levi, the Patriarchal Priesthood of
Abraham and the higher priesthood of Melchizedek, side by side
and simultaneously. Smith and Cowdery and Rigdon didn't
"restore" the authority-principles connected to the Hebrews in the

---

[64]Book of Mormon, Alma 13, cited in Vogel, *Joseph Smith: The Making of a
Prophet*, 217.
    [65]Ibid., 214, emphasis added.
    [66]The Nephite apostles and prophets endorsed an undifferentiated heaven and
an undifferentiated hell. That doctrine, described in the Book of Mormon but soon
superceded, had to be forgotten.

old world, or to the Nephites in the New World, or to the historical Christ, the gospel church, the Christian system or the New Testament.

What Joseph Smith didn't know, by modern Mormon reckoning, on April 6, 1830:

- *That elders, high priests, seventies, apostles, patriarchs, bishops and prophets were elders, holding offices appendant to the authority of something that would only later come to be called the Melchizedek Priesthood; that there were high authority elders, bishops and prophets, high priests, seventies and patriarchs.*

- *That deacons, teachers and priests were lower authority officers of something that would only later come to be called the Aaronic Priesthood (the lineal priesthood of the old law), subject to the control of some higher authority that would only later come to be called the Melchizedek Priesthood.*

- *That the lower or Aaronic priesthood was an appendage of the higher or Melchizedek priesthood.*

- *That higher priesthood power would be required to organize the Church and to administer in spiritual things.*

- *That the "authorities and powers necessary to the establishment and development of the Church" were appurtenant to what would only later come to be called the Holy Melchizedek Priesthood after the order of the Son of God.[67]*

- *That there were at least three priesthoods of different ranks.*

Unfortunately, Smith could not have learned these things from anything he read in the New Testament, or in the Book of Mormon.

---

[67]Talmage, *A Study of the Articles of Faith*, 33rd ed., 188.

Since the Nephites held the priesthood, and because it is clear that the priesthood that they held wasn't the Aaronic Priesthood – the priesthood that history would expect them to hold – by what means did those transplanted Hebrews, subject to the law of a carnal commandment, and to the direction of lineage-dependent less-than-eternal priests in the land of their birth, somehow independently manage to acquire higher unitary eternal exclusive metaphysical authority? What was there about them that might have served to suggest that they didn't require a tutorial authority, some lower law to be administered by some lower priesthood for some lesser people?

Melchizedek in the Book of Mormon

If there had been no Alma, there would have been no Melchizedek in the Book of Mormon. Had there been no Epistle to the Hebrews, a New Testament resource assigned to the Apostle Paul, there may have been no Melchizedek in the book of Alma in the Book of Mormon. Although Melchizedek is supposed to have "received the office of the high priesthood according to the holy order of God,"[68] the discussion of his affairs required less than one entire page in Mormonism's more than five-hundred page bible, and he was by no means any kind of towering figure there. His credentials were elaborately embellished in *Joseph Smith and Sidney Rigdon's* "Inspired Translation of the King James Bible," in the several years that followed the publication of the Book of Mormon.

Joseph Smith failed to understand the finer points of what later became three separate orders of priesthood when he "translated" the Book of Mormon in 1829, or when it was published in 1830. And what there was concerning the subject of priesthood after the book was published was visible to the skeptical populace. In the thousand-year history of Nephite civilization, half a dozen references to "Melchizedek," and less than a dozen references to "high priesthood" in the Book of Alma, and perhaps thirty fleeting

---

[68]Book of Mormon, Alma 13:18.

references to "high priest[s]" at Mosiah, Alma, Helaman, Third Nephi and Ether, are all that is said about the power *"to break mountains, to divide the seas, to dry up waters, to turn them out of their course; To put at defiance the armies of nations, to divide the earth, to break every band [and], to stand in the presence of God; . . ."*[69]

The calls to the priesthood, according to Alma, were made "from the foundation of the world" and served to confer priesthood power on faithful men in the preexistence, "and then again on earth."[70] "Every man who has a calling to minister to the inhabitants of the world was ordained to that very purpose in the Grand Council of heaven before this world was."[71] Alma described how men were "ordained unto the high priesthood of the holy order of God" without earthbound ordinations, hierarchical formality or the laying on of hands. What was good for the Nephites in the Book of Mormon was good for the early Joseph Smith. In the beginning, authority depended upon non-literal metaphysical concepts based on righteousness, visionary experiences, foreordinations, commands, dreams, visions and promptings, measured against a by-the-grace-of-God authority by no means exclusive.

Exclusive Authority

The Book of Mormon model – charismatic, metaphysical, unitary authority – was the model applied in Mormonism's remote nascent phase before Joseph Smith met and then embraced Sidney Rigdon. Following Rigdon's imposing early appearance, the nebulous unitary authority-principle evolved to become separate other-worldly hierarchical orders as non-exclusive earthbound bestowals proved hard to defend, inadequate to differentiate the only true

---

[69]McConkie, *Mormon Doctrine*, 2d ed. (1966), 476-77, citing *Inspired Version*, Gen. 14:30-31, emphasis added.

[70]Book of Mormon, Alma 13.

[71]McConkie, *Mormon Doctrine*, 2d ed. (1966), 477. *Teachings of Presidents of The Church – Joseph Smith* (Salt Lake City: The Church of Jesus Christ of Latter-day Saints, 2007), 365.

church on the face of the earth from poorly intended pretenders. Is it to be wondered that "Joseph was [at first] commanded to search the Book of Mormon itself for instructions on how to receive and dispense priesthood authority"?[72]   Metaphysical authority? Charismatic authority? The Book of Mormon model resembles nineteenth-century Protestant theology. That kind of authority was subjective, arguable but not distinctive, and in the very early Mormon Church it was not the "high priesthood."

Many Christians can say with conviction that they were called to the ministry by the grace of God.   Foreordination in the foreknowledge of God did not require angelic ordination by the laying on of hands. This was authority by way of command and spiritual prompting. This kind of authority was, until Rigdon arrived to help Smith abandon non-literal metaphysical process, a source for the charismatic unitary authority, undeveloped as it was, supposed to have been exercised by the male members of the early Church. In the early Church (and until 1835), Joseph attributed these words to God: "'I give unto you a commandment, that you rely upon the things which are written; for in them are all things written, concerning my church, my gospel, and my rock.'"[73] Grant Palmer added this to that: "When Joseph receives a spiritual prompting to begin to baptize and ordain others, he is following the pattern in the Book of Mormon."[74]

The authority exercised by the Nephites in the Book of Mormon did not depend upon angels, ordinations or apostolic keys, and wasn't exclusive. When the Book of Mormon model was abandoned to be replaced by literal, physical angelic ordination, then did what came to be called priesthood come to be called *exclusive*. "In a single stroke ["with detailed accounts of physical appearances by . . . impressive biblical figures"], the new accounts legitimized the leadership's religious authority, giving them exclusive rights and

---

[72]Palmer, *An Insider's View of Mormon Origins*, 223, citing Book of Commandments 15:3 and Doctrine and Covenants 18:3-4.

[73]Book of Commandments 15:3.

[74]Palmer, *An Insider's View of Mormon Origins*, 223, citing Book of Commandments 15:3 and Doctrine and Covenants 18:3-4.

setting them apart from: anyone who claimed a non-literal or metaphysical reception of authority."[75]

The amended notion – basically "dual priesthoods of different ranks" conferred by the literal laying on of hands and promoted by post-Zion's Camp pump-you-up accounts of previously unknown visitations by John the Baptist and Peter, James, and John, figures first described in altered documents – now served to establish Mormonism's legalistic hierarchical authority claims and to bolster the humiliated prophet's then flagging fortunes. These priesthood-concept strengthening amendments traced their paternity to awkward, backdated, falsified, unprovenanced afterthoughts not supported by the original manuscripts in the archives.

The procedures first practiced in the early Church, showed the efficacy, before those retroactive revisions, of *charismatic authority* in David Whitmer's idealized "community of believers." What the Book of Mormon encouraged, and what Joseph Smith and the early Church originally taught and practiced, supported the notion that good men could act for God based upon righteous living, good works, visionary experience, dreams, visions and promptings. This egalitarian authority theory, before it was disparaged, disrespected and rudely dismissed, had the support of the early Mormons: "Righteousness was an absolute requisite for the conferral of the higher priesthood. This 'order came, not by man, nor the will of man; neither by father nor mother; neither by beginning of days nor end of years; but of God; *And it was delivered unto men by the calling of his own voice, according to his own will, unto as many as believed on his name.*'"[76]

Melchizedek the Man

Alma's isolated identification of a "connection between Jesus and

---

[75]Palmer, *An Insider's View of Mormon Origins*, 231, emphasis added.

[76]McConkie, *Mormon Doctrine*, 2d ed. (1966), 478, citing *Inspired Version*, Genesis, 14:28-29, Hebrews 7:1-3, emphasis added.

Melchizedek" was made in the Bible in Hebrews in an Epistle from which the author of Alma (a Book of Mormon prophet) conceptually borrowed.[77] Smith's use of Hebrews in Alma, like the memorialization of King James *errata* in the Book of Mormon, is damning to the scriptures' historical pretensions. "The close association of Melchizedek, *priest* of Salem, and Jesus, *high priest* of the new covenant – an association that occurs exclusively in Hebrews – influenced Smith's dictation of Alma 13."[78] "Alma's dependence on Hebrews 7," according to Dan Vogel, "is not a matter of plagiarism but one of interpretive and conceptual borrowing. Indeed, both Alma and Hebrews stand alone in linking Jews with Melchizedek's priesthood."[79] Alma's dependence upon Hebrews 7 is yet another Book of Mormon anachronism. Alma's Chapter 13 is supposed to have been written in about 82 BC. The only place Melchizedek is found in the Book of Mormon is in Alma Chapter 13, in work supposed to have preceded the birth of Christ. The Book of Hebrews postdates Christ. "The use of tabernacle terminology in Hebrews has been used to date the epistle before the destruction of the temple . . . the most probable date for its composition is the second half of the year 63 or the beginning of 64 [A.D.], according to the Catholic Encyclopedia."[80]

Hebrews calls Jesus a priest "after the order of Melchisedec" (Hebrews 7:11, 17, 21). Alma calls Melchizedek a priest "after the order of the Son."[81] "This reversal resolved a troubling aspect of Hebrews that placed Melchizedek in a position that was superior to Jesus." Melchizedek, according to Alma, although particularly prominent, was but one of a great many ancient patriarchs. "[T]here were many before [Melchizedek], and also there were many afterwards, but none were greater; therefore, of him they have more particularly made mention."[82] Vogel describes the

---

[77]Vogel, *Joseph Smith: The Making of a Prophet*, 217.
[78]Ibid., emphasis added.
[79]Ibid., 215.
[80]"Epistle to the Hebrews" (accessed 11 June 2014), available from wikipedia.com.
[81]Book of Mormon, Alma 13:9, 14.
[82]Ibid., Alma 13:19.

anachronism: "Thus, Alma's [Old Testament] discussion not only conceptually derives from [the New Testament's] Hebrews, it attempts to resolve a perceived problem with the text."[83] "Hebrews associates Jesus with Melchizedek's priesthood, but Alma expands this to include an entire order of priests, a transparent expansion of Hebrews. This procedure foreshadows Smith's subsequent revision of the Bible where he would revise both Genesis 14 and Hebrews 7 to conform to Alma 13."[84]

While speaking of Melchizedek, Jesus and the priesthood, Alma made the case for charisma. Alma postulates that the Lord God ordained priests to his holy order ("which was after the order of his Son") "soon after the Fall." Unlike "the earthly priesthood of the Levites," these ancient priests were not invested by reason of their particular lineage, but "rather, like Jesus they were foreordained by God."[85] On account of their "exceeding faith," because of their "good works" and as Christians. Soon after the Fall of Mormonism's literal Adam, "'the Lord God ordained priests, after his holy order, which was after the order of his Son, to teach these things unto the people' (13:1)."[86] The genius of this explanation, before Joseph Smith settled upon other ingenious alternatives calculated to secure the exclusivity and polarization that only "one true church" required, was this:

> *As opposed to the earthly priesthood of the Levites, Melchizedek's priesthood was therefore spiritual and the result of charismatic experience rather than physical ordination. These ancient priests had not inherited their authority by lineage; rather like Jesus, they were foreordained by God.*[87]

This Melchizedek was not somehow ordained in mortality by the literal laying on of hands of someone having authority; his

---

[83]Vogel, *Joseph Smith: The Making of a Prophet*, 215.
[84]Ibid.
[85]Ibid., 217.
[86]Ibid.
[87]Ibid., emphasis added.

authority was "spiritual," "the result of charismatic experience rather than physical ordination."[88]   Alma explained: "And this is the manner after which they were ordained – being called and prepared from the foundation of the world according to the foreknowledge of God, on account of their exceeding faith and good works (13:3)."[89]

> *To those who questioned Smith's authority to preach or baptize [in the beginning], he could point to Jesus and Melchizedek as examples of priests who were preordained to office. This also explained how non-Levitical priests could arise among the [non-Levitical] Nephites.*[90]

Until Joseph and Oliver turned history on its head to say that they had in some prior manifestation received the Aaronic and Melchizedek priesthoods by angelic ordination from John the Baptist and Peter, James, and John, they claimed charismatic authority, as Alma allowed, without earthly ordination and with Jesus and Melchizedek as their soft authority exemplars. They might have done well to also consider the phenomena surrounding the conversion of an unordained Apostle Paul. As in the case of other highly problematic doctrinal emendations, the long after-the-fact and poorly supported claims of literal ordination in mortality were evolutionary afterthoughts, part of a late design becoming part of the doctrine after the fine points of priesthood were further articulated and better understood.

WILLIAM E. McLELLIN

Apostle William E. McLellin returned to Kirtland, Ohio, from a mission in June, 1836, and was greatly disappointed to find the First Presidency heavily involved with "temporal things." "They had

---

[88]Ibid.
[89]Ibid., citing Alma.
[90]Ibid., emphasis added.

gone to New York," he said, "and run into debt about forty thousand dollars for goods – which was never paid!!!"[91] In July 1872 – long after he left the Church – and in a well-intended letter to Joseph Smith III (McLellin's second letter to the prophet who led the Reorganized LDS Church from 1860 to 1914), McLellin expressed his personal disappointment to the namesake son of Mormonism's founder. He had told Joseph III, in an earlier letter, that his father wasn't the man the son thought that he was, and he had suggested that Joseph III would be well advised not to follow in his famous father's footsteps. David Whitmer, McLellin's much admired mentor, expressed his personal disappointment in an 1887 tract entitled *An Address to All Believers in Christ.*

> *If you believe my testimony to the Book of Mormon, if you believe that God spake to us three witnesses by his own voice, then I tell you that in June, 1838, God spake to me again by his own voice from the heavens, and told me to "separate myself from among the Latter Day Saints, for as they thought to do unto me, so should it be done unto them."[92]*

Whitmer expressed these faith-denigrating sentiments while facing his own mortality the year before he died.

---

[91]William E. McLellin, Letter to Joseph Smith III, July 1872, in *The William E. McLellin Papers: 1854-1880* (eds. Larson and Passey), 490. Forty thousand dollars – *in 1836* – was all the money in the world. Joseph and Sidney avoided their creditors when they left Kirtland, Ohio, for Far West, Missouri, on horseback at night, in the winter of 1837-1838. Joseph Smith, Hyrum Smith, Brigham Young, Heber C. Kimball, and various others, later declared bankruptcies, discharging their debts. Emma Smith told William E. McLellin (whose abilities she held in high regard), when he visited her in Nauvoo, Illinois, in 1847, after the death of her husband, that the debts "proved against the estate of Joseph Smith, in probate court" amounted to "over $200,000, but not a dollar to pay the debt!" (Letter to John L. Traughber, 14 Dec. 1878, in Ibid., 515).

[92]David Whitmer, *An Address to All Believers in Christ: by A Witness to the Divine Authenticity of The Book of Mormon* (Richmond, MO: n.p., 1887; photographic reprint, Concord, CA: Pacific Publishing Company, 1993), 27, emphasis added.

William E. McLellin and Two Priesthoods

In his second letter to Joseph Smith III, William E. McLellin challenged the proposition that there were two separate orders of priesthood. That notion, according to McLellin, was fatally flawed. The word "priesthood," he said, "is not used in the book of M[ormon] in its *Gospel* history" (McLellin's *gospel era* commenced with the visit of the resurrected Christ). "The word," he further said, "is not found but twice in the New Testament outside of the 7th of Hebrews."[93] "The words minister, ministers, or ministering is usually used in the inspired books instead of priesthood."[94] McLellin endeavored to explain why the supposed restoration of the Aaronic Priesthood wasn't biblical. The Aaronic Priesthood, he said, as this text has also so surmised, came to rest in Christ. McLellin distinguished what he called "the *law* dispensation" from what he called the "*gospel* dispensation."[95] "The law dispensation covered the period from Moses to Christ, its rules set forth in the Hebrew Bible as the legal standard against which people were judged."[96] "With Christ came a new dispensation wherein his gospel provided new guidelines for religious thought and action. These guidelines were to be in place until the millennium . . . ."[97] "Behold, the days come, saith the Lord, when I will make a new covenant with the house of Israel and with the house of Judah: . . . ."[98] The Lord's "new covenant" replaced the law of a carnal commandment and the lesser priesthood that administered the law of a carnal commandment. The old law, lineal and less than eternal, and the lesser priesthood that administered the Old Law, carnal and finite, passed away for Christians following Christ.

McLellin argued that the priesthood during the *law* dispensation

---

[93]Letter to Joseph Smith III, July 1872, in *The William E. McLellin Papers: 1854-1880* (eds. Larson and Passey), 491, emphasis added.

[94]Ibid.

[95]William D. Russell, "Portrait of a 'True Believer' in Original Mormonism," in *The William E. McLellin Papers: 1854-1880* (eds. Larson and Passey), 125.

[96]Ibid.

[97]Ibid.

[98]Hebrews 8:8.

had been Aaronic, and that the priesthood during the *gospel* dispensation had been Melchizedek. He believed that the Aaronic Priesthood was superceded by the Melchizedek Priesthood during the *gospel* dispensation. Thus, McLellin concluded that the old law and the lesser priesthood were "no longer in effect."[99] Smith had undertaken to restore a priesthood which had a place in the *law era* in the Old Testament prior to Christ, but that served no useful purpose in the *gospel era* in the New Testament after Christ. The fact that the Aaronic Priesthood was unknown to the Nephites provided yet further evidence that the lesser priesthood was nothing that needed to be restored. McLellin contended that "neither the Book of Mormon nor the New Testament know anything of 'Aaronic priests.'"[100] "The word lesser priest, Aaronic priest, or Levitical priest, is not found in the Book of Mormon," he said.[101]

The old *law* and its inferior ministry was a "shadow of things to come."[102] When the *gospel era* commenced with and after the visit of the resurrected Christ, the substance overwhelmed the shadow of heavenly things. McLellin, a secretary to the founding quorum and one of the most capable early apostles, reasoned as follows: "There is not a word said in both the books the N[ew] T[estament] and book of M[ormon] about Aaronic, or Levitical, or Lesser priests as existing in the Gospel age."[103] According to McLellin, all of the testimony in support of that fallacious claim (Aaronic or Levitical Priesthood "existing in the Gospel age") was contained in the Doctrine and Covenants, a tome which he personally considered to be fatally flawed. Although McLellin believed the Book of Mormon to be the word of God (and favored the seerstone for translation), he vilified the "Book of Doctrine and Covenants," describing it as a

---

[99]Russell, "Portrait of a 'True Believer' in Original Mormonism," in *The William E. McLellin Papers: 1854-1880* (eds. Larson and Passey), 125.

[100]Ibid., 125-26.

[101]Letter to Mark H. Forscutt, 1 Oct. 1871, reproduced at *The William E. McLellin Papers: 1854-1880* (eds. Larson and Passey), 473.

[102]Hebrews 10:1, quoted in Letter to Joseph Smith III, July 1872, *The William E. McLellin Papers: 1854-1880* (eds. Larson and Passey), 491.

[103]*The William E. McLellin Papers: 1854-1880* (eds. Larson and Passey), 491, emphasis added.

"mutilated, changed, mixed up and bungled" creation.[104] Because of its many awkward out-of-order amendments, he thought that unprincipled work belonged to Joseph Smith, Sidney Rigdon, Oliver Cowdery, W.W. Phelps, Frederick G. Williams, and possibly others, rather than to the Lord of Hosts.

Another disturbing issue concerned how Joseph Smith, a Gentile who claimed to be descended from Joseph of Egypt (an unprovable contention), could hold a lineage-dependent less than eternal priesthood conferred by Levite fathers on Levite sons. McLellin was quite certain that Joseph Smith, who had lost his way, had created a "false system."[105] Bothered to distraction by the oppressive new and unprecedented concepts of priesthood, McLellin, a privileged insider, expressed his discontent. In the *law era,* he said, there was never more than *one* high priest at a time. In the Bible (as opposed to the Book of Mormon), Melchizedek was a "priest," but not a "high priest." In the *gospel era* and in the Bible, Christ was *the* only "High Priest," the "anti-type" to the *law era's* lineage-dependent Aaron.[106] McLellin does appear to have taken his lead from the Apostle Paul, the author of the Epistle to the Hebrews.

In his second letter to Joseph III, McClellin disparaged those retroactive reports that sought to say that Joseph and Oliver had actually received two separate orders of priesthood from two separate sets of heavenly messengers by means of angelic ordinations. He described Brother Joseph's heavenly messenger authority-theory as both late and contrived:

> *But as to the story of John the Baptist ordaining Joseph and Oliver on the day they were baptized: I never heard of it in the church for years, altho I*

---

[104]McLellin to Mark H. Forscutt, 1 October 1871, *The William E. McLellin Papers: 1854-1880* (eds. Larson and Passey), 473.

[105]Russell, "Portrait of a 'True Believer' in Original Mormonism," in *The William E. McLellin Papers: 1854-1880* (eds. Larson and Passey), 125.

[106]Letter to Joseph Smith III, July 1872, in *The William E. McLellin Papers: 1854-1880* (eds. Larson and Passey), 491.

*carefully noticed things that were said. And today I
do not believe the story.*[107]

McLellin informed Joseph III that an apostle (McLellin was one)
was not an administrative officer. "When they ministered," he said,
"they did it as Elders." "Prophets were not administrative officers .
. . . Evangelists were traveling elders . . . . Pastors were Bishops or
Priests."[108] "In this way," according to McLellin, "the book of
M[ormon] and the New Testament are reconciled and harmonized.
I can see," he said, "no earthly use for Lesser priests. I can find
nothing for them to do, that the ministry of the 'church of Christ'
could not do better. I hold that Apostles, Elders, Bishops, and
Deacons are all in the Melchesidick Priesthood with Jesus as the
High Priest – holding different stations only . . . ."[109] "Priesthood,"
McLellin reported, "is not an office but an order of ministry."[110]
"Neither Melchisedec or Aaronic priesthood ever had but three . . .
offices in it. And there never existed but one order at any one time
in the church of God, or in the church of Christ since the world
began."[111] The concept of multiple overlapping priesthoods,
according to the secretary of the founding quorum, was awkward
and unprecedented. McLellin argued that the alleged restoration of
two distinct orders of priesthood operating simultaneously had been
a big mistake. "An Aaronic priests's whole duty was pointed out by
the law, and when the law was abolished [by the coming of Christ]
then the rule by which they [Aaronic priests] should act, [and the
law] which defined their duties, was all set aside also, and hence
there was nothing for them to do. The whole order was set aside . . .
."[112] McLellin supported this sensible biblically favored contention
with Old Testament precedent. "All the ministers of the first-born
who started from Goshen to Canaan with Moses, were . . . set aside

---

[107]Ibid., emphasis added.
[108]Ibid., 492.
[109]Ibid.
[110]Ibid.
[111]William E. McLellin, "Reasons Why I Am Not a 'Mormon'" (ca. 1880), in
The William E. McLellin Papers: 1854-1880 (eds. Larson and Passey), 387.
[112]Letter to Joseph Smith III, July 1872, in *The William E. McLellin Papers:
1854-1880* (eds. Larson and Passey), 492.

when the law priesthood was established – offset by the Levites, ..." After the law priesthood ran its course,

> *We have not a hint of the Aaronic or law priesthood's ever acting after the Gospel ministry was instituted by Jesus Christ. I say no hint in the New Testament or book of Mormon.*[113]

> *Jesus Christ set three ~~orders~~ offices of ministers in his church, upon both continents. At Jerusalem it was Elder, Bishop, and Deacon. In the new world it was Elder, Priest, and Teacher. Not first President, Patriarch, Apostles, High Priests, Elders, Bishop, Priest, Teacher, and Deacon.*[114]

> *The office of high Priest ceased in the church when Christ came and took and exercised that office himself. No mention is made of it . . . as existing in the church after Christ came into the world, . . . chose his Apostles and set them to work. The book of Mormon is silent in all its New Testament part of such office.*[115]

> *There were never two priesthoods at the same time in the church of God, or the church of Christ since the world began. Whenever a new priesthood came into existence then the preceding one was done away – set aside entirely as useless.*[116]

-----

[113]Ibid.

[114]McLellin, "Reasons Why I Am Not a Mormon" (ca. 1880), *The William E. McLellin Papers: 1854-1880* (eds. Larson and Passey), 387.

[115]Ibid., 388, emphasis added.

[116]"Why I Am Not a Latter Day Saint," in *The William E. McLellin Papers* (ed. Larson and Passey), 330, emphasis added.

CHAPTER SIXTEEN

From "Authority" to "Priesthood"

Authority is the word we used for the first two years in the Church – until Sidney Rigdon's days in Ohio.[1]

David Whitmer

In the revision of the concept of "authority" from charismatic to literal, from metaphysical to hierarchical, laid the seeds of Joseph Smith and Brigham Young's theocratic tyranny and the roots of a great deception.

Joel M. Allred

It is my province to teach to the Church what the doctrine is. It is your province to echo what I say or to remain silent.

Apostle Bruce R. McConkie, 1981

SIDNEY RIGDON'S EMERGENCE

Joseph's Lord rejoiced when Sidney Rigdon, in the similitude of John the Baptist ("Behold thou wast sent forth, even as John to prepare the way before me . . ."[2]), "visited Joseph Smith, jun., at Fayette, New York," in December 1830.[3] Rigdon, "the first previously ordained minister to join the hierarchy,"[4] was baptized

---

[1]Sidney Rigdon, Joseph's most intimate early friend and counselor, matriculated in a society (Disciples of Christ) that promoted the notion of multiple priesthoods.

[2]Doctrine and Covenants 35:4.

[3]Andrew Jenson, comp., *Church Chronology: A Record of Important Events Pertaining to the History of the Church of Jesus Christ of Latter-day Saints*, 2d ed., rev. and enlarged (Salt Lake City: Deseret News, 1914), 5.

[4]D. Michael Quinn, *The Mormon Hierarchy: Origins of Power* (Salt Lake City: Signature Books in association with Smith Research Associates, 1994), 618.

(at Kirtland, Ohio, in November 1830) by Oliver Cowdery. When Rigdon "came to inquire of the Lord" and Joseph, he was attended by Edward Partridge, a trusted colleague who was described as "a pattern of piety, and one of the Lord's great men."[5]

On December 7, 1830, God introduced "my servant Sidney" to Joseph Smith in a "Revelation given to Joseph Smith the Prophet, *and* Sidney Rigdon."[6] "Listen to the voice of the Lord your God, even Alpha and Omega . . . . I am Jesus Christ, the Son of God, who was crucified for the sins of the world . . . . Behold, Verily, verily, I say unto my servant Sidney, I have looked upon thee and thy works, I have heard thy prayers, and prepared thee for a greater work. Thou art blessed, for thou shalt do great things . . . ."[7] Jesus sent Sidney to Joseph.

Section 35 of the Doctrine and Covenants informed Joseph and Sidney in promising terms of remarkable things to come. Joseph's Jesus promised Sidney power to confer the gift of the Holy Ghost "by the laying on of the hands even as the apostles of old." To the prophet and Sidney he said, "And it shall come to pass that there shall be a great work in the land . . . . I will show miracles, signs and wonders, unto all those who believe on my name . . . they shall cast out devils; they shall heal the sick; they shall cause the blind to receive their sight, and the deaf to hear, and the dumb to speak, and the lame to walk."[8]

The Lord told his coveted new recruit that, "I have sent forth the fulness of my gospel by the hand of my servant Joseph; and in weakness have I blessed him."[9] "[W]atch over him that his faith fail not . . . write for him . . . tarry with him, and he shall journey with you, forsake him not . . . ."[10] "[C]all on the holy prophets to prove his words, as they shall be given him,"[11] "even as they are in

---

[5]Joseph Smith Jr., *History of The Church of Jesus Christ of Latter-day Saints*, B.H. Roberts, ed., 2d ed., rev., (Salt Lake City: The Deseret Book Company, 1978), 1:128.

    [6]Doctrine and Covenants (1957), Section 35 headnote, emphasis added.

    [7]Ibid., 35:1-4.

    [8]Ibid., 35:4-9.

    [9]Ibid., 35:17.

    [10]Ibid., 35:19, 20, 22.

    [11]Ibid., 35:23.

mine own bosom, to the salvation of mine own elect . . . ."[12] "Keep all the commandments and covenants by which ye are bound; and I will cause the heavens to shake for your good, and Satan shall tremble and Zion shall rejoice . . . and Israel shall be saved . . . ."[13] After he had watched and written and journeyed, and when the prophet was dead, Sidney said, "I guided his tottering steps till he could walk alone . . . ."[14]

The complex and melancholy Rigdon's outsize influence on Smith was swift and immediate.[15] On January 2, 1831, the Church held its Third Conference in Fayette, New York. Starting on June 3, 1831, the Church held its Fourth Conference in Kirtland, Ohio. In December 1830, in yet another revelation directed to Sidney *and* Joseph, there came "the first commandment concerning a gathering in this dispensation."[16] "The Saints in the State of New York [Joseph Smith's home] were commanded by revelation to gather to Ohio [Sidney Rigdon's home]."[17] This second joint revelation provided for nothing less than the redirection of the movement. "And again, a commandment I give unto the church, that it is expedient in me that they should assemble together at the Ohio . . . ."[18] The first conferral of "high priesthood" power followed Rigdon's 1830 visit to Joseph Smith by about six months. The early authority-principle changed at the Fourth Conference of the Church on June 3, 1831, a Conference held at a large log schoolhouse in Kirtland, Ohio, close to Isaac Morley's farm. Years later a disenchanted David Whitmer placed Sidney Rigdon at the

---

[12]Ibid., 35:20.

[13]Ibid., 35:24, 25.

[14]"The First Idea of the Book of Mormon," *The Salt Lake Daily Tribune*, vol. 18 no. 18 (5 November 1879).

[15]In 1830, Sidney Rigdon was the most prominent convert of the first proselyting mission first supposed to have been directed toward the Lamanites (Native Americans then located near the border of Missouri).

[16]Doctrine and Covenants 37 (1957), Headnote. On February 16, 1832, just slightly less than two years after the Church was organized, Joseph Smith and Sidney Rigdon jointly received the revelation of the three degrees of glory, which later became Section 76 of the Doctrine and Covenants. One year later Smith and Rigdon, working together and without the benefit of manuscripts, completed their inspired translation of the King James Bible.

[17]Doctrine and Covenants Sec. 37; Jenson, comp., *Church Chronology*, 5.

[18]Doctrine and Covenants 37:3; Jenson, comp., *Church Chronology*, 5.

center of Mormonism's priesthood/authority convention.[19]   That
Book of Mormon witness described the capable Rigdon as the
architect of the priesthood.

> *This matter of "priesthood," since the days of Sydney*
> *Rigdon, has been the great hobby and stumbling-*
> *block of the Latter Day Saints.   Priesthood means*
> *authority and authority is the word we should use. I*
> *do not think the word priesthood is mentioned in the*
> *New Covenant of the Book of Mormon. Authority is*
> *the word we used for the first two years in the church*
> *– until Sydney Rigdon's days in Ohio.*[20]

Whitmer opined that Joseph Smith allowed himself to become the
instantly influential Rigdon's "priesthood" intern.   After the
biblical primitivist Rigdon joined the Church, the organization
chart fleshed out. When Rigdon became a Mormonite, there were
no high priests. With the passage of time, instead of three offices of
equals (elders, teachers and priests), there came eight or nine offices
of rank. Mormonism's early commendable "aversion to ranking"[21]
vanished in increments. According to the offended Whitmer, "The
office of Elder is spoken of all through the New Testament as being
in the church, but not one High Priest."   The institutional
acceptance of higher and lower authorities and offices operated to
change what Whitmer chose to describe as a previously loving
spiritual landscape. Whitmer reported that there was but one high
priest "in the [gospel] church upon the eastern continent."
"Behold," he was sorry to say, "it is solemn mockery before God to
have established in the church today this important office of which

---

[19]"In the latter part of this month [January 1831] Joseph Smith, jun. and wife,
in company with Sidney Rigdon and Edward Partridge, left Fayette, N.Y., for
Kirtland, Geauga Co., O., where they arrived about the first of February."
(Jenson, comp., *Church Chronology*, 5). Joseph relocated Emma and the New
York Mormons to Kirtland at the urging of Rigdon and because of a revelation.

[20]David Whitmer, *An Address to All Believers in Christ: by A Witness to the*
Divine Authenticity of The Book of Mormon (Richmond, MO: n.p., 1887;
photographic reprint, Concord, CA: Pacific Publishing Company, 1993), 64,
emphasis added. "In no place in the word of God does it say that an Elder is after
the order of Melchisedec, or after the order of the Melchisedec Priesthood. An
Elder is after the order of Christ."

[21]Quinn, *The Mormon Hierarchy: Origins of Power*, 28. In the Bible (as
opposed to in the Book of Mormon) Melchizedek wasn't a High Priest.

Christ alone is worthy."[22] The Apostle Paul, in the epistle to the Hebrews, had spoken to the heart and mind of David Whitmer. With the passage of time, Mormonism's high priesthood embraced high authority elders, high priests, seventies, apostles, patriarchs and prophets.

Michael Quinn opines that because of the Book of Mormon, "everyone in 1831" would have understood that "high priesthood" meant "high priest." But that may be far from certain. "The June 1831 conferral of 'high priesthood,'" according to Quinn, "clearly included ordination [to] the office of high priest. Until the revelation dated September 1832 (but not published until 1835 [D&C 84][23]), Joseph Smith and others saw the higher priesthood as encompassing one office exclusively."[24] But that may be far from certain.[25] The minutes of that Fourth Conference of the Church on June 3, 1831, described "high priesthood" without using the terms "high priest" or "office of high priest."[26] Other offices in the alleged similitude of the gospel Church, and in the alleged

---

[22]Whitmer, *An Address to All Believers in Christ*, 64.

[23]Section 84 was dated September 1832, which was twenty-nine months after the Church was organized and forty months after the May 15, 1829, date awkwardly (and retroactively) assigned by the Church to the miraculous baptisms of Joseph Smith and Oliver Cowdery by John the Baptist. The tardy revelation wasn't published, even then, until six years after those events. Section 84 of the 1835 edition of the Doctrine and Covenants, although supposed to have been dated 1832, was not published in *The Evening and the Morning Star* in 1832 or 1833 (although other revelations received in September 1832 [Doctrine and Covenants 29] and October 1832 [Doctrine and Covenants 65] were). Section 84 was not published in the Book of Commandments (in 1833) or anywhere else until 1835, when it became part of the first edition of the Doctrine and Covenants. After June 3, 1831, and until Section 84, "Joseph Smith and others [according to Quinn] saw the high priesthood as encompassing one office exclusively [high priest]. The lesser priesthood applied to the offices of deacon, teacher, priest, elder and bishop." (Quinn, *The Mormon Hierarchy: Origins of Power*, 29).

[24]Ibid.

[25]A respected Mormon scholar (Greg Prince) avers that while "previously ordained elders" received the "high priesthood" in June 1831, they didn't receive the office of high priest. Quinn is forced to admit that until April 1832 (nearly one additional year), the original minutes from the Fourth Conference in June 1831 continued to list men as "elders," which was what they had been to start, despite their ordination to the high priesthood. (Ibid.). Both Michael Quinn and David Whitmer described the ordinations of high priests.

[26]Ibid.

similitude of the Old Testament, were added later.[27] What Joseph Smith described in the *Times and Seasons* in 1844, after things had settled, was not a new and different kind of office, but rather a new and different kind of authority with a new and different kind of a name. By then it was seen to have become a separate "authority" (order, arrangement) of a different and higher power and rank.

Prior to June 1831, lower priesthood (non-Melchizedek) elders were ordained and about two thousand members were baptized and confirmed before the attributes and elements of overlapping "priesthoods" were formulated, understood and addressed.[28] "By 1835 Smith and Cowdery had good reason to be vague about the introduction of Melchizedek Priesthood. Doctrinal statements published from 1835 on could not comfortably be retrofitted to unaltered documents of the 1830 church."[29] When Sidney Rigdon and Joseph Smith began to promote the concept of greater and lesser priesthoods, earlier articulations emphasizing authority rather than priesthood and treating authority as unitary had to be dismissed. Written out of the minds of the members. When the nature of the authority principle tardily changed, those earlier foundational narratives became a snare and a delusion. In 1835, particularly in 1835, previously published revelations (Book of Commandments 1833, *The Evening and the Morning Star,* 1832-33) were awkwardly altered. The first edition of the Doctrine and Covenants in 1835 retroactively "altered pre-1831 revelations to make a distinction between the Aaronic and Melchizedek priesthoods, and to classify the offices of elder and apostles as part of the latter."[30] Until 1831, "Mormons regarded the office of elder separately from 'high priesthood.'"[31] It was a non-Melchizedek

---

[27]Rigdon – the Disciple of Christ, the Reformed Baptist, an Old Testament scholar and a *protégé* of Thomas and Alexander Campbell and Walter Scott – promoted the restoration of all things.

[28]Rigdon quickly knew just how important he was. "5 July [1832]. Second Counselor Rigdon [colleague to First Counselor Jesse Gause] tries to seize control of the church and is disfellowshipped until 28 July when he is re-ordained a high priest. This is the first instance of apostasy by a general authority." (Quinn, *The Mormon Hierarchy: Origins of Power*, Chronology, 619).

[29]Ibid., 30.

[30]"Priesthood (Latter Day Saints)" (accessed 6 April 2014), available from https://en.wikipedia.org/wiki/ Priesthood_(Latter_Day_Saints); Internet, 10.

[31]Quinn, *The Mormon Hierarchy: Origins of Power*, 30. Brigham Young: "The Twelve Apostles had been ordained, and every one of them happened to be high

lower authority office.

The first unmistakable use of the terms "Melchizedek Priesthood" and "Aaronic Priesthood" in anything unaltered may not have occurred until 1835 in the Doctrine and Covenants (in what is now Section 107). That section is seen to report that, "The office of an elder comes under the priesthood of Melchizedek."[32] When the doctrine got ahead of the facts, when the leaders were forced to revisit the facts, history surrendered to creative theology. David Whitmer saw the aggressive Rigdon, Joseph's God appointed "spokesman,"[33] as the instigator of a priesthood/authority dilemma.

> *This matter of the two orders of priesthood in the Church of Christ, and lineal priesthood of the old law being in the church, all originated in the mind of Sydney Rigdon. He explained these things to Brother Joseph in his way, out of the old Scriptures, and got Brother Joseph to inquire, etc. He would inquire, and as mouthpiece speak out the revelations just as they had it fixed up in their hearts.*[34]

No one should have known that better than Whitmer, a strongly credentialed Mormon founder who shouted his defiance.

> *This is the way the High Priests and the "priesthood" as you have it, was introduced into the Church of*

---

priests excepting Brother Heber C. Kimball and myself; we were elders." Brigham Young regarded the office of elder as separate from the "high priesthood," something he confirmed when he said that he and Kimball "had never been ordained to the high priesthood." (Brigham Young Sermon given 25 May 1877 [the year of his death], *Deseret Evening News* [2 June 1877], 1; Doctrine and Covenants 84; all quoted in Ibid.).

[32]Doctrine and Covenants 107:7.

[33]Quinn, *The Mormon Hierarchy: Origins of Power*, 620. "(12 Oct. [1833]). A revelation appoints Rigdon as 'a spokesman to my servant Joseph.'" Whitmer, of course, was one of the Three Witnesses to the Book of Mormon.

[34]Whitmer, *An Address to All Believers in Christ*, 64, emphasis added. Whitmer reported that there were "no High Priests in the church of Christ of old, and none in the church of Christ in these last days until almost two years after its beginning – when the leaders began to drift into error . . . ." That office, the office of High Priest, according to Whitmer, the epistle to the Hebrews, the Apostle Paul and traditional Christianity, belonged to Christ alone.

Christ almost two years after its beginning – and after
we had baptized and confirmed about two thousand
souls into the church.[35]

Background

Many important events were concluded before Joseph Smith's first
known meeting with Sidney Rigdon. In May 1829, about a year-
and-a-half before Cowdery baptized Rigdon, Joseph and Oliver
baptized each other, finding their authority in a command received
from a stone carefully placed in Joseph's hat. By the use of the
stone, Joseph, a treasure-seeking seer, was supposed to be able to
perceive things invisible to the natural eye. What did they receive
by way of a command conveyed to the two of them in Joseph's
fortune-telling glass? In his money-digger's stone? "Authority."
Generic unitary non-literal "authority." Not "two orders of
priesthood," or the "lineal priesthood of the old law." Not
something then called Aaronic, Levitical, "carnal," or "priesthood."
An older, wiser Joseph later claimed that they were promised
additional authority that would enable them to bestow the gift of
the Holy Ghost, and in June 1829, at Peter Whitmer's house, Smith
and Cowdery supposed that they received additional authority –
charismatic, metaphysical non-literal authority – in consequence of
yet another stone considered command. At that early time, no one
said anything about heavenly messengers, angelic ordinations, the
lineal priesthood of the old law, dual priesthoods of different ranks,
or even "priesthood."

They prayed for the gift they were promised but hadn't received.
After requesting this blessing in the upper story of "Mr. Whitmer's
house," and before much time had passed, "the *word of the Lord,*
came unto us, in the chamber, commanding us; that I should ordain
Oliver Cowdery to be an Elder in the Church of Jesus Christ; And
that he also should ordain me to the same office . . . ."[36] This
instruction had nothing to do with Peter, James, and John, or with

---

[35]Ibid., 64, emphasis added.
[36]*The Papers of Joseph Smith: Volume 1, Autobiographical and Historical*
Writings, ed. Dean C. Jessee (Salt Lake City: Deseret Book Company, 1989), 1:299,
emphasis added.

a "voice . . . in the wilderness between Harmony, Susquehanna county, and Colesville, Broome county on the Susquehanna river . . . ."[37] And nothing at that time (in 1829) served to suggest it had anything to do with what only much later came to be called the Aaronic Priesthood, and even later still with what came to be called the Melchizedek Priesthood.

After the "word of the Lord" commanded them to ordain each other to the office of "Elder" (God "gave them this greater authority in the Whitmer home in June 1829"[38]), they thought they had what they needed to build and develop the Church. Once again no one mentioned John the Baptist, Peter, James, and John, the "lineal priesthood of the old law," "priesthoods," "priesthood" or "angelic ordination." Until September or October 1834, which was more than five years later, there were no documented ordinations by heavenly messengers. On (and for some time after) May 15, 1829, the devil didn't catch and bind them, their faces didn't contort demon-like, they weren't inhabited by evil spirits, didn't see the Savior, and were not unable to speak.

Before Joseph met Rigdon and started to say that there were separate orders of priesthoods ("dual priesthoods of different ranks"), "Joseph Smith, jun., and Oliver Cowdery ordained each other Elders – the first Elders in the Church – according to commandment from God."[39] "They then [on April 6, 1830, by *Church Chronology* reckoning] laid hands on all the baptized members present, 'that they might receive the gift of the Holy Ghost and be confirmed members of the Church.' The Holy Ghost was poured out upon them 'to a very great degree.' Some prophesied and 'all praised the Lord and rejoiced exceedingly.'"[40] That was all supposed to have occurred more than one year before twenty-three lower authority elders received the high priesthood for the first time at Kirtland, Ohio, at the Fourth Conference of the

---

[37]Doctrine and Covenants 128:20; *Teachings of Presidents of the Church – Joseph Smith* (Salt Lake City: The Church of Jesus Christ of Latter-day Saints, 2007), 101, emphasis added.

[38]Grant H. Palmer, *An Insider's View of Mormon Origins* (Salt Lake City: Signature Books, 2002), 218.

[39]Jenson, comp., *Church Chronology*, 4.

[40]Ibid.

Church on June 3, 1831. Prior to June 3, 1831, "authority" (not yet "priesthood") was unitary, and prior to June 3, 1831, none of those previously ordained elders (forty-four of them) held the high priesthood. Two thousand early members were confirmed before those events by elders (and probably by teachers and priests) who are known not to have held the high priesthood. Prior to June 3, 1831, the metaphysical authority, the only authority they made claim to have had when they baptized and confirmed "about two thousand souls into the church," wasn't the high priesthood. The events that transpired at the June 1831 conference made that perfectly clear.

Joseph didn't understand when the Church was organized (on April 6, 1830), or before Rigdon came on board, that "authority" wasn't a unitary concept. Or that the "authority" he supposed that he received, by way of a command through the stone he had previously used to tell fortunes and locate buried treasures, would come to be identified with John the Baptist and the "Aaronic/ Levitical Priesthood" (the "lineal priesthood of the old law"). All of this speaks volumes about the alleged errands of John the Baptist and Peter, James, and John only very much later (in 1834 and 1835) resupposed to have occurred in May or June of 1829.   "No contemporary narrative exists for a visitation to Joseph and Oliver by Peter, James and John."[41] There is no date, there is no location, there is no high priesthood ordination prayer, and there are few if any details. B.H. Roberts, Mormonism's preeminent intellectual, reported in the History of the Church (he was the editor) that: "[T]here is no definite account of the event in the history of the Prophet Joseph or, for matter of that, in any of our annals . . . ."[42]

After the Church was organized, Rigdon convinced Smith to reconfigure his previously stated early authority principle. "Very early in his ministry, Joseph Smith, Jr. began to advocate the position that priesthood does not come directly from God through the Holy Spirit [by way of command], as many Protestants believe [and as he at first had said], but [rather] through a line of direct or

---

[41]Palmer, *An Insider's View of Mormon Origins*, 229.
[42]Roberts, ed., *History of The Church of Jesus Christ of Latter-day Saints*, 1:40 n.

apostolic succession."[43]   This developing point of view, dismissing
the teachings of his earliest ministry as reflected in the Book of
Commandments, followed the supposed supernatural visitations of
John the Baptist and Peter, James, and John, first described to the
members of the Church in 1834 and 1835.   "The Latter Day Saints
[now] generally believe that priesthood originates with Jesus, and is
passed to others through a line of succession. Only one who holds
the priesthood can pass it to another."[44]   Other alternative
explanations, including the once important Patriarchal Priesthood,
a lineal monarchical concept, are now also seen to have been
abandoned.   The modern Mormon priesthoods are linear,
hierarchical, unique, physical and exclusive. With the passage of
time, other conventional explanations, the only explanations
available to the early Saints, have been dismissed.   And the
documents that described them have been altered.

When Joseph Smith and Oliver Cowdery baptized, confirmed and
ordained each other and others, and when they and others then
baptized and confirmed about two thousand new members (and
ordained no less than forty-four elders) – before and without the
bestowal of "priesthood" – they hadn't met John the Baptist or
Peter, James, and John, nor had they said they had. No one said
they had, and the elders they had ordained didn't hold the high
priesthood. Before Smith met Rigdon, Mormonism didn't have
"high priesthood," "high priests" or multiple overlapping "orders"
of priesthood ("dual priesthoods of different ranks"), and
"authority," which was what they said that they did have, wasn't
passed to others through some lineage-based line of succession.
Only later (but not really until 1835) did what they said they had,
"authority," come to be more than only generally identified with
"the lineal priesthood of the old law." Only later ("It was sometime
between January and May 1835 that Peter, James, and John were
first mentioned as the restorers of apostolic keys to Joseph and
Oliver."[45]) did the office of elder come to be publicly identified with
another and higher power.

Before 1835, although it was understood that what had been called

---

[43]"Priesthood (Latter Day Saints)" (accessed 6 April 2014); Internet, 5.
[44]Ibid.
[45]Palmer, *An Insider's View of Mormon Origins*, 230.

"authority" had been enhanced by something called "priesthood" (since June 3, 1831), it wasn't understood that the source of the power they conferred upon each other on May 15, 1829 (an angelic disposition that wasn't reported until October 1834) was "the lineal priesthood of the old law." Some kind of ancient authority embraced from "out of the old Scriptures." No one knew that ancient Israel's controversial law of a carnal commandment, the "tutorial" authority that administered the law of Moses to Hebrews in anticipation of the coming of Christ, had somehow (and for some unknown reason) survived to have been restored. Not until 1835 did Joseph unmistakably (and publicly) declare by means of revelations (D&C 27, 84 and 107) that John the Baptist's authority supposed the reinstatement of ancient Judaism's widely disrespected "Aaronic, or Levitical Priesthood," the lineal priesthood of the old law, the law of a carnal commandment.

The early members of the Church, including Joseph Smith, Oliver Cowdery and David Whitmer, were at first dependent upon non-exclusive charismatic lower "authority." Lesser non-Melchizedek authority. It was initially thought by advantaged insiders (Joseph Smith, Oliver Cowdery, Lucy Mack Smith, David Whitmer, William E. McLellin), and in the Book of Commandments (Chapter 15:6-7), that commands received through Joseph's supernatural stone had been the spiritual source of the founders' "authority." Thus Joseph and Oliver were first baptized on May 15, 1829 – by way of command – without any contemporaneous reference to the presence of John the Baptist, or any thought of Peter, James, and John. That early baptism, the authority for which was referenced by means of the glass looker's stone, was unattended by heavenly messengers and earthbound.

At the Fourth Conference of the Church in June of 1831, the first to be held in Ohio, where Rigdon lived and God said gather, Joseph made a mid-course correction. There is, he said, a new kind of high authority.[46] That important insight wasn't then connected to Peter,

[46]Shortly before his death and long after that Fourth Conference in June 1831, Joseph Smith referred to what he called "3 grand orders of priesthood," a reordering seen to include what he then called the Patriarchal Priesthood, a happy thing for the Smiths. ("James Burgess notebook, August 27, 1843; Franklin D. Richards, 'Scriptural Items,' undated entry concerning Smith's lecture of August

James, and John, or to any other heavenly messenger. Before that 1831 Conference (the first to be held in Sidney Rigdon's Ohio), no one seems to have publicly discussed angelic ordination, the lineal priesthood of the old law, the law of a carnal commandment, linear hierarchical authority, "dual priesthoods of different ranks," Melchizedek elders, seventies, high priests, patriarchs, or even "priesthood." No one knew that the office of elder belonged to some other kind of authority that would only later come to be called "priesthood." Or that any of those other then unknown offices did. Who knew then, more than one year after the Church was organized, that a lower order of authority (till then the only order of "authority") would be reconfigured to become the "lineal priesthood of the old law"? Who knew then that the lineal priesthood of the old law was eternal, something supposed to continue "forever,"[47] side by side with "the priesthood . . . after the holiest order of God"? That perfectly preposterous assumption (*restoration and eternal life for ancient Israel's temporal tutorial law of a carnal commandment*) described in a revelation supposed to have come from Jesus Christ would have shocked the biblical Messiah, the author of Hebrews and gospel Christians. The Aaronic/Levitical Priesthood was nothing to be "restored." Furthermore, in its modern manifestation it bears little if any resemblance to its justifiably maligned but biblically defined carnal prototype.

With the passage of time, the powers of a new and different kind of authority – at first only generally associated with a mysterious biblical figure by the name of Melchizedek – would be deceitfully applied in altered documents with ruthless efficiency. The evolutionary process at work in creating these new orders (as opposed to restoring them) can be carefully traced to pre-1831

27, 1843, Archives of the Historical Department of the Church of Jesus Christ of Latter-day Saints, MS d4409," quoted in "Priesthood (Latter Day Saints)" [accessed 6 April 2014]; Internet, 3). "Smith taught that this order of priesthood was passed from father to son and held by Abraham and the biblical patriarchs." (*Teachings of Presidents of The Church – Joseph Smith* [2007], sec. 1, 38-39; *see* "Priesthood (Latter Day Saints)" [accessed 6 April 2014]; Internet, 3). It seems important to ask: When did the Hebrew church, or the Christian system, or the Nephite church ever surrender governance to *three* separate overlapping orders of priesthood?

[47]Doctrine and Covenants 84:18.

manuscripts and documents that were backdated and falsified. Joseph and Sidney broke a few eggs to make this omelette.

Rigdon had been exposed to priesthoods of different ranks through his association with Alexander Campbell, one of the founders of the Disciples of Christ. "The Disciples of Christ, from which many early members of the Church converted . . . had developed its own priesthood doctrines, influenced by Alexander Crawford, a Scottish minister living in Canada."[48] "In 1827 [three years before Sidney Rigdon (who joined the Disciples of Christ in 1821) left Alexander Campbell in 1830 to join Joseph Smith and the Church of Christ], Crawford had described the existence of three distinct priesthoods: a patriarchal priesthood (which he also called a priesthood after the "order of Melchisedec"), an Aaronical priesthood (originally held by Aaron), and a priesthood held by Jesus Christ."[49] Crawford regarded Melchizedek "as a greater priest than Abraham [because Abraham paid tithes to Melchizedec]." Crawford thought Melchizedek ("Melchisedec") "was one of the key players in the order of the patriarchal priesthood. Crawford also considered the patriarchal priesthood and the Aaronical priesthood as branches of the Levitical priesthood." "Alexander Campbell and the Disciples of Christ were influenced by Crawford's ideas . . . ." In what was a then not so unitary direction. "Campbell taught his understanding of priesthood [which differed "somewhat" from that of Crawford] 'to many of his followers [Rigdon being one] who [then became] part of the Mormonite community and continue[d] to believe the same doctrine.'"[50] These lapsed "Disciples" continued to believe in multiple priesthoods operating in the same faith community simultaneously. This all laid the groundwork for, and furnished raw material toward, the awkward changes forced upon the Latter Day Saints by what is now easily seen to have been the alteration of previously published documents in 1834-35.

---

[48]Matthew C. Godfrey, "A Culmination of Learning: D&C 84 and the Doctrine of the Priesthood" (accessed 18 January 2016), available from https://rsc.byu.edu/archived/you-shall-have-my-word/culmination-learning-dc-and-doctrine-priesthood; Internet, 5.
[49]Ibid.
[50]Ibid.

Rigdon's Progression

On "25 Jan. [1832] Smith is ordained President of the High Priesthood [not President of the Melchizedek Priesthood] by Rigdon at the Amhurst, Ohio conference. This was in response to a Nov. 1831 revelation added without explanation to an 1835 revelation on priesthood."[51] By 5 July 1832, after one and one-half years as a highly visible leader, Mormonism's prized early recruit brazenly attempted to seize control of the Church and was disfellowshipped.[52] One year after Rigdon's brief disaffection, and his ensuing reinstatement, and by July of 1833, Smith and Rigdon completed their inspired translation of the King James Version of the English Bible, embellishing the credentials of Melchizedek and altering something more than 3,400 verses. This "translation," editing unsupported by original archival resources, introduced suspicious (unprovenanced) new passages to the Biblical lexicon.[53]

"In 1833 Smith announced a revelation appointing Sidney Rigdon as his 'spokesman.'"[54] In a revelation given to Joseph Smith at Kirtland, Ohio, on March 8, 1833, Sidney Rigdon, Frederick G. Williams and Joseph Smith were jointly informed that it would be "your business and mission . . . All your lives, to preside in council, and set in order all the affairs of this church and kingdom." Joseph reported that Jesus spoke to the Presidency in these terms: "And again, verily I say unto thy brethren, Sidney Rigdon and Frederick G. Williams . . . they are accounted as equal with thee in holding the keys of this last kingdom."[55] On "19 Apr. [1834]. Smith authorizes

---

[51]Quinn, *The Mormon Hierarchy: Origins of Power*, 618.

[52]In the diary of Reynolds Cahoon, "Cahoon described Rigdon's unsuccessful effort to seize control of the church: 'Thursday 4 O clock Met with some of the Br for Meting [sic] and at the meting Br Sidney remarked that he had a revelation from the Lord & said that the kingdom was taken from the Church and left with him . . . .' When Joseph returned Sidney 'repented like Peter of Old' and the ship was quickly righted. 'Rigdon,' it seemed, 'tired of being third in command [behind Joseph Smith and Jesse Gause].'" [Cahoon, quoted in Quinn, *The Mormon Hierarchy: Origins of Power*, 42].

[53]Smith and Rigdon's inspired translation, an exercise in their early ministry, eliminated references to a plurality of Gods and supported in various important and undeniable ways Joseph Smith's early (and extreme) monotheism. See, *e.g.*, Luke 10:23, "Inspired Translation."

[54]Quinn, *The Mormon Hierarchy: Origins of Power*, 617.

[55]Doctrine and Covenants 90:6.

first counselor Rigdon to preside over the church in his absence."[56] On "24 Oct. [1837]. An appeals court confirms the conviction and $1,000 fine each of Smith and Rigdon for operating an illegal bank."[57] On January 12, 1838, "Smith and Rigdon flee Kirtland to escape law suits."[58] In 1839 Joseph Smith and Sidney Rigdon share a cell at the Liberty Jail. These resourceful colleagues are for the longest time joined at the hip.

THE TRIUMPH OF PRIESTHOOD POWER

By means of the word of God (delivered by the Spirit of God) and by command, righteous men may in theory claim to attain the power to act for God. That egalitarian sentiment is looked upon with favor in the Book of Commandments, and in the Book of Mormon. *"Behold my grace is sufficient for you: You must walk uprightly before me and sin not."*[59] Those who are righteous and follow God "with full purpose of heart" may partake of his power. Before the authoritarian orders of overlapping priesthoods overwhelmed the unitary concept of *"authority,"* the Book of Mormon, which may be said to have featured a kinder gentler concept, was translated and published. The Joseph Smith who said that he translated the Book of Mormon from golden plates with the Urim and Thummim (not the stone) by the gift and power of God had not yet grasped the incredible possibilities of what was at first respectfully called *"authority."* By the grace of God authority! By the voice of God authority! Nor had the prophets who graced the pages of Joseph's Golden Bible, which wasn't exactly "Priesthood 101," thought those possibilities through.

David Whitmer told his readers in *An Address to All Believers in Christ* that the Church lost its way when Joseph Smith introduced arbitrary priesthood concepts "out of the old Scriptures" promoted by the influential Rigdon. Whitmer, himself a God-appointed witness, said that Rigdon manipulated the prophet's revelations. This early important principal concluded that the communications

---

[56]Quinn, *The Mormon Hierarchy: Origins of Power*, 621, Selected Chronology.
[57]Ibid., 627.
[58]Ibid.
[59]Book of Commandments 15:34, emphasis added.

that changed the authority principle were not the work of God. In February 1832, fourteen months after December 1830, the month Smith and Rigdon were supposed to have initially met, Joseph Smith and Sidney Rigdon *jointly received* a revelation that changed the face of the faith and pointed the Church in a new and previously uncharted direction. It was what has been called "the beautiful doctrine of the three glories," a vision in which Joseph and a now very important Sidney jointly claimed that they "beheld the glory of the Son on the right hand of the Father" and saw "the holy angels and they who are sanctified before His throne."[60] Brigham Young told the Saints that when Joseph Smith received this vision in February 1832, that Smith held the "aronic" priesthood. In less than five months after the vision of the three degrees of glory "given to Joseph Smith the Prophet, and Sidney Rigdon" at Hiram, Ohio (D&C Section 76, headnote), and just shortly after the two colleagues described that incredible vision, a difficult Sidney tried to seize control of the Church and briefly apostatized.

The three degrees of glory described in Joseph and Sidney's vision, a universalist view of the afterlife, and the spirit world they chose to then describe, were concepts first articulated by Emanuel Swedenborg, a Swedish cleric who left his mark on many prominent Christians before Joseph and Sidney were born.[61] Now the amended concept of three degrees of glory abruptly replaced the undifferentiated heaven and hell previously described on the gold plates and in the Book of Mormon. Now the nature of natural men, the nothingness of the creatures described in the Book of Mormon,[62] is abruptly interrupted in favor of the more generous concept of gods in embryo, divinely invested disciples waiting upon

---

[60] Jenson, comp., *Church Chronology*, 7.

[61] Smith and Rigdon's vision of the three degrees of glory was a "universalist rejection of heaven and hell" (Quinn, *The Mormon Hierarchy: Origins of Power*, 618) that awkwardly overruled the Book of Mormon's conventional version of an undifferentiated heaven and hell. The revelation was roundly condemned by various early Saints, some of whom were excommunicated for harboring doubts.

[62] "For the natural man is an enemy to God, and has been from the fall of Adam, and will be forever and ever, unless he yields to the enticings of the Holy Spirit . . . ." (Book of Mormon, Mosiah 3:19). "And they had viewed themselves in their own carnal state, even less than the dust of the earth." (Ibid., Mosiah 4:2). "For behold, if the knowledge of the goodness of God at this time has awakened you to a sense of your nothingness, and your worthless and fallen state – I say unto you . . . ." (King Benjamin, quoted in Ibid., Mosiah 4:5).

their exaltation.   Shortly after the vision of the three degrees of glory, Rigdon, as just previously described, was disfellowshipped. On July 28, 1832, after he had counted his delegates and repented, he was welcomed back.

Book of Mormon Ordination

Modern Mormonism's priesthood line of authority profile is not as simple as it sometimes seems.

> *In the Bible God's command to his prophets authorizes them to carry out various assignments and to ordain others. Moses was called by God's voice out of a burning bush, and it was God's spirit that commanded him to ordain Aaron. The voice of God called Samuel to be a prophet and judge and to anoint Saul and David as kings. Isaiah, Jeremiah, Ezekiel, and Zechariah, as well as Lehi in the Book of Mormon, were called by the voice of the Lord in dreams and visions. Following the biblical pattern, Lehi ordained other Nephites.*[63]

Abinadi, living with Lamanites led by the "wicked" King Noah at Lehi-Nephi (the Lamanite stronghold), a believer and unordained, said the Lord commanded him to preach. Abinadi converted Alma, who then converted two hundred others. "By God's command alone, Alma baptized and ordained followers and organized a church." Alma and Helam then baptized each other. These Book of Mormon precepts were firmly in place before the arrival of Rigdon. Without the benefit of any priesthood-conferring heavenly messenger, or of a line of succession, without priesthood ordination by the laying on of hands, "Alma took Helam, . . . and went and stood forth in the water, and cried, saying: O Lord, pour out thy Spirit upon thy servant, that he may do this work . . . and . . . the Spirit of the Lord was upon him, and he [Alma] said: Helam, *I baptize thee, having authority from the Almighty God . . . .*" After that, "Alma, *having authority from God,* ordained priests."[64]

---

[63]Palmer, *An Insider's View of Mormon Origins*, 221, emphasis added.
[64]Ibid., 221-22, emphasis added.

> *The [nonexclusive] Nephite model is a consistent one*
> *in that "the Spirit of the Lord" authorizes men to*
> *baptize and ordain each other and to organize a*
> *church.　This corresponds exactly to the Book of*
> *Commandments pattern for receiving authority. There*
> *are periods during which ordinations occur in an*
> *orderly succession, but when the chain is broken,*
> *another prophet is called by God's voice or by his*
> *Spirit to begin the cycle anew.*[65]

So it was with Jesus and the twelve Nephite disciples.　Jesus "laid his hands upon them," but that was not the only part of the ritual. Jesus told them, and blessed them, to "call on the Father in my name in mighty prayer."　If they didn't do this, and/or until they did, they couldn't expect to confer the gift of the Holy Ghost "upon" those "upon" whom they should lay their hands.[66]　According to the Book of Mormon model, the elders ordained priests and teachers "after they had prayed unto the Father in the name of Christ." When the oral (metaphysical) element was completed, "they laid their hands upon them, and said: In the name of Jesus Christ I ordain you to be a priest" (or a teacher).[67]　"And after this manner [metaphysical bargaining] did they ordain priests and teachers, according to the gifts and callings of God unto men . . . ."[68]

It was by this kind of oral authority, in a process that was mixed, and not merely by the laying on of hands, that Jesus commissioned twelve Nephite disciples "to bestow the Holy Ghost and to ordain others."　He also reaffirmed the authority of Nephi, the son of Helaman, to baptize.

> *These recitals in the Bible and in Joseph's revelations,*
> *including those in the Book of Commandments, are*
> *consistent.　God calls a man by voice or by spirit to*
> *open a gospel dispensation or to commence a mission*
> *of preaching repentance.　This call authorizes the*
> *individual to baptize and ordain others.　In none of*

---

[65]Ibid., emphasis added.
[66]Book of Mormon, Moroni 2:2.
[67]Ibid., Moroni 3:2-3.
[68]Ibid., Moroni 3:4.

these scriptural writings do we find other-worldly beings laying hands upon mortals to bestow priesthood authority.[69]

The priesthood described in the Book of Mormon is sparing and generic. "[T]he Lord God ordained priests, after his holy order, which was after *the* order of his Son" to teach *his* commandments to *his* people.[70] These high priests were "called and prepared from the foundation of the world according to the foreknowledge of God, on account of their exceeding faith and good works . . . ."[71] Melchizedek, "to whom Abraham paid tithes,"[72] was but one of them. The "high priests" were called and ordained to "the high priesthood of the holy order of God."[73] This order of authority was "high," oblivious to rank, without beginning or end eternal. It wasn't Melchizedek's priesthood. Melchizedek was a high priest in "the high priesthood of the holy order of God." The Book of Mormon's priesthood had nothing to do with Levi, Aaron, John the Baptist, Peter, James, and John, Elias or Elijah, or others like them. The office of "high priest" was not recognized in the Mormon Church until after Sidney Rigdon joined Joseph Smith in the leadership. Sidney Rigdon was himself a high priest.

Smith's and Cowdery's Ordinations

While both Joseph and Oliver claimed to have seen angels, and while that claim was reported in the newspapers, they initially said that their authority came "directly from God, not through angelic ministration."[74] Years after the Church was organized, this was rethought and replaced with a different more authoritarian approach. What had first been metaphysical became now literal,

---

[69]Palmer, *An Insider's View of Mormon Origins*, 223, emphasis added.

[70]Book of Mormon, Alma 13:1, emphasis added.

[71]Ibid., Alma 13:3.

[72]Ibid., Alma 13:14, 15.

[73]Ibid., Alma 13:6. According to the Latter-day Saints, the "*Priesthood after the Order of the Son of God*" is referred to as the Melchizedek Priesthood in order to avoid "the too frequent use of the name of the Son of God." ("Priesthood (Latter Day Saints)" [accessed 6 April 2014]; Internet, Internet, 1).

[74]Quinn, *The Mormon Hierarchy: Origins of Power*, 19.

"more impressive, unique, and physical."[75]   The "authority" principle, before Rigdon and as it was originally practiced, was not dependent upon the literal physical bestowal of "priesthood authority" by the laying on of hands of "other-worldly beings."

"When Joseph receives a spiritual prompting to begin to baptize and ordain others, he is following the pattern in the Book of Mormon."[76] "[E]arly missionaries declared that they were called of God but did not say that their authority originated with heavenly messengers. Accounts of angelic ordinations from John the Baptist and Peter, James, and John are in none of the journals, diaries, letters, or printed matter until the mid-1830's."[77] On the day the Church was organized, on and at all times before April 6, 1830, nothing appeared to suggest that Joseph Smith and Oliver Cowdery "had received authority by angelic ordination."[78]   In none of Mormonism's scriptural writings (Joseph's Revelations, Book of Commandments) "do we find other-worldly beings laying hands upon mortals to bestow priesthood authority."[79]   In the "diaries of early convert and apostle William E. McLellin from 1831 to 1836," McLellin "never mentioned that the church claimed angelic priesthood restoration."[80]

In a September 7, 1834, letter published in the October issue of the *Messenger and Advocate*, Oliver and Joseph described receiving the priesthood under the hands of an unnamed angel.[81]   "Shortly thereafter, this angel was [separately] identified as John the Baptist.[82]   Simultaneously, a statement [an unprovenanced statement] about Peter, James, and John appearing to Joseph and Oliver was added to an earlier revelation."[83]   October 1834 was more than five years after a baptismal event on May 15, 1829, which was described one way in 1829 and another more glorious and physical way in 1834.   Latter-day Saints took charismatic

---

[75]Palmer, *An Insider's View of Mormon Origins*, 232.
[76]Ibid., 223.
[77]Ibid., 223-24.
[78]Ibid., 220.
[79]Ibid., 223.
[80]Ibid., 224.
[81]Ibid., 226.
[82]Ibid., 228.
[83]Doctrine and Covenants 27:8, 12-13.

metaphysical authority off the table in the mid-1830s in the nineteenth century, after they had used it for the first five or six years to their early advantage. Latter-day Saints took the lineage of the fathers, patriarchal authority, off the table in the twentieth century. They bet the farm on angelic ordination effectuated in an unbroken line of succession by the laying on of hands. In that unprecedented concept, a thin reed, their investment is seen to have become complete and entire.

"Authority" vs. "Priesthood"

"[B]y degrees the [priesthood restoration] accounts became more detailed and . . . miraculous. In 1829 Joseph said he was called by the Spirit; in 1832 he mentioned that angels attended these events; in 1834-35 the spiritual manifestations became literal . . . [with the] physical appearances of resurrected beings."[84] Until the Fourth Conference of the Church in 1831, Mormons had neglected to call "authority" by the opprobrious Catholic name of "priesthood." "Later accounts applied the term retroactively [in altered documents], but the June 1831 conference marked its first appearance in contemporary records. The term 'authority' frequently appeared, but not 'priesthood.'"[85] It is important to repeat that,

> *So far as can be told now, before 1831 men were called to church offices [three church offices] – elders, priests and teachers – given authority and licensed without reference to a bestowal of priesthood. At the June [1831] conference, the word "priesthood" was used and priesthood was bestowed as if it was an addition to previous authority.*[86]

Not yet Aaronic. Not yet Melchizedek. Not yet identifiably separate. Richard L. Bushman reports that the minutes of the 1831 Conference and John Whitmer's history *"noted ordinations to 'the*

---

[84]Palmer, *An Insider's View of Mormon Origins*, 228-29.
[85]Richard Lyman Bushman, with the assistance of Jed Woodworth, *Joseph Smith: Rough Stone Rolling* (New York: Alfred A. Knopf, 2005), 157.
[86]Ibid., 157-58, emphasis added.

High Priesthood,' also known [but not definitively until in and after 1835[87]] as the Melchizedek Priesthood, named for a mysterious biblical figure from the time of Abraham."[88] The Book of Mormon, supposed to contain "the fulness of the everlasting Gospel," failed to specifically identify the high priesthood as the "Melchizedek Priesthood." Suddenly, without much clarification, there is something decidedly new in the Mormon mix, something allowed to remain maddeningly unexplained. This was history without roots, priesthood without provenance. Joseph Smith, living in Ohio and collaborating with Rigdon, now (years into his ministry) introduces the "high and holy priesthood." Bushman noted that "priesthood was an alien concept to Yankee Christians . . . ."[89] The unequivocal use of the term "Melchizedek Priesthood," although alluded to in an 1832 revelation that wasn't published until 1835,[90] followed the Conference and a still later revelation (D&C 107) in 1835.[91]

To admit that Mormon men previously ordained to the office of elder (including Joseph Smith) did not receive the "Holy Priesthood after the Order of the Son of God" until June 1831, to admit that Lyman Wight, the first Mormon man ordained to hold the office of High Priest, did not receive "the Holy Priesthood after the Order of the Son of God" until June 1831, to admit that forty-four men previously ordained to the office of elder by the authority of Joseph Smith and Oliver Cowdery did not receive "the Holy Priesthood after the Order of the Son of God" until June 1831 was to admit that the Melchizedek Priesthood was not the order of authority in force and effect on April 6, 1830, when Oliver Cowdery ordained Joseph Smith to his office as Prophet, Seer and Revelator of the Church of Christ, by Mormon reckoning, then and now, the highest office on earth. The Fourth Conference of the Church, which was all about issues of authority ("additional authority"), failed to

---

[87]Doctrine and Covenants 107:1-7.
[88]Bushman, *Joseph Smith: Rough Stone Rolling*, 158, emphasis added.
[89]Ibid., 157.
[90]Doctrine and Covenants, Section 84.
[91]Quinn's "harmonization of discrepancies" opines that early Mormonism, unlike later Mormonism, didn't really have "two priesthood orders" but rather "two different religious authorities: a divine calling and a conferred authority." The first was a nonexclusive egalitarian impulse, and the second was an unreported secret. That scholar's underlying assumption seems to be that either authority works. (Quinn, *The Mormon Hierarchy: Origins of Power*, 32).

identify two separate orders of priesthood. In the gold plates part
of Joseph's 1832 Holographic Account of his first encounter with
deity, he is seen to have continued to describe unitary priesthood.
In that first and most contemporaneous account, there is no
discussion of dual priesthoods of different ranks. Brigham Young
told the members of the Church that Joseph Smith held the
"aronic" priesthood when he received the vision of the three
degrees of glory in February 1832. The elders ordained by Joseph
Smith and Oliver Cowdery before and after the Church was formed
on April 6, 1830, and prior to June 3, 1831, did not hold the
Melchizedek Priesthood, nor did they say that they did.

Altering the Revelations

David Whitmer criticized Smith and the other leaders of the
Church (after Smith's death) for tampering with the revelations,
for proceeding like ordinary secular authors editing secular galleys.
The amending process enabled editors to attribute their words to
God. Whitmer considered this cynical process to be a violation of
the ethics of discipleship.

> *You have changed the revelations from the way they
> were first given and as they are to-day in the Book of
> Commandments to support the error of Brother
> Joseph in taking upon himself the office of Seer to the
> church. You have changed the revelations to support
> the error of high priests . . . . You have altered the
> revelations to support you in going beyond the plain
> teachings of Christ in the new covenant part of the
> Book of Mormon.*[92]

"How any person can be so blind in the face of all this evidence as to
still uphold the Book of Doctrine and Covenants is more than I can
understand." These concerns, among others, were deal-breakers
for the former President of the Church in the state of Missouri; for
Joseph's earliest designated successor; for one of early
Mormonism's most faithful stalwarts, and one of the faith's

---

[92]Whitmer, *An Address to All Believers in Christ*, 49, emphasis added.

founders. Whitmer was the man who knew too much. "You who are now living didn't change them [the revelations], but you who strive to defend these things, are as guilty in the sight of God as those who did change them."[93] What was true of them then, as Whitmer opined, is true of them now. Indefensible things are vigorously defended and never changed; disciples who were misinformed, upon learning the truth, continue to offend.

Another Look at the Lower Priesthood

The Nephites, a civilization supposed to have been tutored in the meridian of time by the preexistent Savior, didn't have two separate orders of priesthood. They completely failed to ever even acknowledge the lineal priesthood of the old law. How could expatriate Hebrews say nothing about the Aaronic/Levitical Priesthood over the course of a thousand years? How could pre-Christianity Hebrews have referred to their anticipated Messiah, before the incarnation, by his Greek name "Christ," by that to say the Anointed One? How could Hebrews with origins in the old world fall totally silent about the elements, oddities and constraints of the lineal priesthood of the old law?

By means of a surprising revelation that wasn't published until 1835, the Lord informed Joseph's nineteenth-century followers that ancient Judaism's ossified law of a carnal commandment, because it was eternal, applied to them. It wasn't eternal and didn't apply to the Nephites, a civilization described in the Book of Mormon. By this strange revelatory account, the priesthood the Lord confirmed upon Aaron and his seed in ancient Israel before the exodus of Lehi, was now supposed to continue *forever* in the Church of Jesus Christ of Latter-day Saints side by side and simultaneously with "the priesthood which is after the holiest order of God."[94] That didn't happen in the Nephite Church, or in the Christian system in the gospel church. The author of Hebrews made it his particular task to liberate gospel Christians from the smothering restrictions of ancient Jewish ritual, taking his lead from the great High Priest of his profession, the only High Priest in the gospel Church, the

---

[93]Ibid.
[94]Doctrine and Covenants 84:18.

Mortal Messiah, Jesus Christ. New order Christians, Hebrews following Christ, didn't need to know four hundred ways a Jew could make a living, or fifty different ways not to celebrate the Sabbath. While BCE Hebrews in the New World could have left this blood-letting ritual behind, they couldn't have left it alone, not for a thousand years. And yet it appears that that is just exactly what they did. References to the law of a carnal commandment among those Hebrews are just as scarce as evidence of the very existence of Hebrews in the Western Hemisphere.

Only if the Book of Mormon is a theological and not an historical construct can these incredible errors and omissions ever be explained. Ministering meant something altogether different to Jesus, and to the Apostle Paul, than it did to Smith and Rigdon. God nailed ancient Israel's oppressive Levitical Priesthood to the cross exactly as the Bible reports.[95] Smith and Rigdon, men reasoning "out of the old Scriptures," did not. The New Testament rudely dismissed ancient Israel's law of a carnal commandment. Early Christians could not have believed that the lineal priesthood of the old law, the subject of so much justifiable antagonism, was destined to somehow continue as an essential (then suddenly eternal) part of the Christian system. Joseph's revelator crossed a line to say that the lineal priesthood of the old law "continueth and abideth forever with the priesthood which is after the holiest order of God (*D&C* 84:18)." And Joseph and Sidney crossed a line to say that that oppressive ancient order, God forsaken in retrospect, had somehow been restored.

> *If therefore perfection were by the Levitical priesthood, (for under it the people received the law,) what further need was there that another priest should rise after the order of Melchisedec, and not be called after the order of Aaron? For the priesthood being changed, there is made of necessity a change also of the law . . . . For he of whom these things are spoken pertaineth to another tribe, of which no man gave attendance at the altar. For it is evident that our Lord sprang out of Juda; of which tribe Moses spake*

---

[95]Colossians 2:14.

nothing concerning priesthood.[96]

The priesthood and the law, according to the epistle to the Hebrews, were both "being changed" with Christ. God took the hated lineal priesthood administered by that old law "out of the way."[97] He blotted out "the handwriting of ordinances" that were against the early Christians ("*contrary to us*"). "Let no man . . . judge you in meat or in drink, or in respect of an holy day, or of the new moon, or of the sabbath days . . . ."[98] "Wherefore if ye be dead with Christ from the rudiments of the world, why as though living in the world, are ye subject to ordinances, (Touch not; taste not; handle not; Which all are to perish with the using;) after the commandments and doctrines of men?"[99]

Parley P. Pratt, a powerful figure in the early Church, was one of the first leaders to recognize that the Nephites didn't hold the Aaronic Priesthood; that it wasn't eternal and meant nothing to them. It obviously didn't continue and abide "forever with the priesthood which is after the holiest order of God," among the Nephites. There were Nephites who neglected to consider the law of a carnal commandment before there was a Rigdon, who chose to try and restore the onerous requirements of a tired old law that God took "out of the way." A law that had run its course. "[T]he Aaronic Priesthood," according to Pratt, "is no where pretended to in the Book of Mormon."[100] The Book of Mormon was published before Rigdon was able to say, "I guided his tottering steps till he could walk alone . . . ." For he had tottered before Rigdon arrived. The members of the gospel church in the old world, like the members of the Nephite church in the new world, "were not ordained to the Aaronic Priesthood," an order of authority about which the Book of Mormon is conspicuously silent.[101] Pratt, the author of "A Voice of Warning" (a volume of extraordinary importance in the nineteenth-century Church and a book that is

---

[96]Hebrews 7:11-14, emphasis added.

[97]Colossians 2:14.

[98]Ibid., 2:16.

[99]Ibid., 2:20-22.

[100]*Writings of Parley Parker Pratt*, 209, quoted in Jerald Tanner and Sandra Tanner, *Mormonism – Shadow or Reality?* (Salt Lake City: Utah Lighthouse Ministry, 1987), 180.

[101]Ibid.

still in print), discussed those unsettling issues simultaneously:

> *Members of the early Christian Church were not
> ordained to the Aaronic Priesthood, neither is there
> any mention of the Aaronic Priesthood in the Book of
> Mormon.*[102]

That is an incredibly important admission. It means that the
Aaronic Priesthood wasn't needed, served no purpose and wasn't
"restored." For more than a thousand years in the Western
Hemisphere, multiple overlapping priesthoods were never seen to
coincide. The Aaronic Priesthood isn't mentioned in the Book of
Mormon, the product of an early design, because the restoration of
the Aaronic Priesthood was part of a late design. The lineal
priesthood that administered the hated provisions of the old law
wasn't restored, nor either eternal or missed. In the case of higher
authority, two prominent modern dissidents concluded that "All
evidence points to the fact that the Melchizedek Priesthood did not
come from the hands of Peter, James and John in 1829, but rather
from the mind of Sydney Rigdon in Ohio in 1831."[103] If that is seen
to be true, if Rigdon "explained these things to Brother Joseph in
his way out of the old Scriptures . . . " in and after 1830, and if
Joseph's counselor prompted him to act, what is left to be said?
Joseph and Oliver *didn't hold* the Melchizedek Priesthood, and
couldn't have held the Levitical Priesthood, on April 6, 1830.

WIGHT AND COWDERY

Modern Mormon Priesthood

By 1842, orders of "Priesthood" and issues of authority were at the
heart and center of the Mormon universe – the firm theological
support for the unblushing contention that the Mormon Church, a
tiny blip on a gigantic screen, was the only true and living church
on the face of the earth. Every convert was supposed to have been
baptized with John the Baptist's authority, and every confirmation
looked to the higher power of Peter, James, and John. Every

---

[102]Ibid., emphasis added.
[103]Ibid., emphasis added.

theological debate caused the Mormons to raise the question with so-called Christians: "By what authority do you preach?" By their reckoning only Mormons could baptize, confirm, ordain, curse, bless or seal in such a way as to have those sacraments recognized by a loving God in the afterlife. Every Mormon priest or elder could trace his divine authority back to John the Baptist, and some to Peter, James, and John. At the same time every priesthood holder could also trace his divine authority back to Oliver Cowdery – the excommunicated counterfeiter who ordained Joseph Smith to the office of elder – and to Lyman Wight, the violent, reckless man (and the first ordained high priest) who ordained Joseph Smith to the "high and holy priesthood." The Latter Day Saints bet the farm on the amended other-worldly ministrations of John the Baptist and Peter, James, and John. The Mormon embrace of *exclusive* physically conferred supernatural authority was seen to become complete and entire. Any fall back to some "divine calling" kind of default authority, whether lineal or not, is impossibly foolish.

Latter-day Saints believe that,

> *No one may officiate in any ordinances of the Church of Jesus Christ of Latter-day Saints unless he has been ordained to the particular order or office of Priesthood, by those possessing the requisite authority. Thus, no man receives the Priesthood except under the hands of one who holds that Priesthood himself; that one must have obtained it from others previously commissioned; and so every bearer of the Priesthood today can trace his authority to the hands of Joseph Smith the Prophet, who received his ordination under the hands of the apostles Peter, James, and John; and they had been ordained by the Lord Jesus Christ.*[104]

Note that this influential scholar and apostle, James E. Talmage, doesn't acknowledge Oliver Cowdery or Lyman Wight. Or any of the metaphysical priests: Moses, Samuel, Isaiah, Jeremiah, Ezekiel,

---

[104]James E. Talmage, *A Study of the Articles of Faith: Being a Consideration of the Principal Doctrines of The Church of Jesus Christ of Latter-day Saints*, 12th ed. in English (1924), 189.

Zechariah or Lehi; Abinadi, Alma, Helam, Melchizedek, Jesus, the Nephite disciples, Barnabas or the Apostle Paul. Or the about two thousand Mormons who were baptized and confirmed before anyone is known to have considered the possibility of linear hierarchical priesthood. Nor does Talmage consider the lower authority elders, priests and teachers given authority and licensed without reference to a bestowal of priesthood prior to the Fourth Conference of the Church held in Kirtland, Ohio, in June of 1831. The higher priesthood, by modern reckoning, is conferred by a male higher priesthood holder upon a lower priesthood intern by the laying on of hands. Mormon men, we may suppose, may hope to trace their priesthood back to Jesus Christ, in every case, through Smith and Cowdery and Wight. Wight and Cowdery, seriously degraded Saints, are not singled out as objects of modern emphasis, and their contributions to the priesthoods are ignored and dismissed. So too are those of the architect Rigdon. No one gets to Jesus but through Oliver Cowdery, Lyman Wight and Joseph Smith. And no one gets to Jesus without deference to the worldly theology of the brooding Rigdon.

Oliver Cowdery was baptized by Joseph Smith on May 15, 1829. Joseph Smith was baptized by Oliver Cowdery on May 15, 1829. Oliver Cowdery was the first member of the Mormon Church. He was *ordained* to the office of elder by Joseph Smith on April 6, 1830. Joseph Smith was *ordained* to the office of elder by Oliver Cowdery on April 6, 1830. On April 6, 1830, Oliver Cowdery, who hadn't received the high priesthood, and couldn't have received the low priesthood, purported to ordain Joseph Smith to the highest office on earth. Joseph Smith ordained Lyman Wight, "The Wild Ram of the Mountains," to the high priesthood after the order of the Son of God at Kirtland, Ohio, on June 3, 1831. Lyman Wight ordained Joseph Smith to the high priesthood after the order of the Son of God at Kirtland, Ohio, on June 3, 1831. All roads to Jesus lead through Lyman Wight and Joseph Smith. Those unprovenanced ordinations occurred several years before John the Baptist and Peter, James, and John emerged, by way of support, and signify confusion.[105]

---

[105]Lyman Wight didn't say that Joseph got the authority to ordain him to the higher priesthood from Peter, James, and John, nor did Joseph Smith at that time.

All roads to Jesus lead through Oliver Cowdery, Lyman Wight and Joseph Smith, reckless men who were not exactly ornaments of society. Every Latter-day Saint who purports to hold the lower priesthood received his authority through Oliver Cowdery and Joseph Smith, because Cowdery baptized Smith and ordained him to the offices of elder and prophet. Cowdery is an irreducible founder. Every Latter-day Saint who claims to have received the "high and holy" priesthood got what he got through Oliver Cowdery, Lyman Wight and Joseph Smith, because in every lineage there is a Cowdery and a Wight and a Smith.

Oliver Cowdery

Joseph Smith published his second authorized history of the Church, with the help of a committee, in 1842. Oliver Cowdery had been excommunicated in 1838. Described as alienated and evil, his life threatened by the Mormons, his family dispossessed and his possessions in the street, Cowdery escaped Far West, Missouri, in 1838 with little but his life. Oliver Cowdery – the man who said he had seen the angel and the golden plates, the scribe for the translation of the Book of Mormon, the man who said he saw the Savior, Moses, Elijah and Elias and heard their voices, the man who said that he received the Aaronic Priesthood from John the Baptist and the Melchizedek Priesthood from Peter, James, and John, the first person baptized and the first elder ordained – was estranged from Smith and out of the Church. The first Mormon, the first elder, the man who preached the first sermon, and "one of the presidents of this church" had been consigned to the buffetings of Satan in the flesh. He would leave the Mormons and join the Methodists, and he would enjoy a brief flirtation with an early and important alternative to Brigham Young, another prophet, James J. Strang.

Oliver lost faith in a Missouri Zion. He was determined to sell his Missouri property in defiance of a revelation from Joseph's God, the Lord who said that he should not. If he had continued to believe in Joseph's revelations (and prophecies), he could never have

---

The provenance of the high and holy priesthood was obscure and undetermined in 1831.

insisted upon selling his consecrated inheritance. It was said of Cowdery, after everything he said that he had seen, that he refused to live according to the economic order of the Church. Cowdery, who was married to Elizabeth Whitmer, joined all of the other Whitmers and Hiram Page, another Whitmer brother-in-law (seven of the eleven witnesses to the Book of Mormon) on their way out of the Church. He left Joseph Smith with an angry accusation: Joseph Smith, the prophet of God, he said, had a "dirty, nasty, filthy affair" with Miss Fanny Alger, a teenage household helper who lived in the home the prophet shared with his legal wife and her children.

All of the living Book of Mormon witnesses, everyone who wasn't a Smith, eight in all including Martin Harris, and many other important early apostles and leaders, voted their disappointing convictions with scampering feet. Every living Book of Mormon witness but Cowdery, all of the Whitmers and Hiram Page, together with Emma, Lucy and William Smith,[106] William Marks, Martin Harris, William E. McLellin, John C. Bennett, George Miller, and scores of others, high ranking officers, passed on Brigham Young to form an association with James J. Strang, who later became yet another polygamist and scared many of those hopeful followers off. Strang's movement got off to an impressive start. Oliver Cowdery's father (William from the Wood Scrape) and brother (Warren Cowdery) became disciples of Strang and a friendly Oliver ("almost persuadeth thou me . . .") moved to Wisconsin to be close to his family and one of Joseph's numerous putative successors. These disciples initially accepted Strang, and not Brigham Young, as Joseph's interim heir.[107]

Although out of sight after 1838, rudely excommunicated and apprehensive, Cowdery was far from forgotten. The man had been a fly on the Mormon wall, and he had had co-conspirators when he

---

[106]Initially, according to William Smith, all of the Smiths except Hyrum and Samuel's widows followed Strang.

[107]Restoration scholars (John Hamer, Steve Shields) estimate "that well over 400 groups are extant within the LDS restoration movement. From this perspective, the Church of Jesus Christ of Latter-day Saints [the Brigham Young remnant] is not a continuation of the original church Joseph Smith founded, but rather, its largest schism." (Lindsay Hansen-Park, "Does 'Mormon' Still Equal Polygamy?" *Sunstone*, 181 [Summer 2016]: 5).

defected, rudely dispossessed, shocked but unrepentant. Rigdon – who had replaced Cowdery in the prophet's affections – micromanaged the details of the prophet's decision to abandon his formerly trusted co-president colleague. It was Rigdon who drafted the threatening ultimatum (called the "Danite Manifesto"), a document that warned Cowdery and his notable associates out of Far West, Missouri, within seventy-two hours at the risk of the loss of their lives.

Cowdery and a number of other prominent dissidents had reached a tipping point. He and they refused to "be controlled by an ecclesiastical power of revelation whatever in their temporal concerns." Had they not seen with their own eyes what happened to the Lord's bank at Kirtland? Cowdery and the Whitmers, republicans of convenience, did then seem to suffer from the Mormon pandemic "too much bondage." The clever Cowdery, proceeding unleashed, was an unpredictable force who couldn't be taken for granted. He was out there, somewhere, equipped to contradict the prophet in respect to the details of many important events. Although that was not to be expected, the issue of priesthood became too important to Smith to tempt providence, further change settled equations, or to invite further discord. After 1838, the stories told by Mormonism's co-founders could not be correlated. The new republican Cowdery, a renegade disciple, claimed constitutional rights in a telling confrontation with the representatives of the theocracy. He filed lawsuits in support of his claims to property in the state of Missouri. For the Latter-day Saints the disputations mirrored the future.

Lyman Wight

Wight "was baptized into the Reformed Baptist (later Disciples of Christ or Campbellite) faith by Sidney Rigdon in May 1829."[108] He "was baptized a member of the Church of Christ by Oliver Cowdery in 1830."[109] Wight, the leader of the Mormons (and of the

---

[108]Lyman Wight (accessed April 14, 2017), available from https://en.wikipedia.org/wiki/Lyman_Wight; Internet, page 2 of 6.
[109]Ibid.

Danite Band[110]) in Daviess County, Missouri, recruited about twenty members of the organization later known as Zion's Camp. In 1837, Apostle David W. Patten (Mormonism's Captain Fearnaught) accused Wight, who had baptized more than one hundred people (many of whom had followed him to Missouri), "of teaching false doctrine." He was tried before the High Council in Far West, Missouri, and was found guilty. He was reinstated after making amends and later replaced Patten, who died at the Battle of Crooked River, as an Apostle.[111]

"In 1838, . . . Lyman Wight was brought before the High Council at Far West, Missouri, on a charge of 'disgracing the Church' because of his frequent intoxication. Apostle Thomas B. Marsh [after April 6, 1838, the President of the Church in Missouri] warned that unless Wight confessed his sins before the high council his membership would be revoked."[112]   On Tuesday 4 March, 1845, James Emmett, Lyman Wight and others who had "transcended" their bounds and lost their "kingly authority," men who had been dismissed, were replaced on the notorious Council of Fifty by other members who had come to "take their crowns."[113]   Wight was discharged on 4 February, 1845, for "'following his feelings' rather than the Council of [Brigham] Young and the other apostles."[114] Wight, "The First High Priest" to be ordained, and the man who ordained Joseph Smith, was excommunicated, as Martin Harris, David Whitmer and Oliver Cowdery also were, in his particular case for apostasy, on December 3, 1848.

---

[110]As the head of the notorious Danites in Daviess County, Missouri, Wight led the raid on Millport that terrorized the settlers there. "The old settlers and their families fled and Wight and his men looted their property and burned their homes to the ground." (Ibid., pages 4-5 of 6).

[111]Ibid., page 4 of 6.

[112]*The Joseph Smith Papers: Administrative Records, Council of Fifty Minutes, March 1844-January 1846*, Matthew J. Grow, Ronald K. Esplin, Mark Ashurst-McGee, Gerrit J. Dirkmaat, and Jeffrey D. Mahas, volume ed. (Salt Lake City, UT: The Church Historian's Press, 2016), 139 n 421.

[113]Volume Introduction, Council of Fifty Minutes, in Ibid., 278, cf. Council of Fifty, "Record," 27 February 1845.

[114]Editorial Comment, Ibid., 438.

Character

Cowdery and Wight, like Joseph Smith himself, were egregiously flawed. None of these three leading Mormon men were role models, but all of them claimed to have had revelations. Cowdery and Wight were forced to leave or left the Church – Cowdery at the strong request of more than eighty highly prominent Mormon men, including Hyrum Smith, nearly every one of them, if not every one of them, a member of a violent secret society (Mormonism's notorious "Danites"). Mormon thugs. Wight, like Brigham and James J. Strang, aspired to lead the Church, or some remnant of the Church, after the death of Joseph Smith. He had "revelations," as other pretenders also did, and led yet another remnant of the Church off to yet another place of gathering in the independent unannexed territory of Texas. Let the most prominent authorities in the Mormon Church tell us in a contemporaneous report what kind of men co-founder, witness and co-President Oliver Cowdery, Book of Mormon witness and Missouri President David Whitmer, and Apostle Lyman E. Johnson actually were. Rigdon, the First Counselor in the First Presidency, at that moment second only to Joseph, with the prophet's consent, described Oliver Cowdery, David Whitmer and Lyman E. Johnson – for himself, the Church, Hyrum, Joseph and posterity – at Far West, Missouri, in June 1838. More than eighty influential leaders signed this document and adopted these recitals:

> *Oliver Cowdery, David Whitmer, and Lyman Johnson,*
> *united with a gang of counterfeiters, thieves, liars, and*
> *blacklegs of the deepest dye, to deceive, cheat and*
> *defraud the saints out of their property, by every art*
> *and stratagem, which wickedness could invent; . . . .* [115]

Among some five important consecrated men – Oliver Cowdery, David Whitmer, John Whitmer, W.W. Phelps, and Lyman E.

---

[115]Rigdon, quoted in "Document Showing The Testimony Given Before the Judge of the Fifth Judicial District of the State of Missouri, on the Trial of Joseph Smith, Jr., and others, for High Treason and Other Crimes Against that State," Senate Document No. 189 (Washington D.C.: Blair & Rives; photomechanical reprint of 15 February 1841, Salt Lake City: Utah Lighthouse Ministry), 8, emphasis added.

Johnson, hall-of-fame founders and early Mormon elite – it was reported that there were unrepentant "criminals," "treacherous thieves," "character assassins," "base liars," "promise breakers," "practitioners of iniquity," "counterfeiters," "blacklegs," "cheaters and defrauders."[116]

In 1848, after being out of the Church for ten years, Cowdery was rebaptized.   Brigham Young, whose brother was married to Cowdery's half-sister, took the devious rascal back. In 1850, and without coming to Utah, Cowdery died at the home of his brother-in-law, David Whitmer, in Richmond, Missouri.   Cowdery's counterfeiting fingerprints are on every priesthood officer's priesthood provenance,[117] and on every page of the Book of Mormon, "the most correct of any book on earth." Every Mormon man or boy received his priesthood, one way or another, under the spiritual hands of the discredited Cowdery. No present day elder or priest gets to John the Baptist, Peter, James, and John, or to the Lord Jesus Christ, without the inextricable assistance of Oliver Cowdery, Joseph Smith and Lyman Wight.

EPILOGUE

The supposed restoration of the Melchizedek Priesthood by Peter, James, and John in May or June of 1829 – a matter of critical importance in Mormon theology – remains an undocumented, uncorroborated event not even mentioned in the Articles and Covenants of the Church of Christ, in the journals, diaries, letters or printed matter of those early record keeping Saints, in the Preface to the Book of Mormon, or in any of the sixty-five reve-lations published in the Book of Commandments at Independence, Missouri, in 1833.   "No contemporary narrative exists for a visitation to Joseph and Oliver by Peter, James and John in May or June of 1829."[118]   "[T]here is no definite account of the event in the history of the Prophet Joseph or, for matter of that, in any of our

---

[116]Ibid., 8-9.
[117]Ibid., 6-9.
[118]Palmer, *An Insider's View of Mormon Origins*, 229.

annals . . . ."[119] The priesthood restoration events are awkwardly described in retroactive emendations to falsified revelations and manuscripts. Smith's mid-course corrections occurred long after members first supposed that they had been exercising unitary authority in a charismatic way. The injustices associated with the nineteenth-century Church and its "infallible priesthood" – the dark thought control that characterized the Missouri period and life in Utah, and the hardships experienced across the spectrum by well-intentioned Saints – had their genesis in the claimed reality of unsupported events surrounded by deception.

The Aaronic and Melchizedek Priesthoods were not identified, named or described until after Smith abandoned New York for Kirtland, Ohio, in 1831, to be close to the man who was to become his sinister *consigliere* for most of the rest of his natural life.

In 1841, Joseph Smith and Nauvoo Stake President William Marks ordained Sidney Rigdon to be, like Joseph Smith already was, a "Prophet, Seer and Revelator" to the Church of Jesus Christ of Latter-day Saints. He had fairly earned that most remarkable honor. The Mormon Priesthood was the lengthened shadow of the ubiquitous Rigdon.[120]

---

[119]Roberts, ed., *History of the Church of Jesus Christ of Latter-day Saints*, 1:40 n.

[120]Richard S. Van Wagoner, *Sidney Rigdon: A Portrait of Religious Excess* (Salt Lake City: Signature Books, 1994; paperback 2006), 338; see, *e.g.*, 284-85. In "the first revelation on the First Presidency to be officially published (now Doctrine and Covenants 90) . . . Rigdon and [Frederick G.] Williams 'are accounted as equal with thee [Joseph Smith] in holding the keys of this last kingdom.'" (Quinn, *The Mormon Hierarchy: Origins of Power*, 43). "I [William Marks] laid my hands on Brother Sidney with Brother Joseph and he [Joseph] ordained him a 'prophet and a seer and revelator,' and to be equal with him in holding the keys and authority of this kingdom." (*Latter Day Saints Messenger and Advocate* [Pittsburgh] 1 [1 March 1845]: 129-30, quoted in Van Wagoner, *Sidney Rigdon*, 357). Sidney Rigdon was then supposed to have become the spiritual equal of the most important man on earth.

CHAPTER SEVENTEEN

God's Editors

If nothing can be said to be constant, what can be said to be true?

Joel M. Allred

At no time in its long, tortured journey has Mormon concern for Mormon history been any more pronounced.

Joel M. Allred

It is alleged, and it is not to be taken lightly, that many Mormon leaders, historians and scribes have concealed, suppressed and altered significant facts. In that they have betrayed the laity, those who value truth and the larger world.

Joel M. Allred

THE LDS STANDARD WORKS

The Doctrine and Covenants is a ruthlessly amended compilation of the officially published revelations, almost entirely those of Joseph Smith, basically the words of Smith's nineteenth-century revelator to nineteenth, twentieth and twenty-first century Saints. The Pearl of Great Price included the First Vision (Joseph Smith History), the Articles of Faith, Smith's translation of part of the gospel of Matthew and pseudepigraphic messages from Moses, Enoch and Abraham. The Book of Mormon is "an account of the former inhabitants of this continent . . ." and (according to Joseph Smith in the Pearl of Great Price) contains "the fulness of the everlasting Gospel . . . as delivered by the Savior to the ancient inhabitants."

These books, including the not-so-perfect Bible, comprise the "standard works." They are scripture and canonized (in the case of the Bible with reservations).

The King James Version of the English Bible was egregiously plagiarized in the Book of Mormon by the Mormon prophet, errors and all, then criticized for its inaccuracy, then remodeled by Joseph Smith and Sidney Rigdon without archival support. Their lengthy spiritual revision (completed in 1833) was thought at the time to have been a matter of the highest priority. That notwithstanding, for most of their nearly two-hundred year history Latter-day Saints have chosen to use a Bible trusted only insofar as it was translated correctly by fallible scholars to a Bible revised by Smith and Rigdon without historical resources while both were supposed to be duly inspired. That the Christian Bible is flawed, translated inaccurately by scholars lacking the spirit and power of God, is an article of the Mormon Faith. "We believe the Bible to be the word of God as far as it is translated correctly." The Book of Mormon, translated by the spirit and power of God, and "the word of God," is the most correct of any book on earth. One of those books has a dignity the other is unable to match. Joseph Smith said, "I beli[e]ve the bible, as it read when it came from the pen of the original writers." Additional words along those lines were added to the Manuscript History.[1] A Mormon scholar noted that there are "3,400 verses in which it [Smith and Rigdon's Inspired Translation] differs from the King James Version, many of which throw greater light upon the teachings of Jesus and the apostles."[2]

---

[1]Manuscript History addition: "Ignorant translators, careless transcribers, or designing or corrupt priests have committed many errors." Joseph Smith Jr., *History of The Church of Jesus Christ of Latter-day Saints*, B.H. Roberts, ed., 7 vols., 2d ed., rev., (Salt Lake City: The Deseret Book Company, 1978), 6:57.

[2]Robert J. Matthews, "Joseph Smith's Inspired Translation of the Bible," *Ensign* (December 1972). Bruce R. McConkie: "*The Joseph Smith Translation, or Inspired Version, is a thousand times over the best Bible now existing on earth.*" ("The Bible, a Sealed Book," in *A Symposium on the New Testament, 1984*, 5, quoted by Andrew C. Skinner, "Restored Light on the Savior's Last Work in Mortality," *Ensign* [June 1999], 15, emphasis added). "The Church of Jesus Christ of Latter-day Saints has never published the entire Joseph Smith Translation of the Bible. ... In 1979 the LDS Church published an edition of the King James Version with hundreds of JST footnotes and a seventeen-page appendix containing JST excerpts . . . ." (Robert J. Matthews, *Joseph Smith Translation of the Bible* [BYU, Harold B. Lee Library, 1992, accessed 30 September 2013], available from

Mormonism's "standard works" are rich with meaning for Latter-day Saints (as Mormons greatly prefer to be called). The Latter-day Saint scriptures are explained in meaningful ways by men "inspired of God" (primarily laymen ordained to that authority respectfully described as the "Holy [Melchizedek] Priesthood after the Order of the Son of God"). Latter-day Saints accept their peculiar Mormon scripture as the word of God. The standard works represent dependable truth to thoroughly committed believers surrounded by controversy and threatened by confusion in an unbelieving world.

"We Require No Defense"

The Latter-day Saints are able to say, and have sometimes chosen to say, that "their religion requires no defense."[3] God tells them through the spirit that the Church is true. The Mormon God reserved the right to alter reality retroactively. That thoroughly flexible principle, honored by the laity, surrounded multiple accounts of the First Vision, the supposed restoration of the priesthood and the attributes of the Book of Mormon's Messiah with backdated addenda.

Sterling M. McMurrin, in life a cultural Mormon with a towering intellect, nevertheless reported that "in practice they have commonly made serious efforts to construct effective arguments in response to the critics of their religion . . . ."[4] "There is," according to McMurrin, "something private, subjective, and inevitably elusive about theophanies. They cannot be repeated and cannot become public experience and knowledge and are therefore in a sense unarguable. But a book is something else – it is a public object. It

---

eom.byu.edu/index.php/Joseph_Smith_Translation_of_the_Bible_[JST]; Internet, 9 pages).

[3]"To argue with a man who has renounced the use of authority and reason . . . is like administering medicine to the dead . . . ." (Thomas Paine, *The American Crisis: Common Sense* [essay addressed to Sir William Howe] [Nu Vision Publications, LLC, 2008], 338).

[4]Sterling McMurrin, "Brigham H. Roberts: A Biographical Essay," in Brigham H. Roberts, *Studies of the Book of Mormon*, ed. and with an introduction by Brigham D. Madsen, with a biographical essay by Sterling M. McMurrin (Urbana and Chicago: University of Illinois Press, 1985), xv.

can be printed and reprinted, translated and sold, placed on a shelf and read . . . ."[5] A book can be weighed and measured and criticized.

What was true of the Book of Commandments (the precursor to the Doctrine and Covenants), and what is true of the Book of Mormon, is true of the Doctrine and Covenants and the Pearl of Great Price. All of those works can be weighed and measured and criticized. Orson Pratt, an apostle steeped in certainty, offered this supremely confident nineteenth-century challenge to the Book of Mormon's detractors:

> If, after a rigid examination, it be found an imposition, it should be extensively published to the world as such; the evidences and arguments on which the imposture was detected, should be clearly and logically stated, that those who have been sincerely yet unfortunately deceived, may perceive the nature of the deception, and be reclaimed, and that those who continue to publish the delusion, may be exposed and silenced, not by physical force, neither by persecutions, bare assertions, nor ridicule, but by strong and powerful arguments – by evidences adduced from scripture and reason.[6]

While Pratt boldly speaks of the Book of Mormon, his words apply with equal force to Mormon history, to the First Vision, to the Doctrine and Covenants, to the *Lectures on Faith*, to the books of Moses, Enoch and Abraham, and to various other scriptures and doctrines. Unfortunately, dissenters who have "clearly and logically stated" their "evidences and arguments" haven't been all that well received. Mormon scholars who have challenged these resources have been rather roughly consigned to the buffetings of Satan. "[S]incerely yet unfortunately deceived" Latter-day Saints have not

---

[5]Ibid., xvi.

[6]Orson Pratt, *Divine Authenticity of the Book of Mormon*, no. 1, part of Orson Pratt, *A Series of Pamphlets, with Portrait to which is appended A Discussion (held in Bolton between Elder William Gibson and Rev. Mr. Woodman), also A Discussion (held in France between Elder John Taylor and three reverend gentlemen)* (Liverpool, UK: Franklin D. Richards, 1851), 1.

so much cared to "perceive the nature of the deception, and be reclaimed," nor have they treasured being exposed and silenced by strong and powerful arguments "adduced from scripture and reason." Pratt, who was excommunicated in the early days of the Church for "insubordination" (then reclaimed on a dubious technicality and rebaptized), spoke insincerely. His invitation to discover the truth and pass it carefully on was rhetorical hyperbole.

THE CURIOUS CASE OF JESSE GAUSE

Author's 1957 printing of the 1921 edition of the Doctrine and Covenants (headnote), Section 81: "REVELATION given through Joseph Smith the Prophet, at Hiram, Ohio, March 1832. – Frederick G. Williams called to be a High Priest and a Counselor in the First Presidency of the Church."[7]

For one hundred and fifty years, and until 1981, the Church declared – in Section 81 of the *Doctrine and Covenants* – that Joseph Smith received a revelation calling Frederick G. Williams "to be a high priest in my church, and a counselor unto my servant Joseph Smith, Jun.; . . . ." It is now (but not until 1981) acknowledged that the original revelation dated March 1832 had nothing to do with Williams, a transitional figure who did later become a counselor in yet another First Presidency. The 1832 revelation attributed to Williams for fifteen decades was actually first directed in its specific entirety to a now nearly invisible early Mormon convert by the name of Jesse Gause. Gause, a converted Shaker, was ordained a Counselor in the First Presidency of the Church of Christ (Mormon) on March 8, 1832. When Gause (whose service was short) "denied the faith," the name of Frederick G. Williams was substituted for that of Jesse Gause in the verbatim text of the specific revelation Joseph's Lord had previously directed to Gause. All of the blessings and promises[8] that first pertained to Gause now

---

[7]Doctrine and Covenants 81 (1957 edition), emphasis added.

[8]The precise words of a revelation directed to Jesse Gause that were redirected to Gause's successor, Frederick G. Williams: "I . . . will bless him [Joseph], and also thee [Jesse Gause], inasmuch as thou art faithful . . . in doing these things thou wilt do the greatest good unto thy fellow beings, and wilt promote the glory of him who is your Lord . . . . And if thou art faithful unto the end thou

pertained to Williams with supposedly equal force, as if the March 1832 revelation in all of its particulars had always been directed to Williams. "For more than a century, the *Doctrine and Covenants* wrongly attributed section 81 to Gause's successor as counselor, Frederick G. Williams. However, the 1981 edition acknowledges that Smith directed this revelation of 15 March 1832 to confirm Gause's appointment as counselor and to command him to proselytize 'among thy brethren' [meaning his former Quaker brethren]."[9]

"In the Kirtland Revelation Book, Smith recorded his selection of two older men as counselors: 'March 8, 1832. *Chose this day and ordained brother Jesse Gause and Broth[er] Sidney [Rigdon] to be my councellers of the ministry of the presidency of th[e] high Pri[e]sthood.*'"[10] Michael Quinn reports that "the 1832 event remained absent from official church histories until the 1980's."[11] This author's 1957 printing of the Doctrine and Covenants does not address a later clarification. "The misidentification of this revelation in its first publication [and for nearly one hundred and fifty years] was intentional since Gause was named in the original text and index to the revelation in the Kirtland Revelation Book, 17-18."[12] This casual approach to the misuse of revelation may be seen in this: "HIRAM PORTAGE CO OHIO MARCH 15TH 1832 VER{E[<i>}LV Verily I say unto you my servant ~~Jesse~~ Frederick G. Williams listen to the voice of him who speaketh, to thee the word of the Lord your God . . . ."[13] The remainder is personal directed first to Gause and then redirected to Williams.

On the day Jesse Gause was ordained to the office of First

---

shalt have a crown of immortality, and eternal life in the mansions which I have prepared in the house of my Father. Behold, and lo, these are the words of Alpha and Omega, even Jesus Christ. Amen." (Doctrine and Covenants [1957], 81:3-7).

[9]D. Michael Quinn, *The Mormon Hierarchy: Origins of Power* (Salt Lake City: Signature Books in association with Smith Research Associates, 1994), 41-42.

[10]Joseph Smith's Kirtland Revelation Book, 10-11, quoted in Quinn, *Origins of Power*, 41, emphasis added.

[11]Quinn, *Origins of Power*, 41.

[12]Ibid., 299 fn 15.

[13]*The Joseph Smith Papers: Revelations and Translations Volume 2: Published Revelations*, eds. Robin Scott Jensen, Richard E. Turley Jr., and Riley M. Lorimer (Salt Lake City: Church Historian's Press, 2011), 446-47, emphasis added.

Counselor in the first First Presidency, March 8, 1832, Sidney Rigdon was also ordained to the office of Second Counselor in the First Presidency, the Presidency of the high priesthood.   In February, 1832, just before the March 8, 1832, ordination of a First Presidency comprised of Joseph Smith, Jesse Gause and Sidney Rigdon, Joseph Smith Jr. and Sidney Rigdon jointly received the revelation presently known as Section 76 of the Doctrine and Covenants. In this vision, according to the *Church Chronology*, "the beautiful doctrine of the three glories was explained." "In this vision Joseph Smith, jun., and Sidney Rigdon 'beheld the glory of the Son on the right hand of the Father,' and 'saw the holy angels and they who are sanctified before His throne.'"[14]   Joseph Smith was then inspired to choose Jesse Gause (who was older than Rigdon) and the influential Rigdon to be his counselors in the first First Presidency of the Church of Christ (Mormon). The *Church Chronology's* only reference to Jesse Gause is in April of 1832 and has nothing to do with his brief tenure as a Counselor in the First Presidency of the Mormon Church.   The *Chronology* refers to Gause as having traveled with Joseph Smith and others on a "second journey to Missouri."

Frederick G. Williams *was not* "called by revelation" to be "a

---

[14]Andrew Jenson, comp., *Church Chronology: A Record of Important Events Pertaining to the History of the Church of Jesus Christ of Latter-day Saints*, 2d ed., rev. and enlarged (Salt Lake City: Deseret News, 1914), 7. The "beautiful doctrine" of the "three glories" had been explained [before the birth of Joseph Smith and Sidney Rigdon] by the Swedish mystic Emanuel Swedenborg, who labeled the highest glory the Celestial Kingdom, and also said that it (the highest glory) was divided into three divisions, the uppermost being where God lived. Swedenborg said that a man had to be married to get there. Swedenborg's three divisions – the Celestial, the Spiritual and the Natural – were compared in his book "*Heaven and Hell*" to the "sun, moon and stars." Swedenborg described an interim spiritual state, preceding a final disposition of status, as modern Mormons now also do. Section 76 bears many striking similarities to the much earlier work of Swedenborg. Joseph Smith was familiar with Swedenborg, having mentioned him on at least one occasion, and so most likely was his revelatory co-collaborator, the more broadly-versed Sidney Rigdon. The Inspired Translation of the King James Bible, the Book of Mormon, Section 76 of the *Doctrine and Covenants*, and certain elements of various other revelations reflect virtually undeniable evidence of Smith's borrowings from the earlier works of Swedenborg (1688-1782). Swedenborg lived and died and published before Joseph Smith was born. Had there been no Swedenborg, the Mormon concept of the afterlife would have been very different.

Counselor to Joseph Smith, jun." in March of 1832, nor were *his* blessings enumerated in that revelation as the *Church Chronology* and the revelation said that he was, and they were.[15] Sidney Rigdon *was* called to be a Counselor to the prophet Joseph Smith in March 1832, something the *Church Chronology* didn't admit. Smith's selection of Jesse Gause and Sidney Rigdon is documented in the manuscript of the revelation found in the Kirtland Revelation Book. To avoid mention of Gause (a dissenter), the *Church Chronology* failed to also mention Rigdon. The *Chronology* falsely avers that "Frederick G. Williams [was called] to be a Counselor to Joseph Smith, jun.," in March of 1832.[16] That terse entry deceitfully explains how Frederick G. Williams' name appeared in a revelation the Lord specifically directed to Gause. As the *Church Chronology* is silent about Gause's ordination as a Counselor in the First Presidency, it then also fails to mention his apostasy and excommunication. The fall from grace of the first First Counselor in the first First Presidency of the Church of Christ was nothing if not noteworthy. Its omission from an official chronology of Mormonism's most important events is unacceptable.

Only three of the twelve apostles selected to the founding Quorum of the Twelve were not at one time or another disfellowshipped or excommunicated.[17] Most of them were so sufficiently visible that their offenses, unlike those of the nondescript Gause, couldn't hope to escape detection. Gause's excommunicable offense is not announced in the *Church Chronology*. Gause's excommunication is not announced in the *Church Chronology*. Williams' 1833

---

[15]Ibid., 8. The *Church Chronology* cites Doctrine and Covenants 81 (the revelation to Gause) as evidence of Frederick G. Williams' appointment.

[16]Ibid.

[17]In addition to the recalcitrant apostles, "Rigdon was disfellowshipped on 6 July 1832." His offense: trying to take over the Church. His restitution: "Smith ordained Rigdon to the high priesthood 'the Second time' on 28 July after he had 'repented like Peter of old.'" (Joseph Smith Jr., *The Personal Writings of Joseph Smith*, ed. Dean C. Jessee [Salt Lake City, UT: Deseret Book, 1984], 247, quoted in Quinn, *Origins of Power*, 42). On March 17, 1839, Frederick G. Williams, Thomas B. Marsh, William W. Phelps, George M. Hinkle and others "were excommunicated" during "a conference held at Quincy, Illinois." (Jenson, comp., *Church Chronology*, 16). The first three Counselors in the First Presidency (Jesse Gause, Sidney Rigdon and Frederick G. Williams) were all excommunicated (Gause, Williams) or disfellowshipped (Rigdon) over time. Rigdon and Williams later returned.

appointment was conveniently backdated to March of 1832,[18] and the *Chronology's* anachronistic description of Frederick G. Williams' appointment in March 1832, before Gause's Missouri trip with Joseph in April 1832, is yet another falsified recital. The March 1832 call – described in the *Church Chronology*, as pertaining to Williams – pertained verbatim to Gause. The historical entry in the *Chronology*, like the entries (headnote and text) in section 81 of the Doctrine and Covenants, simply substituted the name of Williams for the name of Gause wherever the name of Gause belonged. The *Church Chronology* promulgates (in its Second Edition published in 1914) at least six obvious deceptions:

(1)   *It fails to mention the March 8, 1832, ordinations of Jesse Gause and Sidney Rigdon as Counselors to the prophet Joseph Smith in the First Presidency of the Church of Christ.*

(2)   *It describes Frederick G. Williams as having been called as a Counselor to Joseph Smith in March of 1832, in the revelation described as Section 81 of the Doctrine and Covenants, when in fact Jesse Gause was called to serve as a Counselor to Joseph Smith in the revelation described as Section 81 of the Doctrine and Covenants.*

(3)   *It omits any reference to a founding First Presidency comprised of Joseph Smith, Jesse Gause and Sidney Rigdon.*

(4)   *It fails to mention the ordination, apostasy and excommunication of Jesse Gause, the first First Counselor in the first First Presidency of the Church of Christ.*

(5)   *It falsely reports that Joseph Smith operated without a First Presidency until March 18, 1833.*

---

[18]Jenson, comp., *Church Chronology*, 8, citing Doctrine and Covenants 79, 80, 81.

(6)   *It fails to describe Jesse Gause as having ever been a Counselor in the First Presidency of the Church of Christ.*[19]

McLELLIN VOTES NO

William E. McLellin, one of the most literate members of the founding Quorum of the Twelve and a man friendly to and admired by Emma Smith, was a well situated insider eyewitness to what he called the mutilation of the Doctrine and Covenants. "In November, 1831, I presided in a council in Joseph's translating room, in which it was first determined to print the revelations at all."[20] In that council "it was determined [that] the time had come for them to be printed, and go to the world, contrary to the Lord's directions!" The council was a multiple-day event with McLellin powerfully privy to everything that transpired. The thoughtful apostle described what he considered to be a great offense. Ordinary men (members of committees) changed the revelations to their liking.

> *J. Smith, O. Cowdery, and S. Rigdon, were appointed a committee to prepare the revelations for the press. In doing so they took out of them, added to them, and altered them just to suit their then supposed enlightened view. Thus altered and changed, O. Cowdery and J. Whitmer were appointed a committee to carry them to Zion [Independence, Missouri], in order for them to be published in the "Book of Commandments." J. Smith, S. Rigdon, and N.K. Whitney visited Zion in April, 1832. W.W. Phelps, O. Cowdery, and J. Whitmer are the committee of publication. And they were still to examine said altered revelations before publication, and alter again when necessary. Many councils were held by these*

---

[19]Jenson, comp., *Church Chronology*, Introductory page, *The First Presidency* vi, 7-9.

[20]McLellin letter to Mark H. Forscutt, 1 October 1871, *The William E. McLellin Papers: 1854-1880*, eds. Stan Larson and Samuel J. Passey, foreword by George D. Smith (Salt Lake City: Signature Books, 2008), 473.

men, while here in Zion.[21]

Feeling betrayed, McLellin left the Church in 1836, then returned, but not for long. In about 1880, after a lifetime to reflect, he further explained some of the reasons why he did what he did. One of them, an unsettling factor for this former Secretary of the Quorum of the Twelve, was that *"J. Smith materially altered his own revelations."*[22] During the council's sittings, "it was determined to have all his revelations printed, and he [J. Smith], O. Cowdery, and S. Rigdon were appointed a committee to read over, and prepare them for the press." When those revelations were modified, according to McLellin, they then became the collaborative production of that faith-promoting committee. *"[T]hey* seemed to think themselves authorized to alter and change what *they* claimed to be the revelations of the Lord, to an alarming extent. *They* altered words, sentences and paragraphs. *They* took out passages and added others so as to entirely change the sentiment, and thus made them read very different."[23] Who could find the hand of the Lord in that? And that – as offensive as it was – was not the end of it.

> *[T]he revelations were [then] sent to Jackson Co. Mo. by O. Cowdery and John Whitmer, during the winter of 1831 and 2, for publication. J. Smith visited Mo. in the spring of 1832, and in council it was agreed that the printers Phelps, Cowdery, and Whitmer should examine, alter and correct them again before printing them. They printed 160 pages, in a small book, called "Book of Commandments."*[24]

Several separate committees, including men who didn't receive the revelations, substantively altered the text repeatedly. Another committee altered the text of other documents (Joseph Smith's *History of the Church*) long after the prophet was dead. "I am astonished," the disillusioned McLellin reported, "that sane men

---

[21]Ibid., 474, emphasis added.

[22]William E. McLellin, "Reasons Why I Am Not a Mormon" (ca. 1880), *The William E. McLellin Papers*, 413, emphasis retained.

[23]Ibid., emphasis added.

[24]Ibid., 414, emphasis added.

should dare do as those men did with what they considered the Lord's word." McLellin, a student of the Bible, quoted scripture in support of his concern: "Moses said to Israel, 'Ye shall not add unto the word which I command you, neither shall you diminish ought from it.' Deut 4:2. . . ." And Solomon said, "'Add thou not unto his words, lest he reprove thee, and thou be found a liar.' Prov. 30:6."[25]   The Book of Commandments project foundered in the summer of 1833 when an Independence, Missouri, "mob destroyed their building, their press, their bookwork, and the printers had to flee for their lives. I [McLellin] have a copy [of the original Book of Commandments] gathered up among the rubbish by one of the printer boys, and roughly bound."[26]   That untoward event – a setback to be sure – did not yet begin to end the effort, or the cynical corrections:

> *The revelations were then taken back to Ohio, and in Kirtland they formed . . . another committee by adding ~~adding~~ Dr. F.G. Williams to the former one. Here the said to be revelations underwent another awful scathing and alteration, and was published in a book ~~of~~ called "Doctrine and Covenants."*
>
> *If any man had the original as first given and there read the alterations, he could not help being surprised at their changes.*[27]

The reconstituted committee now corrected and further composed the previously recomposed revelations. They added and omitted things; thus, theological considerations were operative. After describing how changing the word of the Lord was a crime ("awful plagues shall fall upon the man who tampers with the word of God"), McLellin then described what happened to some of the men who supposedly did: "Sidney Rigdon died a monomaniac, Oliver Cowdery did not live out half his days, and Joseph Smith was miserably butchered by [a] blackened mob!"   McLellin had been

---

[25]Ibid. "Jesus said, 'Till heaven and earth pass away, one jot or one tittle shall in no wise pass from the law, till all be fulfilled.' Matt. 5:18."

[26]William E. McLellin, "Reasons Why I Am Not a Mormon" (ca. 1880), Passey and Larson, *The William E. McLellin Papers*, 414.

[27]Ibid.

dumbfounded. "Wo be the men who destroyed the revelations of the Lord (or those pretended to be) by their ~~their~~ changes and alterations!"[28] All of this is instructive. Nothing Mormon and written was so sacred as to be impervious to nineteenth-century revision, including the contents of the Book of Mormon, the contents of the Book of Commandments, and the contents of the Doctrine and Covenants.

McLellin watched this unseemly process unfold at the place where he lived, Independence, Missouri. McLellin was closely tied to the Whitmers, including Church Historian John, a most important early figure then. John Whitmer's well-appointed brother David had converted McLellin. Church Historian John was heavily involved with the nineteenth-century preparation for and publication of the revelations as the Facsimile Edition of the *Joseph Smith Papers Project* (published in 2009) clearly attests. The unsettling events that turned the obviously capable McLellin against the Church and its leaders included the alteration of the revelations by printers and committees both prior to and after their publication in the Book of Commandments. Further alterations followed when the 1833 Book of Commandments, thought to be close to safely extinct, was superceded by the cynically altered Book of Doctrine and Covenants in 1835.

In Missouri in April 1832, the "Order of Enoch" was established by Joseph Smith, Sidney Rigdon, N.K. Whitney and some other (Missouri) elders. Nine members of that peculiar order then each received a fictitious name "such as Gazelam, Pelagoram, Ohihah, &c.!" McLellin, impatient with such silly outlandish pseudonyms, expressed profound disgust. "O shame on such nonsense!" he is heard to report. Equipped with *nom de plumes* to protect them against the old Missouri settlers who took offense at some of the revelations printed by the Mormon press, "The committee of publication commenced the work." "*[T]hey* were still to examine said altered revelations before publication, and alter again when necessary."[29] Whatever the revelations were to start, they were markedly different when published. When four hundred words

---

[28]Ibid., 414-15.
[29]McLellin letter to Mark H. Forscutt, 1 October 1871, *The William E. McLellin Papers*, 474.

were added to Chapter 28 of the Book of Commandments – a revelation received by Smith in 1830 – in the Doctrine and Covenants in 1835, without archival support, they were presented to the world as the words of Jesus Christ. Nothing since has ever changed. The awkward amendments have found an important place in the theological firmament. The Lord, we must suppose, added that substantial insert five years after the fact. "None of Joseph Smith's revelations were ever printed or published until June, 1832."[30]

Alterations

The "revelations" in the Book of Doctrine and Covenants "were twice, if not three times *altered* and changed before they came to light in that book."[31] In substantive ways that changed the message. After he had seen what he saw, the Doctrine and Covenants meant nothing to William E. McLellin. The alterations by editors, committees and printers soured the apostle on priesthood. McLellin later reported that the Book of Mormon didn't describe Aaronic or Levitical priests, and that the office of a High Priest and the powers of the priesthood were not described in the Book of

---

[30]Ibid., 473. The reckless publication of the revelations did much to foment the violence that caused the Mormons to be expelled from Independence, Missouri, the site that the Lord was supposed to have designated as the center place of Zion, the place of the gathering, and the land of the Mormons' "inheritance." A provocative revelation published in *The Evening and the Morning Star* referred to the "old Missouri settlers" as "enemies" of the children of God. The facilities of *The Evening and the Morning Star* (published at Independence from June of 1832 to July of 1833) were "destroyed by mob violence." (Ibid., 473). "W.W. Phelps & Co." edited and published the *"Star."* After publication in the *"Star," some* of the edited revelations given "until September, 1831" were also printed "in regular course" and "as far as they were given" in the "Book of Commandments." The *"Star"* was republished in Kirtland (under the title *Evening and Morning Star*), starting in January, 1835, after the Church had dropped the name of Christ from its title (it is now the "Church of the Latter Day Saints"). That millennialist revision offended the Christ conscious McLellin, then also his friend and mentor David Whitmer. (Ibid., 473, McLellin to Forscutt). "All *its* numbers, until October 1836, were," according to McLellin, "printed in the interest of the church of *Latter Dayites*" and not the Church of Christ. (Ibid., emphasis added). The society's aggressive millennial aspirations did for a time take precedence over the honor and glory of Christ.
[31]Ibid., 473, emphasis retained.

Mormon after Jesus personally ministered on this continent. He claimed that the word "priesthood is not found in the Book of Commandments, as far as printed in this city in 1833." McLellin then finally concluded that, *"all the support you have for two priesthoods in the church in the gospel age you have to take from that altered, mutilated, changed, mixed up, and bungled Book of Doctrine and Covenants."*[32] His brusque response to the Doctrine and Covenants was resolute and unsparing.

In a letter to Mark H. Forscutt in 1871, McLellin reported that he had in his possession copies of the old *"Stars"* as printed in Independence, and a hard to get copy of the Book of Commandments. The possession of those resources and other original documents, plus his positions of prominence, permitted McLellin to speak with authority about the contents of those early revelations. While he honored the Book of Mormon, and showed respect for the mystical powers of Joseph's controversial peepstone, he held the Book of Doctrine and Covenants in utter contempt. McLellin hadn't wanted the revelations to be published in the Book of Commandments. Had God not specifically said, "Keep these things from the . . . world"?[33] The publication of some of the revelations in *The Evening and the Morning Star* served to inflame the old settlers (non-Mormons) in Independence, Missouri, where William E. McLellin also continued to live after he left the Church.

"In 1831," McLellin reported, "I wrote off a number of the revelations as originally given, and have them now. They were materially altered, (seen by comparison) before printed at all."[34] They were repeatedly changed before they were "brought to light." Is it to be wondered why the twentieth-century Church desperately feared the twentieth-century production of the McLellin papers? McLellin had first-hand knowledge of the publication process, handwritten copies of the original revelations, copies of the "old 'Stars'" where the revelations were initially published, and a roughly-bound copy of the 1833 *Book of Commandments* (a precious artifact retrieved from the rubble left after the destruction of the printing office at Independence, Missouri).

---

[32]Ibid., emphasis retained.
[33]Ibid., 473-74.
[34]Ibid., 474.

After Cowdery, leaving Missouri, traveled to Kirtland to consult the leadership (following the destruction of the printing press at Independence), and after he then traveled to New York to purchase another press and fixtures, the Independence, Missouri, editions of the *"Star"* were reprinted in Kirtland, with yet further alterations, in the *Evening and Morning Star*, a Kirtland publication with a slightly different name. McLellin blew the whistle on a deceptive process: *"They professed* to reprint the *Stars*, but did so in a very altered condition."[35] The apostle found the edits overwhelming. This blatant tampering with what he had by now come to consider only "pretended" revelations, and the contaminated product that then emerged, first distressed then alienated the capable McLellin.

Now, in Kirtland – after the already extensive early alterations that preceded the publication of the Book of Commandments in 1833, followed by the destruction of the Missouri press and printing office – the editorial committee was reconstituted. "In September, 1834, J. Smith, O. Cowdery and F.G. Williams were appointed a committee *to fix up the revelations again* in order to have them printed"[36] again. By August 1835, "they had completed their labors, and submitted them to a general assembly." William E. McLellin left the society of the "Latter Dayites" (Christ was out of the name) in 1836. He briefly returned before leaving again and was excommunicated in 1838. *At that time, and for more than a century forward, the only way out of the Church, whether one was born into the society or caught in the gospel net, was by the humiliating process of excommunication.* In those particular times, the names of wayward Saints were exposed in some of the publications of the early church.

McLellin, who was uniquely positioned to know the true facts, and a person in possession of various hard-to-get original documents, drew the following unsettling conclusions about the revelations published in the Doctrine and Covenants:

> *I think there is scarcely a revelation printed in that book but that is altered and changed.*

---

[35]Ibid., emphasis added.
[36]Ibid., emphasis added.

I have counted more than twenty material alterations in one revelation, by comparing it as printed here [in Independence] and in Kirtland . . . .

Thus they come to us in their mutilated condition, three times altered and changed, and fixed. In their present condition who can have confidence in them?[37]

Appendix F at the back of the book depicts the mutilation of some of the revelations by the men who were charged to prepare and publish them.

THE REVELATIONS

The Typographical Error Theory of Revelatory Readjustment

When the revelations described in *The Evening and the Morning Star* published in Independence, Missouri (Mormonism's Independence periodical) in 1833 were revised and reprinted in the *Evening and Morning Star* in Kirtland, Ohio (one of Mormonism's Kirtland periodicals) in 1836, the editors of the *Evening and Morning Star* (by modern Mormon reckoning) "revised the revelations found in *The Evening and the Morning Star*, changing wording and sometimes order and position on the page."[38] That cosmetic contention is the time-honored apologetic explanation for the alteration of the revelations as they were received. "Rigdon and Cowdery attributed the necessity of changing God's printed word to such minor factors as transcription errors, poor copy, or sloppy printers."[39] The four hundred and fifty words that altered the

---

[37]Ibid., 474-75, emphasis added. "Now if the Lord gave these revelations he said what he meant, and meant what he said. And no additions or subtractions could make it plainer. Man's additions would only bring the curse of God sooner or later, as it did do. But they had to alter or to fix them up to suit their advanced views. The idea conveyed to our minds is that the Lord grew in wisdom and knowledge; so that his revealments must be . . . altered to suit the advanced intelligence."

[38]*The Joseph Smith Papers: Revelations and Translations Volume 2: Published Revelations*, 195.

[39] Richard S. Van Wagoner, *Sidney Rigdon: A Portrait of Religious Excess* (Salt Lake City: Signature Books, 1994; paperback 2006), 162.

innocent provisions of Chapter 28 of the Book of Commandments published in the Independence periodical in March 1833, when it was republished in the Kirtland periodical in May 1836 (and in the Doctrine and Covenants in 1835), concerned a great deal more than semantics, word order, transcription errors, poor copy, sloppy printers and position on the page.   When the revelation was recomposed to be reprinted in the Kirtland periodical, and in the first edition of the Doctrine and Covenants, the changes were monumentally substantive, backdated and falsified.

In 2011 in the *Joseph Smith Papers*,[40] the problem is ignominiously admitted in a Mormon publication for what is probably the first time. "The first issue of the reprinted newspaper, which appeared [in Kirtland] under the slightly modified title *Evening and Morning Star*, was published in January 1835. *Though touted as a reprint that would correct typographical and other errors, Evening and Morning Star actually contained significant changes to the revelation texts.*"[41] "In the first issue, editor Oliver Cowdery explained the revisions *he was making* in the reprinted versions of the revelations . . . ."[42] Note that a man who didn't receive the revelations was making the revisions, a process that the Church now (but not until 2011) admits involved "*significant changes to the revelation texts.*" Cowdery blamed the incredible revisions on "typographical and other errors."[43] "On the revelations [to be reprinted in the retitled

---

[40] *The Joseph Smith Papers: Revelations and Translations Volume 2: Published Revelations*, 198.

[41] Ibid., emphasis added.

[42] Ibid., emphasis added.

[43] It was a technique Cowdery would apply one month later, in February 1835, in yet another vitally important context. In the 1834-35 History prepared by Oliver Cowdery (under the personal supervision of Joseph Smith), Cowdery first explained that the now-famous Palmyra revival occurred in 1820. That was the date much later assigned to that revival in the canonized provisions of the 1838-39 Pearl of Great Price Account of Joseph's First Vision of the Father and the Son, the "hinge pin" upon which the whole cause turns. In a later installment of the 1834-35 History (one of eight) of that vitally important history, he then clarified that earlier text to say that it had not. "You will recollect," he told his audience, "that I mentioned the time of a religious excitement, in Palmyra and vicinity to have been in the 15th year of our brother J. Smith Jr's age – *that was an error in the type – it should have been in the 17th. –*" "year of our brother J. Smith Jr.'s age." In this Cowdery made a change of incredible importance blaming an earlier and inaccurate assertion (a revival in 1820) on a typographical error. "*You will please remember this correction, as it will be necessary for the full understanding of what*

Evening and Morning Star at Kirtland beginning in January 1835]
we merely say, that we were not a little surprised to find the
previous print [the publication of the revelations printed in *The
Evening and the Morning Star* at Independence in 1832 and 1833] so
different from the original." That is to say that we did not detect
before the revelations were published in Independence, Missouri,
that the word of God as reflected in the text of those publications
was "so different from the original" (the text previously and for
years supposed to have been printed correctly). The thought is
utterly preposterous.

The clever Cowdery has said that typographical errors were
significant. Significant errors necessitated significant corrections.
"We have given them [the revelations published in Missouri and the
original manuscripts from which they were printed] a careful
comparison, assisted by individuals whose known integrity and
ability is uncensurable." In this Cowdery describes the work of the
undenominated members of a committee. The careful comparison
of the previously published revelations to the original manuscripts
was conducted, according to this, by Cowdery and estimable but
unnamed assistants. This new (since December 1834) co-president
of the Mormon Church is forced to admit that he had participated
in the previous publication of the supposedly typographically
imperfect revelations. "[W]e cast no reflections upon those who
were entrusted with the responsibility of publishing them in
Missouri, as our own labors were included in that important service
to the church, and it was our unceasing endeavor to have them
correspond with the copy furnished us." Cowdery concludes, after
the "careful comparison" of the previously published revelations to

---

will follow in time. This would bring the date [of the Palmyra revival] down to the
year 1823" (thus associating the Palmyra revival with the vision of the Angel
Moroni in what Cowdery [and Joseph] then called 1823). (Oliver Cowdery,
"Letter IV To W.W. Phelps, Esq." [Oliver Cowdery and Joseph Smith's 1834-35
History], *Messenger and Advocate*, vol. 1 no. 5 [February 1835], 78, emphasis
added). In 1835, Cowdery, under the personal supervision of Smith and claiming
typographical error, denied that the Palmyra revival occurred in 1820 (thus failing
to precede the vision of the Father and the Son). In 1834 and 1835 in the first
authorized history of the Mormon Church (which didn't mention a vision of the
Father and the Son), Oliver Cowdery and Joseph Smith placed the Palmyra revival
in 1823. It preceded, they then said, the vision of the angel in charge of the golden
plates.

the original manuscripts, that *"We* believe they [the revelations as just revised and reprinted] are now correct. If not in every word, at least in principle."[44] Note again that men who didn't receive the revelations were charged with their correction. Men who could be trusted not to tell the truth; unknown individuals, editors, "whose known integrity and ability is uncensurable."

David Whitmer, a Book of Mormon witness, challenged Oliver Cowdery's untenable premise. "Some of the revelations," he said, "as they are now in the Book of Doctrine and Covenants have been changed and added to. Some of the changes being of the greatest importance as the meaning is entirely changed on some very important matters; as if the Lord had changed his mind a few years after he gave the revelations, and after having commanded his servants (*as they claim*) to print them in the Book of Commandments . . . ."[45] God and David Whitmer rejected the typographical error theory of revelatory readjustment.

God first:

> *Behold, this is mine authority, and the authority of my*
> *servants, and my Preface unto the Book of my*
> *Commandments, which I have given them to publish*
> *unto you . . . . Behold I am God and have spoken it:*
> *these commandments are of me . . . . Search these*
> *commandments for they are true and faithful, and the*
> *prophecies and promises which are in them, shall all*
> *be fulfilled . . . the record is true . . . .*[46]

David Whitmer second:

---

[44]Notice, *Evening and Morning Star* (Kirtland, OH: June 1832) (Jan. 1835), 16, reproduced at *The Joseph Smith Papers: Revelations and Translations Volume 2: Published Revelations*, 198, emphasis added.

[45]David Whitmer, *An Address to All Believers in Christ: by A Witness to the Divine Authenticity of The Book of Mormon* (Richmond, MO: n.p., 1887; photographic reprint, Concord, CA: Pacific Publishing Company, 1993) 56, emphasis added.

[46]Joseph Smith Jr., comp., *A Book of Commandments, For the Government of the Church of Christ, Organized According to the Law, on the 6th of April, 1830* (Zion, MO:W.W. Phelps, 1833), Preface, 1:2-7, emphasis added.

The revelations were printed in the Book of Commandments correctly. This I know, and will prove it to you. These revelations were arranged for publication by Brothers Joseph Smith, Sydney Rigdon, Orson Hyde and others, in Hiram, Ohio, while I was there, were sent to Independence to be published, and were printed just exactly as they were arranged by Brother Joseph and the others. And when the Book of Commandments was printed, Joseph and the church received it as being printed correctly. This I know.[47]

Confessions

The Church is now forced to admit (in the publication of the *Joseph Smith Papers* in 2011, nearly two hundred years after its founding) that *"very few of the changes in the reprint represent a restoration back to the earliest text, though Cowdery consulted early manuscript sources when reprinting some of the revelations."* The incredible changes made to Chapter 28 of the 1833 Book of Commandments when that particularly pivotal chapter was reprinted in 1835 (in the Doctrine and Covenants) and 1836 (in the *Evening and Morning Star*) are not to be found in the manuscript, and Cowdery could not have consulted them there if he had most desperately tried. They are not included with the chronological facsimiles of the revelations received in August or September of 1830. The incredible revisions to Chapter 28 of the Book of Commandments – absolutely essential to the establishment of the priesthood – were crafted by a committee without archival support after the revelation was published in the Book of Commandments and in *The Evening and the Morning Star* in Missouri in 1833 without them. Two-thirds of Section 27 of the modern Doctrine and Covenants, consisting of more than four hundred words, find no support in the revelation's only manuscript.

God didn't change the revelations in 1835; editors did. Some unknown and unnamed. Joseph's Lord ("Behold I am God and have spoken it: these commandments are of me . . .") in the Preface

---

[47]Whitmer, *An Address to All Believers in Christ*, 56, emphasis added.

to the Book of Commandments published in 1833 stood behind the revelations as initially published without reserve. *"Search these commandments for they are true and faithful, and the prophecies and promises, which are in them, shall all be fulfilled . . . ."* The Church now lamely explains the alterations to those revelations in these terms: "Because the revelations were meant to be used as a guide for the current operations of the church, they were *edited* in 1835 to reflect current organization, doctrine and practice, which had continued to develop since the revelations were first dictated."[48]

History, written in faithful Mormon terms, trumps reality. A God who can wipe away your sins and say they never occurred can rewrite history at the hands of a capable prophet. Joseph Smith, who understood this principle better than most, said that God was "his right hand man."

David Whitmer, like his trusted friend William E. McLellin, knew just how improper this was.

> *In the winter of 1834 they saw that some of the revelations in the Book of Commandments had to be changed, because the heads of the church had gone too far, and had done things in which they had already gone ahead of some of the former revelations. So the Book of "Doctrine and Covenants" was printed in 1835, and some of the revelations changed and added to. By the providence of God I have one of the old Book of Commandments published in 1833.*[49]

The Church is forced to admit (in 2011) that the revelations were changed by editors. If people who didn't receive them changed them, then (by faithful reckoning) the word of God was ignored. The depth and breadth of those incredible alterations, perhaps thousands of them, is depicted in several striking exemplars collected in this book at Appendix F.

---

[48] *The Joseph Smith Papers: Revelations and Translations Volume 2: Published Revelations*, 199, emphasis added.

[49] Whitmer, *An Address to All Believers in Christ*, 56, emphasis retained and added.

Joseph Smith Papers, 2011:

> *Most of the changes made to revelations in the early issues of Evening and Morning Star are also reflected in the same revelations as published in the first edition of the Doctrine and Covenants (1835), and the editing work on that volume, in turn, influenced the presentation of revelations in later issues of Evening and Morning Star.*
>
> *The first six issues of Evening and Morning Star present the full texts of thirteen revelations that were modified before or during the typesetting of the 1835 Doctrine and Covenants, meaning that the changes to some of the revelations were first made to the texts in Evening and Morning Star and later replicated in the 1835 Doctrine and Covenants.*[50]

May one not conclude with Apostle McLellin that there have been too many hands in this pie. "Who can have confidence in them?"[51]

Coming to Grips with Duplicity

What might a thoughtful person learn upon taking the time to be better informed? That these revelations were altered, backdated and falsified. The words of *"Jesus Christ, your Lord, your God and your Redeemer"*[52] were altered as suited the times by editors as suited them. "Accounts of a second priesthood restoration began appearing the year after Cowdery's [and Joseph's] 1834 history." Those claims came to rest in Section 50 (now Section 27) of the 1835 edition of the Doctrine and Covenants,

> *These phrases about John the Baptist and Peter, James, and John had not appeared when the*

---

[50]*The Joseph Smith Papers: Revelations and Translations Volume 2: Published Revelations*, 199, emphasis added.

[51]McLellin letter to Mark H. Forscutt, 1 October 1871, in *The William E. McLellin Papers*, 473.

[52]Book of Commandments, 28:1, emphasis added.

revelation was first published in 1832 in The Evening and the Morning Star or in the 1833 Book of Commandments (BofC, 60).[53] *A recent study [conducted before the publication of the Joseph Smith Papers] has demonstrated that the center portion on priesthood (now D&C 27:6-13) is also missing from the revelation's only manuscript. The added text cannot be found in any document before 1835, nor can any similar wording or concept be found prior to 1834.*[54]

After 1832 and 1833 but before 1835, the Mormon leaders added passages to previously published revelations attributed to Jesus Christ touching upon matters of supreme importance. The issue at the heart of this super-sensitive discovery (the provisions added to the altered Chapter 28 of the Book of Commandments) is the authority of the restored Church. The sparing revelation confined to a single topic in 1833 tripled in size in 1835 when it was expanded to include provocative unprovenanced topics and earlier dates. LaMar Petersen discussed the embellishment of some of the revelations in the context of the restoration:

The important details that are missing from the "full history" of 1834 [Oliver and Joseph's first authorized 1834-35 History] are likewise missing from the Book of Commandments in 1833. The student would expect to find all the particulars of the Restoration in this first treasured set of sixty-five revelations, the dates of which encompassed the bestowals of the two Priesthoods, but they are conspicuously absent . . . . The notable revelations on Priesthood in the Doctrine and Covenants before referred to, Sections 2[55] *and*

---

[53]In 1833 no one knew that Joseph Smith or Oliver Cowdery had ever seen, and neither of them had ever claimed to have seen, John the Baptist or Peter, James, and John.

[54]Quinn, *Origins of Power*, 16, emphasis added.

[55]Supposed to have been spoken by "Moroni to Joseph Smith the Prophet, while in the house of the Prophet's father [Doctrine and Covenants 2013] at Manchester, New York, *on the evening of September 21, 1823.*" Doctrine and Covenants 2, Headnote, emphasis added.

13[56] are missing, and Chapter 28 gives no hint of the Restoration, which, if actual, had been known for four years. More than four hundred words were added to this revelation of August 1829 [September 1830] in Section 27 of the Doctrine and Covenants, the additions made to include the names of heavenly visitors and two separate ordinations. The Book of Commandments gives the duties of Elders, Priests, Teachers, and Deacons and refers to Joseph's apostolic calling but there is no mention of Melchizedek Priesthood, High Priesthood, Seventies, High Priests nor High Councilors. These words were later inserted into the revelation on Church organization and government of April 1830, making it appear that they were known at that date, but they do not appear in the original, Chapter 24 of the Book of Commandments three years later . . . .[57]

Section 20 of the Doctrine and Covenants (previously Chapter 24 of the Book of Commandments) and Section 27 of the Doctrine and Covenants (previously Chapter 28 of the Book of Commandments) do not describe the priesthood, or the messengers, or the message, in their unamended form.

Lyman Wight, the violent angry man who ordained Joseph Smith to the Melchizedek Priesthood, and the first ordained high priest, "was so affected by the alterations that he said: 'The *Book of Doctrine and Covenants* was a telestial law; and the Book of

---

[56]Supposed to have been spoken by John the Baptist to Joseph Smith and Oliver Cowdery at Harmony, Pennsylvania, *on May 15, 1829.* Ibid., 13, Headnote. Sharon I. Banister asks the important question: "Can you explain why Doctrine and Covenants 13 (which tells of Joseph and Oliver's ordination to the Aaronic Priesthood in 1829) was omitted from the 1833 Book of Commandments and not published [in the Doctrine and Covenants] until 1876?" (Sharon I. Banister, *For Any Latter-day Saint: One Investigator's Unanswered Questions* [Fort Worth, TX: Star Bible Publications, 1988], 51).

[57]LaMar Petersen, *Problems in Mormon Text*, 7-8, quoted in Jerald Tanner and Sandra Tanner, *The Changing World of Mormonism: A Behind-the-Scenes Look at Changes in Mormon Doctrine and Practice* (Chicago, IL: Moody Press, 1979), 443, emphasis retained and added.

Commandments . . . was a celestial law.'"[58]   Wight, an 1841 apostle
and before that a priesthood insider, later apostatized.   David
Whitmer and William E. McLellin both described the mutilation of
the Book of Commandments.   These discrepancies were not isolated
circumstances, but repeated problems with a discredited process.
"Similar interpolations were made in the revelations known as
Sections 42 and 68 . . . ."[59]

> *Upgrading revelations and retrospectively editing the
> past are hallmarks of early Mormonism. Thousands
> of substantive alterations were made between the time
> many revelations were received, their first publication
> in various sources, and later propogations in the Book
> of Commandments (1833) and various editions of the
> Doctrine and Covenants since 1835.*[60]

UNPUBLISHED, UNKNOWN, UNSEEN

Soon after the communitarian Rigdon met Joseph Smith at Fayette,
New York, in December of 1830, and in fact at and after the third
conference of the Church at Fayette, New York, on January 2, 1831,
"revelations regarding economic matters surfaced."

> *Scores of subsequent revelations – many unpublished,
> uncanonized, and unknown to modern Mormons –
> were uttered during this period. Substantial textual
> changes later made by Smith, Rigdon, and others
> resulted in a convoluted narrative of nineteenth-
> century church financial policy. Complicating the
> account, neither Smith nor Rigdon were competent
> financial leaders, yet they considered their judgment
> superior to worldly wisdom. Their naivete brought the*

---

[58]Wight, quoted in Van Wagoner, *Sidney Rigdon*, 162 fn 10, citing Joseph Smith, Jr., *History of The Church of Jesus Christ of Latter-day Saints*, B.H. Roberts, ed., 7 vols., 2d ed., rev., (Salt Lake City: The Deseret Book Company, 1978), 2:481.
[59]Petersen, *Problems in Mormon Text*, 7-8, quoted in Tanner and Tanner, *The Changing World of Mormonism*, 443.
[60]Van Wagoner, *Sidney Rigdon*, 129 fn 5 (citing the "Kirtland Revelation Book"), emphasis added.

church to the brink of financial ruin more than once.[61]

FALSIFYING HISTORY

Mormonism's modern detractors are many times better informed than their nineteenth-century predecessors. At no time in its long, tortured journey has Mormon retreat from Mormon history been any more pronounced. Latter-day Saints love logic and proof, until logic and proof defeat them. Propositions that promote the faith are quickly advanced and warmly embraced. Adventurers, trained and not, made the rubble bounce in North and South America's ruins looking for something calculated to demonstrate the historicity of the Book of Mormon. These disappointingly unproductive investigations are almost never discussed in the twenty-first century Church. The scientist who discovers evidence of a strain of wild barley in ancient Arizona in support of one of the many anachronistic claims made in the Book of Mormon is a hero of the faith.

People who challenge so-called "faithful facts" are labeled "anti-Mormons," "apostates," "evil" and "enemies." Bertrand Russell, one of the deans of philosophy, said: "Find more pleasure in intelligent dissent than in passive agreement, for, if you value intelligence as you should, the former implies a deeper agreement than the latter."[62] Things that are perfectly obvious, things that should never be ignored, can't be discussed in Church or taught in the seminaries, or explained to investigators and converts. The Mormon laity practices an unfortunate unhealthy form of self-censorship. A prominent Professor from Brigham Young University (now deceased) described his approach to biography in these terms: " . . . I will tell the truth and nothing but the truth but not necessarily the whole truth."[63] A prominent senior Mormon

---

[61]Van Wagoner, *Sidney Rigdon*, 84-85, emphasis added.
[62]Bertrand Russell, "A Liberal Decalogue," *The New York Times Magazine* (16 December 1951).
[63]Richard D. Poll, *History and Faith* (Salt Lake City: Signature Books, 1989), 104, quoted in Brigham D. Madsen, *Against the Grain: Memoirs of a Western Historian* (Salt Lake City: Signature Books, 2002), 359.

apostle (now deceased) added this to that: "Some things that are true are not very useful."[64] It is alleged, and is not to be taken lightly, that many Mormon leaders, historians and scribes have not only failed to tell the whole truth but have concealed, altered and suppressed significant facts. In that they have betrayed the laity, those who value the truth and the larger world. It is a sad fact, call it the "curse of the faithful," that if the Church isn't true, most of the members do not want to know. Truth isn't always "useful" and doesn't always "matter."

"In early 1907 the First Presidency issued a major address in which they specifically denied the use of duplicity in any of their dealings. 'Enlightened investigation,' they said, had always been the goal of the Church."[65] But the Church has still never officially published all of the revelations. The failure of generations of authorities to do something so honest and simple is incomprehensible. What interest could anyone possibly have in concealing what is supposed to be the word of God? The Church's nearly nineteen-decade suppression of journals, diaries, stones, minutes, letters and notes in mountain retreats and secret vaults is disrespectful to those who have earned the right to know the truth.[66] It is reported that modern Mormon

---

[64]Boyd K. Packer, "Do Not Spread Disease Germs!" Brigham Young University Studies (Summer 1981), 259.

[65]B. Carmon Hardy, *Solemn Covenant: The Mormon Polygamous Passage* (Urbana, Chicago: University of Illinois Press, 1992), Appendix 1, 363.

[66]Joseph Smith instructed William Clayton to destroy the Minutes of the Council of Fifty. Clayton buried them in his garden in Nauvoo, and the Church soon claimed possession of them. These foundational narratives reflecting the treasonous objectives of the early leaders, and the disingenuous aims of the theocracy, were concealed and suppressed from everyone for the best of all good reasons from 1844 to 2016. In those now reluctantly published materials, the base instincts of those early leaders, the Hebraic origins of the American Indians, the insidious aims of the theocrats, the pitiful subservience of the members of the council to the King, Priest and Prophet of the Kingdom of Israel on Earth, are on full display for all the world to see. Scholars who only now are finally permitted to see those provocative materials should be permitted to see William Clayton's unpublished diaries, Sidney Rigdon's succession speech, Brigham Young's George D. Watt shorthand discourses, the unexpurgated diaries and journals of George Q. Cannon, Matthias Cowley and Franklin D. Richards, and the materials included in dozens of other cynical retentions. George Q. Cannon was the *de facto* leader of the Mormon Church during the administrations of Wilford Woodruff and Lorenzo Snow. "Those trafficking in deceit, warned . . . Cannon lost the spirit of God as well as the trust of men." (*Journal of Discourses*, 24:225, George Q. Cannon, 1880,

leaders are advised not to keep journals or diaries. Mormons forgive and excuse their flawed messengers. They pridefully describe them as rough stones rolling, or as lions of the Lord, in spite of their follies, and remaster them. They accept their teachings as the words of life and salvation and measure themselves against them.

Latter-day Saints have been willing to assume that while their leaders lied to them (and to all the world) for decades about polygamy, that they somehow told the truth about other less important things. Latter-day Saints must somehow hope to distinguish "faithful" from "unfaithful" history, determining that the one can exist where the other does, and that they are somehow able to make the necessary distinctions. A person needs to be very wise to distinguish what is true from what is not. Their "rough stones rolling" are deceivers to be forgiven and followed, charlatans and disciples. Latter-day Saints ignore and excuse their faults, praise their positive qualities, and build unexamined lives around their dubious teachings. When their mentors exclude, ignore, alter, suppress, conceal, neglect, forget, confuse, distort or torture truth, when the hearts and minds of the people are shackled from infancy to the teachings of offenders of enormity, and investigators aren't told the truth, the great story of life sadly becomes "a tale told by an idiot, full of sound and fury signifying nothing."

THE "HISTORY OF THE CHURCH"

Many things cause consternation in Mormon circles, not the least of

---

excerpt from Hardy, *Solemn Covenant: The Mormon Polygamous Passage*, Appendix 1, 363). In December 1869, fully twelve years after the murders at Mountain Meadows, Cannon, who "had known the truth for more than a decade," continued to blame the Mountain Meadows Massacre on the Indians" ("he claimed the citizens from Cedar City heard rumors of a battle but arrived too late to help"). (Will Bagley, *Blood of the Prophets: Brigham Young and the Massacre at Mountain Meadows* [Norman, OK: University of Oklahoma Press, 2002], 270). The still unpublished journals of William Clayton, who shadowed Smith and reported the details of his life, are not available to scholars and will not be published with the *Joseph Smith Papers*. The suppression of the unpublished journals is an admission that the conduct of the Mormon prophet is not "an open book." The careful study of the society's founders does not lead "to faith and strength and virtues."

which are concerns about the integrity of the *History of the Church*. People feel betrayed when they are exposed, after years of devoted service, to the seamy side of the faith. When Joseph Smith's six-volume *History of the Church* was first presented to the members of the Church – good people who wanted to be good Christians – years after his death, exorbitant claims were made for the integrity of the process and the authenticity of the faith-promoting materials therein then exposed. Members of the Church were told that a busy Joseph Smith "quite thoroughly supervised the writing of his history, with the result that more complete historical data have been written and preserved respecting the coming forth of the work of God in these last days than any other great movement whatsoever."[67] There had been, his executors reported, "no attempt to 'cover up' any act of his life . . . ." The "history and doctrine" of the Church had "been carefully preserved" and "published."[68] No other movement had ever come close to so complete a disclosure. Those same reporters carried Joseph Smith's 1832 Holographic Account, the Minutes of the Council of Fifty, Clayton's journals and various other suppressed resources across the plains in their wagons. But now they say, "[T]he manuscript annals of the Church are astonishingly free from errors of dates, relation of facts, or anachronisms of every description."[69] The editors of the production boasted that:

> *The History of Joseph Smith is now before the world, and we are satisfied that a history more correct in its details than this was never published . . . . We therefore, hereby bear our testimony to all the world unto whom these words shall come, that the History of Joseph Smith is true, and is one of the most authentic histories ever written.*[70]

It is to the continuing shame of Church historians George A. Smith,

---

[67]Roberts, ed., *History of The Church of Jesus Christ of Latter-day Saints*, Preface, iv, v.

[68]John A. Widtsoe, *Joseph Smith – Seeker After Truth* (Salt Lake City: Deseret Book, 1951), 250, quoted in Banister, *For Any Latter-day Saint*, 186.

[69]Roberts, ed., *History of The Church of Jesus Christ of Latter-day Saints*, Preface, v.

[70]Ibid., Preface, v-vi, emphasis added.

Wilford Woodruff and others that this elegant introduction so
wanting in veracity needs now to be recounted. It is a stain upon
the reputations of careless men who fudged the truth then led the
Church in turbulent times. These sobering platitudes, so terribly
incorrect and offered without remorse, have misinformed
generations of well-intended disciples. It is now known that "the
narrative [*Joseph Smith's History of the Church*] was written to
August 5, 1838," at the time of the Mormon prophet's death on
June 27, 1844. "The . . . *History* was finished in August 1856
seventeen years after it was begun."[71] Large portions of that
"carefully preserved" history "were not dictated [by Joseph Smith
as the History said that they were] but were written by scribes and
later transferred into the first person to read as though the words
were Joseph's."[72] As if he personally spoke such words when in fact
he clearly did not.

There is no offense, no matter how egregious, unable to invite some
clumsy apologetic response. No one ever thinks to say that they are
sorry. Paul R. Cheesman, LDS scholar: "Liberty was taken by
historians in those days to put the narrative in the first person, even
though the source was not as such."[73] That is an astonishing
insight. A lawyer friend of this author, a master at the deposition,
likes to say, "I love it when they deny the obvious." Sharon I.
Banister makes this further ancillary point: "Dr. Davis Bitton [a
faithful Mormon historian]" reports that "for researchers in early
Mormon history Rule Number One is 'Do not rely on the DHC
[*Documentary History of the Church*]; never use a quotation from
[that source] without comparing the earlier versions.'"[74] Ms.
Banister asks her audience this: "Since only about 40% of 2,200
pages were completed at the time of Joseph Smith's death, could he
have 'thoroughly supervised the writing of his history' as the
Preface to the History states"?[75]

---

[71]Dean C. Jessee, "The Writings of Joseph Smith's History," *BYU Studies
Quarterly*, vol. II issue 4, Article 8 (October 1971), 466, 472.
[72]Marvin Hill, "Brodie Revisited: A Reappraisal," *Dialogue* (Winter 1972): 76,
quoted in Banister, *For Any Latter-day Saint*, 191.
[73]"An Analysis of the Kinderhook Story" (BYU Library, March 1970), quoted
in Ibid.
[74]Davis Bitton, "B.H. Roberts as Historian," *Dialogue*, Vol. III, No. 4 (Winter
1968): 32, quoted in Ibid.
[75]Ibid.

Joseph Fielding Smith made this outsized claim during his tenure as the master of LDS theology: *"The most important history in the world is the history of our Church, . . . it is the most accurate history in all the world."*[76] In 2013, faced with rising protests over the falsification of its history, and in new Mormon papers supposed to "offer an unvarnished look at Joseph Smith," the Church claims to be coming clean (think 1907). Richard Turley Jr., assistant LDS Church historian, describing a new 640-page book of early historic documents to be published as part of the Joseph Smith Papers project, says that the aim of the entire project is transparency. "We are laying it all out," Turley said. "You get Joseph Smith straight up without any intervening interpreters like historians or biographers."[77] God save us from the insights of the well informed.

We shall learn in 2013 and beyond in newly published collections and unsigned undated essays what we should have learned from 1830 on from honest people with honest concerns. We shall learn in the eighth or ninth generation of our servitude what our grandfather should have learned before he joined the Church in 1832. It is way too late to try to start to solve this unconscionable problem; the horse is out of the barn. Many good and faithful Saints have perished in their ignorance. May we say with Mooby on the Internet, "and it came to pass and it came to pass and it came to pass and it came to pass and it came to pass and it came to pass and it came to pass and it came to pass and it came to pass and it came to pass (deep breath) and it came to pass."

---

[76]Joseph Fielding Smith, *Doctrines of Salvation*, ed. Bruce R. McConkie, vol. 2 (Salt Lake City: Bookcraft, 1955), 199, quoted in Ibid., 198.
[77]Peggy Fletcher Stack, "New Mormon papers offer an unvarnished look at Joseph Smith," *Salt Lake Tribune* (5 September 2013).

SIDNEY RIGDON

David Whitmer: *"This matter of the two orders of priesthood in the Church of Christ, and lineal priesthood of the old law [ancient Israel's law of a carnal commandment] being in the church, all originated in the mind of Sydney Rigdon. He explained these things to Brother Joseph in his way out of the old Scriptures, and got Brother Joseph to inquire, etc." "He would inquire, and as mouthpiece speak out the revelations just as they had it fixed up in their hearts – . . . ."*

David Whitmer: *"Remember that we had been preaching from August 1829, until June, 1831 – almost two years – and had baptized about 2,000 members into the Church of Christ, and had not one high priest. During 1829 [before Rigdon became a member of the Church], . . . we were told by Brother Joseph that an elder was the highest office in the church."*

ANGELIC ORDINATIONS

The Aaronic Event

This event, supposed to have occurred on May 15, 1829, was not reported to the members of the Church until October 1834.

The Melchizedek Event

This event, supposed to have occurred in May/June 1829, was not reported to the members of the Church until August 1835.

The 1834-35 First Authorized History of the Church "confirms the idea of one priesthood at the church's organization [on April 6, 1830] and indirectly suggests that Smith and he [Cowdery, scribe] had not yet encountered Peter, James, and John or the 'higher' priesthood . . . ."

"No mention of angelic ordinations can be found in original documents until 1834-35. Thereafter accounts of the visits of Peter, James, and John by Cowdery and Smith remain vague and contradictory." (D. Michael Quinn)

RIGDON ON THEOCRACY

"When God sets up a system of salvation, He sets up a system of government. When I speak of a government, I mean what I say; I mean a government that shall rule over temporal and spiritual affairs."

RIGDON ON VIOLENCE

The Salt Sermon (17 June 1838): *It is "the duty of this people to trample [dissenters] into the earth, and if the county cannot be freed of them any other way, I will assist to trample them down or erect a gallows on the square of Far West and hang them as they did the gamblers at Vicksburg and it would be an act at which the angels would smile in approbation."*

The First Extermination Order (4 July 1838): *"We take God and all the holy angels to witness this day, that we warn all men in the name of Jesus Christ, to come on us no more forever; for from this hour, we will bear it no more, our rights shall no more be trampled upon with impunity. The man or the set of men, who attempts it, does it at the expense of their lives. And that mob that comes on us to disturb us, it shall be between us and them a war of extermination, for we will follow them, till the last drop of their blood is spilled, or else they will have to exterminate us; for we will carry the seat of war to their own houses, and their own families, and one party or the other shall be utterly destroyed. – Remember it then all Men! ...*

"We this day then proclaim ourselves free, with a purpose and a determination, that never can be broken, "no never! no never!! NO NEVER!!!"

RIGDON ON THE REMOVAL OF THE UNWANTED

"[W]hen a county, or body of people have individuals among them with whom they do not wish to associate and a public expression is taken against their remaining among them and such individuals do not remove it is the principle of republicanism itself that gives that community a right to expel them forcibly and no law will prevent it."

A CASE IN POINT: THE FAMILY SMITH

"The Smith's did not stay in Vermont long enough for Hyrum [Hiram, a Masonic name, until 1826] to graduate from Dartmouth. In her autobiography, Lucy Mack Smith wrote that the family left Vermont because of crop failure . . . . What Lucy did not record is that for an unknown reason they had moved from Lebanon, New Hampshire, to Norwich, Vermont, and lived there less than a year before they were formally 'warned out' on March 15, 1816. The town exercised its legal option not to let them stay there as transients, with no visible means of support. The Smiths then settled in the Palmyra area of upstate New York." ("Secret Combinations: Evidence for Early Mormon Counterfeiting," Kathleen Kimball Melonakos, 101)

AMONG THE MORMONS,
EDITORS MULDER AND MORTENSEN

Missouri 1838: *"[T]he Mormon community at Far West [Missouri] was plagued by dissent. Even old intimates like Oliver Cowdery and David Whitmer, two Book of Mormon witnesses, were read out of the church. In June Sidney Rigdon delivered what was afterward called his 'salt sermon,' in which he made clear he considered the dissenters salt that had lost its savor and fit only to be literally trodden under foot. On the strength of that, eighty four churchmen signed a document ordering the dissenters to leave Caldwell County within three days or suffer a 'more fatal calamity.' It was the beginning of an effort by a close band of misguided loyalists called Danites to enforce loyalty, to separate the chaff from the wheat within the church, ironically applying to their own brethren the same terrorizing tactics the Missourians had applied to the Mormons."*

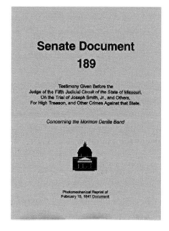

"THE DANITE MANIFESTO," FAR WEST, MISSOURI, JUNE 1838

DRAFTED BY FIRST PRESIDENCY FIRST COUNSELOR SIDNEY RIGDON.
SIGNED BY EIGHTY-FOUR PROMINENT MORMON MEN,
INCLUDING HYRUM SMITH.

"To Oliver Cowdery, David Whitmer, John Whitmer, William W. Phelps, and Lyman E. Johnson, greeting:

"Whereas the citizens of Caldwell county have borne with the abuse received by you at different times, and on different occasions, until it is no longer to be endured . . . having exhausted all the patience they have, . . . the decree has gone forth from our hearts, and shall not return to us void. Neither think, gentlemen, that, in so saying we are trifling with either you or ourselves; for we are not . . . for out of the county you shall go, and no power shall save you. And you shall have three days after you receive this communication to you, including twenty four hours in each day, for you to depart with your families peacably . . . [U]nless you heed us . . . and attend to our request, it ["vengeance sleepeth not"] will overtake you at an hour when you do not expect . . . for you there shall be no escape; for there is but one decree for you, which is depart, depart, or a more fatal calamity shall befal you."

1844 Sketch of Joseph Smith holding a Bible, Image source: http://www.supportingevidences.net/joseph-smith/

Brigham Young by Charles Roscoe Savage [Public domain], via Wikimedia Commons

A PROPHET'S MINDSET

Joseph Smith, 1838: *"If the people will let us alone, we will preach the gospel in peace. But if they come on us to molest us, we will establish our religion by the sword. We will trample down our enemies and make it one gore of blood from the Rocky Mountains to the Atlantic Ocean. I will be to this generation a second Mohammed, whose motto in treating for peace was 'the Alcoran or the Sword.' So shall it eventually be with us – 'Joseph Smith or the Sword!'"*

Joseph Smith, 1844: *"I am a committee of myself . . . . When I get any thing from God I shall be alone." ". . . From hence forth let it be understood that I shall not associate with any committee . . . ."*

A PROPHET'S MINDSET

Brigham Young, Council of Fifty Minutes: *"We have elected our prophet to be our Prophet, Priest and King, but did we choose him? Or did he choose us? Jeses [sic] said, ye have not chosen me but I have chosen you. Our prophet [Joseph Smith] has chosen us, and what this people receives through him is law."*

Brigham Young, Council of Fifty Minutes: *"He [Brigham Young] cannot see the difference between a religious or political government, . . . what would be the necessity to get up a constitution to govern us when we have all the revelations and laws to govern us, and punish us according to our crimes. We may say we will have a constitution because it is fashionable, but he would rather have the revelations to form a constitution from, than any thing else we can get . . . . He would rather have the pure revelations of . . . Jesus Christ as they now stand, to carry to the nations than any thing else. He dont want the legs, nor the head, nor the back bones, nor anything else of the old horse."*

Brigham Young, 1866: *"God is the captain of this company, the general of this army of Saints, and the President of this Church, its ruler and dictator. If I am the instrument which He chooses to use in the prosecution of His great work, it is all right. I am just as willing as any other man to be used."*

WILLIAM E. McLELLIN

A FOUNDING APOSTLE AND A SECRETARY TO THE QUORUM OF THE TWELVE

William E. McLellin, Image source: https://commons
wikimedia.org/wiki/ File:Williamemlellin.gif

"A Levitical priest never lived or ministered among the Nephites from Lehi to Moroni. And from the day Jesus set up his kingdom, no high priest ever lived among them on either continent."

"You say a revelation was given in 1829, 'respecting [angelic] ordinations.' It was not given in 1829, nor until 1835, when the first book of Doctrine and Covenants was compiled. I know what I say."

"I am well aware that the history of Joseph does say he was ordained to the Aaronic priesthood by John the Baptist; I don't believe it . . . . No angel or spirit ever ordained a man to any office since the world began! ... I heard Joseph tell his experience of his ordination and the organization of the church, probably, more than twenty times, to persons who, near the rise of the church, wished to know and hear about it. I never heard of Moroni, John, or Peter, James and John.""

"Jesus stood in Aaron's stead; he was anti-type to Aaron. He is the only High Priest of the gospel age."

1833: *"After the mobbing here [at Independence in Jackson County] in 1833 . . . they held a council in Kirtland, comprising the highest authorities of the church, and determined on <u>war</u>; and sent Orson Hyde and John Gould all the way to Zion to tell the men to stand up and fight if oppressed by a mob. 'Fight in defense of pure religion.' We <u>did</u> fight, and that was the great reason why the church was driven from this county and never allowed to return again."*

1834: *"[T]he day they [the Zion's Camp militia led by Joseph Smith] reached Clay Co[unty], about seventy were taken with Asiatic Cholera, and fourteen died. Joseph disbanded his men, and most of them returned home. Thus all their calculations of redeeming Zion by the <u>sword</u> were blasted; and evil, and only evil, attended that warrior tramp of some one thousand miles, on a fool's errand . . . ."*

"Suffice it to say, when any one wants to know why I left you [spoken in a letter to Joseph Smith], I tell them, 'It was because I lost faith in the Heads of the church.'"

"I visited Mrs. Emma Smith in Nauvoo, in 1847. She told me plainly and frankly that her husband did receive and deliver the polygamic revelation himself, and she knew he practiced its provisions. And she said she knew he had committed adultery with girls previous to that [before the revelation]."

SOVEREIGNTY

THE SECRET COUNCIL OF FIFTY:
"THE KINGDOM OF GOD AND HIS LAWS"

"The name of the council [the Council of Fifty] was discussed and the Lord was pleased to give the following Revelation, 'Verily thus saith the Lord . . . , this is the name by which you shall be called, The Kingdom of God and his Laws, with the keys and power thereof, and judgment in the hands of his servants. Ahman Christ."

THE GOVERNMENT OF GOD

"By 1842 JS [Joseph Smith] was connecting the prophecies of Daniel 2 [". . . the Gospel shall roll forth" like the stone "hewn from the Mountain without hands . . . untill it hath filled the whole Earth"] with the establishment of a theocracy. In July of that year he lectured on 'the prophecies of Daniel which foretold that the God of heaven would set up a kingdom in the last days.' Two weeks later the 'Times and Seasons' published an editorial titled, 'The Government of God,' which recounted historical and biblical forms of government and argued that 'it has been the design of Jehovah, from the commencement of the world, and is his purpose now, to . . . take the reigns of government into his own hand' and that only this form of government would alleviate the degraded condition of humankind." (Council of Fifty Minutes, 50 n 118).

Elder George J. Adams: *"He wanted a perfect code of laws right from the throne of God."*

Elder Levi Richards: *"We want laws to govern us, which are 'thus saith the Lord.' God has said of the last days that he would rule all nations with a rod of Iron which is the word of God."*

Elder George A. Smith: *"He believes that by using . . . all our efforts, before we are aware, we will be governing the world."*

ORSON SPENCER

"[O]ur course is to take care of ourselves, and to legislate like other nations as to what punishment we shall inflict on our enemies."

Orson Spencer, 1802-1855. Image source: https://ldsscriptureteachings. org/2016/11/23/the-faith-of-catherine-and-orson-spencer/

ERASTUS SNOW

"[T]hat <as> the Iron would not mix with the clay no more would the principles of eternal truth mix with the dogmas of Sectarianism, nor the principles of the kingdom of God amalgamate with the injustice and oppression of the kingdoms of the world."

Erastus Snow, Image source: http://www.tbpetersen.com/family/document.asp? BC1=Family%20History&Title=Erastus%20 Fairbanks%20Snow

BISHOP GEORGE MILLER

In 1839, Miller, a convert, was baptized by John Taylor. Miller became the Second Bishop of the Church (an office equivalent to today's Presiding Bishop).

Council of Fifty Minutes: *"The idea he wishes to advance, is, never to throw objections in the way of any thing proposed by the proper source. He expects to be always in perfect subjection to [p. [100]] those whose place it is to govern whether his views agree with theirs or not."*

Bishop George Miller

ERRORS OF MAGNITUDE

Parley P. Pratt: *"Members of the early Christian Church were not ordained to the Aaronic Priesthood, neither is there any mention of the Aaronic Priesthood in the Book of Mormon."*

David Whitmer: *"A Levitical Priest never lived or ministered among the Nephites from Lehi to Moroni. And from the day Jesus set up his kingdom, no high priest ever lived among them on either continent."*

Revelation, 22-23 September 1832 [Doctrine and Covenants 84]. Image source: *The Joseph Smith Papers*,
http://www.josephsmithpapers.org/paper-summary/revelation-22-23-september-1832-dc-84/2

ETERNAL LIFE FOR ANCIENT ISRAEL'S LAW
OF A CARNAL COMMANDMENT?

The Postulate: *". . . Abraham received the priesthood from Melchizedek, who received it through the lineage of his fathers, even till Noah . . . ."* Abel received the priesthood *"by the hand of his father Adam, who was the first man – Which priesthood continueth in the church of God in all generations, and is without beginning of days or end of years. And the Lord confirmed a priesthood also upon Aaron and his seed, throughout all their generations, which priesthood also continueth and abideth forever with the priesthood which is after the holiest order of God."* (Doctrine and Covenants 84:14-18).

"[W]hat advantage would there be in tracing your lineage to a system of law (the Levitical Priesthood) which the Bible says 'was nailed to the cross'?"

"Why would the Levitical priesthood be restored after Christ had 'become the guarantee of a better agreement'?"

"The Old Testament gives much detail about the Levitical Priesthood. If all the leaders from Adam through Abraham belonged to another, greater priesthood, can you explain why it is nowhere described in the Old Testament?" (S.I. Banister)

IN THE EYES OF THE BEHOLDER

GORDON B. HINCKLEY

"TRUE TO THE FAITH," CONFERENCE ADDRESS, APRIL 1997:

"What a wonderful thing it is to have behind us a great and noble body of progenitors! What a marvelous thing to be recipients of a magnificent heritage that speaks of the guiding hand of the Lord, of the listening ear of His prophets, of the total dedication of a vast congregation of Saints who loved this cause more than life itself!"

"Permit me to quote to you from Wallace Stegner, not a member of the Church but a contemporary at the University of Utah who later became professor of creative writing at Stanford and a Pulitzer Prize winner. He was a close observer and a careful student . . . . 'They built a commonwealth, or as they would have put it, a Kingdom . . . . [T]he story of their migration is more than the story of the founding of Utah. In their hegira they opened up southern Iowa from Locust Creek to the Missouri, made the first roads, built the first bridges, established the first communities. They transformed the Missouri at Council Bluffs, from a trading post and an Indian agency into an outpost of civilization, [and] founded settlements on both sides of the river . . . . Their guide books and trail markers, their bridges and ferries, though made for the Saints scheduled to come later, served also for the Gentiles.'"

WALLACE STEGNER

Wallace Stegner, the "Dean of Western Writers," the author of "Mormon Country" and "The Gathering of Zion: The Story of the Mormon Trail," expressed these critical opinions in a private letter to his friend Dale Morgan, another western historian. "Nearly one hundred years after [Illinois] Governor Ford's observation that Nauvoo was 'a government within a government' . . . , Stegner opined 'that Mormons in Utah operated what approximated a police state.'"

"More and more I come to a condition of astonishment at the parallelism in methods between Utah in the early days, and any totalitarian state today. The whole thing is there – private army, secret police, encirclement myth, territorial dynamism, self sufficiency, chosen people, absolute dictatorship operating through party rule, group psychology, esoteric symbols and distinguishing uniforms (garments), New Order and all." (Robert Newton Baskin, by John Gary Maxwell)

Image source: https://en.wikipedia.org/wiki/File:Wallace_Stegner.jpg

MITOSIS

"A GLARING ERROR OF TRANSLITERATION MADE CORPOREAL"

Joseph Smith, 1836: *"After this vision had closed [a vision of Elias who "committed the dispensation of the gospel of Abraham"], another great and glorious vision [a vision of Elijah] burst upon us; for Elijah the prophet, who was taken to heaven without tasting death, stood before us and said: Behold, the time has fully come, which was spoken of by the mouth of Malachi – testifying that he should be sent, before the great and dreadful day of the Lord come – To turn the hearts of the fathers to the children, and the children to the fathers, lest the whole earth be smitten with a curse – . . . ." (Doctrine and Covenants 110:13-16)*

Joseph Smith thought that Elias (the Greek name for Elijah) and Elijah (the Hebrew name for Elijah) were different names supposed to describe two separate persons. That colossal error ("a glaring error of transliteration made corporeal") casts doubt upon all of the visions.

Elijah Contends against the Priests of Baal, by Jerry Harston

THE LAST GASP OF THE LAW OF ADOPTION

Brigham Young: *". . . Young revived the ritual of adoption, which had stirred so much controversy within the church during the exodus. Since reaching the Great Basin, Young had rarely spoken about the ritual of adoption. Like his communitarian vision [the idea of equality] and his identification of Adam as humanity's God [the only God with whom the Saints had to do], . . . the 'law of adoption' retained its significance in his mind. 'Men will have to be sealed to Men,' . . . 'untill the Chain is united from Father Adam down to the last Saint.' In St. George, Young allowed the Mormons to resume that work. Church members without faithful parents could be sealed to prominent Church leaders who, as heirs of the priesthood, could link them back to Adam." (John G. Turner) Wilford Woodruff, another prophet, abandoned the adoption ritual before the end of the nineteenth century. Let every man, Woodruff said, be "adopted to his father." In the modern Church, the communitarian vision, the law of adoption and the Adam/God doctrine – three important early doctrines – have been dismissed.*

THE EGYPTIAN PAPYRI, JOSEPH SMITH TO CHARLES FRANCIS ADAMS

1844: *"'That is the handwriting of Abraham, the Father of the Faithful,' said the prophet, 'This is the autograph of Moses, and these lines were written by his brother Aaron. Here we have the earliest account of the Creation, from which Moses composed the First Book of Genesis.'"*

Charles Francis Adams, Public Domain,
https://commons.wikimedia.org/w/index. php?curid=581910

THOMAS DICK

Thomas Dick introduced Joseph Smith to the mathematics of the heavens, to time, space and quantity, to an infinity of stars and distances. "He [Smith] was groping for a new metaphysics that would somehow take account of the new world of science." From this maelstrom Joseph created the story modern scholarship has turned upside down and inside out for its unconscionable duplicity – the Book of Abraham.

"As the Book of Mormon had solved the question of the origin of the red man, so the Book of Abraham dispatched the problem of the origin of the Negro." Postulating that all Egyptians inherited the curse of a black skin and thus the denial of a right to the priesthood, Smith sided with the southern states. "[W]e have no right," he concluded, "to interfere with slaves, contrary to the mind and will of their masters."
(Fawn McKay Brodie)

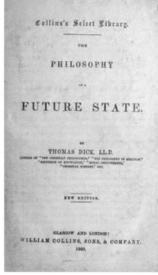

EZRA BOOTH: THE LOST TEN TRIBES

"The condition of the ten tribes of Israel since their captivity, unto the present time, has . . . given rise to much speculation among the learned. But after all the researches which have been made, the place of their residence has never been satisfactorily ascertained." According to Ezra Booth, "these visionaries [Mormonism's founders] have discovered their place of residence to be contiguous to the north pole; separated from the rest of the world by impassable mountains of ice and snow. In this sequestered residence, they enjoy the society of Elijah the Prophet, and John the Revelator, and perhaps the three immortalized Nephites – By and by, the mountains of ice and snow are to give way, and open a passage for the return of these tribes, to the land of Palestine."
(Ezra Booth)

JOSEPH SMITH ADDRESSING THE LAMANITES

"The Book of Mormon identified the Indians of the Americas as the 'Lamanites,' the cursed, dark-skinned descendants of the wicked people who had wiped out the righteous Nephites several centuries after the birth of Jesus. God had tasked the Mormons with bringing the modern-day Lamanites back to the true faith. 'The Savages are not yet grafted in the Olive Tree,' Young explained upon his departure from Winter Quarters in 1847. 'They are now as a withered branch before the Lord.' Once the Lamanites fulfilled their Israelite lineage by embracing the gospel, God would remove the curse he had placed on them, they would become 'a white and a delightsome people,' and they would assist in building the millennial kingdom. The Book of Mormon suggested and Joseph Smith had taught that the 'remnant of the house of Jacob' would marshal themselves, and shall become exceedingly angry, and shall vex the Gentiles with a sore vexation! ... The redeemed Lamanites would become, Young explained a few years later, 'the Lord's battle axe!"

"Joseph the Prophet Addressing the Lamanites."
Lithograph by H. R. Robinson, 1844.
Image from Church History Library, Salt Lake City.

"Converted Indians . . . would serve as God's foreordained vehicle of millennial judgment against the United States and its people." ("Brigham Young: Pioneer Prophet," John J. Turner, 209)

Early Mormons are thus seen to have envisioned a Mormon-Indian alliance in support of the use of force to establish a theocracy led by a prophet of God. Before DNA science humbled the brethren, every Indian was a Lamanite, by that to say a Hebrew. The Doctrine and Covenants (the voice of Joseph's God) refers to the Native Americans as Lamanites no less than eleven times. [D&C 3:18, 20; 10:48; 19:27; 28:8, 9, 14; 30:6; 32:2; 49:24; 54:8]. With the Book of Mormon cruelly disemboweled by molecular biology, the Lamanites, as a "remnant" of the Hebrews and the "battle axe" of the Lord, must now be seen to have disappeared. Their genetic signature, it is supposed, can no longer be found. DNA science can identify the 40,000 year old tracings of the Neanderthal in the human genome, but all evidence for the middle eastern origins of Mormonism's North American Hebrews has, according to Mormonism's twenty-first century scholarship, been rendered indistinguishable with the mixing of the races and the passage of time.

Sioux Indian Tribe. Image source. https://www.pinterest.com/pin/187603140701439415/

COUNCIL OF CHIEFS:
THE "REMNANT OF THE HOUSE OF JACOB"

Brigham Young, Early: *". . . I tell you in the name of the Lord when we go from here [Nauvoo, Illinois], we will exalt the standard of liberty and make our own laws. When we go from here we dont calculate to go under any government but the government of God. There are millions of the Lamanites who when they understand the law of God and the designs of the gospel are perfectly capable of using up these united States. They will walk through them and lay them waste from East to West. We mean to go to our brethren in the West & baptise them, and when we get them to give hear to our council the story is told."* (Council of Fifty Minutes, 268)

THE FAILURE OF THE INDIAN INITIATIVE

Brigham Young, Late: *Brigham Young said that "he had approached the Lamanites with an open mind" when he joined the Church, but that familiarity had bred contempt. In the end his "natural disposition and taste" came to loathe "the sight of those degraded Indians." His feelings of revulsion overwhelmed the expectation that he would convert them, and that they would co-exist. "Although he had initially responded to conflicts by calling for restraint, he eventually initiated military reprisals wholly disproportionate to alleged Indian crimes. Perhaps at moments of stress, Young's disgust at the Indians present condition made it easier for him to authorize their deaths," which he sometimes did with brutality. (Brigham Young's racial history is discussed in John G. Turner's seminal biography of the Mormon leader at chapter 8). His conduct in the Great Basin, in the face of conditions on the ground, stood the prophecies of Joseph Smith and the teachings of the Book of Mormon on their head. The book's promise that Native American Hebrews would reclaim their territories and their previous glory by the shedding of Gentile blood were sorely misconceived and (like so very much else) came to naught.*

Image source: https://thegodguy.files.
wordpress.com/2012/11/a-
emanuel-swedenborg-ii.jpg

Emanuel Swedenborg, *a Swedish mystic, introduced concepts of the afterlife (three tiers of glory, realms likened to the sun, the moon and the stars), elements of marriage (required to reach the highest degree in the celestial division), and the concept of the spirit world (a transitional stage between heaven and earth). Swedenborg lived and wrote and died years before Smith and Rigdon were born. Swedenborg's masterpiece Heaven and Hell "became an American bestseller in the 1820s." Section 76 of Mormonism's Doctrine and Covenants describing the three degrees of glory is the lengthened shadow of Emanuel Swedenborg.*

LOSING A LOST TRIBE: NATIVE AMERICAN, DNA AND THE MORMON CHURCH BY SIMON G. SOUTHERTON

For writing a book, Simon Southerton, a PhD and a molecular biologist who had been a Mormon Bishop, was excommunicated. The book discussed the intricate relationship between Native Americans, DNA science and the Mormon Church. Southerton denied that Native Americans enjoyed an Hebraic lineage (Semitic origins), a charge directed against the central principle of the Book of Mormon. His scholarship directly challenged the historicity of the "most correct of any book on earth," Mormonism's Golden Bible. He was not allowed to speak of his findings at a disciplinary proceeding.

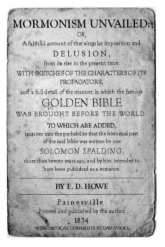

EZRA BOOTH DISCUSSES "THE GATHERING OF ZION"

The Letters of Ezra Booth, an early convert to Mormonism who had formerly been a Methodist clergyman, were originally published in the Ohio Star, then later reproduced in E.D. Howe's 1834 exposé, "Mormonism Unvailed." Booth, who traveled to Missouri, aptly described the notion behind the gathering of Zion: "The plan is so ingeniously contrived, having for its aim one principal point, viz: the establishment of a society in Missouri, over which the contrivers of this delusive system, are to possess unlimited and despotic sway."

HEBER C. KIMBALL

Brigham's Other Prophet: *The Mormons "ultimately viewed political sovereignty as resting with the Mormon priesthood. 'I love my president,' Heber Kimball said of Brigham Young . . . . 'He is not only the president here, but he is the president of the states and kingdoms of this world no matter if they have not elected him.' Kimball urged church members to honor their sovereign. 'It is for me,' he said, 'to be obedient to B[righam] Young as to God, as I was to Joseph.'" (John G. Turner)*

A Mormon Prayer: *"Bless Brigham Young, bless him; may the heavens be opened unto him, angels visit and instruct him; clothe him with power to defend thy people and to overthrow all those who rise up against him; bless him in his basket and in his store, multiply and increase him in wives, children, flocks, and herds, horses and lands – make him very great," etc. (T.B.H. Stenhouse)*

Brigham Young: *"Responding to reports (probably false) that the late president Zachary Taylor had opposed even territorial government [in Utah] for the Mormons, Young observed that 'as incidental providence would have it, he is in hell and we are here.' He warned future presidents that if they opposed the Saints they would soon make Taylor's new home more cramped." "Old Zachary is in hell, and I am glad of it." (John G. Turner)*

FAC-SIMILE OF MORMON MONEY.

Robert Kent Fielding: *"No amount of shifting of blame could obscure the fact that a prophet had failed in a grand project . . . . As the Sheriff appeared ever more regularly with summons and as . . . one after another of the leaders faced the humiliating prospect of publicly acknowledged incompetence and bankruptcy, the discipline and sense of responsibility, which are the heart of all organizations, broke completely and plunged Mormondom into ecclesiastical anarchy."*

"Six of the apostles came out in open rebellion."

William E. McLellin: *"The Witnesses [Oliver Cowdery, David Whitmer and Martin Harris] had quit Smith during their bank troubles in Kirtland, in 1837, and Cowdery and David Whitmer had removed to Far West."* The Latter-day Saints who were evicted *from Independence, Missouri, congregated, as reassembled, at Far West in Caldwell County, Missouri, and in the Counties known as Carroll and Daviess, then and further in and at various other locations to the vexation of the state's "old settlers."*

William E. McLellin: *"Now, sir [William E. McLellin to Elder Davis H. Bays, 24 May 1870] they [the heads of the church] went on in their speculations in Kirtland, until the winter of 1837. Joseph and Sidney had to run away from there between two days [meaning at night], hid in a wagon."*

Bankrupt Saints: *On and/or after April 18, 1842, a month-and-a-half after the federal Bankruptcy Act became effective, Joseph Smith, Hyrum Smith, Samuel H. Smith, Sidney Rigdon, Vinson Knight, Elias Higbee, Reynolds Cahoon, Henry G. Sherwood, John P. Green, Jared Carter, Amos Davis, William P. Lyon, and some other leading Mormon men, declared themselves insolvent and filed petitions seeking to be certified bankrupt. Smith's listed debts totaled $73,066.38, not including a U.S. government obligation of $4,866.38, for the purchase of a steamboat. In early June, hearings Calvin A. Warren processed the bankruptcy applications of at least fifteen Mormons at the court in Springfield, Illinois. (J.S.P. Journals, 2:51 n 191). Bankruptcy notices were published in "The Wasp," a Mormon publication, beginning May 7, 1842.*

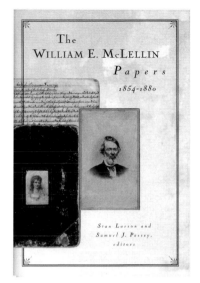

The William E. McLellin Papers, Stan Larson and Samuel J. Passey, editors

A FOUNDING APOSTLE LEAVES THE CHURCH

*In 1836, McLellin, who was then a missionary (while "far in the woods," "praying –
full length on my face – "), reported that "a still small voice said to me, 'Get up and go
home.'" When the Apostle, one of six who left the Church in 1836, heard that voice
again, after rejecting it once, "It went through me with a shock." When McLellin
reached Kirtland at near the last of June, he found that "the Presidency" had gone to
New York to purchase "$40,000 worth of goods" (an average family at the time made
$400 a year). He had returned in time to see "six wagon loads of these goods rolled
into Kirtland," enough to fill two stores.*

*"Soon," he said, "fine dressing and fine parties were the go . . ." followed by that fine
ride to Cleveland, some "fifteen couples hired fine carriages [with] fine harness and
fine horses" to show big for "Joseph Smith, the Mormon prophet, and his company."*

*After that excursion, in McLellin's eyes the ride of shame, "They still continued their
parties and their drinking to excess, until I sickened, and, with a heavy heart, left the
place and church, and wended my way to Illinois, with my companion and two little
children. I wrote a letter to J. Smith and sent him my license . . . ."*

William E. McLellin: *McLellin, who presided over the Council that in 1831 decided to
print "Joseph's revelations," came to conclude that the many amendments to the
Doctrine and Covenants caused that book to become "a relic of folly." "I have no use
for that book . . . ." The committee changed the revelations "so much that a man would
scarcely know them to meet them in a brush-heap!"*

TAKING MEASURE OF BRIGHAM, THE PROPHET, PRIEST, AND KING OF THE UTAH CHURCH

SLAVERY

"I am a firm believer in slavery," Young declared. "Inasmuch as I believe in the Bible, inasmuch as I believe in the ordinances of God, in the Priesthood and order, and decrees of God, I must believe in slavery." Young believed that Africans were cursed by God "with dark skin and servitude"; that a well-treated slave was better indentured than free; and that the institution of slavery was "good" for the slaves, and "good" for their owners. (John G. Turner)

"Any man having one drop of the seed of Cane in him Cannot hold the priesthood, & if no other Prophet ever spake it Before I will say it now in the name of Jesus Christ."

"[I]f any man mingles his seed with the seed of Cane, the ownly way he Could get rid of it or have salvation would be to Come forward & have his head cut off & spill his Blood upon the ground."

BLOOD ATONEMENT

One less frequently described element of the Celestial law to be applied when Mormons ruled themselves, and then the world, was a concept that came to be known as "blood atonement," a notion first described by the Prophet Joseph Smith. "He [Brigham Young, "The chairman" of the Council of Fifty after the death of Joseph Smith] will tell the plan whereby murderers can obtain salvation, for there is only one sin which can have no remedy and that is the sin against the Holy Ghost." The chairman then explained the higher law, "a plan whereby Missouri [the state that rejected the theocracy twice (in 1834 and 1838) and cast the Mormons out] might be saved. If [Lilburn W.] Boggs and the ring leaders of the mob who exterminated the Saints would come to Nauvoo and cast themselves at our feet, and say that they had sinned a sin unto death, and they are willing to submit to the law, let their heads be severed from their bodies, and let their hearts blood run and drench the earth, and then the Almighty would say they should finally be saved in some inferior kingdom. If when a man comes here who is guilty of murder – we would cut off his head, it would be a million times better for him, than it would to let him live." (Council of Fifty Minutes, 351 n 521).

Brigham Young taught the Mormons "that some sins were so serious that the perpetrator's blood would have to be shed for the individual to receive forgiveness."

VIOLENCE

Commenting on the castration of Thomas Lewis (whose entrails were hung by a nail in the school house), which occurred upon the order and under the hands of Bishop Warren Snow, the rejected previously married and much older suitor of the Welsh immigrant's sweetheart, Young said this: "I would prefer that any child of mine should lose his life in atonement for his sins [Lewis was supposed to have been accused of crimes] than lose eternal salvation." Siding with the bishop, one of Brigham's "B-hoys" (a group of early Mormon enforcers), Brigham said, "I will tell you that when a man is trying to do right & do[es] some thing that is not exactly in order I feel to sustain him." (John G. Turner). Snow, who helped Brigham (and Moroni) select the site for the Manti Temple, "kept his bishopric." The young woman, the stricken victim of that particularly brutal encounter, was forced to be sealed to Bishop Snow.

"Young believed biblical law mandated death for extramarital sexual relations." (John G. Turner)

ON MARITAL SUPPORT

Like Joseph Smith, because busy with his "ecclesiastical and political difficulties," many of Brigham Young's more than fifty wives, plural and/or polyandrous, were forced to rely "on the charity of family, friends, or other church members" for their sustenance. (John G. Turner)

ON THE DISAFFECTED

"Scores of disaffected Mormons left [what was then] the [Utah] territory with the 1857 spring thaw. 'The fire of the reformation,' journaled Hosea Stout, 'is burning many out who flee from the Territory, afraid of their lives.' Young saw this as removing the church's spiritual dross. 'The Territory this season,' he wrote George Q. Cannon in July, 'has taken an emetic,' spewing out 'Lawyers, Loafers, Special Pleaders, Apostates, Officials, and filth.'" (John G. Turner).

COUNCIL OF FIFTY

"The chairman [Brigham Young] . . . vacated his seat for a few minutes and called upon councillor George Miller to give the new members their charge, which was done in a very lucid and condensed form. After which councillor Miller called upon them to manifest whether they were willing to conform to the regulations of the council [including death for the disclosure of their membership, and/or for the disclosure of the secret contents of their deliberations]. They all signified their assent." "Being requested to express their feelings more fully, Joseph Young [Brigham's brother] said he was willing that they should cut of his tail behind the ears if he failed to comply, or betrayed his trust."

"The minutes of the council of Feby 4-1845 were then read & accepted by unanimous vote, after which the Recorder moved that the minutes be destroyed. All voted in the affirmative and the clerk put them in the stove and burned them up. [p. [381]]"

When the council was organized, the men "agreed to look to some place where we can go and establish a Theocracy either in Texas or Oregon or somewhere in California . . . ." Brigham Young, Chair: "The time has come when we must seek out a location. The yoke of the gentiles is broke, their doom is sealed, there is not the least fibre that can possibly be discovered that binds us to the gentile world."

"PROPHET, PRIEST, AND KING . . ."

"The clerk was then called upon to state to the new members the relationship of Pres

Young as standing chairman to this council, head and lawgiver &c, after which on motion a vote was taken of the whole house and all voted to sustain Pres Young in his place as standing chairman, Prophet, Priest, and King &c."

JEWS

"There are Jews here. They are not our friends. Do not trade with them. They do not believe in Jesus Christ."

LAWGIVERS

"Inasmuch as president Joseph Smith is gone within the vail President Young is now our lawgiver, and when he is absent the one that stands in his place is our lawgiver."

BRIGHAM MUST THINK FOR THE PEOPLE "CONSTANTLY"

When confronted in the Great Basin by a superior federal force, Brigham essentially said, "Trust me!" In such difficult times, independent thought, according to Young, was something people couldn't afford. "[A]gainst an enemy [the American government] with superior numbers, firepower and resources, they could not afford dissent or a lack of common purpose.... Unity [obedience] was so crucial, he explained, that the Saints should not let their minds form their own supplications during Sunday meetings or prayer circles. He observed that his request for perfect unity and obedience was inimical to the American exaltation of independent thought." (John G. Turner) Such notions "must be checked in this people," he said. The right to dissent is not protected. The Saints must "recognize his words as the 'voice of God to this people,'" he said. The tyranny of the leaders over the minds and spirits of their minions had long since become complete and entire, a force with which every Latter-day Saint must learn to contend. This is the great Mormon pandemic. It is the curse of the faithful, too much bondage.

AS TO THE TYRANNY OF THE GENTILES

Council of Fifty Minutes, Chairman Brigham Young:
"As to suffering any more of the oppression and tyranny of the gentiles, he is just bent and sworn to it, that just so soon as we can secure our women and children and put them where they will be safe, we will put our warriors into the field and never cease our operations untill we have swept the scoundrels off from the face of the earth."

THE IMPORTANCE OF POLYGAMY

"Young...connected plural marriage [polygamy[with exaltation into the celestial kingdom. 'The Lord Almighty created you and me...to become a God like himself.' Each resurrected and exalted Saint would, like Adam had once done, 'organize an Earth, people it, redeem it, and sanctify it.'" A member's "future glory" depended upon "the embrace of plurality...." (John G. Turner)

Brigham Young, By Charles Roscoe Savage - L. Tom Perry Special Collections, Harold B. Lee Library, Brigham Young University, Public Domain, https://commons.wikimedia.org/w/index.php? curid=11303236.

CHAPTER EIGHTEEN

History Is an Institution's Resume

I never told you I was perfect; but there is no error in the revelations which I have taught.

Joseph Smith

History exposes the settled past and predicts the uncertain future.

Joel M. Allred

PREQUEL

In 1835, in a revelation that survived to become Section 27 of the modern Doctrine and Covenants, Joseph Smith introduced John the Baptist, Peter, James, and John, and concepts of the priesthood to the members of the Church.[1]

> These phrases about John the Baptist and Peter, James, and John had not appeared when the revelation was first published in 1832 in The Evening and the Morning Star or in the 1833 Book of Commandments (BofC, 60). A recent study has demonstrated that the center portion on priesthood (now D&C 27:6-13) is also missing from the revelation's only manuscript. The added text cannot

---

[1]"In June, 1829, by divine appointment, Peter, James, and John came to Joseph Smith and Oliver Cowdery and conferred upon them the Melchizedek Priesthood. (D&C 27:12-13)." (Bruce R. McConkie, *Mormon Doctrine*, 2d ed. [Salt Lake City: Bookcraft, 1966], 478). As authority for that confident (and foundational) proposition, the author of *Mormon Doctrine* relies upon the unprovenanced provisions added to Section 28 of the Book of Commandments (first published in 1833) in the 27th Section of the Doctrine and Covenants (first published in the 1835 edition as Section 50).

*be found in any document before 1835, nor can any
similar wording or concept be found prior to 1834.*[2]

When more than four hundred and fifty words were added to about
two hundred words in what had been Chapter 28 of the 1833 Book
of Commandments[3] – when the revelations in the Book of
Commandments were embellished and republished in the first
edition of the Doctrine and Covenants in 1835 – those revisionary
contents were backdated to say that they had been received in
August and September of 1830,[4] dates said to apply to the
manuscript of a revelation first published in its original form
without them.

Section 27 of the Doctrine and Covenants (first published as Section
50 in the first edition of the Doctrine and Covenants in 1835) was
supposed to restate the provisions of Chapter 28 of the Book of
Commandments (the precursor to the book of Doctrine and
Covenants). When what became Section 27 was republished, it
contained unprovenanced provisions pertaining to the added
subject of priesthood. Those new and unfamiliar amendments were
backdated and falsified. "The student would expect to find all the
particulars of the Restoration in this first treasured set of sixty-five

---

[2]D. Michael Quinn, *The Mormon Hierarchy: Origins of Power* (Salt Lake City:
Signature Books in association with Smith Research Associates, 1994), 16,
emphasis added. Quinn cites *History of the Church,* 1:40 n; Woodford, "Historical
Development of the Doctrine and Covenants," 1:393-403. Before September or
October 1834, no one knew Joseph Smith and Oliver Cowdery would later claim
that they secretly received the Aaronic/Levitical Priesthood from a resurrected
personage before the Church was formed. Until 1835, no one knew Joseph Smith
and Oliver Cowdery would claim they secretly received the Melchizedek
Priesthood from other resurrected personages before the Church was formed.

[3]No one has ever discovered or thought to describe an original manuscript in
facsimile form seen to support the four hundred and fifty words first assigned to
the Mormon god in Section 50 (now Section 27) of the 1835 edition of the Doctrine
and Covenants.

[4]There was no Doctrine and Covenants in August or September of 1830, or
until 1835, and nothing before Section 27 of the Doctrine and Covenants is seen to
suggest that the Lord had previously sent Peter, James, and John to deliver divine
authority to Joseph Smith and Oliver Cowdery. If those apostles had appeared in
"1829, May-June," as the Church now allows itself to suppose, the Book of
Commandments would have to have said so four years later (in 1833) in one or
another of the sixty-five revelations included there in the order in which they were
received.

revelations [the Book of Commandments in 1833], the dates of which encompassed the bestowals of the two Priesthoods, but they are conspicuously absent . . . . Chapter 28 gives no hint of the Restoration which, if actual, had been known for four years. *More than four hundred words were added to* this revelation of August 1829 in Section 27 of the *Doctrine and Covenants*, the additions *made to include* [for the first time] the names of heavenly visitors and two separate ordinations."[5]

Members are supposed to believe that Jesus spoke more than four hundred and fifty-words that were not included in the revelation's only manuscript, or in any other manuscript, that he described heavenly visitors who were not included in the revelation's only manuscript or described in the Book of Commandments in 1833, after which he then revealed the restorations of two different priesthoods by John the Baptist and Peter, James, and John.

The original manuscript failed to mention Moroni, the Book of Mormon, the "fulness" of the everlasting gospel, the stick of Ephraim, Elias, Elijah, the restoration of all things, Zacharias, Joseph, Jacob, Isaac, Abraham, Michael or Adam, John the Baptist, Peter, James, and John, priesthood, ordinations, especial witnesses or the apostleship.[6] The greatly remodeled revelation, which introduced the Saints to all of those people and things in the

---

[5]LaMar Petersen, *Problems in Mormon Text*, 7-8, quoted in Jerald Tanner and Sandra Tanner, *The Changing World of Mormonism: A Behind-the-Scenes Look at Changes in Mormon Doctrine and Practice* (Chicago, IL: Moody Press, 1979), 443, emphasis retained and added.

[6]If Peter, James, and John are retroactively supposed to have ordained Joseph Smith and Oliver Cowdery to the "apostleship" in May or June of 1829, why wasn't anyone else ordained to the apostleship until 1835? If these foundational events actually occurred in 1829, as only later described in unprovenanced materials first made public in 1835, why weren't they described when the text of the original revelation was published in the Book of Commandments in 1833? Or in *The Evening and the Morning Star*, where the text of the original revelation was published in 1833? Why wasn't all of that added text described in the chronological facsimiles of the original manuscripts published by the Church of Jesus Christ of Latter-day Saints in the *Joseph Smith* Papers in 2009? Why wasn't any archival resource found to support the extravagant claims contained in Section 27 (Section 50 in 1835) of the Doctrine and Covenants in 1835? The center portion on priesthood (now Doctrine and Covenants 27:6-13), which is routinely cited by faithful Mormon scholars (see McConkie in footnote 1), is "missing from the revelation's only manuscript."

60

CHAPTER XXVIII.

A Commandment to the church of Christ, given in Harmony, Pennsylvania, September 4, 1830,

LISTEN to the voice of Jesus Christ, your Lord, your God and your Redeemer, whose word is quick and powerful.

2 For behold I say unto you, that it mattereth not what ye shall eat, or what ye shall drink, when ye partake of the sacrament, if it so be that ye do it with an eye single to my glory;

3 Remembering unto the Father my body which was laid down for you, and my blood which was shed for the remission of your sins:

4 Wherefore a commandment I give unto you, that you shall not purchase wine, neither strong drink of your enemies:

5 Wherefore you shall partake of none, except it is made new among you, yea, in this my Father's kingdom which shall be built up on the earth.

6 Behold this is wisdom in me, wherefore marvel not, for the hour cometh that I will drink of the fruit of the vine with you, on the earth, and with all those whom my Father hath given me out of the world:

7 Wherefore lift up your hearts and rejoice, and gird up your loins and be faithful until I come:— even so. Amen.

The passages in this revelation, Chapter 28, published in the Book of Commandments in 1833, are faithful to the uncorrupted text of the original manuscript published by the Church of Jesus Christ of Latter-day Saints in the Facsimile Edition of The Joseph Smith Papers in 2009.

60

CHAPTER XXVIII.

A Commandment to the church of Christ, given in Harmony, Pennsylvania, September 4, 1830,

LISTEN to the voice of Jesus Christ, your Lord, your God and your Redeemer, whose word is quick and powerful.

2 For behold I say unto you, that it mattereth not what ye shall eat, or what ye shall drink, when ye partake of the sacrament, if it so be that ye do it with an eye single to my glory;

3 Remembering unto the Father my body which was laid down for you, and my blood which was shed for the remission of your sins:

4 Wherefore a commandment I give unto you, that you shall not purchase wine, neither strong drink of your enemies:

5 Wherefore you shall partake of none, except it is made new among you, yea, in this my Father's kingdom which shall be built up on the earth.

6 Behold this is wisdom in me, wherefore marvel not, for the hour cometh that I will drink of the fruit of the vine with you, on the earth, and with all those whom my Father hath given me out of the world:

7 Wherefore lift up your hearts and rejoice, and gird up your loins and be faithful until I come: Even so. Amen.

[left margin handwritten:] and take upon you my whole armor, that ye may be able to withstand the evil day, having done all, that ye may be able to stand. Stand, therefore, having your loins girt about with truth, having on the breastplate of righteousness, and your feet shod with the preparation of the gospel of peace, which I have sent mine angels to commit unto you; Taking the shield of faith wherewith ye shall be able to quench all the fiery darts of the wicked; And take the helmet of salvation, and the sword of my Spirit, which I will pour out upon you, and my word which I reveal unto you, and be agreed as touching all things whatsoever ye ask of me,

[boxed handwritten insert:] and ye shall be caught up, that where I am ye shall be also.

[right margin handwritten:] Moroni, whom I have sent unto you to reveal the Book of Mormon, containing the fulness of my everlasting gospel, to whom I have committed the keys of the record of the stick of Ephraim; And also with Elias, to whom I have committed the keys of bringing to pass the restoration of all things spoken by the mouth of all the holy prophets since the world began, concerning the last days; And also John the son of Zacharias, which Zacharias he (Elias) visited and gave promise that he should have a son, and his name should be John, and he should be filled with the spirit of Elias; Which John I have sent unto you, my servants, Joseph Smith, Jun., and Oliver Cowdery, to ordain you unto the first priesthood which you have received, that you might be

[bottom handwritten:] called and ordained even as Aaron; And also Elijah, unto whom I have committed the keys of the power of turning the hearts of the fathers to the children, and the hearts of the children to the fathers, that the whole earth may not be smitten with a curse; And also with Joseph and Jacob, and Isaac, and Abraham, your fathers, by whom the promises remain; And also with Michael, or Adam, the father of all, the prince of all, the ancient of days; And also with Peter, and James, and John, whom I have sent unto you, by whom I have ordained you and confirmed you to be apostles, and especial witnesses of my name, and bear the keys of your ministry and of the same things which I revealed unto them; Unto whom I have committed the keys of my kingdom, and a dispensation of the gospel for the last times; and for the fulness of times, in the which I will gather together in one all things, both which are in heaven, and which are on earth; And also with

Book of Commandments – Chapter 28
Compare Doctrine and Covenants – Section 27

The retroactive additions to Chapter 28 of the Book of Commandments published in the Doctrine and Covenants in 1835, as reflected here with the permission of Sandra Tanner, corrupted the text of the original manuscript and backdated revisions which find no support in the materials ("Revelations and Translations") assembled in chronological order in the Facsimile Edition of The Joseph Smith Papers *published by the Church in 2009. "The distance between traditional accounts of LDS priesthood beginnings and the differing story of early [altered] documents points to the retrospective changes made in the public record to create a story [an unprovenanced story] of logical and progressive development . . . ." (D. Michael Quinn)*

first edition of the Doctrine and Covenants in 1835 – without archival support – was enhanced, reconfigured and backdated. Section 27 (Chapter 28 of the Book of Commandments) was retroactively tripled in size. An extremely important foundational document, which first said nothing about them, now made reference to all those different persons and to all those different subjects. Not one word in the 1830 manuscript printed in the Book of Commandments in 1833, and now (since 2009) published with the facsimile edition of the original manuscripts, concerned angelic ordination, the priesthood or the apostleship, John the Baptist, or Peter, James, and John.

In 1835 the twice already published commandment (Book of Commandments, 1833; *The Evening and the Morning Star*, 1833), supported by the original manuscript in the archives of the Church (the only manuscript), was fundamentally altered, embellished to become a differently numbered essentially unrecognizable expansion of the original revelation (Book of Commandments, Chapter 28, xxviii) in Section 27 of the Doctrine and Covenants (Section 50 in 1835). That new section now contained unprovenanced recitals antagonistic to the provisions of the manuscript. Those passages were added to a falsified revelation, the later improvised recitals of which improperly received the benefit of the 1830 revelation's earlier date.

Visions, Dreams and Promptings

Joseph Smith discussed visions, dreams and promptings with such easy familiarity as to suggest that his spiritual insights were never too sacred to be openly described or somehow better kept to himself. He did not hesitate to publish sixty-five of his revelations in 1833, against the wishes of some of his colleagues. The late backdated disclosures of significant events years after the fact in altered documents, and the lame excuses offered in support of these products of some late design, provide evidence of fabrication. It has long been known that Smith's revelations were revised and altered as suited the times before and after publication, and that other revelations were never officially published. Materials perceived as faith promoting have been published on a fast track; controversial materials have been consigned to obscurity, concealed and suppressed, kept out of sight and never seen. Mormon doctrines, changeable propositions, were threatened by Mormon history. If the malleable doctrines were destined to prosper, history had often to change.

Latter-day Saints are unrepentant revisionists. If history is not to their liking, it can be revised. George Orwell might just as well have described the Mormon Church: "The past is whatever the records and memories agree upon. And since the Party is in full control of all records, and in equally full control of the minds of its members, it follows that the past is whatever the Party chooses to make of it."[7] Anything can be revised, abandoned, incorporated, enhanced, denigrated, denied, maximized or minimized. And is.

> *Perhaps the main barrier to understanding the development of Mormon theology is an underlying assumption by most Church members that there is a cumulative unity of doctrine. Mormons seem to believe that particular doctrines develop consistently, that ideas build on each other in hierarchical fashion. As a result older revelations are interpreted by referring to current doctrinal positions. Thus, most members would suppose that a scripture or statement at any point in time has resulted from such orderly change. While this type of exegesis or interpretation may produce systematic theology and while it may satisfy those trying to understand and internalize current doctrine, it is bad history since it leaves an unwarranted impression of continuity and consistency.*[8]

---

[7]George Orwell, "The Theory and Practice of Oligarchical Collectivism" (part 2, chapter 9) in *1984* (Signet Classic, 1950), 263; "1984 by George Orwell: Essential Passages" (accessed 12 December 2013), available from http://www.enotes.com/ topics/1984/quotes; Internet. "It also follows that though the past is alterable, it never has been altered in any specific instance. For when it has been recreated in whatever shape is needed at the moment, then this new version *is* the past, and no different past can ever have existed." (Ibid., 263-64).

[8]Thomas G. Alexander, "The Reconstruction of Mormon Doctrine: From Joseph Smith to Progressive Theology," *Sunstone*, 5:4 (July-August 1980), 24 (24-33).

For Latter-day Saint theology, history is a nagging problem. Mormons mold facts to their liking. D. Michael Quinn describes this unfortunate mentality matter of factly.

> *Significant changes have been made in the published texts of LDS scriptures and in church documents published by official histories. These changes retroactively introduced concepts, people, names, and structures which did not exist in the original revelations and historical documents. In some instances these unannounced changes altered or reversed the original meaning of the various statements.*[9]

That is sympathetically said and greatly understated. Doctrine and Covenants Section 27 may be seen as a foster child for these kinds of developments. The vitally important concepts of priesthood were introduced to the members of the Church by means of tardy unprovenanced emendations to foundational documents, like those reflected in no less than thirteen revelations modified from other revelations already previously published without them. These alterations found their place in that "altered," "mutilated," "changed," "mixed up" "bungled" 1835 first edition of the Doctrine and Covenants.

> *The Book of Commandments [1833] [sixty-five revelations] gives the duties of Elders, Priests, Teachers, and Deacons and refers to Joseph's apostolic calling but there is no mention of Melchizedek Priesthood, High Priesthood, Seventies, High Priests, nor High Councilors. These words were later inserted into the revelation on Church organization and government of April 1830, making it*

---

[9]D. Michael Quinn, *The Mormon Hierarchy: Origins of Power* (Salt Lake City: Signature Books in association with Smith Research Associates, 1994), 5, emphasis added. "Beginning with Smith and Cowdery, church leaders regarded these retroactive changes as necessary because the original documents did not adequately anticipate Mormonism's later developments." (Ibid., 5). The duplicity was institutional and started with the founders. Quinn's many resources are described at note 25, pp. 272-75.

appear that they were known at that date, but they do not appear in the original, Chapter 24 of the Book of Commandments three years later . . . .[10]

The additions were backdated; the dates were fudged. While Mormons accept Christianity's Bible with reservations, only "as far as it is translated correctly,"[11] they accept the Book of Mormon with its multitudes of post-translation dated revisions, and its blatant plagiarism of the King James version of the Bible, as the most correct of any book on earth. In Mormon theology, the Book of Mormon has a higher dignity than Christianity's Bible. The Book of Mormon is "the keystone of our religion."[12] "Take away the Book of Mormon and the revelations," Joseph said, "and where is our religion? We have none . . . ."[13]

CHANGING THE UNCHANGEABLE

The text of the first edition of the Book of Mormon has been changed in one way or another thousands of times. Someone unprepared for such unsettling revisions would be unpleasantly surprised if asked to compare the first edition of the Book of Mormon (1830) to the current edition of the Book of Mormon. The Church tries to explain thousands of changes by saying they "were made by Joseph Smith" – as if he could change the unchangeable whenever he wanted without the plates – or by saying the changes weren't substantive. That does not augur well for the original translation, for Joseph Smith, or for the "gift and power of God" (to whom, make no mistake, the book is assigned in its entirety). Who would expect to see thousands of changes in "the most correct of any book on earth"? Why would anyone choose to covertly alter a

---

[10]LaMar Petersen, *Problems in Mormon Text: A brief study of certain changes in important Latter-day Saint publications including the Book of Mormon, Book of Commandments, ... the priesthood and Mormon concepts of deity* (n.p.: author, 1976), 7-8, quoted in Tanner and Tanner, *The Changing World of Mormonism*, 443, emphasis retained and added.

[11]Pearl of Great Price, Article of Faith 8.

[12]Book of Mormon, 1st ed. (Doubleday, 2004), ix, Introduction.

[13]Joseph Smith Jr., *History of The Church of Jesus Christ of Latter-day Saints*, B.H. Roberts, ed., 2d ed., rev., (Salt Lake City: The Deseret Book Company, 1978), 2:52, Conference Minutes (April 21, 1834).

book "translated by the gift and power of God" as Joseph Smith is known to have done in 1837? And why would anyone familiar with Mormonism's Articles of Faith not expect that the Book of Mormon – as opposed to the King James Bible – had been translated correctly? Smith and Rigdon's "Inspired Translation" of the King James Bible, intended to correct the scriptural corruptions of fallible scholars, was configured without the support of gold plates, peepstones, stovepipe hats or ancient manuscripts.

When a general assembly of the Church convened at Kirtland, Ohio, in August 1835, Oliver Cowdery introduced the "Book of doctrine and covenants of the church of the Latter Day Saints"[14] on behalf of a committee composed of Joseph Smith, Sidney Rigdon, Oliver Cowdery and Frederick G. Williams. "Although this new scripture had not yet been returned from the bindery on 17 August 1835, a general church committee was convened to introduce the publishing committee's labors."[15] The Church of Christ (early Mormon) changed its name to the Church of the Latter Day Saints in 1834, the same year the Mormon militia (Zion's Camp) marched to the state of Missouri to put the "old settlers" ("Missouri flotsam") in their godforsaken place. The new title, while omitting the name of Christ, overtly emphasized the millennial aspirations of the nineteenth-century society. The issue at Kirtland in August was the publication of some revelations. The matter came down to the members as follows:

> *Rigdon . . . spoke briefly, after which Elder John Smith, leader of the Kirtland high council, "bore record that the revelations in said book were true, and that the lectures [the Lectures on Faith] were judiciously arranged and compiled, and were profitable for doctrine." The entire work was then canonized by common consent.*[16]

---

[14]Richard S. Van Wagoner, *Sidney Rigdon: A Portrait of Religious Excess* (Salt Lake City: Signature Books, 1994; paperback 2006), 162.

[15]Ibid.

[16]Roberts, ed., *History of The Church of Jesus Christ of Latter-day Saints*, 2:244, cf. Van Wagoner, *Sidney Rigdon*, 162 fn 8, emphasis added. The *Lectures on Faith*, designated by the First Presidency in 1835 as "the Doctrine of the Church of the Latter Day Saints," were located in the first part of the "Book of Doctrine and

The trusting church membership, which had not yet examined the completed work, was unaware of a number of textual changes between the publication of the Book of Commandments and the new book of scripture (fifteen times the number of all changes that would subsequently be made in all Doctrine and Covenants editions from 1835 to 1921).[17]

At Kirtland in 1835, uninformed Latter Day Saints raised their arms to the square. The compliant members accepted and canonized a book none of them had read. The *Lectures on Faith* "*Prepared by the Prophet Joseph Smith*" (and Rigdon), the first part of the *Book of Doctrine and Covenants*, the doctrine part of the *Doctrine and Covenants*, joined the revelations at that assembly as divinely sanctioned sacred Mormon scripture.

The Book of Commandments and the printing office were destroyed by an angry mob in Missouri in 1833. A few copies of the book survived. William E. McLellin's personal copy was pieced together from remnants picked from the rubble by a printing boy and roughly bound. The revelations in the 1833 Book of Commandments, which were then supplemented, rewritten and republished in the Book of Doctrine and Covenants in 1835, were treated like any secular author's galley by editors acting in concert as a committee. When they were republished in the Doctrine and Covenants, they were greatly enhanced, back-dated, altered and falsified. All "official" Mormon history, both then and now, is suspect. Because so much of it has been revised, altered and modified, the study of Mormonism's origins is a minefield, difficult terrain to be negotiated with considerable caution. The Church has only just (2009) admitted that the revelations contained in the Book of Commandments were altered (and not just by Joseph Smith) before they were republished in the Doctrine and Covenants.

Covenants." "The second part of the book, the portion that comprises current editions, was labeled 'PART SECOND Covenants and Commandments.'"

[17]Van Wagoner, *Sidney Rigdon*, 162 fn 9, emphasis added. *See*, e.g., Melvin J. Petersen, "A Study of the Nature of and the Significance of the Changes in the Revelations as Found in a Comparison of the Book of Commandments and Subsequent Editions of the Doctrine and Covenants" (M.A. Thesis, Brigham Young University, 1955).

Earlier it was said that "Joseph Smith, being the one who received these revelations and had them recorded likewise would have a right to add or to substract [subtract] from, or change, the revelations and did so in some cases. Therefore, there will be some differences between those early publications and the current Doctrine and Covenants."[18] That unsatisfying explanation made a mockery of the translation process. Committees, acting in concert and unannounced, introduced "concepts, people, names and structures which did not exist in the original revelations . . . ." In that they "altered or reversed the original meaning" of scriptures received, and/or translated from golden plates, "by the gift and power of God."

Joseph Smith reported, "I never told you I was perfect; but there is no error in the revelations which I have taught."[19] Mormonism's founder could not withstand cross-examination on that indefensible point. Jehovah (Jesus), in support of Joseph and the Book of Commandments, is supposed to have said, "Search these commandments, for they are *true and faithful*, and the prophecies and promises which are in them, shall all be fulfilled. What I the

---

[18]Letter to T.G. Whitsitt from Joseph Anderson, Historical Department, The Church of Jesus Christ of Latter-day Saints, July 29, 1974, emphasis retained. "When one examines the publications by Wilford Wood [including the 1833 *Book of Commandments*, and the original 1830 edition of the Book of Mormon], one must be aware of what actually went on following those publications. For example, *Joseph Smith made many corrections* in the 1837 and the 1840 editions of the Book of Mormon. The corrections are explained in the preface and title pages of those editions." (Ibid.). Not quite.

[19]Roberts, ed., *History of The Church of Jesus Christ of Latter-day Saints*, 6:366. The Church initially tried to suppress the publication of the Book of Commandments, a rather scarce commodity. It may have thought in 1835, when it made many indefensible amendments, that the book (because it was destroyed) was so close to extinct it couldn't be referenced. For quite some time, copies of the 1833 edition were not available to critics. If none of the spared copies were available, comparisons with the altered contents of the 1835 first edition of the Doctrine and Covenants would have been difficult. The Tanners described their efforts to obtain a copy of the book: "For many years the Mormon leaders tried to suppress the *Book of Commandments*. They would not allow us to obtain photocopies of the book from Brigham Young University. Fortunately, however, we were able to obtain a microfilm of the copy at Yale University and had the *Book of Commandments* printed by photo-offset. Even though the newspapers in Salt Lake City would not allow us to advertize this book we were able to sell all of the copies in a short time." (Tanner and Tanner, *The Changing World of Mormonism*, 43).

Lord have spoken, I have spoken . . . ."[20] It is all on the Lord. If these are revelations, he is the author of them, and of that. "If the 'commandments' are *true and faithful*,'" Sharon I. Banister asks, "would you expect the revelations published [in the Book of Commandments] in 1833 to read the same two years later in the Doctrine and Covenants?" "Is it probable," the scholar further inquires, "that God would command Joseph Smith to publish [his] commandments to the 'inhabitants of the earth,' then afterwards have him change many of them"[21] in fundamental and incomprehensible ways? "If a prophet can 'add to, subtract from or change' revelations so that their meanings differ from one edition to the next, of what validity are the original revelations?" If nothing can be said to be constant, what can be said to be true? "Does a person who did not receive the revelation (originally) have the right to alter that revelation?"[22] "Is there any indication in the Doctrine and Covenants that the revelations (as they now read) were given at a time other than stated?"[23] In nearly two hundred years, has the backdating and falsification of these revelations ever been admitted? Has the institutional Church ever forthrightly confessed to the specifics of this calculated duplicity and asked to be forgiven? Or honestly acted to correct the falsified text?

The Church – its founders, leaders, historians and scholars – has been utterly dishonest in creating (and perpetuating) this untrustworthy tapestry. With the help of many brothers and sisters, men and women for whom the truth doesn't matter, it has concealed, suppressed, altered, amended, obscured and ignored stubborn facts with reckless impunity. Brazen amendments have disgraced allegedly sacred documents in order to accommodate faith-promoting falsehood. It will hardly do to lay some of this out in a series of unsigned undated hard to find position papers that barely scratch the surface in the twenty-first century.[24]

---

[20]Book of Commandments, Chapter 1:7, emphasis added.

[21]Sharon I. Banister, *For Any Latter-day Saint: One Investigator's Unanswered Questions* (Fort Worth, TX: Star Bible Publications, 1988), 159-60.

[22]Ibid., 161.

[23]Ibid., 160.

[24]Church Historian Elder Steven Snow (2013): "My view is that being open about our history solves a whole lot more problems than it creates." (Steven Snow, *Religious Educator*, 14 no. 3 [Brigham Young University, 2013]: 1-11). It is

EMENDATIONS:
SELECTED EXEMPLARS

Book of Commandments Chapter 6;
Doctrine and Covenants Section 7

In Section 7 of the Doctrine and Covenants, Joseph and Oliver "inquired through the Urim and Thummim as to whether John, the beloved disciple, tarried in the flesh or had died."[25] In the headnote to Chapter VI of the Book of Commandments (which then later became Section 7 of the Doctrine and Covenants), it was reported that the revelation was "Translated from parchment, written and hid up by [John the Beloved] himself."[26] That is yet another stunning coincidence worthy of more attention than it is now known to receive. Gold Nephite plates, gold Jaredite plates, brass Hebrew plates, the Old Testament on metal plates as early as 600 BC; a dead and bloody Laban; reformed Egyptian inscriptions; Egyptian papyri dictated, written upon and/or autographed by Abraham, Moses, Aaron and Israel's Egyptian Joseph; the fifteen hundred year history of the Jaredites on twenty-five metal plates; altered Hebrew; breastplates, peepstones, stovepipe hats, wooden submarines, magic daggers, parchments and witch hazel rods? A pre-Columbian sword? Three hour earthquakes? A nine-foot tall white Lamanite by the name of Zelph interred in Illinois? Adam and Eve, Cain and Abel in Missouri? Elias and Elijah, different prophets? Isaiah and Esaias, different prophets? Adam and Michael, different persons? "Nephi" and "Moroni," different names in different resources for the same angel? Kinderhook plates? A Greek psalter identified as an Egyptian dictionary? Lost books from Abraham, Moses and Enoch? When does all of this incredible chicanery spell deceit?

> *[Joseph] had experimented with the idea of "revealing" a lost book of the Bible and had dictated to Cowdery a fragment said to have come from a parchment buried by St. John. Then without benefit*

---

the twenty-first century and the Church at its highest level is still trying to decide whether or not to tell the truth.

[25]Doctrine and Covenants, Section 7, headnote.

[26]Book of Commandments, Chapter 6.

of either plates or parchment he had revealed a conversation between God and Moses that, he said, had been omitted from the Old Testament because of the wickedness of the Hebrews. Now he revealed a third lost book, the history of Enoch, whom according to the Bible God had "translated" into heaven without his ever having died.[27]

After Chapter VI was published in the Book of Commandments (in 1833), and before it was revised and republished in the Doctrine and Covenants (in 1835), one hundred and nine words were added to the text. These kinds of awkward changes to the revelations piqued the interest of one intrepid scholar. Is it from God, or is it from Joseph Smith? Wasn't God's control of this modern translation process "iron clad"? "Are God's revelations true and accurate when given?"

Does the fact that Joseph Smith added 109 words to Doctrine and Covenants 7 after he "translated from parchment" (and printed it) indicate that he did not translate it correctly in the first place?

If Joseph Smith translated the full text of the revelation [preserved on a fragment from St. John's parchment] in the beginning, why did he print only half of it in the 1833 Book of Commandments?

What indication is there in the current section heading that almost half of this revelation was given at a time other than stated?[28]

---

[27]Fawn M. Brodie, *No Man Knows My History: The Life of Joseph Smith the Mormon Prophet*, 2d ed., rev. and enl. (New York, NY: Alfred A. Knopf, 1972), 96. "The parchment of John at first consisted of only three verses published as section 6 in the [1833] Book of Commandments. It was greatly enlarged in the [1835] revised Doctrine and Covenants, as Section 7. The Book of Moses and the Book of Enoch were published separately in 1851 in a pamphlet called The Pearl of Great Price." (Ibid., *fn).

[28]Banister, *For Any Latter-day Saint*, 161, 166, emphasis added.

Book of Commandments Chapter 15;
Doctrine and Covenants Section 18

In the beginning the Book of Commandments assigned divine priority to the Book of Mormon, supposed to contain "the fulness of the everlasting Gospel . . . as delivered by the Savior to the ancient inhabitants."[29] In Chapter 15 of the Book of Commandments, the supreme importance of the Book of Mormon was fully defined.

1833 Book of Commandments:

> [B]ehold I give unto you a commandment, that you rely upon the things which are written [in the Book of Mormon]; for in them are all things written, concerning my church, my gospel, and my rock.

> Wherefore if you shall build up my church, and my gospel, and my rock, the gates of hell shall not prevail against you.[30]

As Joseph articulated imaginative new doctrines that crossed traditional Christian frontiers, that 1829 revelation was seen to have become too restrictive. With the publication of Section 18 of the Doctrine and Covenants in 1835, a correlating committee altered that earlier commandment in order to reduce the supreme importance of the Book of Mormon, "the keystone of the faith."

1835 Doctrine and Covenants:

> [B]ehold, I give unto you a commandment, that you rely upon the things which are written [in the Book of Mormon]; For in them are all things written concerning *the foundation of* my church, my gospel and my rock.

> Wherefore, if you shall build up my church, *upon the foundation of* my gospel and my rock, the gates of hell shall not prevail against you.[31]

---

[29]The Pearl of Great Price, Joseph Smith – History 1:34.
[30]Book of Commandments, 15:3-4.

In a book that influenced a generation of Latter-day Saints, Joseph Fielding Smith – the LDS Church Historian, the son of a prophet father, a grand nephew of Joseph Smith, a future prophet and theologian of last resort – offered this insight: "Before the Church could be organized it was essential that there be revealed such matters as pertained to the organization of the Church [as an aside, one might think of (1) the Aaronic Priesthood, (2) the Melchizedek Priesthood, (3) an account of the First Vision of the Father and the Son]." The disclosure of such organizational matters, according to Joseph Fielding Smith, was supposed to have been accomplished "between the time the witnesses viewed the plates of the ancient record and the 6th of April, 1830 . . . . It was also stated that the *Book of Mormon* contained 'all things written concerning the *foundation* of the Church and the Gospel.'"[32] Joseph Fielding Smith recognized that the commandment (which didn't specifically mention the Book of Mormon by name) concerned the Book of Mormon, but his comment ("the *Book of Mormon* contained 'all things written concerning *the foundation* of the Church and the Gospel") tracked the altered revelation (*D&C* 18:3-5), not the original revelation (*BofC* 15:3-4).[33]

Before Joseph Fielding Smith honored the alterations, David Whitmer voiced his concerns about those 1835 amendments. "The change in this revelation is of great importance," he said, "the word 'them' ["for in them are all things written"] refers to the plates – the Book of Mormon . . . ."[34] Whitmer, long before Joseph Fielding Smith, understood the command in its original form to mean that the society of the Saints was to rely upon the Book of Mormon where "all things" concerning the Church and the Gospel were written just as the Book of Commandments initially said. Without the reservations that surfaced in 1835 in the first edition of the book of Doctrine and Covenants.

---

[31]Doctrine and Covenants 18:3-5, emphasis added.

[32]Joseph Fielding Smith, *Essentials in Church History* (Salt Lake City: The Church of Jesus Christ of Latter Day Saints, 1922), 72, quoted in Banister, *For Any Latter-day Saint*, 166, emphasis added.

[33]Banister, *For Any Latter-day Saint*, 166-68, emphasis added.

[34]David Whitmer, *An Address to All Believers in Christ: by A Witness to the Divine Authenticity of The Book of Mormon* (Richmond, MO: n.p., 1887; photographic reprint, Concord, CA: Pacific Publishing Company, 1993), 58.

The revelation initially commanded the members of the Church to rely upon what was written on the plates and translated in the Book of Mormon. That instruction, to hold the book as the source of dependable truth, was an early warm and comforting first principle. When the revelation-altering committee ("God's editors") changed the revelation sometime between 1833 and 1835, it no longer referred to "all things written, concerning my church, my gospel, and my rock," but rather to "things concerning *the foundation* of the church, *or the beginning* of the church . . . ." Whitmer recognized that wasn't what the unamended revelation had intended. Now there was no firm foundation, no unequivocal model or guide, no rule-based superstructure.

This new and unfortunate unlimited flexibility replaced the sanctity of the law ("walk in my statutes and keep my commandments"[35]) with the commandments of men. Arbitrary discretion took the place of golden rules. Now there were "new offices," "new ordinances," "new doctrines," whatever the times and the all-powerful prophet saw fit to require. For faithful Latter-day Saints, the truth is what the prophet says that it is. This important amendment and some of the other earliest revelations vested authoritarian discretion in an absolute leader. Joseph Smith ended up owning his constituents, body and soul, then and now. One man, and then his successors, rose to control this increasingly uncomfortable universe.

Whitmer saw folly in that: "I was present," he said, "when Brother Joseph received this revelation [Chapter 15 of the Book of Commandments] *through the stone*: I am one of the persons to whom it was given, therefore I know of a surety that it was changed when printed in the *Doctrine and Covenants* in 1834 [1835]. Likewise concerning all these changes of which I will speak [because there were many others], I know that these changes were made. I was present when nearly all the early revelations were received. There are several of the old Books of Commandments yet in the land; bring them [bring that scarce resource] to light and see for

---

[35]Joseph Smith's 1832 Holographic Account, in Joseph Smith Jr., *The Personal Writings of Joseph Smith*, ed. Dean C. Jessee (Salt Lake City, UT: Deseret Book, 1984). 6.

yourselves that these revelations were changed . . . ."[36] David Whitmer's defection was not the product of drift and indirection.

Book of Commandments Chapter 28;
Doctrine and Covenants Section 27

Improbable origins, the devil is in the details

Most Latter-day Saints see the evolution of the modern priesthood through a glass darkly. In his meticulous study of the *Origins of [Mormon] Power*, D. Michael Quinn reports that, "The evolution of authority, priesthood, ordained offices, and presiding quorums traced in this study is not obvious to those acquainted with official LDS doctrine and history."[37] *"Significant changes have been made in the published texts of LDS scriptures and in church documents published by official histories."*[38]

Sometime between 1833 (when the Book of Commandments was published) and 1835 (when the Doctrine and Covenants was published), *Section 27* of the *Doctrine and Covenants* (which was first published as *Chapter 28* of the *Book of Commandments*) would be completely rewritten, added to and supplemented to make it appear as if the original revelation received in Harmony, Pennsylvania, "Circa August 1830," had described visitations by John the Baptist and Peter, James, and John, heavenly messengers come to confer "dual priesthoods of different ranks." The original revelation did not describe those messengers, or those visitations, or those priesthoods. Those alleged visitations and the strikingly

---

[36]Whitmer, *An Address to All Believers in Christ*, 58-59, emphasis added. "They changed this revelation in order to sustain these new doctrines. *If they had not made this change, the plain language of the original revelation would have condemned the Book of Doctrine and Covenants* . . . . These changes were made by the leaders of the church, who had drifted into error and spiritual blindness." (Ibid., emphasis added). *"Through the influence of Sydney Rigdon, Brother Joseph was led on and on into receiving revelations every year to establish offices and doctrines which are not even mentioned in the teachings of Christ* . . . ." (Ibid., 59, emphasis added).

[37]Quinn, *Origins of Power*, 5; see, e.g., 272 fn 24.

[38]Ibid., see, e.g., 272-75 fn 25, emphasis added.

altered revelation invented to awkwardly support them were fabricated.

The leaders of the Church didn't know about the Melchizedek Priesthood in 1829 and 1830 when the first elders were ordained and the Church was spiritually and legally organized. (The word "priesthood" wasn't used in the Church, in the revelations or the sermonizing until that Fourth Conference held at Kirtland, Ohio, in June 1831). By altering Chapter 28 of the Book of Commandments, a revelation faithful to its archival resource, then backdating the alterations, the founders recreated the original record, rewriting history after the fact to make it seem as if they knew things they didn't know at the time. Chapter 28 of the Book of Commandments, a revelation supposed to have been received in 1830, then published twice in its original form in 1833, was revised and republished in a strikingly different form as Section 50 of the 1835 first edition of the Doctrine and Covenants. In later editions and printings, Section 50 was renumbered to become Section 27. Those retroactive alterations to what was supposed to be the word of God, alterations to earlier text that didn't support them, made it seem as if the leaders of the Church knew about John the Baptist, the Aaronic Priesthood, the Melchizedek Priesthood and Peter, James, and John, in 1830. The backdated alterations to a previously published but different revelation got the benefit of the previously published but different revelation's earlier date. New concepts (in this case nothing less than the announcement of the restorations of two different priesthoods by separate sets of heavenly messengers) added to older previously published revelations were backdated to make it seem as if they weren't new concepts added to older previously published revelations, without the least regard for the integrity of those earlier resources.

The proof for the supposed 1829 priesthood ordinations of Joseph Smith and Oliver Cowdery, according to the *Church Chronology*, speaking before evidence of unconscionable duplicity ever really surfaced, is "the word of the Lord Jesus Christ" as it is found in Sections 20 and *27* of the Doctrine and Covenants.[39]   Section 27

---

[39]Can anyone imagine that Peter, James, and John appeared to Joseph Smith and Oliver Cowdery in "1829, May-June," without there having been some reference to that incredible occurrence in any of the sixty-five revelations

identified Joseph's God as its revelatory source: *"Listen," it said, "to the voice of Jesus Christ, your Lord, your God, and your Redeemer . . . ."*[40] Is it not perfectly clear that the Mormon God is supposed to be the ultimate author of this unmistakably altered resource? The cynical amendments to what became the 27th Section of the Doctrine and Covenants, published in the first edition of the Doctrine and Covenants in 1835, tripled the size of their prototype, Section 28 of the Book of Commandments published in 1833. With the benefit of that startling reconfiguration, Section 27 then became a foundational narrative emphasizing apostles and especial witnesses. In the 20th Section of the Doctrine and Covenants, the other revelation supposed to support the priesthood, Jesus said that Joseph and Oliver had been ordained to be apostles and elders. Section 20 doesn't mention angelic ordination, John the Baptist, or Peter, James, or John. That awkward task was left to Section 27.

The reconstituted Section 27, brought to light in 1835, purports to describe a visit of John the Baptist, who is now supposed to have ordained Joseph and Oliver "unto the *first* priesthood which you have received," by that to say a priesthood after the order of Aaron. It then purports to further describe another entirely separate previously unknown visit by Peter, James, and John "by whom I have ordained you and confirmed you to be apostles, and especial witnesses of my name . . . ." Here are revisionary words attributed to Jesus by a committee after the fact. Here is Mormon priesthood and its core principle (angelic ordination) encircled with deception.

---

published in chronological order in the Book of Commandments more than four years later in 1833? Or that Joseph and Oliver said just exactly nothing about that remarkable event on April 6, 1830, the day the Church was officially organized? Or more than five years later when Joseph Smith and Oliver Cowdery jointly created the first authorized history of the Church of the Latter Day Saints? A carefully crafted history published in eight carefully crafted installments over a period of two years (1834-35) that failed to mention Peter, James, and John or a great first vision of the Father and the Son? Cowdery and Smith waited five, then finally more than six years, to say what they finally said about the reception of unequal orders of heavenly power ("dual priesthoods of different ranks") by way of unprecedented angelic ordinations at the hands of separate sets of heavenly messengers.

[40]Andrew Jenson, comp., *Church Chronology: A Record of Important Events Pertaining to the History of the Church of Jesus Christ of Latter-day Saints*, 2d ed., rev. and enlarged (Salt Lake City: Deseret News, 1914), xxii, citing Doctrine and Covenants 27, emphasis added.

Twenty-first Century Insights: The Joseph Smith Papers

Chapter 28 of the Book of Commandments (published in 1833) is described as "A Commandment to the church of Christ, given in Harmony, Pennsylvania, September 4, 1830." It consisted of seven sparing verses and filled about three-quarters of a single page. Chapter 28 of the Book of Commandments, as published in the March 1833 issue of *The Evening and the Morning Star*, "closely corresponds to the version in chapter 28 of the Book of Commandments." So closely, in fact, that "It is unknown whether this version [*The Evening and the Morning Star* version] or the version in the Book of Commandments was set in type first."[41] Had the newspaper edition been versified (it was not), it would have consisted of seven verses and filled three-quarters of a single page.[42] Chapter 28 of the Book of Commandments, when it was honestly published in 1833, and as reflected in the original manuscript, the only manuscript, concerned but one subject, the sacrament, and consisted of less than two hundred words.

Before the Book of Commandments (the Missouri publication in 1833) and *The Evening and the Morning Star* (another Missouri publication in 1833) were monumentally altered and republished in the Doctrine and Covenants (an Ohio publication in 1835) and in the renamed *Evening and Morning Star* (another Ohio publication in 1836), both of the primary publications omitted *all* (Book of Commandments 28) *or elements of* (Doctrine and Covenants 27) the following language from the original manuscript: "A Revelation to the Church given at Harmony susquehann[a]h County State of Pennsylvania given to Joseph the Seer at a time that he went to purch{◊s\ase} wine {it\for} Sacrament & he was stoped by an

---

[41] *The Evening and the Morning Star* in March 1833 and the Book of Commandments in 1833 published provisions faithful to the contents of the original manuscript, the archival resource brought to the attention of ordinary people in the *Joseph Smith Papers* published in 2009. The altered revelation was unfaithfully published in the first edition of the Doctrine and Covenants in 1835, and in the *Evening and Morning Star* in 1836. Those tardy altered contents found in the amended Section 27, although also attributed to Jesus Christ, had (and have) no archival provenance.

[42] *See*, e.g., *The Joseph Smith Papers: Revelations and Translations Volume 2: Published Revelations*, eds. Robin Scott Jensen, Richard E. Turley Jr., and Riley M. Lorimer (Salt Lake City: Church Historian's Press, 2011), 72, 277.

{a\<A>}ngel & ~~he~~ he spok to him as follows Saying ~~L~~ Listen to the voice of Jesus Christ . . . ."[43]   That original material, insofar as it is partially covered in what is now Section 27 of the Doctrine and Covenants, is synthesized in a sparing provision in a deceptive headnote, which describes a *"Revelation given to Joseph Smith, the Prophet, at Harmony, Pennsylvania, August, 1830."*

It is clear from these early resources (the Book of Commandments and *The Evening and the Morning Star*) that this revelation (now Section 27), before it was reconstituted by editors and republished in a different form in the first edition of the Doctrine and Covenants, had been a narrowly drawn sparing instruction pertaining to a single subject, the sacrament.   The amended revelation (*D&C* 27 – the first four paragraphs of which were later reported in the headnote to this author's 1957 edition of the Doctrine and Covenants to have been written at the time ["August 1830"], and the remainder [including the strikingly substantive backdated additions] in the September following[44]) – now provides that "He was met by a heavenly messenger, and received this revelation . . . ."

The original revelation, the provenanced part of the modern revelation as reflected in the original manuscript, described the substance of the sacrament (*Book of Commandments*: "it mattereth not what ye shall eat, or what ye shall drink"), and the symbolism attached to the sacred ordinance (*Book of Commandments*, "Remembering unto the Father my body which was laid down for you, and my blood which was shed for the remission of your sins . . ."). In the original revelation, that part of the altered revelation supported by the manuscript, Joseph was instructed not to purchase wine or strong drink from his enemies. He was told that the emblems of the ordinance ("what ye shall eat, or what ye shall drink") should be "made new among you" ("you shall partake of none, except it is made new among you"), "in this my Father's

---

[43] *The Joseph Smith Papers: Revelations and Translations: Manuscript Revelation Books, Facsimile Edition*, ed. Robin Scott Jensen, Robert J. Woodford, and Steven C. Harper (Salt Lake City: Church Historian's Press, 2009), 40-41. The headnote to Doctrine and Covenants 27 described the encounter with the angel and the revelation that followed.

[44] Doctrine and Covenants (1957), Section 27, headnote.

kingdom which shall be built up on the earth." Finally, Joseph was told that "the hour cometh" when Jesus Christ "your Lord, your God and your Redeemer" shall take the sacrament with you and others "on the earth." Until then, "lift up your hearts and rejoice, and gird up your loins and be faithful until I come: even so Amen."[45] That was the substance of an unembellished revelation containing less than two hundred words that didn't mention messengers, ordinations, especial witnesses, the apostleship or priesthood when it was repeatedly published in 1833. And as it is described in the original (and only) manuscript in 1830, a manuscript presently found in facsimile form in *The Joseph Smith Papers* (since 2009). Everything else described in Section 27, more than four hundred and fifty additional words, is editorial comment added years after the fact without archival support.

Although the Book of Commandments refers to a Commandment given in Harmony, Pennsylvania, on September 4, 1830, although *The Evening and the Morning Star* refers to "A Commandment Given, September 4, 1830,"[46] although the headnote to the author's 1957 edition of Section 27 of the Doctrine and Covenants describes the first four paragraphs of the revelation as written in August 1830 and "the remainder in the September following," the editors of the *Joseph Smith Papers* have now determined that both versions (*original*: Book of Commandments 28; *The Evening and the Morning Star* and the 1830 manuscript, and *falsified*: Doctrine and Covenants 1835, *Evening and Morning Star* 1836) "should be dated circa August 1830."[47]

The original manuscript and the other facsimiles published in chronological order in the *Joseph Smith Papers* in 2009 do not support a headnote in the 1957 edition of the Doctrine and Covenants that says the first four paragraphs were received "in August 1830" and "the remainder in the September following." That curious claim, we may speculate, may have been intended to make it seem to say that a greatly embellished Section 27 was more than a sparing Section 28 had been because it consisted of two

---

[45]Book of Commandments, 28.
[46]*The Joseph Smith Papers: Revelations and Translations: Volume 2: Published Revelations* (2011), 72, 277.
[47]Ibid., 277 fn 50, 51.

separate revelations delivered at two separate times which, for reasons that make no sense, were later combined. The headnote could be envisioned as an awkward attempt to explain away the fact that Chapter 28 of the Book of Commandments in 1833 had been completely remodeled before it was republished as Section 27 of the Doctrine and Covenants in 1835, where it was backdated and falsified. More than four hundred and fifty (450) words were added to Chapter 28 of the Book of Commandments in Section 27 of the Doctrine and Covenants after 1833 and before 1835. Those crude embellishments, when included in the reconstituted Chapter 28, ultimately survived to become Section 27 of the Doctrine and Covenants (after 1835 in future editions and printings). The original manuscript, as reflected in Chapter 28 of the Book of Commandments, contained less than two hundred words. When it was altered and republished in 1835, without archival support, that new and unprovenanced revelation contained six hundred and fifty words and had tripled in size.

The Doctrine and Covenants' Expansion

For nearly one-hundred and eighty years, and until long after perspicacious scholars discovered evidence of editorial dishonesty, the Church has perpetuated this unconscionable deception. In the face of a crisis of confidence among the ranks of the knowledgeable misinformed, and confronted with incontrovertible evidence of historical deception by scholars faithful and not, the Church has been forced to reveal materials that expose massive substantive duplicity. In 2009, as part of the uncomfortable process of confronting a history-based rebellion, the Church (late and reluctantly) ("the truth is not always useful") published in facsimile form the verbatim transcripts of the revelations published in the Book of Commandments in 1833, and in *The Evening and the Morning Star*, in 1832 and 1833. The sixty-five revelations in the Book of Commandments were published in chronological order. The approximately four hundred and fifty words added to Chapter 28 of the Book of Commandments after 1833 and before it was republished (and backdated) as Chapter 27 of the Doctrine and Covenants in 1835 are not found in the original manuscript, or in any of the many other chronological facsimiles. For them there is no archival support. Although attributed to God himself, they are the words of God's estimable uncensurable editors. And they didn't surface to dramatically change the earlier revelation until 1835.

The *Joseph Smith Papers* are intended to put the best possible face on a nasty problem – the long suppression of the notorious facts concerning the society's difficult past, the frailties of its founder and the uneven nature of his important work. The history of the Church is profoundly discredited in these submissions. It isn't "clear and open," as some of the leaders say, and doesn't lead "to faith and strength and virtues."[48] There is a crisis in the ranks. The issues are fundamental, and Mormonism's chickens are coming home to roost. The belated disclosure of unsettling things to multigenerational Latter-day Saints betrayed by multigenerational leaders is a desperate attempt by desperate men to make the best of a bad thing. A careful examination of the *Joseph Smith Papers*[49] published in 2009 is seen to reflect the calculated substantive alteration of Chapter 28 of the 1833 Book of Commandments.

If one part of a revelation delivered in two parts (in August and September of 1830) had followed another – as the 1957 headnote suggests – and if the two parts had been combined – as the headnote also reports – both parts would be found in facsimile form somewhere in the facsimile edition of the chronologically arranged original manuscripts for the months of August and September 1830. Sadly, they are not. There is no archival support for that four hundred and fifty word expansion. The substantive emendations made in the 1835 edition of the Doctrine and Covenants are not supported by the materials found in the Facsimile Edition of the *Joseph Smith Papers* published in 2009. Materials supposed to have followed the first four verses of the revelation in 1830 would have been published when the revelation was published in *The Evening and the Morning Star* four years later in March 1833. They were not. The so-called "remainder" supposed to have been written "in the September following" would have been found with the

---

[48]Jennifer Dobner (Associated Press), "Pres. [Gordon B.] Hinckley answers myriad questions about the LDS Church," *Deseret News* (25 December 2005).

[49]*The Joseph Smith Papers: Revelations and Translations: Manuscript Revelation Books, Facsimile Edition*, 40-43.

chronological facsimiles of the original manuscripts for the month of September 1830, then published in *The Evening and the Morning Star* in 1833, then published in the Book of Commandments in 1833. They were not. The supposed amendments are not found with the facsimiles of the original manuscripts for August *or* September of 1830. They were not published in *The Evening and the Morning Star* in 1833, and they were not published in the Book of Commandments in 1833.

Changing the Word

Joseph Smith made a foundational narrative out of Chapter 28 of the Book of Commandments – a revelation about a single subject (the sacrament) dated September 4, 1830 and originally published in 1833 – in what is now Section 27 of the Doctrine and Covenants, a revelation containing information about many different subjects originally published in 1835. What was one thing in 1833 became something different and unrecognizable in and after 1835. Book of Commandments, Chapter 28: "[M]arvel not, for the hour cometh that I will drink of the fruit of the vine with you, on the earth, and with all those my Father hath given me out of the world: Wherefore lift up your hearts and rejoice, and gird up your loins and be faithful until I come . . . ."[50] When Section 27 was published (meaning when an altered version of Chapter 28 of the 1833 Book of Commandments was published in the Doctrine and Covenants in 1835), the backdated revelation contained eighteen lengthy verses, most of them entirely new. Those new passages now described the priesthood, priesthood power, the keys to the ministry, the restoration of orders of authority, and the dispensation of the fullness of times. They fleshed out an inconspicuous revelation that concerned nothing but the sacrament. The revisions followed what soon became a comfortable, often repeated pattern. The changes made to the founding stories were grand and glorious and monumentally substantive. They followed Mormonism's embellishment model "by becoming more physical, impressive,

---

[50]Book of Commandments, 28:6-7.

unique, and miraculous . . ." in the retelling.[51] *In the retelling.*

When republished, the revelation was transfigured to describe much more than the sacrament. In this new manifestation it concerned kingdom building, the gathering together of all things, the Savior's second coming, promises and blessings. It is now about *the messengers of the restoration*, ancient patriarchs with whom the Savior and Joseph will drink the fruit of the vine on earth (meaning to share the sacrament) (a clever segue). The backdated revelation purports to identify messengers, previous visitors never previously mentioned, some of whom (but not all of whom) were retroactively supposed to have come before August and September of 1830 to reveal "the fulness of my everlasting gospel"? These new unprovenanced faces, with whom the Savior promises to drink the fruit of the vine of earth, names and faces abruptly added to the earlier revelation (the original of which didn't include them), now include *Moroni, Elias, Elijah, John the Baptist, Peter, James, and John, Michael or Adam, Joseph, Jacob, Isaac and Abraham.*

The Lord left all these things out in 1830 when the revelation was first received, in 1833 when it was published in *The Evening and the Morning Star*, in 1833 when it then became Chapter 28 of the Book of Commandments, and in 2009 when the original manuscript was published in its unamended form in the facsimile edition of the *Joseph Smith Papers*. In 1835 Joseph and others added information about the previously unknown missions of John the Baptist and Peter, James, and John to an earlier revelation that had already been published in its faithful form three different times.

In 1834-35, the Church abandoned its "by the grace of God" authority in favor of angelic ordination. The conferral of the priesthood now depended upon the literal physical transfer of divine authority by heavenly messengers by the laying on of hands. By this reckoning, by person-to-person transfer, the society dismissed metaphysical authority conferred because of a command or spiritual prompting. In 1834-35, a society that had previously operated under various non-exclusive claims to spiritual power, by

---

[51]Grant H. Palmer, "Joseph Smith's changing view of God as seen in his First Vision accounts," Outline of a Lecture given at the Salt Lake City Library (6 November 2013).

cutting many corners for the longest time, changed grids. By altering previously accepted equations, the Latter-day Saints no longer validated the proposition that a subjective command or prompting provided the kind of authority needed to do what God wanted to be done. The founders bet the farm on angelic ordination.

Visitors?

Section 27, as altered, describes Elias and Elijah (Elias at 27:6; Elijah at 27:9). Neither of those verses and neither of those names existed in the text of the original revelation when it was first received in 1830. Joseph Smith didn't know that Elijah and Elias (Hebrew and Greek names for the same person) weren't two separate persons, and neither did his revelatory Lord. "Thus for Joseph Smith, the Greek name referred to one prophet and the Hebrew name referred to another."[52]   Joseph didn't know this,

---

[52]Joseph made another mistake concerning Michael and Adam. On April 3, 1976, the Church Section of the *Deseret News* reported that "Two revelations received by former Presidents of the Church were accepted as scripture Saturday afternoon, April 3, by vote of Church membership . . . ." The new scriptures to be arranged as part of the Pearl of Great Price included an "account of the Prophet Joseph Smith's vision of the Celestial Kingdom received Jan. 21, 1836." In describing the revelation, the *Deseret News* reported Joseph said that, "The heavens were opened upon us and I beheld the celestial kingdom of God . . . . I saw Father Adam and Abraham, and my father and my mother, [and] my [unbaptized, unendowed] brother, Alvin . . . ." The problem with that was this: In the original revelation, as recorded in Joseph Smith's diary, Joseph saw *Adam and Michael*, two different persons. "I saw," he said (before that revelation was remodeled), "father *Adam*, and Abraham *and Michael*, and my father and mother, [and] my brother Alvin . . . ." (Joseph Smith's Diary, 21 January 1836, 136). (Tanner and Tanner, *The Changing World of Mormonism*, 62-63). The leaders of the Church deleted the words "*and Michael*" from the revelation ("without any indication") before it was canonized in 1976. That was important because Joseph Smith taught his followers that Adam was Michael. ("And the Lord appeared unto them, and they rose up and blessed *Adam, and called him Michael*, the prince, the archangel. [Doctrine and Covenants 107:54, emphasis added].") ("And also with *Michael, or Adam*, the father of all, the prince of all, the ancient of days.") (Doctrine and Covenants 27:11.) "Thus it is clear that if Adam is Michael, Joseph Smith could not have seen "*Adam*, and Abraham and *Michael*." "Moroni," "Nephi," "Elijah," "Elias," "Isaiah," "Esias," "Adam," "Michael" – the prophet is disconcertingly confused. "[C]urrent [modern] Mormon leaders have canonized a falsified revelation." (Quotes from Tanner and Tanner, *The Changing World of*

Jesus didn't know this, Jesus didn't tell him this, and the most important man on earth failed to figure it out. In that controversial Section 27, along with so many other incongruities, one Elijah is presented as two separate identifiable entities. "In D&C 27:6-9," not to be trusted unprovenanced passages bedeviled by amendment, "'Elias' and 'Elijah' are treated as distinctly different prophets."[53] That error attributed to the Lord by Joseph Smith and Oliver Cowdery speaks to their folly. Although the distinction (calling them two persons) is clear at 27:6-9, erroneous passages added to an earlier revelation, it is infinitely clear at D&C 110:12-13. Hear that in this:

> *After this, <u>Elias</u> appeared [at the Temple at Kirtland, Ohio, on April 3, 1836], and committed the dispensation of the gospel of Abraham, saying that in us and our seed all generations after us should be blessed.*

> *After this vision had closed [the vision of Elias], another great and glorious vision burst upon us; for <u>Elijah</u> the prophet, who was taken to heaven without tasting death, stood before us and said,*

> *Behold the time has fully come, which was spoken of by the mouth of Malachi . . .*

Even before Joseph and Oliver said that they saw Elijah *and* Elias in seclusion behind the veil at the Kirtland Temple, they said

> *We saw the Lord standing upon the breastwork of the pulpit before us, and under his feet was a paved work of pure gold, in color like amber. His eyes were as a*

Mormonism, 62, 63). Michael, by modern Mormon reckoning, was the name by which Adam was known in the premortal life. Joseph Smith clearly identified Adam as Michael. (Doctrine and Covenants 128:21). On this occasion the prophet appeared to forget, and the Church covered the problem up.

[53]Richard Packham, "Elijah and Elias" in "A Linguist Looks at Mormonism: Notes on linguistics problems in Mormonism" (first published April 20, 2003; last revised March 2, 2011; accessed 15 January 2014), available from http://packham. n4m.org/linguist.htm; Internet, 10-11. "At Romans 11:2-3, Paul quotes 'Elias' with the words of Elijah from 1 Kings 19. 10, 14."

flame of fire; the hair of his head was white like the pure snow; his countenance shone above the brightness of the sun; and his voice was as the sound of the rushing of great waters, even the voice of Jehovah, saying: I am the first and the last, I am he who liveth, I am he who was slain; I am your advocate with the Father . . . .[54]

Richard L. Bushman: "Warren Cowdery reported that Joseph said there had been additional visitors behind the veil that day. Moses appeared, and then Elias, followed by Elijah. Each personage presented 'keys' – that is, the power and right to perform certain acts on God's behalf: Moses, to gather Israel; Elias for the gospel of Abraham [the Smith family's patriarchal inheritance]; and Elijah for turning the hearts of the fathers to the children and children to the fathers, in fulfillment of a prophecy in Malachi."[55] A man who saw Elias and Elijah, one after the other and reported it twice, probably didn't see the Lord or Moses even once. A man who said he saw Elias followed by Elijah might be willing to say almost anything. Such a man may not have held his glorious Lord in high regard. One of Joseph's biographers, speaking of the prophet, his mother and his home, captured this: "Her religion [Lucy Mack Smith's religion] was intimate and homely, with God a ubiquitous presence invading dreams, provoking miracles, and blighting sinners' fields. Her children probably never learned to fear Him."[56]

Chicanery

When Chapter 28 was published in the Book of Commandments in 1833, it didn't mention *Moroni, Elias, John the Baptist, Elijah, Joseph, Jacob, Isaac, Abraham, Michael or Adam, or Peter, James, and John.* It said nothing about the restoration of the keys of the ministry. It didn't mention the "fulness of my everlasting gospel" or the "restoration of all things spoken by the mouth of all the holy prophets since the world began." Nor did it describe dual

---

[54]Doctrine and Covenants 110:2-4, emphasis added.
[55]Richard Lyman Bushman, with the assistance of Jed Woodworth, *Joseph Smith: Rough Stone Rolling* (New York: Alfred A. Knopf, 2005), 320.
[56]Brodie, *No Man Knows My History*, 5.

priesthoods of different ranks, the ordination of Joseph Smith, the ordination of Oliver Cowdery, the "keys of my kingdom," the gathering of all things "in heaven" or "on earth," or the "dispensation of the gospel for . . . the fulness of times." It said nothing about apostles, "especial witnesses" or apostleship.

Sections 27:6-13, provisions enormously important to the issue of priesthood, were not included in the original manuscript. Why do the revelations in Chapter 28 and Section 27 not look alike and read the same? Why is Section 27 of the Doctrine and Covenants greatly embellished and differently sized? What does Jesus say about John the Baptist, Peter, James, and John, angelic ordination, the Aaronic or Melchizedek Priesthood and the First Vision in Chapter 28 of the Book of Commandments in 1833? *Nothing.* What does Jesus say about John the Baptist, Peter, James, and John and the priesthood in an amended Section 27 of the Doctrine and Covenants in 1835? *"Remember I sent them, and they ordained you (wink, wink)."*

Unsupported Emendations:

> **1. Aaronic:** *I will drink of the fruit of the vine with you on the earth, and with . . . John [whom] I have sent unto you, my servants, Joseph Smith, Jun., and Oliver Cowdery, to ordain you unto the first priesthood which you have received that you might be called and ordained even as Aaron . . . .*[57]

> **2. Melchizedek:** *I will drink of the fruit of the vine with you on the earth, and with . . . Peter, and James, and John, whom I have sent unto you, by whom I have ordained you and confirmed you to be apostles, and especial witnesses of my name, and bear the keys of your ministry . . . .*[58]

In this substantively altered 1830 (backdated) account first published in 1833, the Lord doesn't say that he will send John the Baptist and Peter, James, and John to restore dual priesthoods of

---

[57]Doctrine and Covenants 27:5, 8 (1835), emphasis added.
[58]Ibid., 27:5, 12 (1835), emphasis added.

different ranks, but that he had already sent them (before 1830). That must have come as a shock to anyone who ever read the original manuscript of a revelation received in 1830, Chapter 28 of the Book of Commandments published in 1833. God's editors revised the revelation years after the fact (sometime between 1833 and 1835) to say that the Lord had sent two separate sets of messengers to restore two separate authorities. Section 107, dated April 1835, an important revelation concerning the priesthood, fails to mention either event. It doesn't mention John the Baptist and it doesn't mention Peter, James, and John. The words of the Lord in Section 27 (wherein God himself is supposed to have said in 1830 that "I have sent" *John*, and *Peter, James, and John*) are backdated and falsified.

Book of Commandments Chapter 44 ;
Doctrine and Covenants Section 42

Chapter 44 of the Book of Commandments, a revelation supposed to have been received on February 9, 1831, described elders, priests, teachers and bishops. It didn't describe high priests and a high council. Joseph Smith was ordained to the high priesthood by Lyman Wight at Kirtland, Ohio, on June 3, 1831, when that greater authority was conferred upon the Church's lower authority elders, including Joseph Smith, for the first time. There were no high priests on February 9, 1831; there was no high council on February 9, 1831. Lyman Wight was the first ordained high priest of the Church of Christ, and there was no high council when he was ordained on June 3, 1831. The first members of the high priesthood were ordained at the Fourth Conference of the Church at Kirtland, Ohio, on June 3, 1831. When Chapter 44 was reprinted in the *Evening and Morning Star* in February 1835, and when it was reconfigured to be republished in the Doctrine and Covenants in 1835 (where it is presently Section 42) – true to form and too – it was "more physical, impressive, unique . . . [and] miraculous," enhanced, backdated and falsified. It was greatly more grand and glorious than it had previously been. Now it did mention high priests and a high council, as additional elements among other changes. The headnote to Section 42 of the Doctrine and Covenants neglects to mention an "update," by that to say the addition of substantive backdated amendments.

The Church has been forced to admit that the revelation was revised in 1835 but doesn't go further to say that no one could know that because of the deceptive headnote. The revisions, which changed the meaning of the revelation, were unannounced, and the altering additions got the benefit of the altered revelation's earlier date. These kinds of deceptions discredit Mormon scholarship, particularly priesthood scholarship, and betray the laity.

Doctrine and Covenants 68;
The Evening and Morning Star (October 1832)

Doctrine and Covenants Section 68 (a "Revelation given through Joseph Smith the Prophet, at Hiram, Ohio, November 1, 1831") wasn't published in the Book of Commandments in 1833, but was published in *The Evening and the Morning Star* in 1832. When it was published in the Doctrine and Covenants in 1835, it purported to describe the Aaronic and Melchizedek Priesthoods ("dual priesthoods of different ranks"). The references to those two different priesthoods thus appeared to have been included in a revelation dated November 1831. The first publication of this revelation in *The Evening and the Morning Star* in October 1832, unlike the second publication of this revelation in the Doctrine and Covenants in 1835, did not describe the Melchizedek Priesthood, nor either a "First Presidency of a Melchizedek Priesthood," nor either the "literal descendants of Aaron." It didn't pertain to "firstborn . . . sons of Aaron," to "a legal right to the bishopric," to a "right of the presidency," to "keys or authority," to "literal descendants of Aaron," nor to the "authority" of the "Melchizedek Priesthood" to "officiate in all the lesser offices" when "no literal descendant of Aaron can be found."

Joseph Smith Papers (Revelation Book 1)

Wording after italicized revisions (by Oliver Cowdery) on the manuscript page. Introductory:

And now conc[e]rning the items in addition to the
Laws & com=mandments they are these there
rema[i]neth hereafter in the due time of the Lord
other Bishops to be set apart unto the church to
minister even according to the first wherefore it
shall be an high priest who is worthy & he shall be
appointed by a confrene of *the presidency of* high
priests *{*/*}*.[59]

*JOSEPH SMITH PAPERS, EDITOR'S NOTE: BETWEEN
THIS POINT AND ANOTHER ASTERISK FIVE LINES
BELOW, THE 1835 DOCTRINE AND COVENANTS
CONTAINS THE MATERIAL INCLUDED HERE AND
ADDITIONAL TEXT NOT FOUND IN [CHRONOLOGICAL
FACSIMILES REPORTED IN] REVELATION BOOK 1.*[60]

The following materials, which were added to the Doctrine and
Covenants in 1835 (materials described in the *Joseph Smith Papers*
as "*ADDITIONAL TEXT NOT FOUND IN REVELATION BOOK 1*"), cannot
be found in the manuscript of the Revelation dated 1 November
1831. This important content is not "found" in any of the
manuscripts published in the *Joseph Smith Papers* in 2009, or in *The
Evening and the Morning Star* (where the revelation was initially
published in October 1832), or in the *Book of Commandments*
(published in 1833). The following provisions, which are not found
in the original manuscript, like the original manuscript, were never
published in the Book of Commandments.

*And if they be literal descendants of Aaron they have
a legal right to the bishopric, if they are the firstborn
among the sons of Aaron;*

*For the firstborn holds the right of the presidency over
this priesthood, and the keys or authority of the same.*

---

[59] *The Joseph Smith Papers: Revelations and Translations: Manuscript
Revelation Books, Facsimile Edition*, ed. Robin Scott Jensen, Robert J. Woodford,
and Steven C. Harper (Salt Lake City: Church Historian's Press, 2009), 198, 201,
including corrections to the manuscript by Oliver Cowdery.

[60] Ibid., 201, emphasis added.

No man has a legal right to this office, to hold the keys of this priesthood, except he be a literal descendant and the firstborn of Aaron.

But, as a high priest of the Melchizedek Priesthood has authority to officiate in all the lesser offices he may officiate in the office of bishop when no literal descendant of Aaron can be found, provided he is called and set apart and ordained unto this power, under the hands of the First Presidency of the Melchizedek Priesthood.

And a literal descendant of Aaron, also, must be designated by this Presidency, and found worthy, and anointed, and ordained under the hands of this Presidency, otherwise they are not legally authorized to officiate in their priesthood.

But, by virtue of the decree concerning their right of the priesthood descending from Father to son, they may claim their anointing if at any time they can prove their lineage, or do ascertain it by revelation from the Lord under the hands of the above named Presidency.[61]

Verses 16 to 21 of Section 68 of the Doctrine and Covenants (as just above described), because they were retroactively created after the supposed fact, are not found in the *Joseph Smith Papers* (*Revelation Book 1*) as part of the manuscript of this revelation principally penned by Oliver Cowdery and dated November 1831. Furthermore, the Melchizedek Priesthood isn't referenced in the manuscript of the subsequently altered revelation. Because none of the interpolations described in verses 16 to 21 of Section 68 of the modern Doctrine and Covenants were described in the manuscript of the revelation supposed to have been delivered at Hiram, Ohio, the revelation was rewritten in 1835 to say that they were. In their book, *The Book of Commandments Controversy Reviewed* (p. 81), "Clarence and Angela Wheaton state that '323 words were added

---

[61]Doctrine and Covenants 68:16-21, emphasis added.

and 21 left out'" when the revelation first printed in *The Evening and the Morning Star* in October 1832 only very much later survived to become section 68 of the Doctrine and Covenants in 1835.[62]

In all of this, yet another important revelation at the center of issues of authority was altered and backdated without archival support. What didn't exist in 1831 was falsely said to exist in 1831 in 1835. The references to the Melchizedek Priesthood were alterations among alterations to the original text. The 1831 revelation was substantively altered to include specific references to the Melchizedek Priesthood when the Doctrine and Covenants, published in 1835, superceded the revelation first printed in *The Evening and the Morning Star* in October 1832.[63] In the modern Doctrine and Covenants, Section 68, in a revelation dated November 1, 1831, Doctrine and Covenants 68:15 and 19 are now seen to refer to "the Melchizedek Priesthood." The "original text of the 1831 revelation did not contain that priesthood phrase . . . ." The reference to the Melchizedek Priesthood "was a retroactive addition in 1835."[64] It was added to the text without archival support when Section 68, like so much else, was reconfigured, backdated and falsified.

CONCLUSION

Things not understood until long after September of 1830 (*Book of Commandments* Chapter 28) now appeared to have been understood in August and September of 1830 (*Doctrine and Covenants* Section 27). The word of the Lord was substantively changed by adding "passages" to the first edition of the Doctrine and Covenants in 1835 that altered and amended the March 1833 issue of *The Evening and the Morning Star,* the 1833 *Book of Commandments* and the manuscript found in facsimile form at Revelation Book 1 of the *Joseph Smith Papers* (published in 2009). What happened there,

---

[62]Wheatons, quoted in Tanner and Tanner, *The Changing World of Mormonism*, 43.

[63]*See*, e.g., Quinn, *Origins of Power*, 15.

[64]Quinn, *Origins of Power*, 15.

with Section 27, happened at other places with other foundational narratives.

Ordinary Latter-day Saints would have to be incredibly alert to catch such well concealed deceptions. For someone investigating the Church, then trusting their teachers in respect to the clarification of the mysterious details of the underlying theology, unearthing these disconcerting discrepancies would be almost impossible. Need it be said how dishonest this is? Need it be said that the creators of these deceptions were deceivers in their time? Need it be said that those who now do nothing to correct them are deceivers in our time? The modern Church profits every day from these uncorrected deceptions. It is to the shame of the leaders that these unconscionable alterations continue to betray the faithful. That will not change for so long as these canonized backdated falsified provisions are permitted to remain untended in their various deceitful places.

CHAPTER NINETEEN

Kirtland Implodes

A tree is best measured when it is down....

Carl Sandburg

The truth will set you free, but first it will piss you off.

Gloria Steinem

PREQUEL

Before Joseph turned out the lights at Kirtland, Ohio, a disgusted apostle left the Church. Many years later, in a letter to Joseph III (Joseph Smith's namesake prophet son), William E. McLellin described the mindset that preceded the meltdown.

> In the spring of 1836 I took a mission south and returned the last of June; but only returned to find the Presidency to a great extent absolved in temporal things. They had gone to New York and run into debt about forty thousand dollars for goods–which was never paid!!! They brought on a kind of stuff they called French Cordial. It would intoxicate. I myself saw your father so much under its influence that he could not walk strait! You may doubt what I say, but it matters not. They formed a kind of an association and kept it up until they went into that swindling Kirtland banking concern, about which so many *lies* were prophesied. Popularity, and drinking, feasting and hilarity was the order of the day. The Presidency and leading men got up a ride to Cleveland, some 15 couple[s]. Fine dressing,

fine carriages, fine harness and horses as the
country produced were hired, and they set out.
They drove into Cleveland and through the streets
round and round to show Big. People inquired who
is this? O its Joseph Smith–the Mormon Prophet!
They put up at a first class hotel, called in the wine
&c. Some of them became high, and smashed up
things generally. Next morning their bill was over
two hundred dollars.   No matter–we are Big-
merchant-men of Kirtland. Next day on their way
home they took dinner at Euclid, and imbibed so
freely that when they started home they commenced
running horses, turned over and smashed up one
buggy so they had to haul it home in a wagon. But
no confessions were ever required or made. All
seemed to go swimingly! But I sickened! I left!! I
could tell much more.[1]

SMOKE AND MIRRORS:
THE KIRTLAND SAFETY SOCIETY

It is a negotiable instrument. In the upper right hand corner is an
artist's rendering of a small but vibrant community. To the left of
what is an attractive village is a steamboat blowing white smoke on
a waterway. To the front of the rendering partially obscuring the
view of the idyllic village is a locomotive trailing freight cars and
billowing dark smoke. Steamboat, locomotive, railroad tracks,
freight cars, homes, granaries, smoke. Here one sees the emblems
of industry, Mormonism gathering momentum. The white well-
ordered village stands behind or to the side of everything. For in
support of this handsome instrument, one is encouraged to look
back at that village, a place of industry and enterprise, to the
security of a bank established by a revelation from God, and to the
veracity of the officers of that bank – Sidney Rigdon, President, and
Joseph Smith, Treasurer and First Cashier.

---

[1]Letter to Joseph Smith III, July 1872 in *The William E. McLellin Papers:*
1854-1880, eds. Stan Larson and Samuel J. Passey, foreword by George D. Smith
(Salt Lake City: Signature Books, 2008), 490, emphasis retained.

What is this curious instrument more exactly? It is Mormon money. The Kingdom of God has pledged its credit and issued its currency. Joseph informed that inveterate diarist and future prophet Wilford Woodruff and others that he had received a revelation "about the society" in "an audable voice."[2] A revelation delivered to a prophet of God in "an audable voice" is of a higher dignity than a revelation received by a prophet of God through the impressions of the Spirit. An organization described in "an audable voice" has a higher dignity than an organization the divine existence of which is merely implied. "Audable" words trump spiritual promptings. "Audable" means unmistakable; doubts must disappear. "And whatsoever they [the prophets] shall speak, when moved upon by the Holy Ghost shall be scripture, shall be the will of the Lord, shall be the mind of the Lord, shall be the word of the Lord, shall be the voice of the Lord, and the power of God unto salvation."[3] For those who followed "the Commandments the Lord had given this morning" (January 6, 1837), the prophet said, "all would be well." Listening very carefully and finding himself powerfully impressed, the faithful Woodruff prayed that the Kirtland Safety Society would "become the greatest of all institutions on EARTH."[4] Many other Latter Day Saints prayed to the same effect before subscribing to the Kirtland Safety Society's capital stock.

Just exactly what is "The Kirtland Safety Society"? Well, as it turns out, it is not really a bank. It was ultimately described by its founders as an "anti Banking Co." Then, pray tell, what is an "anti Banking Co."? It is something that looks and acts like a bank but isn't a bank, something operating in violation of Ohio law without a charter and in defiance of provisions "forbidding private companies to issue money."[5] The Kirtland bank "set up expectations for redeeming notes in hard money."[6] Why isn't it a bank and why doesn't it have a charter? Because the Ohio legislature, "which

---

[2]Richard Lyman Bushman, with the assistance of Jed Woodworth, *Joseph Smith: Rough Stone Rolling* (New York: Alfred A. Knopf, 2005), 334.

[3]Doctrine and Covenants 68:4.

[4]Woodruff, *Journals*, 1:111-12, 119-20, quoted in Bushman, *Joseph Smith: Rough Stone Rolling*, 334, emphasis retained.

[5]Bushman, *Joseph Smith: Rough Stone Rolling*, 331.

[6]Ibid., 330.

knew the pitfalls of underfunded banks," refused to allow the
Society's application to be chartered.   So the "Kirtland Safety
Society anti Banking co." is a kind of undocumented organization
that was supposed to be a bank until the Ohio legislature refused to
allow its incorporation.   "The Mormons adjusted [to their
legislative defeat] by organizing themselves into an 'anti-banking'
company and, spiting the legislature, stamped the word 'anti'
before the word 'banking' and began issuing notes."[7]

It is 1837 and the Latter-day Saints are printing notes bearing the
marketable signatures of Sidney Rigdon (President) and Joseph
Smith (Treasurer).   This money is payable to "W. [Warren]
Parrish," who succeeded Smith as Cashier, "or [to the] bearer."
Joseph Smith, Sidney Rigdon and Warren Parrish are the officers,
but Joseph's God is the indispensable sponsor of Ohio's interesting
new Mormon anti-bank. In all of this we see what little regard God
had for the Ohio legislature. These wonderful notes issued over the
signatures of the prophet and his first counselor are to be
exchanged for real money when opportunity allows. They promise
to eliminate the debts of the Church and those of its leaders. What
is the destiny of this organization described by God to Joseph Smith
in "an audable voice"? This great anti-bank, like Aaron's rod, will
swallow up all of the other banks. It will "grow and flourish, and
spread from the rivers to the ends of the earth, and survive when all
others should be laid in ruins."[8] God said so. Joseph said God said
so. In "an audable voice."

Who are the owners of the Lord's bank?   In the beginning,
subscribing Latter-day Saints owned much of the bank's stock –
leaders like Parley P. Pratt and Heber C. Kimball. Most of the
subscribers   obtained   "Kirtland   Safety   Society   Anti-Banking
Company" capital stock by pledging their Kirtland real estate at
grossly inflated values. The "Kirtland Safety Society Anti-Banking

---

[7]Ibid.
   [8]"According to Warren Parrish, who succeeded Joseph as cashier of the bank,
in a letter dated March 6, 1838, published March 24, 1838 in *Zion's Watchman*.
This letter was certified to be a statement of fact by Luke Johnson and John F.
Boynton (former apostles) and Sylvester Smith and Leonard Rich (former
seventies)," all as quoted in Fawn McKay Brodie, *No Man Knows My History: The
Life of Joseph Smith the Mormon Prophet*, 2d ed., rev. and enl. (New York, NY:
Alfred A. Knopf, 1972), 195 fn.

Co." had a capitalization of four million dollars. The largest chartered bank in the State of Ohio, operating with the permission of the legislature, had a capitalization of two million dollars.[9] "As usual, Joseph thought big. Capital stock was set at $4 million, though the roughly 200 stock purchasers put up only about $21,000 in cash."[10] "Subscriptions to the capital stock ranged from $1,000 to $500,000, most of the subscribers paying in Kirtland boom-town lots at five and six times normal value . . . . Joseph estimated his own land in Kirtland at $300,000 . . . ."[11] An astronomical amount by any reckoning.

The hybrid bank, which also accepted specie for capital stock, encouraged the improbable speculation that the notes could be redeemed for real money. If that had been the case, Heber C. Kimball, who paid $15.00 in cash for $50,000.00 in shares, would have been a very rich man in a very rich community. "Now began the most exuberantly prosperous fortnight in Kirtland's history. Everyone's pockets bulged with bills. Local debts were paid off at once, and Joseph sent couriers east to pay the huge obligations of the Kirtland mercantile firms." C.G. Webb, who was close to Joseph and a tutor to his children, Oliver Olney and Cyrus Smalling described chicanery. Inside the bank vault "were many boxes each marked $1,000." These boxes were actually filled with "sand, lead, old iron, stone and combustables," topped off by a "layer of bright fifty-cent silver coins. Anyone suspicious of the bank's stability was allowed to lift and count the boxes." According to Webb, "The effect of those boxes was like magic . . . ." The beautiful but worthless paper "went like hot cakes. For about a month it was the best money in the country."[12]

A "wicked course"

The bank that would "spread from the rivers to the ends of the

---

[9]Adams, "*Kirtland Bank*," 477, quoted in Bushman, *Joseph Smith: Rough Stone Rolling*, 330 fn 31.

[10]Bushman, *Joseph Smith: Rough Stone Rolling*, 330.

[11]Brodie, *No Man Knows My History*, 195.

[12]C.G. Webb interview with W. Wyl, *Mormon Portraits*, quoted in Brodie, *No Man Knows My History*, 196-97, citing also Olney and Smalling.

earth," the bank that would "grow and flourish," swallow up all other banks and "survive when all others should be laid in ruins," grew and flourished from January 2 to January 27, 1837, for slightly less than one month. "[T]he bank failed within a month. Business started on January 2. Three weeks later the bank was floundering."[13] In May 1837, months after the society started, a banking crisis caused hundreds of banks across the country to fail. The Kirtland Bank "collapsed" about four "months" before the crisis in May.[14] By February 1, 1837, Mormon money was selling for approximately twelve and a half cents on the dollar. The Kirtland Safety Society would continue to issue its worthless notes for another five months until the month of June. The Prophet would not renounce the failed enterprise until some time in August.[15] Sidney Rigdon and Joseph Smith resigned as officers of the private entity issuing money and operating without a charter in violation of the laws and statutes of the state of Ohio. "In June, faced with complete collapse, both resigned. In August, Joseph publicly disavowed the Kirtland notes in the Church newspaper. The bank staggered on until November, long since moribund."[16] Now Warren Parrish – Joseph's duly appointed successor as the Cashier of the Safety Society – resigned his office, criticized the prophet, assailed his banking methods, disparaged the doctrines and left the church. Parrish described the prophet's duplicity:

> *I have been astonished to hear him declare that we had $60,000 in specie in our vaults and $600,000 at our command, when we had not to exceed $6,000 and could not command any more; also that we had but about ten thousand dollars of our bills in circulation when he, as cashier of that institution, knew that there was at least $150,000.*[17]

Thirteen lawsuits were brought against Joseph Smith between June 1837 and April 1839, and he was arrested seven times in four

---

[13]Bushman, *Joseph Smith: Rough Stone Rolling*, 330.
[14]Brodie, *No Man Knows My History*, 198.
[15]Ibid., 197-98.
[16]Bushman, *Joseph Smith: Rough Stone Rolling*, 330.
[17]Warren Parrish, letter to *Zion's Watchman* (published March 24, 1838), quoted in Brodie, *No Man Knows My History*, 197, emphasis added.

months.[18] He was fined for illegally operating a bank without a charter.[19] The prophet's followers raised large amounts of money to bail him out, and six of the thirteen lawsuits were settled. "In the other seven the creditors either were awarded damages or won them by default."[20] Many other claims, for many other borrowings, were never filed in court.[21] What faithful Saint among those about two hundred subscribers, who were still in the church, would want to sue the prophet in a court of law? "[L]oyal Mormons left no itemized account of their own claims."[22] A list of nine other debts, reflecting new borrowings after 1839, reached the then colossal amount of $73,000.00. These nine obligations did not include various unresolved Kirtland, Ohio, debts.[23] Seizing upon a brief window of opportunity afforded by the passage of the poorly considered but well received bankruptcy law of 1841, an act quickly repealed, Joseph Smith, his brothers Hyrum and Samuel Smith, and various other leading Mormon men, discharged their debts in bankruptcy. The prophet and Hyrum "joined the stampede" and skipped on their obligations to both Gentiles and Saints.[24] Other debts, which were not discharged, and complications involving issues also unresolved, were Joseph's legacy to Emma Smith and his children, who were plagued by his debts, massive amounts of debts, for many years after his death.

In the April Conference at Kirtland, desperate to save the Lord's bank, Aaron's great rod, and to avoid the financial collapse of the Church, Joseph encouraged "our brethren abroad" to come with their money and "take these contracts" that were "entered into for lands on all sides . . . ." He closed his remarks with what the *Messenger and Advocate* described as a prophecy. "*This place must be built up, and will be built up, and every brother that will take hold and help secure and discharge these contracts shall be rich.*"[25] Parley P. Pratt described one previously highly favored disciple's personal

---

[18]Brodie, *No Man Knows My History*, 201.
[19]Ibid., 198.
[20]Ibid., 201.
[21]Ibid.
[22]Ibid., 199.
[23]Ibid., 266.
[24]Ibid.
[25]*Latter-day Saints Messenger and Advocate*, April 1837, 488, quoted in Brodie, *No Man Knows My History*, 202.

dilemma. In a letter to Joseph preserved by Warren Parrish, Apostle Parley P. Pratt, the "Archer of Paradise," said in part:

> *And now dear brother, if you are still determined to pursue this wicked course, until yourself and the church shall sink down to hell, I beseech you at least, to have mercy on me and my family, and others who are bound with me for those three lots (of land) which you sold to me at the extortionary price of 2,000 dollars, which never cost you 100 dollars. For if it stands against me it will ruin me and my helpless family, as well as those bound with me; for yesterday, President Rigdon came to me and informed me, that you had drawn the money from the bank, on the obligations which you held against me, and that you had left it to the mercy of the bank and could not help whatever course they might take to collect it; notwithstanding the most sacred promises on your part, that I should not be injured by those writings. I offered him the three lots for the writings; but he wanted my house and home also.*
>
> *Now, dear brother, will you take those lots and give me up the writings, and pay me the 75 dollars, which I paid you on the same? Or will you take the advantage of your neighbor because he is in your power . . . . If not I shall be under the painful necessity of preferring charges against you for extortion, covetousness, and taking advantage of your brother by an undue religious influence . . . . Such as saying it was the will of God that lands should bear such a price; and many other prophesyings, preachings, and statements of a like nature.*[26]

What are Joseph's crimes? Following a "wicked course." Sinking the Church "down to hell." Selling lots for twenty times more than he paid, violating "sacred promises" not to injure Pratt, extortion, greed and the exercise of "undue religious influence." Joseph told

---

[26]Parley P. Pratt to Joseph Smith, May 23, 1837, Brodie, *No Man Knows My History*, 202-203, emphasis added.

subscribers, according to Pratt, that "it was the will of God that lands should bear such a price." Joseph, unamused by Parley's plight, informed the Saints that any Saint who brought a lawsuit against a brother would be excommunicated from the Church. He then ordered Pratt to stand trial before the Kirtland High Council on May 29. Pratt did appear, "But the council itself was racked with schism, and the meeting broke up in disorder."[27] Pratt's brother Orson and apostle Lyman Johnson brought charges "against Joseph for lying, extortion and 'speaking disrespectfully against his brethren behind their backs.' It took months for the Pratts to recover their composure and return to the fold."[28]

Mary Fielding, a recent convert who then later became one of Hyrum Smith's plural wives, noted that Joseph's critics "reviled him in meetings." Parley P. Pratt preached that Joseph "had committed great sins." When Rigdon chose to defend the Prophet, Pratt left in protest. Cowdery attempted to effect a reconciliation. When Orson Pratt, Parley's scholarly brother, also unloaded on Joseph, Mary Fielding left in protest.[29] "Heber C. Kimball claimed that by June 1837 not twenty men in Kirtland believed Joseph was a prophet."[30] In that same year, 1837, Joseph Smith altered a number of passages in the Book of Mormon in order to change the nature of God.

The Sky Is Falling

Joseph Smith and his people are not being tormented by old settlers or threatened by mobs, but rather by creditors and disenchanted followers. The problems concern greed and larceny and doctrine. The prophet is now threatened by the filing of six civil lawsuits in Chardon, Ohio, for debts he cannot hope to pay. The collapse at Kirtland is precipitated by wild and unsustainable speculation. The brethren are about getting rich quick, liquidating debt, smoke and mirrors and selfishness.

---

[27]Roberts, ed., *History of The Church of Jesus Christ of Latter-day Saints*, 2:486, quoted in Brodie, *No Man Knows My History*, 203.
[28]Bushman, *Joseph Smith: Rough Stone Rolling*, 337.
[29]Ibid., 337-38.
[30]Ibid., 332.

A convert by the name of Burgess "persuaded church leaders" that a large sum of money was concealed in the cellar of a Salem, Massachusetts, home.[31] A then desperate Joseph leaves everything else in disarray to travel to Salem and see. The alleged cache is nowhere to be found. A "revelation" will "put the best face on a misbegotten venture."[32] "I the Lord your God am not displeased with your coming this journey, notwithstanding your follies . . .".[33] The headnote to the revelation will not mention the purpose for the trip, Burgess, the money or the cellar. It will simply say that, "The Prophet with one of his Counselors and two other elders had journeyed from Kirtland, Ohio, to Salem, Massachusetts; and, at their destination had entered upon the work of teaching the people from house to house, and preaching publicly as opportunity presented."[34] "[T]here are more treasures than one for you in this city," the Lord had said.[35] The treasures, the "one" and the "more," have never been further identified. After the treasure-hunting excursion in Salem, which came to the attention of "the Lord our God," Joseph took a five-week missionary tour to Canada.[36] Hoping to return to find that absence makes the heart grow fonder, he will return to find his kingdom had divided.

The excommunications of Oliver Cowdery and David Whitmer (brothers-in-law) in Missouri in 1838, following the excommunication of Martin Harris, "completed the work of apostasy among those who had seen the angel, and heard the testimony about 'the plates,' and their translation into English."[37] There were fights in the temple where the Savior, Moses, Elias and Elijah were supposed to have appeared to Joseph and Oliver on April 3, 1836. The melee was between dissidents opposed to the

---

[31]Ibid., 328.

[32]Ibid.

[33]Doctrine and Covenants 111:1. In the author's 1957 copyrighted printing of Section 111 of the Doctrine and Covenants, David O. McKay, Trustee-in-Trust, the headnote differed from the headnote described in the 2013 edition. The headnote described in 1957 is the headnote described in these footnotes and in this text.

[34]Ibid., 111, Headnote.

[35]Ibid., 111:10.

[36]Brodie, *No Man Knows My History*, 204-205.

[37]T.B.H. Stenhouse, *The Rocky Mountain Saints: A Full and Complete History of the Mormons, from the First Vision of Joseph Smith to the Last Courtship of Brigham Young* (New York, NY: D. Appleton and Company, 1873), 75.

prophet and members who were not. In that awful brew, after his trip to Canada and with his back against the wall, a rested Joseph faced harsh adversity with steely resolve. His cause was notably advanced by the thundering oratory of his perennially ailing (but long-lived) ally, Sidney Rigdon. Rigdon bitterly attacked the dissenters. The former President of the Kirtland Safety Society "anti Banking co." found conspiracy and calumny everywhere and reported what he found before leaving the temple with assistance, exhausted by the stern expression of his towering rage. Rigdon saw the dissenters – flawed human beings, hypocrites, adulterers, counterfeiters, cheats and thieves and swindlers – as candidates for damnation. They had formerly been beloved founders, apostles, witnesses and scribes, a band of brothers. What happened in the temple, following Sidney's inflammatory speech could best be described as a fracas. Disillusioned Saints, like Warren Parrish, John F. Boynton, Luke Johnson and others, found in Joseph and the Church less than they had hoped. They had given their lives to a great disappointment.

Taking Flight

The debate challenged the momentum of the seven-year-old Church. "With the mercantile firms bankrupt, the steam mill silent, and land values sinking to an appalling low, Kirtland was fast disintegrating."[38] Faced with many lawsuits, and with the prospect of charges connected to banking fraud, Joseph and Sidney abruptly left Kirtland at night in a frantic dash to reach safety in Missouri. Their enemies followed them, they said, and their lives were threatened. Joseph had had a prophetic vision for Kirtland that was splendidly described by Wilford Woodruff in one of his meticulous journals.

> *Joseph presented to us in some degree the plot of the city of Kirtland . . . as it was given him by vision. It was great marvelous & glorious. The city extended to the east, west, North and South. Steam boats will come puffing into the city. Our goods will be*

---

[38]Brodie, *No Man Knows My History*, 205.

conveyed upon railroads from Kirtland to many places
& probably to Zion. Houses of worship would be
reared unto the most high. Beautiful streets was to be
made for the Saints to walk in. Kings of the earth
would come to behold the glory thereof & many
glorious things not now to be named would be
bestowed upon the Saints.[39]

Joseph's inspired vision for Kirtland verbally resembled the artist's rendering of the negotiable instrument, that currency of the Kingdom of God identified with the Kirtland Safety Society. The vision was not unlike the Mormon money. Kirtland's actual destiny was more accurately described by Fawn McKay Brodie.

Meanwhile [after the nighttime flight of Joseph and
Sidney] the good news came from Kirtland that many
dissenting Saints, disgusted by the rantings of the
apostates in the temple, had rejoined the faithful and
were planning to come to Zion. Joseph's going had
left a void that they had found intolerable . . . .

Six hundred Saints finally pooled their resources and
started for Zion in the longest wagon train that
Kirtland had ever seen. The gentiles shook their
heads in wonder . . . . The departure of this group
reduced Kirtland to the sleepy village it had been
when Joseph arrived in 1831. Near-by Cleveland
eventually became a vast metropolis, its suburbs
reaching out across the hills almost to the temple
doors, but the Mormon city, bereft of the virile spirit of
its leader, withered into a museum piece.[40]

"On the night of January 15-16, three days after Joseph's flight," the building that lodged the printing press had burned.[41] **Some said that Joseph fired the Kirtland press in order to avoid scandalous criticism. And the destruction certainly seemed providential.**

---

[39]Wilford Woodruff, quoted in Bushman, *Joseph Smith: Rough Stone Rolling*, 331, emphasis added.
[40]Brodie, *No Man Knows My History*, 210, emphasis added.
[41]Ibid., 207.

While much was unclear about the issues at Kirtland, one thing was not, Joseph had stolen away under cover of night and abandoned hundreds of Kirtland Saints. The prophet was gone and wouldn't be back. Kirtland, Ohio, was toast. Warren Parrish, Joseph's Kirtland, Ohio, Clayton, "had come to believe the worst of Joseph and Sidney," his early Mormon mentors.

> *I believe them to be confirmed infidels who have not the fear of God before their eyes . . . . They lie by revelation, run away by revelation, and if they do not mend their ways, I fear they will at last be damned by revelation.*[42]

---

[42]Ibid., emphasis added.

Appendices

WITNESSES: *MORMONISM UNVAILED,*
E.D. HOWE, PAINESVILLE, OHIO, 1834

MANCHESTER RESIDENTS GROUP STATEMENT

Manchester Residents Group Statement, Eleven Residents[1]: Overseer for Manchester road district No. 30 (Pardon Butts); Overseer for Manchester road district No. 30 (Hiram Smith); Laborer (Sylvester Worden); Farmer (Horace Barnes).

CREDENTIALS OF INDIVIDUALS WHO
OFFERED STATEMENTS

Barton Stafford Statement, Certified Before Thomas P. Baldwin, Judge Wayne County: Barton Stafford was a fisherman and a farmer from a prominent family who lived in Manchester, New York, south of the Smiths on Stafford road. He had known the Smith family from 1820 to 1831, which was "when they left this neighborhood." Thomas P. Baldwin, who authenticated Stafford's statement, was a Judge in the Wayne County judiciary from 1830-1835, a vestryman in Palmyra's Zion Episcopal Church, and a member of Palmyra's Mount Moriah Masonic Lodge.[2]

Joseph Capron Statement: Joseph Capron, a shoe maker, lived just south of the Smiths on Stafford Road. His name appears immediately before the name of Joseph Smith Sr. in the 1830 census. Capron was taxed for the five acres of land (Manchester Lot 1) upon which the Smith's lived. Capron first became acquainted with Joseph Smith, Sr., in 1827 when Capron seemed to have moved to Stafford Road, where he acquired the deed to his land from Squire Stoddard in 1833.[3]

---

[1]"Manchester Residents Group Statement, 3 November 1833," Dan Vogel, ed., *Early Mormon Documents* (Salt Lake City: Signature Books, 1999), 2:18-21.
[2]"Barton Stafford Statement, 3 November 1833," editorial note, Ibid., 2:22-23.
[3]"Joseph Capron Statement, 8 November 1833," editorial note, Ibid., 2:24-25.

G. W. Stoddard Statement, Concurred in by Richard Ford: G.W. Stoddard was a farmer. Stoddard may have been baptized into the First Baptist Church of Palmyra in 1820, disfellowshipped for immoral conduct and profane swearing in 1823, then reinstated in 1825. Stoddard was acquainted with Martin Harris for about thirty years. Richard Ford, who is seen to have concurred with the statement of Stoddard, was a butcher. Ford moved to Palmyra in the 1820s and died at Palmyra at the age of ninety-five.[4]

Abigail Harris Statement: Abigail Harris is thought to have lived near Palmyra in the 1820s and was a sister-in-law of Martin Harris. She was married to Peter Harris, the brother of Lucy Harris, the wife of Martin Harris. (Lucy Harris, Martin's wife, was a Harris before she married Martin). Abigail's husband, a former sailor, became a Quaker minister after his move to Palmyra.[5]

Lucy Harris Statement: Lucy Harris, a daughter of Rufus and Lucy Harris, married her first cousin, Martin Harris, in 1808. Pomeroy Tucker described Mrs. Harris as "a Quakeress of positive qualities." Lucy and Martin Harris separated when Martin Harris followed Joseph Smith to Ohio.[6] Martin Harris later remarried twenty-two year old Caroline Young, a daughter of Brigham Young's brother John. She was thirty-one years younger than Martin, but they had seven children together.

Henry Harris Statement, Notarized by Jonathan Lapham, Justice of the Peace[7]: Henry Harris' statement, which was neither signed nor dated, was notarized in Ohio. Harris became acquainted with the family of Joseph Smith, Sr., in 1820.[8]

Roswell Nichols Statement: Roswell Nichols probably became acquainted with the Smith family in April 1829 when he and his wife Mary Durfee moved into a house from which the Smiths had been evicted. After the eviction, the Smiths were forced to move

---

[4]"G.W. Stoddard Statement, 28 November 1833," editorial note, Ibid., 2:29-30.

[5]"Abigail Harris Statement, 28 November 1833," editorial note, Ibid., 2:31.

[6]"Lucy Harris Statement, 29 November 1833," editorial note, Ibid., 2:34.

[7]"Henry Harris Statement, circa 1833," Ibid., 2:77.

[8]Ibid., 2:75. "It is unknown if this Henry Harris is related to Martin Harris."

into a small cabin they had previously occupied with Hyrum. Nichols was a close neighbor to the Smiths before the Smiths abandoned Manchester for Ohio. They lived as neighbors for about two years.[9]

Peter Ingersoll Statement – Certified before Thomas P. Baldwin, Judge, Wayne County Court; further authenticated by Durfey Chase. Peter Ingersoll, who traveled to the home of Isaac Hale in Harmony, Pennsylvania with Joseph and Emma, said that he had been a close friend of the Smith family. Lorenzo Saunders reported that Ingersoll's "land joined the Smith farm on the north," and it is quite possible that Ingersoll lived in the cabin occupied by the Smiths before they built their own cabin on their Manchester land. Joseph Jr., according to Martin Harris, worked for Ingersoll after getting the plates. Ingersoll became acquainted with the Smiths in 1822, and lived in their neighborhood until about 1830.[10]

David Stafford Statement – Notarized by Fred K. Smith, Justice of the Peace, Wayne County, New York ("appeared before me")[11]: David Stafford was taxed for twenty acres on Manchester Lot 3, the next lot south of the Smith's farm on Stafford Road. He had been acquainted with the family of Joseph Smith Sr. for several years (in 1833).[12]

William Stafford Statement – Certified, Under Oath ("personally appeared before me"), by Thomas P. Baldwin, Judge, Wayne County Court[13]: William Stafford was the man after whom Palmyra's Stafford Street (where the Smith's lived) was named. He was one of the first settlers of Palmyra. "Later he moved farther south on Stafford Road, locating in Manchester on a farm about a mile south of what subsequently became the Smith's land." Pomeroy Tucker described him as "a respectable farmer in comfortable circumstances." Stafford, like the Smiths, was a treasure seeker and owned a peepstone. He became acquainted with Joseph Smith, Sr.,

---

[9]"Roswell Nichols Statement, 1 December 1833," editorial note, Ibid., 2:37.
[10]"Peter Ingersoll Statement, 2 December 1833," editorial note, Ibid., 2:39-40.
[11]"David Stafford Statement, 5 December 1833)," editorial note, Ibid., 2:58.
[12]Ibid., 2:56.
[13]"William Stafford Statement, 8 December 1833," Ibid., 2:63.

and his family, in 1820. The Smiths lived in Palmyra about a mile and a half from his residence.[14]

Joshua Stafford Statement: Joshua Stafford lived on Stafford road about two miles south of the Smiths. He appeared to have been a treasure-seeking colleague of the Smiths. This Stafford became acquainted with the family of Joseph Smith, Sr., in about 1819 or 1820.[15]

Willard Chase Statement – Notarized before Fred K. Smith, Justice of the Peace, Wayne County[16]: Willard Chase was a carpenter and joiner by trade. Lorenzo Saunders, Willard's brother-in- law, described him as "a true Wesleyan preacher," and Lucy Mack Smith called him "a methodist class leader." "[H]is obituary reported that he was 'formerly a Minister of the Wesleyan Methodist Church, and was an earnest and zealous worker for many years.'" Chase, like the Smiths, was a treasure seeker. Willard Chase became acquainted with the Smith family in 1820.[17]

Parley Chase Statement: Parley Chase knew the Smiths "both before and since they became Mormons."[18]

PALMYRA RESIDENTS GROUP STATEMENT – FIFTY-ONE SIGNERS

Palmyra residents' group statement (endorsed by fifty-one signers), 4 December 1833.

Spokesmen

George N. Williams was a store keeper and an elder in Palmyra's Western Presbyterian Church, the church attended by Lucy Mack

---

[14]Ibid., editorial note, 2:59-60.
[15]"Joshua Stafford Statement, 15 November 1833," Ibid., editorial note, 2:27.
[16]"Willard Chase Statement, circa 11 December 1833," Ibid., 2:74.
[17]Ibid., 2:64-65.
[18]"Parley Chase Statement, 2 December 1833," Ibid., 2:47.

Smith and Joseph's siblings, Hyrum, Samuel and Sophronia Smith.[19]

Lemuel Durfee Jr. was a son of Lemuel Durfee who became the owner of the Smith farm in 1825. Durfee Jr. was a prominent Quaker, a supervisor of Macedon in 1857 and a creditor of Joseph Smith, Sr.[20]

Edward S. Townsend was married to Ruth Durfee, a sister of Lemuel Durfee, Sr. Townsend took over a rope business in Palmyra in 1828, and served as a trustee of Palmyra's Democrat School.[21]

Christopher E. Thayer was a clerk.[22] *Levi Thayer and Joel Thayer*, who were twin brothers, were in an ashery and pork-packing business. The Thayer brothers owned several buildings along the Erie Canal, ran several canal boats and evidently had dealings with the Smiths.[23]

Richard S. Williams is thought to have been the son of a Palmyra merchant by the name of Zebulon Williams.[24]

Pliny Sexton, a Quaker and a jeweler by trade, erected the James Jenner block in Palmyra, a block that housed several businesses, including a furniture factory and store. In 1844, he established the Palmyra Bank.[25]

Martin Butterfield worked in the hardware business and manufactured rope. Elected to the United States House of Representatives in 1859, he served one term as a Republican. He is listed in *Who Was Who in America*, 1967, and in the *Biographical Directory of the United States Congress*, 1989.[26]

---

[19]"Palmyra Residents Group Statement, 4 December 1833," Ibid., 2:49 fn 4.
[20]Ibid., 2:49 fn 5.
[21]Ibid., 2:49 fn 6.
[22]Ibid., 2:50 fn 7.
[23]Ibid., 2:50 fn 9, 2:54 fn 42.
[24]Ibid., 2:50 fn 10.
[25]Ibid., 2:50 fn 11.
[26]Ibid., 2:50 fn 12.

Stephen P. Seymour, with a partner, opened a hardware store in Palmyra in 1837. In 1870, he became the vice-president of the First National Bank of Palmyra.[27]

John Hurlbut Jr. was the son of one of the early settlers in Palmyra, and an elder in the Presbyterian Church.[28]

Haskill Linnell was associated with Palmyra's Western Presbyterian Church in 1828 (Lucy, Hyrum, Samuel and Sophronia Smith's congregation).[29]

James Jenner ran a furniture factory and store in the James Jenner block on Palmyra's main street. He was a stockholder in the Palmyra Hotel built in 1837 and a leading member of Palmyra's Western Presbyterian Church (Lucy, Hyrum, Samuel and Sophronia Smith's congregation).[30]

Stephen Ackley owned commercial property in downtown Palmyra and was listed as the fire warden in 1828.[31]

Josiah Rice is identified as a deacon in the Free Congregational Church of Sodus, Wayne County, New York.[32]

Thomas P. Baldwin was a Wayne County Judge, a vestryman in Palmyra's Zion Episcopal Church and a member of the Mount Moriah Masonic Lodge.[33]

Durfee Chase was a leading "homeopathic" physician, Grand Master of Palmyra's Mount Moriah Masonic Lodge in 1822 and 1823, and a high priest in Palmyra's Eagle Chapter.[34]

---

[27]Ibid., 2:50 fn 13.
[28]Palmyra Highway Tax Record (Palmyra, New York).
[29]Vogel, ed., *Early Mormon Documents*, 2:51 fn 16.
[30]"Palmyra Residents Group Statement, 4 December 1833," Ibid., 2:51 fn 17.
[31]Ibid., 2:51 fn 18.
[32]Ibid., 2:51 fn 19.
[33]Ibid., 2:51, 23 fn 6.
[34]Ibid., 2:51-52 fn 23.

Wells Anderson was a boot and shoe store owner at the east end of Palmyra's Main Street in about 1820, and Palmyra's Town Assessor in 1829.[35]

Nathaniel Beckwith was the co-owner of a mercantile business. According to local historian Thomas Cook, "few of the early families to make a home or homes in this village were more closely connected with the commercial and social life here than that of the Beckwiths." Beckwith was a senior warden in Palmyra's Mount Moriah Masonic Lodge.[36]

Philo Durfee was a merchant and a "highly respected gentleman and extensively known." He was an Assessor in 1834-35.[37]

Giles S. Ely was a businessman associated with Palmyra's Western Presbyterian Church in 1828.[38]

Robert W. Smith was the foreman in the Jessup shoe factory on Main Street. He was a member of Palmyra's Western Presbyterian Church and a Grand Master in Palmyra's Mount Moriah Masonic Lodge.[39]

Pelatiah West ran a saddle and harness shop. He was an elder in Palmyra's Presbyterian Church.[40]

Phineas Stiles was a graduate of Yale University, the pastor of Palmyra's Western Presbyterian Church first installed in 1817, and the pastor of the neighboring Sodus church from 1827-1831.[41]

David Strong Jackway, a hatter by trade, owned a 500 acre farm with his father, William, and seems to have been a member of Palmyra's Western Presbyterian Church.[42]

---

[35]Ibid., 2:52 fn 24.
[36]"Palmyra Residents Group Statement, 4 December 1833," quoting T. Cook 1930, 109, 119; McIntosh 1877, 141, 143, Ibid., 2:52 fn 25.
[37]"Palmyra Residents Group Statement, 4 December 1833," Ibid., 2:52 fn 26.
[38]Ibid., 2:52 fn 27.
[39]Ibid., 2:52 fn 28.
[40]Ibid., 2:53 fn 29.
[41]Jesse Townsend to Phineas Stiles, 24 December 1833, Ibid., 3:20-23.
[42]"Hiram Jackway Interview, 1881," editorial note, Ibid., 2:113.

Henry Jessup was an elder in Palmyra's Western Presbyterian Church. He was a member of the committee that investigated the inactivity of Lucy, Hyrum and Samuel Smith in March of 1830. Jessup ran a Palmyra tannery with George Palmer from 1814 to 1828. Charles Butler of Geneva, New York called Mr. Jessup a "highly respectable citizen."[43]

Linus North was a Presbyterian minister.[44]

Thomas Rogers II was one of the three founders of the Palmyra Manufacturing Company in 1827.[45]

William Parke was a deacon of the First Baptist Church of Palmyra. He is listed as a Trustee in the village minutes for 1828.[46]

Josiah Francis is listed as the overseer of road district three in the Palmyra Village in 1829.[47]

Hiram K. Jerome was a lawyer practicing in Palmyra in 1824, and later a judge of the Wayne County Court. He also ran a grain and pork business in a large warehouse along the Erie Canal. He was a stockholder in the Palmyra hotel completed in 1837. He was selected as a vestryman in Palmyra's Zion Episcopal Church in 1828.[48]

George Beckwith was "a successful merchant in Palmyra for fifty-five years." He owned a carpet store and a mercantile business with an older brother. He was a stockholder in the Palmyra Hotel. He served at one time as the President of the Wayne County Bank in Palmyra. Beckwith was a leading elder in Palmyra's Western Presbyterian Church. He was sent, together with others, to investigate the Smiths' absence from the Presbyterian Church.[49]

---

[43]"Lucy Smith History, 1845," Ibid., 1:307-08 fn 106.
[44]"Palmyra Residents Group Statement, 4 December 1833," Ibid., 2:53 fn 31.
[45]Ibid., 2:53 fn 32.
[46]Ibid., 2:53 fn 33.
[47]Ibid., 2:53 fn 34.
[48]Ibid., 2:54 fn 36.
[49]Ibid., 2:54 fn 37.

Hiram Payne was a member of Palmyra's Humanity Lodge.[50]

Phillip Grandin was a county collector,[51] and possibly a relative of E.B. Grandin, the publisher of the Book of Mormon.

Lovell or Lovewell Hurd, who married Sally Smith in 1825, was the landlord and keeper of Palmyra's Eagle Hotel, and the Secretary of Palmyra's Mount Moriah Masonic Lodge.[52]

Asahel Millard was a builder. His projects included Palmyra's Western Presbyterian Church, the Palmyra Hotel and the Union School.[53]

Azel Ensworth was a physician and the owner of a public house or tavern.[54]

Israel F. Chilson may have been a farmer. He was taxed for 100 acres on Manchester Lot 68 in 1833.[55]

---

[50]Ibid., 2:54 fn 39.
[51]Ibid., 2:54 fn 40.
[52]Ibid., 2:54 fn 41.
[53]Ibid., 2:55 fn 43.
[54]Ibid., 2:54 fn 44.
[55]Ibid., 2:55 fn 45.

Appendix   B

BETTER THAN JESUS JOSEPH

"I boast that no man ever did such a work as I."

While delivering a sermon on Sunday, May 26, 1844, the Mormon prophet, under fire and charged at law, was out of sorts. Nauvoo was beginning to feel a lot like Kirtland. In a withering barrage leveled against formerly prominent and previously well-regarded Mormon men, the supreme leader was full of himself and overblown. "I have suffered more than Paul did." "I," like Paul, he said, "have been in perils, and oftener than anyone in this generation." "The Lord has constituted me so curiously that I glory in persecution."[1] "God is in the still small voice." Joseph Smith is the King, Priest and Prophet of the Kingdom of Israel on Earth, the Lieutenant General of the Nauvoo Legion, the Prophet, Seer and Revelator of the Church of Jesus Christ of Latter-day Saints and a candidate for the Presidency of the United States of America. Called, chosen, ordained.

> *I have more to boast of than ever any man had. I am the only man that has ever been able to keep a whole church together since the days of Adam. A large majority of the whole have stood by me. Neither Paul, John, Peter, nor Jesus ever did it. I boast that no man ever did such a work as I. The followers of Jesus ran away from Him; but the Latter-day Saints never ran away from me yet.*[2]

Here Joseph described Jesus as a figure among figures. Here he grouped Jesus with men like Paul, Peter, John, and himself, and reported that none of those other men, including Jesus, had ever done what he had done. *He had succeeded, he said, where all of them had failed.* Joseph's followers had more faithfully followed

---

[1]Joseph Smith Jr., *History of The Church of Jesus Christ of Latter-day Saints*, B.H. Roberts, ed., 2d ed., rev., (Salt Lake City: The Deseret Book Company, 1978), 6:408.

[2]Ibid., 6:408-9, emphasis added.

him than Jesus' followers had faithfully followed him. Smith had inspired a loyalty in the Latter-day Saints that Jesus hadn't inspired in the members of the gospel church. The members of the gospel church hadn't followed the leader of the gospel church with the kind of devotion with which the members of the Mormon Church had followed the leader of the Mormon Church. It wasn't enough that Smith was the most important man on earth to them. He aspired to be greater than Christ.

The apostolic church had been a tiny blip on a gigantic screen. The church founded by Jesus Christ in the meridian of time was seen to fail. The primitive and only true church, as distinguished from its vastly more successful and prolific Roman counterfeit, the "*mother of harlots*," had lasted but a hundred years or so. The church organized by Jesus died an ignominious death in a sinkhole of corruption. It was extinguished by apostasy. The Savior founded a church that failed, after which he abandoned the world for seventeen hundred years.

And what did Joseph Smith find when he commenced his ministry, following that prolonged period of spiritual darkness? A defeated Messiah supposed to say that "the world lieth in sin ~~and~~ at this time and none doeth good no not one . . . ."[3]; that all of the churches were "wrong"; "that all their creeds were an abomination in his sight: that those professors were all corrupt; that: 'they draw near to me with their lips, but their hearts are far from me, they teach for doctrines the commandments of men, having a form of godliness, but they deny the power thereof.'"[4] So far had they fallen. So far had they strayed from their Heavenly Master's fold. So disappointed was their great but rejected Messiah. This failure, according to Smith, was the predicted result of some great eternal plan. The conditions assigned to this inexplicable demise were the building blocks of what was destined to become a grand and glorious restoration.

That is Mormonism's millennial message: Christ's original church expired after an historically insignificant season; it had quickly

---

[3]*The Personal Writings of Joseph Smith*, ed. Dean C. Jessee (Salt Lake City: Deseret Book, 1984), 1832 Holographic Account, 6.
[4]Pearl of Great Price, JS-History 1:19.

gravitated to become infected by a condition of unimaginable debauchery. Joseph Smith's *"restored"* Church of Jesus Christ of Latter-day Saints – teaching Jesus' original principles, organized like Jesus' original church, bolstered by Jesus' authority but managed by the indefatigable Smith – was destined to succeed where the primitive church directed by Jesus and managed by those who were close to him had failed. This new society, founded by Joseph Smith, would never experience the kind of humiliation Joseph said that Jesus had. Those who followed Jesus "ran away" from him; those who followed Joseph never would.

Joseph Smith taught the Savior something about how to inspire loyalty and build a more permanent church. What Joseph did Jesus hadn't been able to do. The principles and the organization and the inspiration that failed the best efforts of Christianity's Messiah, his apostles and the leaders of the gospel church did not fail Joseph Smith in the better than gospel church he then restored. Well could such a successful man be heard to say, *"I boast that no man ever did such a work as I."*

"How I do love to hear the wolves howl!"[5] *the prophet said that month before he was brutally murdered at the tender age of thirty-eight. "I shall always beat them."*[6]

---

[5]Smith Jr., *History of The Church of Jesus Christ of Latter-day Saints*, 6:409.
[6]Ibid., 6:408.

STATEMENT: RICHARD L. BUSHMAN
DECEMBER 16, 2013

I am very much impressed by Joseph Smith's 1832 History account of his early visions. This is the one partially written in his own hand and the rest dictated to Frederick G. Williams. I think it is more revealing than the official account presumably written in 1838 and contained in the Pearl of Great Price. We don't know who wrote the 1838 Account. Joseph's journal indicates that he, Sidney Rigdon, and George Robinson collaborated on beginning the history in late April, but we don't know who actually drafted the history. It is a polished narrative but unlike anything Joseph ever wrote himself. The 1832 history we know is his because of the handwriting. It comes rushing forth from Joseph's mind in a gush of words that seem artless and uncalculated, a flood of raw experience. I think this account has the marks of an authentic visionary experience. There is the distance from God, the perplexity and yearning for answers, the perplexity, and then the experience itself which brings intense joy, followed by fear and anxiety. Can he deal with the powerful force he has encountered? Is he worthy and able? It is a classic announcement of a prophet's call, and I find it entirely believable.[1]

There are no persecution claims in Joseph Smith's 1832 Holographic Handwritten Account, his first account of his first encounter with Deity. Joseph didn't ask the Lord "which of all the sects was right," and the Lord didn't answer him and say "that they were all wrong." Joseph was not "seized upon by some dark

---

[1]Richard L. Bushman, "Dear Forum Members" statement, "Richard Bushman – Reddit – Ask Me Anything" (16 December 2013, accessed 13 January 2014), available from www.mormonthink.com/glossary/richard-bushman-ama. htm; Internet, 2.

power," and God didn't say, "This is *My Beloved Son. Hear Him!*"
Joseph's mother, two of his brothers and one of his sisters did not
join the Presbyterian Church; there was no Methodist minister;
there was no great Palmyra revival, and Joseph wasn't told not to
join any of the sects.

Bushman's insights:

1.   The 1832 account, partially written by Joseph Smith in
his own hand, then dictated to Frederick G. Williams, is more
revealing than the official account "contained in the Pearl of Great
Price," which was "presumably written in 1838."

2.   We know who wrote (and dictated) the 1832 account,
but "We don't know who wrote the 1838 Account."

3.   According to Joseph's journal, Joseph collaborated on
beginning the 1838 Account with Sidney Rigdon and George W.
Robinson.   It can not be determined "who actually drafted the
history," but the "polished narrative" is "unlike anything Joseph
ever wrote himself."

4.   The 1832 account, "artless and uncalculated," was too
spontaneous to have been contrived. The holographic account is an
excitable narrative, free from constraints and straight from the
source. Spoken with conviction, the 1832 account "has the marks of
an authentic visionary experience." "It is a classic announcement of
a prophet's call, and I find it entirely believable."

5.   The unpolished narrative abounds with factors that
serve to reveal the nature of the prophet's untended mind (a
scenario "rushing forth . . . in a gush of words" reflecting "a flood
of raw experience"). There is "distance," "perplexity," "yearning"
– followed by the homely epiphany – then "joy," "fear" and
"anxiety." Is he up to the task? "[W]orthy"? "[A]ble"? "Can he
deal with the powerful force he has encountered"?

By way of contrast:

Bushman reports that we do not know exactly when the Pearl of Great Price account was written, or with certainty by whom, because it was the collaborative effort of at least three men (Bushman fails to describe James Mulholland, a most important scribe) and was so "unlike anything Joseph ever wrote himself." The 1832 less lavish most contemporaneous of the two accounts is closer to Joseph Smith (handwritten), "more revealing" (straight from the source), better dated (1832), and more like other things ("artless and uncalculated") Joseph "wrote himself."

In summary, the 1832 account has a date and a provenance. It is the only account of the First Vision ever written by the prophet in his own hand and the name of its author, "because of the handwriting," is never in doubt. Because it was spontaneous, "artless and uncalculated," because it was unpolished and distinctively Joseph, Richard Bushman concludes that it is "authentic," "believable," and "more revealing" than the "official account presumably written in 1838 and contained in the Pearl of Great Price." Professor Bushman doesn't choose to declare that the 1832 Account fails to describe a vision of the Father and the Son, but rather only an account of a vision of the Son, a matter of enormous importance, or that Joseph Smith was a monotheist who hadn't yet separated the deities when that most contemporaneous and only handwritten account was drafted in 1832.

Richard L. Bushman prefers Joseph Smith's *"entirely believable"* hundred-year-suppressed 1832 account of his first encounter with one deity (a spirit: *"crucifyed," "omnipotant," "omnipreasant"*) to Joseph Smith's 1838-39 "polished" fourth Pearl of Great Price account of his first encounter with two deities (anthropomorphic personages: *"This is My Beloved Son. Hear Him!"*).

HIGH PRIESTHOOD TIMELINE:
THE PATH TO JUNE 3, 1831

What allegedly happened before anyone publicly described the Aaronic or Levitical Priesthood, the Melchizedek Priesthood, the Patriarchal Priesthood, Levi, Aaron, John the Baptist, Melchizedek, Peter, James, and John, Abraham, Elias, Elijah, angelic ordination, priesthood restoration or multiple overlapping priesthoods of different ranks? What happened while the Church was organizing and operating under the subjective unitary control of generic (charismatic) elders, teachers and priests, "given authority and licensed without reference to a bestowal of priesthood"? Before the word "priesthood" was "used in Mormon sermonizing or modern revelations"? Before the concept of "authority" was identified with "the lineal priesthood of the old law"? Before the concept of authority was identified with "the high and holy priesthood after the order of the Son of God"? Before there was a high priest? Before June 3, 1831, when the authority of the "high priesthood" "was manifested and conferred for the first time" upon about half of some forty-four previously ordained elders?

Spring of 1820:	Scenario 1: A fourteen-year-old Joseph saw the Father and the Son on the morning of a beautiful, clear day early in the spring of 1820 [xxi][1] (first publicly reported in 1842). The vision of the Father and the Son.
1821 or 1822:	Scenario 2: Joseph saw the "crucifyed" Lord in "a piller of ~~fire~~ light above the brightness of the sun" "in the 16th year of

---

[1]This and certain other citations in this section (as marked in the text by roman numerals and numbers), unless and except as otherwise specified, are from Andrew Jenson, comp., *Church Chronology: A Record of Important Events Pertaining to the History of the Church of Jesus Christ of Latter-day Saints*, 2d ed., rev. and enlarged (Salt Lake City: Deseret News, 1914). Some such references for the purpose of better order are more fully reported as footnotes.

[his] age"[2] (first publicly reported in 1965). The vision of the Trinitarian Son.

1823, 1824, 1825: No less than seven visits with "Nephi" or "Moroni," one or the other, the angel in charge of the golden plates.

March 20, 1826: Joseph ("crystal gazer," "glass looker," "fortune teller," "money digger") is tried and found to be a "disorderly person" and an "impostor" in the court of Justice Albert Neeley in South Bainbridge, New York (in proceedings authenticated by primary documents first obtained in 1971). The Bainbridge Trial.

September 22, 1827: Joseph takes physical custody of the golden plates from the angel Moroni [xxi] in the year of his marriage to Emma Hale.

1828 Bushman, "Joseph Smith Chronology": Joseph "Translates [the] Book of Mormon with Martin Harris."[3]

June 1828: Bushman, "Joseph Smith Chronology": One hundred and sixteen pages of the translation of the Book of Mormon are lost.[4]

July 1828: Joseph Smith received the first revelation to be published in the Book of Commandments.[5]

---

[2]1832 Holographic Account, History 1832, *The Personal Writings of Joseph Smith*, ed. Dean C. Jessee (Salt Lake City: Deseret Book, 1984), 6.

[3]Richard Lyman Bushman, with the assistance of Jed Woodworth, *Joseph Smith: Rough Stone Rolling* (New York: Alfred A. Knopf, 2005), Chronology, xiii.

[4]Ibid.

[5]Jenson, comp., *Church Chronology*, 3.

May 1829:	Joseph Smith received additional revelations to be published in the Book of Commandments.[6]
May 15, 1829:	Scenario 1: Joseph Smith and Oliver Cowdery are commanded by the Lord by way of instructions given through a stone concealed in Joseph's hat "to baptize and ordain each other" (first publicly reported in June 1829).
May 15, 1829:	Scenario 2: Joseph Smith and Oliver Cowdery are visited by John the Baptist, a heavenly messenger supposed to have ordained them to "the lineal priesthood of the old law." The messenger instructs them to baptize each other. "Immediately after being baptized, the Holy Ghost fell upon them in great measure and both prophesied"[7] (first publicly reported in 1834 and 1835).
May 25, 1829:	Samuel H. Smith, Joseph Smith's younger brother, is baptized by Oliver Cowdery in Harmony, Pennsylvania.[8]
April–June 1829:	Bushman, "Joseph Smith Chronology": Joseph "Translates *Book of Mormon* with Oliver Cowdery."[9]
May-June 1829:	Joseph Smith received additional revelations to be published in the Doctrine and Covenants in 1835 (Sections 11, 14, 15, 16).[10]

---

[6]Ibid.

[7]Ibid.

[8]Ibid.

[9]Bushman, *Joseph Smith: Rough Stone Rolling*, Chronology, xiii.

[10]Jenson, comp., *Church Chronology*, 3.

June 1829:   Bushman, "Joseph Smith Chronology": "Translation of *Book of Mormon* completed."[11]

June 1829:   The word of the Lord came to Joseph Smith and Oliver Cowdery "in the chamber" of Mr. Whitmer's house, commanding Joseph Smith to "ordain Oliver Cowdery to be an Elder in the Church of Jesus Christ," and Oliver to ordain Joseph Smith to be an Elder in the Church of Jesus Christ, after which "they were to ordain others, as it should be made known unto them from time to time" [xxi-xxii]. "[T]hey were commanded to defer these ordinations until 'such times as it should be practicable to have their brethren, who had been and who should be baptized, assemble together'" [xxii]. Note: On April 6, 1830, the day the Church was officially formed, "The Holy Ghost was poured out upon them 'to a very great degree.' Some prophesied and 'all praised the Lord and rejoiced exceedingly.'"[12]

June 1829:   An angel showed the plates of the Book of Mormon to the Three Witnesses, after which they were then shown by Joseph Smith to the Eight Witnesses.[13] A revelation was given to Joseph Smith, Oliver Cowdery and David Whitmer "making known the calling of Twelve Apostles in these last days," and containing "instructions relative to building up the Church of Christ, according to the fulness of the gospel."[14] The actual organization of and the first ordinations for

---

[11]Bushman, *Joseph Smith: Rough Stone Rolling*, Chronology, xiii.
[12]Jenson, comp., *Church Chronology*, 4.
[13]Ibid., 3.
[14]Ibid.

the founding Quorum of Twelve Apostles did not occur until 1835.

March 26, 1830:   Quinn, "Selected Chronology of the Church of Jesus Christ": "The *Book of Mormon* is first advertised for sale. A few days later Joseph Smith . . . gives Oliver Cowdery . . . the brown 'seer stone' with which Smith discovered the gold plates (according to Brigham Young) and translated the *Book of Mormon* into English (according to Smith's wife Emma, Cowdery's wife Elizabeth, Martin Harris, David Whitmer, Hyrum Smith and William Smith who witnessed the translation process). Smith had previously used this seer stone in his family's quest for enchanted treasure."[15]

April 1830:   "An important revelation on Priesthood and Church Government [The Articles and Covenants of the Church of Christ, not yet denominated "Priesthood"] in general [and generic] was given through Joseph Smith . . . ."[16] This revelation failed to mention heavenly messengers (angelic ordinations), dual priesthoods of different ranks, Levi, John the Baptist, the Aaronic Priesthood, the Melchizedek Priesthood, or Peter, James and John. The publication of this revelation followed the date the Church later assigned to the priesthood ordinations ("*Fri. 15 [May 1829]*; "*1829, May-June*") by almost one year. It was the first revelation published in *The Evening and the Morning Star* in June 1832, and the only revelation to be published twice (yet again in June 1833).

---

[15]D. Michael Quinn, "Selected Chronology of the Church of Jesus Christ," *The Mormon Hierarchy: Origins of Power* (Salt Lake City: Signature Books in association with Smith Research Associates, 1994), 615.

[16]Doctrine and Covenants 20, quoted in Jenson, comp., *Church Chronology*, 4.

April 6, 1830:   The Church was legally organized with elders, teachers, and priests (and the prophet was ordained). "[T]hou shalt be . . . an elder of the church through the will of God the Father, and the grace of our Lord Jesus Christ,"[17] without the conferral of something only later called priesthood. The Church Chronology reported that Joseph Smith and Oliver Cowdery ordained each other on this day to office as elders. They "then laid hands on all the baptized members present, 'that they might receive the gift of the Holy Ghost and be confirmed members of the Church.'" "This [earlier] commandment [given to Joseph Smith and Oliver Cowdery to defer ordinations until 'such times as it should be practicable to have their brethren, who had been and who should be baptized, assemble together'"] was complied with on April 6, 1830, the day the Church was organized. On that occasion Joseph Smith laid his hands upon Oliver Cowdery and ordained him to the office of Elder, after which Oliver ordained Joseph to the office of Elder" [xxii].

April 6, 1830:   "The Church was commanded by revelation to keep a record, and Joseph Smith jun., was named by the Lord a Seer [a "translator"], a Revelator, a Prophet, an Apostle of Jesus Christ, etc." Smith was then ordained to the office of Prophet, Seer and Revelator by Oliver Cowdery,[18] without any mention of something only later called "priesthood."

April 1830:   Scenario 1, Newel Knight exorcism: The first miracle of this dispensation was performed for Newel Knight. Under the

---

[17]Book of Commandments 22:1.
[18]Jenson, comp., *Church Chronology*, 4.

Prophet's administration the devil was cast out of Brother Knight.[19] Two different dates have been assigned to this event.

June 1830:

Bushman, "Joseph Smith Chronology": Smith "Receives [a] vision of Moses."[20] Quinn, "Selected Chronology of the Church of Jesus Christ": "This month Satan also appears to Smith as 'an angel of light and is exposed by the Archangel Michael . . . . Smith dictates a revelation on the 'vision of Moses' which describes a visionary deception by Satan anciently.'"[21]

June 1830:

"The Church held its first conference at Fayette. Several of the brethren were ordained to the Priesthood [a modern claim; "priesthood" is a word that was not used by name until 1831]; the Holy Spirit was poured out in a miraculous manner; many of the Saints prophesied and Newel Knight and others had heavenly visions."[22] Joseph was arrested, "charged with setting the country in an uproar by his preaching, tried and acquitted in South Bainbridge, Chenango County, New York." Immediately after the second South Bainbridge trial (the first trial had occurred in March 1826), he was "again arrested, tried and again acquitted at Colesville." There is no mention in the Church Chronology of any visitation by Peter, James, and John in association with the founders' round trip from Harmony, Pennsylvania, to Colesville, New York, after those trials in June or July of 1830. But

[19]Ibid.

[20]Bushman, *Joseph Smith: Rough Stone Rolling*, Chronology, xiii.

[21]Quinn, "Selected Chronology of the Church of Jesus Christ," *Origins of Power*, 616.

[22]Jenson, comp., *Church Chronology*, 4.

here, after Joseph and Oliver returned to Colesville to confirm members who had been baptized, but whose confirmations had been interrupted by the trials, they were "driven away by a mob." They did visit Colesville again to confirm some newly baptized members.[23]

June 1830:	**Scenario 2, Newel Knight exorcism: Quinn, "Selected Chronology of the Church of Jesus Christ": ". . . Smith performs the church's first miracle by casting the devil out of Newel Knight who afterward sees a vision of the Father and the Son."[24] (The Church Chronology reported this event in April 1830).**
June 30 – July 1, 1830:	**Quinn, "Selected Chronology of the Church of Jesus Christ": "Smith is acquitted in two trials at Colesville, New York, for using a treasure-digging 'peep' stone and performing an exorcism."[25]**
July 6, 1830:	**Quinn, "Selected Chronology of the Church of Jesus Christ": Unannounced (until 1835), "Priesthood restoration by Peter, James and John occurs shortly after dawn near Harmony, Pennsylvania, as Smith and Cowdery are fleeing a mob at Colesville, New York."[26] This is after the Church is officially formed.**
June-Sept. 1830:	**Joseph receives additional revelations (which were later published as Moses 1; Doctrine**

---

[23]Ibid.
[24]Quinn, "Selected Chronology of the Church of Jesus Christ," *Origins of Power*, 616.
[25]Ibid.
[26]Ibid.

and Covenants 24, 25, 26, 27, 28, 29, 30 and 31).[27]

September 1830:   The second conference of the Church is held over a period of three days at Fayette, New York; David Whitmer, Peter Whitmer Jr., John Whitmer and Thomas B. Marsh are called by revelation to preach the gospel.[28]

October 1830:   Oliver Cowdery, Parley P. Pratt, Peter Whitmer Jr. and Ziba Peterson are called by revelation to preach the gospel to the Lamanites.[29] (Many explicit references in the Doctrine and Covenants, not less than a dozen, and hundreds of references by speakers in sermons, diaries, notes and prayers refer to the Native Americans as Lamanites).   The Book of Mormon is "Written to the Lamanites who are a remnant of the house of Israel [and Hebrews]; and also to Jew and Gentile . . . ."[30] It is intended that the Lamanites shall accept the gospel and assist the Mormons in their quest to establish "The Kingdom of God" (a nineteenth-century theocracy).

Bushman, "Joseph Smith Chronology": "Missionaries leave on mission to Western Indians."[31] Quinn, "Selected Chronology of the Church of Jesus Christ": "Cowdery and others of the 'Lamanite mission' leave New York Oct. 1830 and preach to the Catteragus tribe in New York, the Wyandot tribe in

---

[27]Jenson, comp., *Church Chronology*, 4-5.
[28]Ibid., 5.
[29]Ibid., *Church Chronology*, 5.
[30]Book of Mormon, Title Page.
[31]Bushman, *Joseph Smith: Rough Stone Rolling*, Chronology, xiii.

	Ohio, the Shawnee tribe in Missouri, and the Delaware tribe in what is now Kansas."[32]
November 1830:	Quinn, "Selected Chronology of the Church of Jesus Christ": A large branch of the Church is established at Kirtland, Ohio. Oliver Cowdery baptizes Sidney Rigdon.[33] Rigdon is the man who presses for priesthood. (It is unlikely that Joseph knows anything about dual priesthoods of different ranks when Rigdon is baptized).
November 4, 1830:	Quinn, "Selected Chronology of the Church of Jesus Christ": "Smith uses his white seer stone to dictate a revelation to Orson Pratt. This stone is often referred to as the 'Urim and Thummim.'"[34] Several of the early revelations are received with the aid of the stone.
December 1830:	Sidney Rigdon and Edward Partridge, from Ohio, visit Joseph Smith at Fayette, N.Y. [5]. Rigdon had been a charismatic minister in a Reformed Baptist Movement inspired by Alexander Campbell, Thomas Campbell, Walter Scott and others. He is an advocate of the "ancient order" committed to the restoration of primitive Christianity.[35]

---

[32]Quinn, "Selected Chronology of the Church of Jesus Christ," *Origins of Power*, 615.

[33]Ibid.

[34]Ibid., 616.

[35]"It is quite possible that the idea of restoration came from him [Rigdon]. Restoration in the Book of Mormon refers to the restoration of Israel, the return of Israel to its favored place in God's eyes, not the restoration of the New Testament church. Rigdon who was a restorationist along with Campbell could very well have turned Joseph's thinking in that direction." [Richard L. Bushman, "Dear Forum Members" statement, "Richard Bushman – Reddit – Ask Me Anything" (16 December 2013, accessed 13 January 2014), available from www.mormonthink.com/glossary/richard-bushman-ama.htm; Internet].

December 1830 – February 1831:	Many additional revelations are now given (to be ultimately published as Doctrine and Covenants Sections 35, 36, 37, 38, 39, 40, 41, 42, 43, 44).[36]
May 1829 – June 3, 1831	Elders, teachers and priests baptized and confirmed "about 2,000 members into the Church of Christ . . . ." Bushman: "So far as can be told now, before 1831 men were called to church offices . . . given authority and licensed without reference to a bestowal of priesthood."[37] Before 1831, there were no high priests in the Church of Christ.[38]
February 4, 1831:	Quinn, "Selected Chronology of the Church of Jesus Christ": "Edward Partridge is ordained to the office of bishop without high priest ordination . . . he is traditionally regarded as presiding bishop over the entire church . . . ."[39]
June 3, 1831:	Bushman, "Joseph Smith Chronology": "Ordination to high priesthood."[40] Previously ordained elders now receive ordination to the high priesthood (not yet called the Melchizedek Priesthood) for the first time. Charismatic authority, held by the previously ordained elders, is not high authority.
	Quinn, "Selected Chronology of the Church of Jesus Christ": "The Melchizedek Priesthood [not yet called the Melchizedek

---

[36]Jenson, comp., *Church Chronology*, 5-6.

[37]Bushman, *Joseph Smith: Rough Stone Rolling*, Chronology, 157-58.

[38]David Whitmer, *An Address to All Believers in Christ: by A Witness to the Divine Authenticity of The Book of Mormon* (Richmond, MO: n.p., 1887; photographic reprint, Concord, CA: Pacific Publishing Company, 1993), 64.

[39]Quinn, "Selected Chronology of the Church of Jesus Christ," *Origins of Power*, 617.

[40]Bushman, *Joseph Smith: Rough Stone Rolling*, Chronology, xiii.

Priesthood] and the office of high priest are conferred on [twenty-three of forty-four] previously ordained elders at the Conference on this day. *Lyman Wight, the first ordained high priest, ordains Smith to that office [and/or to the high priesthood].*"[41]

Joseph Smith, together with other men previously ordained to the office of elder, receives "the High Priesthood" at the Fourth Conference of the Church on June 3, 1831, at Kirtland, Ohio. Smith is ordained by Lyman Wight. The Church Chronology and Mormon scholar B.H. Roberts described this occasion as the first ordination of high priests. Lyman Wight, according to Quinn, becomes the first ordained high priest in the Church of Christ.

How could that be? It seems not to have occurred to Joseph Smith (or to Oliver Cowdery) on May 15, 1829, or on April 6, 1830, to say that they had received the "priesthood" from John the Baptist by the laying on of hands in a glorious never-to-be-forgotten encounter on May 15, 1829. Before April 6, 1830, Joseph Smith didn't ever say that he received the lower priesthood under the hands of John the Baptist, or the higher priesthood under the hands of Peter, James, and John. Or that "authority" was lineal. Joseph Smith didn't know on April 6, and wouldn't know until sometime after his post-1830 collaboration with Rigdon, that the Church of Christ was going to be governed by different orders of the priesthood.[42] Before Rigdon, no one knew that an ancient charismatic inductee by the name of Melchizedek (Melchesedec) would lend his uncommon name to an authoritarian order. The list just described (High Priesthood Timeline) serves to show what the Church purported to accomplish while governed by nothing more than an undocumented

---

[41]Quinn, "Selected Chronology of the Church of Jesus Christ," *Origins of Power*, 617, emphasis added.

[42]See Doctrine and Covenants section 20, Articles and Covenants of the Church of Christ published in *The Evening and the Morning Star* in June of 1832, and again in June of 1833, in support of this contention.

claim to generic unitary charisma. The Church's generic unitary charisma was not the high authority supposed to have been conferred on non-Melchizedek lower authority elders at the Fourth Conference of the Church on June 3, 1831.

How could that be? Joseph Smith didn't know on April 6, 1830, that the office of elder was an appendage of some higher priesthood, or that there was a higher priesthood, or that there were orders of priesthood. He didn't know that some lower order of priesthood, not yet described or named, was an appendage of some higher order of priesthood, not yet described or named. Joseph's Lord hadn't yet seen fit to say that "the second priesthood" is called the lesser priesthood "because it is an appendage to the greater, or the Melchizedek Priesthood . . . ."[43] "Could the 'appendage' exist prior to the conferment of the Priesthood to which it is appended?" "If the office of an elder comes under the Melchizedek Priesthood and that priesthood was not given until June 1831, on what basis did elders exist in the church in its first year?"[44]

On May 15, 1829, and on April 6, 1830, Joseph Smith didn't know that "authority" would come to be identified with ancient Judaism's primitive law of a carnal commandment, or that the law of a carnal commandment did not include the power to bestow the gift of the Holy Ghost by the laying on of hands. Or that the "authority" then exercised by the members of the Church was destined to be replaced by the Aaronic or Levitical Priesthood, the same onerous order that misadministered priesthood and the law in ancient Israel. Smith didn't know that the Aaronic Priesthood didn't include the power to ordain Oliver to the office of elder. Cowdery didn't know that the Aaronic Priesthood didn't include the power to ordain Joseph Smith Prophet, Seer and Revelator to the Church of Christ. So Joseph Smith and Oliver Cowdery, assuming authority neither of them then had, proceeded to ordain elders, asserting "authority," and to confirm members of the Church by the laying on of hands for the gift of the Holy Ghost, asserting "authority," generic undenominated charismatic unitary authority.

---

[43]Doctrine and Covenants 107:13-14.
[44]Sharon I. Banister, *For Any Latter-day Saint: One Investigator's Unanswered Questions* (Fort Worth, TX: Star Bible Publications, 1988), 50.

Angelic ordination was unknown to those April 6 Mormons, and to their leaders, and to the New Testament, the Book of Mormon and the Book of Commandments. Dual priesthoods of different ranks were unknown to those early Mormons, and to their leaders, and to the New Testament, and to the Book of Mormon. Everything the leaders of the Church were supposed to have done from the earliest beginnings until June 3, 1831, was done under the aegis of generic unitary non-exclusive charisma, undocumented authority not yet called what it was supposedly reconstituted to later become (the Aaronic/Levitical Priesthood). On that day, June 3, 1831, the high priesthood "was manifested and conferred for the first time upon several of the Elders." Until that day, although forty-four men had been ordained to the office of elder, none of them held "the Holy Priesthood." After that day their authorities said twenty-three of them did.

FAILED PROPHECIES AND PROMISES[1]

DOCTRINE AND COVENANTS

PROMISE: Search these commandments, for they are true and faithful, and the prophecies and promises which are in them shall all be fulfilled.

PROMISE: What I the Lord have spoken, I have spoken, and I excuse not myself; and though the heavens and the earth shall pass away, my word shall not pass away, but shall all be fulfilled, whether by mine own voice or by the voice of my servants, it is the same.[2]

THE NEW JERUSALEM

PROMISE: Independence, Missouri, is the City of Zion and the site for the temple.[3]

Independence, Missouri, did not become the center place of Zion, or the site for the city of Zion, or for the temple, or a place "for the gathering of the saints."

PROMISE: Those Saints then presently emigrating to Ohio would be redirected, when land had been purchased and the foundation of the city had been laid, to the place of the New Jerusalem.

Ohio became a pit stop.   The city of the New Jerusalem, to be constructed at the place then called Independence, Missouri, became the place of the Latter Day Saints' inheritance. The Saints then emigrating to Ohio would tarry there only until land had been purchased and the foundation of the city had been prepared. When the place of the New Jerusalem had been prepared, emigrants in Ohio would be redirected to the promised land.

---

[1]The prophecies and promises cited in this appendix are all italicized.
[2]Doctrine and Covenants (1957), 1:37-38.
[3]Doctrine and Covenants (2013), 57, Summary, verses 1-3.

PROMISE: The Lord will tell you when the city of the New Jerusalem shall be prepared. When it is prepared you shall gather there, where you shall be his people and he shall be your God.[4]

His servants did tell his people when the place of the city of the New Jerusalem had been prepared, and when he did they sacrificed to travel there, but all attempts to gather in the state of Missouri ultimately failed. The Missouri settlers were not his people in their sacred place, nor either was he their God there. The city of the New Jerusalem was never built, and the land where it was supposed to stand, the land of the Saints' supposed inheritance, could not be kept.

PROMISE: The New Jerusalem, to be called "Zion," shall be a land of peace, a city of refuge and a place of safety for the people of God. The glory and the terror of the Lord shall be there, and the wicked will not come. The people to be gathered in the holy city shall come from every nation under heaven, and shall be the only people not at war one with another. The righteous shall come to Zion singing songs of everlasting joy.[5]

The New Jerusalem, to be called Zion, was a place of persecution and not a land of peace, a city of refuge or a place of safety for the people of God. The glory and the terror of the Lord was not there, and the wicked came and went at will. The Saints of God did not come from every nation under heaven to gather in the holy city, were not the only people not at war one with another, and did not come to Zion singing songs of everlasting joy.   The Saints involuntarily abandoned the holy city, while desperate and in despair.

PROMISE: The Saints shall gather to stand upon Mount Zion, which shall be the city of the New Jerusalem.[6]

The land of Missouri and the site for the city was not a mountain. The Saints did not gather to stand upon Mount Zion in the city of the New Jerusalem in the land of Missouri. Mormonism's New

---

[4]Doctrine and Covenants (1957), 42:9.
[5]Ibid., 45:66-71.
[6]Ibid., 84:2.

Jerusalem, the Lord's "one place" for the gathering of his Saints, would never be built there.

COMMAND: The Lord's faithful followers should gather together in holy places to worship him.[7]

THE TEMPLE

PROMISE: The New Jerusalem shall be built beginning at the temple lot appointed by the finger of the Lord.[8]

PROMISE: The temple shall be reared in this generation. This generation shall not all pass away until the house of the Lord is built. A cloud shall rest upon the temple and the glory of the Lord shall fill the house.[9]

PROMISE: The kingdom of heaven is at hand and the Lord is coming quickly. The Saints are instructed to gird up their loins because when they do he will suddenly come to his temple.[10]

The kingdom of heaven was not at hand and the Lord did not come quickly. The Saints did gird up their loins, but the temple was not "reared in this generation." A cloud did not "rest upon the temple," which wasn't built, and the glory of the Lord didn't "fill the house." That generation did all pass away before the house of the Lord was built. The Saints did not build and the Lord did not "suddenly come to his temple."

PROMISE: A place lying westward, upon a lot not far from the courthouse, at what is now called Independence, Missouri, is the spot selected by God for the construction of a temple to be built in the city of Zion, to be called the New Jerusalem.[11]

---

[7]Ibid., 101:22.
[8]Ibid., 84:2-4.
[9]Ibid., 84:4-5.
[10]Ibid., 36:8.
[11]Ibid., 57:3.

The temple was not built at a spot appointed by the finger of the Lord at a place lying westward not far from the court house in the center place of Zion called Independence in Jackson County, Missouri. The city of Zion was never built. The temple was not constructed at the divinely selected spot. The place "now called Independence," identified as the center place for the city of Zion, did not come to be called the "New Jerusalem."

PROMISE: The Saints would build a temple at a spot consecrated and dedicated unto the Lord by his servant Sydney Rigdon. [12]

The land selected by the Lord was consecrated and dedicated unto the Lord by Sidney Rigdon, the First Counselor in the First Presidency of the Mormon Church, but the temple site was involuntarily abandoned and the temple was never built.

THE PROMISED LAND

PROMISE: The Lord gave them a land of promise, a land flowing with milk and honey, a land upon which there should be no curse when he returned. [13]

The Saints purchased the land the Lord selected with consecrated funds. The Lord did not provide them a "land of promise," "flowing with milk and honey," as he said that he would, or protect their titles, as they expected him to; the land was cursed, and the Lord did not return.

PROMISE: Missouri, now the land of your enemies, is the land of promise, the land of your inheritance, and the place where the city of Zion will be built. God has appointed and consecrated the land of Missouri as the place for the gathering of the Saints. [14]

The publication of the revelations in Independence, Missouri, by W. W. Phelps, describing Missouri as the place of the Mormon's inheritance, but for now the land of their "enemies," did not sit well

---

[12]Ibid., 58:57.
[13]Ibid., 38:18.
[14]Ibid., 52:5, 42; 57:1-2.

with Missouri's inhabitants. Although Missouri was appointed to be the land of the Mormon's inheritance and the place where the city of Zion was to be built, the members of the Church were unable to keep the land or build the city. Missouri thus remained the land of the Mormons' enemies. Joseph said that God appointed and consecrated the land of Missouri as the place for the gathering of the Saints, and as the place where the city of Zion and the temple would be built, but the Saints who sacrificed to gather there were roughly evicted, and God did not protect them.

PROMISE: The land to be acquired by the members of the church in Missouri will be their everlasting inheritance.[15]

While the Saints acquired land in Independence, Missouri, and in the regions round about, they could not hold the land. The site selected for the city of the New Jerusalem, and for the building of the temple, did not become the everlasting inheritance of the faithful Saints.

COVENANT: You shall have that land for the land of your inheritance, if you seek it with all your hearts.[16]

The Mormon settlers sought the land of their inheritance with all of their hearts, but the Lord did not protect their entitlements as he said that he would. The land was lost when the Mormons abandoned the state of Missouri in 1839.

COVENANT: You shall have the land of your inheritance for yourself and your children forever – while the earth shall stand. And you shall have the land of your inheritance again in eternity – no more to pass away.[17]

The children of Israel have not had the land of their inheritance for themselves and for their children, forever – while the earth shall stand. No one should believe that the part of this promise respecting issues of eternity ["no more to pass away"] will be any

---

[15]Ibid., 38:19-20.
[16]Ibid., 38:19.
[17]Ibid., 38:20.

more valid than the part of this promise respecting issues of time ["while the earth shall stand"]."

PROMISE: The Lord, whose words are sure and shall not fail, declares that his Saints shall obtain an inheritance in the land of Zion in these last days ["the willing and obedient shall eat the good of the land of Zion in these last days"] The rebellious shall be "cut off out of the land of Zion, and shall be sent away." They shall not inherit the land.[18]

The Lord's words were not sure and did indeed fail. His Saints did not obtain an inheritance in the land of Zion, and their days were not the "last days." The willing and obedient did not eat the good of the land of Zion in those last days. The rebellious were not "cut off out of the land of Zion" or "sent away" and did inherit the land.

PROMISE: There is no other place than the land of Missouri, no center place other than that now called Independence, no other spot for the temple than that lot lying westward not far from the courthouse. The gathering of the children of Israel shall occur in the land of Missouri, because there is no other place appointed than that which the Lord has appointed, and because there shall be no other place appointed than that which the Lord has appointed for the work of the gathering of the Lord's Saints. The gathering of the Saints will occur in the state of Missouri.[19] *"Zion shall not be moved out of her place, notwithstanding her children are scattered." "[A]ll flesh is in my hands; be still and know that I am God."*[20]

None of these great promises have ever been fulfilled.

PROMISE: The time for the harvest is come. The gathering of the Saints will continue; the Lord will build up his Saints unto his name at holy places; his word "must needs be fulfilled."[21]

---

[18]Ibid., 64:30-35.
[19]Ibid., 101:16-20.
[20]Ibid., 101:17, 16. No other spot on earth can take the place of Zion – the place where the serpent tempted Eve, the place where Adam walked and talked with God.
[21]Ibid., 101:64.

The time for the harvest had not yet come. The time for the gathering of the Saints, to the only place appointed by the Lord for the work of the gathering of his Saints, has not commenced or continued. The Lord did not build up his Saints unto his name at holy places, and the word of the Lord was not fulfilled. While the Mormon army (Zion's Camp) assembled and prepared to march, the Saints were instructed to continue to gather. "Therefore, a commandment I give unto all the churches, that they shall continue to gather together unto the places which I have appointed."[22] The Saints were unable to gather "unto the places" the Lord had "appointed" in the land of Missouri, and God did not protect them. All flesh was not in his hands. Zion was moved out of her place and her children were scattered.

PRESERVING ZION

PROMISE: The Lord promises the faithful that they shall be preserved and rejoice together in the land of Missouri, and says he cannot lie.[23] *"I, the Lord, promise the faithful and cannot lie."*

PROMISE: The Lord holds Zion in his own hands.[24]

The place chosen for the construction of Zion could not be kept and was never reclaimed. Faithful Saints did not rejoice together in the land of Missouri, and the Lord didn't hold Zion in his own hands. He did not preserve the faithful, and his promises to them have not been kept.

PROMISE: Zion shall flourish, and the glory of the Lord shall be upon her. The Lord hath spoken it.[25]

PROMISE: Zion shall be an ensign unto the people, who shall flock to her out of every nation under heaven. The Lord hath spoken it.[26]

---

[22]Ibid., 101:67, emphasis added.
[23]Ibid., 62:6.
[24]Ibid., 63:25.
[25]Ibid., 64:41, 43.
[26]Ibid., 64:42, 43.

PROMISE: The day shall come when the nations of the earth shall tremble, because of Zion, and shall fear because of her terrible ones. The Lord hath spoken it.[27]

In nearly two hundred years the nations of the earth have not trembled because of Zion or feared because of her terrible ones. Zion did not flourish. The glory of God was not upon her. She was not an ensign unto the people and they did not flock to her out of every nation under heaven. No one trembled because of Zion, or feared because of her terrible ones. What Joseph's Lord has spoken did not come to pass.

PROMISE: The rising generations shall grow up on the land of Zion. They shall possess the land from generation to generation, forever and ever.[28]

The rising generations did not grow up on the land of Zion. They did not possess the land from generation to generation, forever and ever.

THE LAST DAYS

PROMISE: The Lord, whose words are sure and shall not fail, tells his Saints that these are the last days.[29]

Those days were not the last days. The Lord's words were not sure and did in fact fail.

PROMISE: October 1830 is the eleventh hour and the last time that the Lord shall call laborers into his vineyard.[30]

October 1830 was not the eleventh hour or the last time the Lord should call laborers into his vineyard.

---

[27]Ibid., 64:43.
[28]Ibid., 69:8.
[29]Ibid., 64:30-31.
[30]Ibid., 33:3.

PROMISE: Those laborers shall lift their voices and cry repentance unto a crooked and perverse generation preparing the way for the second coming of Jesus Christ.[31]

Various crooked and perverse generations have come and gone, unprepared for the second coming, an event that hasn't yet occurred.

PROMISE: Those called to serve in the 1830's will enjoy the riches of eternity and the riches of the earth if wary of pride. The Lord's faithful laborers will be pruning the vineyard for the last time.[32]

Those called to serve in the 1830s enjoyed poverty, persecution, slander   and   disrespect,   cold   and   hunger,   deprivation, disappointment and death. Although wary of pride, they did not enjoy the "riches of eternity and the riches of the earth." The faithful laborers described in this great but broken promise were not pruning the vineyard for the last time.

PROMISE: The sound must go forth from Zion in the land of Missouri to the uttermost parts of the earth.[33]

The sound of the gospel did not go forth from Zion in the land of Missouri to the uttermost parts of the earth. Missouri's Zion had to be abandoned.

THE REDEMPTION OF ZION

PROMISE: The evicted Saints will return and Zion will be redeemed. The Saints shall build, and what they build shall belong to them. They shall plant vineyards and they shall eat the fruit.[34]

PROMISE: If the Saints do all that the Lord says that they shall do, they shall never cease to prevail until the kingdoms of the world are

---

[31]Ibid., 34:6.
[32]Ibid., 38:39, 39:17.
[33]Ibid., 58:64.
[34]Ibid., 101:100-101.

subdued under the Lord's feet. Then the earth shall be given to the Saints, as their possession, forever and ever.[35]

The Mormons have made incredible sacrifices and performed untold numbers of deeds of valor, but have never prevailed against the kingdoms of the world. The evicted Saints did not return and Zion was not redeemed. The Saints did build, but what they built did not belong to them. They planted vineyards but didn't eat the fruit. The kingdoms of the world were not subdued under the Lord's feet and the earth has not been given to the Saints, as their possession, forever and ever.

PROMISE: The Lord has decreed that those who have been scattered shall return to the lands of their inheritances and build up the waste places of Zion. After much tribulation "cometh the blessing." The scattered brethren shall be gathered and blessed in the land of Zion.[36]

PROMISE: Zion, the land of Missouri, the center place of which is Independence, and the spot for the temple, shall be redeemed and restored and never again thrown down.[37]

The Missouri Zion was thrown down, has never been redeemed and will not be restored. Those who were scattered did not return to the lands of their inheritances, did not build up the waste places of Zion and were not gathered there or blessed. After much tribulation, the blessing did not come.

GOD'S WRATH

PROMISE: The Lord will pour out his wrath upon the enemies of the Saints without measure and in his own time. The oppressors will not be punished until the measure of their iniquities fills their cups.[38]

More often the enemies of the Saints poured out their wrath upon the Saints. The oppressors of the Latter Day Saints, while their

---

[35]Ibid., 103:7.
[36]Ibid., 103:11-13.
[37]Ibid., 103:13.
[38]Ibid., 103:1-3.

iniquities may have filled their cups, have never been punished for their transgressions. The Lord did not pour out his wrath upon the enemies of the Saints without measure on the earth in human time as the Saints had reason to suppose that he would.

PROMISE: The season of the chastening of the Saints, while necessary, shall be brief ("for a little season"). The Lord has decreed, if the Saints do what he asks them to do, that they shall begin to prevail against his enemies from this very hour.[39]

The season of the chastening of the early Mormons was not brief. Although they did what the Lord asked them to, they did not begin to prevail against the Lord's enemies from that very hour, or ever at all. There would be additional difficulties in Missouri, Iowa and Illinois. The Lord's decree has never been enforced.

THE ARMY OF GOD

PROMISE: The redemption of Zion must come by power – by the arm of flesh.[40]

The redemption of Zion did not come by power. The Mormon militia failed to fight and was dispersed. Zion was not redeemed by power, "by the arm of flesh," or ever at all.

PROMISE: God's angels and God's presence shall precede the Mormon force to the battlefield. The Saints are promised that in time they shall possess the goodly land.[41]

God's angels and God's presence did not precede the Mormon army to the battlefield. There was no battle, and there was no battlefield. After a march of a thousand miles, the Mormon troops surrendered the land of their inheritance to their "enemies." The Saints did not in time possess "the goodly land." The promise was not kept.

---

[39]Ibid., 103:4-6.
[40]Ibid., 103:15.
[41]Ibid., 103:19-20.

PROMISE: The Saints shall curse their enemies, those who come to drive them from the goodly land, which God has consecrated to be the land of Zion. Those the Saints shall curse the Lord will also curse. The Saints shall avenge the Lord of his enemies to the third and fourth generation of those that hate him.[42]

PROMISE: The Mormons should prepare to keep the commandments the Lord had given them "concerning the restoration and redemption of Zion."[43]

Zion's Camp failed to fight and then surrendered. The consecrated land was not preserved. The Lord didn't curse those the Saints had cursed, and the Saints did not avenge the Lord of his enemies to the third or fourth generation of those who hated him. The capitulation ignored the commandments the Lord gave "concerning the restoration and redemption of Zion." None of these great promises were ever kept. Those the Saints were told to curse drove them from the goodly land.

PROMISE: The lord of the vineyard's servants would go up unto the land of Zion; "break down the walls of the Lord's enemies; throw down their tower, and scatter their watchmen."[44]

PROPHECY: The Mormon troops were promised the glory of the Christian martyrs and the victories of the ancient Hebrew legions.[45]

The Mormon troops did not gain the glory of the Christian martyrs or the victories of the ancient Hebrew legions, and surrendered Zion. They went up to the land of Zion but did not "break down the walls of the Lord's enemies; throw down their tower, and scatter their watchmen."

---

[42]Ibid., 103:24-26.

[43]Ibid., 103:29.

[44]Ibid., 101:57. "And inasmuch as they gather together against you, avenge me of mine enemies, that by and by I may come with the residue of mine house and possess the land." (Ibid., 101:58).

[45]Fawn M. Brodie, *No Man Knows My History: The Life of Joseph Smith the Mormon Prophet*, 2d ed., rev. and enl. (New York, NY: Alfred A. Knopf, 1972), 147.

PROPHECY: Within three years, Zion shall be redeemed. September 11, 1836, is the official date set for the redemption of Zion. The Saints shall march again to Jackson County and there shall not be a dog to open his mouth against them.[46]

Zion was not redeemed within three years, or on September 11, 1836, or ever at all. The Saints did not march for a second time to Jackson County, as Joseph said that they would, and the prophecy that there should not be as much as a dog to open his mouth against them would never be tested.

PROMISE: God does not now require these Mormon soldiers to fight the battles of Zion. God will fight the battles redemption requires.[47]

God first required then did not require the Mormon military force to fight the battles of Zion. God failed to fight the battles redemption required as he said that he would, and Zion was not redeemed.

RECKONINGS

PROMISE: The sword of the Lord's indignation shall fall in behalf of his people – without measure and upon all nations when the cup of their iniquity is full. In that day all Israel shall be saved; those that have been scattered shall be gathered; those who have mourned shall be comforted, and those who have given their lives for the name of the Lord shall be crowned.[48]

PROMISE: Fear not for Zion for her fate is in my hands ("Be still and know that I am God"). Zion shall not be moved out of her place, notwithstanding her children are scattered. Those who remain in the land of Missouri, and are pure in heart, shall return to their inheritances. There, they and their children shall sing songs of

---

[46]Reed Peck Manuscript, Quincy, Illinois, 18 Sept. 1839, in the possession of Fawn McKay Brodie in 1945 (now at Henry E. Huntington Library, San Marino, California), Ibid., 157.

[47]Doctrine and Covenants (1957), 105:14.

[48]Ibid., 101:9-15.

everlasting joy and build up the waste places of Zion. That what the prophets have said might be fulfilled.[49]

The fate of Zion was not in the Lord's hands. The sword of the Lord's indignation did not fall without measure in behalf of his people, and all Israel has not been saved. Those who were scattered were not gathered, those who mourned were not comforted, and Zion was moved out of her place. Zion's children did not sing songs of everlasting joy, or return to build up the waste places of Zion. The pure in heart did not return to their inheritances. And what the prophets said was not fulfilled.

PROMISE: The day of wrath shall come upon the wicked, the rebellious and the unbelieving as a whirlwind. Let the wicked take heed, let the rebellious fear and tremble, let the unbelieving hold their lips, for on the day of wrath all flesh shall know that he is God.[50]

In Missouri the wicked, the rebellious and the unbelieving did not fear or tremble, but instead claimed and kept the land. Faithful and obedient believers were not protected in their possession and were evicted from their New Jerusalem. The rebellious and unbelieving did not hold their lips on a day of wrath that never came and did not know that he was God.

PROPHECY: The time is near when desolation is to cover the earth. The time is near when the sun will be darkened, when the moon will turn to blood, when the stars shall fall from heaven and the earth shall reel to and fro. If the Saints are not sanctified and gathered to the places God has appointed, they must fall.[51]

The Saints have not gathered to their holy places in the promised land, nor have they been sanctified there. The sun has not been darkened, the moon has not turned to blood, the stars have not fallen from heaven and the earth hasn't reeled to and fro. The time when desolation was to cover the earth wasn't near.

---

[49]Ibid., 101:16-19.

[50]Ibid., 63:2-6.

[51]Journal History, 21 Apr. 1834, cited at Richard S. Van Wagoner, *Sidney Rigdon: A Portrait of Religious Excess* (Salt Lake City: Signature Books, 1994; paperback 2006), 149 fn 22 (citing Smith).

PROMISE: The sword of the Lord's indignation will fall on behalf of his people in Missouri. What the Lord has said shall come to pass.[52]

PROMISE: Those who stood against the gathering and Zion were enemies of God and would be punished in their persons and in their posterity.[53]

PROMISE: The destroyer shall destroy and lay waste the enemies of the Lord. In not many years the enemies of the Lord shall not be left to pollute his heritage, or to blaspheme his name, upon the lands the Lord had consecrated for the gathering together of his Saints.[54]

The destroyer did not lay waste the enemies of the Lord. The enemies of the Lord were left to pollute the Lord's heritage, and to blaspheme the Lord's name, upon the lands the Lord had consecrated for the gathering together of his Saints. The Saints were unable to gather, and the Lord did not protect them in their possession. The enemies of the Mormons were not punished in their persons and in their posterity. And what the Lord said did not come to pass.

> *When a prophet speaketh in the name of the Lord, if the thing follow not, nor come to pass, that is the thing which the Lord hath not spoken, but the prophet hath spoken it presumptuously . . . .*[55]

---

[52]Doctrine and Covenants (1957), 101:10.
[53]Ibid., 103:24-26.
[54]Ibid., 105:15.
[55]Deuteronomy 18:10, emphasis added.

AMENDING THE WORD

From Jerald Tanner and Sandra Tanner,
The Changing World of Mormonism: A Behind-the-Scenes Look
At Changes in Mormon Doctrine and Practice
(Chicago, IL: Moody Press, 1979).
Used by permission, Sandra Tanner,
All rights reserved.

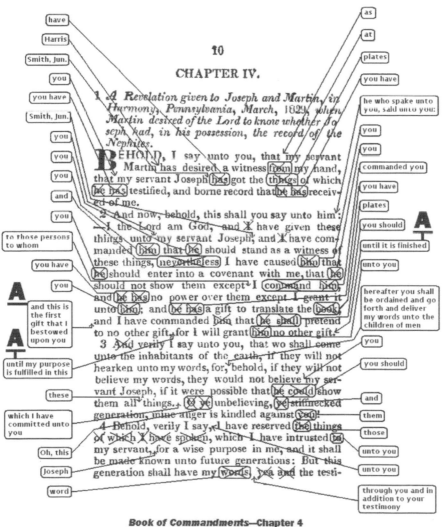

Book of Commandments—Chapter 4
Compare *Doctrine and Covenants*—Sec. 5:1-11

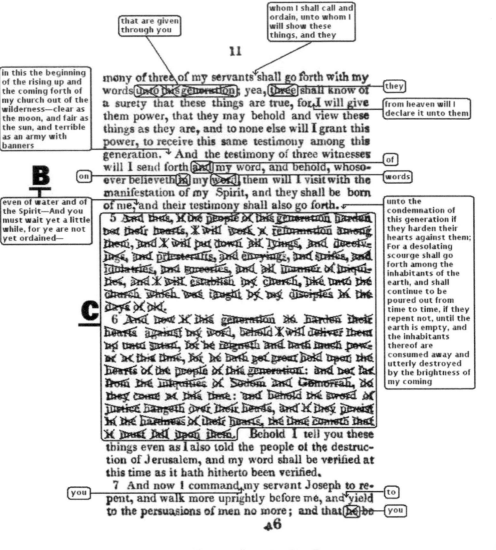

11

that are given through you

whom I shall call and ordain, unto whom I will show these things, and they

in this the beginning of the rising up and the coming forth of my church out of the wilderness—clear as the moon, and fair as the sun, and terrible as an army with banners

even of water and of the Spirit—And you must wait yet a little while, for ye are not yet ordained—

they

from heaven will I declare it unto them

of

words

unto the condemnation of this generation if they harden their hearts against them; For a desolating scourge shall go forth among the inhabitants of the earth, and shall continue to be poured out from time to time, if they repent not, until the earth is empty, and the inhabitants thereof are consumed away and utterly destroyed by the brightness of my coming

...mony of three of my servants shall go forth with my words unto this generation; yea, three shall know of a surety that these things are true, for I will give them power, that they may behold and view these things as they are, and to none else will I grant this power, to receive this same testimony among this generation. And the testimony of three witnesses will I send forth and my word, and behold, whosoever believeth on my word them will I visit with the manifestation of my Spirit, and they shall be born of me, and their testimony shall also go forth.

5 And thus, if the people of this generation harden not their hearts, I will work a reformation among them, and I will put down all lyings, and deceivings, and priestcrafts, and envyings, and strifes, and idolatries, and sorceries, and all manner of iniquities, and I will establish my church, like unto the church which was taught by my disciples in the days of old.

6 And now if this generation do harden their hearts against my word, behold I will deliver them up unto satan, for he reigneth and hath much power at this time, for he hath got great hold upon the hearts of the people of this generation: and not far from the iniquities of Sodom and Gomorrah, do they come at this time: and behold the sword of justice hangeth over their heads, and if they persist in the hardness of their hearts, the time cometh that I must fall upon them. Behold I tell you these things even as I also told the people of the destruction of Jerusalem, and my word shall be verified at this time as it hath hitherto been verified.

7 And now I command my servant Joseph to repent, and walk more uprightly before me, and yield to the persuasions of men no more; and that he be

you   to   you

46

Book of Commandments—Chapter 4
Compare Doctrine and Covenants—Sec. 5:11-22

D

I8

CHAPTER VI.

1 *A Revelation given to Joseph and Oliver, in Harmony, Pennsylvania, April, 1829, when they desired to know whether John, the beloved disciple, tarried on earth. Translated from parchment, written and hid up by himself.*

AND the Lord said unto me, John my beloved, what desirest thou? and I said Lord, give unto me power, that I may bring souls unto thee.— And the Lord said unto me: Verily, verily I say unto thee, because thou desiredst this, thou shalt tarry till I come in my glory:—

2 And for this cause, the Lord said unto Peter:— If I will that he tarry till I come, what is that to thee? for he desiredst of me that he might bring souls unto me: but thou desiredst that thou might speedily come unto me in my kingdom: I say unto thee, Peter, this was a good desire, but my beloved has undertaken a greater work.

3 Verily I say unto you, ye shall both have according to your desires, for ye both joy in that which ye have desired

[Marginal annotations:]

For if you shall ask what you will, it shall be granted unto you.

over death

until

desired

desired

that he might do more, or

unto him:

live and

and shalt prophesy before nations, kindreds, tongues and people

mightest

[Box at bottom, marked E:]

yet among men than what he has before done. Yea, he has undertaken a greater work; therefore I will make him as flaming fire and a ministering angel; he shall minister for those who shall be heirs of salvation who dwell on the earth. And I will make thee to minister for him and for thy brother James; and unto you three I will give this power and the keys of this ministry until I come.

E

Book of Commandments—Chapter 6
Compare Doctrine and Covenants—Sec. 7:1-8

19

CHAPTER VII.

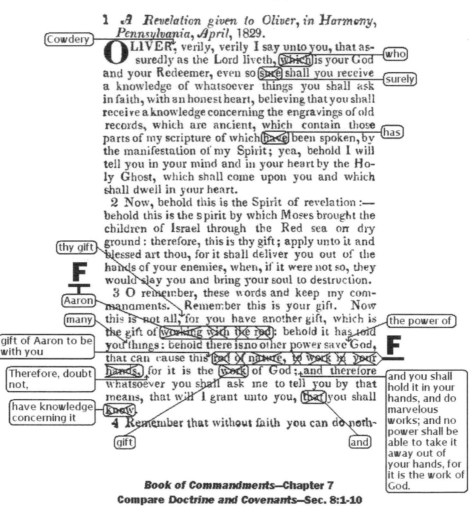

1 *A Revelation given to Oliver, in Harmony, Pennsylvania, April,* 1829.

OLIVER, verily, verily I say unto you, that assuredly as the Lord liveth, which is your God and your Redeemer, even so sure shall you receive a knowledge of whatsoever things you shall ask in faith, with an honest heart, believing that you shall receive a knowledge concerning the engravings of old records, which are ancient, which contain those parts of my scripture of which have been spoken, by the manifestation of my Spirit; yea, behold I will tell you in your mind and in your heart by the Holy Ghost, which shall come upon you and which shall dwell in your heart.

2 Now, behold this is the Spirit of revelation :— behold this is the spirit by which Moses brought the children of Israel through the Red sea on dry ground : therefore, this is thy gift; apply unto it and blessed art thou, for it shall deliver you out of the hands of your enemies, when, if it were not so, they would slay you and bring your soul to destruction.

3 O remember, these words and keep my commandments. Remember this is your gift. Now this is not all, for you have another gift, which is the gift of working with the rod : behold it has told you things : behold there is no other power save God, that can cause this rod of nature, to work in your hands, for it is the work of God; and therefore whatsoever you shall ask me to tell you by that means, that will I grant unto you, that you shall know.

4 Remember that without faith you can do nothing.

Labels:
Cowdery · who · surely · has · thy gift · Aaron · many · gift of Aaron to be with you · Therefore, doubt not, · have knowledge concerning it · the power of · and you shall hold it in your hands, and do marvelous works; and no power shall be able to take it away out of your hands, for it is the work of God. · gift · and

Book of Commandments—Chapter 7
Compare Doctrine and Covenants—Sec. 8:1-10

22

CHAPTER IX.

1 *A Revelation given to Joseph, in Harmony, Pennsylvania, May, 1829, informing him of the alteration of the Manuscript of the fore part of the book of Mormon.*

N OW, behold I say unto you, that because you delivered up so many writings, which you had power to translate, into the hands of a wicked man, you have lost them, and you also lost your gift at the same time, nevertheless it has been restored unto you again: therefore, see that you are faithful and continue on unto the finishing of the remainder of the work as you have begun. Do not run faster than you have strength and means provided to translate, but be diligent unto the end, that you may come off conquerer; yea, that you may conquer satan, and those that do uphold his work.

2 Behold they have sought to destroy you; yea, even the man in whom you have trusted, and for this cause I said, that he is a wicked man, for he has sought to take away the things wherewith you have been intrusted; and he has also sought to destroy your gift, and because you have delivered the writings into his hands, behold they have taken them from you: therefore, you have delivered them up; yea, that which was sacred unto wickedness. And behold, satan has put it into their hearts to alter the words which you have caused to be written, or which you have translated, which have gone out of your hands; and behold I say unto you, that because they have altered the words, they read contrary from that which you translated and caused to be written; and on this wise the devil has sought to lay a cunning

Marginal annotations:
- given unto you
- G T
- by the means of the Urim and Thummim,
- and your mind became darkened
- continue
- Pray always
- has sought to destroy you
- hath
- those
- is now
- of translation
- or labor more
- enable you
- that you may escape the hands of the servants of Satan
- wicked men

35

Spirit in many instances, that the things which you
have written are true:

3 Wherefore you know that they are true; and if
you know that they are true, behold I give unto you
a commandment, that you rely upon the things
which are written; for in them are all things written, concerning my church, my gospel, and my
rock.

the foundation of

upon the foundation of

4 Wherefore if you shall build up my church, and
my gospel, and my rock, the gates of hell shall not
prevail against you.

5 Behold the world is ripening in iniquity, and it
must needs be, that the children of men are stirred
up unto repentance, both the Gentiles, and also the
house of Israel:

6 Wherefore as thou hast been baptized by the
hands hand of my servant, according to that which I have
commanded him:

Joseph Smith, Jun.

7 Wherefore he hath fulfilled the thing which I
commanded him.

8 And now marvel not that I have called him
unto mine own purpose, which purpose is known in
me:

9 Wherefore if he shall be diligent in keeping my
commandments, he shall be blessed unto eternal
life, and his name is Joseph.

Cowdery

10 And now Oliver, I speak unto you, and also
unto David, by the way of commandment:

Whitmer

11 For behold I command all men every where
to repent, and I speak unto you, even as unto Paul
mine apostle, for you are called even with that same
calling with which he was called.

12 Remember the worth of souls is great in the
sight of God:

13 For behold the Lord your God suffered death

Redeemer

B2

Book of Commandments—Chapter 15
Compare Doctrine and Covenants—Sec. 18:2-11

52

or he may receive it from a conference. No person is to be ordained to any office in this church, where there is a regularly organized branch of the same, without the vote of that church; But the presiding elders, traveling bishops, high councilors, high priests, and elders, may have the privilege of ordaining, where there is no branch of the church that a vote may be called. Every president of the high priesthood (or presiding elder), bishop, high councilor, and high priest, is to be ordained by the direction of a high council or general conference.

if occasion requires

he is to

or lay on hands; They are, however

and he is to be ordained

And said conferences are

whatever

to

duties

certificate

may

and take the lead of meetings; But none of these offices is he to do when there is an elder present, But in all cases is to assist the elder.

38 The teacher's duty is to watch over the church always, and be with them, and strengthen them, and see that there is no iniquity in the church, neither hardness with each other, neither lying nor back-biting, nor evil speaking;

39 And see that the church meet together often, and also see that all the members do their duty;

40 And he is to take the lead of meetings in the absence of the elder or priest, and is to be assisted always, and in all his duties in the church by the deacons;

41 But neither the teachers nor deacons have authority to baptize nor administer the sacrament, but are to warn, expound, exhort and teach, and invite all to come unto Christ.

42 Every elder, priest, teacher or deacon, is to be ordained according to the gifts and callings of God unto him, by the power of the Holy Ghost which is in the one who ordains him.

43 The several elders composing this church of Christ, are to meet in conference once in three months, or from time to time as they shall direct or appoint, to do church business whatsoever is necessary.

44 And each priest or teacher, who is ordained by a priest, is to take a certificate from him at the time, which, when presented to an elder, he is to give him a license, which shall authorize him to perform the duty of his calling.

45 The duty of the members after they are received by baptism.

46 The elders or priests are to have a sufficient

when there is no elder present; But when there is an elder present, he is only to preach, teach, expound, exhort, and baptize, And visit the house of each member, exhorting them to pray vocally and in secret and attend to all family duties. In all these duties the priest

if occasion requires

said conferences

to be done at the time. The elders are to receive their licenses from other elders, by vote of the church to which they belong, or from the conferences

or deacon,

shall entitle

Book of Commandments—Chapter 24
Compare Doctrine and Covenants—Sec. 20:49-68

58

CHAPTER XXVI.

1 *A Revelation to Emma, given in Harmony, Pennsylvania, July, 1830.*

HEARKEN unto the voice of the Lord your God, while I speak unto you,

Smith

EMMA, my daughter in Zion, a revelation I give unto you, concerning my will :

2 Behold thy sins are forgiven thee, and thou art an elect lady, whom I have called.

3 Murmur not because of the things which thou hast not seen, for they are withheld from thee, and from the world, which is wisdom in me in a time to come.

for verily I say unto you, all those who receive my gospel are sons and daughters in my kingdom.

and if thou art faithful and walk in the paths of virtue before me, I will preserve thy life, and thou shalt receive an inheritance in Zion.

4 And the office of thy calling shall be for a comfort unto my servant Joseph, thy husband, in his afflictions with consoling words, in the spirit of meekness.

while there is no one to be a scribe for him,

5 And thou shalt go with him at the time of his going, and be unto him for a scribe, that I may send Oliver, whithersoever I will.

my servant,

Cowdery,

Smith, Jun.

6 And thou shalt be ordained under his hand to expound scriptures, and to exhort the church, according as it shall be given thee by my Spirit :

7 For he shall lay his hands upon thee, and thou shalt receive the Holy Ghost, and thy time shall be given to writing, and to learning much.

8 And thou needest not fear, for thy husband shall support thee from the church :

9 For unto them is his calling, that all things might be revealed unto them, whatsoever I will according to their faith.

10 And verily I say unto thee, that thou shalt lay aside the things of this world, and seek for the things of a better.

11 And it shall be given thee, also, to make a selection of sacred Hymns, as it shall be given thee,

Book of Commandments—Chapter 26
Compare Doctrine and Covenants—Sec. 25:1-11

Bibliography

SOURCES CITED

Allen, James B., "Eight Contemporary Accounts of Joseph Smith's First Vision: What Do We Learn from Them?" *Improvement Era* (April 1970).

—— "The Significance of Joseph Smith's 'First Vision' in Mormon Thought," *Dialogue: A Journal of Mormon Thought*, vol. 1 no. 3, (Autumn 1966).

Alexander, Thomas G., "The Reconstruction of Mormon Doctrine: From Joseph Smith to Progressive Theology," *Sunstone*, vol. 5 no. 4 (July-August 1980).

Anderson, Joseph, Letter to T.G. Whitsitt, Historical Department, The Church of Jesus Christ of Latter-day Saints (July 29, 1974).

Bachman, Tal, "What kind of man are you, Epi? My Open Letter" (27 January 2014) (accessed 1 February 2014), available from http://exmormon.org/phorum/read.php?2,1149508,1151145; Internet, 2 pages.

Backman, Jr., Milton V., *Joseph Smith's First Vision: The First Vision in Its Historical Context* (Bookcraft, Inc., 1971).

Bagley, Will, *Blood of the Prophets: Brigham Young and the Massacre at Mountain Meadows* (Norman, OK: University of Oklahoma Press, 2002).

Banister, Sharon I., *For Any Latter-day Saint: One Investigator's Unanswered Questions* (Fort Worth, TX: Star Bible Publications, 1988).

Bennett, John C., *The History of the Saints: Or, an Expose of Joe Smith and Mormonism* (Boston: Leland & Whiting, 1842; photomechanical reprint of 1842 original, Salt Lake City: Modern Microfilm Company).

Beverley, James A., *Mormon Crisis: Anatomy of a Failing Religion* (Pickering, Ontario, Canada: Castle Quay Books, 2013).

Blood Atonement and the Origin of Plural Marriage – A Discussion, correspondence between Elder Joseph F. Smith, Jr., of the Church of Jesus Christ of Latter-day Saints, and Mr. Richard C. Evans, Second Counselor in the Presidency of the "Reorganized" Church (Salt Lake City: The Deseret News Press, 1905).

Brodie, Fawn McKay, *No Man Knows My History: The Life of Joseph Smith the Mormon Prophet*, 2d ed., rev. and enl. (New York, NY: Alfred A. Knopf, 1972).

Brown, Samuel, "The Prophet Elias Puzzle," *Dialogue*, vol. 39 no. 3 (Fall 2006).

Bushman, Richard Lyman, "Dear Forum Members" statement, "Richard Bushman – Reddit – Ask Me Anything" (16 December 2013, accessed 13 January 2014), available from www.mormonthink.com/glossary/richard-bushman-ama.htm; Internet, 46 pages.

—— With the assistance of Jed Woodworth, *Joseph Smith: Rough Stone Rolling* (New York: Alfred A. Knopf, 2005).

Cheesman, Paul R., "An Analysis of the Accounts Relating Joseph Smith's Early Visions" (Master of Religious Education Thesis, Brigham Young University, 1965).

Cowdery, Oliver, [His] transcription of a blessing signed, "Oliver Cowdery, Clerk and Recorder, Given December 18th 1833 and recorded in this book October 2 1835," *Patriarchal Blessing Book 1* (LDS Church Archives), 12.

Cowdery, Oliver (and Joseph Smith), "Letter to W.W. Phelps, Esq." (Oliver Cowdery and Joseph Smith's 1834-35 History), *Messenger and Advocate*, vol. 1 no. 1 (October 1834): 13-16.

——— "Letter III To W.W. Phelps, Esq." (Oliver Cowdery and Joseph Smith's 1834-35 History), *Messenger and Advocate*, vol. 1 no. 3 (December 1834): 41-46.

——— "Letter IV To W.W. Phelps, Esq." (Oliver Cowdery and Joseph Smith's 1834-35 History), *Messenger and Advocate*, vol. 1 no. 5 (February 1835): 77-80.

"Dean C. Jessee" (accessed 18 October 2013), available from https://en.wikipedia.org/wiki/Dean_C._Jessee; Internet, 9 pages.

Deseret News (Salt Lake City, UT).

Dobner, Jennifer (Associated Press), "Pres. [Gordon B.] Hinckley answers myriad questions about the LDS Church," *Deseret News* (25 December 2005).

"Document Showing The Testimony Given Before the Judge of the Fifth Judicial District of the State of Missouri, on the Trial of Joseph Smith, Jr., and others, for High Treason and Other Crimes Against that State," Senate Document No. 189 (Washington D.C.: Blair & Rives; photomechanical reprint of 15 February 1841, Salt Lake City: Utah Lighthouse Ministry).

Ehat, Andrew F., and Lyndon W. Cook, *The Words of Joseph Smith: The Contemporary Accounts of the Nauvoo Discourses of the Prophet Joseph Smith* (Provo, UT: Religious Studies Center, Brigham Young University, 1980).

Ensign (Salt Lake City, UT: Church of Jesus Christ of Latter-day Saints, 1971-present).

"Epistle to the Hebrews" (accessed 11 June 2014), available from https://en.wikipedia.org/wiki/Epistle_to_the_Hebrews; Internet, 8 pages.

The Essential Brigham Young, with a foreword by Eugene E. Campbell (Salt Lake City: Signature Books, 1992).

Evening and the Morning Star (Kirtland, Ohio: December 1833 to September 1834).

The Evening and the Morning Star, 1.8 (Independence, MI: June 1832 to July 1833).

Faulring, Scott H., *An American Prophet's Record: The Diaries and Journals of Joseph Smith* (Salt Lake City: Signature Books and Smith Research Associates, 1987).

Fielding, Robert Kent, "The Growth of the Mormon Church in Kirtland, Ohio," Ph.D. Diss. (University of Indiana, 1957).

"The First Idea of the Book of Mormon," *The Salt Lake Daily Tribune*, vol. 18 no. 18 (5 November 1879).

"First Vision: 'Bedrock Theology,'" *Church News* (9 January 1993).

Gibbons, Francis M., *Joseph Smith, Martyr, Prophet of God* (Salt Lake City: Deseret Book Co., 1977).

Gibson, Doug, "The last years of William B. Smith, a mix of persistent hope and pity," *Standard Examiner* (Ogden, Utah, 21 May 2014).

Givens, Terryl L., *By the Hand of Mormon: The American Scripture that Launched a New World Religion* (*n.p.*: Oxford University Press, Inc., 2002; reprint, New York, NY: Oxford University Press paperback, 2003).

Godfrey, Matthew C., "A Culmination of Learning: D&C 84 and the Doctrine of the Priesthood" (accessed 18 January 2016), available from https:rsc.byu.edu/archived/you-shall-have-my-word/culmination-learning-dc-and-doctrine-priesthood; Internet, 14 pages.

Gunnison, Lieut. John W., *The Mormons, or Latter-day Saints, in the Valley of The Great Salt Lake: A history of their rise and progress, peculiar doctrines, present condition, and prospects, derived from personal observation, during a residence among them* (Freeport, NY: Books for Libraries Press, 1852, 1972).

Hansen-Park, Lindsay, "Does 'Mormon' Still Equal Polygamy?" *Sunstone*, 181 (Summer 2016): 4.

Hardy, B. Carmon, ed., *Solemn Covenant: The Mormon Polygamous Passage* (Urbana, Chicago: University of Illinois Press, 1992).

Hill, Donna, *Joseph Smith: The First Mormon* (USA: Doubleday & Company, Inc., 1977; reprint, Salt Lake City: Signature Books, 1977, 1982, 1999).

Hill, Marvin S., "Brodie Revisited: A Reappraisal," *Dialogue* (Winter 1972).

—— *Quest for Refuge: The Mormon Flight from American Pluralism* (Salt Lake City: Signature Books, 1989).

Hinckley, Gordon B., "Messages of Inspiration from President Hinckley," *Church News* (1 February 1997).

The Holy Bible, Containing the Old and New Testaments (translated out of the original tongues: and with the former translations diligently compared and revised, by His Majesty's special command; specially bound for The Church of Jesus Christ of Latter Day Saints, Deseret Book Company, 1956).

Howard, Richard P., RLDS Church Historian, *Restoration Scriptures: A Study of Their Textual Development*, 2nd ed. (Independence, MO: Herald Publishing House, 1995).

Howe, Eber D., *Mormonism Unvailed: Or, A Faithful Account of That Singular Imposition and Delusion* (Painesville, OH: E.D. Howe, 1834; reprint, New York: AMS Press Inc., 1977).

Improvement Era (Salt Lake City, UT: Church of Jesus Christ of Latter-day Saints, 1897-1970).

Jenson, Andrew, comp., *Church Chronology: A Record of Important Events Pertaining to the History of the Church of Jesus Christ of Latter-day Saints*, 2d ed., rev. and enlarged (Salt Lake City: Deseret News, 1914).

Jessee, Dean C., "The Early Accounts of Joseph Smith's First Vision," *BYU Studies* 9, no. 3 (Spring 1969).

—— "How Lovely Was the Morning," *Dialogue: A Journal of Mormon Thought* 6, no. 1 (Spring 1971).

—— "The Writings of Joseph Smith's History," *BYU Studies Quarterly*, vol. II issue 4, Article 8 (October 1971).

The Joseph Smith Papers: Administrative Records, Council of Fifty Minutes, March 1844-January 1846 , Matthew J. Grow, Ronald K. Esplin, Mark Ashurst-McGee, Gerrit J. Dirkmaat, and Jeffrey D. Mahas, volume ed. (Salt Lake City, UT: The Church Historian's Press, 2016).

The Joseph Smith Papers: Revelations and Translations: Manuscript Revelation Books, Facsimile Edition, ed. Robin Scott Jensen, Robert J. Woodford, and Steven C. Harper (Salt Lake City: The Church Historian's Press, 2009).

The Joseph Smith Papers: Revelations and Translations Volume 2: Published Revelations, eds. Robin Scott Jensen, Richard E. Turley Jr., and Riley M. Lorimer (Salt Lake City: Church Historian's Press, 2011).

Journal of Discourses, 26 vols. (Liverpool, England: F.D. Richards, 1855-1886).

Kirkland, Boyd, "Jehovah As Father: The Development of the Mormon Jehovah Doctrine," *Sunstone* (1984).

Larson, Stan, "Another Look at Joseph Smith's First Vision," *Dialogue: A Journal of Mormon Thought*, vol. 47 no. 2 (Summer 2014).

Lee, John D., *Mormonism Unveiled; Or, The Life and Confessions of the Late Mormon Bishop, John D. Lee* (St. Louis, MO: Bryan, Brand & Company; New York, NY: W.H. Stelle & Co., 1877; photomechanical reprint of the original 1877 edition, Salt Lake City: Modern Microfilm Co.).

LeSueur, Stephen C., *The 1838 Mormon War in Missouri* (Columbia: University of Missouri Press, 1987).

livy (anonymous contributor), "My Personal Ninety-Five Thesis," posted on "Recovery from Mormonism discussion forum" (5 March 2014; accessed 6-7 March 2014), available from exmormon.org/phorum/read.php?2,1193688, quote=1; Internet, 1 page.

"Lyman Wight" (accessed April 14, 2017), available from https://en.wikipedia.org/wiki/Lyman_Wight; Internet, 6 pages.

Madsen, Brigham D., *Against the Grain: Memoirs of a Western Historian* (Salt Lake City: Signature Books, 2002).

Matthews, Robert J., "Joseph Smith's Inspired Translation of the Bible," *Ensign* (December 1972).

—— *Joseph Smith Translation of the Bible [JST]* [BYU, Harold B. Lee Library, 1992, accessed 30 September 2013], available from eom.byu.edu/index.php/Joseph_Smith_Translation_of_the_Bible_[JST]; Internet, 9 pages.

McConkie, Bruce R., *Mormon Doctrine*, 2d ed. (Salt Lake City: Bookcraft, 1966).

Messenger and Advocate (Kirtland, Ohio 1834-1836; Salt Lake City: Utah Lighthouse Ministry, photo reprint of Early LDS Magazine).

Metcalfe, Brent Lee, ed., *New Approaches to the Book of Mormon: Explorations in Critical Methodology* (Salt Lake City: Signature Books, 1993).

Morgan, Dale, *Dale Morgan on Early Mormonism: Correspondence & A New History*, ed. John Phillip Walker, with a Biographical Introduction by John Phillip Walker and a Preface by William Mulder (Salt Lake City: Signature Books, 1986).

Mulder, William, and A. Russell Mortensen, eds., *Among the Mormons: Historic Accounts by Contemporary Observers* (New York, NY: Alfred A. Knopf, 1958).

Orwell, George, "The Theory and Practice of Oligarchical Collectivism" (part 2, chapter 9) in *1984* (Signet Classic, 1950), 263; "1984 by George Orwell: Essential Passages" (accessed 12 December 2013), available from http://www.enotes.com/topics/1984/quotes; Internet, 2 pages.

Packer, Boyd K., "Do Not Spread Disease Germs!" Brigham Young University Studies (Summer 1981).

—— "What Every Elder Should Know – and Every Sister as Well: A Primer on Principles of Priesthood Government," *Ensign* (February 1993).

Packham, Richard, "Elijah and Elias" in "A Linguist Looks at Mormonism: Notes on linguistics problems in Mormonism" (first published April 20, 2003; last revised March 2, 2011; accessed 15 January 2014), available from http://packham.n4m.org/linguist.htm; Internet, 37 pages.

Paine, Thomas, *The American Crisis: Common Sense* (essay addressed to Sir William Howe) (Nu Vision Publications, LLC, 2008).

Palmer, Grant H., *An Insider's View of Mormon Origins* (Salt Lake City: Signature Books, 2002).

—— "Joseph Smith's changing view of God as seen in his First Vision accounts," Outline of a Lecture given at the Salt Lake City Library (6 November 2013).

Palmyra Highway Tax Record (Palmyra, New York).

"Patriarchal Priesthood" (accessed 20 November 2014), available from https://en.wikipedia.org/wiki/Patriarchal _priesthood; Internet, 3 pages.

Petersen, LaMar, *The Creation of the Book of Mormon: A Historical Inquiry* (Salt Lake City: Freethinker Press, 2000).

—— *Problems in Mormon Text: A brief study of certain changes in important Latter-day Saint publications including the Book of Mormon, Book of Commandments, ... the priesthood and Mormon concepts of deity* (n.p.: author, 1976).

Petersen, Melvin J., "A Study of the Nature of and the Significance of the Changes in the Revelations as Found in a Comparison of the Book of Commandments and Subsequent Editions of the Doctrine and Covenants" (M.A. Thesis, Brigham Young University, 1955)

Pratt, Orson, *Divine Authenticity of the Book of Mormon*, no. 1, part of Orson Pratt, *A Series of Pamphlets, with Portrait to which is appended A Discussion (held in Bolton between Elder William Gibson and Rev. Mr. Woodman), also A Discussion (held in France between Elder John Taylor and three reverend gentlemen)* (Liverpool, UK: Franklin D. Richards, 1851).

—— *An Interesting Account of Several Remarkable Visions and of the Late Discovery of Ancient American Records* (Edinburgh: Ballantyne and Hughes, 1840).

"Presiding Patriarch" (accessed 16 July 2014), available from https://en.wikipedia.org/wiki/Presiding_Patriarch; Internet, 6 pages.

"Priesthood (Latter Day Saints)" (accessed 6 April 2014), available from https://en.wikipedia.org/wiki/Priesthood _(Latter_Day_Saints); Internet, 11 pages.

Prince, Gregory A., "Joseph Smith's First Vision in Historical Context: How a Historical Narrative Became Theological," *Journal of Mormon History*, vol. 41 no. 4 (October 2015).

"Proceedings Before the Committee on Privileges and Elections of the United States Senate in the Matter of the Protests Against the Right of Hon. Reed Smoot, a Senator from the State of Utah, to Hold His Seat," 59th Congress, 1st Session, Senate Document No. 486, 4 vols. (1 vol. index) (Washington; Government Printing Office, 1906).

Quinn, D. Michael,

—— *Early Mormonism and the Magic World View* (Salt Lake City: Signature Books, 1987).

—— *The Mormon Hierarchy: Extensions of Power* (Salt Lake City: Signature Books in association with Smith Research Associates, 1997).

—— *The Mormon Hierarchy: Origins of Power* (Salt Lake City: Signature Books in association with Smith Research Associates, 1994).

Rees, Robert A., "Seeing Joseph Smith, The Changing Image of the Mormon Prophet," *Sunstone*, Issue 140 (December 2005).

Richards, LeGrand, *A Marvelous Work and a Wonder* (Salt Lake City: Deseret Book Company, 1976).

Roberts, Brigham H., *A Comprehensive History of the Church of Jesus Christ of Latter-day Saints*, 6 vols. (Provo, UT: Brigham Young University Press, 1965).

—— *Studies of the Book of Mormon*, ed. and with an introduction by Brigham D. Madsen, with a biographical essay by Sterling M. McMurrin (Urbana and Chicago: University of Illinois Press, 1985).

Russell, Bertrand, "A Liberal Decalogue," *The New York Times Magazine* (16 December 1951).

Salt Lake Tribune (Salt Lake City, UT).

Scott, Latayne C., *The Mormon Mirage* (Grand Rapids, MI: Zondervan, 2009).

"Sermon delivered at Nauvoo temple grounds on March 10, 1844 – Sources: Wilford Woodruff journal, James Burgess notebook, Franklin D. Richards 'Scriptural Items,' Joseph Smith diary (Willard Richards), Thomas Bullock diary and the John S. Fullmer papers" (accessed 26 January 2016), available from http://www.boap.org/LDS/Parallel/1844/10Mar44.html; Internet, 20 pages.

Skinner, Andrew C., "Restored Light on the Savior's Last Work in Mortality," *Ensign* (June 1999).

Smith, George D., *Nauvoo Polygamy . . . But We Called It Celestial Marriage* (Salt Lake City: Signature Books, 2008).

Smith Jr., Joseph comp., *A Book of Commandments, For the Government of the Church of Christ, Organized According to the Law, on the 6th of April, 1830* (Zion, MO:W.W. Phelps, 1833).

—— trans., *The Book of Mormon: An Account Written by the Hand of Mormon, Upon Plates Taken from the Plates of Nephi* (Salt Lake City: The Church of Jesus Christ of Latter-day Saints, 1957).

—— trans., *The Book of Mormon: Another Testament of Jesus Christ*, first English edition (Palmyra, NY: n.p., 1830; reprint, New York, NY: Doubleday, 2004).

—— comp., *Doctrine and Covenants of the Church of Jesus Christ of Latter-day Saints: Containing Revelations Given to Joseph Smith, the Prophet, with Some Additions by His Successors in the Presidency of the Church* (Herald Publishing House, 1835).

—— comp., *Doctrine and Covenants of the Church of Jesus Christ of Latter-day Saints: Containing Revelations Given to Joseph Smith, the Prophet, with Some Additions by His Successors in the Presidency of the Church* (Salt Lake City: The Church of Jesus Christ of Latter-day Saints, 1957; reprint 1981; reprint 2013).

—— *History of The Church of Jesus Christ of Latter-day Saints*, B.H. Roberts, ed., 7 vols., 2d ed., rev., (Salt Lake City: The Deseret Book Company, 1978).

—— *[Inspired] Translation of the Bible.*

—— *Lectures on Faith: Prepared by the Prophet Joseph Smith, Delivered to the School of the Prophets in Kirtland, Ohio, 1834-35* (Salt Lake City: Deseret Book Company, 1985).

—— *The Papers of Joseph Smith: Volume 1, Autobiographical and Historical Writings*, ed. Dean C. Jessee (Salt Lake City: Deseret Book Company, 1989).

—— *The Papers of Joseph Smith: Journal, 1832-1842*, ed. Dean C. Jessee (Salt Lake City: Deseret Book Company, 1989-1992).

—— *The Pearl of Great Price: Being a Choice Selection from the Revelations, Translations, and Narrations of Joseph Smith, First Prophet, Seer and Revelator to the Church of Jesus Christ of Latter Day Saints* (Liverpool, UK: F.D. Richards, 1851).

—— *The Personal Writings of Joseph Smith*, ed. Dean C. Jessee (Salt Lake City: Deseret Book, 1984).

Smith, Joseph Fielding, *Doctrines of Salvation*, ed. Bruce R. McConkie, 3 vols. (Salt Lake City: Bookcraft, 1956).

—— *Essentials in Church History* (Salt Lake City: The Church of Jesus Christ of Latter Day Saints, 1922).

—— comp., *Teachings of the Prophet Joseph Smith* (Salt Lake City: Deseret News Press, 1938).

Southerton, Simon G., "A House Divided – Book of Mormon Apologetics in the 21st Century," 17 May 2013 (accessed January 26, 2016), available from http://simonsoutherton.blogspot.com/2013/05/a-house-divided-book-of-mormon.html; Internet, 7 pages.

—— *Losing a Lost Tribe – Native Americans, DNA, and the Mormon Church* (Salt Lake City: Signature Books, 2004).

—— *My Court of Love*, July 18, 2005 (accessed 10 September 2013), available from http://www.mormoncurtain.com/topic_simonsoutherton.html#pub_1293847311; Internet, 30 pages.

Snow, Steven, *Religious Educator*, 14 no. 3 (Brigham Young University, 2013).

Stack, Peggy Fletcher, "No apology? Really? Mormons question leader Dallin H. Oaks' stance," *Salt Lake Tribune*, 30 January 2015.

Stenhouse, T.B.H., *The Rocky Mountain Saints: A Full and Complete History of the Mormons, from the First Vision of Joseph Smith to the Last Courtship of Brigham Young* (New York, NY: D. Appleton and Company, 1873).

Stout, Hosca, *On the Mormon Frontier: The Diary of Hosea Stout, 1844-1861*, ed. Juanita Brooks, vol. 2 (Salt Lake City: University of Utah Press and Utah State Historical Society, 1964, 1982).

Talmage, James E., *A Study of the Articles of Faith: Being a Consideration of the Principal Doctrines of The Church of Jesus Christ of Latter-day Saints*, 12th ed. (Salt Lake City: The Church of Jesus Christ of Latter-day Saints, 1943); 24th ed.; 33rd ed. (Salt Lake City: The Church of Jesus Christ of Latter-day Saints, 1955).

Tanner, Jerald, and Sandra Tanner, *The Changing World of Mormonism: A Behind-the-Scenes Look at Changes in Mormon Doctrine and Practice* (Chicago, IL: Moody Press, 1979).

—— *Mormonism – Shadow or Reality?* (Salt Lake City: Utah Lighthouse Ministry, 1987).

Teachings of Presidents of the Church – Joseph Smith (Salt Lake City: The Church of Jesus Christ of Latter-day Saints, 2007).

Testimony of Benjamin Winchester, Council Bluffs, Iowa, 27 November 1900 (Spalding Stories Library, Special Collections, accessed 9 September 2013), available from http://www.solomonspalding.com/docs/1900winc.htm; Internet, 20 pages.

Times and Seasons (Nauvoo, IL: 1839-1846).

Toscano, Paul James, *The Sacrament of Doubt* (Salt Lake City: Signature Books, 2007).

Turner, John G., *Brigham Young: Pioneer Prophet* (Belknap Press of Harvard University Press, 2012).

Tuttle, Bishop Daniel Sylvester, *Missionary to the Mountain West: Reminiscences of Episcopal Bishop Daniel S. Tuttle, 1866-1886*, foreword by Brigham D. Madsen (Salt Lake City: University of Utah Press, 1987).

Van Wagoner, Richard S., *Mormon Polygamy: A History* (Salt Lake City: Signature Books, 1986).

—— *Sidney Rigdon: A Portrait of Religious Excess* (Salt Lake City: Signature Books, 1994; paperback 2006).

Vogel, Dan,

—— ed., *Early Mormon Documents*, 5 vols. (Salt Lake City: Signature Books, 1996-2003).

—— *Joseph Smith: The Making of a Prophet* (Salt Lake City: Signature Books, 2004).

Walker, Charles L., "Diary" (Harold B. Lee Library, BYU, 1855-1902).

Walters, Wesley P., "Joseph Smith's Bainbridge, N.Y., Court Trials," reprinted by permission from the *Westminster Theological Journal* 36, no. 2 (Winter 1974) (Salt Lake City: Utah Lighthouse Ministry, 1974 and 1977).

Widtsoe, John A., John A. Widtsoe, *Joseph Smith – Seeker After Truth* (Salt Lake City: Bookcraft, 1951).

—— "What Manner of Boy and Youth Was Joseph Smith?" *Improvement Era*, vol. 49 no. 8 (August 1946).

Whitmer, David, *An Address to All Believers in Christ: by A Witness to the Divine Authenticity of The Book of Mormon* (Richmond, MO: n.p., 1887; photographic reprint, Concord, CA: Pacific Publishing Company, 1993).

The William E. McLellin Papers: 1854-1880, eds. Stan Larson and Samuel J. Passey, foreword by George D. Smith (Salt Lake City: Signature Books, 2008).

Wood, Wilford C., *Joseph Smith Begins His Work, Volume I: Book of Mormon, 1830 First Edition: Reproduced from uncut sheets* (USA: Wilford C. Wood, 1962; lithographed, Salt Lake City: Publishers Press, 1995).

Wunderli, Earl M., *An Imperfect Book: What the Book of Mormon Tells Us About Itself* (Salt Lake City: Signature Books, 2013).

Young, Brigham, *Discourses of Brigham Young*, selected and arranged by John A. Widtsoe (Salt Lake City: Deseret Book Company, 1925).

—— Sermon given 25 May 1877, *Deseret Evening News* (2 June 1877).

Index

Man, can become gods, 33, 36-37; creation of, 10-11, 16-18.

Manasseh, 454.

Manchester (New York), xviii, xix, xx-xxii, xxx-xxxi, 18, 542 n 55; affidavits of residents, xxviii-xxix, xli; Residents' Group Statement, xxviii n 30, xxix n 32.

Manuscript History (Joseph Smith Jr.), xxix, 92, 93-96, 105, 112-14, 231.

Marriage, 143-44, 149-50, 461; to Lamanites endorsed, 319.

Marsh, Thomas B., 526 n 17.

A Marvelous Work and a Wonder (Richards), 246-247 n 54.

Mary (mother of Jesus), 10, 14, 15, 44-45; mother of God, 10, 14-15.

Matthews, Robert, 49, 92, 119; vision disclosed (1966, 1971), 51, 65 n 51, 92, 94. *See also* Joshua the Jewish Minister.

McConkie, Bruce R., 174-76, 192, 426-27, 461-62, 464, 481, 420 n 2; high priesthood restoration, 551; Peter, James, and John visit Smith and Cowdery and confer the Melchizedek priesthood "upon them" (June 1829), 551 n 1.

McKean, James, 177.

McLellin, William E., 237, 280-81, 474-80; alterations of revelations, 192, 540, 544; considered Doctrine and Covenants flawed, 477-78; departure from the church, 589-90; priesthood, 160, 163, 233-34, 476-80; voiced opposition to altered revelations, 528-35, 541.

McMurrin, Sterling M., 141, 142 n 7, 521-22.

M'Kune, Hezekiah, xxxviii.

Melchizedek, 159-60, 164, 172, 226, 228, 231, 253, 269-70, 450-53, 456 n 33, 465, 471-74; from charisma and the voice of God to Melchizedek and priesthood,

275; in the Book of Mormon, 464-65; scriptural status, 254.

Melchizedek Priesthood, 132, 139-41, 156, 158, 173, 223-50, 406, 408, 449-80; an anachronism "before 1832 and even up to 1835," 433; conferred by Peter, James, and John, (1829), 192, 225, 230; church organized without, 158, 160, 162, 225, 255-56, 275, 284-86; conferred by the word of the Lord, 192-93; described, 444; early authority claims, 264-67; empty ordinations, 258-61; eternal order, 453; foundational significance, 255-56; the Fourth Conference, 162, 275 (first conferred), 267-74; higher priesthood, 157, 162, 168, 176, 224, 228-29, 275, 277-78; "holy priesthood," 432, 450; missing from early documents, 160, 192-94; necessary to establish church, 444-45; new covenant and new order, 456-59; no account for three apostles' visit, 490; no restoration prayer, 230, 245; not present on 6 April 1830, 445; offices, 157, 162, 227, 229, 253-54, 467, 479-80, 542; origins, 486; product of late design, 204, 205; revelations, 193 (backdated and of unspecified date or time), 195, 196-97 (modern contentions), 223, 225, 445 (retroactive date assigned); restoration of, 152-54, 162, 192-93 (the missing documentation), 223-50, 486 (altered); revisions to, 223-50; significance of *1829 May-June* not recognized (1832), 433; sinful ordinations, 261-63; time and place issues, 200-2; title missing in early scriptural resources, 434; yours to use, 487.

Messenger and Advocate (Kirtland, OH), 113, 152 n 27, 223, 227, 236, 237-38 n 37, 239, 242, 298, 536-7